HOW PROGRESS ENDS

How Progress Ends

TECHNOLOGY, INNOVATION,
AND THE FATE OF NATIONS

CARL BENEDIKT FREY

PRINCETON UNIVERSITY PRESS
PRINCETON & OXFORD

Copyright © 2025 by Princeton University Press

Princeton University Press is committed to the protection of copyright and the intellectual property our authors entrust to us. Copyright promotes the progress and integrity of knowledge created by humans. By engaging with an authorized copy of this work, you are supporting creators and the global exchange of ideas. As this work is protected by copyright, any reproduction or distribution of it in any form for any purpose requires permission; permission requests should be sent to permissions@press.princeton.edu. Ingestion of any IP for any AI purposes is strictly prohibited.

Published by Princeton University Press
41 William Street, Princeton, New Jersey 08540
99 Banbury Road, Oxford OX2 6JX

press.princeton.edu

GPSR Authorized Representative: Easy Access System Europe - Mustamäe tee 50, 10621 Tallinn, Estonia, gpsr.requests@easproject.com

All Rights Reserved

Library of Congress Cataloging-in-Publication Data is available

ISBN 9780691233079
ISBN (e-book) 9780691235073

British Library Cataloging-in-Publication Data is available

Editorial: Hannah Paul, Josh Drake
Production Editorial: Elizabeth Byrd
Jacket: Karl Spurzem
Production: Erin Suydam
Publicity: James Schneider (US), Kate Farquhar-Thomson (UK)
Copyeditor: Rebecca Faith

Printed in the United States of America

10 9 8 7 6 5 4 3 2 1

For Ann-Marie, with eternal love,
and for Victoria and Immanuel, for making me feel reborn

CONTENTS

Preface: Planning and Progress   ix

1	The Mechanics of Progress	1
2	China's Reversal of Fortune	25
3	The Rise of Europe	48
4	Prussia's Visible Hand	86
5	Tsars and Zaibatsus	125
6	Innovation in America	147
7	War, Peace, and Progress	184
8	The Age of Planning	219
9	Growth with Gulags	251
10	Centralization Crumbles	276
11	The Great Flattening	302
12	The Great Leap Backward	330
13	The Veneer of Progress	371
	Epilogue: Moravec's Paradox	392

Acknowledgments 399

Notes 401

Bibliography 463

Index 515

PREFACE

Planning and Progress

"I HAVE been over into the future, and it works."[1]

Those words, penned by journalist Lincoln Steffens shortly after accompanying an American delegation to meet Lenin in 1919, seemed almost prophetic in 1957, when the Soviet Union launched the world's first satellite, *Sputnik I*, into orbit. This milestone, along with Soviet cosmonaut Yuri Gagarin becoming the first human to journey into outer space just four years later, took the entire world by surprise. Uncomfortable questions arose as many in the First World began to wonder if Steffens was right—had the Soviets devised a superior recipe for progress after all? This self-doubt came amid a long-standing scholarly debate on the viability of centrally planned economies—an argument that had raged since the 1920s between Austrian school economists like Ludwig von Mises and Friedrich von Hayek, who cast doubt on the efficiency of planned economies, and post-Keynesian and neo-Marxian economists like Oskar Lange and Abba Lerner, who proposed that a central planning board could indeed effectively simulate market dynamics.[2]

The extraordinary leap of the Soviet economy appeared to vindicate Lange and Lerner's views. In the 1961 version of his economics textbook, Paul Samuelson, a Nobel Laureate and one of the most influential economists of his time, even projected that the Soviet Union's national income might surpass that of the United States as early as 1984, but more likely by 1997.[3] And Lange, emboldened by recent advances in computing, doubled down in 1967 on his predictions about the superiority of central planning: "Let us put the simultaneous equations on an electronic computer and we shall obtain the solution in less than a second. The market process with its cumbersome *tâtonnements* appears old-fashioned. Indeed, it may be considered as a computing device of the pre-electronic age."[4] Not only was the Soviet Union racing ahead of the United States in technology, or so it seemed, but technological progress itself appeared to bolster the case for the Soviet planning model.

In retrospect, it is ironic that the Soviet Union collapsed just as the computer era dawned. Despite being well aware of the wonders of Silicon Valley, the Soviets failed to replicate it, and not for want of trying. After a visit to Leningrad's Special Design Bureau of the Electronics Industry in 1962, premier Nikita Khrushchev prioritized the development of computers, which he declared to be "our future." In fact, Alexander Shokin, the bureaucrat running the industry, soon convinced Khrushchev to build an entire new cluster devoted to churning out semiconductors. The city of Zelenograd, conceived as the perfect scientific settlement (a less sunny Silicon Valley), was the result. But while the new cluster was home to some of the world's finest scientists, the institutions underpinning it could not have been more different from those of California. Whereas the Valley's inventors job-hopped from one start-up to another, establishing a series of concurrent experiments, Zelenograd's efforts were orchestrated entirely from Shokin's ministerial desk in Moscow. With the State Planning Committee sitting on top of seven industrial complexes, managing some 12 million planning indicators, the Soviet economy functioned much like the giant, top-down, preprogrammed computers it was trying to build.[5]

One paradoxical result of the computer revolution is that it complicated planning. As Hayek had recognized, the planning challenge was not so much in calculating or computing the answers to a set of equations with known data but generating that data (much of which is tacit and hard to codify) in the first place. The planning committee and industrial ministries depended on accurate information to function. For standardized operations, this presented no serious challenge because the authorities could benchmark performance across factories. But during this time of technological turbulence, there were no benchmarks, which made it significantly harder to plan, monitor, and hold fellow comrades accountable. Even honest factory managers, those not seeking to personally benefit from the authorities' reduced capacity for oversight, struggled to adjust to changing realities as production decisions were dictated from the top. Factory managers could make suggestions to Party bureaucrats, but the more radical an idea was, the higher up the hierarchy it had to travel for approval, which slowed progress across the board. Meanwhile, in corporate America, the direction of travel was the opposite: the coming of the computer age went hand-in-hand with decentralization. As the eminent computer scientist Marvin Minsky put it in 1982, when *Time* magazine declared the PC the "Machine of the Year" on its front cover, "The desktop revolution has brought the tools that only professionals have had into the hands of the public. God knows what will happen now."[6]

Current discussions about artificial intelligence (AI) echo this uncertainty. Indeed, if you are reading these pages in China, you may just wonder if Lange was simply ahead of his time. While the early days of computing involved rigid, rules-based systems—resembling a strict central planner whose guidelines addressed a steadily diminishing fraction of scenarios encountered—recent years have witnessed a shift to more adaptive deep neural networks, which learn from the vast data generated by human activity. This shift, as Jack Ma, the founder of Alibaba, recently suggested, implies that with the help of AI, "our perception of the world will be elevated to a new level . . . as to allow us to finally achieve a planned economy."[7] Or, in the words of Yuval Noah Harari, technology now favours tyranny, with a notable fusion of oversight and innovation. In the case of China, the quest to amass data for surveillance has driven innovation in AI for commercial markets while reinforcing the Party's grip on power.[8] As Xi Jinping's regime tightens its control over significant segments of the economy and elevates the role of AI technologies in society, "Can China now achieve the Soviet dream of authoritarian technological leadership?" a student once asked me in class. This book is my attempt to answer her question.

The tide of technological change has unfailingly brought with it a myriad of surprises. This book is about why some societies have adjusted successfully in its wake, whereas others have foundered. Understanding these dynamics is important, not only because they shed light on the wealth and poverty of nations over the past two millennia but also because they illuminate pressing current issues, such as the potential for China to surpass the United States in technology, or whether the United States is poised to maintain its position at the forefront of global innovation. To be clear, this is not a work of prediction. Rather, as we journey from the earliest civilizations to the modern era, my aim is to unearth insights into the nature of technological progress and its cessations, providing a framework for thinking about what happens next. If the future is different from the past, we should at least be able to explain why.

To construct a nuanced theory of progress, we must first confront several pivotal questions: Why was economic growth sluggish for millennia, despite sparks of genius from Aristotle, Galileo, and Newton? Why did the Industrial Revolution first take off in eighteenth century England and not in Song China, despite the latter's early technological lead? Why did certain societies, such as Imperial Germany and Meiji Japan, swiftly catch up with England while others did not? What explains episodes of extraordinarily rapid advancement, sometimes spearheaded by autocratic regimes like the USSR, followed by periods of lacklustre growth or even collapse? And how can we account for the endurance of America's technological leadership for more than a century—a run that has defied numerous predictions that it would be overtaken by the Soviet Union in the 1960s and Japan in the 1980s?

Conventional theories of wealth and poverty around the world can at best answer some of these questions. Many scholars, for example, have emphasized with varying success how geography shapes economic outcomes. The glaring limitation of such theories is their inability to explain reversals of fortune—the geography of the Soviet Union was the same when it was growing rapidly in the 1950s and in the 1980s before it collapsed. Nor do we have any reason to believe that Soviet culture markedly changed—another factor that is often emphasized in economic development. Cultural attributes and beliefs, such as the

Protestant work ethic that Max Weber credited for Northern Europe's wealth or the Confucian values that some historians argue hindered China's progress, change too slowly to adequately explain rapid economic booms followed by periods of decline. Institutions, like laws and regulations, are more prone to sudden change and may hold more explanatory power in this regard, but institutional theories emphasizing universal factors are similarly incomplete. Both the USSR and China, for example, saw decades of very rapid growth without secure private property rights. Like all works covering centuries of history, this book is inevitably incomplete too, but illustrating how institutional and cultural factors *interact* with technology at different stages of economic development adds an important dimension to our understanding of economic progress.

In the pages that follow, my narrative begins with an exploration of the mechanics of progress (chapter 1), which I then take to historical record (chapters 2–12) in loose chronological order, zooming in on key technological breakthroughs, from the steam engine, to electricity, computers, and AI. The broad takeaway outlined in chapter 13 is that despite the popular belief that China and the United States are locked in a fierce innovation rivalry, in reality, both countries are edging toward stagnation. To alter this trajectory, we must draw the right lessons about the nature and drivers of progress.

Carl Benedikt Frey,
Oxford, 26 February 2025

HOW PROGRESS ENDS

1

The Mechanics of Progress

> If a baron stole horses from a neighbor, the increase in the size of his cavalry would be far more certain than if he tried to discover better methods of breeding, knowledge that might help enemies more than it contributed to their discoverer.[1]
>
> —WILLIAM J. BAUMOL AND ROBERT J. STORM

ARGUMENTS ABOUT technological progress and economic development often fall along a familiar divide, an intellectual echo of a Cold War now more than thirty years behind us. They either exalt decentralized systems, in which small firms experiment and proliferate with little interference from the government, or they extol centralized bureaucratic systems, in which strong states direct the economy through rational, industrial policy. Such arguments are bound to come up short, for they mistakenly assume that the optimal form of economic governance is invariant across time and place. Instead, I argue, these two ideal types each have their own ecological niche; that is, they are each well suited to different environments.

Stated simply, centralized bureaucratic management is most advantageous for *exploiting* low-hanging technological fruit and spearheading technological catch-up, while decentralized systems are better for *exploring* new technological trajectories, which is the only way to make progress once the technological frontier is reached. Over time, a system that was optimal in one stage of development will, almost inevitably, prove ill-suited for what lies ahead. When this happens, it must either adapt or perish. This also means that the primary sources of stagnation that threaten progress will look quite different, depending on the form of governance and the prevailing stage of development. Future chapters will show how these ideas can help us understand the rise and fall of different societies throughout the past two millennia, but in this opening chapter I hope to show how they arise naturally from what we know about the various drivers of technological progress.

Prohibiting Innovation

On January 17, 1920, the Volstead Act marked the start of national prohibition in America. In historical memory, the movement to prohibit alcohol is most strongly associated with women's groups and Protestant denominations, but its most ardent proponents included another, perhaps more surprising sect: economists. Among the most vocal was Irving Fisher, a prominent scholar and former president of the American Economic Association (AEA). When Fisher organized a roundtable discussion on the subject, during the AEA Annual Meetings of 1927, he was unable to find a single economist to argue the case against it. All economists present agreed that alcohol was harmful, not just to health but also to economic efficiency. As one participant put it during the session:

> In addition to the time lost, there was the loss in individual efficiency of operation when the worker returned, even though he was able to come haltingly back to his job without actual absence. There is also an unmistakable array of evidence that accidents to men and materials on account of unsteady nerves and muscles reached a very high total as compared with the present day. Liquor is an enemy to health and skill. To this must be coupled the fact that thousands of workers were actually thrown out of a job, entailing great loss in the industrial aggregate, through increased turnover and lowered efficiency on the part of the man in question.[2]

In the age of mass production, such a loss of efficiency could be detrimental. The viability of just about every manufacturing business depended on its ability to churn out more goods at a lower cost and ever-faster pace. Drinking slowed workers down and increased the chance of costly mistakes. Yet the AEA participants were on the wrong side of history. All the Volstead Act achieved was to make alcohol consumption part of the shadow economy and turn Al Capone into one of the richest men in America. And as the demand for illegal liquor skyrocketed, cocktails gained popularity to disguise the bitter taste of bathtub gin with juices, herbs, and sweeteners.[3]

Much like during the COVID-19 pandemic, the poor, crammed into small apartments, endured the greatest hardships. Indeed, for the wealthy, the Roaring Twenties were perhaps the greatest, gaudiest spree in American history, as famously depicted in F. Scott Fitzgerald's *The Great Gatsby*. Even before prohibition went into force, the upper classes commonly stockpiled alcohol for legal home consumption. President Woodrow Wilson, for instance, moved his stash of alcoholic beverages to his private Washington residence at the end of his term, while his successor, Warren G. Harding, took his own large supply to the White House. The disappearance of the saloon, meanwhile, disrupted ordinary people's daily lives and social networks. And by bringing the habit of drinking back into the shadows of people's homes, prohibition would have far-reaching consequences for the advancement of industry.

The saloon had a long social tradition in America. In the words of one contemporary, it was "the rooster-crow of the spirit of democracy," rivalled only by the church as the place where the working class met after work.[4] As is evident from saloon names like "Mechanics' Exchange" and "Stonecutters' Exchange," many establishments catered to people in specific occupations or industries.[5] Skilled workers and craftsmen went there not just to drink but to socialize and exchange ideas. And because these workers were responsible for developing the most inventive contrivances of the era, it should be no surprise that innovation took a hit as saloons across the country were forcibly shut down. Taking advantage of the fact that U.S. states introduced prohibition at different times, economist Michael Andrews found that such bans were followed by an

18 percent decline in patenting. Not only did collaborative innovation suffer, but patenting among solo inventors also plummeted as they ceased to socialize at the saloon and were suddenly exposed to fewer ideas. The rate of patents only rebounded to its prior level half a decade later, once people rebuilt their social networks.[6]

Although decisions are always easier to judge with the benefit of hindsight, economists of the Roaring Twenties should have been able to anticipate the costs of this antisocial policy. *Principles of Economics* (1890), the dominant economic textbook of the time, had been in circulation for nearly three decades. In it, Alfred Marshall—one of the founding fathers of neoclassical economics and perhaps the most influential economist of his generation—famously wrote that "each man profits by the ideas of his neighbours: he is stimulated by contact with those who are interested in his own pursuit to make new experiments; and each successful invention, whether it be a new machine, a new process, or a new way of organizing the business, is likely when once started to spread and to be improved upon." Good ideas, Marshall argued, are swiftly absorbed because they are in the "air" where creative people live and work: "if one man starts a new idea, it is taken up by others and combined with suggestions of their own; and thus it becomes the source of further new ideas."[7]

Marshall's writings, of course, focused on the social networks of industrial districts. But drinking establishments performed the same function during the Scientific Enlightenment, which preceded the rise of modern industry, though their importance faded in Europe as coffeehouses sprung up across the continent.[8] Historian Brian Cowan has shown in some detail how this bitter Turkish beverage came with a "culture of curiosity" that accompanied a growing and increasingly interconnected commercial world.[9] In Britain it first took root in academic circles. Oxford, with its vibrant experimental scientific community and unique strength in orientalist scholarship, provided particularly fertile soil for coffee consumption, although London, where a national virtuoso community began investigating this peculiar new beverage, was not far behind.[10] On the other side of the Atlantic, however, neither teahouses nor coffeehouses became as popular. The same role was filled by taverns and saloons.[11]

The importance of social networks for innovation is no mystery. As Montesquieu wrote in his 1748 classic, *The Spirit of the Laws*, "commerce cures destructive prejudices."[12] Contact with other people turns the unfamiliar into the familiar, so that regular trading relationships make the prejudices that come with isolation disappear along the way. Higher trust, in turn, reduces what economists call transaction costs and allows societies to scale up beyond the family or even the nation.[13] Much early learning happens within the family, but over time, parents worldwide have outsourced more of the socialization process to schools, preschools, and other institutions, albeit at different speeds.[14] Google cofounders Sergey Brin and Larry Page, for instance, both had the fortune of having parents working in science and technology. Yet as they grew up on different sides of the Iron Curtain—Brin was born in Moscow, Page in the Midwest—it was Stanford that brought them together in 1996.[15] While vertical learning, by which skills and knowledge are passed down within the family over generations, dominated knowledge-transmission for much of human history, horizontal learning now rules supreme. In one of the most cited studies in sociology, published in 1973, Stanford's Mark Granovetter demonstrated that a network with a plethora of weak ties generates a greater circulation of information and ideas than a network with a few strong ones.[16] From an innovation point of view, this is paramount, because the possibilities for new discoveries expand when populations become more interconnected. In a world where wealth is derived from ideas rather than land and objects, one of our most important resources is our social network, which acts as our "collective brain."[17] And when networked people are free to explore, they test more technological pathways.

As the case of prohibition illustrates, innovation happens in serendipitous ways, which is probably why Irving Fisher and his peers ignored it. They were more concerned that prohibition would reduce what economists call "static efficiency." Benjamin Franklin's dictum that "time is money" captures the essence of the concept. Static efficiency is achieved when machinery and labour are put to optimal use, so that as much as possible is produced at a given point in time. Under this logic, time spent at the local saloon was wasted—even if those barroom conversations sparked ideas that would increase productivity in the future. The AEA roundtable participants simply reasoned that because alcoholism makes factory discipline harder to maintain, such that the hierarchical system of mass production starts to crumble, the economic consequences of failing to act would be dire. Yet the real engine of economic growth, which distinguishes modern societies from their earliest ancestors on the African savannah, is dynamic efficiency—the kind of efficiency that comes with technological progress over time. And this kind of progress necessarily requires a loss of static efficiency. If all everyone did was repetitive assembly, hour after hour, few new ideas would emerge. We have to sacrifice some output today to explore and develop new technologies that allow us to do things better tomorrow.

The Making of mRNA

The remarkable journey that led to the vaccines that rescued humanity from the COVID-19 pandemic is a testament to this point. Although the most efficacious vaccines were produced in a matter of months, the breakthrough technology behind them had been decades in the making. At the heart of this story is Katalin Karikó, a Hungarian biochemist whose pioneering research made the coronavirus vaccines of BioNTech and Moderna possible. Karikó, who joined BioNTech in 2014, had been studying RNA molecules since the 1980s, but her funding dried up in Hungary. Undeterred, she emigrated to the United States and took up a post at Temple University in Philadelphia—a feat that required overcoming a host of obstacles, including strict currency controls, because Hungary remained behind the Iron Curtain. Yet even in the United States, where there were significantly more funding opportunities, she found that harnessing mRNA to fight disease was "too far-fetched for government grants, corporate funding, and even support from her own colleagues."[18]

As a result, Karikó was constantly on the brink of running out of funding. As she later recalled in an interview, "Every night I was working: grant, grant, grant . . . And it came back always no, no, no."[19] After spending six years on the faculty at the University of Pennsylvania, she was denied tenure in 1995. Without any research funding coming in to support her research, her superiors believed mRNA was a dead end. But Karikó remained convinced that mRNA held the key to future therapeutics. It was a stroke of luck that brought her together with Drew Weissman in 1997, who had recently joined the university to work on dendritic cells, which are critical to the body's immune system. They met not while drinking at the saloon, but during an equally serendipitous activity—taking turns on a Xerox machine, which they both used for reading scientific papers. They began talking about their work and, eventually, in Wiessman's words, "decided to try adding her mRNA to my cells."[20]

The early results were not encouraging. They even suggested that it might be impossible to turn RNA molecules into therapeutics, which helps explain why mRNA research remained a scientific backwater for so long. "It was too inflammatory, too difficult to work with," so people probably just gave up, Weissman explains. But Karikó and Weissman did not, and in 2005 a breakthrough came at last. By making chemical modifications to mRNA, they discovered that they could insert it into the dendritic cells without triggering an immune response. This would allow them to trick the cells into thinking that the molecules had been made inside the body instead of the lab, which in theory meant that the technology could be used for therapeutic purposes. In retrospect, this discovery should have turbocharged their careers, but even after the publication of their findings, their funding applications kept being rejected. Part of the challenge was that the technology was still in an experimental phase, and so its applications were still uncertain. A meeting between Karikó and an intellectual property officer at her university is telling in this regard. The officer kept asking, "What's it good for?" without getting a clear answer.[21]

Although the patent was finally granted, the decisive next step was taken in 2008 by another scientist, Derrick Rossi, a researcher at Harvard Medical School who was trying to use mRNA to make stem cells. He had never heard of Karikó and Weissman at the time. Their 2005 research paper had gone largely unnoticed, even in the scientific community. Instead, Rossi was inspired by Shinya Yamanaka, a Japanese scientist, who, like Karikó, would go on to win the Nobel Prize in Medicine.

Yamanaka had demonstrated that it was possible to turn human cells into an embryonic stem cell-like state by inserting four genes. The problem was that the genes he inserted ended up back in the DNA, which increased a person's risk of cancer. Rossi figured that by using mRNA instead, it would be possible to reprogram human skin cells to act as though they were stem cells. But he soon ran into the same problem that had long vexed and perplexed Karikó and Weissman: "The cell was responding as though a virus was coming in, they were killing themselves."[22] Looking for a solution, Rossi stumbled on their 2005 paper, and with some chemical modifications, he made their approach work. To turn his discovery into a medical reality, however, Rossi needed funding, and like Karikó, he benefited from weak ties, as he was introduced to Noubar Afeyan—a venture capitalist who would found a company, Moderna, to commercialize the science behind mRNA.[23]

This path to discovery could not have been choreographed or planned. Suggesting otherwise would be taking "an essentially creationist approach to an essentially evolutionary phenomenon," to use Matt Ridley's phrase.[24] Chance played a big role, just as it did in America's saloons before prohibition. Yet it is also true that what happened thereafter followed a much more predictable pattern. If the chain of events that culminated in Karikó and Weissman's discovery, not to mention Rossi's application of it, would have been impossible to conceive beforehand, the development and rollout of the coronavirus vaccine concerned a much narrower challenge. And because the challenge could be clearly defined, research efforts could be planned accordingly and executed at staggering speed.

On a Friday in late January 2020, Ugur Sahin, the cofounder and CEO of BioNTech, learned that a new coronavirus had been discovered in China. The following Monday, he summoned his board to make an announcement: BioNTech, which had previously focused on the next generation of cancer treatments, would make developing a COVID-19 vaccine its new priority. What he called Project Lightspeed started at

BioNTech's laboratories in Mainz just days after the SARS-CoV-2 genetic sequence was first made public. From that point forward, the task was "to remove all elements of chance" by making innovation a regular process of disciplined attack, as the comedian W. C. Fields once quipped.[25] By late February, twenty vaccine candidates had been identified, of which four were selected for a trial in Germany.[26]

Taking a candidate into production, however, required the capacity to test, develop, produce, and distribute vaccines at mass scale, which neither Moderna nor BioNTech possessed. To overcome this deficit, BioNTech partnered with pharmaceutical giant Pfizer, while Moderna relied on Operation Warp Speed, a government program set up by the Trump administration.[27] If the process of exploration was largely a horizontal activity, exploitation was almost entirely vertical: it required large-scale bureaucracy and managerial hierarchies to succeed.

From Hayek to Weber

The case of mRNA also underlines another critical point about technological progress, which is that every breakthrough begins life facing ubiquitous uncertainty. We simply cannot know if something new will catch on until someone has taken the risk of investing in it. In 1999, for example, the venture capital firms Sequoia Capital and Kleiner Perkins each invested $12.5 million in Google and made a fortune. When Sequoia sold its stake six years later, it was worth over $4 billion and had returned 320 times the initial investment. Yet such numbers simply underscore that Google was not a sure bet in 1999. Other companies like Yahoo! and Altavista dominated the search engine space at the time, and several experienced venture capitalists decided not to invest. When Google's marketing manager, Susan Wojcicki, asked one of Bessemer Venture's partners to meet with Page and Brin, who had rented space in her garage, he allegedly joked, "How can I get out of this house without going anywhere near your garage?"[28]

In the uncertain world of discovery, not even the smartest people can be expected to get things right every time. But Bessemer Venture's failure to see the promise of Google's search engine did not contain its rise. Brin and Page were fortunate to operate in a decentralized economic system where many investors could bet on different technologies. Had Brin's family not left Soviet Russia, chances are he would not be the cofounder of Google, just like Karikó is unlikely to have pioneered mRNA in socialist Hungary. Behind the Iron Curtain, as we will explore in later chapters, inventors needed permission for almost anything, and if they were turned down by the state bureaucracy, they had few alternative options. So, fewer bets were naturally made. This helps explain why *none* of the great *commercial* inventions of the twentieth century were made in planned economies.[29] Decentralized systems allow for thousands of barren trials so that one might eventually succeed; centrally planned ones do not. As Friedrich von Hayek put it, the dispersed nature of what people know cannot be overcome "by first communicating all this knowledge to a central board which, after integrating all knowledge, issues its orders." It must be solved by "some form of decentralization."[30]

Hayek, of course, was writing at end of World War II, when bureaucratic planning had reached new commanding heights, even in the West. But his insights remain as relevant today. As then, there are many instances where experts are better placed to make decisions about what must be done, pandemics and the climate crisis being two prominent examples. Yet in other cases, where no real consensus has been formed, the decision to rely on expert opinion merely shifts the problem to selecting the experts. And when a field or a discovery is new, this is a particularly difficult task. Karikó and Weissman's seminal paper was long unknown, not only to the outside world but even within the scientific community. In fact, their tenacity depended on ignoring the expert naysayers. To make mRNa work, in Hayek's words, they had to go through a "voyage of exploration into the unknown."[31] And because exploration requires sacrificing time and resources today in hopes of greater gains tomorrow, government planners and corporate managers alike struggle to oversee and motivate inventors who hold deeper expertise than anyone else. So it is not surprising that, as MIT's Daron Acemoglu and collaborators have shown, companies operating at the cutting edge choose to decentralize decision making.[32] When dealing with radically new technologies, whose benefits and applications are uncertain, bureaucratic planning almost always fails.

Hayek's teacher, Ludwig von Mises, surely agreed. Writing in 1944, von Mises opened his book *Bureaucracy* with the following line: "Nobody doubts that bureaucracy is thoroughly bad and that it should not exist in a perfect world."[33] If this was true, the world he observed around him certainly did not change for the better. Even when the war ended, bureaucratic management persisted, not only through state control of strategic industries but in the private sector as well. A paradox of the postwar era is that it symbolizes the historic confluence of oppressive factory work, cascading productivity, and shared prosperity in the West, as well as oppressive political regimes and rapid growth in the centrally planned economies of the East. This age of planning produced America's *Golden Age*, Germany's *Wirtschaftswunder*, Italy's *il miracolo economico*, France's *Les Trente Glorieuses*, Spain's *el milagro*, not to mention Japan's and Korea's great leaps, or indeed that of the Soviet Union. Around the world, "the visible hand of management replaced what Adam Smith referred to as the invisible hand of market forces," to borrow Alfred Chandler Jr.'s memorable phrase.[34]

Of course, even Smith's pin factory, depicted in *The Wealth of Nations* (1776), had a visible hand of its own. In it, pin-making was divided into many small sequential steps, allowing workers to specialize more narrowly and so boost productivity. But everything was done inhouse, not through the invisible hand of the market. In a pure market system, there would be no managers overseeing production. Each step would be handled by individuals buying and selling to one another based on changing prices. For instance, in pin production, the wire-drawer would auction off the wire to a buyer, who would then take it to be cut, and later sell the cut pieces to a specialist in sharpening. At each stage, new bids, payments, and transport would be involved—just to move from one part of pin-making to the next.[35] Of course, no factory in the world is organized this way and for good reason: any gains from the division of labour would be swamped by endless rounds of haggling, transporting, and quality checks. That, as Ronald Coase explained in "The Nature of the Firm" (1937), is why companies and hierarchies exist. They let people cooperate under ongoing contracts rather than one-off transactions, and they permit the use of new technologies, like factories, on a massive scale.[36]

To some students of history, this example might seem like a familiar tale. Indeed, one of the hidden truths about the capitalist enterprise is that its internal organization bears a striking resemblance to the crude material balance calculations used by Soviet planners. Inside the firm, there are no market prices to signal where time and resources are best allocated. Instead, individuals are given objectives that they strive to fulfill in exchange for a fixed salary, job security, and the prospect of career advancement. Employees engage in trading favours and disfavours to climb the ranks of the bureaucracy, while superiors use social engineering tactics, exert pressure, and shape incentives, much like an authoritarian state, though workers in a market system generally have many more outside options, and so they can leave at will.[37] Moreover, one of the market economy's great strengths, as Coase emphasized, is the ability of firms to choose between a bureaucratic command-and-control system and a system based on horizontal transactions. Under the Soviet planning system, there was no such choice. And in a decentralized system, firms are ultimately subject to market discipline, with those that incur losses shrinking or vanishing—a fate not shared by state-run bureaucracies that are permitted to operate at a loss. Yet it is also true that governments at times operate under intense geopolitical competition, which has its own disciplining effect. The Soviet Union, for instance, effectively exploited many technologies made in the West, and even made some strides of its own, while competing with America for global hegemony.

As our examination of the historical record in subsequent chapters will show, in the end, innovation is not only about ideation but also about converting these ideas into practical and reliable products that are available and affordable to the masses. And when efforts shift from exploration to exploitation, vertical lines of command trump horizontal lines of exchange. During the late nineteenth century, for example, independent inventors were the primary explorers of new technologies, and they relied on licensing their discoveries to the major corporations of the day, such as General Electric, DuPont, and AT&T, who turned these patents into marketable products.[38] As these technologies matured, competition shifted from innovation to price, spurring centralization and consolidation, transforming what Hayek called a "market economy" consisting of individual actors and small firms into an economy of command-and-control organization in large companies connected by market exchange.

The simple insight, that centralization and consolidation naturally follow periods of decentralization, has profound implications for economic development. It means that the economic organization that excels at inventing the industrial future is not necessarily the most suitable for catching up to an existing target. In fact, backwardness creates opportunities for latecomers to leapfrog exploration and imitate innovators' successes, since they can use centralizing institutions from the onset.[39] Latecomers, in other words, can take different paths to prosperity. The Crown of England did not gather a group including barons, bishops, bankers, and tinkerers to create the modern world, but after Britain had spearheaded the Industrial Revolution, that is effectively what Japan did with the Meiji Restoration.

To see how this transition from exploration to exploitation favours fundamentally different forms of organization, consider the postwar period, which, as noted, was a time when capitalism around the world bureaucratized. Many of the technologies underpinning global growth were made in America before the war and invented through decentralized exploration. Few breakthroughs have transformed the world more than the automobile, and no place had a more remarkable impact on its ascent than Detroit, Michigan. In the early twentieth century, the dynamism of the Motor City was strikingly similar to that of Silicon Valley in the age of computers. In both places, job hopping was the norm, which allowed ideas to spread like fire from one firm to another. Many inventors and engineers who left incumbents did so to set up their own shops.[40] Yet if one obscure start-up deserves to be singled out, it would surely be the company of Henry Ford, which managed to survive the early shakeout and went on to build some of the wonders of the world. When the Highland Park factory, with its moving assembly line, opened on Manchester Street in 1910, the *New York Times* marvelled, "it offers a striking illustration of the solidity of this pioneering company and the methods it adopts for the care of its customers."[41] Indeed, Highland Park soon produced the Model T at a sufficiently low price for it to become the people's vehicle.[42]

Testifying to American technological leadership, as well as to the transition from exploration to exploitation, was the remarkable stream of visits from foreign delegations to Ford's new factories. In the 1930s, countless Italian, German, Russian, and Japanese delegations spent weeks, months, and sometimes years at Ford's new and vertically integrated River Rouge factory. In June 1937, Ferdinand Porsche led his own group of Volkswagen engineers to Detroit on a state-sponsored mission as the protégé designer of Adolf Hitler, whose ambition was to produce a German "people's car." Rather than searching for new ideas, Porsche was on the hunt for machinery and skilled technicians for his own factory, which was already in the planning stage. Around the same time, the Italian carmaker Fiat led another delegation, including Vittorio Bonadè Bottino, a leading architect in Fascist Italy, tasked by Benito Mussolini with designing the enormous Mirafiori factory at the outskirts of Turin. There were also convoys of Soviet bureaucrats, who through an extensive technology transfer agreement created Russia's own "River Rouge" with the opening of the Gorky Automobile Factory (Gaz) in 1932.[43] As H. J. Freyn, a prominent consultant who had spent an extensive period in the Soviet Union advising on industrial development, astutely put it during a Taylor Society gathering in 1931: "a modern business enterprise can scarcely be operated or managed by applying the principles of democracy."[44] Fascists on the right and communists on the left heralded a new century of central authority and planning.

For theorists of the interwar period, like Karl Polanyi, there was a sense of a momentous institutional reversal as laissez-faire imploded and gave way to a new age of competitive technological upgrading orchestrated by activist governments. Mussolini, who started out as the editor of an Italian socialist newspaper *Avanti!*, only to become the first leader of the fascist world, was at least consistent in his views on decentralization. "The Doctrine of Fascism," an essay he published in 1932, is emblematic for its attacks on liberalism, individualism, and democracy as "outgrown ideologies of the nineteenth century."[45] Yet a closer look at the nineteenth century reveals a similar pattern of development. While England had clearly been moving closer to laissez-faire, latecomers also leveraged the advantages of backwardness by adopting technologies invented in Britain, as Alexander Gerschenkron famously observed.[46] And they relied heavily on the symbiotic relationship between big business and the state to do so.[47]

Take Prussia, where Karl vom und zum Stein, Karl August von Hardenberg, and their successors prompted a revolution from above and used a variety of means to drive industrial catch-up. They handed over government-purchased technologies to private companies and created institutions to mobilize scarce resources, "all in order to pressure Prussian industry to modernize its production method."[48] Similarly, after Bismarck's unification, Germany—justly regarded as a liberal autocracy—did much to spur the growth of big business, which was capable of absorbing and exploiting new technologies at greater pace and scale than their British competitors. Max Weber, writing in the wake of these developments, unsurprisingly emphasized both the role of bureaucracy and capitalism in western civilization. The well-defined hierarchical structures of bureaucracy, he noted, "are capable of attaining the highest degree of efficiency and is in this sense formally the most rational known means of exercising authority over human beings."[49]

Yet despite Weber's admiration for the superior efficiency of bureaucracy, he also feared that its spread could stifle the dynamism of capitalism and thwart innovation over the long run. And in this he was right. While much of the productivity growth over the centuries can be attributed to incremental product and process improvements by large, established organizations, these alone are insufficient.[50] Breakthrough innovations are the foundation upon which such incremental advancements are built.[51] One can improve a horse carriage in terms of design and functionality, but eventually one needs a radical innovation to create a motorcar or progress will stall. And tellingly, none of the leading makers of either bicycles or horse carriages became leading producers of automobiles. Great leaps in technology usually come from challengers, as is evident from the endless churn among the companies that make up the S&P 500.[52]

In recent times, this phenomenon has played out in various industries, from the development of highly effective COVID-19 vaccines by startups, to the rise of e-commerce championed by an outsider like Amazon, to the transformation of the media landscape by the likes of X (formerly, Twitter), Meta, and YouTube. Even in capital-intensive industries such as space and electric vehicles, established players such as Boeing, Lockheed Martin, GM, and Volkswagen have been outpaced by challengers like Elon Musk's SpaceX and Tesla. The same appears true at the forefront of artificial intelligence, where startups like OpenAI and Anthropic are now challenging Meta and Google. In theory, large companies have the financial strength to make bigger and riskier bets. But in reality, they tend to play it safe.[53] As Chicago's Ufuk Akcigit and Harvard's William Kerr have shown in a detailed study of patented inventions, challengers have a competitive advantage in spawning major technological breakthroughs.[54] Today's tech giants may still innovate, but their growth comes at a cost. As they absorb more of the world's top talent, those they hire become less inventive than they previously were at startups.[55]

Weber understood why. Bureaucracy thrives on stability, not risk.[56] As technologies mature and processes become standardized, managers gain greater control over production and efficiency. But when a field is still evolving and experimentation is key, measuring performance becomes much harder. In these uncertain conditions, strict oversight can backfire—surveillance discourages collaboration, keeping workers focused on narrow, well-defined tasks instead of exploring new ideas.[57] Centralized bureaucracies that operate on clear rules and predictable workflows therefore struggle when conditions change. Projects requiring multiple layers of approval or broad internal consensus rarely push boundaries. True innovation often requires breaking rules, not following them, as recent research has borne out. When Lingfei Wu and colleagues analysed some 65 million scientific papers, patents, and software projects from the postwar years to the internet era, they found that solo inventors and decentralized teams consistently generated more disruptive ideas and technologies, whereas larger and hierarchical ones focused on developing existing ones. Like large movie studios, they produced sequels instead of new narratives.[58]

Challengers tend to prevail for another strategic reason. Incumbents are often reluctant to pursue new breakthroughs for fear of putting existing revenues from older technologies at risk. Kodak is a classic example. Although they moved into research on computers in the 1960s and developed a digital camera in 1975, the product was dropped. Executives feared cannibalizing the company's main source of income: its photographic film business. As a result, in January 2012, after a long period of struggle, Kodak filed for Chapter 11 bankruptcy. To protect revenues in the short run, management ended up sacrificing the company in the long run. Even the great inventor Thomas Edison was implacably hostile to the alternating current (AC) systems that George Westinghouse was developing because they challenged the direct current (DC) system of his own General Electric (GE). And when an industry is dominated by a few behemoths, like GE, there is a real risk that conservatism inside one company ends up reducing the pace of innovation in the economy as a whole.[59]

To be sure, Edison's concern was not just that GE faced a lower return on investment relative to outsiders with no rents to cannibalize.[60] It was also a matter of pride and recognition. It is therefore perhaps unsurprising that young inventors, who are less intellectually invested in the status quo, are typically more creative.[61] Even in science, where the profit motive is less prevalent, established scholars act as guardians of the existing order. Recent research shows that it often takes the passing of a star for outsiders to challenge the leadership in a field and so advance the frontiers of our knowledge. Max Planck was on to something when he suggested that science progresses one funeral at a time.[62] Over the long run, progress entails creative destruction in both science and technology.[63]

The Road to Stagnation

A longstanding debate in the field of economics has revolved around the existence of hierarchies. While neoclassical economists such as Roland Coase and Oliver Williamson have argued that corporations help achieve economies of scale and drive down costs, thus increasing the accessibility of goods to the populace, neo-Marxians like Stephen Hymer and Stephen Marglin have suggested that hierarchies emerge as a means of power and resource monopolization at the expense of society. According to the latter group, the growth of corporations has resulted in a loss of human welfare.[64] They echo the words of historian Eric Hobsbawm: "It is often assumed that an economy of private enterprise has an automatic bias towards innovation, but this is not so. It has a bias only towards profit."[65]

Yet these views are not mutually exclusive. In fact, they are both essential if we want to understand the rise and fall of growth. Early in the technology lifecycle, exploration thrives in a decentralized environment. Startups, independent inventors, and small teams experiment, iterate, and push the boundaries of what's possible. But once a prototype proves viable, the focus shifts. The next challenge is scaling production, cutting costs, and increasing efficiency—and this is where centralization and corporate consolidation take over. At first, this comes with tangible benefits to society. As the eminent Joseph Schumpeter pointed out, the capitalist achievement did not consist of providing "more silk stockings for queens but in bringing them within the reach of factory girls in return for steadily decreasing amounts of effort."[66] Beyond driving down consumer prices, consolidation streamlines research and development, reducing wasteful duplication across competing firms. Indeed, as a vaccine's efficacy nears 100 percent, further investment in incremental improvements yields diminishing—or even negative—returns, diverting finite resources away from other critical areas. At this point, the easy gains are gone, and the focus shifts once more from perfecting production to protection. When this happens, big companies stop innovating and start lobbying. Instead of investing in productive pursuits, they resort to anti-competitive tactics and pressure the government for regulation that shields them from competition.[67] One does not need to be a cynic to think that it is no coincidence that politically connected companies take out fewer patents.[68]

Economist Mancur Olson made perhaps the clearest argument about how vested interests can strangle progress. His conclusion was short but sour: when interest groups entrench themselves across industries, stagnation follows.[69] A recurring theme of this book is that decentralization is necessary for further progress as a country approaches the technological frontier, but this is rarely in the interest of incumbents who dislike competition and favour the status quo. Stagnation happens when institutions fail to adapt to new technological realities or create the space to explore new avenues of progress, generally because incumbents seek to prevent competition from outsiders. In fact, the capacity for institutional change in the wake of new technological realities can go far in explaining why America has been the technology leader for over a century.

However, latecomers do not need to reinvent the wheel. They can skip the costly trial-and-error phase by adopting technologies developed elsewhere, often with state intervention accelerating the process. Indeed, what is entirely absent from Olson's account is precisely the role of the state. Yet, constant revolution from above took the Soviet Union—where Stalin's terror made sure that no interest groups could organize safely—some way toward the technological frontier under intense pressure from geopolitical competition.[70] Just as special interests can lobby governments to thwart competition in the private sector, states can check the clout of private enterprise, a policy Xi Jinping has vigorously pursued since surging to power in 2012. The challenge for powerful autocrats is a different one. To stay in power they must invest heavily in surveillance technologies that allow them to control the private sector and society to prevent mobilization against the regime. This might, under specific circumstances, give the economy a boost in the short run, as some Sputniks are delivered, but it also risks undermining its dynamism over the long run.

Plan of the Book

To see these forces at play, our journey through time and space begins in ancient China, which created the world's first state bureaucracy. Chapter 2 shows how the state itself acted as a catalyst for progress but with a specific purpose: to collect taxes and wage war. The state's investments in technologies to make production easier to monitor and tax cemented its power, but it also suppressed the kind of grassroots innovation upon which sustained progress depends. In stark contrast, the early absence of surveillance technologies in Europe made bureaucratic governance unattainable. Therefore, as will be explored in chapter 3, when the Roman Empire collapsed, it disintegrated into hundreds of competing territories. This left Europe politically fragmented and economically decentralized but with a common belief structure derived from Christendom wiring its collective brain.[71] So whereas in China, one hegemonic state managed to centralize control, which limited the technological options that were explored, decentralized competition in Europe meant that the authorities failed to suppress heterodox ideas, as inventors and intellectuals were able to move around and exploit political and cultural divisions.[72] Indeed, as the Qing dynasty clamped down on intellectuals and launched the literary inquisition, Europe experienced a period of scientific enlightenment that reached its apex with the rise of modern industry.

The Industrial Revolution, of course, did not just happen anywhere in Europe. It first took off in Britain, where engineers like John Smeaton, James Watt, and Marc Isambard Brunel turned ideas into viable blueprints, prototypes, and products. This process only began later elsewhere in Europe, in large part because the craft guilds, who found their political clout and incomes threatened by the rise of the factory system, put up considerable resistance. But in England, where markets were early to integrate, much thanks to acts of Parliament, decentralized competition between cities undercut local guilds and their capacity to halt the forces of creative destruction. The success of the Industrial Revolution in England hinged not only on secure private property rights; such rights were equally secure in the Dutch Republic, often hailed as the first modern economy. What truly set England apart was the capacity of Westminster to bypass interest groups that stood to lose from industrialization.

On the Continent, the path to modernity required less exploration and was thus more predictable. These industrial latecomers could grow by importing technologies from across the English Channel and leveraging centralizing institutional arrangements to scale up production swiftly. Chapter 4 shows how Prussia, having invested heavily in the capacity of the state, did precisely this. Besides overriding the blocking power of crafts guilds and underwriting a decentralized system of private property rights, like in Britain, the Prussian bureaucracy actively expedited the rise of big business. The kind of "organized capitalism" that emerged in Imperial Germany encouraged the growth of mammoth enterprise on a scale that British laissez-faire was unable to match. Even in Tsarist Russia, a personal autocracy with backward market institutions, state power was able to achieve some noteworthy growth. But relative to the Wilhelmine Empire, and even Meiji Japan, which unlike Russia had embraced meritocratic recruitment into the civil service, progress under Tsarism was less impressive (chapter 5). Catch-up growth is not automatic, and when the private sector is lagging, it heavily depends on the bureaucratic capacity of the state to implement its policies as well as its willingness to direct this capacity toward productive ends. Yet where a society successfully catches up to its peers, when it approaches the technological frontier, this model runs into diminishing returns and eventually serious trouble.

In chapter 6, we turn to the United States, which was the only nation to overtake Britain before the Great War. Unlike European latecomers, America embraced weak rather than strong government, which served as an institutional foundation for broad-based exploration. In addition to permitting tariff-free trade across a decentralized federal system, America also embraced a patent system in which the fee to obtain a patent was a few percent of the amount charged in Britain, making intellectual property rights available to a large swathe of the populace. By the mid-nineteenth century, America had developed a market for technology unmatched anywhere in the world and quickly became a hub for European talent. In the absence of a strong state, the primary challenge the country faced was exploiting emerging technological opportunities. This deficit, however, was frequently solved through public–private partnerships, which by giving birth to giant corporations effectively substituted for the incapacity of the federal government. However, to check the growing power of mammoth enterprise and safeguard competition, America needed, and eventually succeeded in bolstering the capacity of the state. This regulated yet decentralized system allowed the United States to break out of what Mark Twain and Charles Dudley called the Gilded Age.

Chapters 7, 8, and 9 provide a whirlwind tour of progress from World War II to the Yom Kippur War. This journey shows how rapid growth in the postwar years centred on technological opportunities created before global conflict broke out, most notably in America, where independent inventors had been the drivers of progress. It was their deeds that culminated in the Second Industrial Revolution, including electricity and the internal combustion engine. The war itself (discussed in chapter 7) dampened innovation and shifted its aim from productive to destructive applications. Yet it also bolstered the capacity of governments and large corporations to capitalize on existing technologies at scale. Chapter 8 shifts the focus from America to Japan and Western Europe, whose institutions were already set up for technological catch-up. Once global trade resumed, these lagging economies gained access to American technology and swiftly narrowed the gap. Under these circumstances (covered in chapter 9), even centrally planned economies behind the Iron Curtain made considerable strides. Whether through state planning, public holding companies, or conglomerates, bureaucratic management characterized this era, enabling latecomers around the world to exploit America's stockpile of technology—though the extent of their success varied.

Chapter 10 shows how fortunes shifted as the returns from the Second Industrial Revolution petered out. With smokestack industries crumbling, organized capitalism disintegrated as well. The centralizing institutions that persisted in Western Europe, Japan, and other latecomers had been a good fit for catch-up, but the technological uncertainty brought by the looming computer age demanded decentralization. In France, planning worked well in the age of mass production, but in the brave new world of technological turbulence, bureaucrats faced a harder task. Meanwhile, in the European South, where state holding companies reigned, the computer age brought little but two lost decades. And with the system they had built under fire, bureaucrats became more prone to capture by vested interests and more likely to prop up dying industries. Yet nowhere was the earthquake more noticeable than in the USSR. As long as quantity was the measure of success, government bureaucrats could easily monitor performance, and the Soviet system performed tolerably well. However, without the space for decentralized exploration, it soon ran into problems. A comparison with China is particularly revealing. Despite being authoritarian, China remained regionally decentralized, permitting it to better navigate the computer age than its older Soviet comrade.

Chapter 11 turns to the question of why the Computer Revolution ended up being an American affair. Indeed, in the 1980s, it was widely believed that Japan was at the cusp of overtaking the United States. The reason the computer was born in America rhymes well with the story of how the Industrial Revolution was born in Europe. The federal system was not only a laboratory for democracy but also for technological change, because it allowed inventors to seamlessly move from one state to another, and this created space for exploration. While Boston and Detroit—once at the forefront of the Second Industrial Revolution—were dominated by hierarchically run incumbents, the computer age was made in Silicon Valley where institutions supported decentralization and exploration. The Computer Revolution was powered by new companies, and America's commitment to entry helps explain why the United States ended up leading the way. For instance, IBM's decision to unbundle software after an antitrust suit created space for new firms like Microsoft to enter the market. While Japan's powerful conglomerates clung to hardware, missing the rise of software, American firms took the opposite path—shifting toward open systems that connected industries across borders, ultimately driving a new era of economic integration with China.

Although Chimerica was the key beneficiary of the computer age, chapter 12 argues that continued progress cannot be taken for granted in either country. In China, Xi Jinping appears to be establishing a nested dictatorship of loyalists, and over time a bureaucracy rooted in loyalty rather than competence diminishes the state's ability to drive progress. Furthermore, Xi's strategy of rule and divide might secure his power, but it is also undercutting the regional decentralization that has been the engine for Chinese growth since the 1980s. This increasingly hierarchical system inevitably means that more decisions are being made at the top, exacerbating Hayek's knowledge problem as the Middle Kingdom approaches the technological frontier. Just as dynastic China invested heavily in surveillance technologies, making the economy and society easier to manage and control while cementing autocracy in the process, China today is using AI with the same effect, which is likely to have similarly stagnating results. Meanwhile, America's economic strength has long depended on new companies upending old ones. Yet incumbents have recently lobbied to suppress competition. Despite their differences, both superpowers share a troubling trend: faltering productivity over the past decade.

Chapter 13 concludes by offering a reminder that progress is fragile in autocracies and liberal democracies alike, while the Epilogue provides a brief look forward to where we are headed in the age of AI.

2

China's Reversal of Fortune

[M]ost societies that have been technologically creative have been so for relatively short periods.... It is as if technological creativity was like a torch too hot to hold for long; each individual society carried it for a short time.[1]

—JOEL MOKYR

IN 1792, Lord George Macartney—a distinguished public servant who had previously served as envoy-extraordinary to the court of Catherine the Great in St. Petersburg—led a large British delegation to Beijing. His mission was to establish reciprocal embassies in Beijing and London and ensure wider British access to commercial ports along the Chinese coast. At the time, European traders only had one point of access to the market of the Middle Kingdom: the port of Canton. This restriction on entry was part of a long list of regulations that Chinese authorities had devised to keep foreigners—or "West Sea barbarians," as Chinese officials called them—at bay. Not only was it unlawful to teach barbarians from Europe the Chinese language, it was also illegal to sell them many books about China or to communicate with them except through specially licensed local merchants.[2]

In hopes of convincing China to relax these long-standing restrictions and open their markets for trade, Macartney did his best to showcase Britain's scientific and industrial prowess, bringing with him an array of manufactured goods, artillery pieces, and even a hot-air balloon. However, his Chinese hosts were little moved by these efforts and, after bestowing gifts upon him and his entourage, suggested it was time for him to depart.[3] When Macartney protested that they had not even entered negotiations and reiterated the wish of King George to establish diplomatic relations, he was summoned to the Forbidden City in full ceremonial dress, where he received the answer to his petition. The emperor rejected every substantive request and singled out the proposal of having a Chinese ambassador residing in London as particularly absurd: "[S]upposing I sent an Ambassador to reside in your country, how could you possibly make for him the requisite arrangements? Europe consists of many other nations besides your own: if each and all demanded to be represented at our Court, how could we possibly consent?" As for Macartney's proposals of forging closer trading relations, the edict noted that the Celestial Court had already allowed Britain "full liberty to trade at Canton for many a year," and that anything more would be "utterly unreasonable." The emperor also dismissed the supposed benefits of trade to China: "[S]trange and costly objects do not interest me. . . . As your Ambassador can see for himself, we possess all things."[4]

It was a humiliation for British diplomacy, but it was the last time Britain would accept such a dismissal. Historian Alain Peyrefitte sums up the British sentiment after Macartney's failed mission: "If China remained closed, then the doors would have to be battered down."[5] During the Opium War of 1839–1842, the "cannons once dismissed by Macartney's mandarin handlers operated with brutal effect."[6] What happened thereafter we know all too well. The Qing government was forced to accept the Treaty of Nanking (1842), which ceded Hong Kong to the British Crown, and required China to accept free trade through a system of "treaty ports." Two decades later, following the Taiping Rebellion (1850–1864) and the deaths of more than 20 million people, one European power after another forced China to sign similar treaties and to allow opium to enter the country. At the dawn of the Great War, there were no fewer than eighty treaty ports operating as a result of what would later be known in China as the "unequal treaties," signed under the threat of military action.[7]

The unequal treaties are often interpreted as a reflection of the West's industrial supremacy. Less often noted, however, is just how surprising this asymmetry looks from the long sweep of history. Of all the pre-industrial civilizations, none appeared more technologically advanced than China.[8] In the eleventh century, the wonders of Chinese technology were perhaps most visible in the city of Kaifeng, located along the Yellow River's southern bank in Henan Province.[9] The city clock, standing thirteen meters tall and designed by the polymathic scientist and statesman Su Song, did not just show the time but also contained a variety of astronomical measures. It was, moreover, powered by water and used an advanced escapement mechanism that was unheard of in Europe at the time.[10]

This was the golden age of the Song dynasty (960–1279 A.D.), when industries as diverse as shipbuilding, iron, paper, and printing flourished; the invention of true porcelain reinvigorated the ceramics industry; and key technologies like the compass were introduced—about a century before it surfaced in Europe.[11] This era also witnessed the invention of movable type printing, which would take Johannes Gutenberg four more centuries to introduce to Europe. But even before the Song dynasty, China was well ahead of Europe. They were, for instance, casting iron in 200 B.C., a technology that only arrived in Europe around 1400. These technologies, Francis Bacon later remarked, "changed the face and state of things throughout the world," first in literature, and then in warfare and navigation.[12] Indeed, as the late Joseph Needham's magisterial survey of *Science and Civilization in China* makes clear, for most of recorded history, China led the way in technology.

This early technological advantage was intimately related to China's highly centralized economic and political system. Many Chinese discoveries were made to meet the demand of the state or were developed under its control. As Daron Acemoglu and James Robinson astutely observe, "The famous water clocks were built by and for government officials. Agricultural innovations and irrigation were state projects, and so were the advances in metallurgy."[13] These efforts did not bring about an Industrial Revolution, yet they were sufficient to support the doubling of the population of Song China and to improve material standards to such an extent that by around 1090, China was the most prosperous place on the planet, well ahead of England.

How, then, did China fall behind its European rivals? To understand this shift in fortunes, we need to track the rise and fall of the Chinese state.

Genesis of Bureaucracy

The origin of China's bureaucracy dates all the way back to the Western Zhou dynasty (1047–772 B.C.).[14] At the time, many civil service jobs were still assigned on a hereditary basis, but over time, fierce military competition favoured selection on aptitude over privilege.[15] And to describe the competition as fierce would be something of an understatement: During the subsequent 294-year Spring and Autumn period (771–475 B.C.), when Chinese states fought more than 1,211 wars, there were only 38 years of peace. Although the subsequent Warring States era (475–221 B.C.) saw fewer wars, it was only because some 110 political units had been extinguished.[16] During this age of political fragmentation, with local leaders vying for talent, Chinese creativity and innovation blossomed.[17] This period included, for instance, writers as diverse as Confucius, Mozi, Mencius, and Sun Tzu. By the end of this era, however, the existing sixteen states had been reduced to seven, and these seven states would ultimately consolidate under the Qin dynasty—putting China firmly on a state-led path of progress.[18] As the renowned historian of China, Richard von Glahn, explains:

> By the late Warring States period, two distinctive patterns of economic development had emerged. In the thickly settled heartland of the North China Plain, central government authority weakened after the division of Jin into the three separate states of Wei, Hann, and Zhao in 453 BCE. In this region local cities and their merchant and artisan classes enjoyed considerable autonomy from their royal overlords. Private entrepreneurship stimulated industrial and commercial expansion. In the peripheral states of Qin, Chu, Qi, and Yan, by contrast, autocratic rulers established the bureaucratic institutions to

control economic resources that became the hallmarks of the fiscal state. In these states industrial production was concentrated in state-managed workshops and officials exercised much tighter control over trade. The latter pattern of strong state control of the economy would prevail after the formation of a unified empire under the Qin in 221 BCE.[19]

The rise of the Qin dynasty can be attributed in no small part to the state-building efforts of one of its senior ministers, Shang Yang. Born amid the Warring States era, Shang recognized that the absence of consolidated power came with turmoil and sought to create a comprehensive system of territorial control subordinated to a central government. Almost two millennia before Hobbes wrote *Leviathan*, Shang noted that "the greatest benefit to the people is order." And order, he reckoned, could only be achieved when the state is strong and the people are weak.[20] To deliver on this insight, he established a professional civil service with promotion based on merit, undercutting the privileges of the old aristocratic elite, and further diffused aristocratic power by mandating that all sons inherit their father's estate in equal proportions. Shang also recognized that kinship networks reduced people's reliance on the government. Through a new doctrine—later to be known as *Legalism*—he and other Qin state builders deployed various tactics to tie individuals directly to the state, and in doing so, they challenged the Confucian ideal of the joint family.[21] A prime example was the introduction of a poll tax mandating that households with multiple sons pay double tax or live separately when the sons came of age.[22]

In their quest to steer the economy, the Qin bureaucrats took a range of measures, both relying on and enhancing the capacity of the state. They standardized Chinese written script, introduced unified coinage, imposed a uniform system of weights and measurements, and constructed an extensive network of roads emanating from the capital, Xianyang. Through numerous expansive irrigation initiatives, such as the Zhengguo Canal in Henan that provided water for over 180,000 hectares, the Qin ensured a consistent flow of water and made agricultural production more dependable, thereby facilitating easier supervision and taxation by external authorities. They also set up a population register, which recorded people's residence and provided the emperor with vital information about the taxable resources of his subjects, in addition to their land and dwelling needs.[23]

The register also enabled the government to better enforce the Qin legal code, which made unauthorized relocation an offense punishable by convict labour servitude. Social stability, elites believed, required geographical and occupational immobility, even if it held back the growth of the private sector by thwarting the circulation of knowledge and ideas. Indeed, not unlike in the era of Chairman Mao, artisans were assigned to workshops by the government, and merchants were restricted to trading only in designated marketplaces under the watchful eye of state officials.[24] Under this system, most productive assets, including foundries, workshops, mines, and forests, were controlled by the state. For instance, the treatise on statecraft commonly attributed to Lü Buwei catalogues twenty departments deemed necessary for the functioning of government that are devoted to everything from calendrical sciences and prognostication to responsibilities over slaves, maps, chariots, oxen, palaces, and wine.[25] By the time of the Han dynasty in 200 B.C., this powerful imperial bureaucracy comprised 130,285 individuals. Adjusted for population, this implies one bureaucrat for every 440 citizens—an impressive number by any premodern standard.[26]

Yet, as has often been remarked, while China was the first civilization to create a modern state, it created one that was unconstrained by a rule of law or democratic accountability. No councils or assemblies existed to limit its power—a legacy that has shaped Chinese civilization to the present day. Virtually all invaders who conquered part of China— whether the Manchus, Mongols, or Tanguts—at first sought to keep their own traditions and institutions, but they soon found that administrating this vast territory was eased by top-down bureaucratic governance.[27] Zhou-style feudalism, in which a family or clan established a local power base outside the control of the central government, recurred from time to time, but early centralization always eventually succeeded in perpetuating itself. Just like the Han dynasty picked up where Qin left off, the founders of the Sui and Tang dynasties (618–907 A.D.) saw the Han state as their political blueprint.[28]

Why did this process of strong centralization manifest itself in China but not in Europe? The European experience is discussed in chapter 3, but one reason that centralization occurred in China is that once the Chinese state was in place, rulers faced few constraints on using it to cement their power. Historian Ray Huang points out: "None of the deterrents to unlimited exercise of imperial power—including Confucian morality, reverence for the standards set up by imperial ancestors, public opinion, or the influence of senior statesmen—had the effect of law. If the emperor chose to defy all these and was determined to exercise his absolute power to the full, there was no way of checking him."[29] This pattern of unchecked authority has been traced back to a stunning astronomical event in the year 1059 B.C., which established the notion that the legitimacy of Chinese emperors derives from a "Mandate of Heaven."[30] As internal court documents demonstrate, top officials consistently used this idea as a way of instilling a simple idea: anger the people and you risk losing power. This created a sense of moral accountability, but it did not involve rulers asking people what they wanted.

Although this belief surely served to solidify autocracy, it does not explain how Chinese rulers built a functioning bureaucracy in the first place. And, as we shall see, the simple fact that Chinese emperors developed and sustained bureaucratic autocracy over millennia, while their European counterparts did not, can go some way to explaining why the Industrial Revolution first happened in Europe. The fundamental factors behind these different patterns of political development are therefore well worth investigating.

State of Surveillance

One popular explanation for China's developmental path, put forward by Karl Wittfogel in *Oriental Despotism*, is that societies relying on irrigation and flood control must centralize decision-making to coordinate agricultural production, and that these early institutions lay down the foundations for autocracy.[31] However, this theory faces several significant difficulties. As the Nobel laureate Elinor Ostrom subsequently observed, many societies achieved irrigation and flood control in a decentralized manner.[32] In fact, Chinese bureaucracy first emerged in the north, which depended on rain-fed agriculture rather than irrigation. In the south, where irrigation was more widespread, bureaucratic control only became established in the era of the Qin and the Han, when Chinese autocracy was already a millennium old. Furthermore, although centralized flood control was critical in the Loess plain of the north, as the Yellow River often changed course, centralized flood control was only implemented after autocracy ruled.[33]

A more convincing theory, advanced by NYU's David Stasavage, centres on the development of high-yield agriculture—that is, the adoption of sophisticated farming methods to optimize crop yield. In the Loess plateau, the cradle of early Chinese dynasties, vast expanses of fertile land were highly concentrated, whereas in Europe soil deposits were much smaller and plots geographically dispersed.[34] The discovery of technologies to support farming at scale thus paid more handsomely in China than in Europe, much to the detriment of democracy in the former. Just as Soviet planners would later embrace the system of mass production, which simplified managerial oversight by providing standardization and clear performance benchmarks, in ancient China agricultural output suddenly became easier for outside bureaucrats to monitor and tax due to the routinization of farming techniques. This turn of events set China on a trajectory of state-driven advancement as rulers developed a bureaucracy capable of raising revenue, which, in a self-reinforcing cycle, they then used to support innovations that further cemented their power.[35]

Consider, for example, the effect of technologies for understanding the soil that were pioneered by the Far and Middle East. In China, the *Tribute of Yu*, or *Yu Gong*, narrates the tale of Yu the Great, the inaugural emperor of the Xia dynasty. According to this classic of Chinese literature, Yu meticulously assessed each of his nine provinces, setting varied tax rates based on soil quality. The tale of Yu may be steeped in myth, but the early Chinese comprehension of soil is genuine.[36] If a central bureaucracy can map the soil accurately and assess the potential tax base, why bother to draw upon a council or assembly for local information? Unlike European medieval kings who convened assemblies to gauge optimal taxation, an arrangement that leveraged local knowledge and hence required sharing power, Chinese monarchs utilized detailed soil maps, a capability most European states only achieved in the nineteenth century.[37]

Devoid not only of the technology for soil mapping, but also irrigation, fertilizers, and sophisticated crop management, Europeans instead sustained their growing population by clearing marshlands, swamps, and forests, and expanding into new territories.[38] Yet such a strategy presented a dilemma for rulers: without a history of production on newly cleared land, assessing potential output and setting appropriate taxes was challenging.[39] This issue was exacerbated by Europe's prevalent "slash and burn" farming techniques. Here, plots were cultivated for a brief time and then abandoned for extensive fallow periods, as cultivators moved on to virgin lands. Although ploughing reduced the time land was left fallow, Europe did not widely adopt the heavy plough until the first millennium, again lagging behind China, where it had been in use for millennia.[40]

Beyond these advancements in agriculture, China's development of information technologies similarly enhanced administrative governance while eroding democratic principles, akin to the present-day impact of China's internet and AI surveillance systems. Initially, the primary function of writing was to document economic transactions, especially in societies that needed to store crops and thus maintain records.[41] In China, however, the centralized state quickly imposed a single writing system.[42] This allowed bureaucrats to correspond across the extensive empire and to create population registries, which, as previously mentioned, became crucial for the Qin state to gather data on individuals and their assets for purposes of taxation.[43] Moreover, by undercutting the information advantage of locals, writing served as a catalyst to centralized political organization.[44] For example, after the state of Chu defeated the Zhou dynasty in 957 B.C., the royal administration promptly shifted to a more hierarchical structure, capitalizing on technological advancements in recordkeeping. Alongside the existing Three Ministries overseeing Lands, Construction, and Horses—each staffed with a multitude of scribes and clerks—the Royal Household and the Secretariat were introduced as distinct governmental divisions. They soon epitomized the era's growing focus on bureaucratic oversight.[45] In contrast, after the fall of the Roman Empire, Europe saw the decline of Latin as a unifying language and the corresponding development of distinct regional languages (although Latin continued to be used among educated elites, which helped spread scientific knowledge and ideas).

In short, the ability of the Chinese government to infiltrate civil society and execute its policies relied heavily on technologies that bolstered bureaucratic governance. Without these, Chinese authoritarianism would probably have resembled that of Russia, which lacked the technological advancements that facilitated bureaucratic progress. As a result, Russian autocratic governance always rested on weak state foundations and only maintained power due to the existence of an even weaker society; the Tsars wielded what the sociologist Michael Mann called "despotic power," rather than bureaucratic power.[46] Indeed, in contrast to Western Europe, where the information problem was addressed by town councils and assemblies, Russia had very few towns across a vast expanse of land. As late as 1814, the time depicted by Leo Tolstoy in *War and Peace*, when the Russian Empire, having just defeated Napoleon in a march on Paris, stood at its apex, Tsar Alexander I governed half of Europe's lands but only a quarter of its populace. In Asia, the Romanov Empire covered more than a third of its landmass but contained only 3 percent of its people.[47] Whereas the riches of towns and cities would become important sources of tax revenue to nobles across Western Europe, in Russia the cost of taxing their equivalents outweighed the benefits of establishing rival power centres that could threaten the Tsars' despotic authority. So instead of relying on local councils and assemblies for revenue collection, Russian elites cautiously refrained from granting them autonomy and instead gradually sought to build a bureaucratic state, albeit a weak one.[48]

The Needham Puzzle

As the preceding sketch suggests, various technological innovations in China both emerged under and further strengthened the state's autocratic rule. Under the stewardship of the renowned chief minister Wang Anshi, for instance, the central administration spearheaded more than 11,000 irrigation and flood control initiatives, not to mention the monumental Grand Canal, which spans 40 meters in width and stretches 1,776 km, connecting Beijing in the north to Hangzhou in the south.[49] Established by the state over a millennium ago, this canal became the linchpin of an elaborate water transportation system.[50] The result was a large and unified empire, which sped up the diffusion of new technologies. For example, in response to the 1012 A.D. drought in the Yangtze River valley, Emperor Zhenzong was able to take advantage of the vastness of his territory to introduce drought-resistant rice varieties. He even sent envoys to the Fujian Province, which had been severely affected, where they instructed local farmers how best to cultivate the new *Champa* rice seed.[51]

The beneficiaries of these infrastructural systems were not just state-run factories but private entrepreneurs as well, who suddenly reached larger markets.[52] Following the creation of China's unified writing system, ideas now traveled on horseback by letter just as fast as goods. Although the Song dynasty did limit the dissemination of political ideas, similar to present-day China, it promoted the advancement of printing technology at the same time, making sure that technological manuals had a wider reach.[53] Leveraging the power of the state, Chinese emperors were able to hasten technology adoption, curtail local monopolies, and expand markets, all of which opened the floodgates for more competition and investment by the private sector too.

This history makes clear that the conventional story about economic growth in Europe is, at best, incomplete. According to this theory, checks on the autocrat were essential for secure property rights and investment, which fueled economic development and growth. In China, however, there were no representative assemblies to check the power of the monarch, yet the country was nevertheless able to promote the development and diffusion of technologies that powered economic growth, as the case of the Champa rice vividly illustrates. Economist Justin Lin has argued that such experimental learning was aided by larger populations, which helps explains why great civilizations of the antiquity—like Mesopotamia, Egypt, and China—did better than Europe at the time.[54] But population size only matters if people are connected. By building infrastructure, creating a standard writing system, and nurturing a shared elite culture, the Chinese state made it easier for technologies and ideas to travel.

Over time, however, China would eventually cede its place at the technological frontier. As Needham's compilation of key inventions shows, China retreats as the global innovation leader in the fourteenth century, after which no major discovery is made in the Middle Kingdom.[55] Having retreated technologically, China soon fell behind in economic terms too. While there were certainly vast differences in income within China, just as within Europe, China as a whole was substantially poorer than the most developed parts of Europe by the fifteenth century. And by the turn of the eighteenth century, even its most advanced region, the Yangtze Delta, had fallen behind the West.[56] A century later, Europe had also overtaken China in terms of its share of global industrial output (figure 2.1). The question of why China, despite its early technological superiority, did not produce an industrial revolution, and even ended up being overtaken by the West, has aptly been called the "Needham puzzle."[57]

Why, then, did China falter? China excelled in spreading ideas over its vast territory, but over the long run the kind of ideas that people spread is more important to progress. One of the great paradoxes of Chinese development is that its drive to make bureaucratic recruitment more impersonal and meritocratic ended up stifling grassroots innovation. The rise of the Chinese state surely encouraged scale, but it came at the price of diversity of thought.

Consider the civil service examination system that emerged to select candidates for official positions in the days of the Qin (and gradually became more systematic under the Song) when it was opened to most male commoners. At the provincial level, people gathered to take a test

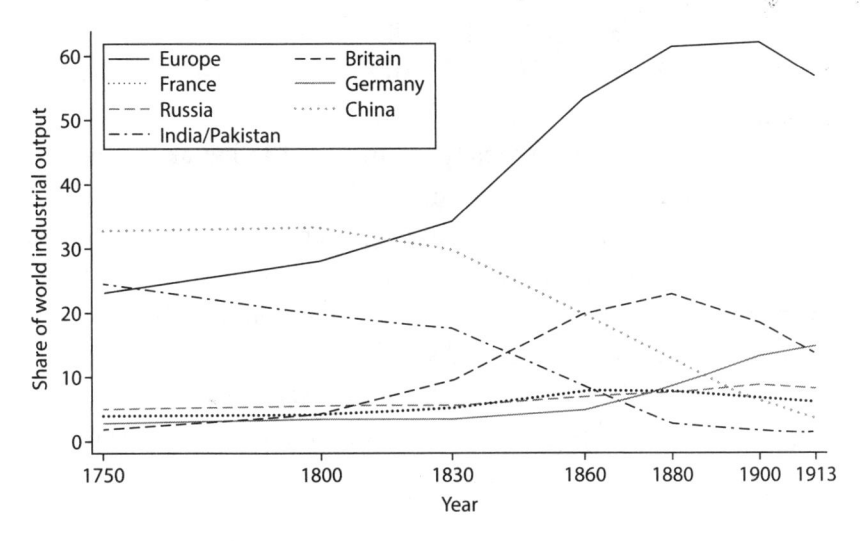

FIGURE 2.1. Global industrial output, 1750–1913
Source: Bairoch, "International Industrialization Levels from 1750 to 1980," 269.

over three days and two nights. About 95 percent of the applicants failed, but the few who passed could travel to Beijing for the metropolitan exam, where roughly the top 10 percent would fill 300 positions and could go on to work for the central ministries.[58]

The incentives to do so were compelling. The pursuit of public office was an important pathway to prestige, wealth, tax benefits, and even legal exemptions: civil servants could not be arrested, tortured, or investigated without permission of the emperor, nor did they have to worry about the harshest punishments inflicted on commoners, like flogging, exile, or death. But above all, public office was an escalator of social mobility for those who attained it.[59] As a result, the competition for office produced "a remarkable consistency of objectives, incentives, and mobility strategies across social strata."[60] Farmers and craftsmen, rich and poor, all used the means they had to invest in education and climb the socioeconomic ladder. However, by focusing on Confucian ideology, these examinations reinforced cultural beliefs emphasizing a hierarchical and patrimonial structure, which placed the emperor at the top, and directly tied the family to the state.

This system created political stability but also serious obstacles to reform and continued progress.[61] Instead of consolidating their influence, local families competed for jobs in the bureaucracy. This funneling of ambition upward made society too fractured and weak to mobilize and hold the government accountable. More fundamentally, as Lin notes, it meant that if Galileo had lived in China, he would have been a bureaucrat and not a scientist.[62] Skewed incentives encouraged China's most able youths to pursue a career within the government bureaucracy, which required passing the civil service examination and investing heavily in Confucian education. Under this system, China did well as long as technological progress was incremental and served the state. Yet this also meant that the Middle Kingdom would have no scientific revolution.

While this explanation helps clarify why many talented individuals in China failed to become scientists, inventors, and entrepreneurs, it also raises a new question: why didn't more experimentation happen within the bureaucracy itself? After all, did not the U.S. government launch Advanced Research Projects Agency (ARPA), which laid some of the foundations for the modern internet? And in Song China, did not renowned scholars, like Su Song, also climb the ranks the bureaucracy? The number of scientists among office holders, however, was very few. And as chapter 7 will show, the success of ARPA depended on a *decentralized* system of universities for talent and reporting channels that allowed it to circumvent much of the bureaucracy of government.[63]

Another reason for China's fading technological innovation is that much like ARPA, which was set up in response to the Soviet launch of *Sputnik I*, Chinese modernization was driven by interstate competition, and as competition faded, so too did the engine of Chinese growth. Consider, for example, the Song dynasty's response to the devastating military defeat to the Tanguts in the 1040s.[64] Under the young Emperor Shenzong, Wang Anshi initiated a set of far-reaching "New Policies" to drive progress and consolidate the power of the central government at the same time. Determined to recruit a cadre of loyal and professional civil servants, Anshi made merit-based examination a key priority, undermining the old aristocracy in the process. In addition, by focusing the curriculum on Confucian thought, he sought to create a society, though still divided by kinship, "united in one mind and common moral purpose."[65] To spur innovation, Anshi created a number of mission-oriented agencies, including the State and Trade Bureau and the Finance Planning Commission, which were allowed to operate outside the sclerotic bureaucracy, unconstrained by civil service protocols, similar to ARPA in the twentieth century.[66] This kind of "bureaucratic entrepreneurship" entailed recruiting managerial talent and giving them a great deal of latitude to test the waters.[67] They engaged in government procurement, extended credit to petty retail shopkeepers, and sometimes seized control over factory operations.[68]

Conversely, when the Chinese state withered away, so did the fortunes of its empire. The end of the Song era illustrates this clearly. After disruption by the Mongols (under the leadership of Genghis's grandson Kublai Khan) a period of turmoil ensued. Amid mass revolts in the 1350s, the Mongols and their Yuan Empire was overthrown by Zhu Yuanzhang, who founded the Ming dynasty in 1368 after a long and bloody civil war. Zhu moved to take advantage of the existing state bureaucracy to consolidate power, but in the process, he undermined it. For one thing, he abolished the position of prime minister, which had been the chief of the civil service under previous governments, and so handed more power to himself. By ending the civil service examination system, he made it possible for appointments to be based on loyalty rather than competence.[69] To make things worse, he also brought much of the private sector under his control while cutting commercial ties with foreign lands. Following the so-called sea ban of 1371, overseas trade would be prohibited until the sixteenth century, and the ban would be reimposed periodically thereafter. This is truly remarkable since China, the birthplace of the magnetic compass, was at the frontier in both naval warfare and shipping. In 1420, the Ming navy possessed 1,350 combat vessels, of which 250 ships were long range and another 400 large floating fortresses. True, the fleet of privately managed vessels was unquestionably smaller, but it had already established profitable trade links with Korea, Japan, much of Southeast Asia, and even East Africa.[70] And needless, to say, the taxable revenues from those endeavours supported the Chinese state.[71]

Under admiral Zheng He, China also undertook a series of official overseas expeditions between 1405 and 1433, sending hundreds of ships and tens of thousands of men to ports "from Malacca and Ceylon to the Red Sea entrances and Zanzibar." But the 1433 expedition turned out to be the last one. Three years later, yet another imperial edict was issued, this time banning even the construction of seagoing ships, only to be followed up by another order forbidding the mere existence of ships with more than two masts. So, Zheng He's warships were left to rot away. Despite the vast opportunities for both trade and territorial expansion, "China had decided to turn its back on the world."[72]

The question, of course, is why? Though there are plausible strategic reasons, such as the continued albeit fading threat of the Mongols, which prompted Ming rulers to concentrate scarce resources in exposed areas, this cannot explain why the emperor felt the need to clamp down on all maritime trade.[73] A better explanation is the conservatism of the Confucian bureaucracy, which again acted to promote stability at the expense of progress. In principle, nothing prevented the Chinese from hiring foreign engineers and scientists. Nor were there real obstacles to sending ambassadors and spies to London and Amsterdam to learn about Western technology, as did the Russians and eventually the Japanese. However, Chinese bureaucrats not only resented the wealth accumulated by merchants, but they believed trade incentivized the toiling masses to shift their attention away from more virtuous activities like serving the state or ploughing the land. Foreign trade seemed the most dubious of all commercial activities, because it was harder for the state to control. This is neither to suggest that the Ming emperors disliked all forms of progress nor that they tried to undermine every entrepreneurial endeavour, but the policy reversal from the Song era is quite remarkable. Historian Paul Kennedy notes: "The Ming rebuilding of the Great Wall of China and the development of the canal system, the ironworks, and the imperial navy were for state purposes, because the bureaucracy had advised the emperor that they were necessary. But just as these enterprises could be started, so also could they be neglected. The canals were permitted to decay, the army was periodically starved of new equipment, the astronomical clocks (built c. 1090) were disregarded, the ironworks gradually fell into desuetude."[74] In the absence of any major external security threats, the Ming dynasty did not have to embrace progress to ensure political stability. Its emperors could cement their power by building an increasingly personal autocracy, even if it weakened the state.[75]

A Patronage Economy

New threats eventually emerged, but the replacement of the Mings by the Manchus, who formed the Qing dynasty in 1644, did not reverse China's relative decline.[76] In 1736, when Abraham Darby's ironworks at Coalbrookdale were taking off, the blast furnaces of Honan and Hopei had been almost entirely abandoned. To consolidate power, the Qing had clamped down on private commerce, a decision that significantly eroded their tax base. To make matters worse, they further eroded the Chinese bureaucracy from within.[77] By choosing not to undertake cadastral (property tax) surveys after 1713, they effectively decided not to tax new production sites. Rather, they sought to raise revenues in less invasive ways. As tax revenues fell, beginning in the 1680s, the Kangxi emperor resorted to selling examination certificates en masse, effectively making elite membership a matter of wealth, with 350,000 degrees sold by 1800.[78] As a result, the whole system became profoundly personalized, with the emperor exercising unrestrained authority in matters of appointment, promotion, and demotion.

This approach kept internal peace among the elites in the short run, but it also made the Qing regime highly exposed to internal rebellion and external threats over the long run, as the state lumbered under increasing fiscal difficulties. By embarking on a program of ambitious territorial expansion both north and west—spreading its wings deep into Mongolia, Tibet, and modern-day Xinjiang—the Qing controlled twice as much territory as the Ming, who themselves had controlled a much larger territory than the Song. As the Chinese population grew, however, so too did the cost of monitoring. At the same time, China's tax revenue intake continued its downward trajectory under Qing rule (figure 2.2). In fact, as the population expanded, by 1850 per capita tax revenues had fallen to less than half of its 1700 level.[79]

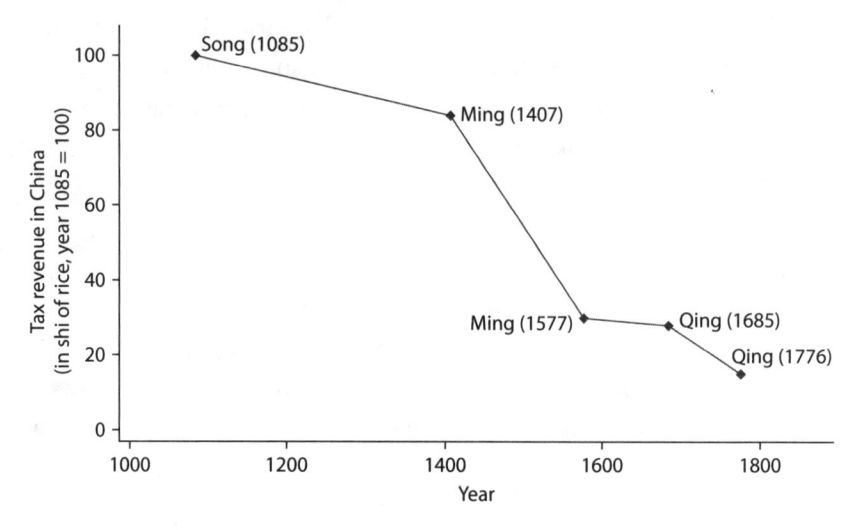

FIGURE 2.2. Fiscal state capacity in China, 1085–1776
Source: Brandt, et al., "From Divergence to Convergence," 45–123, Table 2. Compiled by Liu, "Wrestling for Power."

Territorial expansion created formidable challenges for the Chinese bureaucracy. Because newly conquered areas were further away from Beijing, the Qing regime had less knowledge of local assets and tended to tax provinces further away more lightly, as Hayek would have predicted.[80] The task of governing far-flung regions was entrusted to imperially appointed officials at a time when information could not travel faster than the horses carrying it. Indeed, before railroad technology arrived, it took some 30 days to travel from the capital to Shenyang; about 50 days to Xi'an, Wuhan, or Nanjing; and some 90 days to Guangzhou.[81] The difficulty of monitoring meant that local officials often pursued their own self-interest, even at the expense of the emperor. They exaggerated the severity of bad harvests, colluded with local landowners to remove land from the tax rolls, diverted public funds into their own pockets, and outright resisted taxation. For instance, in one episode, recounted by historian Madeleine Zelin, when a magistrate collecting overdue land taxes in Shanghai ordered the arrest of defaulters, among them a village headman whose job it was to pursue tax evaders, riots broke out.[82]

Keenly aware of such practices and challenges, Chinese emperors sought to limit the costs of tracking compliance in several ways. Confucian ideology, with its detailed codes guiding the behaviour of the population—officials included—fostered obedience and served to uphold the chain of command, even if monitoring from the top was absent. But a number of institutional arrangements were also critical to ensure compliance and direct the loyalties of officials toward the throne. Not only were bureaucrats barred from serving in their home district, but frequent rotations also made sure that they did not develop loyalties to the district they served, which in turn mitigated the risk of collusion against the emperor. Early on, the short-lived Qin dynasty even introduced a high-level supervisory agency called the *Censorate*, which "dispatched roving observers to serve as the emperor's eyes and ears by circumventing routine official channels to report episodes of official malfeasance directly to the throne."[83]

Despite these legacies, however, the later Qing's fiscal and bureaucratic capacity was severely limited when pitched against other Great Powers. In 1750, at the dawn of the British Industrial Revolution, total Chinese tax intake was well above that of the Ottoman, Russian, Spanish, French, and Dutch empires, but in per capita terms, it lagged behind all of them (figure 2.3). As England began to industrialize, it even overtook China in terms of total revenue collected.[84] Deprived of revenues, the Qing bureaucracy slowly withered away. Around 1800, when European powers had approximately one government worker for every 600 to 800 citizens, China maintained a ratio of one civil servant for every 32,000 people.[85] Meanwhile, the number of counties ruled by magistrates—occupying the lowest rung of the state hierarchy—had barely changed since the days of the Han dynasty. Even with its much larger population, Qing China consisted of 1,360 counties relative to 1,180 under the Han rule and 1,230 in the Song era.[86]

In the Qing days, these counties were grouped into 180 prefectures, under eighteen provinces, each run by a governor. Given the country's population of around 300 million by the end of the seventeenth century, the average magistrate was left to manage some 230,000 people, with over a million people residing in some of the larger coun-

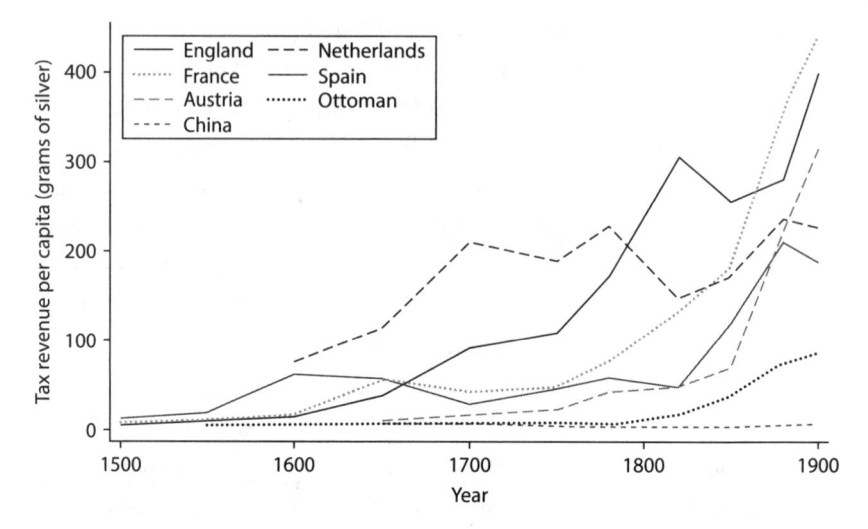

FIGURE 2.3. Comparative fiscal state capacity around the world, 1500–1900
Source: Karaman and Pamuk, "Different Paths to the Modern State in Europe."
For China: Brandt, et al., "From Divergence to Convergence," 45–123, Table 3.

ties. The difficulty of governing these vast populations was compounded by the broad responsibilities assigned to the magistrates. When it came to law enforcement, the magistrate was "the detective, prosecutor, judge, and jury all rolled into one," in addition to overseeing public works, defense, and policing.[87] Consequently, the central Qing government was merely "registering and checking the actions of various provincial administrations [rather] than ... assuming a direct initiative in the conduct of affairs."[88] The sheer size of the empire, limited revenues, and long communication lines acted as breaks on the scale and scope of official activity.[89]

Faced with a mountainous administrative burden, local magistrates became dependent on the local gentry, which reinforced the pressure for a low-tax regime, as the case of nineteenth century Xinhui in Guangdong makes clear.[90] When the Qing state sought to impose taxes on domestic trade, the local palm-leaf guild forcefully resisted, making it impossible for the local magistrate to survey the palm growing areas being taxed.[91] Unable to raise revenue, all levels of government began to grant kinship groups, merchants, and guilds unwritten but enforceable monopoly rights in return for taxable income. As economic historians Loren Brandt, Debin Ma, and Thomas Rawski note, "Such practices, which essentially amounted to official sales of market control in exchange for informal revenues . . . may have acted as a long-term brake on innovation."[92]

Furthermore, this approach to governing, which involved rewarding behaviour that supported the state's aims and punishing actions that threatened to undermine its political clout, required a high degree of imperial discretion, including control over the legal system. Like ancient Rome, the emperor was the source of law, which left much of economic and social life to be governed and regulated by family, clan, and village elders. But unlike Western Europe, where the Roman Empire mercifully collapsed, there was no army of autonomous legal professionals to protect private property and other rights in Imperial China. Rather, legal specialists were viewed with suspicion.[93] Under the Ming dynasty, "incitement to litigate" was even criminalized; the Qing went even further and banned the occupation of "litigation master"—a job resembling that of a lawyer today.[94] Also in contrast to Europe, there was never a period when local barons in China grew sufficiently powerful to force the emperor to embrace a constitutional compromise, like the Magna Carta in England. As political scientist Francis Fukuyama observes, "Local power holders never had the legal legitimacy that they did in feudal Europe. . . . [W]hen the hereditary aristocracy in later years tried to gain power in China, it was not by building a localized power base but by capturing the central government."[95]

The consequences of this Imperial dominance were far-reaching. Without legal formalization, private property rights were insecure and risked confiscatory intervention by the state, which prompted many property holders to "seek shelter under an umbrella of political power."[96] Within these networks, built around families and lineages, most transactions occurred through personal patron–client ties rather than through an impersonal market of equals. This situation would persist well into the twentieth century and to some extent still holds true today. According to historian Prasenjit Duara, during the decades leading up to World War II, "neither the market nor the state fully regulated economic relationships." This arrangement left room for powerful figures to protect citizens from predatory local governments, who received loyalty in return and sought to build their stock of political capital this way.[97] The trouble with this so-called patronage economy was—and still is—that it is not scalable beyond personal relationships, which constrains not only commercial transactions but more importantly the flow of ideas. Put differently, the persistence of the clan in China acted as a break on the interconnectedness of its collective brain.[98] And to make matters worse, it further weakened the bureaucracy from within. The wealth of salt merchants, for example, derived from state-granted monopolies in exchange for taxable revenues. These merchants then invested substantial resources to climb the imperial bureaucracy, where they used their power to hire friends and family in the salt administration, which further strengthened their monopolies.[99]

With the public fractured along kinship lines, the growth of civil society was also constrained.[100] With families competing for jobs in the civil service bureaucracy, no unified bourgeoisie emerged in China to challenge the government or hold it accountable.[101] Consider the commercial city of Hankou on the Yangtze River, which is now part of Wuhan. While Hankou became a bustling metropolis in the late eighteenth century, to which merchants and artisans flocked, its guilds and other associations were based on individuals' places of origin. People coming from all over China—whether salt merchants from Huizhou, or tea merchants from Canton and Ningbo—formed kinship groups from various regions or towns. Rather than working together, they engaged in incessant disputes. For example, an incident unfolded in 1888, embroiling Anhui and Hunan guildsmen in a dispute over a pier. The ensuing conflict reached a crescendo when the local magistrate, upholding the interests of the Anhui merchants, ruled in their favour, triggering a retaliatory attack by the aggrieved Hunan faction. The dragon boat races, once a cherished tradition evoking communal celebration, escalated into violence as the Cantonese clashed with their counterparts from Hubei. Authorities were compelled to intervene and impose a ban on the races. In this way, the nature of mercantile activity in China impeded the emergence of a shared local identity.[102]

It is easy to see how, relative to an environment of local cronyism, a centralized meritocratic bureaucracy, capable of raising taxes, maintaining order, and investing in critical infrastructure, can act as an escalator for growth. During the Song era in particular, the transition toward greater centralization proved transformative. It helped break up local monopolies, encouraged market integration, and spread technological knowledge far and wide. It also gave the state more power to directly promote progress through large-scale irrigation projects and state-run factories that triggered waves of new investment. But while Chinese rulers leveraged the technologies of the time to consolidate power in ways that European monarchs could only dream of, the information, communication, and transportation technologies of the time did not permit them to "reach very far into Chinese society."[103] As a result, state leaders were unable to control their subjects, while kinship structures and the Chinese family remained remarkably resilient. Indeed, much of Chinese history can be seen through the lens of a power struggle between centralized state power and various kinship groups.

The other central strand we can extract from the preceding history concerns how the state reacted to threats to political stability. When Chinese emperors perceived the main threat to the regime to be internal, the government sought to divide civil society and co-opt vested local interests, rewarding loyalty with bureaucratic appointments, while at the same time centralizing more economic activity under the control of the state, even if it came at the expense of growth and innovation. When the chief threat was foreign competing powers, on the other hand, rulers felt the need to provide more freedoms to private entrepreneurs, strengthen the meritocratic selection of bureaucrats, and drive technological progress through state-sponsored projects, which often happened in response to military defeat or a widespread sense that the Middle Kingdom had fallen behind. As will be discussed in chapter 3, however, even at its most innovative, China was unable to bring about anything like a broad-based industrial revolution.

3

The Rise of Europe

There is nothing more difficult to take in hand, more perilous to conduct, or more uncertain in its success, than to take the lead in the introduction of a new order of things. Because the innovator has for enemies all those who have done well under the old conditions, and lukewarm defenders in those who may do well under the new.[1]

—NICCOLÒ MACHIAVELLI

EVEN AT the height of their power, the Romans never managed to build a bureaucratic state comparable to that of Han China. This was, in part, because they lacked the tools to track what their populations were producing and tax them accordingly—tools that European monarchs would still be deficient in a full millennium after the fall of Rome.[2] Without these technologies, scaling up while leaving local structures intact was the only way of governing. Instead of disarming former enemies, Rome pursued a strategy of indirect rule over the places they conquered; they encouraged them to maintain their armies and sought to integrate their war machines into its network of warrior communities.[3] It was, in other words, Europe's technological backwardness that gave political decentralization a chance. And it was this decentralization—underpinned by the family policies of the Latin Church, competition between states, and increasingly autonomous cities—that ultimately supercharged Europe's technological and economic growth.

True, many premodern empires were heavily reliant on the cooperation of local elites, but Rome was particularly decentralized. Each city typically had a curia, a local council of about a hundred members, responsible for its governance and tax collection.[4] These decentralized institutions, though functional for local administration, were not designed for managing a global empire. Change was thus inevitable. The empire would either fragment, or it would centralize—a question that resolved itself when Julius Caesar declared himself dictator for life in 44 B.C., an act leading to his assassination.

The Roman Empire, which emerged from the ashes of the republic with the accession of Caesar Augustus soon thereafter, was ruled by the emperor and his inner circle, with a tiny bureaucracy to implement policy.[5] Not until Diocletian's reign (284–305 A.D.) did significant state-building efforts begin. And even then, the bureaucracy remained thin. By the time the first credible figures exist, around 400 A.D., Rome had just over 30,000 full-time civil servants (about one-quarter of the number of bureaucrats working in the Han Empire centuries earlier), and they were responsible for governing an enormous empire, spanning the praetorian prefectures of Italy (including parts of Africa), Gaul (comprising also Britain and Spain), Illyricum (consisting of Greece, Crete, and the Balkans), and Byzantium.[6]

From Rome to León

Whatever state the Romans did create, it collapsed in Western Europe after the empire's fall. But what Edward Gibbon regarded as "the greatest, perhaps, and most awful scene in the history of mankind," may also have been, as the Stanford historian Walter Scheidel has argued, "our biggest lucky break since an errant asteroid cleared away the dinosaurs."[7] According to Scheidel, the collapse of Rome was critical for the competitive state system that emerged in Europe. It meant that European fragmentation persisted along with the continent's decentralized political tradition—a tradition exemplified by Germanic politics. Already when Julius Caesar crossed the Rhine during his campaign to conquer Gaul, he noted how German tribes elected their leaders through assemblies in times of war and how the powers of their chiefs were limited in peacetime. The best description however of the decentralized system of German rule surely comes from Tacitus's book *The Germania*, written in 98 A.D., which notes that, "On matters of minor importance only the chiefs debate; on major affairs, the whole community."[8]

Given this background, it is unsurprising that when the Romans left, and the Kingdom of the Franks emerged, this decentralized model of organization reasserted itself at the local level. What vanished was the central structure binding these localities together. Instead of using formal taxation to collect revenue, the Germanic kingdoms began to grant land in exchange for service, an arrangement that paved the way for even greater local autonomy. Even during the reign of Clovis (481–511 A.D.)—often called the real founder of the Frankish state and the best-known ruler of the Merovingian dynasty—governance remained remarkably decentralized.

This pattern persisted under the successor dynasty of the Carolingians, which took over in 751 A.D. Broadly speaking, the Carolingian bureaucracy was made up of two types of officials: counts and emissaries, known as *missi dominici*. The counts were administrative units inherited from the Roman *pagus* (a term that survives in the French word for country, *pays*). During the reign of Charlemagne, when the power of the Franks peaked, there were some six hundred counts north of the Alps.[9] To safeguard against collusion and vested interests capturing the local branches of the state, the Carolingians originally refused to appoint natives of the region to rule the count. Yet, by 802 A.D., in an attempt to tie them directly to the state, locals were appointed to run their own counties. While these local leaders were appointed by and served at the pleasure of the emperor, the limited capacity for monitoring meant that, in effect, central rulers were forced to cede authority to locals. It was thus only a matter of time before count positions became hereditary,[10] and a feudal order arose.[11] This order required that local elites could be brought together in councils or assemblies for decisions to be made. Even Charlemagne had to consult with locals, which restricted his ability to mobilize resources for war: because most nobles were reluctant to sacrifice their own men and resources, any expansionary efforts needed to generate new territory and bounty to attract aristocratic support.[12]

Holding the Carolingian kingdom together was the *missi dominici*, a very slim bureaucracy. Efforts by historian Victor Krause to compile the activities of *missi* yielded a list of a mere 108 undertakings.[13] Even if this list is not exhaustive, extrapolations suggest that in an empire of 1.5 million square kilometres and ten million people, there were no more than a few dozen *missi* at any given point in time.[14] Given the weakness of the state bureaucracy, local councils and assemblies were critical for monarchs to collect local information.[15] Without the inheritance of a central administration and the technologies to support bureaucratic development, European rulers were left with no other option than relying on members of society to provide the information they needed to collect revenue, which meant governing through consent and negotiating with various interest groups. Even aspiring autocrats, like Philip the Fair of France, who ruled from 1285 to 1314, had little bureaucratic or fiscal capacity to support his ambitions. Compared to the Song dynasty in 1086 A.D., or even the Caliphate in 850 A.D., French and English monarchs as late as 1300 were only able to extract minimal revenues—about a tenth of what their counterparts in the East extracted, as a percentage of GDP.[16]

As a way of collecting more revenue, the grand councils convened by kings gradually evolved into meetings of the *estates*, which initially comprised the nobility and the clergy. However, faced with fiscal pressures to fund war, these gatherings were extended to involve representatives of different groups and their interests from the various cities. This marked the beginnings of Parliament, where not just royal councils, but also independent bodies, played an active role in the negotiation and authorization of taxation. The cradle of Parliamentarism was León, which held the first gatherings of magnates, bishops, and elected city representatives in 1185. From there it spread across the Iberian Peninsula to Sicily, France, and England, where the Magna Carta, signed by King John and his barons in 1215, marked a milestone in the formation of medieval parliaments: alongside charters like the Hungarian Golden Bull, the Unions of Aragon and Valencia in Spain, and the Pact of Koszyce in Poland, it compelled monarchs to seek formal consent for their initiatives.[17]

However, not all estates turned into national institutions like the English Parliament. While *Parlement de Paris* initially covered the entire kingdom of France, the French monarch was forced to devolve authority to regional parliaments during the Hundred Years' War, giving rise to those of Toulouse, Rouen, Guyenne and Gascony, Burgundy, and Provence, which came to represent local rather than national interests. This limited their ability to check the power of the Crown. Moreover, and unlike today, parliaments across Europe were only called into session by rulers, most often when the monarch needed additional tax revenue. As a result, the frequency with which parliaments gathered varied greatly across Europe. While parliamentary activity in the North Sea countries surged in the sixteenth and seventeenth centuries, it declined elsewhere on the Continent.[18] In Spain, for example, where trade was a monopoly of the Crown of Castille, the discovery of gold and silver in the New World created new sources of income for the monarch and thus reduced its dependence on Parliament for taxation. In England, in contrast, where Parliament had successfully blocked attempts by both the Tudor and Stuart monarchs to create a royal trading monopoly, the rise of the Atlantic economy enriched merchants outside the royal circle. Their growing political clout would be critical for Britain's later industrial takeoff.[19] Besides increasing their ability to constrain the Crown from ruling arbitrarily, this economic structure empowered those who stood to benefit from industrialization.[20]

Clans, Corporations, and Cities

The political divergence between Europe and China was not, however, driven merely by differences in state formation. The ascent of representative assemblies crucially depended on the so-called communal movement, which was largely a bottom-up process, despite being shaped by the most powerful and enduring legacy of the Roman Empire: the Latin Church. When the Roman Emperor Constantius II made uncle–niece marriages punishable by death in 339 A.D., it was in response to Christian sentiments and marked the beginnings of a process by which the Latin Church used marriage as a source of patriarchal power. By prohibiting marriages between both blood and affinal kinfolk—including primary relatives, key in-laws, first cousins, and siblings-in-law, as well as godchildren—the Church, with considerable success, promoted marriage by choice and encouraged married couples to form independent households. Indeed, as Jonathan Schulz, Joseph Henrich, and their collaborators have shown, the family policies of the Latin Church served to undermine kinship in Europe over time.[21]

These policies put Europe on a different trajectory than China and the rest of the world, where kinship remained the predominant form of social organization for many centuries. In forging Christendom, the West gradually replaced tribalism with a unified Christian identity that connected individuals from distant parts of Europe.[22] Hence, the answer to the famous *Monty Python* quip, "What have the Romans ever done for us?" is that they laid the foundations for what can be regarded a European culture. What mattered was not so much particular Christian values, but that people began to draw less of a distinction between the kinship ingroup and the rest of society. In the East, kinship persisted much longer; consequently, the Byzantine Church did not pave the way for a scientific or industrial revolution. Conversely, in the West, breakdown in kinship institutions led to the broadening of social networks. Freed from the constraints of familial responsibilities, individuals gained the autonomy to select their friends, life partners, and business associates, thereby fostering decentralized exploration and the exchange of ideas.

This freedom also led to the formation of voluntary groups, educational institutions, and chartered towns, which collectively served to curb the authority and rent-seeking capacity of the ruling elite, such as princes, dukes, and kings. Moreover, in contrast to those who lived in kinship-based societies, individuals who were dissatisfied with their present situation had the option to leave, a choice many embraced; indeed, the competitive nature of chartered towns, vying for the brightest intellectuals, engineers, and artisans, encouraged unconventional thinkers to relocate.[23] This newfound mobility was a key driver of the communal movement, which was defined by the growing political autonomy of nascent European towns and cities and more democratic forms of governance, with assemblies playing a crucial role in representing a broader spectrum of the populace.[24]

The communal movement first took off in northern Italy, where central princely authority had collapsed and left a power vacuum in the late eleventh century. From there, it spread north to the Low Countries, through the Rhineland, and west to southern France. In some cases, communes were established by citizens themselves through a sworn oath. In other instances, they were given a charter by a prince or a bishop. For many revenue-strapped monarchs, the lure of tapping into the taxable commercial transactions generated by the communes was simply irresistible. Backed by a steady stream of income, the Western European communes were even successful in issuing debt—a step the Crown would be unable to take until the sixteenth century.[25]

Beyond developing novel financial powers, these cities also served as laboratories for legal experimentation. For example, having been granted a set of town privileges by the Holy Roman Emperor Otto I, the city of Magdeburg began to develop its own charter laws, impersonal legal rights, and civil administration. These institutions would become known as the "Magdeburg Law" as they spread first to cities along the River Elbe and then to over a hundred cities, from Saxony to the Grand Duchy of Lithuania. Meanwhile, cities like Lübeck, Bruges, and Amsterdam, which all competed for talent, responded by introducing their own charters. The result was the creation of a vast trade federation—the Hanseatic League.

This sharply contrasts with China during the Song dynasty, which saw a commercial revolution but without autonomous cities. As discussed in the previous chapter, Chinese rulers directly taxed commerce through their bureaucracy.[26] But the European experience can similarly be contrasted with the Islamic world, where the fertile river valleys of Egypt and Mesopotamia supported state-building through the intensification of agriculture. As in China, this made efficient land surveying for taxation purposes easier and ensured that political power stayed centralized with the sovereign and his administration, even when Muslim armies invaded Sasanian Iraq and created the Islamic Caliphate. It also led to impressive growth (by the standards of the day) in the early Middle Ages: in 800 A.D., when London was a small town of just 10,000 beset by internal conflicts among Anglo-Saxon tribes, Baghdad stood as a bustling metropolis with over 300,000 people at the heart of an Abbasid empire that spanned the terrain from the desert of modern-day Algeria to Pakistan's mountains.

Thus, Islam was not intrinsically conservative or against commerce. Islamic partnerships were, in fact, innovative in supporting market activities, such as small-scale, one-off trading ventures. Yet these partnerships could be easily dissolved by any partner and offered limited protection for investors, making them unsuitable for large-scale or long-term commercial relationships. These limitations were not a major issue in the Middle Ages, but they became increasingly relevant in the early modern period as new technologies emerged and the scope and scale of trade expanded, necessitating more robust and enduring organizational structures. Hence, as with China, by 1800, the Islamic world would stagnate, both technologically and economically.

London, conversely, evolved into a key node in Europe's decentralized urban network. By 1800, with a population nearing a million, the city stood as the epicenter of the British Empire and a global beacon of affluence, a status epitomized by Samuel Johnson's 1777 remark, "There is in London all that life can afford."[27] What favoured cities like London, and Western Europe in general, was their embrace of institutions geared toward impersonal exchange, adhering to the rule of law, and capable of scaling in response to technological advancements. The most prominent example is the modern business corporation, which first revolutionized trade, then finance, and later transportation and manufacturing. This organizational revolution was a fundamental shift from personal to impersonal cooperation, which significantly reduced the unpredictability of doing business beyond the community.[28]

Outside Europe, the spread of the corporation occurred at a notably slower pace. Business dealings in China, for instance, took place through the clan—a hierarchical kinship-based organization that relied on strong collectivist moral ties to sustain cooperation.[29] Over time, as the forces of competition and creative destruction were unleashed in Europe, corporate China evolved into lineage trusts, whose rentier mindset favored broad portfolios over efficiently run individual firms, which helped keep unprofitable ventures afloat.[30] Meanwhile, Islamic laws and regulations, which supported growth for some time, ultimately hindered the rise of the modern corporation. This, as economic historian Timur Kuran has argued, helps explain why the Middle East, despite its early prosperity, did not spark an oriental industrial revolution. Indeed, the long absence of modern corporations led to a diminished need for other institutions, like standardized bookkeeping, which further entrenched the predominantly personal nature of commerce in the region.[31]

The Republic of Letters

The wealth and autonomy of European cities also gave rise to another important institution: the university. After the establishment of the first *universitas* in Bologna at the end of the twelfth century, universities soon sprung up in cities like Oxford and Paris. It was within the walls of these European institutions that a multitude of revolutionary ideas took root. Galileo, for instance, conducted some of his most significant work at the University of Padua, as did Andreas Vesalius. Padua, which also lists William Harvey and Nicolaus Copernicus among its distinguished alumni, was, at its zenith, "perhaps the most dynamic and successful institution spreading the new Newtonian physics and cutting-edge medicine."[32] And while progressive universities rose and fell, the competitive environment in Europe made it exceedingly challenging for any central authority to suppress innovative ideas. Neither the University of Paris nor the King of France had the power to stop an elector from founding a university in Heidelberg. By 1500, Europe was home to more than sixty universities competing for scholars and students. This competition also created a highly mobile intellectual class dispersed across the continent who established a public sphere known as the Republic of Letters.[33]

The expansion of postal services, initiated by the Tasso family in Italy in the fifteenth century, which eventually linked all of Europe by the seventeenth century, enabled members of this virtual community to share significant discoveries by letter.[34] Much like email today, this allowed intellectuals in remote locations, such as the Croatian mathematician Marino Ghetaldi or Jan Brożek in Krakow, to keep in touch with their peers in Cambridge, Leiden, and Paris. Such ties established bridges between local knowledge networks and served to expand Europe's collective brain. But this process was also aided by new technologies, including Johannes Gutenberg's printing press and the paper mill, which emerged alongside social inventions like Protestantism and the emphasis on literacy and education that it brought about. All of this supported the circulation of books, technical manuals, magazines, and eventually scholarly journals, which were made available in the many libraries across the continent. Suddenly, French scholars could profit from the insights of Newton's *Principia* (1687), despite disruptions from incessant wars between Britain and France.[35]

The Republic of Letters also laid the groundwork for numerous local scientific associations. While English and French monarchies made deliberate efforts during the seventeenth century to promote research through the Royal Society of London for Improving Natural Knowledge and the *Académie royale des sciences* in Paris, most knowledge societies emerged in a bottom-up fashion. European cities, from Vienna to Edinburgh, turned into intellectual bazaars, where thinkers gathered in coffeehouses and bookstores to debate and discuss the ideas of the day.[36] For example, by the beginning of the eighteenth century, there were some 2,000 coffeehouses in London, the most famous being the London Chapter Coffee House—a favourite among the members of the Royal Society.[37] Alongside these informal hubs, formal knowledge societies arose with the purpose of connecting local intellectuals with engineers, entrepreneurs, and tinkerers. The Birmingham Lunar Society, for instance, brought together scientists like Benjamin Franklin and Joseph Black, who would go on to discover latent heat, but also inventors like James Watt and entrepreneurs like Matthew Boulton, whose Boulton & Watt Company would be at the forefront of the revolution in steam power.[38]

By turning measurement, replication, and experimentation into systematic processes, knowledge societies revolutionized the way engineers and mechanics approached invention. Innovation was no longer just about trial and error—it became methodical, structured, and scalable. As Alfred North Whitehead famously observed, "The great invention of the nineteenth century was the invention of the method of invention."[39] Before 1760, engineers were almost invisible in patent records. But by the turn of the century, they accounted for 10 percent of all patents in Britain, and their influence only grew throughout the Industrial Revolution.[40] Suddenly, civil engineers, like John Smeaton and James Brindley, and mechanical engineers, like Henry Maudslay and Joseph Bramah, were pushing the boundaries of their respective fields, while polymaths like James Watt and Marc Isambard Brunel were making contributions across multiple branches of engineering.[41]

When we think of the rise of knowledge societies, Britain often gets the spotlight. But in reality, it was a European affair (figure 3.1).[42] In Germany, many societies were established in response to the Seven Years' War (1756–1763), when rulers needed to rejuvenate their economies following devastating population losses. A first wave came in the late 1760s and early 1770s, when several dukes and princes granted charters to societies with the explicit statutory mission to "improve the local economy for the common good." The *Berliner Mittwochsgesellschaft* (Berlin Wednesday Society), for example, was responsible for the publication of the *Berlinische Monatsschrift* (Berlin Monthly)—Immanuel Kant's magazine of choice, which gained traction for hosting discussions on the pivotal question, "What is Enlightenment?" Other societies took a more hands-on approach. They built vast libraries, packed with the latest technological discoveries, and made them available to all members. Some went even further, funding competitions and cash prizes for groundbreaking inventions. The wealthiest among them even ran demonstration factories, allowing people to see cutting-edge technologies in action. By lowering the cost of acquiring knowledge, these institutions did much to drive innovation forward.[43]

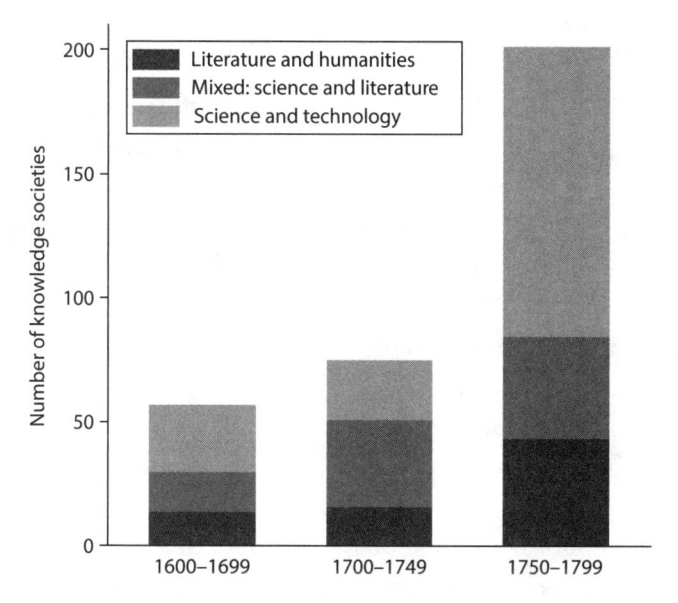

FIGURE 3.1. Number of knowledge societies in Europe, 1600–1800
Source: Mokyr, "The Intellectual Origins of Modern Economic Growth," Figure 5.

In the Far East, meanwhile, people's social networks rarely extended beyond their family or clan, which not only precluded the emergence of knowledge societies but also made people less portable and so hindered the free flow of ideas.[44] In China, artisans were deeply rooted in their familial institutions and places of origin, whereas by the eighteenth century, European cities like Vienna and London had evolved into melting pots, with a significant proportion of skilled craftsmen moving there from other places.[45] Knowledge did not just pass from father to son anymore—it spread sideways, among people from different backgrounds. This shift made collective invention possible, as innovators borrowed, improved, and built on each other's work.[46] As economic historian Robert Allen has documented, in places like England's Cleveland district, where key advances in blast furnace technology were made, competitors openly shared insights.[47]

Exit to Enlightenment

China's collective brain was not only less wired but, as noted in chapter 2, also constrained by a more centralized power structure. In societies where power is concentrated, authorities can more easily manipulate information flows through educational institutions, religious organizations, and media and may detain individuals holding dissenting or inconvenient views.[48] The Middle Kingdom made significant discoveries and, for a period, even spearheaded innovation. But after unification under the Qin dynasty, progress was mostly contingent on state support, which could be withdrawn at will. And when the preferences of the central authorities changed, so did China's fortunes. If Charlemagne, Napoleon, or the monarchs of Habsburg Spain had prevailed in unifying Europe politically, it might have experienced a similar fate. As the eminent Joel Mokyr puts it, "had a single, centralized government been in charge of defending the intellectual status quo, many of the new ideas that eventually led to the Enlightenment would have been suppressed or possibly never even proposed."[49] Indeed, Kant himself believed that Enlightenment needed the absence of authorities guiding peoples' thinking.

The chief virtue of Europe's competitive state system, in other words, was that no central government could crack down on people with a disruptive idea that might shake up the existing order.[50] The Republic of Letters transcended political fractures, and its basic rules of freedom of entry, contestability, transnationality, and transparency created new standards of scientific rigor unencumbered by any central authority. The combination of cultural unity—in the form of Latin and Christian norms—and political pluralism, was a legacy of the Roman Empire and its collapse, which both enabled and safeguarded free discourse.[51] Connectivity boosted the reach of Europe's market for ideas, while polycentrism opened up space for intellectuals and innovators to pursue heterodox endeavours, even if it required moving from one patron, university, or city to another, which they frequently did.

Among émigré scholars fleeing persecution in their homelands, we find some of Europe's most prominent intellectuals, such as Comenius, often considered the father of modern education, who escaped Bohemia for Sweden, Poland, and England. Galileo's defender Tommaso Campanella eventually was freed from Spanish detention and moved to France. Thomas Hobbes, shortly after completing *The Elements of Law*, fled to Paris, where he joined other exiles from England. Pierre Bayle fled France not once but twice—first to Geneva, where he learned about the work of René Descartes, who himself went into exile, and then to Rotterdam. John Locke took refuge in the Dutch Republic until the Glorious Revolution made his return to England possible. And the restless Voltaire spent much of his life moving around. The list goes on.[52]

Escaping heavy-handed political authorities was much harder in China, and even those who successfully did so ended up having little impact, since China and its neighbours had significantly less intellectual interchange. Consider, for instance, the seventeenth-century Chinese scholar Zhu Shunshui—a rare intellectual who could match his European counterparts in his peripatetic nature, as well as in the breadth of his knowledge, which comprised not just Confucian classics but many practical subjects, ranging from crafts to architecture. As a loyalist of the Ming dynasty, he was forced to flee China after its overthrow in 1644. He first sought refuge in Annam, Vietnam, and later moved to Japan, where he gained a significant following and ultimately served as adviser and mentor to the *daimyo* Mitsukuni. But Zhu's works remained unknown in his homeland until their rediscovery in the late nineteenth century.[53]

Meanwhile, Europe's intellectual traditions frequently transcended national boundaries. The sixteenth-century Reformation, for instance, spread to several different countries and even challenged the power of the Catholic Church, thus further fragmenting the continent and making the coordination of repression efforts harder. Ulrich Zwingli, for instance, could skillfully exploit the divisions among the Swiss cantons to promote his reform movement, while John Calvin found asylum in Geneva after escaping from France. And unlike Jan Hus, who met a tragic fate at the stake in 1415 for heresy against the Catholic Church's doctrines—because King Sigismund, who had first acted as his guarantor, later turned him over to the pope and his council—Martin Luther, operating a century later, enjoyed relative safety under the protection of the Electors of Saxony. The nursery of modernity became a fractured terrain, with multiple actors vying for influence, including the state, autonomous cities, nobility and knights, and now also Catholics and Protestants.[54]

To see how religious fractures and the rivalry for talent among European rulers aided technological advancement, consider the Huguenots, who suffered a crushing blow after the Edict of Nantes was revoked in 1685 by Louis XIV, making Protestantism illegal. Protestant churches and schools were shut down, and citizens were forcibly converted to Catholicism. Consequently, rather than facing the prospects of lifelong imprisonment or execution, some 200,000 Huguenots left the country—many of whom settled in Protestant England, Germany, the Netherlands, and Switzerland. In Prussia, the Great Elector Frederick William astutely took advantage of the situation by issuing the Edict of Potsdam and offering his estates as a refuge. By the beginning of the eighteenth century, Huguenots made up some 20 percent of Berlin's population. Upon entering the country, they were granted lucrative exemptions from tariffs and most taxes, free use of abandoned houses, and financial support for setting up businesses and factories, which many of them did. And in doing so, the Huguenots, renowned for being technologically advanced in France, imparted valuable skills and new professions to the local population.[55] In Halle on the Saale, for example, citizens were encouraged to apprentice their children to French manufacturers. Even a century later, empirical studies indicate, German towns with a higher proportion of immigrants still benefited from the knowledge and technology transfer brought by the Huguenots.[56] Friedrich List was right in thinking that "Germany owes her first progress in manufactures to the revocation of the Edict of Nantes, and to the numerous refugees driven by that insane measure into almost every part of Germany."[57]

At the same time, Germany's censorship efforts remained laughably ineffective even as the Prussian state grew in sophistication. Though liberals like Karl Varnhagen von Ense lamented government restrictions on books and newspapers, the political fragmentation of Germany at the time meant that it was virtually impossible to control the traffic in contraband print. Publications banned in one region could easily be printed in another and then smuggled across lightly guarded borders. For instance, Thomas Beck, a card seller from Württemberg, frequently smuggled his prohibited works into the Rhineland by hiding them inside his hat. And Friedrich Engels, the radical son of a wealthy Barmen textile manufacturer, and future collaborator of Marx, boasted in a letter to his friend Wilhelm Graeber in 1839 that he had become "a large-scale importer of banned books into Prussia."[58]

As a general rule, places where elites did not stifle heterodox thinking became hotbeds for eminent innovators and thinkers. Examining historical records of renowned intellectuals born in Europe between the eleventh and nineteenth centuries, economic historians Michel Serafinelli and Guido Tabellini have uncovered a compelling correlation between city-institutions that fostered local autonomy, as well as economic and political freedoms, and the flourishing of creative talent. The transformation of a city into a commune, for instance, came with a remarkable surge in the birth of celebrated individuals, and nearly doubled the likelihood of attracting renowned immigrants.[59]

While free cities in Europe served as havens for intellectuals seeking refuge from censorship and persecution, no such sanctuaries existed in a politically unified China. The "literary inquisition," when the Qing government imposed severe crackdowns on intellectuals, serves as a case in point.[60] Consider the case of Wang Xihou, a sixty-four-year-old dictionary maker who had passed the provincial-level examinations in 1750 and then spent much of his life improving indexing techniques for a new dictionary. When the governor general and the provincial governor examined his work, they found nothing inappropriate. But when the case was passed on to the Qianlong emperor, he decided to punish Wang for not showing enough respect and deference to the dictionary his grandfather, the Kangxi emperor, had once commissioned. The consequences were severe: the provincial governor, who had not aligned with the emperor's verdict, only narrowly escaped execution, more than a hundred individuals faced investigations, and the publishers of the dictionary, along with those who contributed prefaces, were subjected to punishments. Wang himself received the harshest sentence conceivable: nine familial exterminations, including his own. Tragically, all his sons met the same fate, while an additional twenty-one family members were consigned to lives of enslavement.[61]

According to the contemporary Chinese poet Gong Zizhen, the fear of persecution left a deep mark on intellectuals and prompted many to withdraw from public life altogether.[62] This created a social environment of mutual suspicion, which reduced the kind of trust that supported the Republic of Letters and cooperation across family lines in Europe more broadly.[63] Recent statistical analysis of literary inquisitions from the Qing Imperial Archives shows that this wave of repression had long-lasting consequences for the growth of civil society and schooling, which in turn helped solidify Chinese autocracy, even as its bureaucratic capacity in this period diminished.[64] Not only did the centralization of the Chinese empire prevent nonconformist intellectuals from exiting the regime, but it also cemented the hegemony of neo-Confucianism. The reading lists for civil service examinations, for instance, were based on the classical canon, which emphasized literature. Intellectuals were thus steered away from science, technical fields, and controlled experimentation in favour of memorizing the 431,286 characters of the Confucian classics. It is no exaggeration to refer to this system as "a prescription for stagnation," which by focusing on refined literacy and calligraphy strongly favoured the existing order.[65]

Seen in this light, the divergence between Europe and China is no mystery. As Mokyr has argued forcefully, the failure of radically heterodox views to gain traction in China highlights a key difference between the Middle Kingdom and Europe. While Europe had its share of repressive and reactionary regimes, competition between them limited their capacity to impose a single orthodoxy. In contrast, China's institutions lacked the same degree of competitiveness, both in the marketplace of ideas and within the realm of political power.[66] This was also true of Tokugawa Japan and the Ottoman Empire, which were quick to adopt Western firearms but shut out much otherwise useful knowledge. Just as the Ming dynasty sought to prevent the outside world from gaining knowledge about China, in 1485 Sultan Bayezid II, fearful that rebelling scribes and an informed population might undermine his leadership, issued an edict banning the printing of Arabic across his empire—a decision that would have devastating consequences for economic growth and literacy over the following centuries.[67]

Yet these trajectories were not predetermined. Europe could have experienced a similar fate had it not been for the fall of the Roman Empire. Though Rome certainly saw sparks of genius, its elites had very little interest in industrial pursuits, which they even sometimes sought to obstruct. According to a story by Pliny the Elder, Emperor Tiberius had an inventor executed, fearing the possibility that his discovery might put people out of work and cause angry workmen to rebel. And when Emperor Vespasian, who ruled in 69–79 A.D., was shown a machine for transporting columns to the Capitoline Hill, he banned it, declaring: "How will it be possible for me to feed the populace?" He was more concerned about political stability than the cost of construction, which made conserving jobs more appealing than technological progress. Unsurprisingly, then, most progress in mechanics—including the development of cranes, pumps, and water-lifting devices—were made to support the vast construction and hydraulic engineering efforts of the empire rather than to save labour. With its 1,780 great houses, 423 neighbourhoods, 28 libraries, 19 aqueducts, 2 circuses, 886 baths, 144 public latrines, 37 gates, and 1,352 cisterns, Rome was surely an extraordinary place,[68] but technology served Rome's ruling class rather than the expansion of manufacturing.[69] According to classical scholar Moses Finley, Roman elites primarily saw technology as a means of increasing their popularity and safeguarding their political power.[70]

Why England?

The significance of creative, heterodox ideas for Europe's coming technological leap cannot be overstated, but the transformation of these ideas into tangible progress required more than fresh thinking. To drive the economy, inventions had to be made practical and profitable, and economic ends needed to take precedence over political interests, which ruled in Rome as well as ancient China. In the absence of corporate R&D labs geared toward the conversion of new concepts into functional prototypes and marketable products, which would power technological advancement in the twentieth century, progress at this time relied heavily on individuals with practical skills. Artisans, mechanics, engineers, and tinkerers played a pivotal role in this process.[71] Given this, some scholars posit that the abundance and proficiency of such skilled individuals across the English Channel may help explain why Britain took the lead in industrialization.[72]

Undeniably, the value of mechanical skills surged as a wave of intricate machinery entered the factories of England.[73] In particular, Britain had a large supply of millwrights, specialists in water-powered machinery, which remained the backbone of industry until steam power took over in the mid-nineteenth century.[74] Moreover, the cultivation of mechanical skills was bolstered by a well-developed system of apprenticeships, but apprenticeships were not exclusive to Britain. What set the nation apart was the absence of guild restrictions that tied training to specific locales. This freedom of movement enabled individuals to carry their expertise from town to town, fostering a genuinely national labour market. It also meant that the political influence of guilds—whose power had largely faded in Britain by 1700—could not stifle the forces of creative destruction.[75]

As is well known, the rise of the mechanized factory system and the consequent displacement of artisan shops lay at the core of the Industrial Revolution. This process was heralded in the silk industry, which was first to mechanize, but its limited scale prevented it from igniting a full-fledged revolution. Instead, the true bedrock of modern industry was established in the cotton sector. Initially inconsequential, the cotton industry underwent dramatic change during the early years of the Industrial Revolution and by 1830 had evolved into Britain's most substantial industry, when it accounted for roughly 8 percent of the nation's GDP. This meteoric rise was propelled by a cadre of independent entrepreneurs and inventors, including luminaries such as James Hargreaves, Samuel Crompton, Paul Lewis, and John Wyatt. The most important of these pioneers, however, was Richard Arkwright, whose numerous inventions shaped the industry and whose second Cromford mill, established in 1776, held particular significance as a blueprint for subsequent factories. And what Arkwright did for spinning, Edmund Cartwright did for weaving. While Cartwright made notable discoveries in diverse fields, his most significant contribution was undoubtedly the power loom. In collaboration with the Grimshaw brothers, Cartwright established a factory housing several hundred steam-powered looms.[76]

The combined impact of these technologies soon reverberated across the globe, reshaping the fortunes of the textile industry. Before the advent of modern machinery, the global hubs of cotton production were found in the regions of Gujarat, Punjab, the Coromandel Coast, and Bengal in India, as well as the Yangtze Delta in China. However, as industrialization surged ahead, they were overshadowed by burgeoning industrial hubs like Manchester.[77] Concurrently, France, which had once rivalled Britain in the textile industry, also began to trail its rival. By 1850, cotton spinning output per worker in France fell to a mere 40 percent of its British counterpart, with an even larger gap in weaving productivity.[78]

Among the wave of gadgets that entered British factories, the steam engine stands as the crowning achievement. As a general-purpose technology, it revolutionized a range of industries, not only driving machinery but also transforming transportation—its influence similar to the impact of computers and electricity in modern times. In contrast to many inventions of the era, which were born purely from engineering pursuits, the creation of steam power was rooted in discoveries from the scientific revolution. It relied on the insight that the atmosphere has weight and therefore can be used to do work—a discovery made by Galileo's assistant, Evangelista Torricelli, who developed the first barometer in 1643. This discovery paved the way for Thomas Newcomen's steam engine in 1712. Nevertheless, the full transformative impact of the steam engine would only be felt after nearly a century of further tinkering and development.

The most important advance was made by James Watt, whose idea for a separate condensation chamber in 1765 made steam power energy efficient and economically viable. Yet even with this workable design in hand, it took nearly two decades and financial backing from Matthew

Boulton before the first Boulton & Watt engine was successfully installed in 1784. For the next fifty years, steam's impact on the British economy remained modest, with waterpower still serving as the predominant force driving many factories. It took the advent of the railroads for steam-powered productivity to take off.[79]

Before the railroad, many attempts had been made to build steam cars, but steam engines remained too large and bulky, especially for Britain's many unpaved roads. This would change in 1803, when Richard Trevithick unveiled his London Steam Carriage, which used a lighter and smaller engine. This breakthrough, along with the introduction of other significant technologies—like better gears, gauges, and couplings—would eventually culminate in George Stephenson's *Rocket*: the steam locomotive used when the first public line between Liverpool and Manchester opened in 1830. The network swiftly expanded thereafter, covering 6,200 miles by 1850 and 15,600 miles by 1880. This development ushered in an era in which people, literature, correspondence, and news traveled at unparalleled speeds. Businesses flourished, as they could access bigger markets and better information, fueling the rapid rise of factories and machinery.[80] The age of the small artisan workshop was over. In its place, massive industrial enterprises emerged, driven by the logic of scale, efficiency, and speed.[81] As historian David Landes writes, the Industrial Revolution was "like in effect to Eve's tasting of the fruit of the trees of knowledge: the world has never been the same."[82]

The transition to the modern world, however, was hardly a smooth one, because powerful incumbent forces had an interest in protecting the status quo. Attending to these barriers can help explain why Britain, rather than its rivals on the Continent, would make and reap the bounty of these technological breakthroughs. All over Europe, those wanting to be a butcher, a baker, or a brewer could not just open a shop—they had to become a member of a guild. These organizations had controlled urban life since the twelfth century, regulating industries and ensuring that their members maintained high standards. Consumers trusted guilds as brands—a bottle of Burgundy wine or a wheel of Parmigiano cheese carried a seal of quality. But guilds were not just quality control systems. They were also gatekeepers, keeping membership exclusive and making it difficult for outsiders to compete. Extensive training was required to become a master, and even then, the number of new members was kept low.[83] Local rulers, in turn, had no interest in breaking this system, since guilds helped them collect taxes.

Guilds played a complex role in the history of innovation. On one hand, they helped pass down knowledge and skills, ensuring high standards within trades. But they also functioned as cartels, tightly controlling their industries and fiercely resisting any technology that threatened jobs or incomes, including those that made the Industrial Revolution. Indeed, it is no coincidence that new towns like Birmingham and Manchester, which emerged in formerly rural areas free from gilded restrictions, would go on to become Britain's industrial powerhouses.[84] Manchester, for instance, went from a small town of merely 2,000 people in the seventeenth century, ranking eighty-second largest in England, to a bustling city of 300,000 by 1841, ranking behind only Liverpool and London.[85]

By blocking progress, the guilds imposed extraordinary costs on the rest of society. Drawing on two databases of guild activities, economic historian Sheilagh Ogilvie shows that guilds lobbied governments for privileges, restricted competition from nonmembers, and vehemently opposed any innovations when they threatened their profits.[86] At times, when a more powerful guild benefited from a new technology at the expense of a weaker faction, swift adoption followed. One example is the multi-shuttle ribbon frame—a weaving innovation that most guilds in Europe successfully resisted. In the Dutch Republic, though, it spread because some ribbon-weaving guilds supported it. But such cases were rare. More often than not, guilds clung to their privileges, and their opposition to change often turned violent. Consider the destruction of Denis Papin's steam digester in 1705. Even though his friend and mentor, Gottfried Leibniz, had written to the Elector of Kassel, asking for Papin to be granted free passage, no petition was granted. When Papin decided to embark on his journey anyway, the boatmen's guild, who monopolized the river traffic on the Fulda and Weser, smashed the steam engine to pieces when his boat arrived at Münden.[87]

The power of the guilds is best illustrated by the frequency with which the political authorities sided with them.[88] In 1551, the gig mill was banned in Britain over employment concerns. And when the clergyman William Lee traveled to London in anticipation of a patent for his stocking-frame knitting machine, Queen Elizabeth I refused to grant him a patent, fearing that it would bring members of the hosiers' guild to "ruin by depriving them of employment, thus making them beggars." This logic also underpinned the Privy Council's decision to ban a needlemaking machine in 1623, as well as Charles I prohibition on the casting of buckets nine years later. Meanwhile, on the Continent, political authorities took similar steps. Automatic looms were banned in several cities, including the city of Leiden and throughout the provinces in Germany, after riots erupted during the seventeenth and eighteenth centuries.[89]

Although guilds were only abolished in England with the Municipal Corporations Act of 1835, their power began fading much earlier as markets became more integrated. Because their influence did not extend beyond the borders of the city where they operated, competition between cities significantly undermined their power. Even before the railroads, the turnpike trusts created a sizable road network, so that by 1840 Britain had twice the road density of competing powers like Spain and France. This period also witnessed a remarkable leap in stagecoach speeds, with the pace of travel increasing from a modest 1.96 journey miles per hour to a substantial 7.96 journey miles per hour.[90] While it took ten to twelve days to travel from London to Edinburgh in 1750, the same trip could be covered by stagecoach in about forty-five hours by the time of the first railroads in the 1830s.[91] As these changes swept through the country, even well-entrenched cartels such as the shearers' guild—once mighty enough to block the gig mill for decades—found themselves facing fierce new competition. In places like Wiltshire and Somerset, guilds violently resisted progress, but in Gloucester, the shearers discovered a new strategy:

by adopting the mills, they could produce at lower costs and even expand their trade beyond local borders.[92]

Patent records confirm that regions exposed to greater competition were more likely to pursue new technologies, accelerating the decline of guild influence.[93] But this shift also relied on state power and an emerging merchant class. This dynamic first unfolded in Britain, where a cadre of wealthy merchants gained influence within the halls of Parliament, culminating in the Glorious Revolution of 1688, which reinforced parliamentary supremacy over the Crown. The enactment of new legislation, such as the Bill of Rights and the Mutiny Act, effectively erected new defenses against vote and seat buying, and curbed the monarch's ability to govern unchecked by shortening the period for which taxes were granted.[94] As a result, power slowly shifted not only from the Crown to Parliament but also to merchant manufacturers, who stood to gain the most from the rise of modern industry.[95] This turned Parliament into a forum and voice for British commerce, paving the way for the use of land for more productive ends.[96]

For instance, take the turnpike trusts, set up to build roads and boost trade. Backed by acts of Parliament, they had the power to raise funds through bonds and tolls, aiding travel and commerce.[97] Moreover, unlike in France or the Holy Roman Empire, where merchants moving goods along the Rhine had to pay extra tariffs at every border, in England, Parliament kept tolls low and ensured that internal trade remained largely free from such obstacles.[98] Undeniably, the English Parliament had a persistent tendency to enact laws that favoured special interests, often at the expense of the broader public, as exemplified by the notorious Calico Act of 1721, which restricted the import of cotton textiles into England. But the direction of travel is unmistakable. As the eighteenth century unfolded, a notable shift took place whereby numerous special interest groups saw their legislated privileges and monopolies, along with restrictions on workers' freedom to move and choose their jobs, come under mounting scrutiny.[99] Whereas under the Tudor or Stuart monarchs someone like Papin, whose steam digester was destroyed by angry Fulda boatmen, would have encountered significant resistance, this was no longer true after 1688.

The weakening of the guilds in Britain, in other words, was much a deliberate political choice. In the eighteenth century, the polity and judiciary, which had long supported the guilds opposition to technological progress, began to side with the innovators, as the elite establishment came to the realization that British power in Europe depended on the taxable fortunes it could accumulate. Despite protests from spinners, combers, and shearers who petitioned Parliament to ban gig mills and cotton-spinning machines, their demands went unanswered. In 1769, Parliament took an even stronger stance, passing a law that made the destruction of machinery a capital offense. When the Luddite riots erupted between 1811 and 1816, forcing the government to send in the army, they were in part a reaction to the repeal of the 1551 law that had originally prohibited gig mills. Even in the face of violent resistance, the government remained firmly on the side of industrial progress. After the Lancashire riots of 1779, a resolution made the official position clear: while new machines had caused social unrest, they had also brought undeniable economic benefits. To destroy them would not stop technological change—it would only shift its rewards to Britain's rivals.[100]

In France, by contrast, the phenomenon of machine-breaking became inextricably intertwined with the emergence of revolutionary politics, making it virtually impossible for the state to undercut the guilds or to quell the insurrectionary sentiment. In the wake of the storming of the Bastille, unrest spread far and wide. Among those swept up in the fervour were the woollen workers of Darnetal, who descended upon the industrial enclave of Saint-Sever with a resolute purpose: to dismantle and destroy the machines that symbolized their grievances. This act of defiance set off a ripple effect as similar incidents proliferated throughout the nation. George Garnett, a stalwart industrialist, attempted to stem the tide of unrest. Yet, without the backing of the army, his efforts proved feeble. The incapacity of the state to repress France's Luddites undermined the resolve of its entrepreneurs to embark on industrial pursuits.[101] What set Britain apart during the Industrial Revolution was not an absence of resistance to the winds of technological change but rather the unwavering support and resolute alignment of its government with the "party" of innovation.[102]

The tale of how British institutions fostered and safeguarded an environment conducive to innovation and entrepreneurship, while suppressing resistance to mechanization, also stands in sharp relief to the experience of the Dutch Republic. Often referred to as the "first modern economy," the Dutch had a more democratic system. Yet its political institutions were more vulnerable to capture by incumbents and special interests. Guilds in the Netherlands were less restrictive than those in much of Europe, allowing relatively easy entry for newcomers and fostering a thriving artistic scene—after all, Rembrandt, Vermeer, and Hals, despite belonging to guilds, still produced works that define the Dutch Golden Age and the canon of Western art. Unlike in Germany, where guilds imposed strict barriers based on family background, religion, and even lifestyle, Dutch cities became magnets for talent. But while their guilds were more inclusive, they still resisted mechanized industry, fearing that new technologies would threaten jobs and incomes.[103] In 1734, for example, Jacob Jacobi faced considerable hostility while attempting to demonstrate his new dredging machine in Amsterdam. He had arranged with the public works department to conduct a trial but encountered threats from angry craftsmen who warned of stoning his team and burning his equipment. A few years later, in 1743, Daam Schijf designed a mechanized postal vessel that could speed up deliveries between Holland and Venice. But before it could set sail, an angry mob, which had been threatening him for months, surrounded the nearly finished ship. Within half an hour, the vessel was deliberately sunk and destroyed. Meanwhile, in Leiden local blacksmiths and carpenters hindered the completion of Leopold Genneté's water-raising machine by withholding necessary materials.[104]

Notably, the number of guilds on Dutch soil significantly increased throughout the seventeenth century. Indeed, by the late seventeenth century, an estimated 70 to 85 percent of adult male workers in Amsterdam, the heart of Dutch capitalism, were involved in the guild system.[105] And their efforts to lobby local governments for protection, which were far more effective than violent resistance, were widely recognized as a hinderance to economic development. For instance, in prize contests held by learned societies in Holland and Utrecht that focused on the decline of Dutch trade and industry, three out of five winning essays, including one by Leiden cloth manufacturer Jan van Heukelom, identified guild restrictions as a major barrier to innovation.[106]

As figure 3.2 suggests, they had a point. The Dutch initially led the British in patenting, but eventually fell behind. After 1575, a modern patent system was set up in the Dutch Republic, benefiting inventors like Simon Stevin, Cornelis Drebbel, Jan Leeghwater, Corneliszoon van Uitgeest, and Willem Meester.[107] Before the Dutch Revolt, patents were granted as royal favors by sovereigns like Charles V and Philip II—a practice that continued in Britain for some time. But after gaining independence in the early 1580s, the Dutch transferred patenting power to the States General, provincial governments, and towns. Between 1580 and 1620, this system evolved to protect both inventors and the national interest, offering exclusive rights, penalties for infringement, and allowing patent trading. This framework promoted decentralized exploration and collaboration, as demonstrated by the 1586 profit-sharing agreement between Stevin and Johan de Groot, Delft's mayor, for a water-raising mill patent.[108]

Yet Dutch innovation, for the most part, was incremental rather than radical, not least because the latter threatened the power of the guilds. Early on, this permitted faster growth than in the rest of Europe, as the Dutch craft guilds were relatively open to migrants, and helped facilitate improvements to existing technologies. However, it was not enough to ignite an industrial revolution. Meanwhile, Dutch elites, rather than investing in technology, focused on protecting their trading interests by spending vast sums on wars against England and other armed conflicts in Denmark, Brazil, and East Asia. And when the conquest of markets petered out as a source of growth, merchant interests turned to protecting existing revenue streams, which thwarted meaningful reform. The trouble was that in addition to the existence of a States General for the whole republic, each Dutch town and province also had its own assembly. In this system, power ultimately resided in the towns, who tied the hands of their

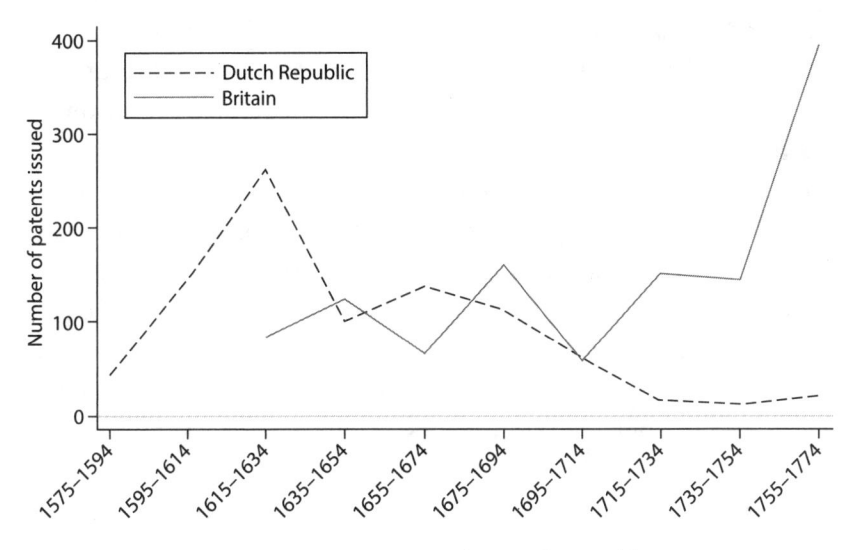

FIGURE 3.2. Patenting in Great Britain vs. the Dutch Republic, 1575–1744
Source: Stasavage, *Decline and Rise of Democracy*, Figure 9.2.

deputies with strict mandates in negotiations.[109] For proposals to pass higher level assemblies, consent from each major town was needed, and in cities like Rotterdam, some 80 precent of new city council members were relatives of existing board members. As nepotism flourished, elite families increasingly appointed their sons to key positions, such as mayors and directors, handing themselves the power to regulate trade, control market access, and decide on citizenship rights.[110] The stagnation experienced by the Dutch Republic was caused, in part, by a cohort of gilded elites who guarded their own fortunes by regulating the economy in their favour.[111]

During the mid-eighteenth century, the rising tide of protectionism became increasingly evident in many Dutch cities. In 1749, for instance, Haarlem introduced a system to monitor frames and looms in the linen ribbon industry to prevent their export. Gouda followed in 1750 with a bylaw against exporting tobacco pipe–making equipment, and in 1755, Delft restricted faience craftsmen from returning to work in the city if they had worked elsewhere. These bans were also accompanied by greater secrecy, as recorded by foreign visitors. In 1776, for instance, French engineer Bonaventure Le Turc was barred from an Utrecht cloth mill, while Prussian travelers in the 1770s and 80s were required to obtain permits to visit Haarlem factories. Similarly, Swedish traveler J. J. Björnståhl failed to access papermaking techniques in the Zaan district, and in 1782, a Danish spy named Ole Henckel, posing as a merchant, unsuccessfully tried to access mills producing blue dye in Zaandam.[112] To be sure, protectionism was more a symptom of Dutch decline than its cause, but it undeniably exacerbated the situation. At a time when gilded interests undermined the force of creative destruction that was unleashed in England, technology suddenly flowed less freely in the Dutch Republic.[113]

Comparing the fortunes of England and Holland makes clear that the improved security of property rights was not, as is often claimed, the decisive factor in propelling English innovation after the Glorious Revolution of 1688. Property rights were equally secure in the Low Countries. What made the difference was that English institutions after 1688 no longer let powerful groups stand in the way of technological change. Unlike on the Continent, British MPs were not bound by mandates. They could make laws as they saw fit, and their constituents could then decide to reelect them or not. Hence, once the British Parliament became supreme, politicians were relatively insulated from local interests. Paradoxically, Britain's technological miracle not only depended on Parliament's ability to protect private property but also on its capacity to override some of those rights when the prosperity of the nation was at risk. The expansion of canals and turnpikes throughout Britain, for example, was accomplished by acts of Parliament that prioritized economic growth over the property and interests of select landowners.[114]

This would have been unthinkable in the Dutch Republic or even in ancien régime France, where, despite its autocratic constitution, local incumbents still had a great deal of blocking power. It took Napoleon to sweep away the old estates-based order, abolish the guilds, and develop the kind of centralized state capable of overruling special interests.[115] Indeed, Napoleon's imposition of the *Code Napoléon* on much of the Rhineland disrupted the power of German local elites and led to the dissolution of the guilds, producing an upsurge in innovation.[116] Recent findings show that as late as 1900, German territories occupied by Napoleon filed twice as many patents as their unoccupied counterparts.[117] The interplay between state power and external pressures, in the form of intense geopolitical competition, proved critical to bypass incumbent interests, which established the conditions for innovation-led growth.

China's Gilded Age

In China, a contrasting trajectory unfolded during the same period. While Europe saw heightened Great Power rivalry in the eighteenth century, China experienced relatively little such competition, which contributed to the continued erosion of the bureaucratic state and an increasing reliance on local elites. The result was that oligarchical politics gained prominence, laying the groundwork for a state of stagnation. Notably, however, by the late Qing dynasty, the Middle Kingdom was freed from the burden of inventing new technologies as a prerequisite for economic growth. Having fallen sufficiently far behind the West, it now had the opportunity to simply adopt pioneering British technologies. Nevertheless, because of diminished state capacity, it failed to do so.

In the 1860s, government agencies in China assumed an active role in the recruitment of foreign talent and the importation of Western technology. These efforts first focused on military projects and then expanded in the following decade to include civilian ventures, such as establishing railroads and telegraph systems connecting major cities, and building shipyards in Shanghai and steel mills in Wuhan.[118] These industrial undertakings were carried out by so-called *kuan-tu shang-pan* enterprises, which were supervised by government officials but run by merchants, in an attempt to attract private capital while keeping ultimate control in the hands of the state.[119] But they were plagued by corruption and excessive interference from officials, which resulted in huge inefficiencies.[120]

The vanishing bureaucratic capacity of the Qing government also meant that attempts to capitalize on Western technologies were systematically thwarted by vested interests. The Chinese guilds (*gongsuo*) not only persisted much longer than their counterparts in Europe but also had almost unchecked control over their crafts.[121] By uniting people with lineage or native-place ties practising the same occupation, the guilds were able to resist any technologies that posed a threat to their livelihoods. When native merchants imported thin sheet brass from Birmingham in the late nineteenth century, for example, local coppersmiths of Fatshan in the Guangdong Province, who hammered out sheets imported in a thicker form, threatened to revolt. A riot was only narrowly averted when the "offending metal" was returned to Hong Kong. In much the same way, the indigenous population responded to a Chinese entrepreneur introducing sewing machines from America by swiftly destroying them.

To avoid unrest, Chinese local authorities typically sided with the guilds, just like on the Continent in Europe. For instance, when a steam-powered cotton mill was established in Shanghai in 1876, the cotton cloth guild promptly passed a resolution prohibiting the production of clothes using machines, and city officials refrained from endorsing the mill due to fears of unrest.[122] Similarly, when a Chinese merchant established mechanized silk-reeling factories in Guangdong, traditional silk weavers responded with riots, prompting the local magistrate to order the closure of the factories.[123]

The formidable power wielded by the guilds largely stemmed from the concessions granted to them by officials in exchange for tax revenues. These arrangements resulted in the emergence of local oligarchs, who united to restrict competition over trade privileges with the state.[124] Notably, in the realm of transportation, the Qing government issued "dragon tickets" and other official notices of approval to the guilds.[125] According to Hosea Ballou Morse, who served in the Chinese Imperial Maritime Custom Service around 1900, "all Chinese trade guilds are alike in interfering with every detail of business and demanding complete solidarity of interest in their members. . . . The result is a tyranny of the many over the individual, and a system of control which must by its nature hinder freedom of enterprise and independence of individual initiative."[126]

The anticompetitive web of relationships Morse observed can go some way in explaining why Chinese industrialization was long delayed. Contrary to Britain, where the influence of guilds gradually waned with the integration of markets and successive governments assertively superseding their authority, China remained on a less dynamic trajectory throughout the nineteenth century. One crucial factor contributing to this disparity was the enormous distances between Chinese cities, which limited the competitive dynamics between them.[127] Before the advent of railroads, the cost of transporting goods, people, and ideas across this vast territory remained exorbitantly high. In addition, China's railroads, like other modern technologies, were held back by the presence of various interest groups, including traditional junk vessel owners and officials benefiting from canal-based rice tribute transportation, both of whom resisted the spread of railways.[128]

As a result, the first railway, connecting Wusong to Shanghai, was constructed by the British company of Jardine, Matheson and Co. only in the 1870s, a full four decades after the inaugural line in Britain. That project, however, was eventually acquired by the Qing government and subsequently dismantled due to opposition from local stakeholders.[129] This episode convinced officials like Li Hung-chang that resistance to the railroads was so strong that a covert approach was needed: when embarking on the construction of a short coal-carrying railroad, Li misleadingly referred to it as a "horse road" and kept the use of steam-powered locomotives secret until operations were underway, when, as one contemporary notes, very few high officials dared to visit.[130] The prevailing belief in China was that railroads, telegraph lines, and other innovations could jeopardize the delicate fabric of social stability by engendering land grabs and disputes, displacing porters and peddlers, and fueling conflicts between local communities and foreign entities. This pervasive sentiment, in turn, significantly influenced the imperial court's ambivalent stance toward reform.[131]

As the new century dawned, China thus found itself lagging behind other major global powers in technological terms. Even the significantly smaller Portugal had constructed nearly three times as much railway length as China, whose network clocked in at a humble 829 kilometres.

China was trapped in a vicious cycle, where entrenched interests stifled railroad development, thus fragmenting markets while fortifying their own power. Despite having comparable levels of market integration as continental Europe around 1750, the Middle Kingdom experienced a notable decline thereafter, a divergence that coincided with the railroad craze in Europe.[132]

Unequal Treaties

China's lack of domestic competition meant that its growth was primarily fueled by integration with the global economy and the arrival of foreign competition.[133] This transformative process commenced within the confines of select urban enclaves, which were forcibly converted into what came to be known as treaty ports. Following the Opium War of 1842, the British Empire established five ports to facilitate its foreign trade with China. As discussed in chapter 2, China soon found itself subjected to additional "unequal treaties" imposed by the United States, Russia, France, Germany, and Japan that ultimately resulted in the establishment of more than eighty treaty ports across the vast empire (figure 3.3).

An unintended consequence of this regrettable colonial endeavour was the modernization of China. As economic historians Loren Brandt and Thomas Rawski point out, "The creation of semi-autonomous treaty ports unleashed a flood of innovation, especially in Shanghai, which anticipated Shenzhen's contemporary role as a magnet for ambitious and entrepreneurial migrants, an entry port for new ideas and a hotbed of institutional innovation."[134] Careful empirical analysis affirms this view: while destabilizing the Qing regime, the opening of these treaty ports significantly increased the number of industrial machines and steam engines and created new businesses.[135] Beyond forging essential connections to worldwide markets and know-how abroad, these ports also became pivotal conduits for domestic technological diffusion.[136]

Chinese modernization was also facilitated by the completion of the Suez Canal in 1869, which drastically cut shipping costs, and the rise of steamships that by the 1880s could annually ferry an impressive 100,000

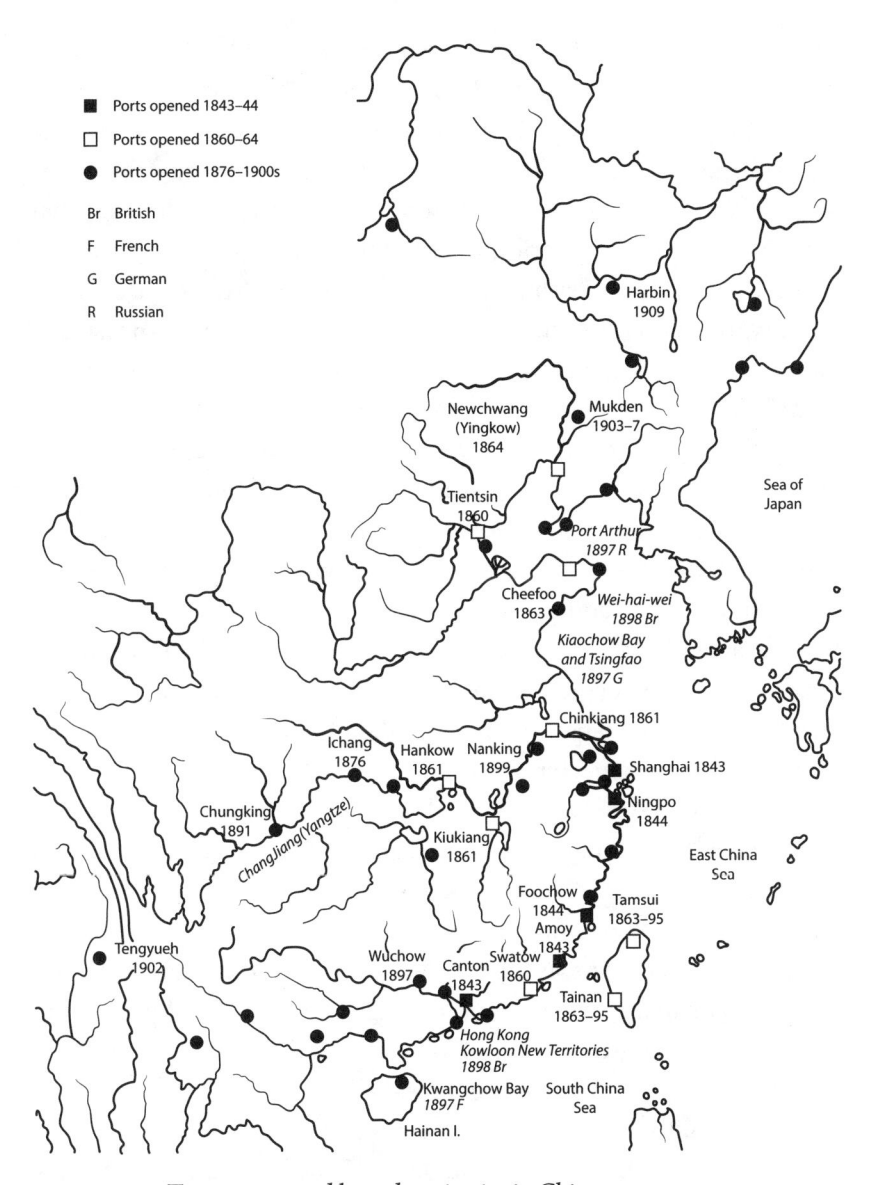

FIGURE 3.3. Treaty ports and leased territories in China
Source: Drawing by author, based on Osterhammel, "Britain and China 1842–1914," Map 8.1.

tons of foreign coal to the thriving port of Shanghai.[137] But the advent of global trade served as a catalyst to China's transformation not primarily by bringing an influx of goods to its shores but by increasing its exposure to innovative ideas and institutions. This era saw the emergence of modern banking entities, the establishment of the Shanghai stock exchange, the creation of the *Zongli Yamen* (China's foreign ministry), and the flourishing of shareholding companies with limited liability. It also witnessed an unparalleled inflow of new knowledge and ideologies—ranging from engineering principles to Marxism to democratic values—often disseminated by Christian missionaries who established schools, medical facilities, and universities nationwide. Meanwhile, success stories of students who returned from overseas training and alumni of Western-style schools in Hong Kong demonstrated that the study of Confucian classics was no longer the only way to climb the social ladder. Overseas Chinese, who were once targeted for official predation, were suddenly welcome for both their wealth and know-how. An 1893 edict, for instance, ordered that "all Chinese merchants . . . may return home to practice their trade upon receiving a pass from the Chinese minister or consul."[138]

Global trade also led to heightened competition, which diminished the sway of local vested interests, as had happened in Britain two centuries earlier, but with a twist: the Chinese state lacked both the inclination and the capability to undermine incumbent interests in the manner of Westminster. In Europe, as the British Empire forged ahead, competing powers found themselves with more to gain and less to lose by introducing new technologies that promised industrial advantages, even if it meant embracing the unsettling forces of creative destruction and internal instability.[139] Economic historians Nathan Rosenberg and L. E. Birdzell Jr. eloquently encapsulate this shift, noting that, "Once it was clear that one or another of these competing centers would always let the genie out of the bottle, the possibility of aligning political power with the economic status quo and against technological change more or less disappeared from the Western mind."[140] As chapter 4 will unveil, this realization prompted governments around the West to assume a more proactive role in propelling technological catch-up. However, the weakened state in China failed to assume the role of a facilitator. Unlike Japan, where Western intervention ignited the Meiji Restoration and ushered in a series of state-sponsored initiatives encompassing technology transfer, manpower training, and sweeping reform, the Qing government resisted the tide of modernization.[141]

The backward Qing dynasty might well have collapsed during the Taiping Rebellion, but it was propped up by the foreign powers, who preferred the enfeebled imperial regime to the rebels. Not until the Sino-Japanese War of 1895—which led to the seizure of Taiwan, the end of Chinese control of Manchuria, and dealt a profound shock to the Chinese public—did a large fraction of the Chinese elite accept that technological conservatism could no longer maintain the political status quo.[142] The ensuing 1896 Treaty of Shimonoseki triggered the Hundred Days' Reform, which advocated a "revolution from above," much like the Meiji Restoration and the Stein-Hardenberg Reforms (see chapters 4 and 5). Yet even these reforms were stopped in their tracks by forces favouring conservatism, notably the influential Empress Dowager Cixi, who had been alarmed over proposals to modernize the civil service in favour of competence over loyalty.[143]

Eventually, however, the imperial court accepted the necessity of change. When the so-called Boxers ("The Righteous and Harmonious Fists") channeled their ire toward European missionaries and, encouraged by Empress Cixi, laid sieged to Western embassies situated within Beijing's imperial core, an eight-nation coalition consisting of Britain, the United States, France, Germany, Italy, Japan, Russia, and Austria-Hungary responded by seizing Beijing, marching through the Forbidden City, and conducting a commemorative ceremony in honour of the late Queen Victoria at the Meridian Gate. The shame of a force of 20,000 foreign troops subduing a nation of 400 million ignited a renewed drive for domestic reforms. By January 1901, a somewhat hesitant emperor issued a proclamation emphasizing the need for change to bolster the state: "The weakness of China is caused by the strength of convention and the rigid network of regulations. We have many mediocre officials but few men of talent and courage.... The appointment of men of talent is restricted by regulations which are so rigid that even men of extraordinary talent are missed."[144] By December 1905, an elite delegation set off to Japan, England, the United States, Germany, and France to study their strides in modernization. Tsinghua University, for example, founded by the Qing court as *Tsinghua xuetang* (Tsinghua Academy) in 1911, began as a preparatory institution for students chosen for further education in the United States.[145]

As a result, elite resistance to modern education, imported technologies, and factories began to wane. The early 1900s saw a "wave of scientific translations" of foreign writings, as well as the first Chinese translation of Adam Smith's *The Wealth of Nations*.[146] But while China reluctantly opened up and began to accept Western thought, its reform movement remained conservative. "[I]mport from the West its practice not its ideas" was the slogan of the reformers, echoing the view that the Qing official Zhang Zhidong put forward in his influential publication "Exhortation to Learning" (1898): "the old learning is the fundamental thing; the new learning is for practical use."[147] Yet, in practice, industrialization and modernization efforts were mostly local rather than national, because the state remained too weak to take on the role of facilitator.[148]

In the absence of a strong state, two distinct patterns of industrial growth emerged: "Treaty-Port industrialization" and "Manchurian industrialization."[149] At China's treaty ports, where successful Chinese industrialists with foreign experience or links to global companies established their businesses, the rise of modern industry happened in a bottom-up fashion. One successful venture would spark further ones through learning by doing, as the case of the Shanghai Dalong Machinery Company illustrates: having first set up a ship repair shop, it then diversified into repair of textile machinery before producing its own machines.[150] In Manchuria, in contrast, industrialization was carried out by the Japanese government and its quasi-official affiliates, like the Southern Manchurian Railroad, whose endeavours were fueled by economic and geopolitical aspirations. The iconic steel mill in Anshan stands as a testament to this process, as the mill only turned profitable after a decade and a half of continuous financial backing from the Japanese government—an investment magnitude unheard of elsewhere on the mainland.[151]

Yet despite its waning strength during the Ming-Qing era, the Chinese bureaucratic tradition never entirely disappeared. In a salient illustration of Max Weber's claim that bureaucracy is "among the social structures that are the hardest to destroy,"[152] the Guomindang regime, spearheaded by Sun Yat-sen and later Chiang Kai-shek, adeptly drew upon China's historic bureaucratic foundations to bolster its power.[153] This involved creating central government institutions like the National Resources Commission (NRC), the Ministry of Finance, and the Cotton Control Commission, as well as augmenting the civil service with a cadre of highly trained professionals, whose prime function soon became modernization when Japan invaded in 1937.[154] Moreover, after the Allied victory in World War II, numerous factories that had been confiscated in Shanghai under Japanese occupation passed into the hands of the Guomindang, endowing the Nationalist government with significant industrial assets.[155]

War, in other words, propelled investment in state capacity, and the state used its capacity to expedite the ascent of modern industry. This process began much earlier in continental Europe, where the emergence of a decentralized competitive state system made the administrative state play a more active role in closing the gap to the British Empire from the onset. To paraphrase Mokyr, in the economic history of the world, England is what the land of Israel is in the history of Christianity: where it all started.[156] But while the Old Testament of industrialization quickly spread to faraway places, followers began to chart their own, distinctive developmental path. Relative to Britain, they relied more on bureaucratic management to drive technological progress from above.

4

Prussia's Visible Hand

The technology of mass production ... favored—and the German literature of the time is filled with the phraseology—integration, coordination, systematization, interlacing, schematization, in a word "planning" on an ever wider and more intricate scale. This language, new for the businessman and the engineer after 1850, was still entirely understandable to the bureaucrats and the politicians of the *Beamtenstaat* who were schooled in the writings of the cameralist Becher, the nationalist List, the administrative reforms of Stein and Hardenburg, and the synchronized militarism of von Schlieffen and von Moltke.[1]

—ROBERT A. BRADY

DURING THE Industrial Revolution, England had raced ahead of its rivals in terms of technological and economic growth. By the end of the nineteenth century, however, the Continent was quickly closing this gap. In Germany, in particular, Prince Otto von Bismarck's unification of the country in the 1870s supercharged its industrial capacity and set the stage for a Great Power competition in the coming decades. To be sure, the economic integration of German states under the banner of the *Zollverein* (a customs union) was already underway, but the crowning of King William I of Prussia as German Emperor in the Hall of Mirrors at Versailles in 1871 created a politically unified Reich for the first time. Before then, the word *Germany* referred to a region with a common language and culture, but consisting of hundreds of political entities.

For the British, this initially was a welcome development. Between 1688 and 1815, Britian and France had been almost perpetually fighting for global supremacy. Many Britons, including the Queen, thus rejoiced to see her traditional Gallic adversary defeated in the Franco-Prussian War of 1870. Within little more than a decade, however, rapid German industrialization and population growth left France behind, and British sentiment shifted. The country now faced German hegemony on the Continent. Stretching over 1,200 kilometres from areas west of the Rhine to the Klaipėda region across the river Neman, which now divides Lithuania and Russia, and over 900 kilometres from the North Sea to the Alps, the new German Empire was more than twice the size of Great Britain. Germany, with its 41 million people, was significantly larger than its British rival, with a population of only 31.5 million, Ireland included.

The real cause for alarm, however, was that German companies were making significant inroads into Britain's industrial preeminence. Indeed, speaking about the matter in 1896, the former British Prime Minister Lord Rosebery argued that Britain was threatened by "one very formidable rival" who "is encroaching on us as the sea encroaches on weak parts of the coast."[2] To make his point, Lord Rosebery cited statistics from a new and much discussed book, *Made in Germany,* by Ernest Edwin Williams, a Welsh journalist and socialist. Williams observed that while English industries were steadily slowing down, Germany was making "marvellous progress." The reasons for this, he argued, were Germany's willingness to protect and support its industries and Britain's commitment to free trade.[3] While England "was throwing wide her gates to the world at large, her sisters were building barriers of protection against her; and behind those barriers, and aided often by State subventions, during the middle and later years of the century, they have developed industries of their own." In his words, Germany had successfully "wormed its way into English manufacturing secrets," "educated her people in a fashion which . . . made it in some branches of industry the superior," and "kept a strict controlling hand on all strings of their businesses."[4] To see the consequences of Britain's failure to adjust to this alleged new reality, Williams urged his readers to undertake the following mental exercise and observe their surroundings:

> You will find that the material of some of your own clothes was probably woven in Germany. Still more probable is it that some of your wife's garments are German importations; while it is practically beyond a doubt that the magnificent mantles and jackets wherein her maids array themselves on their Sundays out are German-made and German-sold, for only so could they be done at the figure. Your governess's *fiancé* is a clerk in the City; but he also was made in Germany. The toys, and the dolls, and the fairy books which your children maltreat in the nursery are made in Germany: nay, the material of your favourite (patriotic) newspaper had the same birthplace as like as not. Roam the house over, and the fateful mark will greet you at every turn, from the piano in your drawing-room to the mug on your kitchen dresser, blazoned though it be with the legend, *A Present from Margate*. Descend to your domestic depths, and you shall find your very drain-pipes German made. You pick out of the grate the paper wrappings from a book consignment, and they also are "Made in Germany," You stuff them into the fire, and reflect that the poker in your hand was forged in Germany. As you rise from your hearthrug you knock over an ornament on your mantlepiece; picking up the pieces you read, on the bit that formed the base, "Manufactured in Germany." And you jot your dismal reflections down with a pencil that was made in Germany. At midnight your wife comes home from an opera which was made in Germany, has been hero enacted by singers and conductor and players made in Germany, with the aid of instruments and sheets of music made in Germany. You go to bed, and glare wrathfully at a text on the wall; it is illuminated with an English village church, and it was "Printed in Germany."[5]

In his fear of British decline, Williams was not alone. The use of the word *decadence* in *The Times* rose constantly throughout the nineteenth century.[6] But fears over German imports peaked during what historian Ross Hoffman has called the "midsummer madness" of 1896.[7] Newspaper columns argued that the economic consequences of foreign goods pouring into Britain were being felt most keenly by the average British worker, who struggled to find new and equally profitable employment as British industry suffered, while orators in the House of Commons eloquently denounced government purchases of Bavarian pencils. Replace "Germany" with "China" and "Britain" with "America," and those writings and speeches could have been made today. Among contemporaries, Arthur Shadwell's *Industrial Efficiency* (1906) lamented that "the once enterprising manufacturer has grown slack [and] has let the business take care of itself, while he is shooting grouse or yachting in the Mediterranean," while the main preoccupation of the British worker has become "football or betting."[8]

With the benefit of hindsight, it is easy to dismiss such alarm as exaggerated.[9] British income per capita, which was almost twice as high as Germany's the day it unified in 1871, remained about 40 percent higher in 1913.[10] This gap, however, reflected Germany's vast and backward agricultural sector, not the state of German industry. In the 1870s, 50 percent of the German workforce was employed in farming, compared to just 22 percent in Britain. Although the agricultural share in Germany had fallen to 30 percent by 1935, it had declined to a mere 7 percent in Britain.[11] One reason, of course, was that the path to modernity in England had begun much earlier.[12] Moreover, Britain's trading empire meant that landed elites had more diversified wealth, making them beneficiaries of urban growth and global markets. This meant that the agricultural protectionist lobby was vocal but weak, which contributed to the Empire's devotion to free trade and ultimately resulted in the repeal of the Corn Laws in 1846.[13]

In Wilhelmine Germany, by contrast, agrarian protectionism ruled. The Prussian three class franchise system, which was established after the 1848 revolution, did extend the franchise by giving tax-paying men the right to vote, but voters were allocated into three classes depending on their tax payments. First-class voters, despite making up less than 5 percent of voters, had more than seventeen times the number of votes of their third-class counterparts, who made up 83 percent of the voting population. In some constituencies, industrialists were able to take advantage of this system and elect MPs who voted for liberal policies. But where large estate owners dominated, they used their political clout to secure generous tariff protection for rye, wheat, and oats—their chief grain outputs.[14] Indeed, while Bismarck famously declared that the German Empire was forged in iron and blood, critics called it an alliance of iron and rye.[15] Such protections, however, came at a significant price for the German nation, as agriculture failed to modernize and mechanize as a consequence. With most of the population stuck in farming, Germany could only hope to create a few islands of progress in an otherwise backward sea. Thus, while volumes have been dedicated to the so-called Victorian Climacteric, debating the English growth failure, seen through this lens, the failure was German—a result of its political system, which held back much needed structural change.[16]

On the other hand, Germany undoubtedly forged ahead as Britain fell behind in some critical emerging and increasingly science-based industries, but they were not yet large enough to leave much of an imprint on the national economy.[17] To many, however, this would have seemed inconceivable just a few decades earlier. When the Crystal Palace Exhibition in Hyde Park, London, was opened by Queen Victoria in May 1851, Britain's technological leadership left visitors from around the world stunned. About half of the space was devoted to exhibits from the host country and her Empire, with France coming in as the second largest contributor. Meanwhile, the official German commission at the exhibition criticized their countrymen for their lack of creativity and imagination. In its own words: "It is clearly not to be expected that Germany will ever be able to reach the level of production of coal and iron currently attained in England."[18] Even the Ruhr, which would become the heartland of German industry, was still insignificant at the time. In the mid-nineteenth century, the world produced some 70,000 tons of steel annually, of which 40,000 tons were produced in Britain.

Fast forward half a century and the tables had turned. In 1910, Ernst Bassermann, a businessman and politician who served as leader of the National Liberal Party through the last years of the German Empire, reported to Kaiser Wilhelm II: "The English really cannot keep up with us any longer . . . without the stream of gold still flowing from the large colonies into the tiny mother country they would soon be a quantity negligible" on the world market.[19] The English, he felt, had become too complacent and conservative. Writing in 1913, the German economist and historian Werner Sombart likewise noted that Germany, thanks to its organizational capabilities and scientific attitudes, had made enormous strides, while the old pathbreaker, England, had lost the spirit of enterprise for their love of luxury, sports, and aristocratic living.[20]

Indeed, Germany's relatively rapid growth led many to believe that it had found a superior recipe for progress. Though Britain's economic liberalism was widely admired, other countries did not strive for minimalist government intervention.[21] On the contrary, throughout most of Europe—in Austria-Hungary as in Poland, in France as in Germany, in Italy as in Russia—the consensus among the elites was that industrialization required a strong state. Liberal reforms, including the abolishment of serfdom and guilds, the establishment of some forms of democratic representation, and the protection of private property rights were mostly part of the industrialist package. But a passive, merely law-enforcing state was not. Rather, the objective of reformers on the Continent, many of them influenced by the writings of Friedrich List, was to weaken traditional society and build a strong state in its ruins. It was widely understood that countries could import British technologies without importing her economic policies.[22] If the British Industrial Revolution had been guided by Adam Smith's invisible hand, Alfred Chandler's visible hand played a much larger role among latecomers.

Continental Emulation

By 1800, Britain's technological lead was already considerable, and the opportunities for catch-up on the Continent were abundant. French as well as German businesses struggled to compete with British goods, which were produced with cutting-edge automation technologies. And almost all steam engines used on the Continent were British imports. The first mechanized German cotton mill, for example, was set up in Ratingen in 1784 using Arkwright's water frame. During the early years of the century, however, access to British technology abroad remained limited by Napoleon's Berlin Decree, which brought into effect a large-scale embargo against British trade. Not until the defeat of Napolean and subsequent Congress of Vienna in 1815, which lifted the blockade, were Prussian entrepreneurs permitted to buy the latest technologies.[23]

True, the export of most machines and blueprints thereof from Britain remained banned until 1842, while the emigration of British artisans—which were needed just as much as machines—was forbidden until 1825. But mercifully, for continental entrepreneurs, these measures were largely ineffective. As one historian points out: "there were so many loopholes and the ingenuity of smugglers and industrial spies was such, that these efforts were in the long run unavailing. By 1825 there must have been two thousand—and perhaps more—skilled British workers on the Continent. Similarly, while we will never know precisely how much machinery crossed the Channel illicitly . . . the sources on the continental countries are full of evidence of the successful purchase and installation of British equipment."[24]

Even so, bringing British foremen, technicians, and craftsmen across the channel was often costly, especially since many did not stay for long. Factory owners frequently poached them from their competitors, and so their already high salaries were pushed even higher. And higher pay did not always translate into better work. Many technicians were used to considerable autonomy and irregular hours, wanted more leisure, became homesick, and drowned their sorrows in alcohol. Aware of their indispensability and possessing a strong sense of national pride, British artisans were also often arrogant and fractious.[25] The German pioneer of industry Fritz Harkort lamented that he could not wait for the day when German moulders were properly trained, so he could send his spoiled British workers back home: "we must even now tread softly with them, for they're only too quick to speak of quitting if one does so little as not look at them in a friendly fashion."[26] At the same time, however, many of the best of the British technicians who went abroad also became industrialists themselves—though often with the assistance of local partners. In France, this included Richard Waddington (cotton), Job Dixon (machine-building), and James Jackson (steel), while in the Prussian and Austrian Empires, James Cockerill (machine construction), William Mulvany (mining), Norman Douglas (cotton), and Edward Thomas (iron and engineering) all became leading figures. Perhaps most famously, in Belgium, John Cockerill (James's brother) made a career of commercializing the innovations of others, with generous support of the Dutch and Belgian governments.[27]

European monarchs and princes did not just compete for British talent—they actively studied Britain's technological progress.[28] Officials were frequently sent across the channel on inspection tours, returning with reports that highlighted the urgent need to catch up. In response, governments took a far more active role in driving innovation than their British counterparts ever had. Besides technical assistance, governments awarded grants to attract skilled immigrants and exempted duties on imported technology. Such efforts to spur catch-up were state-led in Italy, Spain, France, and Russia, but in Prussia in particular, it was symptomatic of a "passionate desire to organize and hasten the process of catching up."[29] The Prussian *Seehandlung* was the first active agency to pursue this task. Under the direction of Christian von Rother, it invested not only in the seaborne trade but also in railways and manufacturing enterprises. And while much technological learning still happened informally, continental Europe pushed further by developing formal training systems—again, with state backing.[30]

At the same time, institutional reforms helped spread technological knowledge more efficiently. During the ancien régime, France sought to encourage the transfer of foreign technologies through a complicated system of exclusive privileges, but following the revolution, the government introduced a modern patent law, inspired by the English system, with the objective of reducing corruption and spurring innovation. Although Germany did not have a unified patent law until 1877—which meant that inventors had to apply for patent protection in each individual state, making patenting extremely expensive—individual German states, like the Grand Duchy of Baden, introduced sweeping patent reform in 1827 to make the system less corrupt and more transparent.[31] These reforms led to an upsurge in patenting, driven by foreign inventors, which proved crucial in enabling technological catch-up in both countries.[32] As statistical analysis of French inventions by economic historian Alessandro Nuvolari and collaborators shows, in the period 1791 to 1844, patents filed by either British inventors, or French inventors personally linked with British ones, were particularly valuable.[33] In water-power technologies, for example, French inventors built on the work by John Smeaton and John Rennie, carried out in England in the eighteenth century, which culminated in the Benoit Fourneyron water-turbine in 1837.[34] Even Britain's most iconic technology, the steam engine, was introduced to France from England by Humphrey Edwards by means of a French patent of importation, where it was improved upon during the 1820s and 1830s.[35]

A Revolution from Above

What laggards needed more than anything else was the capacity to swiftly transfer, absorb, and improve British technology, but large-scale manufacturing required more than just the latest machines.[36] It demanded roads, bridges, ports, and transportation systems, as well as schools for general and technical education, which exceeded the investment capabilities of any single enterprise. And vis-a-vis Britain, this was Germany's comparative advantage.

The German state bureaucracy arrived before modern industry and shaped the country's path to riches to a far greater extent than its counterpart in Britain or, for that matter, America. Indeed, when Max Weber wrote about modern bureaucracy early in the twentieth century, it was the disciplined and technically skilled bureaucracy of his native Germany he had in mind. In contrast to England, where accountable government had first emerged following the Glorious Revolution of 1688–1689, which strengthened parliament and checked the monarch's ability to rule arbitrarily, the Estates in Prussia were weak and divided. Moreover, the widespread destruction from the Thirty Years' War, for which Prussian soil served as centre stage, intensified efforts to centralize power and bolster the state. As Samuel Pufendorf—a jurist from Saxony and the most influential German student of Thomas Hobbes—would forcefully argue, the all-destructive fury of the Thirty Years' War revealed that a strong state was necessary to prevent violence and disorder.

Recent memories of war thus paved the way for a series of strongmen rulers—from the Great Elector Frederick William (1640–1688) to Frederick the Great (1740–1786)—who through the army managed to consolidate the political power of the centralized royal administration.[37] This process began when the Great Elector, in the 1660s, decided to maintain a standing army in peacetime, which he used to undermine the Estates, relying on military force instead of consent to collect taxes. The *Generalkriegskommissariat*, set up in April 1655, was first staffed with officials selected by the monarch but gradually grew into a bureaucracy capable of both tax collection and war, thus paving the way for the creation of a Prussian state that would only be abolished by the Allied Control Council in 1947. Through a set of significant reforms—carried out by Dodo von Knyphausen—the government streamlined and organized the collection of Electoral revenues, encompassing crown land, tolls, mines, and monopolies, across the Hohenzollern territories. In 1689, even after the passing of the Great Elector, von Knyphausen oversaw the creation of the central Brandenburg-Prussian revenue office, which prepared the first comprehensive income and expenditure balance sheet for the fiscal year 1689–1690.[38] Around this time, the commissariat further expanded its role to encompass the welfare of the domestic manufacturing industry. Initiating programs aimed at achieving self-sufficiency in wool-based textiles and mediating conflicts between guilds and emerging businesses, it took on a broader responsibility for the economy, akin to the influential *contrôleur-général*, Jean-Baptiste Colbert in France.[39]

Like the Chinese had done in the days of the Xia dynasty, millennia earlier, Prussian rulers also introduced soil mapping technology for tax collection, thereby undercutting the information advantage of local elites. Previously, because tax-collecting agencies were controlled by the nobility, who often ignored aristocratic landowners understating their taxable holdings, revenues were low and the tax burden disproportionally borne by smallholding peasants. In 1715, Elector Frederick William I commenced a meticulous survey of landholdings, which unveiled approximately 35,000 formerly unreported taxable land units. The provincial domains administration then categorized all holdings based on soil quality. A new so-called General Hide Tax, tailored to soil quality, was instituted across the entire province. These measures, coupled with enhanced transparency and standardized leasing arrangements for crown land farms, yielded the desired upsurge in measured agrarian output and crown revenues. By reducing the need for fiscal negotiations with urban Estate representatives, however, this gain in revenue came at the expense of the autonomy of Prussia's already weak towns. Of the thirty German cities boasting populations of 10,000 or more in 1700, a mere two—Berlin and Königsberg—resided within the bounds of Brandenburg-Prussia.[40] What scholars have described as the intentional destruction of the Brandenburg bourgeoisie by the centralizing forces of the monarchical state, although difficult to quantify, likely left enduring scars. In the words of the Cambridge historian Christopher Clark, "The consequence was a political culture that was strong on obedience, but weak on civil courage and civic virtue."[41]

While the Hohenzollern monarchs were well aware of the importance of an efficient civil bureaucracy for their Great Power aspirations, the shift from a patrimonial bureaucracy based on loyalty to a modern meritocratic one took over a century. It was only in the 1770s that sweeping civil service reform—informed by accounts from Jesuit missionaries of the examination system in China—introduced examinations as the basis for recruitment and promotion.[42] As meritocratic appointments became more common, and education levels rose among the higher ranks of the bureaucracy, Enlightenment ideas soon collided with the traditional privileges of the ruling class. Indeed, a small but increasingly prominent number of individuals had become acquainted with liberal doctrines at the Prussian universities of Königsberg and Halle, where the ideas of Kant, Locke, Smith, and Hume had spread.[43] Consequently, concepts like individual freedom, merit, competition, and equality soon entered the civil service.

In the decades of the French Revolution, however, these ideas did not provide a realizable path to reform in Prussia, as the revolution strengthened reactionary sentiments among the aristocratic elites. The spirit of the Enlightenment, in other words, was not enough to bring about radical reform. What it did create was a blueprint ready to be implemented when the time was ripe, and that time finally came after the Battle of Jena-Auerstadt in 1806, when Napoleon Bonaparte demolished the half-patrimonial Prussian army. A young Georg Wilhelm Friedrich Hegel, who held an appointment at the University of Jena, witnessed Napoleon riding through the city. In the victory of the First French Empire, he saw the triumph of the modern state, organized according to bureaucratic principles.[44]

The ensuing peace of Tilsit came with harsh conditions. Negotiations took place by the river Niemen, where Napoleon and Tsar Alexander of Russia dictated terms, while Prussian King Frederick William had to stand on the riverbank as a mere observer wrapped in a Russian overcoat. In addition to territorial and population losses of half the kingdom, Prussia was forced to pay high reparations. These catastrophic results opened the door to the Stein-Hardenberg Reforms, which aimed to reestablish Prussia as a major power. As historian Elisabeth Fehrenbach writes, the Prussian reformers engaged in defensive modernization "not *with* but *against* Napoleon."[45] These reforms were based on Enlightenment ideas and sought to encourage private enterprise by removing guild restrictions, abolishing serfdom, and transforming feudal tenures into peasant landownership. In the words of historian Reinhart Koselleck, they constituted a "Prussian Magna Carta."[46] They also established occupational freedom and secure private property rights for the first time, which, as in Britian, spurred innovation.[47]

These reform efforts were aided by an increasingly capable civil service. By 1806, more than 80 percent of new councillors (*Räte*) came from non-noble backgrounds.[48] Not only were these councillors generally better educated than their predecessors, but in virtue of their lesser social status, they were also more willing "servants of the state."[49] The hierarchical chain of command both fostered and required a working culture of strict obedience. To enforce such a culture, Prussia put in place a sophisticated network of spies to monitor ministries and departments. Punishments for sloppiness or dishonesty were severe, but these sticks were supplemented by plentiful carrots. High salaries, pensions, and social prestige created a bureaucracy of highly motivated civil servants ready to serve Prussia.[50]

These changes came not from a populist uprising from below, but rather from the noble elite. Karl vom und zum Stein (1757–1831), who led the reform, was an aristocrat and descendant from a family of Imperial Knights. But he was also a follower of the liberal philosopher Montesquieu, whose work he had studied at Göttingen and in England. Similarly, the motto of the Prussian chief minister Karl August von Hardenberg (1750–1822) became "democratic principles in a monarchical government."[51] Together, the two initiated the eponymous Stein-Hardenberg Reforms and transformed the Great Elector's personal dictatorship into liberal autocracy, or *Rechtsstaat*. For instance, Stein's October Edict of 1807 not only abolished the legal privileges of the nobility, but, following the example of the French Revolution, it made positions in the civil service completely open to commoners. Recruitment was soon firmly based on education rather than descendance.[52]

The Stein-Hardenberg Reforms, in short, constituted a "revolution from above," as the Prussian finance minister Carl August von Struensee famously put it.[53] They also constituted a crucial "step forward in German industrialization."[54] The reforms took place on the initiative of a reformist-oriented bureaucracy, under an authoritarian state, which repressed democratic forces in the pursuit of modernization. The abolition of compulsory guild membership for many trades, for example, came without consulting the vested interests who lost out, noble estate owners being the exception. This weakened the democratic balance of power, but excluding the losers, most notably the guilds, made radical reform possible. As economic historians Richard Tilly and Michael Kopsidis note, "German states that successfully centralized power in the post-1648 period at the expense of particularistic interests would have a clear advantage in creating swiftly the institutional framework of a modern market economy after 1800."[55]

A comparison with Baden, Württemberg, and Bavaria further south is instructive. Beginning in 1806, they all undertook a series of reforms to unify the administration of their enlarged territories, along with sweeping financial and economic reforms. However, the absence of modern industry and a politically confident bourgeoisie meant that the premodern parliaments (*Landstände*), controlled by the nobility and clergy, extended privileges like monopoly rights to guilds to encourage manufacturing and commerce. The guilds then used these privileges to restrain competition and innovation. Indeed, all three states kept guild restrictions on entry into various handicrafts in place. The guilds, which represented an important force in local town government, were simply too strong to take on, so the relatively weak German states were forced to continue to guarantee their parasitic privileges to ensure state financing. This came at the price of entrenching an institutional framework hostile to growth. As Tilly and Kopsidis explain, the economies of these southern states "fell well behind those of Prussia and Saxony, industrially, commercially, and in output per capita.... Prussia was not the only state where administrative elites realized that radical reforms were necessary; but it was by far the most important and the only one with a bureaucracy able to implement them."[56]

A strong state, it turns out, was critical to uphold competition in Prussia. As noted in chapter 3, this was also true of Britain, where the central government undercut the guilds, but in Prussia, the state also came to play a more active role in expediting the adoption of technologies invented elsewhere. In a system of competing states, the larger the opportunity for catch-up becomes, the greater the pressure for change from within.

The fruits of Prussia's revolution from above can be seen clearly by contrasting its civil service to that of Britian. In terms of fiscal capacity, the British state in the early nineteenth century was second to none.[57] In terms of bureaucratic civil capacity, however, it trailed both Germany and France (figure 4.1).[58] Indeed, in stark contrast to Prussia, the British civil service grew out of the private sector. The very term *civil service* came not from Westminster but from India, where the East India Company long exercised quasi-governmental authority, to distinguish the company's civilian employees from those running its military operations. It was the experience of the Indian Civil Service (ICS), and the rampant corruption within it, that convinced a young official in its ranks, Sir Charles Trevelyan, that reform was needed. Together with Sir Stafford Northcote, he drafted the Northcote–Trevelyan Report in 1854.

Consisting of just over twenty pages, the report called for an end to patronage appointments, the introduction of examinations as a gateway into the civil service, and higher educational requirements for

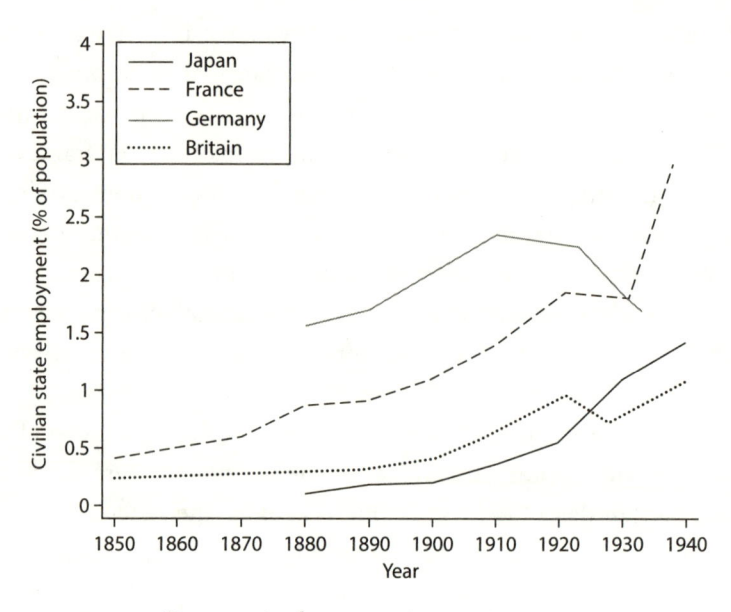

FIGURE 4.1. Comparative bureaucratic capacity, 1850–1940
Source: Vries, Averting a Great Divergence, Tables 30 and 31.

administrative functions, which it proposed splitting from routine clerical duties.[59] In a university system characterized by "lethargy, corruption, and sinecurism," however, education did not necessarily count for much. Richard Chapman, for example, tells a story of how Lord Eldon graduated from Oxford in 1770: "By way of examination he was asked only two questions to test him in Hebrew and History: 'What is the Hebrew for the place of a skull?' and 'Who founded University College?' By replying 'Golgotha' and 'King Alfred' he tells us that he satisfied the examiners who asked him nothing else."[60] The situation only improved in the middle of the century, with sweeping reforms to raise standards—including the Oxford Act of 1854, the Cambridge Act of 1856, and the Universities Tests Act of 1871—the elimination of religious examinations for admission, and the founding of new institutions, like the University of London in 1836.

Yet even with these educational reforms, the proposals of the Northcote–Trevelyan Report saw no immediate implementation. The existing officeholders, whose positions were under threat from merit-based entry, pushed back. The tide first turned with the Crimean War (1853–1856) and devastating British losses at the Battle of Balaclava, which created a furor in the press and generated momentum for an overhaul of the civil service. The British war effort was "a confused heap of mismanagement, imbecility, and disorder, under which the nation's bravery lies crushed and withered," a fuming Charles Dickens wrote at the time.[61] Threats to the lives of both soldiers and civilians created demand for reform that peacetime failed to inspire.[62] As the report suggested, the government implemented a dual-tier system, reserving spots for the elite from Oxbridge while also providing opportunities for the rising middle class. High-ranking roles continued to be influenced by patronage until 1930 when the Warren Fisher Reform curbed arbitrary appointments. Although not very meritocratic by today's standards, these post-Crimean alterations edged Britain nearer to the systems of Prussia and France.[63] However, Germany's head start meant that even by the twentieth century, its state apparatus was not only more meritocratic but also much larger than that of its English rival. As German historian Jürgen Kocka writes, "Rough comparison seems to show that about 1890 the proportionate importance of government employees in Germany was about twice as great as in Great Britain." Most of these employees, Kocka goes on to note, shared "a specific legal status under public law, special privileges in and loyalties to the state, high esteem, and a favourable image associated with power, a sense of duty, hierarchy, formalized procedures and security. They were, so to speak, part of the state and its authority, not merely private citizens."[64]

This German civil service culture shaped industrialization in both direct and subtle ways. In Prussia, the belief that private entrepreneurs did not have the necessary know-how to manage its coal mines persisted up until the 1850s, and so the job was reserved for state-trained civil servants.[65] But while large state-owned enterprises persisted in some sectors, German industrialization was clearly primarily capitalist in character. Entrepreneurs and corporate managers made most strategic decisions, using market shares and profitability as yardsticks.[66] Nevertheless, private companies frequently employed civil servants to introduce methods of bureaucratic management and increase efficiency.[67]

This trend was evident at companies like Siemens & Halske, a pioneering electrical engineering firm that emerged on the Berlin scene in 1847. Within its ranks, many employees boasted prior experience as civil servants, seamlessly transitioning from public to private realms. To see this, consider the company's founder, Werner Siemens, whose formative years were shaped within the confines of a technical military institution in Berlin. Having dedicated over a decade to the military establishment, Siemens possessed an innate familiarity with the principles of disciplined organization. It comes as no surprise then that the Siemens enterprise swiftly embraced a hierarchical structure, replete with meticulously crafted written directives and well-defined channels of communication permeating through every office. As Kocka notes: "This high degree of bureaucratization cannot be explained merely as managerial response to the operational requirements of the enterprise; it also resulted from the acceptance of traditional organizational models developed outside industry."[68] Indeed, just like in the civil service, employees at Siemens enjoyed the benefits of job security, vacation entitlements, and regular monthly salaries—rewards closely tied to their length of service. They regarded themselves as a corporate kind of civil servant, which embraced the concept of managerial hierarchy. Indeed, they were aptly called private civil servants, or *Privatbeamte*.

System Althoff

Beyond its impact on the civil service, Prussia's revolution from above also had major ripple effects on the educational system, which would benefit the advancement of industry in turn.[69] After his triumphant entry into Jena, Napoleon sought to consolidate his dominion over the German lands, and these efforts included the shutdown of more than half of the German universities due to suspected political activities. While the state of Westphalia and its renowned universities, including Halle and Göttingen, suffered severe setbacks, the royal garrison town of Berlin continued to enjoy a certain degree of autonomy in matters of culture and education. Over the following years, the University of Berlin would emerge as the world's leading institution of science. It was a newcomer compared to institutions like Bologna (founded in 1088), Salamanca (1164), Oxford (1167), Cambridge (1209), Vienna (1365), and Heidelberg (1386), but it would surpass them all in its audacious reimagination of the university concept. By the early nineteenth century, notable travelers such as Madame de Stael and astute observers like Victor Cousin would journey to Germany to witness the "greatest achievement of a knowledge hungry people."[70]

At the forefront of this transformation stood Wilhelm von Humboldt, a prominent figure of the German Enlightenment and a lifelong companion of Friedrich Schiller, whose intellectual repertoire encompassed philosophy, linguistics, and diplomacy. It was during a sixteen-month stay in Berlin, between his diplomatic assignments to the Vatican and Vienna, that Humboldt would leave his most impactful legacy in the domain of educational reform. In his unpublished treatise, *The Limits of State Action*, likely penned in 1792, Humboldt envisioned universities that could serve the state most effectively through indirect means. The aim was to foster knowledgeable individuals and conscientious citizens capable of acquiring their respective callings later in life, and his conception of the university revolved around nurturing the innate abilities of individuals. To achieve this, Humboldt argued for the need to bridge social divides and admit students on the basis of talent rather than hereditary lineage or social status. If people's capacities were allowed to flourish autonomously, regardless of class, they would ultimately contribute to the betterment of both the state and society at large.[71]

Leveraging his persuasive powers, Humboldt convinced Frederick William III of a new university model that rested on three fundamental principles: the unity of research and teaching, the safeguarding of academic freedom, and the centrality of the *Philosophische Fakultät*—the idea that all students should begin with classes in arts and science before specializing. *Lehrfreiheit*, the freedom to teach, and *Lernfreiheit*, the freedom to learn, became inseparable principles, and so the task of the state was to protect the freedom of the university rather than impede it. What this meant in practice was that the university needed financial independence so that it would be shielded from direct government influence. Under autocracy, of course, there can be no guarantor of independence from the state itself: what the state could grant it could also take away, as would become evident when Adolf Hitler clamped down on the universities in the 1930s. But in the nineteenth century, the German state afforded its universities wide latitude and acted as a catalyst for science.[72]

To be sure, there remained considerable disagreement over the future of German education and science. For one thing, Humboldt's focus on "pure" theoretical science, like mathematics and physics, meant that there was little room for lab-based science. At first, laboratories were only set up for the purpose of lecture demonstrations and to support academics' private research needs, not for the advancement of new technologies. In the 1830s and 1840s, however, the chemist Justus von Liebig's influence reverberated across Europe and America, as he became a central figure in the burgeoning "international laboratory movement." At the University of Giessen, he welcomed visiting scientists from various German regions, including the illustrious Alexander von Humboldt, Wilhelm's younger brother, as well as numerous international scholars. Yet while the rise of the laboratory symbolized the transition to an era defined by experimental science, many old-guard professors saw this shift as undermining the university's purpose. After the unification of Germany, however, the tensions between academic and industrial cultures gradually dissolved thanks to the efforts of state ministers, like Friedrich Althoff, the head of the University Department in the Prussian Ministry of Education.[73]

Over the following decades, Althoff came to define the university landscape and much of Prussian higher education through what would later be known as the "System Althoff." Initially an associate professor of civil law at the University of Strasbourg, Althoff assumed his leadership post in 1882, where he would remain for the next twenty-five years. Amid changing ministers and rectors, Althoff represented the enduring *Berufsbeamtentum*, the permanent civil service. He earned the nicknames of "czar of Prussian universities" and "Bismarck of German higher education" by mobilizing enormous resources for the university system, with a particular focus on bolstering the University of Berlin. Under his stewardship, the number of institutes at the University of Berlin nearly doubled, the renowned Charité clinic was transformed into a modern hospital, and the city's libraries came to form a network of specialized sites that cooperated in lending and acquisitions. He also attracted esteemed scholars such as Adolf von Harnack, Max Planck, Walther Nernst, Paul Ehrlich, Robert Koch, and Ferdinand von Richthofen to Berlin. But perhaps his most important endeavor was spearheading the establishment of the Kaiser-Wilhelm-Gesellschaft (KWG), later renamed the Max-Planck-Gesellschaft. An umbrella organization that housed several independent research institutions, which would support the work of numerous Nobel Prize winners, the KWG challenged the universities' monopoly on research by unleashing competition for talent.[74]

Yet as important as the contributions of Humboldt, Liebig, and Althoff were to the transformation of Germany into a scientific powerhouse, these efforts to drive education and science from above would not have succeeded without the existence of some critical and decentralizing intuitional underpinnings. During the Enlightenment era, the newly established universities of Halle and Göttingen had already challenged religious orthodoxy and developed curricula aimed at preparing students for a career in the civil service. Notably, at the University of Göttingen, established in 1737, the Hanoverian privy counsellor Gerlach Adolph von Münchhausen championed scholarly freedom by promoting uncensored research and facilitating collaboration between the Academy of Sciences and the university. As a result, Halle and Göttingen attracted scholars from afar—Benjamin Franklin and Samuel Taylor Coleridge included. The University of Berlin, in other words, was not an isolated phenomenon but intricately connected to the broader landscape of German cities. While Berlin enjoyed an astonishing share of state university funding in Prussia, receiving nearly as much as all other universities combined, vibrant universities on the periphery also thrived with substantial support, proving to be formidable contenders, not least in disciplines where they had a history of excellence: Chemistry in Gießen, mathematics in Göttingen, and psychology and cultural history in Leipzig.[75]

Thus, even as German nationalists bemoaned the fragmentation of their country into numerous states, an observer in Württemberg in 1860 recognized the positive consequences of such decentralization: "Germany," in his view, had "become a country second to none with regard to the dissemination of culture and knowledge."[76] In a captivating analysis, Stanford historian Emily Levine highlights the pivotal role of federalist political structures in propelling Germany and the United States to the forefront of global knowledge centres. While other Great Powers on the Continent endeavoured to replicate Germany's achievements, they struggled to foster the robust cultural and intellectual competition that thrived within the decentralized federal German system of higher education.

Compare France, where Paris's marvellous new boulevards were just being rolled out by Georges-Eugène Haussmann. Having long reigned as the eminent hub of scientific thought and progress, the International Exhibition in Paris in 1867 served as an embarrassing reminder that Germany's advancements in research had far outpaced those of the host country. This prompted the French Education Minister Victor Duruy to dispatch envoys to Prussia to assess the competition. At a subsequent conference, organized by Napoleon III, leading scientists such as Louis Pasteur and Claude Bernard made the case to the emperor that he needed to provide the provinces with greater resources so they could develop competing intellectual centres to Paris. Although Minister Duruy supported their plea, aside from the establishment of the *École Pratique des Hautes Études*, little else was accomplished. Not even the devastating defeat by the Prussians in 1870, which surely created a sense of urgency that reform was needed, could overcome centuries of consolidation efforts around Paris. While Louis Liard, the director of higher education in the Ministry of Public Instruction, proposed six universities in strategic locations around France and an autonomous financial structure that would encourage regional fundraising, and scholars such as the historian Jules Flammermont advocated for a decentralized system akin to the German model, these efforts all ultimately fell short, as the stronghold of Paris and limited regional funds hindered the desired transformation.[77]

Britain, meanwhile, encountered similar obstacles in its pursuit to replicate German success. Though scholars like Matthew Arnold, a professor of poetry at Oxford who also worked as a school inspector, deeply admired Humboldt, they faced considerable resistance in reforming the system. At Cambridge and Oxford, colleges remained dedicated to training clergy within religious orthodoxy.[78] The key challenge, according to sociologist Joseph Ben-David, was that there was "no incentive for academic innovations: the two leading universities did not need it, and the rest had limited chances of competing with them."[79] Moreover, the absence of widespread primary education meant that the pool of scientific talent that British universities could draw upon remained relatively limited. Whereas Frederick the Great had issued his General *Landschulreglement* in 1763, England's Elementary Education Act, which established the initial framework for universal schooling, only materialized in 1870.[80] And this Act was primarily concerned with maintaining social order rather than driving the advancement of British industry or science. "The Education Act of 1870," wrote H. G. Wells, "was not an Act for common universal education, it was an Act ... to discipline a growing mass of disaffected proletarians and integrate them into British society. Its object was to civilize the barbarians; as Her Majesty's Inspector for London put it, 'if it were not for her five hundred elementary schools London would be overrun by a horde of young savages.'"[81]

The sequencing of industrialization and educational reform is important here. Britain saw the growth of a new industrial society before schooling became widespread, and since factories heavily relied on child labour, sending children to school meant sacrificing family income—an untenable proposition for many households. In contrast, Germany followed a different path, implementing its elementary educational system before the onset of industrialization, which proved advantageous. As machines grew more complex and technical knowledge advanced, relying on traditional on-the-job training became costly. Germany's well-developed school system ensured a steady supply of skilled workers, giving it a competitive edge. As early as the 1820s, Germany established public industrial and technical schools (*Gewerbeinstitute* and *Gewerbeschulen*), and by 1856, the influential *Verein Deutscher Ingenieure* (VDI) emerged, linking engineers with industry. Meanwhile, Britain's machine tool sector stuck to traditional apprenticeships, lagging behind in formal technical education.[82]

Germany did not stop there. *Gewerbeinstituten* soon evolved into full-fledged technical universities (*Technische Hochschulen*), preparing workers specifically for industrial appointments. In the late nineteenth century, Charlottenburg (Berlin), Munich, Darmstadt, Hannover, Karlsruhe, Dresden, Stuttgart, Aachen, and Brunswick all established technical universities. Enrollment at these institutions exploded between 1890 and 1900, surging by 170 percent, from 5,361 to 14,738 students, even as the overall population grew by just 10 percent. Again, a compelling comparison can be drawn with Britain, where a mere 1,129 engineering students entered university in 1913.[83]

This educational divergence extended beyond engineering. Germany also invested in *Handelshochschulen*, modeled after the business schools emerging in the United States. The first appeared in Cologne in 1898, the same year Chicago Booth was founded, followed by Aachen in 1903, Berlin in 1906, Mannheim in 1907, and Munich in 1910. Although we should not downplay the role played by family wealth and commercial ability in launching industrial careers, many pioneers of industry—like August Borsig, Alfred Krupp, and Werner Siemens—saw their authority as lying in their own technical competence.[84] By the late nineteenth century, salaried managers with university or *Doktor Ingenieur* degrees frequently moved into the *Vorstande* (executive board) and appeared on the Supervisory Boards of German enterprises, which they gradually came to dominate. Britain, in contrast, placed less emphasis on formal technical, scientific, and managerial skills, a gap that would have lasting consequences for its industrial development.[85]

By all accounts, Germany's early investments in education yielded remarkable returns and favourably positioned the nation for the unfolding technological opportunities of the nineteenth century. Statistical analysis by economic historians Sacha Becker, Erik Hornung, and Ludger Woessmann confirms that Prussia's strong education system played a key role in helping the country catch up technologically. Regions with higher levels of education were more successful in adopting and applying Britain's technological advancements.[86] Moreover, Germany's focus on education became even more important during the Second Industrial Revolution, when science-based industries began to take off. In the First Industrial Revolution, Britain had led the way, with skilled craftsmen and visionary entrepreneurs driving innovation in traditional machine industries. But as industrial R&D became more structured, formal education played a bigger role in technological progress. This was especially true in fields like chemicals and electrical engineering, where scientific knowledge was essential. Indeed, industrial giants like BASF, Bayer, and Siemens profited magnificently from Prussia's highly developed system of science and education.[87]

Berlin to Baghdad

Yet to effectively exploit new technological opportunities, German enterprises needed more than skilled scientists, engineers, and managers. They also needed sizable markets. The *Zollverein*, which created a customs union among German states in January of 1834, was important to that end, yet market integration was still hindered by Germany's patchwork transportation network.[88] The presence of waterways like the Rhine and Elbe rivers offered some opportunities for trade, but accessing the North Sea via the Rhine necessitated traversing Dutch territory. And the Congress of Vienna had granted the Dutch the prerogative to levy transit tolls on goods originating from German states, and urban centres such as Cologne and Mainz, where guilds claimed exclusive dominion over shipping employment, wielded transit control rights. Although the advent of steam-powered shipping in the 1820s gradually eroded their monopolistic grip, it was not until the enforcement of the Rhine Shipping Act of 1831, propelled by Prussian pressure, that these guild-imposed impediments to progress were effectively dismantled. Even then, land transportation remained backward, as the German railway network in 1850 measured only half the length of its British counterpart.[89]

This was, in part, due to constitutional restrictions, which prevented the Prussian government from raising the capital necessary to rapidly roll out the public network. To circumvent these constraints, and inspired by the British model, Prussia enacted a new law in 1838 that allowed private joint-stock companies to build railroads. Within a year, the first railroad was built, linking Berlin with the Potsdam residency of the Kaiser. Yet the decision to rely on private companies meant that there was no central plan to link up the network, and that lines were only built where profitable. As a result, sparsely populated communities in the eastern provinces of Prussia were only connected in 1848, when the government began the construction of the *Ostbahn*—a railway line that would link up the Rhineland and the French frontier with Brandenburg and East Prussia.[90]

The very same year, revolution swept across Europe, which brought important changes to German political institutions and paved the way for greater state involvement in railroad construction. As the bourgeoisie joined the landed elites at the centre of political power, Germany's new constitution was unsurprisingly favourable to industrial interests. Speaking to parliament in 1849, banker and MP Friedrich Carl summarized the new consensus as follows: "The previous administration may have been guilty of too frequently withholding approval of the funds that would have sufficed to further cultivate our country. Now, however, we stand behind the government, and we will always approve the means that are designed to improve our transportation, commerce and industry, and agriculture; and though the governmental budget may grow in result, nevertheless, we may see such expenditure as an investment which will yield a good return."[91] Consequently, the Prussian public debt grew by some 90 percent between 1848 and 1865, with much of this spending devoted to railroads, in the form of shareholdings, loans, and interest guarantees. Meanwhile, the Saxon industrial city of Chemnitz also began spending more, albeit for different reasons: railroad construction created new jobs and was seen as a way of undercutting protest from unemployed factory workers.[92]

All the same, the fragmented mosaic of states that aided exploration in Europe during the Scientific Revolution and the subsequent Enlightenment—allowing the intelligentsia to escape the tyranny of the ruler in pursuit of new and controversial ideas (chapter 3)—was clearly a disadvantage when it came to solving coordination problems, scaling up production, and building infrastructure. To help resolve these issues and ensure uniformity of the network across states, the Union of German Railway Administrations was established in 1847, with the aim of regulating the joint handling of freight and passenger traffic. The idea, which had been put forward by Friedrich List a decade earlier, was first implemented in Prussia and then enlarged to include the railways of other German states. However, with member states continuing to compete for traffic, setting uniform freight rates proved nearly impossible until after the political unification of Germany in 1871. To consolidate the German railroads into a single system, the new Chancellor, Prince Otto von Bismarck, created the Imperial Railway Department and put forward the Imperial Railway Act. Nevertheless, some smaller states—especially Bavaria—resisted and successfully defeated the Railway Act three times. In response, Bismarck decided to nationalize the Prussian railroad lines, which accounted for two-thirds of the mileage in the newly unified German Empire. Other states followed suit, and by 1909, only 2,236 of the 38,000 miles' network were still privately held.[93]

As the lines were nationalized, the Railway Traffic Association became the central ratemaking board within Germany. This laid the foundation for an international agreement, signed in 1890, that not only extended the traffic association's rate structure but also introduced standardized routing and scheduling procedures to all neighbouring countries. From then on, German industrialists enjoyed the benefits of a Continental transportation system, which permitted the seamless movement of goods, people, and ideas with greater speed and regularity. Indeed, the integrated Continental railroad network gave German pioneers of industry readier access to European markets than their British or even French counterparts enjoyed. In the East too the transportation advantage was shifting from the English and the French to the Germans. In 1889, for example, the *Deutsche Levante Linie* established a direct steamship service between Hamburg, Bremen, Antwerp, and Constantinople. But the best-known project, of course, was the Berlin-Baghdad Railway, which came to be at the centre of Great Power politics in the run-up to World War I.[94]

The ambition of these mammoth undertakings marked a new age of German commercial power. When the London *Times*, in its edition of October 28, 1898, featured a lengthy review of German commercial activities within the Ottoman Empire during the preceding decade, the pattern was clear. What had once been a domain primarily dominated by France and Great Britain had undergone a remarkable transformation, with Germans emerging as the most dynamic and proactive group in modern day Turkey. The bustling streets of Constantinople were teeming with hundreds of German salesmen, passionately promoting their goods and diligently surveying the markets to discern the needs of the local populace. On these same streets, German bicycles were rapidly displacing their American-made counterparts. Government sales and exchange had also shifted in Germany's direction: notably, the Germania Shipbuilding Company, owned by Krupp, had begun supplying torpedoes to the Ottoman navy, while Ludwig Loewe and Company of Berlin had become instrumental in equipping the Sultan's military forces with state-of-the-art small arms. Indeed, it was against the backdrop of closer ties between the Ottomans and the Germans that Britain's First Lord of the Admiralty Winston Churchill seized without compensation two completed dreadnought battleships ordered by the Turks—a decision that may have led the Sultan to enter the Great War on the side of Germany.[95]

The expansion of German trade was felt keenly within the country's borders as well. The demand for construction materials, particularly iron, served as a catalyst for the ascendance of the Rhenish-Westphalian industrial district and ignited a broader expansion of industrial operations. Before the railroad era, German industry was almost nonexistent. In the mid-1840s, a mere forty-eight cotton spinning mills dotted the entirety of Prussia, employing a scattered workforce of 4,127 individuals across rural regions.[96] Yet as German cities became interconnected through the rail network, companies grew in size and were able to take advantage of new machine tools and steam power to serve larger markets.[97] According to the 1907 occupational census, for instance, in technologically progressive industries—like transportation, chemicals, and electrical engineering—companies with fifty employees or more employed around 70 percent of all workers.[98] That year, the rapidly expanding Krupp enterprise alone employed 64,000 workers, while Siemens-Schuckert employed 43,000, and around 31,000 people worked at AEG.[99] Unlike in Britain, where industrialization preceded the railroad, in Germany it was a key enabler. As business historian Alfred Chandler Jr. has argued, the railroad in Germany allowed "entrepreneurs to make large enough investments in the new production technologies to exploit fully the economies of scale and scope, to build the marketing networks needed to distribute goods on an international scale," just as its educational system made it easier for German companies to "recruit and train the essential managerial teams."[100]

At the same time, German railroads never provided the managerial model for the modern corporation the way the railroads did in America (chapter 6). Instead, this model was provided by the Prussian civil service bureaucracy. In stark contrast to the United States and Britain, the German railroad system functioned as a representative entity of the bureaucratic state.[101] Indeed, under Bismarck's leadership, the nationalization of the railroads led to their formal inclusion within the civil service apparatus. By 1907, four of the five largest enterprises in the Wilhelmine Empire—the Prussian-Hesse State Railway, the German Imperial Postal Service, the Prussian Mining Enterprises, and the Bavarian State Railway—were state-owned, and two of these enterprises were railway companies. Together, they employed almost 1.2 million citizens—more than half of the 2.2 million workers serving Germany's 125 most prominent employers.[102] As Werner Sombart would say, the postal services and the railways were "only the civil sections of the army."[103]

Britain's Backslide

To appreciate Germany's capacity to exploit technologies invented elsewhere, contrast its gains during this period with those of Britain. Although the railroad was pioneered by British inventors, such as Richard Trevithick and George Stephenson, the British network, rolled out with minimal state involvement, ended up being inefficient and disjointed. Corporate Britain failed to harness the technology conceived within its borders. The railroad industry suffered from feeble competition, subpar management, and ineffective corporate governance. This created fertile soil for rent seeking and resulted in roughly 1 percent of national GDP being consumed by the cost inefficiency of British railroads by the turn of the twentieth century.[104] We lack comparable figures for Germany, but by the time of the Great War, Germany had certainly gained a remarkable productivity lead over Britain in transportation and communications.[105] Work by Oxford's Stephen Broadberry shows that Britain performed poorly in high-volume, low-margin industries, where hierarchical organization could deliver substantial productivity gains, and railroads were no exception.[106] Indeed, comparing the hundred largest German manufacturing and mining firms in 1887 and 1907 with a similar British list reveals that German firms were much larger, more diversified, and better integrated.[107]

The triumph of German industry was unmistakable to anybody visiting the massive chemical works of Leverkusen, Ludwigshafen, and Frankfurt, or the huge machinery works and steel mills along the Rhine and in the Ruhr. But most impressive of all was surely Berlin's Siemensstadt, which at the dawn of World War I was, by a fair margin, the world's largest industrial complex.[108] With factories and branches in St. Petersburg, Vienna, and Woolwich, Siemens symbolized industrial prowess on the global stage, standing alongside American giants like General Electric and Westinghouse. German bankers, meanwhile, pursued ambitious ventures to develop assets in foreign lands. Deutsche Bank, for instance, founded the Deutsche Übersee-Bank in 1886, with branches in Argentina, Chile, Bolivia, and Uruguay, while the Deutsche Überseeische Elektrizitäts-Gesellschaft (DÜEG) set up shop in Buenos

Aires in 1898. German companies, in short, were riding the first wave of globalization when steam replaced sail, causing shipping rates to plummet and global markets to integrate.[109]

Their pioneering British competitors were, by contrast, significantly less capable of conquering global markets. Consider steel, which was long known to be a superior form of iron but too expensive to mass produce. A turning point came in 1856, when Britain's Henry Bessemer discovered a way of removing impurities from pig iron through oxidation, which allowed steel to be produced in large quantities at low cost for the first time. A major drawback of the Bessemer converter, however, was its inability to use iron ore containing phosphorus, because non-phosphoric ores were rare and expensive. Again, the solution came from Britain: Sidney Gilchrist Thomas and his cousin Percy Gilchrist soon invented a converter that neutralized the acid effects of phosphoric ore. Their efforts were a testament to British inventiveness, but Britain's early advantage in steel rapidly evaporated as companies on the Continent more effectively harnessed this new process.[110] Hörder-Verein and Rheinische Stahlwerke were the first licensees of the Thomas-Gilchrist process, but others soon followed, and within a mere decade, German steel producers had closed the gap to Britain. Data on steel output shows that around the peak of its dominance in 1879, Britain produced more steel than Belgium, France, and Germany combined, but the output curves crossed in the 1890s, when Germany took the lead.[111]

The divergent fates of the two countries were intimately linked to their different approaches to industrial organization: unlike their British counterparts, German steel giants—like Krupp, the Gutehoffnungshütte, Gelsenberg, and Deutsch-Luxemburg—were all vertically integrated. They controlled coal mines, produced pig iron and raw steel, and turned these materials into finished goods, sometimes even advanced machinery. This full integration guaranteed a steady internal demand for steel, reducing reliance on outside buyers.[112] German steel giants also produced a more diversified range of products, which they could allocate marketing costs across. And to manage increasingly complex operations, they had more capable top executives, often with university and engineering school degrees. British steel managers, by contrast, would obtain comparable qualifications only half a century later.[113]

The story of steel—in which Britain raced ahead only to be overtaken by Germany—was common across a swathe of industries. Even in industries of the Second Industrial Revolution, where German investments in science and engineering gave her the greatest advantage, Britain began with an early lead. The story of William Perkin, who invented the first process for making dyes by chemical synthesis in 1856, is particularly illuminating. At the age of fifteen, Perkin entered the Royal College of Chemistry—now Imperial College London—where he became an assistant to August Wilhelm von Hofmann, who had just developed a hypothesis on how quinine might be synthetized for the treatment of malaria. During his Easter vacation, Perkin performed some experiments in a crude laboratory in his apartment in East London. It was here that he accidentally discovered that aniline could be transformed into a mixture that produced a substance with an intense purple colour, which he soon set out to commercialize as a dye called *mauveine*.

A new industry was born, and it was born in Britain. But following an astonishing turn of events, it is the names of German chemical companies—like Bayer, BASF, Hoechst, and Agfa—that we all remember. As economic historians Peter Lindert and Keith Trance note, Britain created a thriving research field, but these opportunities were not fully exploited—an assessment with which practically every author dealing with chemical entrepreneurship agrees. Though Britain had established a strong lead in chemicals in 1870, it was far behind Germany and America by 1913.[114] The failure of British industry to capitalize on its early advantage assumes even greater significance when one considers that the textile industry, which England pioneered in mechanizing, remained the largest market for dyes before total war descended all over Europe.[115]

The question, of course, is why? One possible explanation is that German entrepreneurs had greater access to much needed financial capital. Banks in Germany, for example, played a much more central role in channelling the nation's capital than their Anglo-American counterparts. Around the time when Wall Street made its appearance to finance railroad expansion in the United States, concentrating much of the nation's money and capital market on Manhattan, Germany created a wholly new financial intermediary—the *Kreditbank*—which soon became central to financing its industrial endeavours.[116] As economic historian Alexander Gerschenkron famously argued, in backward countries such banks played the pivotal role of channelling scarce capital into the modernization of industry and enabling rapid industrial catch-up. Yet as Germany approached the technological frontier, the banks' influence faded. Industrial giants like Siemens could rely on retained earnings from its early investments in telegraph technology to finance its operations. Although Deutsche Bank—whose chairman, Georg Siemens, was a nephew of Werner—helped strategically by facilitating the company's move into electric light and power equipment, banks played a minimal financing role as stock markets developed.[117] Between 1892 and 1913, German innovators in high-tech industries increasingly relied on the Berlin stock market for funding. And Berlin could never match the London Exchange, which remained the world's most important securities market, whether for rail, mining ventures, or industrial shares.[118]

A more plausible explanation for Britain's industrial failure is its shortfall in science and education. Germany boasted a greater number of skilled managers and engineers, as well as accomplished scientists poised to unlock new frontiers of knowledge. And German universities flourished under the patronage of a state that honoured their autonomy and lavished them with ample resources, while federalism fostered an environment ripe for academic competition. Consequently, as the Great War drew to a close, German researchers had been awarded approximately one-third of the total Nobel Prizes, with the University of Berlin serving as home to nearly half of Germany's laureates.[119]

Moreover, the German system excelled at harnessing scientific breakthroughs and swiftly transforming them into commercially viable technologies, which allowed their companies to cement their supremacy in the global marketplace.[120] BASF's venture with Munich professor Adolf Baeyer, proprietor of the patent for the synthetic dye known as indigo blue, is but one of many examples.[121] Cooperation between universities and industrial enterprises was simply "much closer in Germany than in

Britain," as is evidenced in the patent statistics.[122] From 1885 until the turn of the century, Germany registered eleven times more chemical patents than Britain.[123] A glance at foreign patents granted in the United States underscores the trend. By 1890, Britain still had a commanding lead in innovation, accounting for 36 percent of total foreign patents, while Germany accounted for 21 percent. By 1913, however, this picture had reversed, largely because of Britain's poor performance in new industries.[124] Its greatest technological strengths remained textiles, industrial engines, turbines, ships, and telegraphy. Germany, in contrast, dominated in science-based industries like chemicals, pharmaceuticals, and electricity.[125]

A notable commonality, though, is that in both countries, these breakthroughs largely stemmed from independent inventors.[126] In the Wilhelmine Empire, it was the likes of Wilhelm Maybach, Gottlieb Daimler, Hugo Douglas, and Wilhelm Kornhardt who spearheaded discovery and subsequently established companies around their pioneering patents—not to mention Carl von Linde, who invented the first industrial-scale air separation and gas liquefaction processes, paving the way for the first reliable compressed-ammonia refrigerator in 1876. However, the crowning achievement was Nikolaus Otto's seminal gas engine, a marvel that garnered considerable acclaim during the Paris Industrial Exhibition of 1867.[127] Corporate giants, such as Siemens and AEG, on the other hand, accounted for less than 20 percent of the country's electrical engineering patents, despite commanding a substantial share of the sector's employment.[128]

In fact, Britain's continued dominance in older industries—where universities played a lesser role—partly stemmed from the broader opportunities Britain offered to independent inventors. Although the *Zollverein* brought greater economic integration for its members, Germany remained culturally divided between Catholics and Protestants, as well as between various ethnic minorities, notably the Polish in the East and French in the southwest. Within the German Empire, a Catholic Bavaria coexisted with a Lutheran Saxony and a Calvinist Palatinate. And after unification, the culture struggle

(*Kulturkampf*) between Bismarck's government and the Roman Catholic Church, led by Pope Pius IX, only exacerbated these divisions. Yet the educated elites were remarkably fluid, traversing from one university to another, often spanning state borders. This mix of cultural nationalism and political fragmentation encouraged intellectual migration, undeniably advancing German science.[129] However, for the tinkering innovators, the benefits of German unification took much longer to be felt. Data on patent assignments reveal that the border separating Prussia and Saxony reduced technology transfer as much as the border between Prussia and France, despite the shared language and patent law between Prussia and Saxony.[130] Germany's lead in science created new technological opportunities to be exploited, but the state bureaucracy could not make cultural and social cleavages disappear.

British inventors, by contrast, benefited from a vibrant market for technology.[131] Liberated from the burden of transforming their patents into products, English inventors could effortlessly license or sell their innovations through accredited patent agents, of which 245 were soon approved after the 1888 Patent Act required formal registration. This allowed individuals like Frederick Lanchester to take out over 400 patents for his contributions to automobiles and aeronautics.[132] Even in electrical industries, tinkerers made the field, and the efforts of German pioneers, such as Werner Siemens and Johann Georg Halske, were no more innovative than those of Thomas Edison and George Westinghouse in America, or Joseph Swan in Britain. But as the industries they created matured, the competitive advantage shifted decisively toward the Wilhelmine Empire.[133]

Capitalism Bureaucratized

Although many historians like Alfred Chandler Jr. and David Landes have blamed British entrepreneurs for this failure, establishing such claims proves difficult.[134] The crux of the matter is that German and British businesses operated within different contexts, and that German institutions fostered an environment more conducive to large-scale enterprise.[135] What has been aptly described as "organized capitalism" by historian Jürgen Kocka drew upon Prussia's bureaucratic heritage and a range of institutional arrangements that facilitated industrial cooperation, elements that were absent not just in Britain but also in America.[136] A case in point is the year 1897, when the United States Supreme Court deemed anticompetitive agreements illegal under the Sherman Act, while the German high court, the *Reichsgericht*, ruled that contractual agreements on price, output, and market allocation were enforceable and served the public interest.

This ruling allowed German industrial giants to expand their product lines without concern for antitrust regulations. For instance, Siemens, a pioneer in telegraph and cable equipment in Europe, not only competed with General Electric and Westinghouse, but also rivalled AT&T's Western Electric in telegraph and telephone technology. However, the deeper consequence of the ruling was the legalization of cartels, creating barriers that shut out new competitors. Prior to the breakup of IG Farben by the Allies and the imposition of a more rigorous competition regime after World War II, cooperative arrangements among large businesses in Germany were so prevalent that Chandler, echoing Kocka's insights, coined the term "cooperative managerial capitalism" to sharply contrast Germany's economic system with the "competitive managerial capitalism" of America, and the "personal capitalism" of Britain.[137]

Not all German cartel agreements stood the test of time. Many collapsed because some competitors refused to join, enjoying the benefits of price stability without actually limiting their output. Others fell apart due to cheating—companies had a strong incentive to break the rules first, grabbing a larger market share before their rivals could react. But instead of abandoning cartels, German industry made them more sophisticated. When sales agreements failed, firms found ways to pool profits, ensuring that rule-breakers would not gain an advantage by exceeding their quotas. This led to the creation of *Interessengemeinschaften* (IGs)—corporate alliances that went far beyond price-fixing. Companies shared patents, exchanged technological knowledge, and coordinated industrial policies, making it much harder for members to compete independently. Moreover, to assure compliance, members purchased each other's shares.[138] By the turn of the century, IGs had become dominant players—especially in the chemical industry, where two powerful groups controlled 95 percent of Germany's dye production and 80 percent of the global supply. One group consisted of Hoechst, Cassella, and Chemische Fabrik Kalle, while the other included BASF, Bayer, and Agfa. And of course, in 1925, they all became part of IG Farben. Meanwhile, in other key industries, like steel, the direction of travel was similar. The Pig Iron Syndicate, which emerged in 1899 as an umbrella organization of regional cartels, was superseded by the Steel Mill Federation (*Stahlwerksverband*) five years later, which all major producers joined.[139]

The case of steel is instructive more broadly. Cartels, along with protective tariffs, meant that some inefficient firms could remain in business, as they artificially inflated German steel prices above the world level.[140] But by raising input costs for domestic businesses reliant on steel, they also created powerful incentives favouring scale. Firms that integrated backward—producing their own raw materials—could avoid the inflated cartel prices, giving them a major cost advantage. At the same time, key advances in steel-making technology, such as larger furnaces and mechanized material handling, required firms to adopt vertical integration. Stable prices and production levels also made it less risky to invest in expensive new machinery, accelerating the adoption of cutting-edge technologies. And by constantly being subjected to the test of global markets, where tariffs and cartels did not shield them, the prevalence of stagnant "zombie" companies was averted.[141] On the eve of the Great War, when some 70 percent of Germany's half-rolled steel exports went to Britain, the *British Iron and Coal Trades Review* shows that quoted prices for German iron and steel were well below the prices of non-cartelized British producers, despite the higher transportation costs from the Continent.[142]

Whether German corporations competed or cooperated depended on the specific industry and stage of technological development.

Siemens and AEG were bitter rivals in most sectors, yet when it came to electric locomotives for long-distance travel, they chose to work together. In 1890, they even co-financed Accumulatoren-Fabrik Aktiengesellschaft (AFA), which soon became Europe's leading producer of storage batteries. But cooperation tended to be more common in the later stages of technological development. As a technology matured, the opportunities for differentiation diminished, which placed a greater emphasis on price as a crucial competitive weapon, while innovation took a backseat. As one leading business historian notes, "The more standardized the product and the less susceptible it was to rapid technological innovation, the greater the likelihood of cartelization."[143] Here again, the advantage of Germany's cooperative model was in facilitating catch-up rather than driving innovation, which it undermined.[144] Indeed, when IG Farben was finally broken up in 1952, innovation accelerated, and the upswing was driven by separate, unaffiliated companies.[145]

Telefunken and Macroni

To conclude this investigation into Germany's system of bureaucratic capitalism and its ability to drive technological upgrading from the above, consider in detail how this occurred in one striking and particularly important case: the Anglo-German competition for global standards in radio technology.

The first mover in the field was Guglielmo Marconi, who would later share the Nobel Prize in Physics with Karl Ferdinand Braun for his contributions to wireless telegraphy.[146] Marconi, who was born into Italian nobility, did not have any formal education, though his parents hired several private tutors to educate him at home. He began experimenting with radio waves in the attic of his father's country estate at Pontecchio, building his own equipment with the help of the family butler. A breakthrough came the summer of 1895. Marconi found that greater range could be achieved by raising the height of his antenna, and he succeeded in sending wireless signals over one and a half miles. The lukewarm reception of his work in Italy, however, led him to leave for England, whose decentralized system of finance he correctly believed would make it be easier to fund his experiments. In 1897, he established the firm that would become the Marconi Company and was granted the world's first patent for a system of wireless telegraphy. With the unwavering support of the British Royal Navy, he forged ahead in establishing a comprehensive radio network that gave Britain a monopoly over global radio transmissions. This first-mover advantage, coupled with Britain's commanding 60 percent stake in the international undersea cable network, firmly positioned the nation as the preeminent force in international communications.[147]

Meanwhile, in Germany, early progress also happened in a decentralized manner. Independently of each other, Adolf Slaby, a professor of mechanical and electrical engineering at the Technical College Charlottenburg, and Karl Ferdinand Braun, a professor of experimental physics at the University of Strasbourg, had started working on the scientific and technical advancement of wireless telegraphy. Around the same time, at Siemens & Halske, physicist Adolf Koepsel and engineer Carl Rode had joined forces in building their own wireless telegraph system. When Slaby heard of Marconi's early triumphs, he ventured to Britain to witness Marconi's groundbreaking endeavours firsthand. Upon his return to Berlin, he eagerly shared his experiences and became the first individual to replicate Marconi's apparatuses in Germany. With the backing of financial resources provided by Emperor Wilhelm II and operational assistance from the navy, Slaby and his assistant, Georg von Arco, embarked on a series of additional and auspicious experiments during the summer of 1897. Their progress caught the attention of those in power, who directed them to develop wireless equipment capable of bypassing Marconi's patents, which had yet to be granted in Germany at that time. They took out five patents, and in cooperation with AEG and the German navy, developed their own system. Even so, Marconi had successfully leveraged his first-mover advantage to establish his British-backed company as the global standard. Relying on so-called network effects, the Marconi Company pursued a policy of non-intercommunication with other radio operators.[148]

This meant that German corporations, who feared being cut off from global communication, used the British-backed system instead of their native German one. To challenge the British standard, Kaiser Wilhelm

II decreed that Siemens & Halske and AEG, who had previously been competitors, join forces to create a viable German alternative. "The [domestic] rivalry in the field of wireless telegraphy weakens the competitiveness of Germany," the emperor explained, "and gives the Marconi Company the opportunity to reach a worldwide monopoly" that was "not in Germany's interest."[149] The result was the formation of Telefunken, which set out to break the British radio monopoly by selling its technology to emerging markets in South America and Africa. When those efforts failed, the Kaiser launched a series of multilateral efforts, including conferences among Great Powers on radio standards, targeting Marconi's non-intercommunication policy with some success. To close the gap, in other words, the Kaiser leveraged Germany's cooperative and bureaucratic model, much like China is doing vis-à-vis the United States today. In addition to authorizing direct state support for German scientists and engineers, he encouraged them to copy Marconi's designs, financed by contracts with the German military, and ordered Germany's industrial giants to cooperate in pursuit of a national objectives. This culminated in a formidable peer competitor to the Marconi Company.

As this example and the preceding chapter make clear, catch-up growth is far from automatic; it relies on the existence of bureaucratic capacity along with a willingness to direct this capacity toward productive ends—a decision frequently driven by geopolitical competition. As we will see in the next chapter, state-led efforts without this institutional foundation are far less likely to turn technologies invented elsewhere into high levels of growth.

5

Tsars and Zaibatsus

> In England little was done directly, the State being more involved in creating a trading, colonial, and legislative environment in which knowledge and technologies could be exploited.... More direct state *tutelage* occurred in nations of relative economic or industrial backwardness.[1]
>
> —IAN INKSTER

THERE IS some truth to be found in Karl Marx's famous claim that "The industrially more developed country presents to the less developed country a picture of the latter's future."[2] But it is important to recognize that latecomers often forge their own path to the future. The Wilhelmine Empire was no exception in this regard.[3] Unlike England, which embraced laissez-faire principles, states like Russia, Italy, France, Austria-Hungary, and Japan relied more on centralized institutions, albeit to varying degree.[4] Tracing the developmental paths of three of these countries—France, Russia, and Japan—shows how catch-up growth depends on bureaucratic capacity and how the existence of such capacity creates a distinctive set of challenges to further economic and technological progress.

Among these countries the role of the state was relatively subdued in France, which was closer to its long-standing British rival in terms of technological development and had once harbored aspirations of growing the economy by emulating British laissez-faire. However, amid the turmoil of civil conflict, peasant uprisings, and foreign incursions, the Revolutionary regime soon concentrated its efforts on building a bureaucratic state capable of ramping up military production, sidelining its earlier dreams of decentralized growth.

Before the age of revolution, French society was structured into three distinct groups known as "estates." The First Estate comprised the nobility; the Second Estate, the clergy; and the Third Estate, all other members of society. These estates were subject to varying legal standards, with the first two enjoying privileges denied to the broader population. Notably, the nobility and the clergy were exempt from taxation, which left ordinary citizens to bear the brunt of the tax burdens, while also constraining the fiscal capacity of the state.[5] This changed when the delegates of the Third Estate, demanding equal rights, declared themselves the National Assembly on June 17, 1789. The constitution they drafted abolished the privileges of the nobility and the clergy, ended absolute monarchy, and took France some way toward the creation of a professional-bureaucratic state. And as the Industrial Revolution in Britain took off, the French state used its newfound capacity to aid the modernization of industry by incorporating and diffusing technologies invented in Britain. As economic historian François Crouzet writes, the French industrial revolution was a "foreign transplant" that swiftly became "naturalized."[6]

Between 1791 and 1797, a committee of thirty members called the Bureau of Consultation was established to coordinate technological catch-up with its English rival through legal and illegal means alike.[7] French spies and entrepreneurs obtained machinery, while English craftsmen discreetly made their way across the Channel, disregarding Britain's prohibitions and occasionally receiving compensation from the Bureau. Half of its members hailed from the Academy of Science, with the remaining half coming from various other scholarly societies. This group, overseen by six secretaries and a lead secretary, included some of the leading lights of the Continent: notable chemists like Claude Louis Berthollet, Antoine Lavoisier, and Jean Henri Hassenfratz; esteemed mathematicians such as Jean-Louis Lagrange, Pierre-

Simon de Laplace, and Jean-Baptiste Leroy; and innovators like Nicolas Leblanc and Jacques-Constantin Périer.[8]

Most technocrats of the Bureau were of the view that market forces should guide entrepreneurs toward the economy's most lucrative sectors—a belief shared by the Minister of the Interior, Nicolas-Louis François de Neufchâteau. But they also regarded the pursuit of industry to be crucial for defending the Republic against both external military and internal revolutionary threats, and so gave the state a more active role to play than it had in England. In de Neufchâteau's own words, "glory belongs to the ingenious inventor just as it does to the intrepid warrior.... The people must persuade themselves that our manufactures are the arsenal from which will come weapons fatal to the power of Great Britain."[9] To this end, he launched a series of industrial exhibitions to promote the adoption of new techniques and technologies. The most significant exhibition was held at the Champ de Mars in southwestern Paris, with 60,000 livres of public funding allocated to construct sixty-eight arches, designed by François Chalgrin, who would later be known for the iconic Arc de Triomphe. The purpose of the exhibition was to make attendees discover new inventions and motivate the public to buy products "Made in France." Access to the event was restricted to those not wearing foreign-made apparel, and horse owners were obligated to provide proof that their animals had been born in France.[10] The new French state was officially in the business of industrial policy.

Code Napoléon

The interventionist de Neufchâteau era of the First Republic soon carried over to the reign of Napoleon Bonaparte, who did much to make France more meritocratic and remove obstacles to progress. Indeed, reflecting on his leadership, Napoleon once claimed that the introduction of the Civil Code was more important than any of his victories on the battlefield—an assertion with which it is hard to disagree. Up until that time, French law was a byzantine tapestry of regional regulations. Code Napoléon introduced a unified legal framework that solidified the revolution's achievements by removing any legal remnants of feudal hierarchies and privileges. From then on, all citizens were granted equal rights and responsibilities: private property rights were enshrined, feudal restrictions on land were removed, rent-seeking guilds were abolished, and localized lord-governed courts were completely disbanded. These changes paved the way for a standardized civil judiciary system as well as a national burgeoning market economy.[11]

Moreover, while Alexis de Tocqueville may have been right in tracing the early structures of centralized governance to the days of Louis XIII and Louis XIV, fiscal constraints due to wars and royal extravagances prompted the Bourbon monarchs to resort to selling public offices.[12] Once purchased, these offices could be bequeathed to heirs, entrenching landed interests and creating a powerful source of resistance to reform. The revolution, however, resulted in many of these officials losing their positions and, in numerous cases, their lives, making room for a more merit-based state system. This transition, which took shape over the subsequent century, was bolstered by supporting educational structures. By 1794, the revolutionary administration had founded several Grandes Écoles, such as École Normale Supérieure and École Polytechnique, to educate future civil servants.[13]

The successful implementation of Code Napoléon and the more targeted pursuit to rival Britain hinged on these developments. Under the guidance of Napoléon's Interior Minister, Jean-Antoine Chaptal, the state began adopting a more proactive role in the knowledge economy. While Chaptal was an admirer of Adam Smith and agreed with the Smithian idea that the government's main responsibility was to safeguard private property rights and ensure market access, he believed it was equally imperative for the state to coordinate between private stakeholders in the national interest. To forge cooperation among scientists, entrepreneurs, and bureaucrats Chaptal established Chambers of Commerce in two dozen cities and more than 150 *Chambres consultatives de Manufactures* in smaller towns. He was also instrumental in creating the Society for the Encouragement of National Industry (*Société d'encouragement pour l'industrie nationale*, or SEIN) that was tasked with supporting technology transfer, providing vocational training, and spurring innovation through prize competitions, which while privately run on paper, included many government officials as members who had been handpicked by Chaptal. Indeed, Napoleon himself, accompanied by fellow consuls, prefects, and officers, graced the inauguration at *L'Hôtel de Ville de Paris* in 1801.[14]

As usual, however, the primary strength of bureaucrats was not in identifying promising innovations. For instance, in full agreement with Chaptal, the SEIN refused to support critical improvements of Nicolas-Louis Robert's breakthrough paper-making machine, not once but twice. And Robert Fulton, who developed the first commercially successful steamboat, received such a lackluster reception from Chaptal and Napoleon that he eventually ended up leaving France for America, where his invention was soon introduced on the Hudson River.[15] More broadly, SEIN officials often avoided funding projects based on novelty or economic impact. Their priorities were telling: ceramics accounted for 13 percent of SEIN's funding, while fine arts and music received 11 percent—far more than locomotives, which received only 1 percent. Though some awards went to productive innovations, many were granted for imitating foreign products, demonstrating superior craftsmanship, or simply coming from individuals of high moral standing.[16]

These problems were compounded by the highly personalistic and conservative character of the government bureaucracy. Creative entrepreneurs often found themselves at a disadvantage compared to less inventive competitors who had better connections to patrons. These networked individuals could leverage their relationships to gain favourable treatment from state-sponsored institutions, which made it harder for innovators to succeed.[17] Baron Joseph-Marie De Gérando, who served as the SEIN secretary for more than forty years and played a pivotal role in prize distribution, filled the board with his allies, including his own father. Indeed, positions on juries or committees were often conferred as honours rather than based on technological expertise.[18]

The state of the French Empire, in other words, was hardly meritocratic by modern standards. Nevertheless, the slow drift towards Republicanism increased pressure for competence in government. After the 1848 revolution and the brief Second Republic, competitive civil service exams became more common, strengthening the state and aiding industrialization. Public engineers now took on projects like railroad construction.[19] They designed France's first national rail network, approved by Parliament in 1842, and later expanded the system in response to economic downturns in 1857–1859 and 1876–1878, when twelve private rail companies were merged into a massive state-owned company.[20] From 1823 to 1875, the state invested 1.4 billion francs in railways, a figure that grew to 4.5 billion between 1876 and 1913, largely due to the Freycinet Plan of 1878. Named after Public Works Minister and later Prime Minister Charles de Freycinet, the plan saw the government subsidizing private rail companies while also funding construction directly. The result was that France went from laggard to leader in rolling out rail. In 1840, it had just one-fifth the rail infrastructure of Belgium, England, and Germany. By 1913, France had 104 km of rail per 100,000 people, surpassing those three countries (89 km) and far outpacing Italy (54 km).[21]

Yet while France relied more on the state than Britain had, it was also much closer to the frontier than other latecomers.[22] At the Crystal Palace Exhibition in 1851, France outperformed all visiting countries in the number of medals awarded per capita.[23] In the early 1840s, it was also the largest importer of machinery from Britain, underlining its ability to swiftly absorb cutting-edge technologies.[24] And although the French state played a key role in rolling out infrastructure, its effort to drive frontier innovation through SEIN failed spectacularly. Rather, it was individual entrepreneurs and inventors, like Joseph Marie Jacquard, who spearheaded French innovation by capitalizing on the 1791 patent law that, inspired by the English system, abolished the complicated system of "exclusive privileges" under the ancien régime and made patenting more accessible to the wider population (see chapter 4).[25] This stands in contrast to Russia and Japan, where the private sector lagged much further behind and innovation was thus unnecessary for growth. In both cases, the state played a more prominent role in facilitating technological development, but as we shall see, the effectiveness of the state as facilitator hinged on the bureaucratic capabilities of the government apparatus. While the weak Russian state impeded the development of private enterprise, in Japan, the state bureaucracy, like in Germany, was capable of mounting a revolution from above.[26]

From Bismarck to Witte

The Russian path to the future was unquestionably shaped by its long history of state-led development, dating back to the days of Peter the Great. In the early eighteenth century, as historian R. W. Davies notes, Peter used "state power and serf labour to establish the iron industries of the Urals and to build St Petersburg as a window onto Europe."[27] But although his efforts generated a period of catch-up with both Britain and the Dutch Republic, this was followed by a period of profound stagnation in the second half of the eighteenth century. Russia's next big modernization push would not come until after its humiliating defeat in the Crimean War (1853–1856) to the more technologically advanced powers of Britain and France, a conflict that clobbered the state finances and frustrated the military and political ambitions of the Tsars.[28]

In the following decades, most notably under the stewardship of Finance Minister Sergei Witte, who had a long career managing the Odessa railways, the Russian state—together with foreign banks—played an active role in financing the rise of Russian industry. The quest for modern industry was, for Witte, a geopolitical imperative: "in comparison with foreign countries," he observed, "our industry is still very backward." This, he felt, endangered the fulfillment of the daunting political tasks of the Empire.[29] Much like Bismarck, not to mention Lenin and Stalin, he favoured heavy industry over the welfare of the population and relied on the state to drive growth.

But even though Witte saw himself as a Russian Bismarck, and certainly drew inspiration from the Iron Chancellor's strategies to promote industrialization from the above, he operated under different institutional conditions that were much less conducive to modernization. Indeed, within the Tsarist regime, there was a growing divide between traditionalists and modernizers. The traditionalists, like Vyacheslav von Plehve, who served as a director of Imperial Russia's police and later as Minister of the Interior, staunchly opposed any efforts toward liberalization. They viewed the more economically and politically decentralized Western model with deep suspicion, no doubt in part because they realized that such changes would undermine their own political clout. Consequently, modernizers, like Pyotr Stolypin, who later became prime minister, faced significant obstacles as their initiatives were effectively undermined by the traditionalist faction.[30] To navigate this minefield, industrializers like Witte pursued a strategy focused on driving technological progress while avoiding institutional change that could potentially weaken the repressive potency of the Tsarist regime.[31]

As a general matter, this meant that Russian reform initiatives were often long delayed and less than comprehensive.[32] For instance, while serfdom in Prussia was abolished after Napoleon's devastating victory at Jena, similar change only occurred in Russia half a century later in response to the Crimean War debacle. "It is better that this come from the above than from below," Alexander II remarked, echoing the logic behind the Stein-Hardenberg Reforms.[33] However, not until the Stolypin reform, following the revolution of 1905, did Russian peasants gain adequate control over their land to accelerate consolidation and drive productivity.[34] And this reform came too late to alter the fortunes of the Tsarist empire. As the Great War edged closer, after which the Romanov dynasty would cease to exist, approximately three-quarters of the population still worked in agriculture; urbanization was limited, with industry primarily centred around St. Petersburg and Moscow; and the elites were determined to shield whatever industry Russia possessed.[35] When cheaper steam-powered transportation cut the cost at which mechanized English producers could supply cotton and steel to Russian ports, the Tsarist government countered with protective tariffs, apprehensive that they would inadvertently import deindustrialization. In Tsarist Russia, there was nothing comparable to Berlin's Siemensstadt, and considering its enormous landmass, factories were few. Around the turn of the twentieth century, Russian income per capita was still less than one-third that of Germany.[36]

For Witte and fellow industrializers, one problem was that while Peter the Great had opened up the ranks of the bureaucracy to create more competition for important posts, he undercut his own efforts by involving himself in everything. The result was a personal and despotic state with a weak bureaucracy.[37] By the end of the Seven Years' War in 1763, when Russia was finally acknowledged as a major European power, the state employed only 16,500 people—a number only slightly higher than that of Prussia, whose land area was about 1 percent of European Russia's.[38] And in Prussia, the monarchy had the luxury of recruiting from a variety of German universities; in contrast, Moscow University, established in 1755, was the sole equivalent in Russia, and recruitment was hardly meritocratic anyway. Even under the last Tsar, Nicholas II, state employees did not have to pass any civil service examination.[39] Indeed, the Polity data series suggests that Russia in the 1890s was the most authoritarian state in the world, with the lowest possible democracy score.[40] While Fredrick the Great of Prussia had called himself "the first servant of the state" more than a century earlier, the Romanov's were still hesitant to "recognize a state independent of themselves."[41] By the dawn of the twentieth century, Imperial Russia lacked not just a parliament but also a bureaucratic apparatus to check the monarch's power. And, of course, the State Duma (the first representative body of legislative power in the Russian Empire), which was created in response to the 1905 revolution, would be short-lived, dissolved by Nicolas II after 73 days. As historian Dominic Livien puts it, "In these circumstances, the wonder was not that Russian bureaucracy was inefficient but that it functioned at all."[42]

Another issue was that the comparatively weak Tsarist regime had to exert extreme repression to survive. As mentioned in chapter 2, due to the immensity of the Russian Empire and the absence of technologies that enabled bureaucratic governance, the Tsars established a fragile state, whose equilibrium relied on the existence of an even frailer society. This engendered deep-seated mistrust among the landed elites toward capitalist development, because they feared the generation of wealth outside the royal ambit, as well as the congregation of workers in industrial towns, where they could potentially mobilize against the government. Under Tsar Nicholas I, for example, industrial exhibitions were prohibited. And following a wave of revolutionary uprisings across Europe in 1848, legislation was introduced that restricted the number of factories in Moscow by explicitly forbidding the establishment of new textile mills and iron foundries. Railroads, meanwhile, were perceived not only as a revolutionary technological advancement but also as a catalyst for revolutions, a view that turned out to be almost prophetic as Vladimir Ilyich Ulyanov (better known as Vladimir Lenin) arrived in St. Petersburg from Zurich by train seven decades later. Consequently, the sole railroad constructed before 1842, which connected St. Petersburg with the imperial estates at Tsarskoe Selo and Pavlovsk, was justly regarded as the "Tsar's toy"; information pertaining to railroads was even suppressed in Russian newspapers.[43]

As previously noted, the calculus of the Tsarist regime shifted in favor technological progress following Russia's defeat in the Crimean War. The construction of the St. Petersburg–Vienna line via Warsaw in 1862 marked the beginning of extensive railway construction across European Russia that persisted until the Great War. For instance, the establishment the *Grande Société des Chemins de Fer Russe*, backed by the French Pereire brothers, supported the line from Warsaw to St. Petersburg, passing through Grodno, Vilna, and Pskov, with a branch extending to Riga. However, most of the country's rail construction occurred in two waves: the first from 1866 to 1875, and the second from 1893 to 1905.[44] The initial phase focused on establishing main trunk lines connecting the Baltic region to the Black Sea and Sea of Azov coastlines, as well as linking the central region around Moscow. The next wave involved the construction of numerous branch lines and the Trans-Siberian Railway (1891–1903), which connected the capital to Vladivostok on the Pacific coast. During this period, under the leadership of Witte, the Russian state played a key role in accelerating the expansion of the railway network. To bypass bureaucratic obstacles, for example, Witte successfully advocated for the establishment of an interministerial organization, the Siberian Railroad Committee, which would possess the authority to make decisions regarding construction. And to convince Tsar Alexander II to endorse the idea, he proposed that his son, Grand Duke Nicholas Aleksandrovich, receive the chairmanship.[45]

In constructing Russia's rail network, Witte, who had written a sympathetic pamphlet about Friedrich List's "The National System of Political Economy," used tariffs and state procurement to further accelerate the growth of domestic steel and engineering sectors.[46] This contributed to the ninefold increase in the output of heavy industry, as the Russian network expanded at staggering pace.[47] Consequently, by the time of Archduke Franz Ferdinand's assassination, Russia possessed one of the world's largest rail networks, with 70,156 km of track, which would soon facilitate the movement of Russian troops.[48] As historian Alfred Rieber has observed, "Together with the emancipation of the serfs, the construction of a national railroad network helped launch Russia into the industrial age."[49]

However, compared to Wilhelmine Germany or Meiji Japan, the Tsarist regime continued to impose significant restrictions on private sector development. Unlike the Prussian government, which used its power to support private enterprise, allowing German companies to scale up swiftly and conquer global markets, the Tsarist state continued to undermine it, fearing that other centres of power would emerge outside the orbit of the Romanovs. Not only did bureaucrats sow uncertainty by intervening arbitrarily in business dealings, they also used political repression to disrupt informal networks and weaken civil society. The kind of voluntary associations that political scientist Robert Putnam has argued are essential to capitalist growth in general, and which we have seen are critical to innovation in particular, never emerged under Tsarism, or indeed later under Communism.[50] Add to this the uncertainty of property rights, the limited access to capital and skilled workers, and the backwardness of Russian corporation law, and it becomes clear that the impediments to entrepreneurship were formidable.[51] Unlike in America, Western Europe, and Japan, which had embraced incorporation by registration, Russia had a concessionary system of incorporation in which firms needed government grants of special privileges or exemptions to operate, which obstructed the "free establishment of corporations by delaying the granting of charters."[52] This, together with the backward financial markets in the empire, meant that Russia had relatively few companies.[53] And their motives were not just economic: "The concession system represented more than simply a rent-seeking enterprise; it gave the Ministry of Finance the authority to regulate and control large-scale enterprises, which integrated well with the autocratic government's agenda."[54] Just like the Russian government initially supported the endeavors of Swedish industrialist Immanuel Nobel in his development of exploding underwater mines, it withdrew its support after the costly Crimean War. And after his father's bankruptcy, Ludvig (the older brother of Alfred Nobel, founder of the Nobel Prize) devoted most of his energy to convincing Tsar Alexander II of the necessity to build more factories with his assistance.[55] Despite attracting some foreign talent in search of profits, this highly despotic system favoured incumbent loyalists and stifled the forces of competition.[56]

Predictably, state-led industrialization without institutional modernization soon reached its limits. In 1904, when the Russian Empire suffered another humiliating defeat, this time on the Korean Peninsula at the hands of the Japanese, the Russian people took notice of their backwardness and soon took to the streets. As the Russian fleet sailed toward Port Arthur, the press had depicted the Japanese as puny monkeys (*makaki*), scurrying away in fear from the formidable fist of Mother Russia, or as Oriental spiders, mercilessly crushed beneath the weight of a colossal Cossack hat. In a remarkable display of naval prowess, however, the Japanese fleet decisively vanquished the Russian fleet, consigning two-thirds of it—147,000 tons of naval hardware and nearly 50,000 sailors—to a watery grave in the depths of the Korea Strait. In the aftermath of "Bloody Sunday" on January 22, 1905, when the Imperial Guard opened fire on unarmed demonstrators led by Father Georgy Gapon as they marched toward the Winter Palace, a tidal wave of strikes and mutinies presented Russian revolutionaries with a seemingly golden opportunity. Indeed, for a brief period, St. Petersburg was effectively governed by a *soviet* or council of deputies elected by factory workers.

Among them was one Leon Trotsky, who declared that "the Russian fleet is no more [but] it is not the Japanese who destroyed her. Rather, it is the Tsarist government."[57] The peace treaty signed in Portsmouth the following year, mediated by Theodore Roosevelt, earned the otherwise war-hungry American president the Nobel Peace Prize and marked a dark moment in Russian history—the first time an Asian country had triumphed over an industrial European power.

Samurai Bureaucrats

In Japan, too, the seeds of progress were sown amid a backdrop of national humiliation. The Edo period (1603–1868), overseen by the Tokugawa Shogunate, witnessed more than two centuries of political stability. However, this stability was achieved at a significant cost, as the regime enforced strict controls over travel, trade, and freedom of occupation. The port of Nagasaki was the sole gateway for international trade, and even Nagasaki restricted entry exclusively to Chinese and Dutch vessels. Through these restrictions, the Tokugawa regime was able to uphold the existing feudal–agrarian order while perpetuating a climate of isolation and stagnation.[58] As E. Herbert Norman famously remarked, it was "one of the most conscious attempts in history to freeze society in a rigid hierarchical mold."[59]

The lack of improvements in living standards under Tokugawa rule was not the chief concern of Japanese elites. Rather, it was their waning power, which became glaringly evident when U.S. Commodore Matthew C. Perry first arrived in 1853. Backed by imposing warships and modern weaponry, Perry compelled the Shogunate into a treaty that opened Japanese ports to international trade. On his second visit the following year, Perry also brought a model steam locomotive, which he showcased on a circular track to an audience of fascinated spectators. One adventurous passenger, riding on top of the train, clung tightly to the roof, describing the experience "as though it were flying."[60] Eighteen years later, Japan's first railway was inaugurated. The line, which connected Tokyo to the nearby deep-sea port of Yokohama, cut a daylong walk to less than an hour by train. Soon thereafter, railway tracks were laid between Osaka and the port city of Kobe, marking the start of serious efforts to link up the country.[61]

The arrival of American gunboats in Japan, known as the Black Ships incident, was a pivotal event that sparked the most determined effort to acquire Western technology the world had ever seen. Almost immediately after Perry's arrival, the Japanese government established the Institute of Barbarian Books (*Bansho Torishirabesho*) with the mission of developing English–Japanese dictionaries to facilitate technical translations. At that time, however, there were not even Japanese words for key inventions such as railroads, steam engines, or telegraphs. To rectify this situation, the government hired a cadre of professional translators, alongside 2,400 foreigner instructors, to work around the clock to codify the bulk of Western science and technology. These efforts were a boon to Japanese industry, whose productivity and exports subsequently surged, and by 1890, the Japanese National Diet Library (NDL) housed more technical books than either the *Deutsche Nationalbibliothek* or the national libraries in Italy.[62]

The Black Ships incident also led to the Meiji Restoration of 1868, a comprehensive reform effort aimed at revitalizing Japanese power and avoiding the fate suffered by Qing China.[63] This overt display of vulnerability sparked dissent among the regional domains and led to an alliance of Satsuma, Chōshū, Saga, and Tosa, who collectively overthrew the Shogunate and reinstated the Meiji Emperor. This quintessential case of what Samuel Huntington called defensive modernization initiated widespread reforms, including the end of feudalism and the rebuilding of a centralized state capable of instigating industrial initiatives in national defense and economic development alike. Reassured by the Meiji government's guaranteed return rates, Japanese firms swiftly rolled out national rail and telegraph networks, fueling the expansion and modernization of industry in the process. These public–private partnerships persisted right up until the 1906–1907 nationalizations.[64] By that time, Japan's manufacturing output, greatly enhanced by the rapid integration of foreign technologies, equalled that of the United States in terms of its contribution to national income. In less than fifty years, Japan had undergone a remarkable transformation.[65]

A notable difference between Japan and Qing China, where unequal treaties failed to ignite a comparable drive for modernization, lay in the greater state capacity of the Tokugawa regime, fused with its more measured conservatism.[66] Despite both nations experiencing substantial opposition to radical reform, only Japan successfully overrode incumbent interests.[67] Resistance from peasants against the new land tax, public education, and conscription was promptly and forcefully quelled, as were the revolts of discontented samurai's who resented the elimination of their stipends and the right to bear swords. For instance, in the response to the 1877 Satsuma Rebellion, when around 20,000 samurai who had lost their privileges attacked Kumamoto Castle and attempted a march on Tokyo, the government decisively and ruthlessly crushed the revolt, effectively putting an end to the samurai class.[68] The Meiji Restoration, in short, did not merely entail the ascendance of a new business elite that shattered the old feudal structures. Rather, akin to the German experience, it emerged from a younger generation of ambitious and patriotic "*samurai*-bureaucrats."[69]

The parallels to the ascent of the Wilhelmine Empire are plentiful. Like in Germany, the key to rapid industrialization was the creation of a centralized bureaucracy. Also as in Germany, unification was led not by the most economically progressive regions of the country but rather by the most hierarchical and conservative states: Japan's Chōshū and Satsuma regions were more like Sparta than Athens. Whereas in Europe the abolition of feudal privileges and the subsequent formation of a modern state was a long and often violent process, Japan was able to draw upon a legacy of Chinese bureaucratic governance. This inheritance from China endowed Japan with a capable civil service, which would shape its post-1868 economic modernization. Moreover, as an island nation ruled from its inception by one unbroken dynasty—the House of Yamato—Japan had an extraordinarily high degree of ethnic and cultural homogeneity. The imprint of centralized dictatorship under the Tokugawa, combined with the cultural unity of the country, meant that the breakup of feudalism did not lead to a period of localism with competing city-states, as was the case in Europe. The Meiji reformers successfully leveraged traditions that had existed for centuries, like Shinto and emperor worship, to elevate national identity. So, in contrast to many less successful latecomers, Japan did not have to build a nation, just a state.[70]

Societal uniformity had a flip side, however. Unlike their European counterparts, who actively sought to attract British artisans and entrepreneurs, Japan faced limitations in its ability to nurture foreign talent. Although the government brought in engineers and technicians to assist in the construction of railroads and factories, their role was to provide knowledge and skills to the Japanese rather than to become permanent residents, because foreigners were not allowed to settle and meld into society.[71] Consequently, there were no Cockerills, Douglases, or Jacksons ready to build Japanese industry.[72] Western enterprise in Japan only took off in the twentieth century, when multinationals, by exchanging advanced technology for market access, began to forge joint ventures with Japanese partners, most notably in the industries of the Second Industrial Revolution. But early advances in textiles, metallurgy, and railroads were almost entirely accomplished by Japanese entrepreneurs, albeit with imported British machinery.[73] To be sure, foreign technology was sometimes cleverly upgraded, as Sakichi Toyoda's automatic loom bears witness to. (His son, Kiichiro Toyoda, would later establish Japan's largest carmaker, Toyota.) But there were few breakthrough innovations. To paraphrase one scholar, if Japan's experience teaches any single lesson, it is that myriads of simple improvements to established technologies can take a country a long way.[74]

For the most part, this stream of improvements came from the private sector. Yet often it was the state that served as the stimulant by introducing foreign technologies and creating the preconditions for Japanese firms to grow. This state assistance was possible partly because, contrary to the Romanovs in Russia, the Japanese emperor had become merely a symbolic figurehead. The real authority lay in the hands of a select group of senior political figures, such as Itō Hirobumi, Yamagata Aritomo, and Inoue Kaoru. One of their first acts was to establish a Weberian bureaucracy modelled on Prussia. By 1937, over 73 percent of higher-level bureaucrats were graduates of Tokyo University, where the Law Faculty had become the preferred entryway into elite ministries[75]—a stark contrast to the situation that prevailed prior to 1900, when more than 97 percent of those appointed prefectural governor had no formal university education.[76] And as in the Prussian bureaucracy, Japanese officials were screened in a competitive examination system, established in 1887 and strengthened in 1893, making patronage appointments less common.[77]

The role of the bureaucracy in formulating and implementing reforms was significant, again reminiscent of the Prussian experience. The Meiji Constitution, in fact, rejected the English model of parliamentary sovereignty and instead adopted a constitution resembling that of Imperial Germany. This modified Prussian constitution established a hereditary House of Peers and a Diet to be elected by a tiny property-owning elite comprising no more than 1 percent of the population, but it also diverted the business of running government away from elites into the hands of a professional civil service. The rule of bureaucrats rather than the rule of law prevailed.[78]

These parallels between Germany and Japan are not coincidental.[79] Many Japanese officials went to Europe and were particularly impressed with what they saw in the Wilhelmine Empire:

> Ito Hirobumi, Japan's first (and multiple) prime minister, spent two months in Berlin in 1882, meeting the Iron Chancellor, Otto von Bismarck. Among the second generation of Meiji leaders, several studied in Germany for periods of years. Hirata Tosuke, Minister of Agriculture and Commerce and then Interior Minister in the 1890s, was the first Japanese to obtain a German doctorate, in 1875; Hirata also undertook one of several translations of List into Japanese. Kanai Noboru, who studied in Germany in the 1880s under almost all the key scholars of the Historical School, returned to a professorship at Tokyo Imperial University and trained a generation of bureaucrats at what remains Japan's most elite school for government officials. Several important German scholars were also recruited to teach in Japan and to advise the government.[80]

Ministers and senior officials embarked on journeys overseas not solely to familiarize themselves with policy matters. They also sought to acquire knowledge about the latest technological advancements. For instance, when Japanese diplomats traversed the United States and several European nations during the Iwakura mission, the delegation included Okubo Toshimichi, the Minister of Civil Affairs, who was entrusted with the task of identifying opportunities for pilot industrial projects in Japan.

Besides helping to establish pilot projects, the Japanese state also provided minimum profit guarantees for large-scale industrial endeavours. One beneficiary was Mitsubishi, an enterprise established in 1870 by the politically well-connected trader Iwasaki Yataro. Through governmental provisions of vessels and substantial subsidies, the company persevered until it successfully broke the foreign stronghold on shipping.[81] By the turn of the century, Mitsubishi Shipbuilding proudly housed the fourth largest factory in the country.[82] The largest enterprises, however, were the Railroad Agency and the Ministry of Communication, which were run by the state and employed some 240,000 workers collectively.[83] From 1887 to 1936, the government consistently backed around a third of investment projects, with significant resources going into transportation, communication, and heavy industry—areas that were initially spearheaded by the Meiji reformers.[84]

To be sure, the task of the Meiji statesmen was eased by Japan's already well-educated populace, which was notably advanced considering the country's otherwise underdeveloped economy.[85] During the Tokugawa period, Japan had already made considerable progress in education, establishing thousands of schools for commoners and around 1,500 private academies.[86] Yet it was during the Meiji period that, drawing inspiration from Western educational models, the state introduced a comprehensive three-tier system comprising primary schools, middle schools, and universities. From 1880 until the start of World War II, Japan experienced a fortyfold increase in student enrollment in higher education, particularly in scientific and technical fields, while new institutions, like Tokyo's College of Engineering, became among the largest of its kind globally. Nevertheless, relative to Germany, or even England, Japan lagged behind in scientific research, a factor that helps explain the weaker performance of Japanese companies in the industries of the Second Industrial Revolution. Even Japan's universities focused on "application rather than pure science or *Bildung*" and "were keener on integrating existing knowledge in the Japanese system than on creating new knowledge."[87]

However, Japan possessed its own competitive edge: a seemingly boundless reservoir of inexpensive, skilled, and disciplined labour, which quickly adapted to modern machinery and provided a strong foothold in the industries spawned by the First Industrial Revolution. That Japan surpassed Britain as a major exporter of manufactured goods was not solely due to catch-up in productivity; deliberate suppression of real wage growth also played a role in securing a cost advantage.[88] Yet, this advantage was not unique—around the turn of the century, countries like India had similarly cheap labour and comparable levels of factory mechanization. By the early 1930s, however, Japan had tripled its manning ratios, whereas in India they remained unchanged; in other words, Indian factories required many more workers to operate the same number of machines.[89] One reason for this was that Indian workers successfully resisted efforts to increase mechanization.[90] Between 1918 and 1938, the Indian textile industry experienced eight general strikes in Mumbai alone. The early work stoppages concerned wages, whereas the later ones were primarily attempts to resist any rationalisation and reorganization of production. Strikingly, even though the remaining workers would earn higher wages by operating more machines, they refused to cooperate.[91]

While sociologists like Ronald Dore have argued that factory discipline and hierarchical management in Japan were deeply culturally ingrained in the population, the forcefulness of the Japanese state was surely no less important.[92] If similar strikes had paralyzed major cities like Osaka or Tokyo for an extended period, the Japanese government would likely have declared martial law rather than permit such a disruption to the country's paramount export industry.[93] Indeed, Article 17 of the Public Order & Police Law explicitly outlawed strikes and in effect made unions illegal as well. The Japanese police exhibited an unwavering commitment to enforcing these laws, as exemplified by their resolute response to strikes at establishments such as Yawata Steel Works, the Tokyo Streetcar Company, and Mitsubishi Shipyards.[94] In a manner reminiscent of labour repression observed in eighteenth century England, the Japanese state staunchly pursued the elimination of any obstacles holding back industrialization.[95]

These tendencies were further reinforced and solidified by the power of the *zaibatsu*—the large, vertically integrated industrial conglomerates—who did much to advance mechanization and the broader interests of industry.[96] During the 1880s, the sale of many government-operated pilot firms at reduced prices provided emerging zaibatsu with the opportunity to broaden their enterprises, and as in Germany, the path to industrial modernization hinged on a cooperative relationship between the government and major corporations.[97] Here again, this resemblance is not coincidental: in 1930, Kishi Nobosuke, a high-ranking official at the Ministry of Commerce and Industry, traveled to Germany with the purpose of examining how their cartels operated.[98] Following the dissemination of Kishi's findings, the government enacted the Important Industries Control Law, which granted it the authority to enforce agreements among cartels. This consolidation of power within the sphere of business concurrently hindered the advancement of democratic and labour movements domestically while furnishing a useful instrument for assertive military endeavours beyond Japan's borders.[99]

The zaibatsu, in many respects, perpetuated the customs of guild organization and clan monopolies within the framework of the modern era. According to the renowned scholar of Japan William Lockwood, "The spirit of hierarchical organization, of leadership, subordination, and group teamwork, found fresh expression in the new world of corporate finance and industry."[100] Correspondingly, the Big Four zaibatsu—Mitsui, Mitsubishi, Sumitomo, and Yasuda—functioned as colossal family enterprises. The Sumitomo conglomerate, for instance, was governed and owned by a single-family head, whereas Mitsubishi was overseen by two Iwasaki families. Unlike the guilds, the zaibatsu's interests extended beyond local boundaries, encompassing the nation as a whole. By the start of the Great Depression, Mitsui, Mitsubishi, Yasuda, and state-owned Yawata controlled 94 percent of Japan's pig iron production and 83 percent of its steel output. And in other key sectors, their influence was absolute—Mitsui and Mitsubishi split the entire ammonium sulfate market between them, while Mitsui, Mitsubishi, and Yasuda controlled over 80 percent of the cement industry.[101]

Imitators and Innovators

As these family-run conglomerates grew, their influence seeped into the government that had once nurtured their rise. By establishing close relationships with key government officials and funding major political parties, they ensured that their influence reached beyond the economic sphere. Leaders of these conglomerates also moved effortlessly into top roles within governmental bodies, such as the Bank of Japan or the Ministry of Commerce. Moreover, together with the state, the conglomerates created several semiofficial organizations like the Yokohama Specie Bank and the South Manchuria Railway, as well as other ventures called "national policy companies," both within Japan and internationally.[102] Although the zaibatsu were not at the forefront of innovation, innovation was not necessary for growth and exportation; being an adept imitator was enough.[103] However, by relying on technologies borrowed from abroad, often with support from the state, the zaibatsu soon lost their pioneering edge.[104]

As this chapter has illustrated, catch-up growth needs bureaucratic capacity, which helps explain the divergent trajectories of Japan and Russia in this period. Yet in the long-run, an imitation-based strategy ultimately hinges on the innovative breakthroughs and discoveries made by others. And with the emergence of the Second Industrial Revolution, these transformative discoveries increasingly emanated from a more decentralized economy—namely, the United States—which stood alone as the sole nation to surpass Britain in income per capita in the nineteenth century, as well as in innovation.

Clarence Streit's compilation of 1,012 major inventions is particularly illuminating in this regard (figure 5.1). It reveals a remarkable reversal in the relative contributions of Britain and America during the Second Industrial Revolution. In the earlier classic period spanning from 1776 to 1825, Britain held a commanding lead, accounting for 44 percent of all major inventions worldwide. However, between 1875 and 1926, a stag-

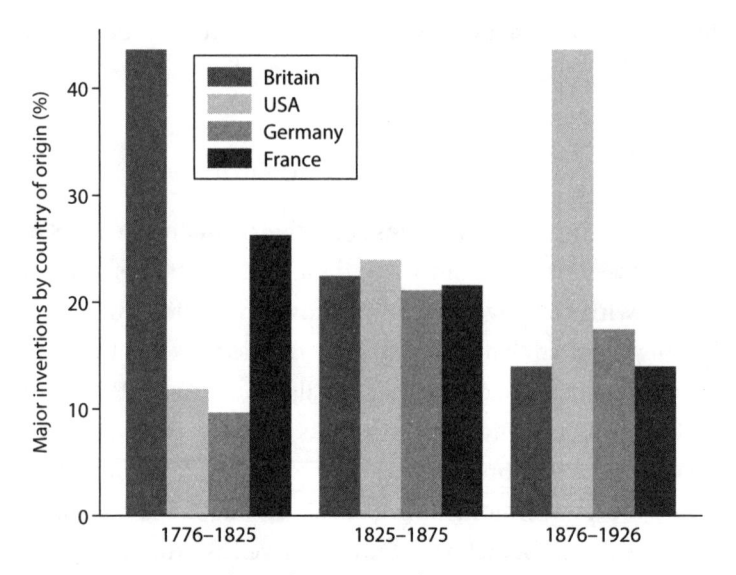

FIGURE 5.1. Breakthrough inventions by country, 1776–1926
Source: Streit, *Union Now*; Magee, "Manufacturing and Technological Change," Table 4.12.

gering 44 percent of all major discoveries took place in America; Britain, France, and Germany found themselves more or less evenly matched following the classic period, with invention shares hovering between 14 and 22 percent.[105] For the rest of the world, this meant that as long as America continued to invent a steady flow of technologies for them to adopt, bureaucracies in latecomer countries could hasten modernization like an ambitious mother pushing her child prodigy. But, to borrow the words of David Landes, while the child grew and developed its own capabilities, "it never overcame the deformity imposed by this forced nurture."[106]

6

Innovation in America

[In America,] People do not enquire concerning a Stranger, What is he? but What can he do? . . . The People have a Saying, that God Almighty is himself a Mechanic, the greatest in the Universe; and he is respected and admired more for the Variety, Ingenuity and Utility of his Handiworks, than for the Antiquity of his Family.[1]

—BENJAMIN FRANKLIN

Americans are constantly driven to engage in commerce and industry. Their origin, their social condition, their political institutions, and even the region they inhabit urge them irresistibly in this direction. . . . This is the characteristic that most distinguishes the American people from all others at the present time.[2]

—ALEXIS DE TOCQUEVILLE

IF IMPERIAL Germany was established on the back of Prussian bureaucracy, what became the United States of America was due to the efforts of its entrepreneurs. Jamestown, established in 1607 as the first permanent colony in North America, began as an entrepreneurial venture of the Virginia Company of London. It also became the first government bailout in the region when it was converted to a Crown colony. But while the settlers were disappointed that "gold did not wash up on the beach and gems did not grow in the trees," they understood the potential for acquiring wealth in other ways in what they made their new home—at times through horrific crimes against the native population.³ Before independence, however, there were few jobs in industry. Even in 1800, 83 percent of Americans worked in agriculture.⁴ There was some overseas trade in tobacco and cotton, but farms primarily produced for their own consumption or for local markets. Similarly, the vast majority of manufactured goods were made at home and sometimes traded with local artisans.

This lack of trade and market access was the result of high transportation costs and low population densities. On the new continent, a population of 5.3 million people was spread across a vast territory of 860,000 square miles, and with the Louisiana Purchase from Napoleonic France in 1803, the United States almost doubled in land area, making it even more sparsely populated despite rapid population growth. Only Philadelphia and New York could justly be regarded as cities, and only 6.1 percent of the population qualified as urban.⁵ As U.S. Secretary of the Treasury, Albert Gallatin, observed in 1810, "by far the greater part of goods made of cotton, flax, or wool are manufactured in private families, mostly for their own use . . . about two thirds of the clothing . . . worn and used by the inhabitants of the United States who do not reside in cities, is the product of family manufactures."⁶

Yet over the course of the next 150 years, American markets, and consequently its industry, would grow in both scope and scale and do so in a distinctive fashion: in contrast to Prussia and other European counterparts, America would be defined by a weak, decentralized government, with a feeble bureaucracy. However, the American government would, more than any other, harness the talents of its innovators through a democratised patent system, and it would overcome its lack of state capacity through public–private partnerships. This formula would be so successful that America would eventually move to the forefront of technological development, even as it gave rise to corporations so powerful that they threatened to thwart competition and innovation.

Federalism and Freedom

From the outset, the German path to modern industry was foreclosed to the United States. Among the Founding Fathers, Alexander Hamilton stood alone in articulating the case for a powerful central administration, which he outlined in a series of articles, later collected as part of "The Federalist Papers." Hamilton, however, was vehemently opposed by the likes of Samuel Adams, Patrick Henry, and Thomas Jefferson, who in his first inaugural address explained America's enduring distrust of bureaucracy and big government: "We may well doubt whether our organization is too complicated, too expensive; whether offices and officers have not been multiplied unnecessarily and sometimes injuriously to the service they were meant to promote."[7]

Many scholars, building from Jefferson's observation, have sought to distinguish the American development path from the European trajectory. Seymour Martin Lipset, a Stanford sociologist, famously argued that because the United States was founded in a revolution against the concentrated power of the British Crown, it possessed a deep-seated scepticism of government, which explains the multiple checks and balances the nation adopted in its new Constitution.[8] To echo the words of political scientist Barry Weingast, "A government strong enough to protect property rights is also strong enough to confiscate the wealth of its citizens."[9] To defuse this threat, Americans adopted a federalist structure of government, which safeguarded against expropriation by the state in a decentralized manner. But it is also true that, beyond the influence of cultural allergies to centralized institutions, initial conditions were inconducive to state building. America had no powerful neighbour to threaten it, and its dispersed rural population meant that the cost of monitoring output to collect taxes would have been very high, particularly before the advent of the railroads and the telegraph.[10]

In any event, decentralization meant that the federal government was highly constrained in its ability to spur American industrialization. The consequences of American state incapacity are perhaps most evident in the domain of trade policy. Having formally declared independence from Britain, individual states tried to make up for lost trade by promoting commerce with France. But although the United States was now principally free to trade with the rest of the world, its options were limited. French merchants offered expensive yet inferior goods and were generally ignorant of American customs.[11] So Americans instead pinned their hopes on a trade agreement with Britain. John Adams was sent to London, only to discover that British officials were completely uninterested in trade negotiations. They had read Lord Sheffield's 1783 pamphlet, which observed that the U.S. Congress was powerless to retaliate against any restrictions on American commerce simply because it could not regulate the trade of its states. And in Paris, Thomas Jefferson encountered similar problems when trying to convince officials to open up the French West Indies to American ships. America had as many trade policies as it had states, so European powers could just dock their ships in the most welcoming ports.[12]

Solving this problem required bolstering the federal state, a task that was nearly impossible under the Articles of Confederation drafted after independence, which severely restricted the powers of any national government. Congress could not, for instance, impose any import duties, which left the federal government unable to finance its operations, defense included. And without any reliable source of revenue, Congress was unable to borrow in credit markets. This made America extremely vulnerable to foreign policy challenges. The growing recognition of these infirmities set the stage for the Constitutional Convention in Philadelphia in May 1787.[13]

The Constitution, which went into effect in March of 1789, was designed to centralize political power—to put in place a federal government that could coordinate laws, defense, and economic policy across the states.[14] Through this new constitution, the Federalists aimed to increase the fiscal and administrative capacity of the state by allowing the federal government to raise taxes to pay for a standing army. Indeed, once the Constitution was ratified, the first action taken by George Washington's federally funded army was to suppress an anti-tax uprising: the Whiskey Rebellion. However, this centralization of power justifiably created anxieties about tyranny and so was counterbalanced by the adoption of institutional checks, such as the separation of powers between the executive and the legislature. The Federalists also needed to make concessions to those concerned about preserving the autonomy of the states, in effect limiting federal powers and establishing the understanding that anything left unspecified in the Constitution would be the domain of the states. Similarly, they were forced to strike a deal with a highly mobilized civil society worried that a more powerful bureaucracy spelled despotism; the result was the adoption of the Bill of Rights.[15]

Despite these concessions, relative to the Articles of Confederation, the Constitution gave considerable new powers to the federal government at the expense of state sovereignty. Take Article I, Section 10, which restricts individual states' dealings with foreign nations and prohibits states from creating their own paper money, in addition to establishing the sanctity of contract, creating the basis for secure private property rights, and upholding free trade by prohibiting restrictions on interstate commerce. Or consider Article II, Section 8, which gives Congress the power "to promote the progress of science and useful arts by securing for limited times to authors and inventors the exclusive right to their respective writings and discoveries." It was this section that allowed the federal government to enact the nation's first patent law in 1790, thus making way for the upsurge in patenting that followed.[16]

The Constitution, in other words, established a decentralized system of secure private property rights (for white men) and ensured that entrepreneurs would have access to a vast internal common market with few impediments. At the same time, it also constrained state power by establishing that no "direct taxes," specifically income taxes, could be collected by the federal government, which left the state with limited funds to provide public goods or solve coordination problems. The main objective of the Constitution was to create more state capacity, but it created plenty of incapacity as well. The American state in 1789 was, for instance, far less powerful than its Prussian counterpart. It had a tiny bureaucracy and provided only a few public services. Given the government's limited fiscal powers, the prime objective of American trade policy between 1790 and the Civil War (1860) was to raise revenue, and import duties accounted for about 90 percent of the federal government's income. Even after the war, tariffs continued to serve as a major source of federal income for some time. Only with the introduction of the income tax in 1913 did their importance for state finances eventually fade.[17]

Some of the Founding Fathers, notably Alexander Hamilton, clearly saw a more active role for government in accelerating the rise of industry, beyond merely acting as a passive enforcer of private property. In his famous "Report on the Subject of Manufactures," published in 1791, he argued that there was a case for government to help industries overcome impediments to their development, including: "the strong influence of habit and the spirit of imitation—the fear of want of success in untried enterprises—the intrinsic difficulties incident to first essays toward a competition with those who have previously attained to perfection in the business to be attempted—the bounties, premiums and other artificial encouragements, with which foreign nations second the exertions of their own Citizens in the branches, in which they are to be rivaled."[18] Such promotion of domestic industry would be best achieved through targeted subsidies, Hamilton pointed out, since protective tariffs support inefficient and efficient producers alike. Indeed, Hamilton was more interested in using the state to encourage the new rather than to protect the old.

Embargoed

Protectionism, however, was what followed, though not for economic reasons. In February 1793, France declared war on Britain. Initially, as British and French commercial ships were diverted to military service, American merchants stepped in to fill the void. In April, President Washington issued a "Neutrality Proclamation," declaring that the United States would not take sides in the conflict. The hope was that this would allow America to continue to trade peacefully. But as the British government began to crack down on American trade with France, U.S. merchant ships soon found themselves in the firing line. Diplomatic solutions failed, and escalation followed. In June 1807, the British navy fired on a U.S. warship off the coast of Norfolk, Virginia. To avoid military conflict, Jefferson responded with a trade embargo. All American ships were prohibited from sailing to foreign ports, while foreign ships were barred from taking on cargo in the United States. Although foreign merchants could, in theory, bring goods into America, very few did as they had to bear the cost of returning empty.[19]

The repercussions were enduring. Though Congress repealed the embargo in March 1809, a series of restrictive measures on imports followed, which culminated in the War of 1812.[20] As a result, American industry was shielded from import competition for several years, until the Treaty of Ghent in December 1814, when the war ended and trade was restored. This shutdown of foreign commerce was the most radical trade policy experiment in American history, and it had large distributive and disruptive effects. One the one hand, it imposed enormous costs on American farmers, fishermen, and merchants, and so most of the population. For American industry, on the other hand, it was a mixed blessing.[21] Commercial industries collapsed, and export-oriented manufacturing industries, like shipbuilding, suffered, while production by import-substituting manufacturers blossomed. Economic historian Douglas Irwin notes:

> While the promotion of domestic manufacturing was not the primary intention of Jefferson and Madison, their trade policies restricted imports so severely that enterprising entrepreneurs started producing manufactured goods to replace those formerly imported. Although he had no desire to see large-scale factories appear on America's shores, Jefferson anticipated that the embargo would provide "indirect encouragement" to small domestic manufacturers. In contrast to his earlier views, he welcomed this development as a way of achieving economic independence. "Our embargo, which has been a very trying measure, has produced one very happy & permanent effect," Jefferson wrote after leaving office in 1809. "It has set us all on domestic manufacture, & will I verily believe reduce our future demands on England fully one half."[22]

For import-competing manufacturers, production spiked during the war, but the gain in output was largely reversed after trade resumed in 1815. Protected by 35 percent wartime duties, small American mills were inefficient, and they were unprepared for the flood of cheaper goods produced by larger and mechanized manufacturers in Britain. Bankruptcies multiplied during 1816, so that half the spindles around Providence, Rhode Island, stood idle. A wave of petitions urging tariff increases soon entered the White House. Under tariff protection, they argued, domestic manufacturing capabilities could be nurtured, shielded from the forces of foreign competition. The government acquiesced to these demands, and the Tariff of 1816 was the first time the federal government used tariffs to protect American industry, rather than as a means of raising revenue or economic warfare.[23]

Yet to suggest that the rise of American industry was the result of protectionism would be mistaken. For one thing, early American progress was mostly made in Britain. What propelled America to the technological frontier was its openness to foreign ideas, technologies, and talent. The first American cotton mill, which was set up in Rhode Island in 1790, used Arkwright's technology, and it was brought in by Samuel Slater, who had been a superintendent of a mill in Lancashire. Because the export of textile machinery was still banned by the British government, Slater was concerned that his possessions would be searched for any descriptions of the technology when he left the country. To prepare for this possibility, he memorized the blueprints of the machines before sailing off to America, where the technology soon spread through Massachusetts and Rhode Island. Gallatin's report on manufactures counts fifteen cotton mills working eight thousand spindles across the United States in 1807, when the embargo came into force. Mercifully, for the growth of American industry, Britain's export ban on machinery was highly ineffective.[24]

If any single person deserves praise for the early ascent of American manufacturing industry, it would be Francis Cabot Lowell—a Harvard-educated merchant who had seen the power loom at work in Manchester and returned to set up the Boston Manufacturing Company together with his friend Nathan Appleton in 1813.[25] Their company specialized in producing power looms, which spread like wildfire and produced a shakeout of the industry.[26] As old spinning mills went under, early adopters thrived. Even if the embargo had supported some smaller spinning mills for a time, none would have survived the onslaught of foreign competition without embracing the loom. As Irwin has shown in some detail, what saved American textile was not the 1816 tariff but pirated British technology and the ability of skilled artisans and entrepreneurs to apply it to local conditions.[27] Among them were the Schofield brothers, who came to America from Yorkshire to build wool-carding machines and would go on to train Paul Moody—a major figure in the development of New England's textile industry; the Scotsman Henry Burdon, who became responsible for many crucial innovations at Springfield Armory, where he made a habit of bringing over immigrant mechanics; and David Thomas, a Welsh immigrant, who was the first to introduce Pennsylvania's iron industry to anthracite.[28]

America, in short, was a magnet for talent. From 1790 to 1890, its population surged from 3.9 to 62.6 million, in large part thanks to an enormous influx of European settlers—many of whom were adventurous, thrifty, and willing to cut family ties in search of a better future and the prospect of free land. Over the same period, the settled area expanded from under 240,000 square miles to nearly 2,000,000, with the centre of gravity of the population shifting 500 miles westward from Washington, DC, to Decatur, Indiana. This westward expansion would only reinforce the pattern of decentralized American development.

In an influential essay, published in 1893, historian Frederick Jackson Turner made the case that American individualism and antipathy toward government could be traced back to the frontier line.[29] A key source of inspiration for Turner's classic was the Census Bureau report on the "Progress of the Nation" from 1890, which noted that the thirteen colonies declaring independence from Britain were "the sources of supply for a great westward migration," as people "swarmed from the Atlantic coast to the prairies, plains, mountains, and deserts by millions during the last century." In this period, frontier states, like Minnesota, Kansas, and Texas, attracted large swathes of young, mobile, and curious émigrés. The migrants who settled there were indeed particularly self-reliant. Even today, these former frontier counties are more opposed to just about any form of government intervention, like redistribution, minimum wages, gun control, and environmental protection.[30] And according to data collected by the World Value Survey, the United States still stands out as the most individualistic country in the world.[31]

America's laissez-faire values can go some way in explaining how it turned into an innovation powerhouse. While individualism checked the capacity of the state, making coordination harder, it also made discovery easier. As economists Yuriy Gorodnichenko and Gerard Roland show in an important paper, both within the United States and across countries, individualism turns out to be a good predictor of innovation.[32] As noted in chapter 3, the dissolution of kinship ties made Europeans more individualistic in their outlook, which supported the flow of knowledge by wiring Europe's collective brain. Individualists are not only more willing to socialize beyond the clan and learn from strangers, but they are also more inclined to deviate from norms and customs, which is in the end what innovation is about. Moreover, they have a greater willingness to move around and thus act as proliferators for ideas. Indeed, of the great American inventors between 1790 and 1846, more than 70 percent of them migrated to two or more states over their career, while many traveled to Europe to exploit opportunities there. By all accounts, these innovators were much more mobile than the general population.[33]

To account for American prosperity, however, the Turner thesis must be modified in important ways. For one thing, American industry and innovation first arose in the Northeast, mostly far away from the frontier—although Maine was a notable exception. Nor was frontier expansion exceptional to the United States. South America, for example, similarly underwent a period of massive territorial expansion, but unlike in the United States, political elites in Argentina, Chile, and Guatemala allocated land from the top-down in a "very oligarchic manner."[34] How the frontier shaped progress depended on the institutions in place. By creating a system of private property rights, along with the largest free-trade zone in the world, the U.S. Constitution provided the backbone of American innovation and entrepreneurship. This system attracted and rewarded people like Heinrich Steinweg, who in Europe constantly struggled against guild regulations, first as a cabinetmaker in Goslar, Sachsen, and then as an organ builder in the German town of Seesen. Eventually, Steinweg left for America, where he established his Steinway & Sons business in New York City, free from guild restrictions. In the absence of a constitution to support exploration, North America would look much more like its Southern counterpart.[35]

One crucial pillar of this decentralized approach to technological innovation was America's patent system. Indeed, Abraham Lincoln, who himself had patented a device to buoy steamboats over sandbars, suggested that the patent system added "the fuel of interest to the fire of genius."[36] This system was largely created through the Patent Act of 1836, which introduced examination prior to the issuing of a patent, created a professional body of patent examiners, and established a library of prior art to aid examinations. The law also required all patentees to publish detailed descriptions of their inventions with the Patent Office, housed in a Greek revival temple. Over time, this created a central storehouse of technical information available to the public that even Charles Dickens admitted was "an extraordinary example of American enterprise and ingenuity."[37]

Not only could anyone travel to Washington, DC, to access the Patent Office files of detailed descriptions of past inventions, but the Patent Office also published an annual list of all patents issued. This list was then reprinted in several private journals, many of which were issued by patent agencies that functioned as intermediaries in the growing market for technology. This was, for instance, the primary focus of *Scientific American*, published by Munn and Company—the largest patent agency of the day.[38] Alongside Munn, several agencies facilitated trade in patents, linking local clients to agents in Washington, DC, and other major hubs. It was this system that allowed a cadre of professional inventors, like Richard Gatling, to specialize in innovation. Over his 60-year long career, Gatling took out patents for everything from machines to guns, which he sold or licensed to manufacturers around the country.[39] Overall, in 1870, at the dawn of the Second Industrial Revolution, an astonishing 83 percent of patents granted were traded.[40]

A Market for Ideas

The U.S. patent system was second to none, which is why Britain's patent reform of 1852 was modelled on her economic rival across the Atlantic.[41] First and foremost, the American system was specifically designed to be more democratic than its European counterparts.[42] The fee to obtain a patent was a mere 5 percent of the amount charged in Britain, making intellectual property rights accessible to a much broader swathe of the population.[43] This helps explain why so many key inventions of the late nineteenth century came from the United States. Though Alexander Graham Bell will always be remembered as the father of the telephone, Antonio Meucci had conceived a similar system years before him, but he could not afford to file a patent in Italy. American inventors were no more ingenious than their peers elsewhere; the barriers to participate in innovation were simply lower.[44]

U.S. institutions still, of course, left much to be desired. Men continued to have legal control of family property and income, which left women unable to enter contracts without their husbands' approval and so deprived the American innovation economy of half its potential. Predictably, in states where coverture was abolished, patenting among married women subsequently surged.[45] American institutions also shackled the vast majority of the Black population.[46] Even with the abolition of slavery and the Fourteenth Amendment, granting African Americans the full property rights afforded other citizens, Jim Crow laws continued to enforce racial segregation in many Southern states until 1965.[47] The primary brunt of these inhumane institutions was borne by Black communities, but the economic costs were inflicted upon the rest of society as well. Recent research by economist Lisa Cook shows that race riots and lynchings, which contributed to uncertainty over property rights, reduced patenting among African Americans.[48] Yet despite the limitations imposed by bigotry and injustice, innovation in America was sufficiently broad-based for scholars to call it "democratized"—by the standards of the day—already in the antebellum period.[49] Samuel Morse, who invented the electric telegraph, was a professional painter. Cyrus McCormick, who developed the mechanical reaper, was a farmer and blacksmith. Isaac Singer, who invented the most popular sewing machine, was an actor. Charles Goodyear, who pioneered vulcanized rubber, was the owner of a hardware store.[50] Most leading inventors of the time were self-taught, and few had any background in science.

Some of these technologies were surely mundane, but they had a profound impact on the U.S. economy. For a family farm, McCormick's reaper made it possible to do "in one day what previously had occupied the harvest season."[51] Even more consequential was Eli Whitney's cotton gin, both for productivity and the expansion of industry. Before its arrival, removing the seed from one pound of cotton fibre took one person one day. Thereafter, one person could handle 300 pounds per day. In 1793, when the cotton gin was invented, the United States produced 1 percent of the world's cotton. By 1830, it produced half. Cotton was the largest single commodity export of America until the outbreak of the Great Depression in 1929, when it accounted for 18 percent of total exports.[52] But regrettably for American society, cotton harvesting remained dependent on cheap and obedient labour. The cotton gin arguably entrenched slavery, which besides depriving millions of their basic human rights, held back the adoption of automation technologies and contributed to the Civil War, costing somewhere between 650,000 and 850,000 men their lives.[53]

The vast majority of inventions in this period, however, were productive rather than destructive. They were also the result of decentralized exploration, which is evident from the virtual absence of corporations in the making of key discoveries. In 1880, almost all patents (95 percent) were taken out by individuals.[54] The railroad companies invented neither steam engines nor locomotives, just as Western Union was not responsible for the invention of telegraphy. Even the technologies of the Second Industrial Revolution, which would lend steam to American growth for the next century, were by and large individual endeavours. These include such famous examples as Edison's incandescent lamp, phonograph, and motion-picture system; Bell's telephone; Stanley's, Tesla's, and Thomson's efforts in electric light-and-power transmission; Fessenden's, de Forest's, and Armstrong's contributions to wireless telegraphy, telephony, and radio; Sperry's electric railways and automobiles; Maxim's helicopter; and the Wright brothers' iconic internal-combustion-engine to power airplanes.[55]

Some, like Edison and Westinghouse, built vast commercial empires around their patents, but most did not. Instead, they were able to continue to pursue more radical ideas, rather than having their talents fettered by bureaucratic management. Tesla, for example, whose eccentricities made him the very model of a mad scientist, sold his patents to Westinghouse, where a team of gifted engineers helped transform his ideas into a practical system. Supported by Westinghouse royalties, he stayed away from corporate activities to focus on bolder projects. Having achieved financial independence, his ultimate commitment was to his own small research laboratory. This gave him a great latitude to focus on problems of his choice, whether power transmission, turbines, or vertical-takeoff airplanes. When he died in 1943, he had taken out over 100 patents.[56]

Scope and Scale

All the same, during the closing decades of the nineteenth century, professional tinkerers were becoming increasingly reliant on corporations as a steady source of demand. These larger companies made their ideas and blueprints practical and available to consumers—including through lucrative export markets during the first era of globalization.[57] Unlike when Britain first industrialized and markets were fragmented, American businesses benefited from a world economy that was highly integrated. Indeed, while the voyages of Columbus and da Gama were surely important events, there was little or no price convergence before the transport revolution of the nineteenth century. If commodity markets are perfectly integrated, prices at home and abroad would be the same, and price data reveal a first discontinuity in that direction around 1820, when steamships, and later railroads, began to proliferate, making a flood of cheaper goods available to consumers around the world.[58]

Market integration was also aided by the globalisation of news services. As major newspapers began to bring stories from across the Atlantic, writers could share their ideas with distant and growing audiences. Karl Marx, for instance, was able to reach some 200,000 Americans through his columns in the *New York Tribune*. Around the same time, globetrotters, like William Howard Russell of the London *Times*, were the first to write about battles, sieges, and uprisings for the reader back home, who could follow his reports of seismic events, such as the American Civil War, as well as his impressions from Egypt, India, and South Africa.[59] The period also witnessed the expansion of the telegraph, which linked up all continents and provided a splendid stimuli to both trade and the transfer of knowledge.⁶⁰ And where the telegraph could not reach, news was carried by steamship. The globalisation that followed the steam age, in other words, was very different from the eighteenth century guns–slaves–sugar triangle trade, which left devastating marks in Africa and the Caribbean while enriching a wealthy few in North America and Europe.⁶¹

True, globalisation was not all about the wonders of modern technology; in Europe, the acceleration of empire also continued to forge closer links with foreign markets. By 1900, several countries had adopted German as their official language, which was also widely spoken across the northern and eastern parts of Europe. The French had an even larger franchise in North Africa, and the French language extended to Rumania and Russia. And of course, Russia itself had a vast multiethnic empire. In a globalized world, these empires were all seemingly well placed to take advantage of the economies of scale that mass production offered. They also benefited because expanding markets facilitated the flow of technology and helped close the technological gap to Britain.

The role of Empire in trade, however, should not be overstated. After all, in the 1870s, when the Second Industrial Revolution began, America did not (yet) have one. Even in Britain, the share of exports destined for colonial markets hovered around a third between 1830 and 1900 with no clear upward trend. The trade effects of empire only really took off in the interwar years, when trade with the Dominions of Australia, New Zealand, the Union of South Africa, Canada, and Newfoundland became more important.⁶² Before then, trade with neighbours dominated, which is hardly surprising, since distance is still a key predictor of trade even in our digital age.⁶³ But the pattern of regional trade was surely aided because European governments also made concerted efforts to reduce the cost of moving goods, people, and ideas on the Continent. International agreements guaranteed unhindered passage on major waterways like the Bosphorus, Suez, Rhine, and Danube. And the International Rail Traffic Association in Berne served to facilitate cross-border flows of people and goods, just as the International Telegraph Union and the Universal Postal Union did for ideas. At times, national governments even joined forces to overcome the tyranny of distance.

To build the St. Gotthard rail tunnel under the Alps in 1882, for example, the Italian and German governments gave the Swiss financial support. In this environment, European companies like Nestlé & Anglo-Swiss, Nobel Dynamite, J. & P. Coats, Royal Dutch Shell, Thomas Cook, Crédit Lyonnais, Deutsche Bank, De Wendel, Rio Tinto, Siemens, and Rothschild were all committed to intra-European trade and travel, and many operated plants or branches in neighbouring countries.[64]

America's advantage over Europe, in other words, was not just its large market for goods, as has often been suggested.[65] In terms of population, America first overtook Britain in the 1850s and Germany in the 1870s. Even by 1900, when the U.S. rail system had been rolled out, it only served 76 million people compared with the 285 million who resided in Europe, in an area only half the size.[66] Yet, as we shall see, despite being slow in making key improvements to develop its internal market, America was early to move down the road of mass production. As economist Erwin Rothbarth has noted, "The ease with which the US industry has been able to install mass production methods is probably due as much to the structure of the buying public as to anything thing else; for the US public is very ready to buy standard articles which are not differentiated by marked individual features. In the United Kingdom, on the other hand, there remains an aristocracy and a middle class impregnated with aristocratic ideas, who reject mass produced articles and insist on articles with individual character."[67] Whereas in Europe, lavishly decorated and custom-made guns were purchased by the wealthy for activities like hunting and shooting, the private market for cheap standardized guns in America was huge, and the road to mass production began in the Colt factories. Samuel Colt, Eli Whitney, Isaac Singer, and Cyrus McCormick, who pioneered the so-called American system—making it possible to assemble products from mass produced interchangeable parts—could not have done so had American consumers rejected mass-produced goods.[68]

The virtues of the American system were widely acknowledged during the 1851 Crystal Palace Exhibition in London. In the words of one visitor, "Nearly all American machines did things that the world earnestly wished machines to do.... Most exciting was Samuel Colt's repeat-action revolver, which was not only marvelously lethal but made from interchangeable parts, a method so distinctive that it became known as the American system."[69] In fact, American machine tools were shipped to Enfield Arsenal in Britain as early as the 1850s, where they laid the foundations for interchangeable parts in Europe.[70] They were also the reason why Ludwig Loewe, and later Heinrich Lanz, two of Germany's most successful machinery makers, came to the United States to learn about new production technologies.[71]

What propelled America to pole position was its institutional commitment to competition alongside its ability to attract and nurture talent. In Europe a patchwork of customs barriers still existed, which were exacerbated by the German Zollverein's 1879 tariff and the French Méline tariff of 1892. In America, on the other hand, the Interstate Commerce Clause prevented individual states from passing laws and putting up tariffs to impede internal trade. When, for instance, the State of New York tried to grant Robert Fulton a steamboat monopoly in 1824, it was struck down. But for American firms to exploit economies of scope and scale, physical infrastructure was also needed. Although the Founding Fathers could ban internal tariffs, they could not defy the laws of physics. Greater distance means higher costs, not least without roads, railroads, and canals.[72]

———

What the United States lacked vis-à-vis Great Powers on the European Continent was a strong state capable of building infrastructure to spur market integration. Indeed, the same Constitution that safeguarded trade continued to hold back internal improvements. By placing limits on federal taxation, the fiscal firepower as well as the bureaucratic capabilities of the federal government were severely restricted. The solution to American state incapacity was found in public–private partnerships, whereby the state provided support, inducement, and at times limited funding to tap into the talent and creativity of the private sector. The Morrill Land-Grant Acts, for instance, allowed for the creation of colleges using the proceeds from sales of federally owned land—a policy which radically expanded access to higher education in America.

The government also facilitated economic growth by providing certain crucial services. Already in 1792, Congress passed the Postal Service Act, which created the central nervous system for the circulation of news across the newly founded country. In addition to giving the federal government control over various regional postal routes, it also gave the public better access to information, which had previously been confined to the elite. This effort to facilitate the flow of information would become critical to the democratization of innovation.[73] Initially, high rates were set to make the postal service self-supporting, but rates were gradually lowered, and as demand surged the number of post offices grew in tandem. From a modest 75 in 1790, the number of post offices swelled to almost 13,500 in 1840, while the number of people served per post office fell from about 43,000 to just over 1,000 in the same period.[74] Thanks to postal subsidization, the number of newspapers in the country also increased significantly, going from 100 in 1790 to over 1,400 in 1840.[75] It was the rise of the post that prompted Tocqueville to remark that: "There is an astonishing circulation of letters and newspapers among these savage woods ... I do not think that in the most enlightened districts of France there is an intellectual movement either so rapid or on such a scale as in this wilderness."[76] Indeed, as Zorina Khan writes, "rural inventors in the United States could apply for patents without serious obstacles, because applications could be submitted by mail free of postage ... [so] it is not surprising that much of the initial surge in patenting during early American industrialization occurred in rural areas."[77] Recent empirical analysis affirms this view: where post offices sprang up, innovation flourished.[78]

Growing up in an otherwise bureaucratic backwater, the post office swiftly became the single largest government employer. In 1841, America's 9,000 postmasters constituted an astonishing 79 percent of the entire federal civilian workforce. Around this time, the United States had five times as many post offices as France, and double the number in Britain, relative to population. In the words of one historian, "for the vast majority of Americans the postal system *was* the central government."[79] Still, in the absence of technological improvements, information could not travel faster than horses could carry it. Eventually, however, with the advent of train travel, delivery times fell rapidly, boosting innovation in the process.[80] In 1800, for example, it would have taken two weeks to travel from New York City to Cleveland and another four weeks to reach Chicago. But with the railroads, the same distance could suddenly be covered in two days. And after a city was connected to the network, patents per capita doubled over the next two decades.[81]

Yet these internal improvements took decades to spread throughout the vast continent. Altogether, between 1824 and 1828, the federal government spent about $2 million on canals and another $7 million on the National Road, whose construction aroused fierce controversy and moved forward at a glacial pace before being abandoned.[82] Initially, states did somewhat better in this regard. While some projects, like South Carolina's Santee Canal, were private endeavours, the most ambitious project was unquestionably the construction of the 364-mile Erie Canal, which was completed thanks to the determination of Governor De Witt Clinton. Although Congress passed an act to fund a canal for New York, President James Madison vetoed the bill because he considered it to be unconstitutional. Instead, the State of New York ended up providing the funds for construction under Clinton's leadership.[83] When the Erie Canal finally opened in 1825, it gave the city of Buffalo on the shores of Lake Erie a direct link to the Atlantic Seaboard via the Hudson River. It was a considerable success: the $9 million investment was quickly recovered, and the return over the first decade was around 8 percent, to say nothing of the greater social return, which was many times higher.[84] For one thing, its opening sparked a marked rise in patenting, as did canal building on the Connecticut and the Merrimack Rivers.[85]

The importance of canals was due in no small part to the advent of the steam engine, which supercharged travel by waterway. In 1807, Fulton introduced the first American steamboat on the Hudson River, and by the time the Erie Canal was completed, the waters were crowded with steamboats. From the Mississippi Valley to the Great Lakes, and eventually to the Atlantic Ocean, steamboats became critical to the movement of goods and people. But for internal transportation, they had serious limitations. Ice sometimes shut down northern lakes and rivers during the winters, while low water was a problem in the West during the summer.

The more transformational application of steam power was yet another British technology that American entrepreneurs eagerly adopted and applied to local conditions: the railroad. Between the opening of the Stockton-Darlington in England, and the operation of the first U.S. railroad between Baltimore and Ohio, there was a lag of just five years. Indeed, America needed the railroads even more than the Europeans did. It had to contend with enormous distances on a relatively empty continent:

> The average U.K. rail haul in 1910 was only 64 km, and in France 190 km, against 402 km in the United States.... The average distance between all nine north-west European 500,000+ population city pairs—London, Birmingham, Glasgow, the Lancashire and Yorkshire conurbations, Amsterdam, Paris, the Ruhr conurbation, and Hamburg—was around 500 km and none of them were 1,000 km apart. The average distance between all seven American cities with that population (New York, Chicago, Boston, Philadelphia, Pittsburgh, St Louis, and Baltimore) was 762 km and Boston to St Louis was 1,670 km.... Of the world's busiest transport nodes, seven—London, Liverpool, Cardiff, Newcastle, Antwerp, Rotterdam, and Hamburg—were in northwest Europe, against only two—New York and Chicago—in the United States.[86]

By 1860, the U.S. railroad network was quite developed in the Northeast and in individual states, but there was no national plan for linking up the country. There were also serious obstacles to overcome: while the Eastern Seaboard had adopted the English 4 ft. 8½ in. gauge, Cleveland and Pittsburgh used a different standard, which in turn differed from the standard in New York and Erie.[87] In addition, many lines did not even touch each other. As historian Maury Klein notes, "When Abraham Lincoln reached Baltimore on his way to Washington for the inauguration, his railroad car had to be hauled by horse from the President

Street depot of the Philadelphia, Wilmington & Baltimore Railroad to the Camden Street station of the Baltimore & Ohio Railroad."[88]

Without the federal government playing any meaningful role, America had built 30,626 miles of railroad. However, this patchwork of lines, none of which reached beyond the Missouri River, left many communities isolated.

Twins of Commerce

Things changed with the Pacific Railroad Act, signed by Abraham Lincoln in 1862, which gave railway companies loans backed by the government, along with large tracts of land, to build out the network. Crucially, this approach circumvented the need for any additional federal expenditure, thereby leaving the size of government and the burden of taxation on the American populace untouched. Section 2 of the Act, for example, bestowed a right-of-way extending 200 feet on either side of the track and thus created substantial benefits for railway companies by granting them unobstructed access to necessary construction materials within this vicinity. Yet the main source of inducement lay in Section 3, which granted these companies the right to claim up to five square miles of land on each side of the rail line for every mile of track—a provision that was doubled in 1864. This incentive structure served as a powerful motivator for the railway companies to swiftly execute the project, as they profited handsomely from the land they could sell once the railroad was completed.[89] Hence, by 1900, the U.S. rail system stood at a proud 311,287 kilometres, making it about a third longer than Europe's west of Russia.[90]

No single innovation created American economic growth, but the railroads certainly gave it a big boost. Following in the footsteps of economic historians like Robert Fogel and Albert Fishlow, several scholars have attempted to estimate the contribution of the railroads to American growth by asking the counterfactual question: How would the United States have developed in their absence? Surely, the cost of moving goods and people would have been higher, but more would also have been invested in developing alternative modes of transportation, like waterways and canals. Taking these alternatives into consideration, both Fishlow and Fogel suggested that the economic impact of the railroads was quite modest.[91] Yet more recent studies show that when improvements to market access are taken into account, the effects are more sizable, especially among the Western states, which suddenly became connected to markets on the Eastern Seaboard.[92] This greatly increased U.S. manufacturing output, such that aggregate productivity would have been 25 percent lower in 1890 had there been no railroads.[93]

Something similar happened in telegraphy, where the rollout was a bureaucratic undertaking, but the exploration was done by independent inventors. The first telegraph was a British invention patented by William Cooke and Charles Wheatstone in 1837, but Samuel Morse patented the first American telegraph just a year later and communicated over it using his own Morse code. An early commercial breakthrough came in 1843 when he received a $30,000 grant from Congress to build an experimental 61 kilometre line between Baltimore and Washington, DC.[94] Only a year later, in May 1844, the message "What hath God wrought" traveled from the Supreme Court chamber of the Capitol building to the B&O's Mount Clare Station in Baltimore and back. Together with his partners, he then sold the patent rights to entrepreneurs seeking to erect lines between other cities. Consequently, the Cleveland and Toledo Telegraph Company was entirely separate from the Ohio, Indiana and Illinois Telegraph Company, which also had a line between Toledo and Dayton.[95]

The result was a fragmented market, which meant low quality and high prices. Messages could easily be distorted, and for companies and private individuals, receiving the wrong information could be a costly affair, not least for those trading on it. When a message was sent from Boston to St. Louis, it would travel over the lines of five firms. The complexity of the system meant that no firm felt the need to take responsibility if the information was transmitted incorrectly.[96] These issues ultimately led to consolidation. Larger integrated networks were simply more valuable than smaller, disjointed ones, in part because bundling the wires between two cities onto a single route was significantly cheaper than operating and maintaining multiple lines. Thus, in the late

1850s, a coalition of six firms established the Treaty of Six Nations, a transient national cartel. Amid the turmoil of the Civil War, only three major entities persevered, paving the way for Western Union's ascent as an unrivalled national monopolist by 1870.[97]

The rise of Western Union, like that of the railroad, was aided by the federal government. When the Telegraph Act was passed by Congress in 1860, the government was authorized to open bids for telegraph construction, and Western Union came out on top. The resulting subsidy, in the form of loans and public land, aimed to finance the construction of a telegraph line extending from the state of Missouri to San Francisco, with an additional branch line to Oregon. The contractors were granted the freedom to select their preferred route, unhindered by regulatory constraints.[98] That same decade, partly because of its government-backed dominance, Western Union absorbed its two largest competitors. By 1890, Western Union operated 19,382 telegraph offices linked by 679,000 miles of line and handled 55,879,000 messages.[99] It was a giant operation that only paled when pitched against the railroads, and arguably the greatest boon of the telegraph was the logistic control of the railroad network that it enabled.[100] Previously, trains had been dependent on using double-track lines, but the telegraph made it possible to safely operate railroads on a single-track system, which allowed two trains to travel in opposite directions on the same track.[101] The nearly perfect symbiotic relationship between two technologies led H. D. Estabrook to call them the Siamese Twins of commerce.[102]

Collusion Course

As markets became increasingly integrated, the modern corporation ascended. Eventually, this would lead to the internalization of much of the innovation process. Early on, however, most American corporations— from the Lowell Machine Shop to giants like the American Bell Telephone Company—continued to rely on technologies invented by outsiders. In 1894, the latter's patent department screened seventy-three patents submitted by independent inventors, while only twelve patents were filed by its own employees. Indeed, T. D. Lockwood, who long served as the head of Bell's patent department, was an ardent opponent of internal R&D: "I am fully convinced that it has never, is not now, and never will pay commercially, to keep an establishment of professional inventors, or of men whose chief business it is to invent," he explained in a letter to Bell's general manager.[103] It was only when Theodore N. Vail became president in 1907, and Bell had become AT&T, that internal R&D became a priority.[104]

AT&T was not a latecomer in this regard. The two other American technology leaders—Westinghouse and Edison Electric (later General Electric)—also pursued a strategy of buying patents from external inventors rather than developing their own R&D facilities.[105] This approach was similarly embraced by Standard Oil, which established a patent department based on the belief that "new ideas and inventions would arise in the main from external sources."[106] The primary objective of the department was to discover and test these ideas, rather than foster creative research internally. In fact, just a handful of American companies, like DuPont, established any in-house R&D facilities worth mentioning before the Great War.[107]

As the century moved forward, however, the trend was unmistakably toward bringing innovation in-house. Yet this transition was hampered by the fact that internal innovation demanded a different breed of inventor. Entrepreneurially oriented independents had to be converted into loyal service professionals, committed to advancing the broader interest of the firm. The financial uncertainty of being a solo inventor surely made secure employment compelling to some, but those who could afford it generally preferred to hold on to their freedom. For the most part, as historian Thomas P. Hughes notes, large bureaucracies did not support the kind of disruptive innovation that "upset the old, or introduced a new, status quo."[108] They were focused on improving efficiency in what they were already doing. In such an environment, the likes of Elihu Thomson (the inventor of alternating current motors) and Elmer Sperry (inventor of the gyrocompass) found that their talents were no longer needed. So, they made the decision to withdraw from, or were compelled to leave, the very companies they had founded. As Sperry explained, "If I spend a life-time on a dynamo I can probably make my little contribution toward increasing the efficiency of that machine six or seven percent. Now then, there are a whole lot of arts that need electricity, about four or five hundred per cent, let me tackle one of those."[109] Even Edison stayed away from the routine and mundane managerial responsibilities of running Edison General Electric. Of the best inventors, only 14 percent ended their careers in stable employment, and those who failed to remain independent often ended up moving "restlessly from position to position."[110]

To attract and keep prima donna inventors, companies began to offer attractive packages, including bonuses for patents, but this created perverse incentives to take out as many patents as possible (a situation not unlike China today; see chapter 12). An invention could either be covered by one strong patent or a dozen minor patents, and inventors naturally went for the latter to the detriment of the firm. To end patent inflation, AT&T and General Electric were forced to stop bonuses and tighten control. This, however, was easier said than done and only worked well in mature industries, where breakthroughs were no longer needed and efforts focused on exploitation rather than exploration.[111]

To understand the quest for control over inventors, consider the railroads. During the nascent phase of the industry, when operations were local and fragmented, the multitude of railway lines acted as simultaneous experiments unfolding across an array of laboratories. At this stage, licensing gave companies the flexibility they needed to test new technologies. But as virgin land along the frontier was absorbed, and there were no new territories to infiltrate, the railroad bonanza faded. Consequently, competition intensified, and so the paramount concern of managers became cost cutting and standardization. Companies no longer wanted to find novelty, but rather to restrict the realm of technical possibilities. To do so, managers began negotiating technical specifications through trade associations externally, which diminished the autonomy of each individual company. Engineers thrived in such an environment, but inventors did not. Indeed, to absorb external discoveries, railroad companies over time established their own machine shops, which soon were capable of refining sourced technologies, whether it was new engines or braking systems. This, however, also brought new tensions. As railroad companies built on technologies from the outside, patents became increasingly interrelated rather than separable, creating fertile soil for litigation.[112]

To undercut the claims of pioneering inventors, the railroad companies joined forces to set up so-called patent pools. The New England railroads were the first to organize in 1866, and the following year many joined either the Eastern Railroad Association (ERA) or the Western Railroad Association (WRA). Members agreed to share valuable information on disputed technologies, which helped lawyers prepare their appeals with some effect.[113] In a rare display of concerted action, frustrated inventors, who found themselves unable to pursue their claims individually, banded together to lobby Congress. The ERA and WRA, they argued, were in violation of U.S. antitrust laws. Their petitions, however, fell on deaf ears, much to the detriment of continued technological progress. Though cartels aided standardization, such as the adoption of the standard railroad gauge, which helped link up the network, railroad patent pools also slowed the pace of innovation from both within and without. As Jeremy Atack, an economic historian notes, "For outside inventors, the pooling of information among the railroads reduced the expected return from invention.... On the inside, collusion stilled the winds of 'creative destruction' that jeopardized the value of existing investment."[114]

In this and many other ways, the railroad industry provided an early glimpse of what would later unfold across almost every major sector. Whereas Prussia's state bureaucracy set the tone for industrial organization there, railroad companies assumed that leadership role in the United States. Coordinating a nationwide flow of passengers and goods required large teams of professional managers, and as markets became more integrated—boosting scope and scale—bureaucratic management methods spread from one industry to the next. Moreover, running huge factories demanded substantial capital, largely in the form of fixed costs that had to be covered regardless of sales volume, whether in boom times or during downturns. And as factories grew, fixed costs climbed accordingly. To distribute those costs across as many units as possible, bigger was simply better.

As firms grew larger, they needed standardized operations and tighter workflow monitoring, which drove them toward centralization. By the mid-1850s, the railroad industry had already rapidly outpaced other sectors, with the Erie Railroad employing a workforce of 4,000, while the largest manufacturing firms like the Pepperell Manufacturing Company in Biddeford, Maine, employed only a few hundred people. By 1900, the Pennsylvania Railroad had expanded to over 100,000 workers.[115] As the modern business firm "acquired functions hitherto carried out by the market," Alfred Chandler Jr. famously observed, "it became the most powerful institution in the American economy and its managers the most influential group of economic decision makers."[116] No one was better placed to see this transformation than John D. Rockefeller, who was at the forefront of it. In his words, the time was ripe "to save ourselves from wasteful competition.... The day of combination is here to stay. Individualism is gone, never to return."[117] In this new age, the Edisons and Sperrys, who had pioneered new industries, were succeeded by a cadre of what Chandler called "a new subspecies of economic man"—the salaried professional manager.[118]

This transformation surely benefited the American consumer. In 1850, the retail landscape was overwhelmingly populated by small family-run stores. Yet, within just one generation, a few retail behemoths emerged among the multitude of smaller outlets. These vast corporations used the national railway system to broaden their merchandise assortments and dramatically cut prices. In 1859, George Francis Gilman started with a modest establishment dealing in hides and feathers; by 1900, this would become the Great Atlantic & Pacific Tea Company (A&P), consisting of nearly 200 stores across twenty-eight states and offering a wide range of products. But the more groundbreaking development during this period was the advent of mail-order business. Pioneers like Aaron Montgomery Ward in 1872, and Richard Warren Sears and Alvah Roebuck in 1886, introduced mail-order services that transformed the shopping experience, especially for rural Americans. Through catalogues, consumers could access an extensive array of products, from basic farm necessities to more unusual items like the

Heidelberg Electric Belt, designed to alleviate anxiety by sending mild electric shocks to the genitals.[119]

Yet scale also introduced new challenges. With the consolidation of industries and the emergence of dominant firms like AT&T, Kodak, DuPont, Westinghouse, and GE, a new concern became apparent: the possibility that conservatism within these corporations could reduce the vibrancy of the wider economy. For these corporate giants, the greater the capital investment, the less desirable competition and its accompanying instability became. Consequently, their focus shifted away from investing in innovation and toward shielding themselves from competitive pressures. To protect their profits, they secretly colluded to carve up markets, manage patents, limit production, and prop up prices. Unlike in Germany, cartels in America had no legal standing, and so members would violate cartel agreements when it suited their interests. In this environment, Standard Oil introduced a groundbreaking solution in 1882: the trust. In essence, a controlling number of shares in several competing firms would be conveyed to a trust, which would be managed by a small group of trustees, thus allowing them to control and coordinate activity between the companies. This institutional invention revolutionized the structure of American business by ingeniously avoiding the legal prohibition against one corporation owning stock in another. This allowed them to bypass restrictions on control and coordination across companies, to the dismay of some onlookers at the time and the enthusiasm of others. By 1904, 440 trusts controlled some 8,664 industrial plants, transportation lines, and utility franchises.[120]

Trustbusting

These giants were growing up at a time when the United States was still a small government society; in many respects, it was still the government of town hall meetings that Tocqueville had described in 1835. As late as 1879, the federal government had a workforce of approximately 20,000 individuals, including everyone from territorial governors and bureau chiefs to lower-level clerks like customs officials—a remarkably small number when juxtaposed with the bureaucracies of European nations, and all the more so given the extensive territory under U.S. governance. Washington, DC, with a population of less than 150,000, was still a small town, and certainly nothing like Paris, London, or Beijing. Only in 1893 did Britain see fit to establish a full embassy in the capital, the first European power to do so.

The relative paucity of government capacity can also be seen in its fiscal feebleness: in the lead up to the Great War, the United States federal government collected less than 3 percent of GDP in taxes, of which the bulk came from tariffs, and in 1915, the United States' national debt stood at $1.191 billion, a sum John D. Rockefeller could have comfortably cleared multiple times using his personal wealth, which had reached $25 billion by 1919.[121] Insofar as there was any government at all, it operated at state and local levels, where corruption was always a concern. Land Office administrators, for example, "strung out along the frontier ... were relatively secure from the prying eyes of Washington bureaucrats," which led to many instances of fraud or simply convenient indifference to the public good. The Land Office Commissioner had implemented an inspection system for local offices, but because inspectors only visited each office annually, local officials could easily hide misconduct.[122]

In an era dominated by artisan workshops and the ingenuity of solo inventors, small and local government worked reasonably well. Yet in the decades following the Civil War, the structure of the American economy changed enormously. Railroads and telegraph lines now united a vast territory, and private entrepreneurs were building industrial empires of unmatched scale. This called into question the core principles of laissez-faire, because these new giants could easily escape the confines of local regulation. Despite the federal courts granting states the authority to challenge mergers, their power was effectively neutered as corporations could either recharter in more lenient states or relocate operations entirely. Consequently, after a brief flurry of unsuccessful antitrust action in the 1880s, the states dialed back their efforts, acknowledging that only federal intervention could address the issue.[123] Yet federal governance, for the most part, depended on personal relationships between office chiefs and their subordinates.[124]

The American elite, much like its European counterpart, was a closely knit and homogeneous group, primarily composed of graduates from Harvard and Yale, members of the banking elite in New York and Boston, and nobles from Virginia's planter aristocracy.[125] The administration under Thomas Jefferson, where 60 percent of senior roles were allocated to landed elites, merchants, or professionals, only looks meritocratic compared with the John Adams administration, when the figure was 70 percent. While social class in America might have been less cemented relative to Europe, political appointments across the Atlantic were similarly a matter of loyalty and patronage rather than merit-based selection. It was a time that can aptly be described as "Government by Gentlemen."[126]

Complicating matters further, in the succeeding decades, a party system emerged that made it easier to gather support by handing out government jobs than by mobilizing voters around specific policy issues. As the U.S. Civil War raged in the country, Senator Charles Sumner joked on the floor of the Senate that "The world seems almost divided into two classes: those going to [Sutter's Mill in] California in search of gold, and those going to Washington in quest for office."[127] The large number of political appointees meant that when the administration changed, so did many officials. When Zachary Taylor was elected president in 1849, he replaced a third of all federal officials during the first year of his administration. Following the 1860 election, Abraham Lincoln complained about the endless stream of patronage requests, though there was little he could do to avoid them. Appointing people to bureaucratic offices was an integral part of winning over allies and building political coalitions—even the military was open to political appointments.[128] This led the satirist Artemus Ward to joke that "the Union Army's retreat at the Battle of Bull Run was caused by a rumor of three vacancies at the New York Custom House."[129]

This made fertile soil for what Mark Twain famously called the Gilded Age. Railway tycoons like Cornelius Vanderbilt and Jay Gould, industrialists like John D. Rockefeller and Andrew Carnegie, and financiers like J. P. Morgan had invested heavily in the technologies that drove economic expansion. The problem was that the fortunes they accumulated gave them considerable political influence. In technology wars of the time, the "robber barons," as the press inaptly called them, considering they did not inherit their wealth, J. P. Morgan being the exception, fought for the control of the latest advances in telegraphy, with Vanderbilt and Gould battling to gain control of Western Union through dubious methods.[130] Their 1869 "war" for control of New York's Erie Railroad, for example, involved "hired judges, corrupted legislatures, and under-the-counter payments.... They used their lobbies to fight their competitors and to beg favors from the government, blurring the line between economic and political competition."[131] Unsurprisingly, the combination of governance through personal networks and vast private fortunes made the government apparatus highly susceptible to capture through payoffs and patronage.[132] It also made the drawbacks of America's public–private partnership model more apparent. For example, in 1850, at the urging of Illinois's Senator Stephen Douglas, the federal government made a 3.75-million-acre land grant to Illinois, Alabama, and Mississippi to fund the construction of the Illinois Central Railroad. The original plan was that the line would follow the eastern bank of the Mississippi River the length of Illinois, but Douglas championed the expansion of the road to New Orleans and a branch to Chicago. Soon thereafter, he settled in Chicago and immersed himself in real estate dealings.[133]

It was the corruption scandals surrounding the construction of the Pacific Railroad, however, that received the most media attention and helped curb the public's enthusiasm for public–private partnerships. The most notorious episode involved Crédit Mobilier, which charged its parent company an exorbitant amount for construction and ultimately led disgruntled stockholders to sue the company. When a newspaper revealed that the "railroad ring" had bribed a congressman in the run-up to the presidential campaign of 1872, the story exploded, underlining the need for reform.[134] Eventually, the scandal would ensnare Vice President Schuyler Colfax and vice presidential nominee Henry Wilson, as well as Speaker of the House James Blaine, and a future president, James A. Garfield.[135]

To check rent seeking, the United States needed a European, Weberian state bureaucracy. The most famous proponent of this idea was future president Woodrow Wilson, who had grown up in Europe, learned German, and felt that the bureaucratic organization of Prussia and France made their governments "too efficient to be dispensed with."[136] In the 1880s, soon after completing his doctorate in political science at Johns Hopkins University, Wilson published an article titled "The Study of Administration." Although Wilson naturally looked to Prussia and France as the hallmarks of bureaucratic government, he deemed them incompatible with the foundational American principles of democracy and its deep-seated wariness of concentrated power. Instead, the Northcote-Trevelyan Report that had been enacted in Britain a decade earlier would serve as the blueprint for reform in America.[137]

In both Britain and Prussia, the impetus for the creation of an efficient and meritocratic bureaucracy had been war, but in the United States the bureaucratization that followed the Civil War turned out to be short-lived. America faced no significant foreign threats, so there was no need for sustained military mobilization. Reform, in the American case, required pressure from the public, which was fed up with corrupt elites. As Mancur Olson famously pointed out, large groups are always hard to mobilize, yet there are times when the public is attentive and united, and thus capable of solving the collective action problem. When this condition is met on rare occasions, it forces governing members to pursue the public will or face electoral retribution.[138]

The inefficacies of government became all too apparent after a series of public scandals that began during the Grant administration. In 1882, *The New York Times* ran a story about the dismissals of appointees who refused to make voluntary contributions to the party's coffers.[139] Later that year, when newly elected President Garfield was shot by a mentally ill office seeker for not being appointed U.S. consul to France, the event fueled the movement in support of reform to the patronage system. However, it took the loss of thirty-nine members' seats in the 1882 midterm election for the ruling elites to fully realize the intensity of the public's disdain for the spoils system. Fearing further public backlash, members of Congress gave up patronage and opted for change. Statistical studies show that Senators and House representatives with an affiliate of the Civil Service Reform League in or near their district were much more likely to support the Pendleton Act—which abolished patronage within the civil service—as were members receiving petitions urging them to support reform.[140] As Senator Preston B. Plumb explained at the time:

> We are not legislating on this subject in response to our own judgment of what is proper to be done, but in response to some sort of judgment which has been expressed outside.... I think popular opinion, so far as it has been given expression to at the late election or at any other election or has been voiced in the public press, has been directed to the condemnation of two particular things, the assessment of officeholders, and the solicitation, and appointments consequent upon the solicitation, of members of Congress.[141]

The passage of the Pendleton Act was a watershed moment in U.S. political history.[142] Besides prohibiting mandatory campaign contributions, which accounted for some three-quarters of total contributions in the post-Reconstruction era, it introduced entrance exams for aspiring bureaucrats. As exams replaced loyalty with merit as the basis for securing political appointments, the American Leviathan became increasingly capable of reacting to the changing economic circumstances, boosting its capacity to regulate monopolies. The Interstate Commerce Act of 1887 to oversee the railroads was the first step in this direction at the federal level, followed by the Sherman Antitrust Act of 1890, the Hepburn Act of 1906, the Clayton Antitrust Act of 1914, and the Federal Trade Commission Act of 1914. The central mission of this legislation was to protect consumers and small businesses by restoring competition. To achieve this, the Sherman Act, in particular, gave the federal government new powers to counteract excessive market concentration.[143]

These acts, as well as the election of reformist presidents, were consequences of the Progressive movement, which mobilized both discontented farmers and the urban middle class against centralizing monopolists. In this period, small business owners, merchants, and farmers organized cooperatives and professional associations to retain their independence and counteract the rise of big business. The Grange—with 1.5 million members at its peak—Greenback, and other populist movements rose to demand regulation over railroads and other technologies. Between 1881 and 1905, there were also 37,000 strikes, predominantly in construction and mining, but the most contentious occurred in key technology industries like railways and steel. The Pullman strike of 1894, for instance, dramatically disrupted the U.S. transportation system until President Grover Cleveland stepped in. That same year, an extensive coal strike halted coal production in Pennsylvania and the Midwest, severely impacting American industry. However, the most violent confrontation occurred during the 1892 Homestead strike near Pittsburgh, where angry strikers targeted Carnegie Steel, a high-tech company of the late 1800s.[144]

Such events soon drew the focus of diligent journalists known as "muckrakers," who assumed an active role in shaping public policy by shedding light on the exploitative practices of the robber barons and their manipulation of politics for personal enrichment. Indeed, as Marc Law and Gary Libecap have shown, muckraking journalists played a key role in tipping the scales toward Progressive Era reform.[145] Among them, Ida Tarbell famously published a nineteen-part exposé in *McClure's Magazine*, accusing Standard Oil of "fraud, deceit, special privilege, gross illegality, bribery, coercion, corruption, intimidation, espionage or outright terror," while Louis Brandeis, dubbed the "people's attorney," warned against "the curse of bigness" and banks gambling with "other people's money." Prominent novelists—such as Upton Sinclair, who exposed the dreadful conditions within Chicago's meatpacking industry—also lent their voices to the muckraking cause.[146]

The reining in of corporate power, however, was hardly a linear process. In response to the Sherman Act, the Supreme Court ruled that cartels, or horizontal agreements to fix prices, were illegal, but that mergers were legal. The result was that many of the entities controlled by trusts merged into holding companies. Thus, somewhat ironically, the invigoration of antitrust led to greater consolidation. In a merger wave that ran from 1894 to 1904, more than 1,800 companies disappeared into larger behemoths. Before the merger mania, companies primarily engaged in vertical integration, acquiring their suppliers and distributors. However, the surge in mergers introduced horizontal integration into the mix, as firms began merging with or acquiring companies in the same industry at the same stage of production. These new giants soon embarked on consolidating and centralizing their operations in ways that the trusts themselves could not. Prominent technology leaders such as DuPont, Eastman Kodak, Otis Elevator, and International Harvester partook in mergers and emerged as formidable entities during this period.[147]

The impetus behind consolidation was not solely scope and scale but also the elimination of price competition.[148] As a result, the great merger movement galvanized the public once more and spurred successive presidents to act. Faced with mounting public outcry, politicians initiated investigations across various levels and branches of government. President Theodore Roosevelt, for example, earned the moniker of "trustbuster," breathing new life into the Sherman Antitrust Act through his lawsuit targeting the dismantling of J. P. Morgan's Northern Securities railroad holding company. Moreover, Roosevelt and his successor, William Howard Taft, embarked on a series of dissolution suits against major corporations, including Standard Oil, U.S. Steel, and the American Tobacco Company.[149]

Yet at the same time as Standard Oil and American Tobacco were being broken up, the Court set out a new standard for antitrust violations, one which would significantly defang the law. Rather than size per se, the concern became efforts to restrain trade unreasonably or unduly. In *United States v. United States Steel Corp*, the Supreme Court held that "the law does not make mere size an offense or the existence of unexerted power an offense."[150] William J. Donovan, the Assistant Attorney General for the Antitrust Division under president Calvin Coolidge, succinctly explained the new position of the Supreme Court as follows: "It is believed that consolidations may in some degree correct the evils of destructive competition and that it [the movement] represents an effort to adjust the relations between production and consumption, supply and demand. It is when these consolidations attempt to eliminate competition, to enhance existing prices, and to exercise permanent control in the industry that they constitute violations of the law."[151] The effects were soon felt throughout the economy. Writing in 1931, economist Willard

Thorp observed, "The shifting emphasis in the interpretation of the Sherman Act from size to behaviour, has greatly lessened its influence as a limiting factor on industrial consolidations."[152]

Consequently, a delicate equilibrium emerged, allowing companies to harness the advantages of mass production technology as long as they did not engage in anticompetitive behaviour. This, in turn, enabled Henry Ford to bring forth the Model T at a price accessible to the masses, and it soon became the quintessential vehicle of the people. More broadly, the unfolding of the Second Industrial Revolution presented ample opportunities where economies of scope and scale held considerable sway, which naturally fostered a trend toward concentration. In 1918, for example, the United States housed some 318,000 corporations. Among them, the top 5 percent claimed a staggering 80 percent of the overall net income, while the bottom 75 percent merely accounted for a meagre 6 percent.[153] Concurrently, factories expanded in size—a trend that would continue through the postwar decades. The economic landscape was characterized by cascading market concentration alongside astonishing leaps in productivity. However, it is crucial to recognize that the symbiotic relationship between productivity and concentration was predicated on the credible threat of displacement, be it through market competition, the emergence of new contenders, or indeed legal action. As we shall see, in Britain where the postwar competition regime was feeble, rising concentration did not go hand in hand with the same rise in productivity[154]

All the same, even in this new age of corporate giants, unpredictable changes in technology continued to be the main threat to incumbents, as the case of Western Union illustrates.[155] Having absorbed its two largest competitors in 1866, it had reached the apex of power, and the scale economies it was able to achieve were surely good for consumers. The volume of messages traversing its lines soared from 5.8 million in 1867 to an impressive 63.2 million in 1900, while transmission rates plummeted from an average of $1.09 to a mere 30 cents per message over the same period. Even with these reduced prices, approximately 30 to 40 cents of every revenue dollar manifested as net profit for the company. Yet despite its monopoly, Western Union found itself disrupted by the telephone, which had important advantages. For one thing, it did not require an operator to translate every Morse code message, and so it democratized the flow of information. Nor was it a strict station-to-station medium. For a company to communicate with ten different people at different places by telegraph, each recipient needed a separate wire connecting them to the sender, creating a jungle of lines along the streets of every metropolis.[156]

Nevertheless, the virtues of the telephone were far from clear. When Bell patented the telephone in 1876, he even referred to it as a "talking telegraph," whereas others saw it as a mere entertainment novelty.[157] And with little infrastructure to support it, the telephone was primarily used for local calling. So, when Bell offered Western Union the patent for $100,000, the company declined, failing to appreciate how this obscure technology would transform communication. In the 1890s, Western Union had a golden opportunity to gain control over AT&T, yet its management, prioritizing higher dividends over expansion, missed the chance to capitalize on the future.[158] Instead, the reverse happened when AT&T bought a 30 percent share of Western Union in 1909. A new monopoly emerged, and despite their best effort in pushing for regulation, the Postal Telegraph and smaller telephone companies were excluded from the centralized AT&T system. Only after the breakup of Standard Oil, when the threat of antitrust action appeared credible,[159] did AT&T issue the "Kingsbury Commitment" to divest its Western Union telegraph subsidiary and allow independent telephone companies to interconnect with its system.[160] In effect, antitrust actions deterred rent seeking that took place at the expense of technological progress. As long as the threat of antitrust remained credible, it incentivised companies to invest in production technologies to increase efficiency, instead of lobbying to thwart competition and innovation at society's expense. As a result, the American middle class gained access to a growing array of consumer goods—a remarkable improvement in the quality of life that would continue despite major disruptions like the Great Depression and World War II.

7

War, Peace, and Progress

If the carboniferous age were to return and the earth were to repeople itself with dinosaurs, the change that would be made in animal life would scarcely seem greater than that which had been made in business life by these monster-like corporations.[1]

—JOHN BATES CLARK

OVER THE course of the last two centuries, the United States has demonstrated a remarkable ability to adapt its institutions in the face of emerging challenges, thereby propelling its technological prowess. This propensity for institutional change was underscored by President Dwight D. Eisenhower in his Farewell Address to the nation in January 1961. Eisenhower astutely acknowledged the profound transformations that had taken place in America during the preceding decades, a period marked by the crucible of unprecedented global conflict. With the weight of World War II still fresh in the country's collective memory, Eisenhower recognized the imperative to avert a recurrence of such a crisis and the necessity of shunning ad hoc national defense measures. A permanent armaments industry, he argued, was necessary. But Eisenhower also left a warning to the American people: "We must not fail to comprehend its grave implications. Our toil, resources and livelihood are all involved; so is the very structure of our society. In the councils of government, we must guard against the acquisition of unwarranted influence, whether sought or unsought, by the military–industrial complex. The potential for the disastrous rise of misplaced power exists and will persist."[2]

Other contemporaries took notice of these dangers as well. In *The Power Elite*, published in 1956, sociologist C. Wright Mills shed important light on the connectedness and coziness of America's political, military, and industrial leaders. Similarly, in his 1967 book *The New Industrial State*, John Kenneth Galbraith coined the term *technostructure* to highlight how a new managerial elite had asserted control over much of the American economy. Two world wars and a depression had bolstered the bureaucratic capacity of both the American state and its industrial enterprise significantly. America was no longer a libertarian's paradise in which progress was predominantly driven by the thrift of solo inventors, as is evident from their steadily diminishing share of new patents.[3]

Before the war, American technological development had largely been confined to the civil domain.[4] One migrant, Lev Davidovich Bronstein, who reluctantly brought his family to New York City for a ten-week stay in January 1917, could not help being impressed with all the novel gadgets, including electric lights, gas cooking, automatic service elevators, and even modern communications technology. For some time, his boys' main interest was the telephone, whose magic they had not encountered either in Vienna or Paris. Among their new friends, one even had a chauffeur, whose mastery of driving, making "the machine obey his slightest command," was a supreme delight to watch.[5] Indeed, before Lev returned to St. Petersburg, where he would become Leon Trotsky, the most spectacular U.S. success story was unquestionably the automobile. By bringing together American inventiveness and mass production methods, the automotive industry gained a considerable lead over French, German, and British rivals, who all took advantage of Ford's open-door policy.

Yet America's advancement in transportation was hardly unique. Even in science-based industries, the early German lead was fading. In chemicals, DuPont was expanding its share of world markets, while Westinghouse and General Electric were pushing the frontier in electrical engineering.[6] As Adolf Hitler wrote in what is known as his "Second Book": "The European today dreams of a standard of living, which he derives as much from Europe's possibilities as from the real conditions of America. Due to modern technology and communications it makes possible, the international relations amongst people have become so close that the European, even without being fully conscious of it, applies as the yardstick of his life, the conditions of American life."[7]

It was against this backdrop of America's technological supremacy that Nazi Germany rushed into war. The emerging dominance of American industry, Hitler contended, would eventually reduce European powers to the status of "Switzerland and Holland." The reason, in his reductionist view, was America's "vast internal market" that enabled car producers to adopt "methods of production that in Europe due to the lack of . . . internal sales would simply be impossible."[8] Fordism, according to Hitler, required *Lebensraum* (territorial expansion), and he was convinced that there was still a window of opportunity for Germany to acquire it. While American technology in the civil domain was second to none at this time, its military capacity still lagged behind. America's intervention in the Great War had come too late for its industry to scale up war production in any meaningful way. Furthermore, many Americans felt that in a free-market economy, the government had no right to suppress consumption and turn butter into guns. They regretted the American intervention of 1917 and were determined not to make the same mistake again. In fact, in 1937, Congress passed a comprehensive neutrality legislation intended to limit armaments production and keep the United States out of other countries' wars.

Thus, in the 1930s, the world's richest economy only had the eighteenth largest army, consisting of 20,000 men, not to mention its small and backward air force.[9] And the consequences would be felt in the battlefield. In the early days of the war effort, American fighter planes were no match for their German and Japanese adversaries. The Lockheed P-38, Bell P-39, Curtiss P-40, Grumman F4F, and Brewster Buffalo found themselves outclassed by their Japanese and German counterparts. But in a sign of the rapid evolution of American military technology in this period, by the later stages of the war, all of these fighters, except for the P-38, ceased production.[10] Examining this period of technological development, we can see how America's approach to the war harnessed its existing system of private enterprise and decentralized system of knowledge production, as well as how the war itself, while reducing innovation, bolstered the capacity of the state and big business to exploit existing technologies on massive scale.

The War Economy

The managed economy that emerged during the war is often given credit for delivering a golden age of American growth over the following decades. In our current age of inequality and stagnation, many prominent voices, like Mariana Mazzucato, have argued for a return to a managed economy as a way to reignite broad-based growth. But while it is often remarked that American technology made great strides thanks to the military, which laid the foundations for postwar prosperity, this state-focused story ignores the fact that the U.S. military modernized swiftly thanks to its advanced civilian industries. For all the nostalgia over the golden postwar years, productivity growth was already impressive in the 1920s. The underpinnings of rapid technological progress had already been established before war broke out in Europe.[11] Economic historian Alexander Field has even called the 1930s "the most technologically progressive decade of the century."[12]

The American war effort, by contrast, only gained steam following President Franklin D. Roosevelt's blistering "Arsenal of Democracy" speech, which was broadcasted by radio to the nation on December 29, 1940. Having promised Winston Churchill to provide Britain with the military supplies it needed to defeat Nazi Germany at Placentia Bay, the Roosevelt administration set out to fulfill its promise, incorporating many of America's leading industrial centres—including Cleveland, Chicago, Detroit, New York, Philadelphia, and Pittsburgh—into the war machine. At the peak of the war effort, defense-related jobs reached an astonishing 40 percent of total employment. In fact, spending on the war was so enormous that in 1944, military expenditure amounted to 80 percent of the entire economy in 1939.[13]

Such mobilization was a daunting task. Car plants had no magic switch that would allow them to shift production seamlessly from automobiles to armaments. For the automobile industry, 1941 was a record year, which witnessed the production of over 3.5 million passenger cars. Only a few weeks later, on February 10, 1942, the last day for civilian output had arrived and the final chassis came down the assembly line. During the war, the American car industry would produce a mere 139 cars.[14] Instead, in car factories across the country, old machinery was ripped out and new machine tools were installed for the production of weapons. It is astonishing to think that in 1939, when German and Soviet troops marched into Poland, the United States produced no more than six medium tanks.[15] From mid-1940 to mid-1945, however, the country produced 86,300 tanks, along with 297,000 airplanes, 64,500 landing vessels, 6,500 other navy ships, 5,400 cargo ships and transports, 17,400,000 rifles, carbines, and sidearms, and vast amounts of artillery and ammunition.[16] This level of production required an enormous amount of resources from the private sector, which accounted for two-thirds of all the military equipment produced during the war. General Motors alone produced a tenth of the total American war machine and hired some 750,000 workers to achieve this, while the Ford Motor Company produced more army equipment than the whole of Italy.[17]

Ford also took on the perhaps most challenging task of all—namely, applying mass production techniques to aircrafts. The feat of assembling millions of parts and fasteners at stations spanning over half a mile surpassed all prior efforts of manufacturing at scale. Many assumed it could not be done, but when Ford's general manager Charles Sorensen was invited to visit the Consolidated aircraft plant in San Diego, set up to produce the B-24 Liberator bomber, he was so appalled by the lack of ambition that he sketched out his own plan that very evening. It would ultimately lead to the construction of the Willow Run factory, with its legendary 5,450-foot assembly line, covering an area of 67 acres. This project, which took mass production to its very limits, almost collapsed under the weight of its ambition. In the end, though, Ford's persistence paid off. During the peak of production in 1944, the factory produced a rate of over 5,000 bombers per year, or roughly one bomber every 63 minutes.[18] Willow Run, despite its challenges, emerged as a powerful emblem of American industrial prowess, exuding a sense of self-assurance and determination. The vast assembly hall, resembling a scene from Fritz Lang's iconic film *Metropolis*, left observers in awe. Aviator Charles Lindbergh aptly dubbed it the "Grand Canyon of the mechanized world."[19]

The American war effort, with its reliance on the ingenuity of private enterprise, was strikingly different from that of the USSR. While America was surely no laissez-faire economy, it was also not a command economy. Besides introducing some price controls and rationing, the President could do no more than authorize temporary and uncoordinated contracts.[20] Hence, much of the American war effort remained voluntary. As Henry Stimson, Roosevelt's secretary of war, wrote in his diary, "If you are going to try to go to war or prepare for war in a capitalist country, you have got to let business make money out of the process, or business won't work."[21] Drawing upon a long tradition of public–private partnerships, this approach substituted for the relative incapacity of the American state compared to the other great powers.[22] American executives, in particular, boasted greater expertise in the intricacies of planning and coordination necessary for the wartime economy than their governmental counterparts. Thus, it was under the guidance of Donald Nelson, a director at Sears-Roebuck, that the War Production Board took shape, embodying the fusion of entrepreneurial spirit and national mobilization.[23]

Efforts to spur military technological development similarly largely happened outside established bureaucratic channels. In preparation for war, President Roosevelt authorized the creation of the National Defense Research Committee (NDRC) in 1940, which later expanded into the Office of Scientific Research and Development (OSRD). And Vannevar Bush, who proposed the NDRC to Roosevelt during a White House meeting in June 1940, certainly had little time for bureaucracy. The former vice president and dean of engineering at MIT was also a cofounder of Raytheon with a profound distaste for government involvement in science and technology. Instead of establishing another level of bureaucracy, Bush wanted to create an entirely new government committee with a clear mandate to develop weapons. The committee, he argued, should not just consist of admirals and generals but also industrial companies, leading research labs, and top universities.[24]

Employing outsiders with no political experience was a bold move, but Roosevelt agreed. By 1942, what had become the OSRD had spent $11 million—an amount that increased tenfold to $114.5 million at its peak in 1945. Overall, the OSRD entered into more than 2,200 R&D contracts with industrial and academic partners during the war, amounting to nearly $8 billion in current (2020) dollars—a quantum leap compared to the federal government's prior investments in science and technology.[25] In 1938, before the outbreak of hostilities in Europe, the combined expenditure of federal and state governments on scientific research barely accounted for 0.08 percent of national income. By 1944, this figure had skyrocketed, reaching nearly 0.5 percent of national income and yielding tangible results for Washington.[26] Progress in radar detection, for example, was critical to breaking the preeminence of the German submarine fleet in the Atlantic. And although the atomic bomb came too late to transform the war in Europe, it hastened Japan's surrender, albeit with devastating consequences. As historian Thomas McCraw writes, "American industrial mobilization as a whole was brilliantly successful. Without question it was the key to victory over Japan, and it was the single most important element in the Allied triumph on the western front in Europe."[27] Despite countless mistakes and turf battles, the American war economy did what it was designed to achieve: produce more guns than the enemy.[28]

Guns and Butter

While World War II underlines America's formidable industrial might, it is also a reminder that not all technologies serve the common good. Civilian Americans, to be sure, did not suffer from the same atrocities that their European and Asian counterparts did from the war itself, but that is not to say that they fared well.[29] The notion that the war economy was "producing more guns and more butter," as Seymour Melman famously suggested, does not fit well with the evidence.[30] The war economy produced neither a carnival of consumption nor an investment boom. What it did produce were bombs, shells, and bullets, and plenty of them. But this came at a price as the American standard of living faltered.

Important work by economic historian Robert Higgs shows that the welfare of average citizens deteriorated considerably as the war commenced. Private investment plunged by 64 percent between 1941 and 1943, never to rise above 55 percent of its 1941 level during the war. Personal consumption fell as well, even though the official data likely overstate the decline. As price controls and rationing were introduced, black markets expanded and unmeasured costs of searching for goods increased in tandem. Much time was wasted orchestrating illicit exchanges of ration coupons or enduring lengthy queues, not to mention the thousands of ways in which consumers were deprived of their cherished freedom of choice.[31] In the pursuit of acquiring those coveted yet dearer commodities, individuals found themselves compelled to toil with heightened intensity, enduring lengthier work hours and embracing riskier occupations. For instance, in manufacturing, which accounted for the majority of new employment opportunities, the average weekly workload swelled from 38.1 hours in 1940 to 45.2 hours in 1944.[32] Meanwhile, the prevalence of night shifts surged, the incidence of work-related injuries escalated, and commuting became an arduous endeavour. With the absence of new automobiles, the black market thrived with exorbitant prices attached to used cars, and those in possession of cars suffered from the rationing of gasoline and tires. Simultaneously, the employment-to-population ratio witnessed a notable rise, soaring from 47.6 percent to 57.9 percent, as teenagers abandoned their studies, women departed from domestic production, and elderly individuals withdrew from retirement.[33]

Even in the domain of science and innovation, the impact of the war was mixed at best. In a bid to safeguard the most cutting-edge American technology from falling into the hands of the Axis powers, the U.S. patent office imposed secrecy orders on approximately 11,000 patents. The impact on innovation was not confined to a mere chilling effect; rather, these restrictions solidified the dominion of established companies, which enabled them to derive substantial returns from prior research and development endeavours. This significantly raised the barrier to entry for aspiring innovators seeking to penetrate the market.[34] And while the mission-oriented approach achieved some of its missions, including developing the atomic bomb before Nazi Germany, the popular idea that "World War II gave us jet airplanes, radar, synthetic rubber, and fabrics—that later unleash peacetime prosperity" does not fit the evidence either.[35] Though it is common to provide examples of technologies developed during the war, this approach ignores the technologies that were not developed or delayed as a consequence. As Fredric Bastiat astutely articulated in his seminal essay of 1850, "That Which Is Seen, and That Which Is Not Seen," every action sets in motion a cascade of effects. Among these effects, the immediate one is readily apparent, as it reveals itself alongside its cause—it is seen. However, the subsequent effects unfold gradually and remain hidden from view.[36] With regard to the war, the innovations that were spawned by it were seen. What remains concealed are the potential discoveries that never materialized due to the war's demands. Yet plentiful evidence shows that the war effort diverted the attention of some of America's brightest minds toward destructive purposes. The Manhattan Project, which became one of the largest projects in the history of the world, absorbed enormous resources, employing 130,000 people at its peak.[37]

To prodigies like Claude Shannon, who would later become the founding father of information theory, the war was certainly a distraction.[38] After receiving his doctorate in the spring of 1940, he spent an academic year at the Institute for Advanced Study in Princeton, but soon moved to Bell Labs in New York City to work on antiaircraft fire control. And there are many cases where the war effort directed resources away from promising technologies. For instance, when Vannevar Bush asked researchers all over the country to propose projects that would help the war effort in the summer of 1940, Norbert Wiener quickly answered with a proposal to build computers. What he outlined was "remarkably close to the electronic, digital computer as we know it today."[39] But with the Blitz raging over London, German U-boats' wreaking havoc in the Atlantic, and limited research dollars, Bush rejected the idea and funds were instead allocated toward more imminent war priorities, including the development of radar, antisubmarine warfare, and antiaircraft fire control. The mission economy, which diverted resources to priority goals, left little room for decentralized experimentation, so instead of developing the next generation of computers, Wiener ended up working on antiaircraft fire control, just like Shannon. While World War II involved enormous R&D expenditures, the urgency of war heavily favoured the mass production of military technologies and placed a low premium on basic research, building on what had already been done inside universities. Even in the case of the Manhattan Project, most basic discoveries, conceived in universities and the labs of private foundations, were already in hand when the making of the atomic bomb commenced.[40]

Crucially, these anecdotal examples fit the data more broadly. Careful studies show that the production of new science and technology books experienced a drastic decline during the war and would not match its prewar level until the late 1950s.[41] The same is true of patenting, which plummeted in spectacular fashion, reached a plateau, and did not rebound until the 1980s (figure 7.1).[42] Remarkably, this occurred despite the influx of exceptional talent from abroad that greatly benefited America. When the Nazis enacted the Law for the Restoration of the Professional Civil Service on April 7, 1933, requiring civil servants of non-Aryan descent to be placed in retirement, many German Jewish citizens left for the United States. By 1944, more than 133,000 German Jewish émigrés had arrived in America, of which an astonishing 20 percent had university degrees. And where they settled, ideas collided, generating new sparks. The areas where these émigrés worked witnessed a 31 percent increase in patent filings by American inventors, underscoring their substantial contribution to scientific and technological advancements.[43]

But even this boost from abroad could not make up for the fact that much technological and scientific talent was drawn into the war effort. Indeed, when America entered the war in 1941, manufacturing productivity predictably collapsed (figure 7.2). If labour productivity in industry had just remained at its 1941 level through 1944, 1.8 million fewer workers would have been needed to produce victory in the latter year. Productivity only reasserted itself after the Paris Peace Treaties of 1947.[44]

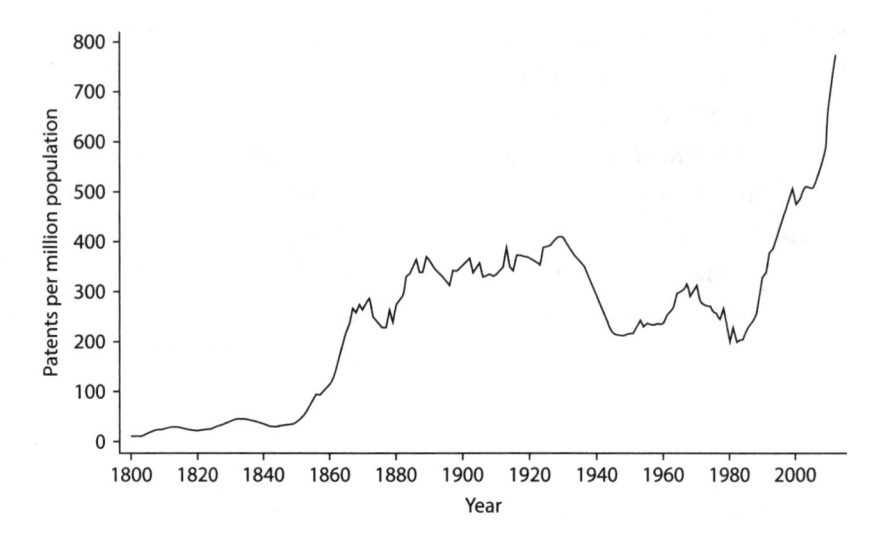

FIGURE 7.1. Patenting in the United States, 1790–2020
Source: U.S. Patent and Trademark Office (USPTO), U.S. Patent Statistics Report.

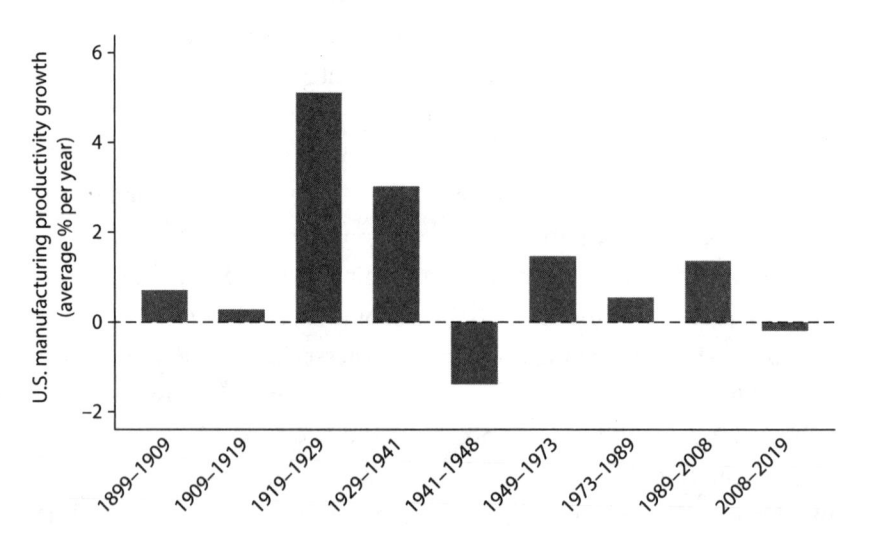

FIGURE 7.2. Manufacturing productivity in the United States, 1899–2019
Source: Field, "Decline of US Manufacturing Productivity," Table 1.

The same pattern can be seen in the value of the stock market. By 1942, Standard & Poor's had fallen by 28 percent, while all exchange traded stocks had plummeted by a staggering 62 percent in nominal terms. By 1944, with the war economy operating at its peak, stocks had still not returned to their 1939 level, even though corporate profits were on the rise. It took the prospect of peace for the stock market to bounce back.[45]

The Endless Frontier

Mercifully, the command regime fell apart when the war came to an end. By 1947, a majority of the controls had been lifted, marking a swift transition from a managed economy to one driven by market forces once again. Nonetheless, the war's impact on the direction and organization of science and technology would endure.[46] Perhaps most importantly, the role that the public sector would play in the coming decades was much larger than it would have been without the war. Leading figures like Vannevar Bush felt that, in the aftermath of the war, significantly more investment in scientific research was needed. In a 1945 report prepared for President Roosevelt, titled "Science: The Endless Frontier," he argued that science now needed to focus on improving living standards and creating jobs rather than defending the nation.[47]

However, Bush was of the view that unlike the Rad Lab or the Manhattan Project, which had clear missions and therefore could be organized in a centralized manner under military control, bureaucracy was unconducive to the kind of scientific breakthroughs that drive long-run prosperity. If applied industrial research is about picking low-hanging fruit, basic science is about building the ladders that allow us to pick the fruit higher up. In his words, "It creates the fund from which the practical applications of knowledge must be drawn." Bush was well-aware that breakthrough discovery typically happens in an unpredictable manner. "It is wholly probable that progress in the treatment of cardiovascular disease, renal disease, cancer, and similar refractory diseases will be made as the result of fundamental discoveries in subjects unrelated to those diseases and perhaps entirely unexpected by the investigator," he noted.[48]

Yet Bush also recognized that the current structure of R&D in the country was unlikely to provide the support necessary for such discoveries. In the nineteenth century, the most foundational discoveries came from solo inventors, but as science became more important and corporate R&D labs gradually took over, their days were numbered. At the same time, with some exceptions, the executives running these labs were disinclined to pursue revolutionary technologies that threatened the company's existing business model. Consequently, as the age of the independent inventor came to an end, innovation became less radical and more routine. To overcome this limitation and sustain progress, America effectively reestablished the role of independent inventors inside universities—a process that had already begun in the late nineteenth century. Indeed, while it has become popular to point to World War II as the crucial turning point for American science, it was closing the gap to Europe much earlier. As depicted in figure 7.3, the percentage of U.S. universities mentioned in the biographies of Nobel Prize winners rose steadily from the 1870s onward and overtook Britain, France, and even Germany well before the war. Similar to the rise of American industry, which owed its momentum to the entry of new companies, the ascent of American science was propelled by the emergence of new universities.[49]

As shown by the insightful work of Columbia's W. Bentley MacLeod and Miguel Urquiola, the United States adopted a comparatively free-market approach to higher education and fostered an environment conducive to the entry of new institutions seeking to meet the demands of prospective students. Cornell and Johns Hopkins are prominent examples, with the former founded to focus on practical pursuits, such as agriculture, and the latter modelled on the German research university, the first of its kind in America. Rather than supplying their customers with a single product, U.S. universities provided a more diverse set of services that attracted different types of people. This diversity was nurtured by both private donations, which propelled the establishment of pioneering institutions like the University of Chicago and Stanford University, and public funds, which played a pivotal role in supporting the emergence of institutions such as the University of California at Berke-

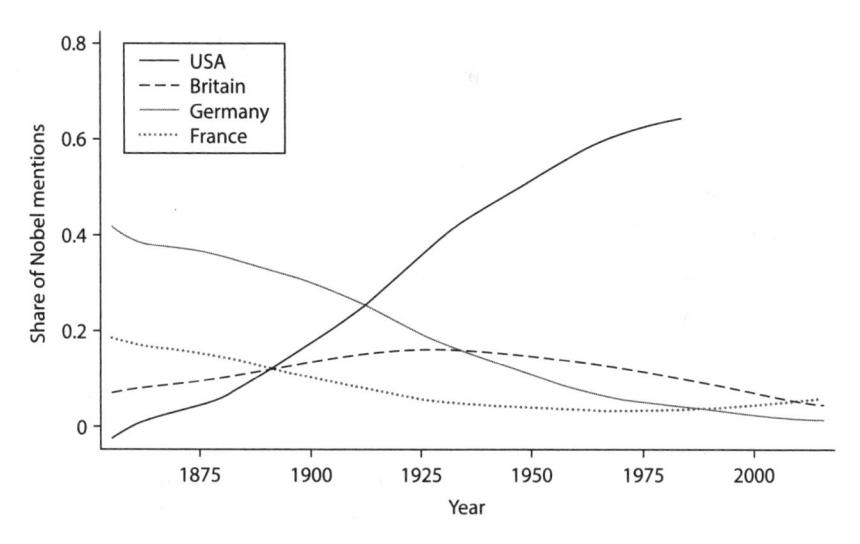

FIGURE 7.3. Nobel Prize spawning universities by country, 1855–2016
Source: Urquiola, *Markets, Minds, and Money*, Table A.1.

ley and the Massachusetts Institute of Technology. Recognizing the shifting landscape, established universities like Harvard and Columbia responded with vigour by establishing science departments and creating professional schools.

These forces were much weaker in Europe, where states controlled the systems of higher education and did not permit easy entry, preventing the emergence of challengers while reducing their allure as magnets for global talent.[50] Whereas German academics were beholden to Fredrich Althoff (see chapter 4), needing his approval just to contemplate a position at a different university, their American counterparts had the freedom to entertain multiple job offers, effectively leveraging the market to their benefit. "The United States have an Althoff at every university. The American university president is such a man," Max Weber declared, when he, accompanied by his wife Marianne, visited the United States in 1904.[51]

What Vannevar Bush did through the establishment of the National Science Foundation (NSF) and its independent board of directors was to harness the decentralized nature of America's university system. He sought to ensure that universities received adequate financial backing and that such funding was acquired through a competitive process. Bolstered by NSF funding and the influx of skilled foreign scientists seeking refuge from oppressive regimes like under Nazism and Communism, the university-based model yielded remarkable returns, and the United States surged to the forefront of global science. Bush nevertheless had some powerful critics, especially as he sought more independence from both the president and Congress. President Harry Truman, for instance, felt unease about giving up control over vast sums of money, while many in the Truman administration thought that Bush himself was becoming too powerful. Though legislation supporting Bush's version of the NSF passed both the Senate and the House in 1947, Truman ended up vetoing it. In addition, senator Harley M. Kilgore of West Virginia, who was an ardent supporter of the New Deal, took issue with Bush's elitist approach to science funding, arguing that it ought to be more distributed to foster economic development across the country. A long debate over NSF legislation ensued, and in the end neither side got it their way. By the time the National Science Foundation Act was finally passed in 1950, many wartime research contracts had already been transferred to mission agencies, like the Atomic Energy Commission and the Office of Naval Research. At first, only limited funding was put behind basic research—the NSF received just $3.5 million in 1952 and $16 million in 1956.[52] It would later surge from $1 billion in 1983 to $9.9 billion in 2023.

Sputnik, Apollo, and Computing

Though Bush's achievement was considerable, in that it created some of the decentralized institutional foundations for innovation that would later follow, the scale of his ambition was tempered by another war, albeit a cold one. When the USSR launched *Sputnik I* into low-Earth orbit in October 1957 and *Sputnik II* a month later, it ignited a space and innovation race with the United States, with many prominent figures calling for a more activist government to counter the Soviet threat and avoid further technological surprises.[53] In particular, dire warnings radiated from Capitol Hill. Democratic Senator Henry M. Jackson called

Sputnik "a devastating blow to the prestige of the United States as the leader in the scientific and technological world," while Lyndon B. Johnson, who acted as Democratic majority leader in the Senate at the time, held several high-profile hearings on the nation's satellite and missile programs, where the lead witness and physicist Edward Teller gave alarmist testimony that landed him on the cover of *Time Magazine*. To Teller and Johnson, Sputnik was a worse defeat than Pearl Harbor, and in arguing so, they invoked a strong sense of wounded nationalism. But underpinning all of this was a deeper concern—namely, that the Soviets had developed a superior system for organizing progress and society more broadly.[54]

Far from being a byword for the failure of socialism, the Soviet Union was regarded by both pundits and academics in the 1950s as one of the wonders of the world. When Nikita Khrushchev turned to Western ambassadors during a speech at the Polish embassy in Moscow, pounded his shoe on the podium and declared, "We will bury you," it was meant as a statement of the superiority of Communism in driving technological change, and it was treated most seriously. During the late 1950s and early 1960s, *Foreign Affairs* published articles on the implications of Soviet technological might as regularly as it does about China today. A prime example of the prevailing alarmism can be found in a 1957 article penned by economist Calvin Hoover, who had firsthand experience living in Moscow. Hoover concluded that the USSR was already outpacing any significant capitalist nation in terms of economic growth, growing at three times the rate of the United States. From this, he concluded that a collectivist authoritarian state possessed greater capabilities for achieving rapid economic expansion than free-market democracies and projected that America would be overtaken by the Soviets as early as the 1970s.[55]

Amid the prevailing alarmism, however, there also existed a genuine desire to comprehend how the Soviet Union had swiftly surged ahead. To regain the edge in space, it was believed, America would need a major push across a wide range of fields. This collective belief created strong congressional support for more funding for science and technology. In January 1958, National Advisory Committee for Aeronautics

(NACA) Director Hugh Dryden published a staff study titled, "A National Research Program for Space Technology," which asserted that, "It is of great urgency and importance to our country both from consideration of our prestige as a nation as well as military necessity that [the Sputnik challenge] be met by an energetic program of research and development for the conquest of space.... It is accordingly proposed that the scientific research be the responsibility of a national civilian agency."[56] Six months later, in July 1958, President Eisenhower signed the National Aeronautics and Space Act, establishing NASA, which began operations on October 1.

The Soviet threat had a unifying effect, bringing Democrats and Republicans together in ways that seem almost inconceivable today. With this broad bipartisan support, America's space efforts quickly expanded. In May 1961, President Kennedy's democratic administration launched the Apollo program, first conceived by the republican Eisenhower government, and publicly committed to landing a man on the moon by the end of the decade. It was an enormous undertaking, costing almost five times as much as the Manhattan Project and consuming a larger share of a much bigger government budget. The Manhattan Project absorbed 1 percent of all federal spending at its peak, whereas the Apollo program peaked at 2.2 percent of the federal budget.[57] In addition to the resources channelled into NASA's civilian projects, the government also created the Advanced Research Projects Agency (ARPA) in February 1958 to develop space technology for the military. Later renamed the Defense Advanced Research Projects Agency (DARPA), the agency grew swiftly to an annual research budget of $3 billion, overseen by some 100 program managers. As the Soviet threat loomed more ominously, successive administrations deemed it necessary to avoid relying solely on entrepreneurs and research universities to spearhead what was seen as essential technological progress.[58]

When the basic research had already been completed, and an objective could be clearly defined, the mission-oriented approach surely had its merits. The Manhattan Project delivered the first atomic bomb, just like the Rad Lab advanced radar technology, and the Apollo program put the first man on the moon. However, the most transformational technologies were either accidental spin-offs or the result of bottom-up initiatives by individual scientists and inventors.[59] The most consequential developments of the postwar era were unquestionably in computing, although its impact on the economy and people's lives would only be felt around the mid-1990s. As late as 1987 Robert Solow famously quipped, "You can see the computer age everywhere but in the productivity statistics."[60] It is indeed quite telling that defense secretary Robert McNamara, whose appetite for facts and figures is legendary, asked ARPA director Jack Ruina about what was going on in just about every area of technology except one: computing. To McNamara and others in the Department of Defense, computers were just gadgets to be used for payroll and accounting, with the exception of some exciting applications like the SAGE air-defense system. As Ruina notes, "People saw that something was there but they were not prepared to invest big money without knowing quite what that something was."[61]

The key to early progress in computing, it turns out, was bringing in outsiders and giving them the freedom to operate at the fringes of the federal bureaucracy. It was Ruina, the first scientist to administer ARPA, who hired J. C. R. Licklider as the first administrator of the Information Processing Techniques Office. And it was Licklider who pioneered the key concepts underlying the internet: decentralized networks to share information and interfaces to support human–machine interaction in real time. As one of his collaborators, Bob Taylor puts it, "He was really the father of it all."[62] In reality, however, he had already laid the foundations for it before joining ARPA. His 1960 *Symbiosis* paper was a "ready-made research agenda" for the entire ARPA program, so it is perhaps unsurprising that Licklider showed little enthusiasm about joining ARPA at first. Why give up his freedom to bury himself in the bureaucratic limbo of Washington? Yet in the end, Licklider saw the opportunity to execute his vision of interactive computing with the financial backing of the Pentagon. Indeed, his initial budget of $10 million annually must have seemed like a fortune.[63]

When Licklider took up his new position, everyone at the Pentagon thought of computers as colossal calculators. His primary objective thus became to convey the potential of interactive computing in revolutionizing both military and civilian life. As he recounts, "every time I possibly could, I got them to say 'interactive computing.' I kept trying to convince them of my philosophy that what the military needs, is what the businessman needs, is what the scientist needs." Remarkably, his efforts bore fruit, as he was granted the freedom to pursue his vision without pressure to focus on military applications alone. In fact, he hardly even saw Jack Ruina, who stuck to his anti-micromanagement philosophy, and met with his newest recruit perhaps once a month. Instead, during the autumn of 1962, Licklider found himself predominantly on airplanes, traversing the nation to attract the most exceptional talent to his cause.

By the spring of 1963, he had begun arranging meetings with the leaders of the groups he was underwriting—including some of the most prominent computer scientists of the day, among them Robert Fano, John McCarthy, Keith Uncapher, Douglas Engelbart, Mitchell Feigenbaum, and Alan Perlis. These meetings, as Licklider would later attest, were characterized by an informal atmosphere reminiscent of the later Homebrew Computer Club meetings that would play a role in the rise of Apple: "There would be lots of discussion, and we would stay up late at night, and maybe drink a little alcohol and such. So we would have one place interact with another place that way."[64]

All the same, Licklider was also quick to grasp that better tools for remote collaboration were urgently needed to transcend geography. With the ARPA community scattered across space, would it become nothing more than a high-tech tower of Babel, producing incompatible machines, languages, and software across different enclaves? Providing the group with the means to exchange data and software regardless of their locations seemed essential. What he proposed as a solution was a network of ARPA-funded sites connected to a national system of time-sharing computers, where programs and data lived on the net. At its core, this was an elaboration on the network of "thinking centres" he had envisioned in his seminal 1960 paper. With the backing of ARPA, in just a few years, his memorandum to the Intergalactic Network became the blueprint for Arpanet, which would eventually evolve into the internet as we know it today. In the words of his biographer, Mitchell

Waldrop, Licklider set in motion "the forces that would give rise to essentially all of modern computing: time-sharing, personal computing, the mouse, graphical user interfaces, the explosion of creativity at Xerox PARC, the Internet—all of it. Of course, not even he could have imagined such an outcome, not in 1962."[65]

The ARPA Model

ARPA has been credited with many breakthroughs of the postwar years, including missile defense, stealth technology, GPS, and artificial limbs.[66] Scholars have thus naturally sought to discern the underlying traits of the so-called ARPA model.[67] However, recent attention has skewed the narrative toward its mission-oriented approach and has thus obscured the true source of its triumph. In reality, the key to ARPA's resounding success lay in its ability to attract talent and its willingness to endow this talent with the necessary resources and unbridled autonomy to develop their ideas.[68] From its early days, as MIT's Pierre Azoulay and colleagues have shown, ARPA fostered a flat organizational structure, populated by elite engineers and scientists from both industry and academia.[69] Unlike other agencies in the federal state apparatus, ARPA enjoyed significant organizational flexibility, with executives reporting to the top, permitting them to operate outside the labyrinthine bureaucracy that entangled the Department of Energy and the Department of Defense. Without question, this free-wheeling "ARPA style of management" was dynamic and nothing like the rigidly stratified hierarchies prevalent elsewhere in the Pentagon.[70] For one thing, within the ARPA framework, program managers were granted great latitude in circumventing the confines of the civil service. Not only could they recruit talent from outside the traditional spectrum, but they were also unburdened by the shackles of Civil Service regulations. This unique freedom enabled ARPA to offer competitive salaries and to hire promising rising stars despite their sometimes limited track records, and they were given sway to build their teams and create connections between researchers with expertise.[71]

In a departure from conventional practice, ARPA managers also served relatively brief terms of three to five years. This policy resulted in a revolving door of talent that infused the organization with a steady stream of fresh ideas. During their short tenure, ARPA managers enjoyed considerable leeway in allocating funds, even without the need for external peer review. Whereas outside experts are generally familiar with the frontier and thus least burdened by uncertainty, the peer review process can inadvertently favour seniority and stifle unconventional thinking. To encourage risky and potentially transformative research, ARPA allowed program directors to make funding decisions based on their own judgment. And herein lies perhaps the key difference between the ARPA model and academic research more broadly. Although American academics relish much autonomy, their work is inevitably subjected to peer review, which, in turn, fosters conformity. ARPA, in contrast, pursued radical novelty and actively sought to evade the perils of groupthink that often accompany collective decision-making.[72]

Ultimately, however, the success of the ARPA model hinged on the decentralized landscape of America's leading universities, which served as the primary wellspring of talent for the agency. Although granting individuals the freedom to explore is undoubtedly crucial for catalysing breakthrough innovations, the more freedom that is given, the more an organization depends on the talent of the individuals it hires. Arpanet, for example, would not have materialized under the weight of micromanagement or with underqualified program staff. America's cutting-edge research institutions, like Stanford and MIT, were a prerequisite for it, and ARPA had to consistently cultivate strong ties to the research community to compete effectively in the race for talent. This challenge was not particular to ARPA—in fact, all pioneering research endeavours of the era invariably revolved around the talent within American universities. Take the Manhattan Project, for instance, where the core scientific endeavours were spearheaded by academic luminaries like Ernest Lawrence and Robert Oppenheimer at Berkeley, Harold Urey at Columbia, and A. H. Compton at the Chicago Metallurgical Laboratory. Or consider the Rad Lab, which was located at MIT. Clearly, ARPA directors were given much greater leeway than their Rad Lab counterparts, but their efforts all built on a competitive system of universities, which no other country could match and cannot be easily replicated.[73]

To be sure, many government officials would have preferred more control, so it is somewhat ironic that the Pentagon—an institution with a highly hierarchical command structure—funded a group of academics who were deeply suspicious of centralized authority. In fact, Arpanet was specifically built to foster decentralization, a point that Licklider's protégé Bob Taylor would emphasize: "My bias was always to build decentralization into the net. . . . That way it would be hard for one group to gain control. I didn't trust large central organizations. It was just in my nature to distrust them."[74] By opting for a structure of limitless nodes, each with its own router, instead of a few centralized hubs, they deliberately made the network hard for the Pentagon or anybody else to monitor and manage. This also meant that nobody, not even Licklider, could foresee how it would evolve. Even in December 1991, when the first American server was installed at the Stanford Linear Accelerator System, and the English computer scientist Tim Berners-Lee made the World Wide Web publicly accessible, the internet revolution was by no means a foregone conclusion. As an enthusiastic observer wrote in 1995, when Internet Explorer was first released together with Windows 95, "The Internet is slow, superficial, chaotic, nerdy, hostile, and largely a waste of time. You just gotta try it."[75]

The Innovation Slowdown

America's university system, with ARPA in the middle of it, laid some important foundations for the coming Computer Revolution and the productivity boom of the mid-1990s that followed. But there was no government mission or plan to create the modern Internet. Nor was contemporary innovation the chief driver of postwar prosperity.[76] As already noted, innovation plummeted during World War II. And while it bounced back after the Paris Peace Treaties, the postwar years saw nothing like the acceleration in inventive efforts that marked the late nineteenth century or indeed the post-1980 era, whether as measured by total patents or breakthrough patents per capita.[77] The large jump in patenting after 1860, as shown in figure 7.1, coincides with the great inventions that made the Second Industrial Revolution. Transformational technologies like electric light (1879) and power (1882), the telephone (1876), and the internal combustion engine (1879) all emerged in this period. For the next half century, they spawned a wave of spin-offs, which gradually entered people's homes, including electric irons (first introduced in 1893), vacuum cleaners (1907), washing machines (1907), toasters (1909), refrigerators (1916), dishwashers (1929), and dryers (1938), to name just a few.

As we have seen, the era that witnessed this remarkable surge in innovation diverged significantly from the institutional landscape of the twentieth century. The postwar decades were characterized by the ascendancy of expansive government and corporate behemoths, whereas the late nineteenth century epitomized the era of the individual inventor. Remarkably, in 1880, 95 percent of patents granted in the United States were attributed to enterprising individuals rather than corporations.[78] In this period, becoming self-made was a badge of success that excited many young men, and sometimes women, who strived to forgo a life of dependency as an employee. Even if most fell short of becoming the next Edison, social mobility was remarkably high in America—both by today's and contemporary European standards. Supported by a patent system that allowed for greater participation in innovation than anywhere else in the world, many inventors who moved up the socioeconomic ladder were immigrants or came from modest family backgrounds.[79]

However, capitalizing on the technological possibilities presented by the Second Industrial Revolution was a different matter. Most inventors lacked the requisite expertise and means to fully exploit their ideas, so they opted to license their technologies to established corporate entities, which possessed the necessary resources to transform these inventions into marketable products. Subsequently, these corporations shifted their focus toward internal development efforts, consolidating their control over the innovation process. As corporate research labs grew larger, the share of patents granted to individuals began to fall. By 1920, individual inventors were only responsible for 73 percent; by 1940, when America became the Arsenal of Democracy, this figure would drop to 42 percent. Soon, technology giants like AT&T, DuPont, IBM, and Kodak brought forth an army of tens of thousands of scientists tasked with refining existing products and spearheading new avenues of business. General Electric, which had sprung up around Edison's early light bulb patents, created its R&D lab to incrementally improve his technology through better filaments. And AT&T established its legendary Bell Labs to exploit Bell's invention of the practical telephone through a series of improvements, including amplifiers, making long-distance calls feasible nationwide. At its peak, in the 1960s, Bell Labs employed 15,000 people, of which some 1,200 had PhDs.[80]

The routinization of innovation was an organic consequence of the breakthroughs witnessed during the late nineteenth century as corporations endeavoured to capitalize on these advancements.[81] However, the institutional and political landscape also underwent transformative shifts that tipped the scales in favour of in-house R&D, thereby casting a shadow over the fortunes of independent inventors.[82] American antitrust enforcement had been vigorous in the decades following the Sherman Act, but Franklin D. Roosevelt's administration embraced a more relaxed approach. For instance, the National Industrial Recovery Act of 1933, which introduced the concept of fair competition, officially encouraged collusion, though it would be struck down by the Supreme Court in 1935.[83] A revival of trust busting would commence in 1941 after a three-year government investigation into the "Concentration of Economic Power." Under Thurmond Arnold, who was put in charge of the Justice Department's Antitrust Division, compulsory licensing—in which companies are required to license their technology to other players—became a common remedy. In fact, the Arnold era marked the beginning of what the legal scholar Jonathan Barnett has called "The Great Patent Grab," when Justice Department officials systematically began to attack the patents held by big business—a pattern that would continue into the 1970s. From 1938 to 1975, a striking 133 compulsory licensing orders were issued (figure 7.4).[84] The government was giving with one hand while taking with the other, encouraging economic concentration through a range of state-sponsored programmes, yet trying to limit the monopolistic consequences of their policies through antitrust at the same time. As economic historians Stephen Haber and

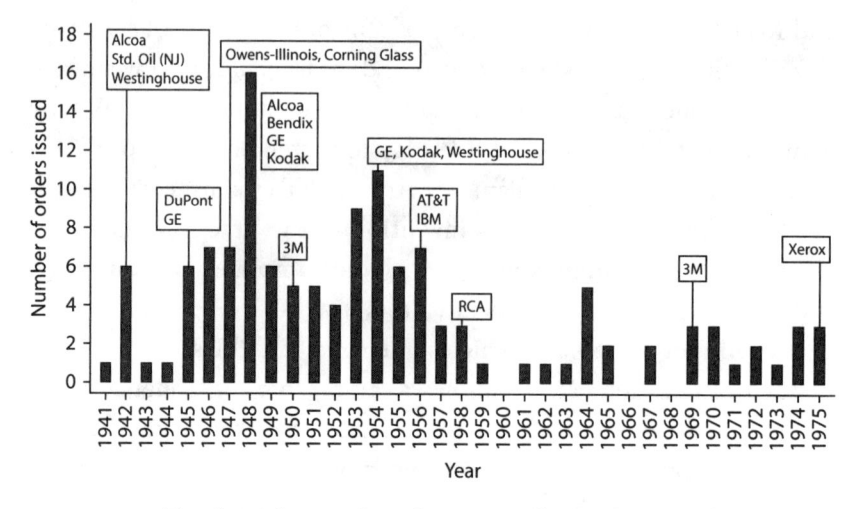

FIGURE 7.4. Timeline of compulsory licensing orders in the United States
Source: Barnett, "Great Patent Grab," Figure 6.1.

Naomi Lamoreaux write, "The result was as close to a managed economy as the US has ever had, and it involved the entire policy apparatus, including the courts."[85]

As firms grew larger, however, the state needed to deter the possibility of anti-competitive behaviour, such as the practice of scooping up potential rivals, and it did so with some success. At Du Pont, for example, growth by acquisition was ruled out by senior management as antitrust rules tightened. Instead, they set out to develop technologies internally, prompting in-house R&D to expand dramatically in the late 1940s.[86] But just as crucially, efforts at empire building also were moderated. Faced with a major antitrust lawsuit that threatened its very existence, AT&T became reluctant to develop a new line of business in transistor products, which would have drawn further attention to its market power. Consequently, the first commercially successful transistor ended up being produced by Texas Instruments (TI) in 1954. And the 1956 consent decree, which forced Bell Labs to license its patents, delivered a splendid stimulus to innovation, as evidenced by recent research.[87]

To be sure, the potential benefits of follow-on innovation must be balanced against the potential disincentives that such antitrust efforts may create for future pioneers. The emergence of the patent system in the nineteenth century introduced a framework of property rights that could be traded within a technology market, which enabled independent inventors to specialize in discovery while leaving the development and commercialization tasks to larger corporate entities. By encouraging companies to pursue organic growth rather than growth through acquisitions, the federal government inadvertently undermined the market for technology that solo inventors relied upon, just like compulsory licensing diminished the returns that first movers might expect from their pioneering efforts. Even so, innovation could still be enormously rewarding. What has changed is that today's innovators generally eschew the path of licensing and instead build companies around their technologies.

In the end, the extent to which startups rely on mergers with large corporations for funding hinges on the development of decentralizing institutions, like the ease of enlisting on the stock exchange and accessing venture capital (VC), which rose to greater prominence as the century drew to a close. Throughout the 1980s and 1990s, the number of initial public offerings (IPOs) outpaced the number of VC-backed acquisitions, as IPOs proved superior in generating returns.[88] By the new millennium, Paul Gompers and Josh Lerner estimate, VC-backed firms accounted for 20 percent of publicly traded U.S. companies, or 32 percent of market capitalization. Indeed, before Amazon's IPO, Jeff Bezos sought financing from the VC firm Kleiner Perkins Caufield & Byers, which invested $8 million for a 13 percent equity stake in 1996. In 1999, Kleiner Perkins also invested in Google, doing so alongside Sequoia, which had previously funded Yahoo!.[89]

As will be discussed in chapter 11, a new generation of entrepreneurs was indispensable to the Computer Revolution and the revival of innovation beginning in the 1980s (figure 7.1). This era coincided with a notable shift in the practices of major corporations, who, partly in response to mounting antitrust concerns, began to "externalize" parts of their business, thereby creating opportunities for fresh contenders to enter the market. In the 1960s, John Kenneth Galbraith could argue that the modern corporation had replaced "the entrepreneur as the directing force of the enterprise with management," but following the stagnation of the 1970s, the tables turned as entrepreneurs reclaimed their central role in American society. The founding of Microsoft by Paul Allen and Bill Gates in Albuquerque, New Mexico, in 1975 marked a significant milestone, and was followed by Steve Jobs and Steve Wozniak establishing Apple (1976), Leonard Bosack and Sandy Lerner making Cisco Systems (1984), Michael Dell founding Dell Technologies (1984), Jensen Huang, Chris Malachowsky, and Curtis Priem starting Nvidia (1993), Marc Andreessen and Jim Clark launching Netscape Communications Corporation (1994), Jeff Bezos constructing Amazon (1995), as well as Sergei Brin and Larry Page developing Google (1998)—all of which went public.[90] This founder movement stands in contrast to the postwar years, when growth was powered by established players who focused on exploiting existing technologies. Antitrust, in this period, played a role in deterring rent seeking among incumbents, but it is more catalytic when new technological opportunities are surfacing because it provides challengers with a realistic chance to upend the existing corporate order, as later happened in the age of computers.[91]

From Sparks to Scaling

Though not marked by an overtly innovative climate, the postwar miracle or so-called golden age of growth undeniably yielded remarkable leaps in productivity. Coming out of World War II, American companies had an abundance of unutilized technologies at their disposal, coupled with newly acquired institutional capacities to promptly implement them. As Robert Gordon documents in *The Rise and Fall of American Growth*, the great inventions of the late nineteenth century—like electricity and the internal combustion engine—delivered their main contribution to productivity between 1920 and 1970 (figure 7.5).[92] It took four decades after the opening of Edison's first 1882 Pearl Street power station in New York for factories and machines to be rearranged in ways that gave a meaningful boost to productivity, just as it took time for electric streetlights and elevators to transform the skyline of Manhattan, or electric streetcars and underground subways to connect suburbs and

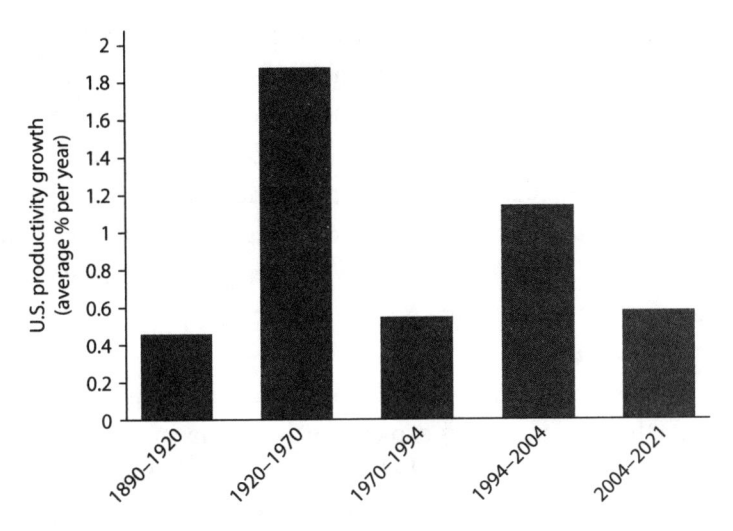

FIGURE 7.5. Productivity growth in the United States, 1890–2021
Source: Gordon, *Rise and Fall of American Growth*. Figure 17-2. Own analysis for later years.

the metropolis.[93] Fully harnessing the enigmatic potential of electricity necessitated complementary investments throughout the nation, at times undertaken by major corporations and at other times facilitated by government programs. Notably, rural electrification gained momentum only after President Roosevelt signed the Rural Electrification Act on May 2, 1936, which provided financial support to local cooperatives that private enterprises had neglected.[94]

The same is true of the internal combustion engine, which spawned the car, truck, tractor, and bus. Although Karl Benz's pathbreaking engine design materialized in 1879, it was not until Henry Ford introduced the moving assembly line in 1913, thereby enabling mass production at a low cost, that automobiles truly gained momentum. The automobile industry went from being so unimportant that it was barely mentioned in the 1900 manufacturing census to being the largest employer in America at the dawn of World War II.[95] And aviation—representing the shotgun marriage of the internal combustion engine and the 1903 aerodynamic design of the Wright brothers—followed a comparable trajectory. Though commercial air travel first took off after World War II, the industry experienced most of its technological progress between 1926 and 1936.[96] As pointed out by Gordon, "nothing after 1936 comes close in its magnitude except for the introduction of jet travel in 1958."[97] The first commercial flight was run by the predecessor company to United Airlines on April 6, 1926—a year before Charles Lindbergh's legendary first-ever solo transatlantic flight, which made him one of the most famous people in the world. Merely six years later, in 1933, the two-engine Boeing 247 could fly from New York to Chicago in 5.5 hours with a quick stop for refueling.

As discussed in chapter 6, early progress in land transportation was also made through grassroots exploration by solo inventors, but exploitation required the visible hand of government or big business to scale and solve complex coordination problems. Consider the Federal-Aid Highway Act of 1956, when Congress authorized almost $34 billion for the construction of the Interstate Highway System. The Act was signed by President and former Army General Dwight D. Eisenhower, who had been stationed in Germany, where he had been impressed by the developed network of high-speed roads known as the *Reichsautobahn*. In the beginning of the twentieth century, the American road network was still a patchwork of dirt tracks. And despite heavy investment in the 1920s and 1930s, when many iconic bridges like the Golden Gate Bridge and Benjamin Franklin Bridge where constructed, there was often still no way of bypassing urban neighbourhoods, which reduced the speed of moving goods and people. The Interstate Highway System changed all of that. Concurrently, the number of cars in the United States doubled in the 1950s, so that by 1960 Americans owned more cars than the rest of the world combined. As *The New York Times* wrote at the time: "the highway program will constitute a growing and ever-more-important share of the gross national product ... [affecting] every phase of economic life in this country."[98]

The greatest contribution to GDP, however, came with the rise of the trucking industry toward the end of the golden age. Truckers were soon seen as the new cowboys of the country, as depicted in blockbuster films like *Smokey and the Bandit,* and their commercial importance could hardly be overstated. By 1997, almost two-thirds of the value of commodities transported by truck were shipped at distances longer than 50 miles, often across state borders. By that time, however, the benefits of highway construction had already begun to diminish. According to some estimates, the interstate highways were perhaps responsible for a quarter of the upsurge in American productivity in the 1950s and 1960s, yet its contribution had largely faded by the 1980s, as had American productivity growth nationwide.[99]

Through the implementation, refinement, and expansion of these earlier breakthroughs, the Second Industrial Revolution powered American growth up until the 1970s. As elucidated by Alexander Field, the period from 1919 to 1973 can be understood as a tale of two distinct transitions. The first involved the electrification and reconfiguration of the factory, whereas the second was the coming of the horseless age, as cars transformed transportation and distribution. What these transitions had in common is that they both depended on a third general purpose technology: the moving assembly line. While electricity and the internal combustion engine spawned a host of new goods and industries, advances in mass production technology were critical to produce refrigerators, cars, television sets, and vacuum cleaners at affordable prices.[100] This form of mass production, meanwhile, was made possible by America's emphasis on the standardization of parts.

As noted in chapter 6, the American manufacturing system had already garnered acclaim for its the capacity to assemble products from identical components, as witnessed during the illustrious 1851 Crystal Palace exhibition, where European observers were astounded by the capabilities of American machinery and production techniques. However, the production of identical parts still eluded the capabilities of machine tools at that time, and achieving standardization necessitated meticulous bureaucratic coordination. The establishment of the National Bureau of Standards (NBS), chartered by the U.S. Congress in March 1901, created a system of uniform parts to reduce waste and speed up production. By setting nationwide standards for everything from incandescent lamps to elevators, the Act greatly aided the electrification of America and is justly regarded as one of the hallmarks of American industrial efficiency.[101] As recounted by the editor of *Scientific American* in 1923, "Once upon a time there were over 150 different styles of electric-lamp sockets. In buying a new bulb it was almost necessary to take your socket out and carry it to the store, to be fitted with a bulb. Today a lamp bought anywhere fits, automatically, a socket bought anywhere else." And with the outbreak of World War II, the NBS swiftly expanded simplification efforts. From 1939 to 1946, recommendations for simplified practices grew over 40 percent, while commercial standards nearly doubled. This push toward standardization outlasted the war itself: the numbers of standards continued to grow, sacrificing product diversity for greater economies of scale.[102]

The pursuit of standards naturally introduced constraints on exploration and radical innovation, but it concurrently bolstered the capacity of industry to engage in mass production. Consider, for example, the millions of universal joints produced during World War II. It was the standardization of parts that facilitated the realization of Vincent Bendix's design for high-speed vehicles, enabling companies without prior expertise in mass production to partake in its manufacture, at a time when war converted the U.S. economy to a maximum production regime.[103] Another testament to this fervent production drive was Henry Ford's Willow Run factory, where a workforce of 50,000 toiled relentlessly. Through the iterative process of learning by doing, Willow Run went from manufacturing seventy-five bombers per month in February 1943 to 432 per month by August 1944.[104] Simultaneously, at Henry Kaiser's shipyards, the time required to construct a Liberty ship from prefabricated components diminished from eight months to an astounding four days.[105]

True, many wartime endeavours had limited relevance in times of peace. After the war, much of what firms had learned producing B-24s and Sherman tanks was scrapped forever, simply because the country stopped making any of those products. The aircraft industry would never again— not even during Vietnam—attempt anything akin to Ford's achievements at Willow Run. Tens of thousands of aircrafts were flown one-way to boneyards in Arizona, like Kingman and Davis-Monthan, while aircraft carriers, naval ships, and submarines were sent to the bottom of the North Pacific Ocean.[106] It was the institutions from the war and the organisational changes they brought about, rather than the mostly destructive technologies developed, that endured. A prominent example is the Training Within Industry (TWI) program. Faced with a scarcity of skilled labour necessary to ramp up production, the National Defense Advisory Commission designed a program to equip American war contractors with effective management training, which enabled them to expedite the acquisition of new production skills by their workforce. Meticulously analysing the pool of nearly 12,000 companies vying for inclusion in this program, economists have documented lasting and positive impacts on the performance of the firms that received training—impacts that transcended the war itself.[107]

The triumph of mass production, in short, depended on the ability of American institutions to adjust as technology progressed and the capacity of the federal government to take on more responsibilities. The institutional arrangements of the late nineteenth century, which supported the market for technology upon which independent inventors relied, laid the foundations for postwar prosperity. When it came to exploiting new technologies, however, those arrangements did little more than secure a large internal market. Scholars like Alfred Chandler Jr. have correctly noted that leveraging economies of scope and scale depended on the ability of corporations to make "three-pronged investment" in production, distribution, and managerial skills.[108] Yet these investments, in turn, depended on complementary institutions. For instance, distribution was reliant on railroads and highways, whose construction was facilitated by the federal government, while mass production profited from stable labour–management relations, a balance that companies on their own struggled to maintain.

Indeed, by the nineteenth century, the United States had experienced the "bloodiest and most violent labor history of any industrial nation in the world."[109] It was the fear of unrest that famously prompted Henry Ford to introduce the $5-per-day program, along with many perks, and several companies followed suit by implementing welfare capitalist schemes. Those arrangements, however, collapsed during the Great Depression, as corporate America struggled for survival and needed to cut costs. It took the National Labor Relations Act of 1935, which guaranteed the rights of unions and centralized collective bargaining, to make labour–management relations more peaceful and predictable. By enlisting unions to play an active role in managing technological change, the legislation greatly aided mechanization and modernization.[110] Looking back at the postwar decades in the 1980s, for example, the Congressional Office of Technology Assessment noted that labour–management relations had played an important role in the introduction of new production technologies. The efforts of unions, they observed, had been focused on minimising the social costs of creative destruction, and so were "directed toward easing the adjustment process rather than retarding the process of change."[111] Their work was greatly helped by the federal government's efforts in education and training, which besides easing adjustment for the workforce, provided the private sector with the skills they needed to build managerial hierarchies.[112]

Here, too, new institutions proved critical. After the Great War, discharged veterans had been given a mere sixty dollars and a ticket home. This understandably led to resentment. In 1932, a massive protest consisting of 43,000 demonstrators, including 17,000 veterans, marched on Washington, DC, demanding compensation. The situation escalated when police opened fire on the crowd and killed two veterans. This incident, and President Herbert Hoover's decision to deploy the U.S. Army against the protestors, probably contributed to his electoral defeat against Franklin D. Roosevelt that year. In an effort to avoid similar unrest as World War II was coming to an end, the Servicemen's Readjustment Act of 1944—known as the GI Bill of Rights—was designed to "ease the transition back into civilian life." The result was an enormous expansion in the number of university-trained engineers and scientists: some 7.5 million veterans took part, of which over 2 million attended college. Around three-quarters of a million people took courses in science. During the 1940s and 1950s, the share of engineers in the Ameri-

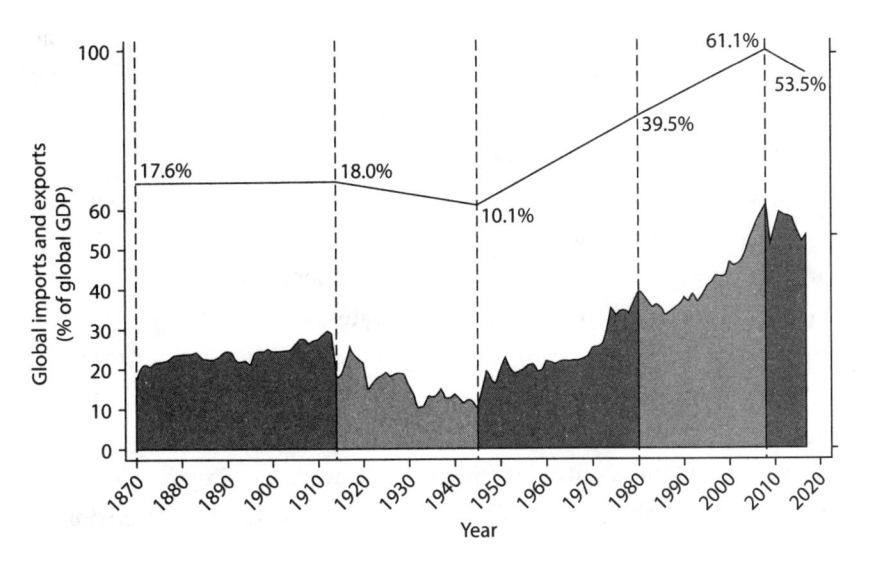

FIGURE 7.6. World trade as a percentage of global GDP, 1890–2020
Source: D. Irwin, D., 2020, The Pandemic adds Momentum to the Deglobalisation Trend. VoxEU, May 5. Based on https://ourworldindata.org/grapher/globalization-over-5-centuries.

can workforce tripled from around 0.5 percent to 1.5 percent of total employment. As new sectors like air travel developed on the back of prewar technologies, millions of jobs were created to meet the rising supply of mechanics and engineers. Alongside the swelling number of administrative office jobs, these technical roles were the backbone of the modern corporation, with its managerial hierarchies geared toward realizing economies of scale as the world opened to trade once more.[113]

Two world wars and the interwar depression had ended the first age of globalization, but after World War II, disastrous protectionist policies were largely reversed. The Bretton Woods Agreement and the Marshall Plan forged nations closer together economically and politically than they had ever been under the League of Nations and the Treaty of Versailles. Concurrently, tariff policy, a long-standing source of contention in American politics, became considerably less divisive as the United States assumed the role of the primary supplier of goods and materials to the allied war effort. As peace ensued, the U.S. export surplus persisted, as the Truman administration made concerted efforts to provide its allies with the necessary resources for postwar reconstruction.[114] These efforts also came with tangible benefits for American companies. Following the reopening of the trading system, the likes of DuPont, General Electric, and IBM were able to exploit their lead abroad and conquer markets in Europe and Japan (figure 7.6). Between 1947 and 1973, cutting-edge industries like electrical machinery, communication, and chemicals recorded some of the fastest rates of productivity growth in the nation.[115] From a comparative perspective, however, American growth in this period was by no means exceptional. In a world where knowledge flowed across borders with ease, countries with a tradition of catching up and centralized institutions were particularly well positioned to absorb the backlog of technologies that had accumulated during the interwar years.

8

The Age of Planning

> Just how and why capitalism after the Second World War found itself, to everyone's surprise including its own, surging forward into the unprecedented and possibly anomalous Golden Age of 1947–73, is perhaps the major question which faces historians of the twentieth century. There is yet no agreement on an answer, nor can I claim to provide a persuasive one.[1]
>
> —ERIC HOBSBAWM

THE POSTWAR ERA was a time of economic convergence not only between the United States and Europe but also with the Eastern bloc (figure 8.1). As the Second Industrial Revolution commenced in the 1870s, America's gross domestic product (GDP) was 25 percent larger than its European counterparts on a per capita basis. By the time the Great War erupted, this gap had expanded to 43 percent. The advent of assembly lines and the electrification of factories, homes, and cities then further widened America's lead, propelling it to an unprecedented 53 percent by the end of the second global conflict. But from 1950 to 1973, even as America experienced the fastest decades-long streak of productivity growth in its history, this trend reversed: Western Europe reduced this gap by an astonishing third in GDP per capita terms, and almost by half in terms of output per hour. Within just a single generation, the economies of continental Western Europe swiftly recovered from the setbacks endured during decades of war and depression.[2]

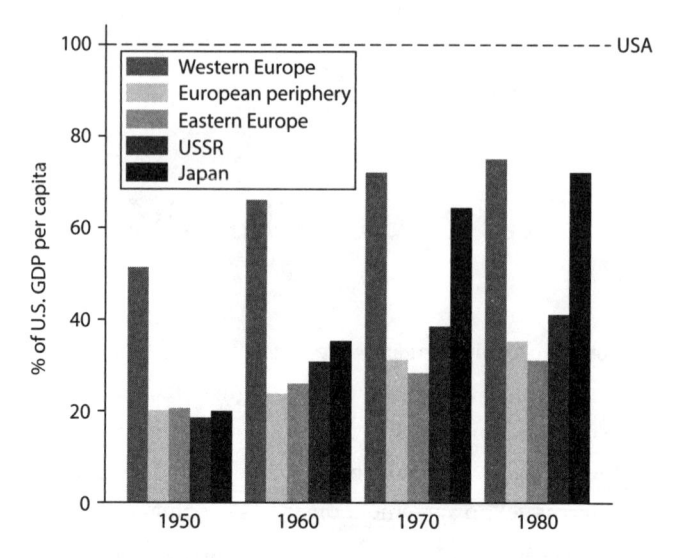

FIGURE 8.1. GDP per capita as a percentage of the United States by region, 1950–1980
Source: Maddison Project Database, version 2013. Bolt and van Zanden, "The Maddison Project."

A period of European resurgence was to be expected simply because the devastation from the war itself had been so large. The Wehrmacht had obliterated many small towns and cities in its march through Poland, Yugoslavia, and the USSR, just like the Luftwaffe's blitzkrieg had devastated entire districts of central London. But the most extensive material destruction in Europe occurred during the bombing campaigns by the Allies in 1944 and 1945, alongside the relentless push of the Red Army from Stalingrad to Prague. In Germany, where cities like Hamburg, Cologne, Dusseldorf, and Dresden suffered immense devastation from carpet-bombing by British and American planes, and Berlin had been reduced to smoking rubble and twisted metal by the Red Army, it took months for electricity, gas, and water to be restored—to say nothing of transport and communication services like rail, telephone, and even mail, all of which also suffered because the country was divided into four occupation zones, run by separate powers.

In France, the situation was also dire. While most cultural landmarks, such as the Eiffel Tower, the Notre-Dame Cathedral, and the Louvre, had thankfully been spared the kind of devastation witnessed in Germany, some 1.8 million buildings were severely damaged, over 70 percent of locomotives were rendered inoperable, and 90 percent of motor vehicles were either defective or idle. When peace finally arrived, industrial output had plummeted to a mere 40 percent of its prewar levels in both France and the Low Countries. These figures only appear favourable when juxtaposed with manufacturing output in Germany and Italy, which stood at less than 20 percent of its prewar level.

Yet for the most part, where roads and bridges and buildings had been damaged or destroyed, they could be repaired or rebuilt quickly. As a result, across Western Europe, prewar income levels were achieved by 1950. The reconstruction effort itself, in other words, cannot explain the postwar miracle. For another two decades, nations as diverse as France, Germany, Sweden, and Japan, not to mention the centrally planned economies behind the Iron Curtain, grew at quite remarkable speeds. Even as federal spending on R&D reached a crescendo in the United States—with vast funds devoted to ARPA as well as the Apollo program—America's lead was fading. Growth was fastest in Germany, Austria, and Italy, but also impressive in Greece, Spain, and Portugal. And it was more than respectable across Eastern Europe, where the heavy hand of central planning meant that there was relatively little variation in economic performance.[3] What all of these countries had in common is that they had a massive backlog of technologies to absorb, which meant their growth potential was significantly higher than that of the U.S. economy.

Hence, Europe's strong postwar performance does not imply a higher rate of innovation. Rather, its growth was largely made in America. As early as 1917, General Electric described the coming wave of electrification as the arrival of "electric servants, dependable for the muscle part of the washing, ironing, cleaning, and sewing. They could do all your cooking—without matches, without soot, without coal, without argument—in a cool kitchen."[4] Although these electric servants would take some time to trickle down to the average worker, they reached American households much sooner than they reached their European counterparts. Refrigerators, for example, which relieved the vast majority of American housewives of considerable burdens by 1940, remained a rarity in most European homes. As late as 1957, only 12 percent of West Germans and fewer than 2 percent of Italians owned a fridge. By 1974, however, ownership had surged to north of 90 percent of households in the Netherlands and West Germany and a staggering 94 percent in Italy, which had also become the leading manufacturer of refrigerators in Europe. The adoption of washing machines was slower, not least because in the mid-1950s more than half of the households in Belgium, Italy, Austria, Spain, parts of France, and Scandinavia still lacked running water, and electricity grids in many areas could not support two large appliances simultaneously. Again, by 1972, most West European homes were fitted with indoor toilets and plumbing, and two-thirds of households had a washing machine. These changes reflected significant investment in public infrastructure, as well as the rising purchasing power of ordinary workers.[5]

Yet the single greatest symbol of European postwar prosperity was unquestionably the arrival of the family car. In America, the prevalence of automobiles was already high by 1940, with 93 percent of households owning a vehicle. This widespread ownership facilitated travel and contributed to a burgeoning culture of road trips and motels. The mobility and freedom associated with car travel in the United States is nicely illustrated in films like *Detour* (1945), which traces the journey of a pianist hitchhiking from New York to Los Angeles. In Europe, in contrast, automobiles were a luxury rarely seen; even in major European cities, the majority of people relied on public transportation, like trains, trams, and buses, or bicycles for private transportation. The Italian film *Bicycle Thieves* (1948), which follows a father in postwar Rome searching for his stolen bicycle, underscores the scarcity of cars during this time. As the 1950s dawned, Spain had only 89,000 private cars, or one for every 314,000 people, while only one in twelve French households owned a car. And in Britain, where car ownership was common by European standards, it was still highly concentrated in London, where many still relied on horses and carts. But this was soon to change: in France, car numbers rose rapidly from less than 2 million to nearly 6 million during the 1950s and doubled again in the following decade. In Italy, which quickly built a formidable automobile industry of its own, ownership surged from just 270,000 cars at the war's start to over 10 million by 1970.[6]

These technologies transformed the lives of commoners around the Continent. As cars proliferated, leisure travel suddenly became mass tourism. Traditional holiday destinations in Northern and Western Europe saw a revival, and new or rediscovered spots began to gain popularity and were often featured in popular culture and glossy travel brochures. The French Riviera, for instance, transformed from a quiet winter retreat for the Edwardian elite into a vibrant, youthful destination, partly due to its portrayal in the 1956 Roger Vadim film *Et Dieu... créa la femme*, which showcased St. Tropez and introduced Brigitte Bardot. Not everyone could afford the glamorous spots on the Riviera, but domestic seaside vacations also became increasingly popular and affordable. Camping, which was already favoured by budget-conscious travelers and nature enthusiasts before the war, burgeoned into a significant industry in the late 1950s.[7]

Most of these changes, whether the electrification of the home, the rise of private entertainment such as televised imports from Hollywood, or personal travel, emanated from America, where everything was mass produced. In the words of historian Tony Judt, "This was the brave new world that the British novelist J. B. Priestley described in 1955 as 'admass'. For many other contemporary observers it was, very simply, 'Americanization': the adoption in Europe of all the practices and aspirations of modern America."[8] And in response to those aspirations, European industries stepped up their game. Before the war, several European car manufacturers, including Porsche in Germany, Fiat in Italy, Renault and Citroën in France, and Morris in Britain, had sought to emulate the success of Henry Ford's Model T in building an affordable, mass-produced vehicle. And when the peace came, they finally did.

Over the coming decades, companies like Fiat, whose engineers had made vigorous use of Ford's open-door policy, swiftly surged ahead. Indeed, by 1966, Fiat's advancements and expertise were internationally recognized, such that Moscow enlisted the company to build new Soviet factories.[9] Montecatini, which merged with the Edison Company, originally set up to exploit Thomas Edison's patents in Italy, also built several factories in the Eastern bloc. From the 1950s until the early 1970s, the so-called industrial triangle, comprising the manufacturing centres of Milan and Turin, and the seaport of Genoa, thrived in large part by absorbing and exporting U.S. technology, as did smokestack industries all over Europe. What Germans call the *Wirtschaftswunder*, and the French *Les Trente Glorieuses*, was primarily the result of exploiting American innovations. But while German Chancellor Ludwig Erhard once described himself as "an American invention," the institutions he represented, that allowed Allied businesses to absorb foreign technology, were European.[10] Despite the wartime destruction, below the surface, the foundations of Europe's earlier catch-up with Britain following the Industrial Revolution remained in place.[11]

The Atlantic Alliance

The stunning growth witnessed in Western Europe was contingent on the ability to acquire or license technology from across the Atlantic. However, it is crucial to view these opportunities within the broader geopolitical landscape, because they were fused with global developments that influenced Europe's access to the cutting-edge technologies of the day. Of particular significance was the security umbrella provided by the United States, which enabled countries to allocate fewer resources toward defense expenditures. Consequently, these freed-up resources could be redirected toward productive investments in emerging technologies. Moreover, successive U.S. administrations, driven by their determination to curb the spread of Communism, played an instrumental role in facilitating technology transfer to their allies.

No one deserves more credit for these policies than George Kennan, an American diplomat who assumed the role of deputy chief of the

Moscow mission in 1944. It was in 1946, responding to the Treasury Department's request for an explanation of recent Soviet actions, that Kennan crafted his now-iconic "long telegram." This text underscored his belief that the USSR would relentlessly pursue the expansion of Communism wherever feasible. The following year, when Kennan's telegram, signed "X" to dissociate it from official government views, was published in *Foreign Affairs*, the Soviet threat seized the public consciousness. Its unequivocal message resonated: "The main element of any United States policy toward the Soviet Union must be that of a long-term, patient but firm and vigilant containment of Russian expansive tendencies."[12] The Truman administration acted upon Kennan's prescription that same year by unveiling the Marshall Plan, officially titled the European Recovery Program, which sought to dilute Soviet influence in Western Europe and served as a cornerstone in the broader framework of containment.[13]

The Marshall Plan was the largest aid transfer in history. A staggering sum of $190 billion (in 2024 dollars)—equivalent to 5 percent of the United States's GDP in 1948—was allocated for the purpose of relief and reconstruction in Europe, and with great effect. Consider Italy, whose GDP per capita when the war formally ended on May 2, 1945, had plunged 38 percent below its 1938 level. A key obstacle to recovery was that the infrastructure upon which mass production depended laid in ruins: 77 percent of roads had been shattered, and 44 percent of the rail network had been rendered unusable. But having received $12 billion in recovery funding, roads, railways, and bridges were swiftly rebuilt. From the Lazio region to Tuscany and up to the Austrian border, the impact of this aid on Italy's modernization was significant. In provinces receiving more funds, recent research shows, farms adopted more tractors, agriculture saw an exodus of workers, and industry expanded faster as markets integrated, which made mass production technologies more profitable.[14]

An often-overlooked part of the Marshall Plan is the technical assistance it provided.[15] In 1949, James Silberman, the Chief of Productivity and Technology Development at the Bureau of Labor Statistics (BLS), toured European factories and came to a striking realization: managerial inefficiencies were a bigger obstacle to productivity than war-related destruction. To tackle this, the U.S. government launched the Productivity Program, an initiative that allowed European companies to send their managers to the United States for hands-on training, exposure to American technology, or both.[16] These study trips, lasting eight to twelve weeks, immersed teams of European managers in U.S. factories producing similar goods. A typical visit included plant tours and direct collaboration with American colleagues. As one Italian manager observed after his 1953 trip, the Italians usually "work twice as long . . . but only finish half the amount of work."[17] The potential for catch-up, in short, was vast.

As part of the package, companies adopting American technology could secure loans matching the market value of the machinery they purchased—at a favorable 5.5 percent interest rate over ten years, compared to Italy's prevailing 9 percent market rate in the mid-1950s. And the dividends from embracing new technologies were nothing short of extraordinary. Take bottle-washing machines: American models could sanitize 200 bottles per minute, while their European counterparts managed just 50 bottles in three minutes. On average, firms benefiting from management training and technology transfers saw their productivity surge by 50 percent over the next fifteen years.[18]

Beyond technology and know-how, the Marshall Plan also opened broader markets for European firms to exploit by accelerating European integration. Postwar globalization owed much to developments in aviation, trucking, and containerization, but political forces were equally significant.[19] Marshall aid was contingent on a collective European strategy for allocating the funds, which American officials hoped would foster a "United States of Europe" as a cohesive and formidable front against the encroaching Soviet Union. Those who came into power after World War II—Konrad Adenauer and Georges Pompidou among them—saw the development of a European political identity as a way of preventing the reoccurrence of war and had ardently championed the cause of integration already during the interwar years.

The Congress of Europe held in The Hague in 1948 reinforced this tradition. During this gathering, France's Foreign Minister Georges Bidault proposed the creation of a European Assembly, which later became the Council of Europe. Additionally, the idea of forming a customs and economic union was put forward. This eventually led to the establishment of the European Coal and Steel Community and the subsequent Treaties of Rome in 1958, which gave birth to the European Economic Community (EEC). Within a decade, a customs union encompassing France, Germany, Italy, and the Benelux countries had been forged. And over the next half century, as the union expanded, the barriers that divided markets melted away, while the blurring of corporate and national boundaries helped make the latest American technology easier for European corporates to access. Though science had been an international activity since the Republic of Letters, knowledge exchange became more systematic after the war, when scientists from IBM, Philips, and Fujitsu could suddenly meet at an international congress to exchange ideas and paper drafts.[20]

A Concerted Economy

Ample technological opportunities were in the "air," as Alfred Marshall would have put it. But seizing these opportunities also required institutions and mechanisms for absorption—the kind of bureaucratic state capacity that Europe was fortunate to have built over the preceding centuries. The prevalence of apprenticeships and vocational training across the Continent, for instance, meant workers were well-equipped to interpret and understand the blueprints and manuals accompanying American machinery. This proficiency in technical skills supported the successful integration of modern technologies into European industries.[21] Indeed, despite suffering devastating destruction during the war, neither Britain nor Europe remerged as blank slates. Among other things, the Great Powers of Europe already possessed banks, like Crédit Foncier, to mobilize scarce capital, and other institutions to coordinate the adoption of British technology, as discussed in chapter 5. In Germany, an economic council (*Wirtschaftsrat*), originally created by Prince Otto von Bismarck, existed to bring together society's organized interests and coordinate between social partners—a process that was aided by big business and high levels of economic concentration; in essence, what Kocka termed "organized capitalism." These centralizing institutions, as discussed previously, were effective in closing the gap to Victorian Britain. And after World War II, they proved to be useful once more, when they facilitated the adoption of American technology.[22]

Similarly, existing efforts to incorporate the labour movement into the bureaucratic process—initially pursued to avert disputes and disruption to the war effort during World War I—played a key role in the economic boom following World War II. In Germany, union activity was permitted under American occupation as early as September 1945, and the newly established trade union associations wasted little time. Almost immediately, they began to assist the council of state ministers (the *Länderrat*) in formulating social and labour market policy. The surge in unionization not only improved working conditions but also brought clear advantages to businesses. With stronger worker representation, employee turnover dropped, strikes became less frequent, and industrial relations stabilized. At a time when mass production depended on a disciplined workforce, these changes were crucial to Germany's economic resurgence.[23]

In Europe, where postwar growth necessitated substantial levels of investment, the benefits of unionization were even greater than in America, particularly due to the looming spectre of Communism. The political landscape in Italy and France was marked by the presence of prominent communist figures, with the Communist Party garnering over a quarter of the votes in the elections held between 1945 and 1946, despite Italy's Christian democrat leader Alcide de Gasperi declaring that Marx and Jesus Christ shared the same message of universal brotherhood and equality. Meanwhile, in Britain, the new Labour government led by Clement Attlee, which displaced Winston Churchill in 1945, included several individuals with radical leanings and swiftly embarked on an extensive program of industrial nationalization. And in Germany, Kurt Schumacher, the leader of the Social Democratic Party (SPD), thought that the postwar period would be an age of revolution, culminating in the abolition of the capitalist system. Even the Ahlen Programme, issued in February 1947 by the main opposition party, the Christian Democratic Union (CDU), declared that "The new structure of the German economy must start from the realisation that the period of uncurtailed rule by private capitalism is over." Two years later, its Düsseldorf Programme reiterated: "the capitalist economic system has not done justice to the vital interests of the German people."[24]

To entrepreneurs and industrialists, in other words, it was by no means clear that these parties would uphold private property rights and shun confiscatory policies. Yet despite such uncertainty, trade unionists and even Communist Party hardliners mostly worked as if it was "a national effort comparable to the resistance."[25] "Produce, produce" and "Work hard first, then ask for concessions" featured among the slogans of France's *Confédération Générale du Travail*.[26] Worrying that strikes and disruptive labour action would drive the middle class into the arms of the Fascist right, the confederation opted for pragmatism and subordinated their revolutionary aspirations. In such an environment, growth and higher living standards became a shared obsession around which governments could easily rally supporters.

There was, nevertheless, a constant danger that increasingly powerful labour unions might prioritize exorbitant wage hikes, thereby impeding crucial investment in industrial projects. In return for wage restraint, postwar governments introduced social security and mandated paid holidays and shorter workweeks. This bargain ensured that profits would be available for modernization, from which labour would also benefit in the future. The key challenge with this arrangement was assuring workers and unions that these profits would genuinely be channelled into investments in productive, job-creating technologies, raising the growth prospects of the nation, rather than be distributed as dividends to shareholders. What this meant in practice was that the parties needed mechanisms to monitor one another's compliance with the agreed-upon terms. Germany's codetermination law (*Montan-Mitbestimmungsgesetz*), which permitted workers to elect representatives to the supervisory boards of large firms, was one such mechanism.

Workers and companies faced a tricky problem however: if one union accepted lower wages to attract investment and create jobs, the benefits might spill over to other industries rather than directly helping their own workers. This created a strong temptation to defect from cooperative wage-setting agreements. To prevent this, Germany's metalworkers' union took the lead in wage negotiations, setting a benchmark for other sectors to follow. But an even more effective solution was to centralize negotiations through trade union federations and employers' associations. Sweden perfected this approach in the 1950s, when the employers' federation (SAF) and the blue-collar workers' umbrella organization (LO) negotiated national wage agreements. These deals struck a balance—ensuring workers received fair wages while allowing companies to reinvest profits. Only after this framework was established would individual unions and employers fine-tune their agreements.[27] As economic historian Barry Eichengreen has argued, Europe's corporatist model kept wages in check, ensured stability, and fast-tracked industrial modernization, speeding up the adoption of U.S. technologies.[28]

Europe's centralized institutions had other advantages, too. Writing in the 1940s, economist Paul Rosenstein-Rodan, trained in the Austrian tradition and highly sceptical of government intervention, formulated what would become a highly influential theory in economic development. In essence, he argued that getting complementary industries up and running simultaneously required a "Big Push." This theory, which represented a significant shift from the tradition in which he was trained, reflected the experience of the postwar recovery.[29] For starters, reconstructing Europe's devastated railroad network depended on the supply of high-quality steel, but steel required access to coal, and transporting coal to Europe's power plant, in turn, required railroads.[30] With one of these links missing, none of these industries could thrive. And amid the scarcity of capital and widespread devastation, scepticism radiated regarding the ability of decentralized markets to effectively mobilize and coordinate investments across various sectors.[31]

In the pursuit of reconstruction, synchronization became imperative, as each investment's profitability depended on the presence of others. Though it was General Charles de Gaulle who declared that the state "must hold the levers of command," France was far from alone in pursuing the path of state-led development.[32] From Bonn to Tokyo, state bureaucracies assumed control over vital technology industries such as steel, railroads, and telecommunications. In Austria, assets seized by the Germans after the Anschluss and later by the Soviets were nationalized, giving the state significant control over high-tech industries. Sweden, by contrast, kept most key sectors in private hands, yet planning remained central. The influential Wallenberg family, whose enterprises employed roughly one in seven Swedish industrial workers, played a pivotal role. Through their holding company, Investor AB, they strategically managed investments across industries, fostering knowledge-sharing between firms.[33]

One would expect that Germany, with its long bureaucratic tradition, would thrive in the age of planning. However, memories of recent abuses of state power weighed heavily on the country, undercutting enthusiasm for either political or economic centralization. While German big business rarely backed Hitler prior to his ascent to the chancellorship in 1933—Fritz Thyssen being a noteworthy exception—extreme concentration of market power in the Weimar era had enabled the Nazis to consolidate totalitarian power once in the driver's seat.[34] So after the war, Walter Eucken's *ordo-liberalism* and the broader Freiburg School, according to which the state should enforce market rules to encourage competition, naturally gained traction.[35] Moreover, as Germany was already leading in a range of high-tech industries, planning had also become harder (and so less effective) relative to its neighbours—though Germany's history of legalized cartels still cast a lingering shadow. While the Allies dismantled IG Farben and enacted the Act against Restraints of Competition (*Gesetz gegen Wettbewerbsbeschränkungen* or GWB) in 1957, German antitrust regulations nevertheless remained more discretionary than those in the United States.[36] Although the number of German cartels never again reached the levels seen during the interwar years, the GWB included explicit exemptions for legalized cartels.[37] Similarly, Allied efforts to break up Germany's banks had no lasting impact, as they maintained a "web of connections" to the governance structures of big business through ownership, voting rights, and positions on supervisory boards.[38]

In neighbouring France, meanwhile, the role of the state loomed larger, especially given the prevalence of small, family-owned businesses and the limited access to advanced technologies. For large-scale industry to take hold companies needed assurances of coordinated investments. And given France's long-standing history of state-guided development, government intervention was not seen as sacrilegious. During World War II, the Vichy regime had already laid the groundwork for centralized planning by creating the Ministry of Industrial Production, which coordinated resources through industry panels in an attempt to solve Hayek's knowledge problem. After the war, Charles de Gaulle, a staunch believer in state-led modernization, built on this legacy. In January 1946, he issued a decree to establish the Planning Commissariat within the Ministry of Economic Affairs, appointing Jean Monnet—a diplomat and former adviser to Franklin D. Roosevelt—as its head.[39]

The resulting Monnet Plan of 1946 sought to create a "concerted economy" (*économie concertée*), where industries would not develop in isolation but through carefully orchestrated coordination. The government, with its control over the banking system, channeled credit strategically into key technological priorities. The Planning Commissariat became more than just a policy office—it served as a negotiating table, bringing together state officials, corporate leaders, and trade unions. This structure did not just link industries—it connected industrialists and workers, ensuring that France's postwar recovery was driven not only by capital but also by cooperation.[40] For Monnet, this system was more than an economic strategy; it was a way to insulate industrial policy from political interference and short-term interests. By placing investment decisions in the hands of technocrats rather than elected officials, the French government sought to create a more rational, long-term approach to economic development.[41] Indeed, for the civil service, it was fairly straightforward to channel resources into well-established technologies—ones that had already proven themselves in the United States and promised predictable returns.[42]

On the periphery, centralization and planning ruled in similar fashion. In Spain, after the collapse of anticipated technological aid from Nazi Germany, *generalissimo* Francisco Franco's drive for self-sufficiency started to mirror the strategy of the Soviet Union, which had backed the Republicans Franco had fought a bloody civil war against. After World

War II, the Franco regime was internationally isolated, branded a "U.N. outcast" due to its fascist ties. The United Nations barred Spain from membership, and the United States initially pursued a policy of diplomatic isolation, hoping it would lead to Franco's peaceful downfall. Meanwhile, Spain's economy remained tightly controlled: most exports required special licenses, and nearly all industrial investments needed government approval. These restrictions stifled competition, prevented new businesses from emerging and allowed established firms to continue using outdated technologies.[43]

However, as Cold War tensions escalated, American policy shifted. Military strategists along with Secretary of State Dean Acheson recognized Spain's strategic importance—it was close enough to reach Soviet targets but far from the main battlefronts in Europe. Thus, in September 1953, the United States and Spain signed the Pact of Madrid, securing American economic aid in exchange for military bases on Spanish soil. This agreement not only strengthened Franco's regime but also made the United States invested in Spain's stability. As *The Economist* observed at the time, "Now that the Americans have an interest in the country, it is reasonable to assume that they will help it get out of the most serious economic difficulties."[44] Although most of aid was spent on commodities, even modest investments in technology led to significant progress in an economy desperately short on capital.[45] Following the example of its neighbors, Spain embraced planning through the *Instituto Nacional de Industria* (INI), a state-owned holding company that coordinated major investments. This strategy helped fuel the so-called "Spanish Miracle" of the 1960s and 1970s, as the country gradually opened to trade.[46] One key success was *Sociedad Española de Automóviles de Turismo* (SEAT), which launched with technology licensed from Fiat, with the INI providing 52 percent of the initial capital.[47]

Meanwhile, in Italy, large corporations, like Fiat, had already begun experimenting with assembly lines before World War II, but they were giants in an age of pygmies. Most Italians still toiled on farms, and those in industry were often employed in tiny workshops with just a handful of workers.[48] After the war, however, with financial and technical support from the Marshall Plan, Italian industry fully embraced the American mass-production model. The ensuing industrial boom pulled waves of farm laborers from the rural south to Turin, Fiat's industrial stronghold: "Southerners would arrive in rags, sleep on park benches or at the train station, and wait as long as it took to get a job in a Fiat plant."[49] Between 1950 and 1973, productivity nationwide soared by over 5 percent annually. In just two decades, Italy's GDP per capita rose from 38 percent to 64 percent of U.S. levels, and from 50 percent to 88 percent of Britain's.[50] As Italy's economy surged, the Fiat 500 became an icon of the era, embodying the shift from an agricultural past to an industrial future.[51]

Again, the institutions underpinning Italy's economic success were largely in place before the war. When Garibaldi and his thousand red-shirted volunteers set sail from Liguria to Sicily on May 5, 1860, the Italian peninsula was mired in poverty and slow growth. Unification brought little immediate improvement—over the next three decades, Italy's GDP per capita grew at barely half the pace of Britain's.[52] Unlike France, which inherited a robust Napoleonic bureaucracy, or Germany, which built on Prussia's administrative traditions, Italy lacked a strong state apparatus.[53] Italian catch-up growth needed new institutions to support economies of scale.[54]

For one thing, decentralized capital markets were poorly developed. So, *Banca Commerciale Italiana*, founded in October 1894, mostly by capital from German banks, helped mobilize scant resources, which it channelled into industrial endeavours like electrical power. It also established close relations with the Edison Company—a relationship that would drive the acquisition of foreign technology and spawn numerous electrical enterprises. To strengthen its hold on the electric power industry, Banca Commerciale further established the Society for the Development of Electric Firms in Italy, dedicated exclusively to funding emerging electrical companies. Using both Societa Edison and this holding company, it successfully sculpted and coordinated electrical industries in Italy.[55] And tellingly, Italy's postwar leap centred on the industrial triangle of the Northwest, the same region that had been the hothouse for growth in the late nineteenth century.[56] Home to pioneers like Società

Edison, this area accounted for 40 percent of Italy's total output in the late 1880s, a share that rose to 54 percent by 1911—marking the country's first "big industrial push."[57]

Initially, Italy's industrial efforts focused on railway expansion.[58] When the country unified in 1861, its rail network covered just 3,900 km—far behind Britain's 18,000 km, Germany's 16,000 km, and France's 12,000 km. But the new Kingdom moved quickly to connect its major cities. At unification, rail lines extended only as far south as Ancona on the Adriatic coast and just below Genoa on the Tyrrhenian side. Yet by 1864, trains reached Bari, and by 1870, passengers could travel from Milan and Turin to Naples or cross the peninsula from Rome to Ancona and from Naples to Bari.[59] But while unification spurred construction, different private companies operated sections of the network. A significant shift in 1885 saw the Railways Conventions delegate management to three primary private firms: *Rete Adriatica* and *Rete Mediterranea*, which divided the peninsula from west to east, and *Rete Sicula*, responsible for Sicily. Then, in 1905, Italy followed Bismarck's lead in Germany and fully centralized its railways under *Ferrovie dello Stato*, a state-owned entity employing around 100,000 people to unify the system.[60]

In the early years, the Italian network relied heavily on foreign-made locomotives.[61] British, then French and German firms dominated the market. By the mid-1880s, Germany's *Maschinenfabrik Esslingen* was sending about half of its locomotive production to Italy. Though imports fell in the 1890s, demand surged again in the early 1900s, as Italian manufacturers gained a larger share of the market. To support this shift, the government used state contracts to boost domestic production—much like Tsarist Russia had done (chapter 5). This strategy ensured a steady demand for Italian-made locomotives while still allowing foreign firms to compete for state contracts, keeping innovation and pricing pressure in check.[62] As economic historians have noted, these policies should be seen within the broader context of Great Power competition in the lead-up to World War I. Yet their legacy extended far beyond that era, with state companies like *Ferrovie dello Stato*, now *Ferrovie dello Stato Italiane*, shaping Italy's industrial landscape until this day.[63]

State control and ownership soon expanded across a wide range of industries, with *the Istituto per la Ricostruzione Industriale* (IRI) leading the way. Founded in 1933 under Mussolini's Fascist regime, the IRI quickly diversified into banking, steel, shipbuilding, telecommunications, airlines, and even television. Originally set up as an emergency measure during the Great Depression, it evolved into a state-run giant under tight political control, with its board appointed by Italy's ruling parties and accountable to the Ministry of State Holdings. By the 1950s and 1960s, it had become the second-largest corporation in Europe, fueling Italy's postwar economic miracle, alongside *Ente Nazionale Idrocarburi* (ENI)—another state holding company, set up from Agip in 1953 to explore for oilfields in the Middle East. By coordinating energy investments, ENI provided the conditions for Italy's new manufacturing giants to import American technology, expand, and thrive.[64]

As noted, this centralizing trend was not unique to Italy. Throughout postwar Europe, the challenge of coordinating interdependent industries was met through planning and bureaucratic expertise. As Eichengreen has argued, this took different forms—industrial conglomerates, state holding companies, and planning agencies in the West, and full-scale nationalization in the East. In a nutshell, Europe's centralizing institutions provided a good "fit" for the technological imperatives of the day, just as they had in the aftermath of Britain's Industrial Revolution. The outcome was an era of unparalleled growth from the conclusion of World War II well into the 1960s, which today's politicians look back at in envy.

Zaibatsu to Keiretsu

If catch-up in Western Europe was enabled by unions making wage concessions to boost productive investment, East Asia achieved similar gains through labour repression. In Japan, workers willingly accepted the introduction of labour-saving machines, and strikes were few. While cultural conformism probably played a role in this relatively compliant labour force, institutional engineering was also important. According to sociologist Totsuka Hideo, postwar Japan developed a style of management that encouraged loyalty among workers to their supervisors, and business took a very hard line against militant unions.[65] For instance, during the 1960 Mitsui Miike coal mine dispute in Kyushu, militants were subsequently fired and the radical *Sōhyō* movement faded. Meanwhile, in Taiwan, strikes and collective bargaining were prohibited under martial law. Unions could only operate under Kuomintang supervision, which, among other things, involved party control over the election of union leaders. And in South Korea, closed shops and strikes were illegal. Leftist forces and unions were quashed by the right wing of the nationalist movement under the U.S.-backed president Syngman Rhee.[66]

Bureaucratic coordination, however, was more important in East Asia, with its historical legacy of state-led development. In Japan in particular, access to American technology eased considerably after its formal surrender in September 1945, which officially ended the war in Asia. The Treaty of San Francisco, signed by forty-nine nations in 1951, reestablished peaceful relations between Japan and the Allied powers and allowed technology transfer to resume. Before the war's onset, Japan had been heavily dependent on Western enterprises for access to machinery, automobiles, and chemicals; its conglomerates had cultivated robust partnerships with Western technology giants like General Electric, Westinghouse, and Siemens. After years of wartime isolation, political leaders embraced a period of grand reopening, comparable to that of the Meiji Restoration, which ignited a period of catch-up after the first Industrial Revolution.[67]

This time around, though, the approach to technology transfer was significantly more systematic. In the nineteenth century, governments mostly attempted to prevent technological leakage. For instance, as previously discussed, the British government, albeit without much success, tried to limit the emigration of skilled artisans until 1825 and put a ban on the export of numerous machines and their designs until 1842. In stark contrast, beginning in the 1950s, successive U.S. administrations actively supported the handover of domestic technology to foreign lands—for compelling political reasons. The looming shadow of the Cold War underscored the importance of ensuring that Japan did not gravitate toward Communism. This strategic need led to the establishment of the Military Assistance Program (MAP), which created channels for technology transfer in a bid to bolster America's newfound ally.[68]

The scope for catch-up growth was enormous. Upon arrival, the devastation that General MacArthur and the U.S. occupation authorities encountered was simply horrific. The atomic bomb dropped on Hiroshima on August 6, 1945, had delivered temperatures exceeding one million degrees Celsius at the blast site, killing over 20 percent of the local population and obliterating the center of the city. The bomb dropped on Nagasaki three days later, with almost double the explosive power of the Hiroshima bomb, caused even more extensive damage. In addition, the Allied strategic bombing had left over sixty Japanese cities shattered beyond recognition. On the night of March 9, 1945, alone, U.S. B-29 Superfortress bombers dropped 1.7 kilotons of napalm incendiaries over Tokyo in just three hours, unleashing a firestorm: "Rivers boiled. Asphalt streets liquefied and burst into flame. . . . Sixteen square miles of Tokyo were reduced to ash. At least 80,000 people were killed in that raid alone . . . it was the deadliest single-day air attack in the history of the world." In the cities under fire, two-thirds of productive capacity was left in ruins, a total of 2.2 million buildings were destroyed, and some 40 percent of the population left homeless. By the end of the war, the U.S. Air Force had destroyed more square miles in Tokyo alone than the Allies took down in the fifteen most targeted German cities.[69]

The MacArthur leadership correctly concluded that, with the economy in shambles, civil unrest was very likely; to avoid such an outcome, Japan's industrial capacity had to be swiftly rebuilt. A blueprint for this effort was provided by the Training Within Industry (TWI) Service, which had successfully trained key personnel in war-related industries and aided the American mass production miracle during the war. When the program concluded in America in 1945, it was extended to the war-torn nations of Europe and Asia. And nowhere was American aid better absorbed than in Japan, where it melded with established institutions and production techniques. Indeed, TWI would serve as the foundation of what would become known as *kaizen*, which means "continuous improvement," the production technique pioneered by the Toyota Motor Corporation in conjunction with the Lean management and Just in Time (JIT) principles of Taiichi Ohno.[70] The TWI methods, which had been developed for large-scale war, when there was no time for experimentation and sweeping innovative changes, recommended many small incremental improvements that could be introduced during the flow of production. This approach served Japanese conditions well, since the almost total devastation meant that it could scarcely afford to waste valuable raw materials. And continuous improvements of American technologies are precisely what it delivered as Japan rose from the ashes of war.[71] Between 1950 and 1967, over 4,000 licenses were purchased by Japanese industry, half of which covered machinery, mostly from America.[72]

The outbreak of the Korean War further cemented the alliance between Japan and America and prompted the United States to expedite the turnover of technology and know-how. Through the Vehicle Exchange programs, the United States provided investment and assistance to Japanese industry, which then supplied the U.S. military with more than 60,000 vehicles. This special procurement program permitted corporate Japan to adopt mass production technology on a scale reminiscent of what Henry Ford had done before the war. In fact, the ordnance depot in Fuchu, where Japanese workers and American supervisors worked side-by-side to rebuild Japan's automotive industry, soon became known as "little Detroit."[73] Propelled by giants like Toyota, Japan— which produced a mere 458 vehicles in 1938—was poised to dominate the global car manufacturing landscape.[74]

Japan's extraordinary recovery was not, of course, due entirely to the largesse of the United States. After all, Japanese producers did not just catch up with the frontier; they soon became powerful challengers in both American and European markets, including in cutting-edge industries like electronics and semiconductors.[75] Eventually, by the 1980s, this reality had trickled down to American corporations, who began inviting Japanese managers to the United States, while American executives queued up to see Japanese factories to learn the "Japanese management way." The Ford Motor Company, which had pioneered mass production and welcomed Japanese companies to River Rouge to learn about American technology and practice, now turned to Japan to improve production processes. The company swiftly put much of what it learned into practice, much thanks to W. Edwards Deming, who was hired to jumpstart the company's quality movement and who, having worked under General MacArthur as a census consultant to the Japanese government, was already familiar with the Japanese way. The result of his efforts was the Ford Taurus, which soon became an all-time bestseller.[76]

Japan's miracle, in other words, was due to the blend of American technology and domestic institutions, which proved remarkably persistent. As during the Meiji period, the government bureaucracy was not a passive bystander in Japan's great leap forward. Even in the postwar era, Japan was run "for the sake of the citizenry" rather than with the "participation of the citizenry."[77] Political scientist Chalmers Johnson's account of Japan's postwar success, for example, highlights the role played by the Ministry of International Trade and Industry (MITI), which gave a meritocratically recruited elite group control over the levers of economic policy.[78] The MITI was, to be sure, a powerful force in the diffusion of foreign-sourced technology, which Japanese firms were quick to absorb and improve on.[79] By forcing IBM and Texas Instruments to license its patents in return for market access, it made the latest technologies available to corporate Japan.[80] In the infamous case of IBM, for example, Sahashi Shigeru, then head of MITI's Enterprises Bureau, told the company that he would "block Big Blue's business unless it licensed its technology to local firms at a maximum 5 per cent royalty," to which they agreed. Moreover, many MITI civil servants retired only to join the upper echelons of private enterprise, where they continued their work to advance Japanese industry.[81]

The cozy relationship between the government bureaucracy and big business that characterized the postwar period in Japan thus looked much like it had prior to the war. The business groups known as *keiretsu*, which emerged after the war, where essentially zaibatsu successors, whose origins dated back to the Meiji era.[82] Before war broke out, the zaibatsu had thrived in large part due to the absence of antitrust regulation.[83] The legalization of cartels and the compulsory participation of members, mandated as early as 1925, had provided fertile ground for their expansion; a law enacted in 1931 even granted the government the power to coerce all companies into joining a cartel. These institutions also proved instrumental in supporting Japan's war machine. By 1938, there were more than 1,538 compulsory wartime cartels operating under direct government supervision, effectively cartelizing the entire economy, and many of Japan's business leaders and bureaucrats "came to appreciate this way of doing business."[84]

The concentrated power of Japanese industry was an early target of the Allied Occupation Command, as it sought to transplant American institutions and social policies to Japan. Take the Antimonopoly Law, enacted in 1947, which had much in common with the Sherman Act. Its first aim was to undercut the zaibatsu, which were seen as obstacles to competition and liberal democracy alike. However, this policy was relaxed almost as soon as Allied Occupation Command returned authority to Japanese officials, and it did not take long for three of the leading zaibatsu—Mitsui, Mitsubishi and Sumitomo—to restructure themselves as keiretsu. They were soon joined by three new keiretsu conglomerates—Fuji, Dai-ichi, and Sanwa—and by the mid-1960s, the six controlled 30 percent of corporate Japan.[85] Ties among the keiretsu firms may have been looser than those of Korea's family-run chaebol, but they were still linked by cross-ownership, personnel, and knowledge exchange. These arrangements hindered radical innovation, as the keiretsu used their power to erect barriers to prevent new companies from entering lucrative markets with better products. They were nevertheless a good fit for the age of mass production, as they provided Japan's corporations with the ability to coordinate across a range of industries.[86]

Miracle on the Han

Japan's East Asian neighbours took similar paths to riches. The influence of Bismarck's industrial state, which in many ways provided a blueprint for the Meiji Restoration, also left its mark on Japan's colonies, Korea and Taiwan, and even China, which began their modernization journeys later. These countries, like Japan, required foreign companies to share critical technologies in exchange for access to domestic markets. Notably, from the 1950s to the 1970s, Korea, Taiwan, and Singapore all experienced remarkable success in the inward transfer of technology, a feat that eluded many other developing nations, such as India.[87] While each East Asian miracle had its distinct nuances, they each shared access to American technology and had the bureaucratic capacity to harness it effectively.[88]

In the case of Korea, the Armistice Agreement in July 1953, which brought an end to the hostilities of the Korean War, served as an important turning point. As Korean soldiers integrated into American Army units through the "buddy system," closer ties were forged, which resulted in increased technology transfer. Subsequent U.S. aid development programs also surely helped sustain the Korean economy throughout the 1950s. But unlike in Japan, there was no "little Detroit." And Korea, with a per capita income of approximately $1,200 at the time, remained one of the poorest countries in the world. Nevertheless, the two countries' journeys into the future still had much in common. As the late Alice Amsden has argued, the state bureaucracy, large conglomerates, and competent salaried managers were the drivers of Korean catch-up.[89] In this sense, it can justly be regarded as a "second Japan," which is hardly coincidental.[90]

Although dynastic Korea had a long tradition of recruiting the Yangban aristocracy to the bureaucracy via an examination system, thereby embedding landed power into the state apparatus, the monarchy remained highly personalistic and patrimonial.[91] Centralizing efforts truly began in the 1870s, when the 1,000-year-old Yi dynasty was disrupted by Japanese gunboat diplomacy, much like the Tokugawa regime had been by Perry's Black ships only two decades earlier. The subsequent Japan–Korea Treaty of 1876 was another example of an "unequal treaty," and it also laid some of the foundations for its later development. Ito Hirubumi, who was tasked with running the Korean protectorate in the early 1900s and was the architect of many key reforms, had also been (as previously discussed) a key figure in the Meiji Restoration. He had traveled extensively in Europe and became fascinated by the Prussian bureaucratic model. So it is not surprising, as Japanologist Mark Peattie has noted, that many of the policies Japan pursued in Korea were "based on the Meiji experience in domestic reform."[92] Although there were some 10,000 officials in the Japanese-Korean government in 1910, this figure reached over 87,500 by 1937, and many of these bureaucrats were Koreans who had been trained by the Japanese.[93] Successive land surveys in this period, leveraging centralizing technologies like soil mapping to grade land according to ownership and productivity, served to bolster taxable revenues while reducing the autonomy of the landed elites, who were also pensioned off from the bureaucracy they had dominated under Yi rule.[94]

When Japan finally retreated from the peninsula in 1945, after decades of colonial occupation, war soon broke out between the Soviet-overseen north and the U.S.-backed south. In the years that followed, North Korea's rapid militarization, fused with a decisive shift in U.S. foreign policy, made growth the key priority in the eyes of the people. Yet rather than using American support to build up Korea's technology base, the corrupt Syngman Rhee government used the funds it received to pay off its cronies and buy support.[95] This sparked a revolution from above as well as from below. But while the so-called April Revolution forced out the Rhee government through social mobilization and popular protest, the outcome was one of consolidated autocracy, as General Park Chung Hee swept into power through a *coup d'état* in 1961. In any event, as Princeton's Atul Kohli has noted, his subsequent efforts were aided by the fact that the basic structures of the Japanese colonial state bureaucracy survived the Rhee government. Many Koreans who had passed the Japanese civil service exam were available and hired into the post-colonial bureaucracy. Yet in addition to this inheritance, Park himself did much to bolster the capacity of the state. During the first ten years of his rule, the bureaucracy nearly doubled in size, growing from 240,000 in 1960 to almost 425,000 in 1970.[96]

To drive the economy, Park believed that state power was needed to guide big business, monitor the population, and repress labour. Having served as a lieutenant in the Japanese colonial military, when it oversaw the massive drive to industrialize Korea and Chinese Manchuria in the 1930s, he was inspired by what he had seen and learned. When in power, he regularly compared his own ambitions to those of Meiji Japan. He was also an ardent student of German development and an amateur historian of rising powers. Less than a year after taking office, he published his own book, *Our Nation's Path: Ideology for Social Reconstruction*, in which he outlined a road map for Korean development that would be state-guided but managed by the private sector. In his own words: "One of the essential characteristics of a modern economy is its strong tendency towards centralization. Mammoth enterprise—considered indispensable, at the moment, to our country—plays not only a decisive role in the economic development and elevation of living standards, but further, brings about changes in the structure of society and the economy."[97] The following year, Park published the modesty titled, *The Country, the Revolution and I*. Containing chapters on "The Miracle on the Rhine" and "Various Forms of Revolution," the book discussed the developmental experience of historical revolutions, and cast his own coup, which he continued to call a revolution, in similar light. In a reference to the river that runs through the capital of Seoul, he promised his compatriots a "miracle on the Han."[98]

To deliver on the promised miracle, Park first sought to bring the cronies of the Rhee government under his control. Leading *chaebol* owners were put under house arrest, and their release required them to agree to participate in Park's first Five-Year Economic Development Plan, as well as to accept his concept of "guided capitalism." The power of the government was also bolstered through Weberian state reform, which ensured that bureaucrats would be recruited through a highly competitive examination system, symbolizing the beginnings of an autocratic yet meritocratic order.[99] Just six months after the coup, the initially sceptical U.S. Ambassador Samuel D. Berger was so impressed that he called Park's reform efforts a "genuine revolution from the top."[100] Park also created Korea's own "pilot agency"—the Economics Planning Board (EPB)—set up as a superministry to coordinate between industries and branches of government, much like Japan's MITI. The EPB, in turn, established the Korean Development Institute, which was managed by a cadre of professional economists holding advanced degrees from leading universities around the world and insulated from public pressure.[101]

Having created the foundations for catch-up growth at home, Park sought to normalize diplomatic relations with Japan and strengthen ties with the United States, dispatching troops to support the American war effort in South Vietnam to secure foreign technology and capital. But those ties were soon put under severe strain. When President Nixon announced the end of large-scale U.S. military presence in the Asia-Pacific region in 1969, it came as a shock to America's allies. It also caused South Koreans to conclude that they would have to fend off their Communist-backed neighbour themselves, just like their South Vietnamese counterparts. Faced with an aggressive North Korea and an unreliable American ally, the domestic political situation was becoming unsustainable. After coming close to electoral defeat in May 1971, Park dissolved the National Assembly and suspended the 1963 constitution. In its place, Park commissioned the *yushin* constitution, handing himself dictatorial powers for life. The new regime focused its efforts on developing heavy and chemical industries, with some success in pursuing foreign technology adoption.[102] Both heavy and chemical industries grew rapidly up until the Asian crises, as did GDP per capita, averaging 7 percent per year between 1963 and 1997.[103]

As in Japan, the Korean economy centered around large conglomerates (the chaebols), like Hyundai, Daewoo, and Samsung, with sales of the ten largest conglomerates accounting for an astonishing two-thirds of GNP by the end of the Park era. That said, while the chaebols gained in influence and power as they grew, they continued to be subject to strong bureaucratic control. By holding on to the levers of the banking system, Korean officials could use a variety of credit instruments to mobilize entrepreneurs for industrial state programs. Unlike the public–private partnerships once forged by the U.S. federal government, the Korean state still maintained control over the business community.[104]

This required bureaucratic capacity to monitor progress, and indeed the Ministry of Commerce and Industry began tracking the performance of the chaebol on a daily basis and holding them accountable to their export pledges.[105] In the words of the late Edward Mason and his collaborators, writing in 1980: "All Korean businessmen, including the most powerful, have been aware of the need to stay on good terms with the government to assure continuing access to credit and to avoid harassment from the tax officials."[106] When the auto giant Shinjin ran into trouble during the oil shocks of the 1970s, for example, the government withdrew support and transferred its holdings to Daewoo Motors. Asia Motors, the Taihan group, and the Korea Shipbuilding and Engineering Company experienced similar fates. Yet as Amsden concluded in her seminal account of Korean development in that era: "The sternest discipline imposed by the Korean government on virtually all large size firms—no matter how politically well connected—related to export targets. There was constant pressure from government bureaucrats on corporate leaders to sell more abroad—with obvious implications for efficiency. Pressure to meet ambitious export targets gave the Big Push into heavy industry its frenetic character."[107]

As the case of Korea illustrates, when geopolitical competition makes progress imperative and bureaucratic capacity is prevalent, autocratic systems may find it easier to override vested interests and spark a revolution from the above. During the Park years in particular, the Chairman of the Board of Korea, Inc., was the government, which allowed business to hold a few directorships.[108] Unlike in Latin America, where the state catered to private interests, East Asian corporations had to dance to the tune of the state.[109] However, after Park's assassination in 1979, South Korea experienced a turbulent transition to democracy, marked by military coups, the Gwangju Uprising, and widespread protests, culminating in the June Democracy Movement of 1987. These events led to constitutional reforms and the country's first direct presidential election in sixteen years, but politics also suddenly came to depend on big business for funding in Korea. To stave off cronyism, and safeguard continued progress, a considerable strengthening of antitrust legislation would be required (see chapter 11).

British Exceptionalism

In contrast to the miracles of Continental Europe and East Asia, the places that fell short during the Golden Age were typically those that were either too isolated from the global technological developments or lacked the capability to leverage them. In Ireland, for example, the reluctance of successive governments to invest in roads and communications technology meant that by the 1950s, the country only had fifty telephones per thousand citizens, compared to 150 in Britain and more than 400 in America. The lack of basic infrastructure, in turn, made economies of scale harder to achieve in a country where mass production was already hindered by its small market size. And to make matters worse, the Fianna Fáil government introduced the Control of Manufactures Act of 1932 and 1934, which restricted access to foreign technology.[110] If equipment was imported, it was imported from Britain, which was no longer the technology leader. In fact, among the major economies, Britain stood as the prime underperformer of the Golden Age.

Of course, the fact that many European economies outperformed Britain is unsurprising: they began the era with lower per capita GDP and a greater backlog of technologies from which they could benefit. However, by 1979, both West Germany and France had not merely caught up to Britain, they had surpassed it (figure 8.2).[111]

In some ways, Britain was a victim of its early industrialization. It was bequeathed a decentralized system of industrial relations, which later hampered the introduction of American mass production technologies. On the employer side, post–World War II Britain had roughly 1,900 associations, the bulk of which were local or sector-specific. Only a handful were national or aimed to represent broader economic interests.[112] On the labour side, there were at least 700 unions, of which most were not affiliated with the Trades Union Congress (TUC), which had limited control over its affiliates anyway.[113] The result of this system, as illustrated by Chancellor Macmillan's failed attempt to coordinate economy-wide wage settlements in 1957, was chaos and even outright resistance both to new technologies and the increasingly rapid pace of work.[114] Even after a triumphant Winston Churchill made a comeback as prime minister, the government caved to the demands of the unions, fearful of social and political unrest: "Seeking to avoid strikes ... the government became an engine of concession rather than change."[115]

Management, meanwhile, faced few incentives to push for progress. Pressure to perform was not high on the agenda, especially in public

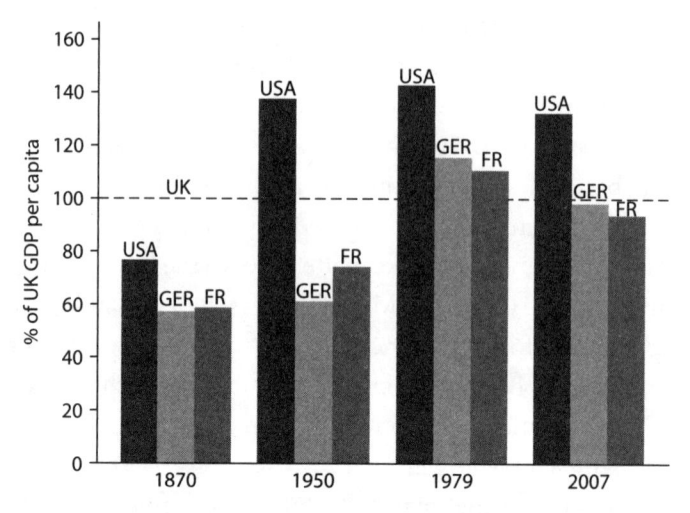

FIGURE 8.2. Percentage of UK GDP per capita by country, 1870–2007
Source: Crafts, "British Relative Economic Decline Revisited," 17–29, Table 1.

companies. The wave of nationalization under the Attlee government had been profound: railroads, coal, gas, electricity, iron, steel, and even the travel agent, Thomas Cook, became state-owned, while the predecessor of British Airways had already been nationalized during the war. Overall, nationalized industry accounted for almost one-fifth of the British economy, and productivity in those sectors was worse than disappointing. Unable to privatize national champions, which would have prompted vehement resistance from the trade union movement, the government resorted to boost investment through a variety of subsidies, which peaked at 10 percent of fixed investment in the 1970s. These efforts, however, were spectacularly unsuccessful.[116] To paraphrase two leading historians of the period, instead of governments picking winners, losers like Rolls Royce, British Leyland, and Alfred Herbert were picking Ministers.[117] By 1974, the government had spent £1.5 billion on aviation alone for a return of £0.14 billion. Winners were selected based on dubious criteria, and financial support provided to failing companies at a level that greatly exceeded what any private investor would have deemed acceptable, British Leyland and DeLorean cars being two prominent examples. Besides automobiles, the long list of failures also included aviation, computers, and nuclear power.[118]

Like elsewhere in Europe, big government and big business in Britain were the hallmarks of the times, but throughout the postwar era, Britain failed to develop anything like the systematic planning of France. The railroad industry, for example, received much funding without any coherent plan. Nor did anything like the "ordo-liberalism" of Germany take root to expose inefficient companies to the discipline of the market. And compared to Italy and Spain, Britain was closer to the frontier, making state-led planning harder. By the mid-1930s, the share of output produced by the largest 100 manufacturing companies had risen to almost one-quarter, while almost one-third of manufacturing output was cartelized. Yet no strong bureaucratic state held firms accountable, nor did much competition come from abroad: cartelization was accompanied by a sharp increase in tariffs, which would remain high up until the 1960s.[119]

The Monopolies and Restrictive Practices Commission (1948), the Restrictive Practices Act (1956), and the Monopolies and Mergers Commission (1965) also failed to revive competition domestically. Enforcement was feeble, few mergers were prevented, and no significant penalties were imposed on attempts to stifle competition.[120] When economic historians Stephen Broadberry and Nicholas Crafts studied the agreements registered in compliance with the 1956 Act, they found that only 27 percent of manufacturing was free of price-fixing, while 36 percent was cartelized. They further discovered a negative correlation between cartelization and productivity performance.[121] Even England's once eminent shipbuilding industry, a symbol of the British Empire, trailed behind its overseas rivals. While British shipyards still relied on skilled craftsmen and flexible practices, competitors in Sweden, Germany, and America capitalized on the latest welding and fabrication technologies and embraced larger-scale mass-production methods.[122] These problems were further amplified by a British wave of protectionism at a time when markets opened up on the Continent. Much of Europe integrated under the EEC, but Britain remained on the sidelines until 1973, leaving its companies sheltered from foreign competition and limiting its market size.[123]

Predictably, without the disciplining force of the market or the bureaucratic capacity of the state to check vested interests, the industrial policies of the postwar era in Britain were counterproductive. As noted earlier, in East Asia, where bureaucracy played a pivotal role in industrial development, exposure to foreign competition proved vital. "In Japan, Korea, Taiwan and China," Joe Studwell astutely points out, "the state did not so much pick winners as weed out losers."[124] Forced to export, firms had to pass the global market test for continued government support. Meanwhile, behind the Iron Curtain, where countries lagged significantly behind Britain, sticks and bureaucratic planning devoid of market competition took growth some way. Yet, the Soviet Union was soon undone by the looming Computer Revolution.

9

Growth with Gulags

> The most radical revolutionary will become a conservative on the day after the revolution.[1]
>
> —HANNAH ARENDT

LIKE WESTERN Europe and Japan, Eastern and central Europe also closed the gap to the United States during the postwar era. And this growth was, once again, largely the product of American innovation. There was, however, one obvious difference between these regions: much of Eastern and central Europe was brought within the Soviet sphere of influence—which up until the fall of the Berlin Wall in 1989 comprised Albania, Bulgaria, Czechoslovakia, East Germany, Hungary, Poland, Romania, and Yugoslavia. Because these countries largely adopted the planning system of the USSR, to understand their rapid growth during this period, we must examine the origins and development of the Soviet system.

While the Soviet economy was born in the Great War, its roots can be traced much further back. Imperial Russia was unquestionably more centralized and authoritarian than other monarchies in Europe. Moreover, as discussed in chapter 5, in the late nineteenth century, under the influence of the economic theories of Friedrich List, Russia's Finance Minister and first Prime Minister Sergei Witte had already adopted a model of state-led industrialization that emphasised the development of heavy industry. Indeed, on the eve of archduke Franz Ferdinand's assassination, Russia boasted one of the largest railroad networks in the world; and according to conventional wisdom, Germany rushed to war in 1914 because Russia was industrializing so rapidly that Germany feared its window of opportunity was closing.[2]

Nevertheless, Tsarist Russia was far from being fully modernized. As historian Peter Gatrell observes, Russia at this time "resembled Germany or Britain in the preceding generation."[3] Tsarist growth was driven by more people and factories rather than by domestic technological advances.[4] But unlike the Habsburg and Ottoman Empires, which would not survive the war, the Russian Empire reemerged, albeit in a different shape. Once the Treaty of Brest-Litovsk was signed in March 1918, Lenin turned his attention not only to a raging civil war but also to Russian modernization. His signature project was the GOELRO plan for electrification, which aimed to spur the construction of power plants and transmission lines to promote the use of electricity in production. With Lenin's backing, Soviet Russia embarked on many other modernization projects, such as a pioneering programme to develop diesel locomotives.[5] His motives and those of Witte were not dissimilar, but as Lenin saw it, the war had made the need to advance Russian technology ever more urgent: "The war taught us much, not only that people suffered, but especially the fact that those who have the best technology, organization, discipline and the best machines emerge on top; it is this the war has taught us, and it is a good thing it has taught us. It is essential to learn that without machines, without discipline, it is impossible to live in modern society. It is necessary to master the highest technology or be crushed."[6]

In many ways, as Polish economist Oskar Lange famously remarked, the Soviet economy was not merely an embodiment of the ideas of Marx and Engels, but a permanent war economy.[7] Above all, it was designed to direct scarce resources toward national priorities by suppressing private desires in favour of patriotic pursuits, as underlined by the two models of economic organisation the Bolsheviks widely admired. One was the German war economy of Walther Rathenau and Erich Ludendorff, with its capacity for mass mobilization through rationing and price fixing. The other was the fusion between Henry

Ford's mass production methods and Frederick Winslow Taylor's emphasis on standardization and hierarchical management. Together, these two models provided key principles upon which the Soviet economy was built.[8]

While Taylorism had been strongly condemned by prominent Marxists, including Antonio Gramsci, for subordinating workers to management, Lenin was a pragmatist: he put Russian modernization ahead of workers interests, at least temporarily. To introduce Taylorism and drive efficiency from the top, he had to crush opposition from Russian trade unions as well as curb workers' power on factory committees. He also had to secure the cooperation of Russian engineers, whom he justified paying salaries five or six times higher than Communist workmen on these grounds: "We must . . . without awaiting help from other countries, immediately increase the forces of production. To do this without bourgeoisie specialists would be impossible," he declared.[9]

Purges and Progress

Yet despite efforts to incorporate the intelligentsia and harness the ingenuity of domestic inventors, Soviet innovation left much to be desired. In his widely cited survey of Soviet technology, Anthony Sutton pointed to only two examples of native Soviet discoveries before World War II: synthetic rubber and an improved boiler for steam power plants.[10] This is probably an exaggeration, but there can be no doubt that the Bolsheviks mostly relied on foreign technologies, which they acquired through several channels.

Occasionally, especially during the late 1920s and early 1930s, friendly foreign inventors wrote to the Red Army and offered to help promote new inventions in the Soviet Union. For instance, the German engineer Rolf Engel, a member of the Association for Space Travel (*Verein für Raumschiffahrt*) and Communist Party sympathiser, proposed bringing a group of German engineers to collaborate with Soviet rocketeers. More common, however, was for domestic inventors to develop ideas they read about in the foreign press. The director of the Gas Dynamics Lab (GDL) in Leningrad reported directly to the Red Army on rocketry developments in the United States and Germany, which were described in great detail by publicly available sources. And when press information was hard to come by, foreign study trips were always an option. In 1936, for instance, the Reactive Scientific Research Institute (RNII) sent its engineers on three separate tours of Western Europe and America.[11] Such easy access made industrial espionage unnecessary, which perhaps explains why such episodes were seemingly rare in the 1930s. And Stalin's 1939 nonaggression pact with Hitler, which gave the Soviets access to the latest German technology in return for neutrality, reduced this need even further.

Yet domestic technological efforts also played a modest role in the country's development. Some inventors were clearly compelled to improve the state of Soviet technology, even in the absence of market incentives. Rather than being driven by passion for the communist cause, however, these innovators pursued their own dreams and sought recognition for their achievements. Thus, when Soviet innovation happened, it most often did so in a decentralized manner. Mark Harrison's fascinating study of Soviet aviation jet propulsion provides a case in point.[12] It shows that, like in capitalist economies, new ideas bubbled up rather than came raining down from above. At times, these ideas came from professional Soviet designers. In other cases, they were brought in by foreign talent or developed by backyard inventors. But no "all-seeing and all-knowing planners" existed to identify and fulfill the technological needs of the nation. As commissar for the aircraft industry, Aleksey Shakhurin, explained to deputy prime minister Nikolai Voznesensky a few months before the German invasion in 1941: "Work on the creation of jet propulsion engines at home in the USSR ... began on the initiative of a few engineers taking the form of inventors' proposals."[13]

The key obstacle to Soviet innovation was not its pool of talent but a system that held back inventors who needed to seek permission for everything.[14] Approval and funding required support from officials, and so inventors needed to build cozy relationships with government bureaucrats to stay afloat, while outsiders found themselves isolated and underfunded. Civilian enthusiasts could write to the Red Army with ideas and proposals, but very few were taken up. And if a proposal was turned down by the defense ministry, only a handful of alternative sources of funding remained. In aviation, for example, inventors could seek support from the Red Army air force, the civil aviation authority, or the Academy of Sciences, but thereafter they quickly ran out of options. And in a system based on privilege, the bulk of funding was captured by a few networked individuals: just four aircraft designers took home 60 percent of funding activity.[15] Moreover, as Harrison writes, outsiders had to overcome a strong status quo bias for established technology:

> To create a demand for new designs they had to build coalitions with soldiers or industrialists to overcome interests vested in markets for products that already existed. In particular, they had to overcome the preference of industry for the undisturbed mass production of weapons in long serial runs, which was often at odds with radical product innovation and the risks and requirements of continual upheaval in production. For example, the aircraft designer P.O. Sukhoi is said to have won success in having his designs adopted only after he took on a partner, E.A. Ivanov, who had the political and bureaucratic skills to push his product through the military and party-state apparatus.[16]

All of this made Soviet invention enormously expensive, as building and nurturing the necessary political connections consumed much time.

Worse yet, once project funds were obtained and the outsider became an insider, they were often able to sustain the flow of resources regardless of the promise of the project. Soviet authorities found it challenging to identify and eliminate unproductive initiatives. And when issues arose, inventors frequently pointed fingers, blaming failure on either the lack of funding or the incompetence of those involved in execution. As one steam-turbine designer complained to the notorious Marshal Mikhail Tukhachevskii, known as the Red Napoleon for his inventive military tactics, the Leningrad Kirov factory was gripped by conservatism and incapable of driving progress. With funding rationed and entry controlled, there was a real danger that bad projects would end up driving out the good ones.

To prevent the pursuit of self-serving interests, the state mounted periodic inquisitions, during which Stalin and his security chiefs—Nikolai

Yezhov and Lavrentiy Beria—sought to "peer into the souls" of their scientists and engineers.[17] But even those who believed they were following the wishes of the Party could find themselves in hot water if the states preferences changed during the course of exploring different technological options. Legendary rocket engineer Sergei Korolev, for example, became a traitor in 1937 only because the Party's agenda had changed; he became a hero again two decades later for the same reason. Such risks, by making it even more important for inventors to ensure that their method prevailed, further elevated the importance of personal relationships and led to bitter fights between inventors and engineers. For instance, Andrey Kostikov, who was unduly favoured by Stalin, took the public credit for the Katiusha rocket launcher, while its true inventor, Georgy Langemak, was arrested by the NKVD and executed on allegations from no other than Kostikov himself.[18]

Political infighting and the concentration of power at the top also favoured consolidation in innovation. Although there is an economic case for eliminating duplication as a technology matures, in the USSR, politics always trumped economics. Larger units and fewer lines of communication served to streamline the command system. For smaller branches, however, this meant a constant danger of being swept up by rival behemoths. In 1938, for example, the commissariat of the defense industry proposed that all work on aviation steam turbines should be centralized in the Central Boiler and Turbine Institute (TsKTI) in Leningrad. While the director of the Special-Purpose Design Bureau (SKB) fiercely resisted this move, which amounted to a hostile takeover of his unit, he predictably lost the battle. Nevertheless, he was fortunate not to be forced out like many of his comrades, who were arrested by the NKVD in the purges of 1936 to 1938, when some were shot and others sent to labour camps.[19]

These purges—which Robert Conquest aptly called the "Great Terror"—were part of Stalin's drive to cement his power and remove any remaining influence of Leon Trotsky, who had been Stalin's primary challenger for the Party leadership after the passing of Lenin. By this time, of course, Stalin was already firmly in power, and Trotsky was living in Mexico, though his polemical criticisms of Stalin—calling him "the gravedigger of the revolution" and "the mediocrity of the Party"— continued to undermine his authority. By all accounts, Stalin's purges had a "devastating effect," not just on Trotsky loyalists but on the scientific community and civil society more broadly. To make matters worse, much of Soviet scientific and technical life fell under the control of Party-backed pseudoscientists, like the plant biologist Trofim Lysenko, who became director of the Institute of Genetics within the USSR's Academy of Sciences and rejected Mendelian genetics in favour of his own ideas, later dubbed *Lysenkoism*.[20] Scientists who refused to renounce genetics were not only dismissed, but hundreds were imprisoned, and several were sentenced to death as enemies of the state.[21] Under such conditions, scientists were understandably inclined to be cautious and conformist rather than innovative and daring.

Thus, while significant resources, both human and financial, were dedicated to advancing Soviet science and technology, the results rarely lived up to the investment. Soviet innovation made some strides during the years of relative freedom under the New Economic Policy (NEP) in the 1920s, but this period of progress was short-lived.[22] By the late 1930s, as centralized state planning replaced the mixed economy under the NEP, progress occurred in piecemeal fashion in a few high-priority sectors, like aviation, where Soviet engineers managed to produce airframes comparable with foreign designs. Yet it was a far cry from the broad-based dynamism the United States experienced in the 1930s, despite the Great Depression. The number of allegedly new technologies registered with the Committee on Inventions, and later the Gosplan, rose from 5,500 in 1929 to 7,000 in 1934, but then fell to a total of 3,900 between 1936 and 1939, when the Great Terror raged.[23] Furthermore, very few of these inventions had any real value: a mere 2 to 4 percent ended up being used in production.[24]

Feeding the Bear

The advancement of the Soviet Union, instead, depended on America. As Sergo Ordzhonikidze, a Georgian top Bolshevik tasked with leading an overhaul of the Soviet R&D effort in 1928, put it: "If indeed we hope to catch up with and surpass American industry, we must absorb those technical achievements which exist in America."[25] Lenin, Stalin, and other Party members correctly saw the United States as the emerging global powerhouse; thus, they equated American technology with modern technology, and Americanisation with modernisation. The logic that followed was straightforward: to compete with the United States, the USSR first had to emulate her, at least in science and technology.[26]

The Soviets, however, desperately needed new talent to undertake this endeavour. During three years of revolution and six years of a bloody civil war, hundreds of thousands of engineers, technicians, and scientists had fled abroad. This deficit was overcome, in part, by a flood of Americans who came in the 1920s. Many of them were committed Communists and Socialists who emigrated to what they regarded as the land of the future, despite efforts by officials in Moscow to discourage immigration through radio broadcasts warning of the harsh conditions. Some, especially after the Great Depression of 1929, traveled to the USSR in search of work and a better life. Still others ventured to the Soviet Union to provide technical assistance under the American Relief Administration of 1921, led by future president Herbert Hoover.

One of the arguably most important figures in the history of Russian agriculture was Harold M. Ware, a committed American Marxist and graduate from the Agricultural College of Pennsylvania. When Lenin appealed for a report on the state of U.S. agriculture to the American Communist Party in 1920, Ware set out to tour American farms, from the South to the Midwest, to the Northwest. When he returned after six months, his report was sent directly to Lenin. Afterward, Ware became active in the Society of Friends of Russia, where he also met Lincoln Steffens, who was the president of a Russian famine-relief group at the time. He managed to persuade Steffens that what Russia needed was mechanized agriculture and to use the funds of his organization to buy tractors and teach Russian peasants how to operate the machines. When they arrived in Russia in 1922, there were fewer than 1,500 tractors in the entire country, many of which were old or unrepairable. They first set out to Perm, in the Urals, where the hunger was particularly acute, and from 1925 to 1932, Ware advised the Soviet government while working as a dollar-a-year man for the Department of Agriculture in Washington, DC (where he later organized a Communist cell during the New Deal era).[27]

Another key figure was William Haywood—also known as Big Bill. To escape a twenty-year prison sentence for obstructing the American war effort, he took refuge in Russia in 1921, where he became the leader of the famous Colony of Kuzbas, set up in Siberia as an experiment to attract American engineers during the New Economic Policy period.[28] Most of the Americans who arrived were members of the Industrial Workers of the World—a radical group committed to revolution and the expropriation of industry—of which Haywood was a founding member. With Lenin's backing, he commissioned Herbert Culvert, a former plant foreman at Ford in Detroit, to return to the United States to recruit engineers and workers. However, Siberian conditions were so harsh that many committed ideologues became disillusioned. Thomas Doyle from Baton Rouge, Louisiana, returned home in 1923, claiming that the colony "was an unfit place for human habitation."[29] To attract additional skilled workers to the northern Urals, new arrivals were allowed to keep 50 percent of output above and beyond their targets.

Something similar happened in the Soviet auto industry, where hundreds of American workers, many of them Communists, arrived in Moscow in 1921, to take over the Moscow Automobile Society (AMO) car plant, which had been set up by the industrialist Pavel Ryabushinsky in 1916 to produce vehicles for the army of Tsar Nicholas II. The plan faced some opposition in Moscow, but Lenin personally endorsed it, arguing that it would help the country gain the technological know-how it so urgently needed. Arthur Adams, a Russian-American who had previously worked for the Ford Motor Company in Detroit, became director of the new cooperative, and by 1923 they were able to produce small trucks for the Red Army. This tiny operation, which later became the Stalin Automobile Works, was an escalator for Soviet progress, as it introduced the Soviets to the latest mass production techniques, including the assembly line.

During this period, the White House itself offered the Soviets little direct support, because the Coolidge administration refused to extend diplomatic relations to the Bolshevik government. However, Washington's decision not to impose export restrictions surely helped the Soviet modernization effort. In 1929, the Amtorg Trading Corporation, founded by Russians in New York City, licensed several of General Electric's patents to the Soviets. The same year, the Ford Motor Company signed an agreement with the USSR to produce automobiles and trucks on the Volga River. Working with Albert Kahn Associates—the industrial architects bureau that had just built Ford's enormous River Rouge plant—the Soviet government built a virtual copy of the plant in Nizhny Novgorod, the GAZ factory, just as another U.S. manufacturer, A. J. Brandt Co., helped expand the AMO factory. "These two giant factories," one study would find, "together with three Khan-designed tractors factories ... provided the heart of the Soviet motor industry." By making these industries the highest priority, the Soviets were able to manufacture 182,400 lorries and 93,400 tractors in 1938 alone, significantly outpacing British production figures of 113,946 lorries and 10,679 tractors, as well as German totals of 87,661 lorries and 12,846 tractors.[30]

Even the hallmark for Stalinist industrialization, the industrial city Magnitogorsk on the slopes of the Ural Mountains, was modelled on the most advanced steel-producing cities at the time: Gary, Indiana, and Pittsburgh, Pennsylvania. But whereas American steel hubs rose from market dynamics, Magnitogorsk was part of Stalin's Five-Year Plans, whose considerations were not just economic.[31] The colossal factories in Stalingrad, Kharkov, and Chelyabinsk, for instance, were built not only to benefit from economies of scale but also for quick transition to tank manufacturing. And the Soviet model, designed for mobilization rather than for innovation, was on the brink of its first significant test.[32]

Wartime Mobilization

On June 22, 1941, German forces launched their surprise attack on Russia, known as "Operation Barbarossa." The most devastating land war in history had begun, and the USSR immediately witnessed the technological and operational superiority of the German forces. With only 3,600 German tanks against an estimated 15,000 Soviet ones, "the Panzer armies cut swathe through the Soviet defenses, virtually destroyed the Soviet tank and air arm, and brought the Soviet Union almost to the point of collapse."[33] By mid-autumn Kiev was taken, Leningrad besieged, and Moscow directly endangered. Yet, in the end, neither Leningrad nor Moscow fell, and it was on the Eastern front that Nazi Germany would ultimately suffer its largest casualties.

Russian forces denied Hitler the lightning victory on which Nazi hopes were pinned, and having come terrifyingly near complete destruction, the Red Army started to build a new modern force almost from scratch. By the end of 1942, the Soviet tank arsenal was already twice as large as Germany's; by the fall of 1943, it was triple the size of the German tank arsenal.[34] These mechanized forces were used with real success, first at Stalingrad in the winter of 1942–1943, and then in the battle at Kursk in the summer of 1943. By that time, the Soviet air force—which now consisted of a new generation of advanced aircraft, like the notorious Sturmovik Il-2 bomber—was also unrecognizable from the one defeated in 1941. The effectiveness of these new forces, however, hinged on seamless coordination and communication. Through the Lend-Lease agreements, the United States provided over 956,000 miles of telephone cable, 35,000 radio stations, and 380,000 field telephones, which became the core of the Soviet communication infrastructure. The United States also delivered 500,000 vehicles, including 77,900 jeeps, 151,000 light trucks, and more than 200,000 Studebaker army trucks.[35]

Nevertheless, in several areas, Soviet mass production led the way in its fight. Throughout the war effort, only one in six combat aircrafts and one in eight armoured motorized fighting vehicles were supplied by the West.[36] Although American motorized vehicles played a part in the push from Stalingrad to Berlin during 1943–1945, the pivotal firepower that halted German advances during 1941–1942 was made in the USSR, under the most daunting circumstances. When the Nazis invaded, the Soviets had to evacuate hundreds of factories under the noses of approaching German forces. With enemy armies only some 150 miles away from Moscow, plants were dismantled piece by piece and taken by train to Siberia. Between July and December 1941, more than 1,500 enterprises were moved to the Urals, Kazakhstan, and the Volga region.

Workers, engineers, and plant managers escaped German forces for the east, where they wrestled with the reassembly of factories in temperatures sometimes reaching −40°C. In his memoirs, the aircraft engineer Alexander Yakovlev provides a vivid first-hand account of the Soviet system in action. The Yak plant, where he had worked, was destined for western Siberia. On arrival, crude wooden barracks were set up for industrial refugees who worked around the clock to get local supplies of electricity, fuel, and water up and running for production.[37]

This remarkable relocation highlights the strength of the command economy: unlike other systems, the Soviet state did not have to collaborate with capitalists or make compromises with labour. Rather, the economy operated on directives, and the growing numbers in the Gulag camps were swiftly mobilized to contribute to the war effort behind barbed wire. As historian Stephan Link writes, "The Soviet command economy was more capable than its German counterpart of enforcing the conditions under which mass production would flourish"—a point also acknowledged by Albert Speer, Germany's Minister of Armaments and War Production. "There is one thing that the Bolsheviks have over us," he noted. "They ruthlessly clamp down and punish even the most minimal infractions against the state interest."[38] During the Nazi era, the German state was the principle and industry the agent, but, as always, industry had a closer eye on its own interests. In 1939, for example, the German corporation IG Farben turned down a request from the Economics Ministry to increase its rayon production for use in tires. And in 1943, amid war, an analysis conducted for the armaments ministry revealed that steel companies continued to produce a broad array of goods intended for civilian use.[39]

In addition, Germany prioritized quality and variety over sheer volume and simplicity. Instead of building tanks that could easily be repaired and mass produced, Hitler demanded cutting-edge technology. The result was the *Tiger* and the *Panther*, which were complex, heavy, and hard to maneuver. To make matters worse, Germany used 2,000 different types of vehicles for Operation Barbarossa, for which the Army Group Centre had to carry over a million spare parts. By contrast, the USSR strategically opted for a limited variety of weaponry, utilizing just two

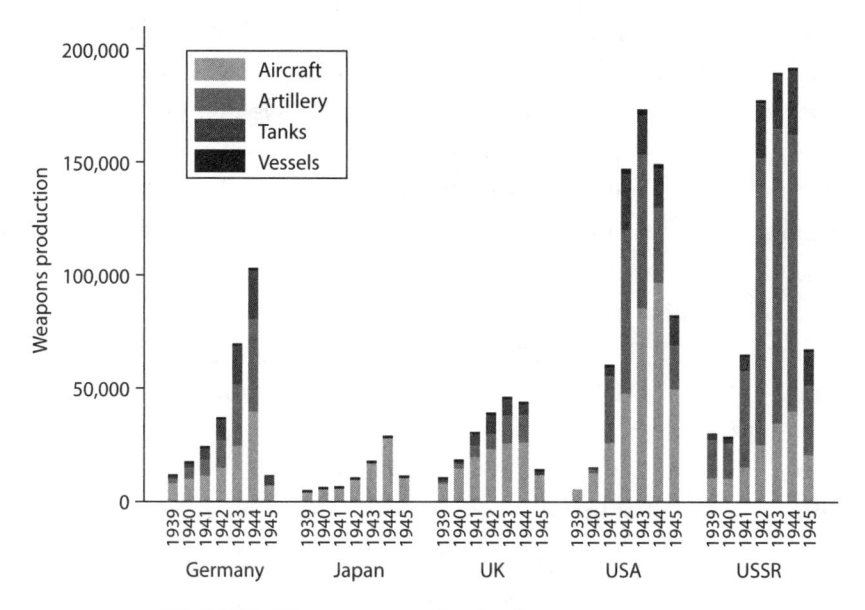

FIGURE 9.1. World War II weapons production by country
Source: Overy, *Why the Allies Won*, 407–408, Figure.

types of tanks during the war. This streamlined approach simplified repairs and maintenance for engineers on the front lines. It was such standardization that allowed the USSR to produce quantities that only a much richer America could match (figure 9.1).[40]

The Command Economy

Central planning, mass production, and mass mobilization were not only central to Soviet survival but also to its subsequent revival. In fact, the story of Soviet growth after the war is almost as remarkable as the story of the war itself. Having suffered 25 million premature deaths and only narrowly escaped total defeat, the Red Army in 1945 occupied Tallinn, Riga, Vilnius, Warsaw, Sofia, Budapest, Vienna, Prague, and Berlin. The massive destruction on the Eastern front meant that the scope for rapid growth was substantial. Between 1938 and 1946, losses of GDP were even larger than in the West, on the order of 50 percent in Yugoslavia and Poland, 40 percent in Hungary, and 25 percent in Czechoslovakia. But except for East Germany, GDP in these countries had returned to prewar levels already by 1950. Thus, like in Western Europe, mere recovery from wartime damage cannot explain the growth miracle after 1950.[41]

A key difference, of course, was that while the West relied mostly on privately run behemoths for the coordination of industry, in Eastern Europe industrial catch-up was completely tasked to the state. This was also the ambition of Tsarist Russia, which sought to control private enterprise and drive industrialization through the state, but the centralized Community Party—consisting of more than 600,000 members—had much greater capacity to run and control the economy. Moreover, by the mid-twentieth century state-led development had a much broader appeal, because the market economy had been widely discredited by the Great Depression, not to mention the rise of National Socialism, which many (incorrectly) believed was the result of big business and the vast concentration of economic power.[42] Throughout Central and Eastern Europe, the template for achieving self-sufficiency was the Soviet economy.[43]

The script for the central planning system went as follows. Most private enterprise was declared illegal, and ownership of all key industries was assumed by the state. Stock exchanges were closed, commercial banks were nationalized, agriculture was collectivized, and workers were prohibited from leaving their respective enterprises without permission. Production decisions were not based on market signals; rather, the plan was set out by the Communist Party, which held the monopoly on expressing the needs and preferences of the working class, including what should and should not be produced. In a cumbersome process that took many months to complete, the planning commission, overseen by the Council of Ministers, made preliminary estimates of how much of each product was required. These estimates were then passed down to the industrial ministries, who developed more detailed plans for their own divisions and assigned each enterprise under their command a corresponding target. These enterprises then reported back results, on which basis the planning office revised its projections.[44]

The resulting complexity was certainly a challenge. Planning documents could run many thousands of pages, and in the absence of a market economy, quantity ruled rather than price. Authorities therefore resorted to rules of thumb, setting quantities that favoured industry over agriculture and heavy industry over consumer goods. This served the war machine well, insofar as resources could be redirected swiftly without economic considerations. When war broke out on the Korean Peninsula, for example, Stalin could simply instruct leaders to boost their targets for heavy industry. But targets came at a price as quality was constantly sacrificed for quantity, and managers, who were rewarded for meeting those targets, were encouraged to hold back production in one year to avoid a higher output target the following year. Shifting managers around between enterprises may have mitigated this perverse incentive to some degree, but output quotas still provided no inducement to save rubles on expensive machines or raw materials. And any company director with good political connections could relax labour discipline to make himself popular with workers, who thus naturally preferred a well-connected party hack to a competent director.[45] In other words, János Kornai's famous soft-budget constraint—in which chronic loss-making enterprises are not allowed to fail—was an endogenous part of the system.[46]

To implement the plan, the Soviet system relied on threats rather than rewards. As a leading Hungarian planner put it in 1952, "Strict measures must be taken to make the plan effective. Those breaking it must receive not only disciplinary punishment but, in more serious cases . . . must be brought to trial."[47] And the outcomes of such trials were not, of course, hard to predict. By the year of Stalin's death in 1953, some 2.5 million people worked in labour camps called gulags, where they were forced into almost impossible endeavours, like the construction of the city of Norilsk in Siberia, which was built on permafrost. However, almost immediately after Stalin's death, some of the worst atrocities were scaled back, as MVD chief Lavrenty Beriia released 1.5 million prisoners, comprising 60 percent of the gulags' inmates. Between 1953 and 1957, the gulags across the country were emptied of prisoners. As it turned out, even repression and coercion had a price, because guarding detainees was expensive, and labour productivity among prisoners was low relative to free workers.[48] Moreover, punishing offenders required obtaining costly information, and managers, for the most part, struggled to tell whether workers were exerting full effort or not. In light of these challenges, the gulag, in its final years, went through a process of "conversion of slaves to serfs," as some camps began to pay prisoners for their labour.[49]

As a result, higher pay for increased effort emerged as the primary incentive mechanism, making piece rates the dominant form of compensation. And after Nikita Khrushchev's denunciation of Stalin at the Twentieth Congress of the Communist Party in 1956, similar reforms spread across Eastern Europe. Yet this simply meant that increases in output often were "rewarded" with reductions in piece rates. Occasionally, this led to open protests, as in Berlin in 1953 and Poznan in 1956. But for the most part, it simply led to an informal change of norms, in which workers would limit their effort. Without the stick, the old joke "we pretend to work, and they pretend to pay," soon became an apt description of Soviet industrial relations (see chapter 10).[50]

Moscow and Mao

The command economy faced other headwinds as well, as the Soviets were becoming more isolated. Although the lessons gleaned from early technology transfers were not forgotten, gaining access to new technologies became harder as the Cold War escalated. Guided by Kennan's strategy of containment, the United States imposed embargoes on the export of high-tech products, which the recipient countries of Marshall aid also were compelled to abide by. Moreover, since the prices set by the planners rarely corresponded with those prevailing in the rest of the world, the Soviet central planning system was largely incompatible with foreign trade. Consequently, Soviet trade with other planned economies dominated. The USSR imported machines and other equipment from the more advanced economies of the GDR, Czechoslovakia, Hungary, and Poland, and they exported engineering products to the relatively backward Bulgaria and Romania in exchange for agricultural goods. This new pattern of trade became an integral part of Moscow's ambition to integrate the Eastern bloc into the planned Soviet economy.[51]

Those ambitions soon also expanded to include what Moscow regarded as its new protégé: Beijing. When the Communist Party of China (CPC) swept into power on the mainland in 1949, they followed the Soviet template of nationalizing industry, though the planning impulse was already present. In some respects, the Chinese story resembles the German one, and these parallels are not entirely coincidental. Around the turn of the twentieth century, Chinese leaders remained sceptical of laissez-faire capitalism and sought to model itself on Germany, which better fit the country's bureaucratic legacy. General Li Hongzhang, renowned for suppressing the Taiping rebellion, viewed Alfred Krupp as the standard of success for Chinese steelmakers to match and held admiration for Otto von Bismarck, even keeping a photograph of the German statesman. Chiang Kai-shek, meanwhile, required his cadets at Whampoa military academy to take exams on how Bismarck unified the German Empire and often praised the educational values of Prussia, emphasizing patriotism, discipline, and order. Chiang even sent his son, Chiang Wei-kuo, to attend the Munich *Kriegsschule*, where he took part in the German Anschluss with Austria in 1938.[52]

Building on China's millennia-old bureaucratic tradition, Chiang established the National Resources Commission (NRC), which was tasked with strategic planning for China's growing civilian and defense industries. In 1936, he also made a deal with Hitler to trade Chinese minerals for German industrial technology—a cooperation that would be short-lived as Hitler chose the more militarily capable Japan as his ally against Stalin, despite protest and pressure from both German investors and Chinese lobbies. This rejection did not, however, thwart the expansion of the NRC. By 1944, its ranks swelled to 12,000 personnel, with an additional 160,000 workers employed in mining, manufacturing, and electricity generation. Some businesses were established as state-owned enterprises, whereas others were nationalized from the private sector. Remarkably, state firms controlled nearly 70 percent of the paid-up capital of registered businesses in China, with the NRC bureaucrats assuming managerial responsibilities for most of them and earning a reputation for competence and professionalism. After the

Chinese Civil War, many stayed on in their current posts and facilitated the transfer of control of state-run companies to the CPC.[53]

Under Chairman Mao, of course, state control went much further. The nationalization of industry, the collectivization of agriculture, the elimination of markets, the assignment of jobs to workers without choice, the imposition of resource quotas, and the centralized setting of wages by the CPC all became the new norm.[54] Like in the Soviet Union, which served as the command economy template, people depended on the Party for everything, including their livelihoods, their children's education, food, housing, and other necessities. Workers wanting to move, for example from Wuhan to Beijing, to take up new work had to apply for permission to move. It was usually denied, and as a result the circulation of knowledge and ideas was impeded. In the few cases that permission was granted, workers found it nearly impossible to find housing, as there was no real estate market. Unsurprisingly, highly desired goods, whether bicycles or washing machines, were also rationed. So were many necessities, including food and clothing, with people receiving monthly coupons that dictated limited quantities of meat, grain, and soap. In an economy that was geared toward heavy industry rather than the well-being of the people, all consumer goods were in short supply.[55]

Similar control was exerted over China's universities, which, before Mao rose to power, were broadly modelled on the Prussian system of higher education. Indeed, Cai Yuanpei, who became Minister of Education in the new Republic of China in 1912, had himself studied philosophy under the tutelage of Karl Lamprecht and Wilhelm Wundt at the University of Leipzig. Despite his background as a Qing bureaucrat who had passed the highest level (*jinshi*) of the imperial civil service examinations, Cai's firm belief was that universities should not function merely as extensions of government but should be endowed with institutional independence and act as centres for "education with a worldview" (*shijieguan jiaoyu*). Later in life, as president of Peking University, Cai brought on board Chen Duxiu and Li Dazhao, both of whom played a crucial role in the introduction of Marxism in China, as well as Hu Shi, China's foremost advocate of liberalism and a disciple of John Dewey at Columbia. In similar spirit, Luo Jialun, who later became the Kuomintang Minister of Education and had studied at the universities of Berlin, Paris, and London, took on the task of leading the National Central University—with its own iconic Brandenburg Gate and an auditorium modelled after that of the University of Berlin—where he recruited exceptional faculty from abroad, such as Luo Rong'an from MIT, to establish the university's mechanical engineering department.[56]

The Communist takeover, however, reversed these efforts, triggering a large exodus of talent, with many academics from the country's top universities leaving for Taiwan, Hong Kong, and the United States. Tsinghua University, once established as a preparatory school for students going to America, saw its foreign ties severed. And after the construction of its new campus, it soon looked more like Moscow State University than any American institution.[57] Throughout the country, decision-making within higher education became more centralized, with the presence of the Communist Party ensuring ideological adherence at every turn. Universities were now tasked with imparting both political and academic knowledge, while research tasks were delegated to elite academies, like the Chinese Academy of Sciences (CAS). Those who refused to align with the new program suffered the consequences. In Nanjing, teachers and professors "were hauled on to a stage, hung up and beaten." At Tsinghua University, Gao Chongxi, a renowned chemist, committed suicide. And in Shanghai, where a total of 237 tonnes of books were destroyed just in 1951, Li Pingxin of the East China Normal University, following vicious acts of denunciation, tried to chop off his own head with an axe and ultimately bled to death.[58]

Such repression was merely a prelude to the Cultural Revolution of the 1960s, when the admission of new students was entirely suspended, intellectuals faced persecution, and universities became hotspots of political contention, with different Communist Party factions wrestling for dominance. By 1970, when universities reopened, the traditional *gaokao* entrance examination had been supplanted by an admissions process prioritizing "mass recommendations" and political allegiance. It was only with Deng Xiaoping's ascent to power in the late 1970s that Chinese universities would regain their autonomy and thrive once more.[59]

The foundation of China's modernization, meanwhile, was anchored in a so-called walking-on-two-legs technology policy. This allowed small backward factories to exist alongside giants forged through the Soviet Big Push strategy, which China copied wholesale. From the 1950s to 1978, China's spending on science and technology was remarkable for one of the poorest countries in the world, peaking at 1.7 percent of GDP in 1964, the same year that the CPC detonated its first atomic bomb. Nevertheless, the country's technological development depended almost entirely on a steady flow of technology from the Soviets.[60] As China scholar Barry Naughton remarks, the very first Five-Year Plan (1953–1957), was drawn up "half in Moscow, half in Peking."[61]

The Sino-Soviet Treaty of Friendship, signed on February 14, 1950, which cemented the People's Republic of China (PRC) as a crucial strategic partner of the USSR, was a particularly significant milestone. While Stalin was a staunch Communist, he was also a pragmatist, and throughout the civil war between the Communists and the nationalists he remained neutral, instead prioritizing the withdrawal of American forces from China. This set the stage for a tense relationship with Mao, as Stalin demanded retention of all prior concessions from the nationalists, including territorial ones, echoing the unequal treaties of the nineteenth century. Nonetheless, for Mao, these compromises were acceptable in exchange for access to Soviet technological expertise.[62]

After the treaty was signed, Russian engineers and specialists began arriving in Beijing and Shanghai in droves. Many of them settled in the plush suburbs of Shanghai, replete with well-maintained parks, golf courses, and tennis courts, and Russia became the first and only foreign language taught in schools, where every detail was copied from the Soviet system. Meanwhile, the Soviet-Sino Friendship Association, with its 120,000 branches, distributed books, magazines, films, and radios to spread the communist message but also valuable technological knowhow. Indeed, what followed has been called the "largest coordinated international transfer of technology in the history of the world."[63] The famous 156 Projects, signed off between 1950 and 1957, covered nearly every heavy industry, from machinery to electricity. The USSR provided blueprints and technical specifications, along with some 6,000 Soviet advisers, while more than 10,000 Chinese students went to study in Russia.[64]

While these efforts were far from frictionless—when Soviet advisers first arrived at the Changchun First Automotive Works in 1955, for instance, their work was delayed by the lack of Chinese translators—they nevertheless yielded tangible results.[65] By the 1950s, the Soviet Union had established itself as a leading producer of blast furnaces, renowned for their excellent quality, and these furnaces soon found their way into Chinese industrial plants in Anshan, Wuhan, and Baotou, marking a significant leap in China's technological capabilities. Unsurprisingly, such advances did not go unnoticed by contemporaneous proponents of bureaucratic planning, including India's Prime Minister Nehru. During a tour of the Anshan steelworks, Nehru marvelled at what he saw, noting that while the technological know-how originated from the Soviet Union, the entire management of the production process was effectively conducted by the Chinese, which allowed them to learn on the job. The British and Americans, he remarked, would never have allowed "Indians to manage the most important mechanism of the enterprises."[66]

More generally, recent studies indicate that, without the extensive support from the 156 Projects, China's per capita growth between 1953 and 1978 might have been nearly 20 percent lower.[67] The effect of Soviet support can also be seen in its absence. While China experienced significant gains in productivity between 1952 and 1957, these advances slowly reversed over the next two decades, until Mao's passing.[68] This productivity slump coincided with the deterioration of Sino-Soviet relations, which were significantly damaged by Khrushchev's 1956 criticism of Stalin—who after all was the Mao of Russia—and reached their nadir in 1959, when Khrushchev's U.S. visit led Moscow to cease its technological aid to Beijing, leaving Mao with limited alternatives amid Western sanctions.[69]

By all accounts, the Soviet rapture had a "catastrophic effect" on Chinese equipment, as Beijing was left trying to reverse engineer technologies from abroad.[70] The country experienced occasional success in these endeavours: for instance, although China's nuclear program was abruptly disrupted when all Soviet assistance was withdrawn, it nonetheless managed to build the bomb with the blueprints at hand. However, for the most part—including in its attempts to ramp up half-finished Soviet-supplied car factories and build a domestic airline—the country failed spectacularly. Its institutions were geared toward absorbing Soviet technology rather than innovation, and when the tap was turned off, stagnation followed.[71]

Soviet Strides

The pivotal role Moscow played for China's fortunes underscores a wider truth: the Soviet Union's journey to the future was a mixed bag. While the nation grappled with the dire consequences of mass collectivization, widespread famines, and sweeping purges that left its populace wearied and traumatized, it still registered commendable labour productivity growth rates, thanks to the effective absorption of American mass production methods and its capacity to mobilize resources at scale. Between 1928 and 1973, productivity saw an average increase of 2 percent per year, with this figure increasing to 3.8 percent from 1946 to 1961.[72] But in an economy where technological efforts were focused on heavy industry and defense, national income does not say much about the material standards of the people. Not all technologies serve the common good, and most of the innovative endeavours undertaken by the Soviet Union were directed toward destructive rather than productive ends. To ensure readiness for future conflicts, the Soviet economy bore a massive and enduring military burden, with significant resources allocated to the development of atomic weapons, rockets, and jet aircraft. Few resources were left over for civilian sectors.

The outbreak of the Korean War in June 1950 only exacerbated this asymmetry, making the Soviet postwar economy even more militarized than it had been before the Nazis and the Japanese took the world to war.[73] Planners, in their quest to prioritize heavy industry over consumer goods, held the belief that they could bypass gradual progress and swiftly ascend to the pinnacle of the technological ladder by producing sophisticated capital goods. However, their grasp fell short of their reach, and Soviet citizens paid the price. The production of consumer goods remained scarce, with preference given to those items that were easiest to fabricate rather than to those consumers truly desired. Even under Khrushchev, who permitted a slightly greater emphasis on the production of consumer goods, the contrast with the American standard of living remained striking. During Khrushchev's visit to the United States in September 1959, Vice President Richard Nixon made a point of highlighting this disparity by showcasing a model ranch house. Yet Soviet journalists "scoffed that the exhibit was a fraud, since such a 'Taj Mahal' could surely be afforded only by millionaires."[74] In Moscow at the time, city dwellers were confined to barracks or communal apartments, sharing kitchens and bathrooms. True, income was more evenly distributed in the Soviet system, but so too was poverty. And the unprivileged masses often found themselves queuing for basic necessities like bread and butter, while the politically connected always found a way to jump the line.[75]

If one were to evaluate the USSR based on the principles of conventional economics as taught in universities today, it would undoubtedly be deemed a failure. But Lenin and Stalin were not students of Economics 101, nor would it have been particularly helpful to the game they were playing. The Five-Year Plans were not meant to maximize consumer welfare. And for the objectives Soviet leaders set out, like the advancement of heavy industry and mass mobilization, central planning worked remarkably well. Like the economies of Western Europe, the nations behind the Iron Curtain were closing the gap to the American frontier.[76] In fact, the strict planning regime could mobilize scarce domestic savings more swiftly than comparably poor market economies could, and it channelled those resources toward the construction of railroads, bridges, and factories and also schools, universities, and research institutes. Despite the inheritance of an illiterate and uneducated peasantry, the Soviets created a fine educational system, which was open to both men and women, of whom many would go on to work in government administration.[77]

To be sure, the history syllabus at Soviet secondary schools demanded that pupils learn that "the downfall of capitalism and the victory of Communism are inevitable," and that this must produce "intolerance towards

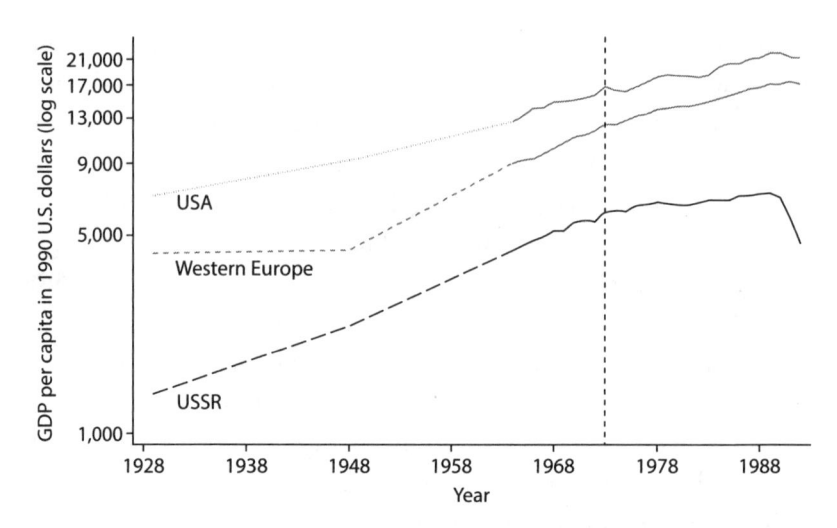

FIGURE 9.2 Soviet GDP per capita growth vs. the West, 1929–1992
Source: Harrison, "Economic Growth and Slowdown," Figure 3.2.

bourgeoisie ideology." However, as one graduate student in Leningrad put it, "Science and engineering are needed for production, but what does history produce?"[78] In this spirit, the primary and secondary school curriculum was heavy on mathematics, while in higher education, the Soviets excelled in science and technical subjects. And although the restricted autonomy of Soviet universities may have fostered fewer groundbreaking discoveries than American institutions, the nation's focused investment in physical capital, and human talent facilitated its technological catch-up. According to research by Wendy Carlin of University College London and her collaborators, in the age of mass production, poorer economies reaped greater benefits from central planning, such as improved infrastructure and education, than they suffered from the absence of market incentives. Conversely, wealthier countries experienced the opposite effect, with the lack of markets hampering long-term growth rates compared to their capitalist counterparts.[79]

Central planning, in other words, constituted a basic trade-off. On the one hand, it provided few incentives to innovate, there was no real threat of bankruptcy, and thus little creative destruction. On the other, it coordinated greater investment in infrastructure, prioritized education, and facilitated scale. The relatively backward economies behind the Iron Curtain could thus continue to grow fast as long as there was a backlog of technologies to exploit and intense geopolitical competition made their adoption imperative (figure 9.2). But as the opportunities for catch up were gradually exhausted, the inefficiencies inherent in central planning vis-à-vis more decentralized economies became all too apparent.[80] A few idealists, motivated by the idea of building socialism, stuck with their ideals, but to the rest of society, it was clear that the attempt to transform *homo economicus* into *homo sovieticus* was failing.

10

Centralization Crumbles

> Assume for a moment that the vision of Marx, Lenin and Trotsky had materialized, the world-revolution was victorious all over the globe, without a spot of capitalism left. In such a case we would never get the computer and the transistor radio, the refrigerator and the supermarket, the internet and the escalator, CD and DVD, digital photography, the mobile phone and all the other revolutionary technical changes.[1]
>
> —JÁNOS KORNAI

BY THE 1970s, the mass production system of the postwar era was falling apart globally. Smokestack industries, which had powered economic growth since the advent of the Industrial Revolution, found themselves experiencing diminishing returns from incremental improvements to production technology. Then, in October 1973, they were dealt a crushing blow. In the response to yet another war between the Arabs and Israelis, the Arab members of the Organization of Petroleum Exporting Countries (OPEC) effectively weaponized oil for the first time by cutting back production and banning exports to targeted nations. As a result, oil prices climbed by some 400 percent. Over the next two years, when American GDP fell by 6 percent and unemployment doubled to 9 percent, behemoth companies that produced big batches of capital goods took the largest hit.

The ensuing period of so-called stagflation—with sluggish growth, high unemployment, and surging inflation—puzzled the leading economists of the day and paralyzed policymakers, who had been absorbed by the Watergate debacle and the fall of Saigon to the Communists. Meanwhile, in the Soviet Union, the surge in oil prices that followed the Yom Kippur War masked the decline of mass production. After the CIA-backed 1953 Iranian coup d'état, which overthrew the democratically elected Prime Minister Mohammad Mosaddegh and reinstalled the Shah, the USSR had lost access to Iranian oil, and the lack of a steady energy supply emerged as a key Soviet weakness in the following years. However, with the discovery of vast oil deposits in the forested swamps of West Siberia in the early 1960s, the Soviets suddenly had plentiful oil, as well as oil money to pay for everything. The sudden abundance of Soviet oil, however, did little to halt the decline of the mass production system, which would soon impact the fortunes of nations both East and West.[2]

The industries that had sprung up in the nineteenth and early twentieth century were heading toward extinction, as were the cities hosting them. A visitor to Sheffield in the 1960s would occasionally note: "Goodness, this is a prosperous city!" But by 1990, as Oxford's Paul Collier notes, "nobody would have said that."[3] Having lost over 150,000 jobs in steel throughout the 1970s, and many more in engineering, the city council itself became the largest employer in town. The same process of deindustrialization was underway in Germany's Ruhr Valley, as well as in Bethlehem, Pennsylvania, once known as the "Ruhr Valley of America." The steel industry that had built the Golden Gate Bridge across San Francisco Bay, made the war effort, and transformed the skyline of America's cities was quickly fading into irrelevance. Faced with growing competition from minimills, which used electrical furnaces to defy economies of scale in favour of greater flexibility, large vertically integrated incumbents all across the Rust Belt experienced relentless decimation. Minimills were simply more productive, which benefited America as a whole but not the people working in integrated mills and the communities in which they lived.

Between 1962 and 2005, the U.S. steel industry shed some 400,000 jobs—equivalent to about 75 percent of its workforce—with dramatic social implications. Pittsburgh, which had been the tenth largest city in America in its heyday, dropped to fifty-second place.[4] In concert, over

1,000 factories across a variety of mass production industries closed during the 1970s, while book titles like *Shutdown at Youngstown, Crisis in Bethlehem,* and *The Deindustrialization of America* were filling the shelves.[5] Industrial decline was the theme of the day, and not just in America. Historian Stephen Kotkin observes:

> This wrenching of industries and communities left an indelible mark on the culture and popular psyche. A cheeky British film entitled *The Full Monty* (1997) retrospectively spotlighted a group of down-and-out steelworkers who hit upon a survival scheme: organize their own potbellied male striptease, recruiting performers from an unemployment queue. The film was set in Sheffield and opened with footage from a bygone civic-booster film about a "city on the move, the jewel in Yorkshire's crown." Now, its idle men were compelled to show their jewels to get by. The film's soundtrack appropriately featured disco, as in the industrial classic, *Saturday Night Fever* (1979), about a blue-collar dancing king, which had helped set off the late 1970s disco craze with the anthem of irrepressible dreams, "Staying Alive." Desperate times brought desperate approaches. In Johnstown, Pennsylvania, "tour buses idle outside the moldering steel mills," wrote a *New York Times Magazine* reporter in 1996. He described how Johnstown was "heading into a future in which the economy will be fed by an ambitious, seemingly quixotic experiment called heritage tourism," which "retails the often unhappy narratives of unlucky places, and is clearly a growth industry."[6]

Monuments of misfortune pervaded places where mass production industries had clustered, and as smokestack industries collapsed, the concerted economy began to crumble as well.

Western Europe, which had grown rapidly during the postwar years, largely by applying American mass production techniques to a widening set of industries, had no choice but to switch to intensive growth based on innovation. But this was easier said than done. The institutions of coordinated capitalism were deeply ingrained on the European Continent, where they had been devised for the task of driving industrial catch-up in the late nineteenth century and then again in the postwar period. However, these institutions were unfit for the technological uncertainty brought by the looming computer age. Bank-based financial systems were good at mobilizing resources for investment in established technologies and physical capital, but they were ill-suited for a moment of technological turbulence, when financial markets could take more and riskier bets. Generous employment protections, which gave workers sufficient security to accept the introduction of mass production technologies, also became a headache for start-ups entering the market. Furthermore, the skills provided by a vocational training system geared to churning out capable factory workers were of little help for the unfamiliar activities spawned by computers, and many of these new jobs required higher education.[7] High top tax rates, meanwhile, blunted the rewards for entrepreneurial risk-taking, and bureaucrats found it harder to monitor production and allocate resources.

In France, for example, indicative planning—which relied on forecasts and output targets to coordinate investment—worked well in the golden age, but at a time of technological upheaval, bureaucrats were confronted with a much more difficult task. In Italy, state holding companies acted as catalysts for catch-up in the era of Fordism but proved inflexible as technology changed, just like in Spain and Portugal, where the heavy hand of the state, clientelism, and restraints on competition bred massive problems. Worse yet, as the existing system came under strain, bureaucrats became increasingly prone to capture by special interests and increasingly likely "to bail out loss-making firms and prop up declining industries."[8] Consequently, in Southern Europe, the Computer Revolution was accompanied by "two lost decades" as businesses failed to adjust.[9]

Some of the forces responsible for Europe's growth deceleration were global in scope, and thus beyond the control of any given government, but productivity nevertheless fell more sharply in Europe than in the United States. The lone exception to this general pattern was Britain, whose deceleration was less dramatic than in Germany and France. Prime Minister Margaret Thatcher's reforms, which undeniably came with significant social costs, also made Britain better placed for the early computer era. One integral part of Thatcher's agenda was EU membership, and during the 1980s, the average effective rate of protection in Britain fell from around 4.7 percent to 1.2 percent, while subsidies providing lifeline support for old industries vanished.[10] While economists have shown that this increased openness partially drove Britain's improved productivity, the relative revival was also rooted in its institutional legacy.[11] British decentralization may have been a poor fit for the age of Fordism, but it was more adaptable to the changes brought by disruptive computer technology, just as it had been in the early days of industrialization. To echo the words of the eminent Nicholas Crafts, "relative social capability varies according to the technological epoch.... [S]uccess in ICT [information and communications technology] diffusion was an unintended consequence of the deregulation and resistance to further pursuit of corporatism in the Thatcher period."[12]

Where prosperity returned, however, it did so in places with less consolidated and less hierarchical industries. It was London, not Manchester, that would lead the way in ICT. Indeed, once-prosperous industrial centres, like in the industrial heartland of the Great Lakes region in the United States, the Midlands in the United Kingdom, and the Ruhr Valley in Germany, are still in despair. As the late Benjamin Chinitz, who advised presidents from Kennedy to Nixon on matters of urban policy, noted already in the 1960s, "you do not breed as many entrepreneurs per capita in families allied with steel as you do in families allied with apparel," where companies are smaller and less hierarchical. The children of salaried executives at GM, DuPont, or U.S. Steel, he continued, were simply less likely to be responsive to opportunities wholly unrelated to their parents' field of work. And in this, Chinitz was right: subsequent research has confirmed that the children from inventive environments are much more likely to become inventors themselves.[13]

One way that a bureaucratized environment might make up for breeding fewer entrepreneurs is through openness to migrants. But here, too, as Chinitz wrote, competitively organized places have an edge: "There is an aura of second-class citizenship attached to the small businessman in an environment that is dominated by big business. It manifests itself in many small ways, such as the kinds of social clubs he can belong to, the residential areas he will comfortably fit into, the business organizations he can join, and so forth."[14] Finally, Chinitz argued, while mammoth companies can raise capital almost anywhere, entrepreneurs are more likely to be able to attract funding closer to home, and large companies are also more likely to locate outside city centres, which impedes knowledge flows and the cross-fertilization of ideas.[15]

Chinitz's casual observations have held up well over the subsequent decades. Economists Edward Glaeser, Sari Pekkala Kerr, and William Kerr have found that, across cities in the United State, coal regions, with their industrial legacy of large hierarchical companies built to exploit economies of scale, have seen less entrepreneurship and slower urban growth in recent years.[16] The same is true of Europe (figure 10.1), where mass production industries depressed the demand for entrepreneurial skills. This hindered experimentation and innovation and contributed to slower growth from around the turn of the 1970s. Even second-generation migrants whose parents came from industrial regions are less likely to become entrepreneurs.[17] In other words, the traits and institutions that once supported command and control activities, like mass production, can hinder the kind of radical innovation that promises to spawn new industries. And when institutions become embedded in hierarchal structures, they create powerful forms of inertia. As economists Matilde Bombardini and Francesco Trebbi have shown, when an industry supports many workers locally, the member of Congress from that district usually votes in line with what the industry wants. And powerful incumbents, along with the people they employ, rarely want radical change that threatens the status quo.[18]

Of all industrial economies, however, the one most exposed as mass production crumbled was the Soviet Union. The USSR's Bethlehem's and Sheffield's, which numbered in the thousands, were even more antiquated than their Western counterparts. Much of Soviet industry was still from early Stalinist industrialization, and the industry that was rebuilt after the devastating destruction of World War II was often constructed according to 1930s specifications and blueprints. More important, for just the same reasons that the political economy of socialism was well-equipped for building rust belts of massive factories, it was particularly ill equipped at taking them down. The central planning system did not permit experimentation, nor did planners, who had a stake in the existing system, welcome change. The USSR, in short, operated like one giant factory town.[19]

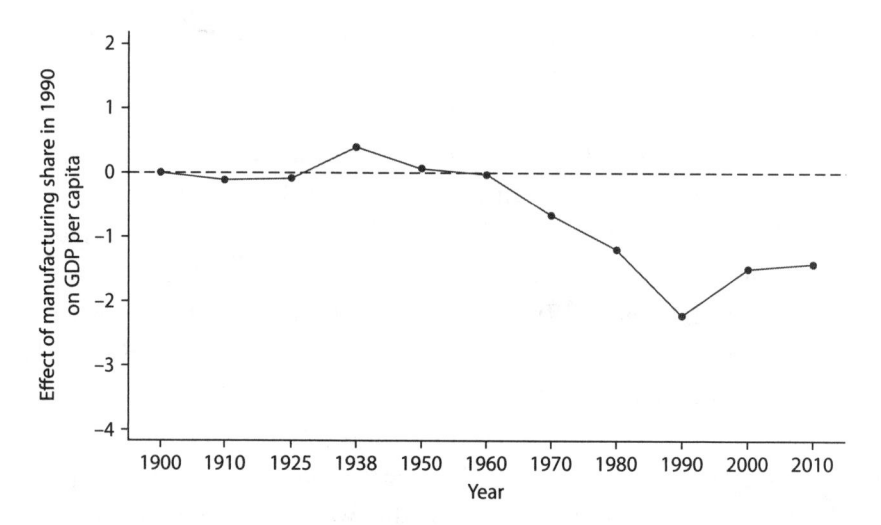

FIGURE 10.1. Deindustrialization and regional growth in Europe, 1900–2015 *Source*: Own analysis, including country FE, based on Rosés and Wolf, "Regional Growth and Inequality in the Long-Run," 17–48."

Science and Secrecy

The rate of economic growth in the Soviet Union tapered-off in the 1960s and dropped abruptly in the 1970s. Explanations for the Soviet slowdown, as well as its eventual collapse, have often focused on the impact of Soviet censorship and the drive to control society. These theories begin from the undeniable fact that technologies were pursued and used more enthusiastically when they served to consolidate political power. For instance, worried that switchboard operators could listen in on calls, the Soviet regime moved swiftly to introduce a self-dialed government network with Stalin personally overseeing the installation.[20] And the Party aggressively promoted technologies that could be used to spread Communist ideology and control the populace. Lenin, of course, was among the first political leaders to leverage cinema for propaganda purposes. In a similar spirit, the Soviets were early to adopt radio and television broadcasting as centralized mediums of communication.[21]

Before the 1960s, the backbone of Soviet radio involved a wired feed, which carried one or two stations from Moscow and, unlike wave receivers, was easy to control. However, with the spread of wave radios, censorship became next to impossible, and enthusiasm for the Party took a considerable hit. The Berlin Wall could stop people from moving across the border, but no walls or barbed wire could stop the radio and television waves traveling right through the Iron Curtain.[22] Though state radio attempted to disrupt the BBC, Deutsche Welle, and Voice of America by broadcasting random noises, citizens could go out in the country to escape jamming and learn the forbidden secrets of Soviet politics and Western life. On television, meanwhile, Soviet authorities permitted translations of some family serials, like *David Copperfield* from Britain and *Les Thibault* from France. Such shows, however, raised uncomfortable questions for the authorities. Soviet families watched as much for clues about Western material life as for entertainment. They keenly observed the characters gathering in well-equipped homes, driving modern cars, appearing in different clothes each day, and choosing their meals from overstuffed refrigerators. Was it all a fantasy?[23] In any event, they would not find the answers on Soviet television, which was still dominated by official views.

More broadly, control over information and communication remained tight across all sectors of Soviet society. Typewriters had to be registered with the police, photocopiers were restricted, and private telephones kept to a minimum. And although the several-million-strong army of Soviet scientists were mostly not active in politics, they could not escape it. Those needing access to foreign publications or even domestic data had to go through their hack political supervisors, who mostly denied such requests. But some restrictions were eased for those who joined the Party, which was prerequisite for career advancement for scientists anyway. As Kotkin explains:

> This dilemma of needing and yet stifling scientific exchange became ever more acute, and a few top apparatchiks broached the possibility of relaxing censorship. But the party's chief ideologue in the Brezhnev period, Mikhail Suslov—a CC secretary since 1949 (under Stalin), and a full politburo member since 1955—pointed out that it was only a matter of months after the removal of censorship in Czechoslovakia that the tanks had to roll in. Who, he asked, was going to send tanks to the Soviet Union?[24]

While the precise magnitude of the censorship effect on Soviet innovation is difficult to judge, such censorship almost certainly had a chilling effect. The KGB's obsession with nonconforming behaviour surely made becoming an inventor unattractive, just as it stifled other creative endeavours.[25] Moreover, because the secret police always had an incentive to exaggerate dangers to strengthen their claim to more resources, good information was sometimes so hard to come by that bureaucrats were forced to rely on intuition more than anything else. Ironically, in many cases, they preferred information from abroad to their carefully crafted Soviet handbooks.[26]

Interpreting Soviet decline through the lens of state repression, however, encounters the trouble of timing. If anything, the USSR and its satellites were much more open and decentralized at the time of collapse than during Stalin's reign, when some years of impressive growth were recorded.[27] Paradoxically, as the holes in the Iron Curtain accumulated, Soviet growth slowed.[28]

A more convincing explanation is that as the Second Industrial Revolution petered out globally, something radically new was needed for continued growth. And that something was the Computer Revolution, to which Soviet contributions were virtually nonexistent.[29] A confidential 1965 report by the Soviet economist Abel Aganbegyan—who would go on to become a key Gorbachev adviser—noted that not even the Central Statistical Administration had a single computer at its disposal, nor did it have any prospect of acquiring one. While the KGB had set up foreign front companies to circumvent Western restrictions on technology transfers, few of their acquisitions had any impact on the Soviet economy. Soviet factories were either unwilling or unable to adopt the latest information systems. By the 1980s, the entire Soviet Union had only 200,000 microcomputers, whereas the United States already had twenty-five million, with that number poised to skyrocket.[30]

Innovation and Planning

In mature industries, where quantity ruled, the Soviet system was at its best. Most cement, for example, which was of great importance to the first Five-Year-Plans, was produced in central Russia and shipped long distances at huge cost to Siberian sites. Socialist planners thus had to balance the cost-savings from the economies of scale that massive plants delivered against the cost of moving the cement over longer shipping routes. They also had to elicit managers' cooperation in maximizing productivity through the right mix of capital, labour, and raw materials. And in cement, they did so very well. According to economist Alan Abouchar, Soviet cement in the postwar era behaved as a "rational industry." Leveraging technological advances in electric power, kiln, and plant size, the Soviet cement industry saw labour productivity double between 1928 to 1950, and more than doubled again by 1968.[31]

Crucially, this form of rational planning required overcoming certain information problems inherent to the system. Coordinating production over long distances involved many hands and the passing along of relevant information. Plant managers could speak authoritatively about what happened on their assembly line, but they also had compelling incentives to inflate their resource requirements and exaggerate capacity constraints. The planning committee and industrial ministries, which depended on the accuracy of the information they provided, could solve this problem by benchmarking performance across factories. But this was only possible where operations were standardized and routine. Assessing the reliability of any information provided thus became significantly more difficult during periods of dramatic changes in technology. In such times, even a rare honest manager struggled to put into practice detailed orders from above about when to replace product lines or machines. Managers could make suggestions before a plan was approved, but they had to ask for permission for everything. And the more radical an idea, the higher up the hierarchy it required approval, and the longer the bureaucratic process took, which slowed progress considerably.[32]

These problems were compounded because exploration requires sacrifice today in order to produce more tomorrow. With bonuses linked to output targets, such sacrifices were predictably few. Whether managers hoped to climb the greasy pole or just wanted to sleep peacefully, they had to comply with the Party plan. If output fell short of monthly targets by a single percentage point, the loss to a factory director's bonus could be severe, ranging from 20 to 50 percent of his base salary.[33] Because loyalty was built by sharing some gains with the team, directors who missed their targets took a political hit as well. There was, moreover, little incentive to take such risks. If a factory increased its productivity, that would merely result in a corresponding increase in future output targets.[34]

Consequently, most R&D was carried out in industrial ministries and research institutes, which received their funding from the central authorities. However, in comparison to factory directors and managers, these researchers knew little about the dull practicalities of business and were generally uninterested in meeting corporate needs. Bureaucrats, of course, recognized this problem and tried to solve it. But contrary to innovation systems in the West, which had begun drifting toward decentralization, the authorities behind the Iron Curtain sought to fix it through even greater centralization. As Barry Eichengreen writes:

> The East German government reorganized R&D as an integrated complex, establishing large-scale research centers within each of its *Kombinate* (industrial holding companies). In Czechoslovakia, where resources for R&D had been allotted to small as well as large enterprises, these were now concentrated in the large ones in the hope that this would lead to the development of innovations of wide applicability. In Hungary the National Office for Technological Development allowed R&D to remain decentralized but sought to coordinate the tasks of the various research institutes. In the early 1970s, the problem of integrating research with production was acknowledged with the establishment of so-called research-production units, but these were of no real significance.[35]

The authorities correctly decided to alter course in response to the lack of innovation, but they were moving in precisely the wrong direction. Even in the planned economies in the East, new ideas mostly bubbled up from below rather than raining down from above, and computers were no exception (chapter 9). For instance, Jacek Karpinski, a Polish engineer and scientist, invented one of the first minicomputers in the early 1970s, but his K-202 never reached the market. Instead, as computers proliferated in the West, where Karpinski could have made a fortune, he later became a pig farmer. The Hungarian floppy disk inventor, Marcell Jánosi, faced a similar fate. While his discovery caught interest from IBM and ended up being reinvented by a Japanese company, central planners in his own country were reluctant to adopt his technology. Clearly, innovators had no guarantees for success in the West either, but in a decentralized system, if a promising innovation is rejected by one potential sponsor, someone else might still be willing to embrace it. Under central planning, in contrast, innovative ideas had to follow official pathways, and though appeals could sometimes be made against unfavourable outcomes, they were rare and even more rarely successful.[36]

Even in areas where the Soviets made notable technological advances, as with *Sputnik I*, these breakthroughs seldom improved people's lives. Whereas in the United States satellites soon found civilian use, unleashing a new era of telecommunication, in the USSR nothing remotely similar ever happened. Targeted action in a highly centralized bureaucratic system might occasionally produce spectacular results, but these developments will lack the robust spillover effects that accompany breakthrough innovations in decentralized systems.[37] Unlike in Soviet civilian sectors, where competition was largely absent, the arms race between the USSR and the West created enormous competitive pressure for military progress. Military R&D focused on clearly defined objectives that required less exploration, which the command economy was well-equipped to achieve. The Ministry of Defense could easily impose its requirements on any supplier, obtain scarce resources whenever needed, and allocate them toward its highest priorities.[38]

Under these conditions, the USSR achieved some striking technological advances, but without broad-based dynamism. This was because barriers to innovation were enormous and the rewards in the unlikely case of success were relatively paltry. Beating the West for the Communist cause, it turns out, was not sufficient motivation for most people, and even for those whom privilege and recognition were enough, the obstacles they faced were significant. Pioneers of semiconductor technology, like Abram Ioffe, received plenty of praise, including the Stalin Prize (1942), the Lenin Prize (1960), and the Hero of Socialist Labor (1955).[39] Even so, despite his prominence, he was removed from his positions during the Great Terror, having been labelled a Zionist.[40] The lack of economic incentives, in short, did not kill Soviet innovation but it surely reduced it. When the USSR finally collapsed, many superstar inventors ended up migrating, and not just anywhere. They settled in countries where top income tax rates were low.[41]

Treats and Terror

These problems could not be overcome simply by spending more rubles on R&D. For one thing, the Soviets had already reached parity with the United States by the 1960s, both in terms of the number of scientists and engineers it employed and in terms of R&D expenditure as a percentage of national income. And by 1975 it had overtaken America on both measures by some margin.[42] Reform was needed, but the innovation challenge was simply too daunting, since it threatened to unravel the entire system.

From the viewpoint of the Soviet bureaucracy, radical innovation increased planning costs, made output harder to track, and made worker productivity more difficult to monitor. Even organizational changes, like moving from mass production toward a more flexible computer-aided manufacturing system, proved challenging. After all, the reason why Soviet industry swiftly abandoned craft production in favour of mass production was not merely to increase output but also to make monitoring easier and so bolster control. The introduction of more flexible production threatened planners with a return to elevated monitoring costs reminiscent of the days of artisan-controlled production.[43] This also risked exacerbating the hidden burden on the Soviet economy: the striking cost of having Party organisations in every workplace and office around the country. Indeed, as industry grew, so did Party membership, which swelled from less than 1 percent of the adult population in the early 1920s to 9 percent in the late 1980s. And predictably, over time, those Party members established their own local power bases.[44]

This created a society in which networks of acquaintances and connections (what the Soviets called *znakomstvo i sviazi*, or ZiS) became increasingly important. Corrupt factory directors and higher officials in the local Party were often partners in crime, with the latter falsely reporting smooth delivery of plans and targets by the people they oversaw.[45] Aware of this, Stalin set up the People's Control Commission to scrutinize the undertakings of government, local administrations, and enterprises.[46] And to align incentives, he relied on terror rather than treats, as the Soviet archives make abundantly clear. According to a background report for Nikita Khrushchev's de-Stalinization speech in February 1956, from 1940 through June 1955, 36 million people were sentenced for criminal offenses, of which 15 million were imprisoned, and a quarter of a million were executed, in a country with an adult population of roughly 100 million. These decisions were not made by an independent judiciary. Stalin regularly intervened personally, forcing a sometimes "reluctant judiciary to prosecute tardy or lazy workers."[47]

However, over time, the loyalty constraint on Party members became as soft as the budget constraints on the firms they managed. While Stalin had pledged that the terror would only intensify as Soviet society marched nearer to the end game of Communism, Khrushchev did not follow through on this commitment. As discipline was relaxed, rent seeking skyrocketed and efficiency crumbled. This led to another cycle of reforms and counterreforms, but they failed to stem the rising tide of regime costs. As economic historian Mark Harrison has pointed out, the dictator's reputation had been irreversibly damaged, and the credibility of the threat that malpractice would be punished would never recover.[48] This turned out to be fatal, as the stability of the existing system rested on the Party's ability to punish cronies and slackers. Worse yet, this loss of state power also meant that lobbies were able to resist any meaningful reforms, which made it impossible for the USSR to shift from a system of mass production to a decentralized system that could encourage innovation. The effects of this lack of bureaucratic capacity can be seen most clearly in the diverging trajectories of China and the USSR after Mao.[49]

Stumbling Bear, Soaring Dragon

In 1989, when the crowds cracked the Berlin Wall and the satellites broke away from the Soviet Empire, the Chinese government declared martial law and launched a massive crackdown on student-led demonstrations in Tiananmen Square. Many pundits have argued that this is the path the Soviets should have taken as well. Indeed, Deng Xiaoping famously called Mikhail Gorbachev an "idiot" for pursuing economic and political decentralization at the same time through *glasnost* and *perestroika*.[50] By dismantling the levers of political power, Gorbachev inadvertently cut the capacity of the Soviet state as the Communist Party imploded and lost control over the reform process, or so the story goes.[51]

This story, however, is at best incomplete. For one thing, it overlooks the fact that Soviet officials were fully aware of what was going on in China and even tried to emulate many of its policies. Having visited China in 1986, Soviet analyst A. I. Iziumov drafted a memo on China's use of special economic zones (SEZs), which he shared with high-level officials inside the USSR's policymaking bureaucracy. He was clearly impressed by what he saw, noting that China had initiated 6,850 foreign invested projects, with a total of $21 billion invested in just seven years. Although many early investments were in tourism and hotels, China was also beginning to integrate into high-tech industries, where they assembled more than 30,000 personal computers for large multinationals. The SEZ that impressed Iziumov the most was Shenzhen, whose early investors were from Hong Kong and Macao, and which, Iziumov reported, had attracted more than $1.1 billion of foreign investment. He also keenly observed how people arriving there introduced new technologies and management practices that helped China get back on its feet.[52]

Moscow followed suit, as the Council of Ministers approved the USSR's own SEZs in December 1988, which local leaders were quick to embrace. In Leningrad, for example, Mayor Anatoly Sobchak soon placed SEZs at the heart of his economic plans to revive the city. Yet, to take full advantage of the contemporary East Asian miracle, as the Chinese had, many felt that the zones should be located on the Pacific. This was the message Gorbachev brought when he traveled to the Siberian city of Krasnoyarsk to set out his plans to revitalize *perestroika*: "we are only at the beginning of the path to the future of the world's great Asian and Pacific region," he declared.[53] The regional capital, Vladivostok, was not far from China, South Korea, and Japan—so it was well-placed to benefit from the growth of the Far East. Nevertheless, geographic proximity and the support of the local population were not sufficient to turn Vladivostok into Shenzhen. It attracted some foreign investment, including from a Chinese timber company and the Korean conglomerate Hyundai. Yet like in Soviet SEZs elsewhere, it was not enough to get agglomeration going. Historian Chris Miller writes:

> In the end, there was no tremendous inflow of foreign capital to the Soviet Union, nor did the USSR and its successors enjoy a manufacturing renaissance spurred by foreign trade and investment. By the early 1990s, special economic zones were associated more with tax evasion than with economic reconstruction. As the central government continued disintegrating in the early years after the collapse of the Soviet Union, local and regional governments in Russia took advantage of special economic zones to help individuals and corporations reduce their taxes, much as offshore banking centers such as Bermuda and the Cayman Islands do for multinational corporations today. A zone created in Ingushetia—a small, conflict-ridden province surrounded by the Caucasus Mountains and located far from international trade routes—was estimated to have cost the Russian government $5 billion in lost tax revenue in 1994. This was no path to economic rejuvenation. Yet abuses such as this are evidence not that the Soviet Union's foreign trade strategy failed but that the central government's ability to enforce basic rules had all but collapsed.[54]

Gorbachev could copy all the Chinese policies he wanted, but he lacked the bureaucratic capacity to implement them. Unlike Deng, he was in constant battle with vested interests. The KGB, for example, was so successful in staving off any cuts to military spending that Gorbachev reminded President George H. W. Bush in 1991, "We need to reduce arms in a way that won't make the army rise up."[55] With the threat of a coup always lurking in the background—and with farm bosses, energy industries, and powerful industrial interests deeply invested in the existing order—it was close to impossible to slash rents and reform the economy.[56]

Indeed, China's revival and the Soviet Union's collapse cannot be explained without understanding their respective institutional legacies. In a series of influential articles, economist Xu Chenggang has pointed to the great paradox of the Chinese political system: despite being authoritarian, it was highly regionally decentralized.[57] In China, local leaders could exercise a great deal of autonomy, which made it possible to adjust to and take advantage of a period of technological turbulence. By contrast, decision-making in the USSR was strictly centralized around the Central Committee of the Communist Party. Under the nomenklatura system, introduced by Lenin after the Russian Civil war in 1923, party officials and state bureaucrats were appointed by higher-level officials along the strictly vertical chain of command, and Soviet industry was organized along production branch lines. From Kiev to Vladivostok, ministries managed all enterprises in one industry across all regions.[58]

The Soviet Union, in other words, was run as a U-form hierarchy. The Gosplan, which sat on top of seven industrial complexes, each in turn supervising several ministries specializing in one particular industry, was responsible for 12 million planning indicators. In contrast, bureaucrats at the State Planning Commission of the Chinese central government were never responsible for more than 1,000. This extreme centralization of the USSR, which gave priority to vertical over horizontal relationships, allowed the country to achieve considerable economies of scale, but it also created siloes that hurt innovation.[59]

From a political standpoint, the appeal of this system is not hard to understand. It allowed Stalin to create a highly nested dictatorship, which allowed him to stay in power for thirty years. Like every dictator, Stalin wanted his subordinates to be loyal to him rather than to each other, so he created formidable institutional barriers to prevent regional leaders from colluding against him.[60] Not only did these officials need permission to visit Moscow, they were even precluded from having representative agents in the capital. To cut personal ties among subordinates, Stalin also increased the rate at which officials circulated between nomenklatura posts. As Irina Bystrova puts it, he pursued a policy of "divide and rule."[61] This kept his diary full of appointments with regional elites who made the pilgrimage to Moscow to seek favours.[62] And much like Vladimir Putin today, his desire to make all decisions meant that he suffered the "dictator's curse."[63] From the viewpoint of his subordinates, the less they decided, the fewer the things for which they could be blamed, so they funneled even trivial decisions up the hierarchy. This strategy of avoidance caused excessive administrative burdens at the top.

After Stalin's passing in 1953, however, elite circulation slowed down. Over the next four years, Nikita Khrushchev and Georgy Malenkov engaged in a fierce political battle for the leadership of the Party. Khrushchev prevailed largely through the support of regional party leaders, to whom he had promised more autonomy and authority over local decisions, which also meant rolling back much of the surveillance by the secret police. In January 1957, Khrushchev set out to deliver on his promises through the *Sovnarkhoz* reform, which made local officials responsible for technological and industrial development in their regions. The result was a massive shift of political power away from the central bureaucracy, which the ministerial lobby in the politburo naturally resisted. But their plot to dismiss Khrushchev from office in June of 1957 failed; instead, Khrushchev was able to call a meeting of the Central Committee, where regional secretaries had a majority, and crushed the so-called Anti-Party Group.[64]

A new, albeit brief, era of decentralization had begun. Under the *Sovnarkhoz* system, regional bodies took on responsibility for local industry, while branch industrial ministries were abolished, turning Soviet industry into an M-form hierarchy. In 1962, to encourage specialization, Khrushchev went further: he separated party units into detached industrial and agricultural bodies. As many historians have pointed out, this caused chaos in management and turned many regional leaders against him.[65] Together with the ministerial lobby at the centre, they helped Leonid Brezhnev oust him. With Khrushchev gone in October 1964, Brezhnev and his allies in Moscow, notably Alexei Kosygin, who became the head of the government, argued that the *Sovnarkhoz* system undermined the power of the central state. The U-form hierarchy of production branch ministries was reintroduced, and so regional party secretaries lost much autonomy and control over industry. In return, Brezhnev pledged not to return to the days of Stalin.

During his time in power, Stalin's purges, mass killings, and rapid rotation of cadres meant that few interest groups could organize, and certainly none powerful enough to block reform or challenge his leadership.

Enterprise managers did not want to risk their careers and even less their lives by missing production targets. However, after Stalin, the Soviet Union embarked on realizing the dream of "socialism with a human face."[66] This vision, which emerged under Khrushchev, meant that bureaucrats and managers suddenly faced few incentives to act effectively. Brezhnev's "stability of the cadres" policy, which postulated no demotions, only further cemented the power of incumbents keen on upholding the status quo. As a result of these reforms, when Gorbachev came to power, he inherited a system in which promotions were based on political connections rather than performance, in a country where firms could not go bankrupt, and where lobby groups played a larger role than ever. As Miller writes, "his powers as head of the Communist Party were weaker than any Soviet leader since the Bolsheviks took power in 1917."[67]

China, meanwhile, had embarked on a different trajectory. During the Cultural Revolution, the Party and the bureaucracy had been shaken up like never before. Mao had not just inflicted Stalinist suffering on his people, but he had also effectively destroyed any special interests by purging many elites, among them Xi Jinping's father, Xi Zhongxun, who spent long periods in confinement in Beijing, and Deng Xiaoping, who was sent to the Xinjian County Tractor Factory in rural Jiangxi. Paradoxically, however, those purges later paved the way for Deng's reforms. In contrast to the USSR, where industry and agriculture received massive subsidies, neither sector was powerful enough to undermine reform in China. Indeed, with Chinese farmers on the brink of starvation, there were few beneficiaries of the status quo, so opposition to change was predictably weak.

In addition, while the *Sovnarkhoz* system Khrushchev created was similar to that of Deng's China, it lacked some essential preconditions for success.[68] First and foremost, yardstick competition between decentralized units only works if the policies being pursued affect local prosperity, but not that of other regions.[69] Unless this condition is met, local leaders face compelling incentives to pursue projects that harm their neighbours and to reject ones that favour them, so they look comparatively better in the eyes of the central authorities. This is precisely what happened in the 1960s, when Tartaria refused to cooperate with

Bashkiria to exploit oil fields along their joint border. The case of Tartaria, it turns out, was far from an isolated example. Economists Andrei Markevich and Ekaterina Zhuravskaya have shown that *Sovnarkhoz* reform only spurred industrialization in diversified regions, whereas growth suffered in highly specialized ones.[70] And herein lies a crucial difference between China and the USSR.[71] For historical reasons, going back to the millennia-old imperial, locally administered *junxian* system, Chinese regions were more self-sufficient than their Soviet counterparts.[72] Even in the modern era, Chinese local governments controlled two-thirds of the country's state-owned enterprises and enjoyed fiscal autonomy well above the OECD average.[73] And predictably, state-owned enterprises in distant locations, far away from the reach of the Party headquarters (and costlier to monitor), were those managed locally rather than by Beijing.[74] China was thus better placed to solve Hayek's knowledge problem than its older Soviet comrade.

As discussed in the previous chapter, the USSR excelled at exploiting economies of scale. The whole Soviet steel industry, for example, was coordinated by the Ministry of Iron and Steel, whose organizational structure mirrored corporate giants like U.S. Steel. Tasks were divided in functionalized departments, and each department supervised specialized enterprises below it, with some success.[75] Even though ownership was public, Soviet steel output grew at one of the fastest speeds in the world, from 14.5 million tons in 1947 to 147 million tons in 1977.[76] In China, in contrast, most steel plants were medium size and under the control of regional governments. Hence, despite starting from a comparable level of output in 1947, the Chinese achieved only half of the growth of Soviet steel. Such poor performance is hard to explain by factors other than differences in organization, as steel in the Middle Kingdom was assigned the highest priority by the central government, and China had considerable iron ore reserves as well as some of the largest coal deposits in the world.[77]

As long as quantity was the goal, the Soviet Union was the envy of the Communist world. But as smokestack industries perished its comparative advantage became a disadvantage. China's M-form hierarchy was simply better at dealing with the kind of rapid change and uncertainty that characterized the era.[78] Without pulling the rug from underneath the entire planning system, China could facilitate progress and reform through local experiments rather than resorting to full-scale experimentation, which turned out to be politically unfeasible. To paraphrase Barry Naughton, the genius of Chinese reform was not that it was gradual, and so avoided Soviet-style shock therapy, as many scholars have argued, but that it was able to swiftly respond to changing conditions. Put simply, there is no benefit to walking slowly if you know where you are going.[79] Having lifted some restraints on rural industry, Deng himself admitted that the buoyant growth that followed "was not something I had thought about. Nor had the other comrades. This surprised us."[80]

China, in other words, did not have a grandiose plan for everything. What it did have was a host of local laboratories for experimentation and the bureaucratic capacity to scale up what worked on the national level. For example, early rural reforms, which allowed for "above-quota" transactions, were the source of the entire Dual-Track approach Deng ended up pursuing. The erosion of central power did not turn China into a full-fledged market economy, but it created space for China to develop new transitional institutions that effectively performed the same function.[81] In the absence of the rule of law, the CPC could act arbitrarily without constraint from the judiciary, which made it difficult to convince entrepreneurs and innovators that they would be allowed to hold on to the fruits of their investments. But as Yingyi Qian and Barry Weingast have argued convincingly, China's devolution of authority created a credible commitment to preserve market incentives. This system, much like federalism in the United States, protected entrepreneurs from the grabbing hand of government.[82] With tens of thousands of local governments competing for investment and talent, leaders where under great pressure to attract foreign companies and inventors to generate revenues and bolster their public finances.[83] They behaved "more like firms than like governments," simply because their careers depended on it.[84] Indeed, those who did well moved up the ranks of the Party. Unlike in the late Qing dynasty, when local elites undermined the power of the state, a strong central state co-opted locals into pursuing the interests of the nation.[85]

Without a system of secure private property rights and an independent judiciary to enforce them, political centralization was necessary for economic decentralization to do its wonders.[86] It provided the backbone of the system that Branko Milanovic aptly has called "political capitalism."[87] While local leaders had a great degree of autonomy, the CPC retained control over the most important resource of all: the personnel of local governments. With the power to select and reward successful local leaders and punish unsuccessful ones, the CPC created incentives similar to those of a market economy.[88] This system was, however, a delicate balancing act. It required giving local leaders sufficient sway to adjust to changing realities but also maintaining a sufficiently strong central state to monitor local progress. And at the frontier of development, where breakthrough innovation is crucial, effective monitoring becomes more challenging, creating fertile ground for cronyism—an issue discussed in chapter 12.

From Dazhai to Shenzhen

Gorbachev was dealt a harder hand than Deng, but China's rise was never a forgone conclusion. Government bureaucracies are only as good as the policies they implement, and it was the Party that set the metrics upon which local officials competed for promotion. Thus, a key factor in China's successful modernization after 1978 was the fixation of the Communist Party on technological advancement and economic growth beyond heavy industry and the military.[89] As in Prussia, where the battle of Jena-Auerstedt was a wake-up call that prompted a revolution from above, in China, the catastrophes of famine and the Cultural Revolution served as the catalyst for reform. By the mid-1970s, it was clear to the CPC leadership that China was losing the technological race not just with the West and the USSR, but also to its neighbouring runaway province: Taiwan. The humiliation China had suffered under the unequal treaties (see chapter 2) remained a source of widespread resentment, and older Chinese leaders were reminded of a saying from decades earlier: "Lagging behind is to get bullied by others."[90] The only choice left for the CPC to gain legitimacy with the Chinese population, and avoid falling further behind rivals both near and far, was to deliver material progress. Economic growth and technological upgrading thus became the national consensus objectives under the leadership of Deng Xiaoping.

China's great leap to prosperity was ignited when Deng visited the Guangdong Province in 1977. Five years earlier, Chairman Mao and President Richard Nixon had signed the Shanghai Communiqué. Facilitated by the Chinese Premier Zhou Enlai and Henry Kissinger, Nixon's secretary of state, this document ended decades of Chinese isolation—no formal diplomatic relations had existed between China and the United States since 1949, when Chiang Kai-shek decamped to Taiwan—and laid the foundations for future cooperation.

In the wake of this agreement, China's modernization plan was simple: import U.S. technology and pay for it with petroleum exports. Specifically, the government proposed importing $6.5 billion worth of modern industrial plants and machines from 1978 through 1985. Hopes were naturally high, but with the onset of the computer age and the downfall of mass production, picking winners became increasingly difficult—not least in the absence of market incentives and prices. And without foreign exchange reserves, licensing foreign technology turned out to be a risky strategy because it depended on export earnings.[91]

Indeed, during Deng's 1977 visit, Guangdong officials complained about the shortage of foreign currency needed to import technology to modernize. At that time, the annual income of a village farmer in Hong Kong was multiples that of a farmer across the border, and Hong Kong factory workers did even better, both in absolute and relative terms. Separating these two groups was a twenty-mile-long barbed-wired fence and thousands of policemen patrolling the area. But that did not deter Chinese youngsters hoping for a better future. In what has been called the "Great Escape to Hong Kong," people crossed illegally in the hundreds of thousands. According to recently declassified government documents, there were 565,000 crossing attempts between 1954 and 1980.[92]

The following year, when Xi Zhongxun visited the region as the newly appointed first secretary of the province, he began his new mission, in the words of the late Ezra Vogel, by "following the political line of the time—that is, pursuing class struggle."[93] Chinese fleeing to Hong

Kong were traitors pursuing a bourgeoisie life, he declared. In an act of bravery, a local party secretary dared to speak up, pointing to the plight of the people in Guangdong who toiled day and night yet struggled to meet their basic needs. This audacity came at a cost as he was promptly dismissed from his position.

As Deng Xiaoping ascended to power, however, the Communist Party's approach to economic policy changed dramatically. Just a few weeks after his election at the Third Plenary Session of the 11th Central Committee in December 1978, Xi received a directive from Beijing instructing him to develop a proposal that would grant Guangdong permission to attract direct foreign investment. As they prepared the proposal, Gu Mu was made director of the newly established SEZ Office and tasked with coordinating the work between Guangdong and Beijing.[94]

In August of 1979, four special economic zones were officially given permission to start operating. These zones, which served as a way to engage in localized experiments rather than introduce sweeping reform to the entire country, went on to deliver beyond expectations. Between 1985 and 1995, Hong Kong and Taiwan lost almost a million manufacturing jobs, of which many migrated to Shenzhen and the broader Guangdong region. When Deng visited again in 1992, during his famous "Southern Tour," he left Shenzhen by boat along the Pearl River. Passing the remains of a Qing dynasty customs house, he noted that while China had been humiliated by western powers in the nineteenth century, that was now a distant memory: "Those who are backward get beaten.... We've been poor for thousands of years, but we won't be poor again. If we don't emphasize science, technology, and education, we will be beaten again."[95] Just as the village of Dazhai had earlier served as Mao's national model for a higher stage of socialist agriculture during the Cultural Revolution, under Deng, Shenzhen became China's archetype for successful modernization. Once a small fishing village, it quickly emerged as a rival to Hong Kong and Singapore as Asia's economic powerhouse—home of a cutting-edge Science and Technology Industrial Park and boasting over 8,000 registered companies.[96]

At a time when computers transformed traditional industries by enabling more flexible production methods and global supply chains

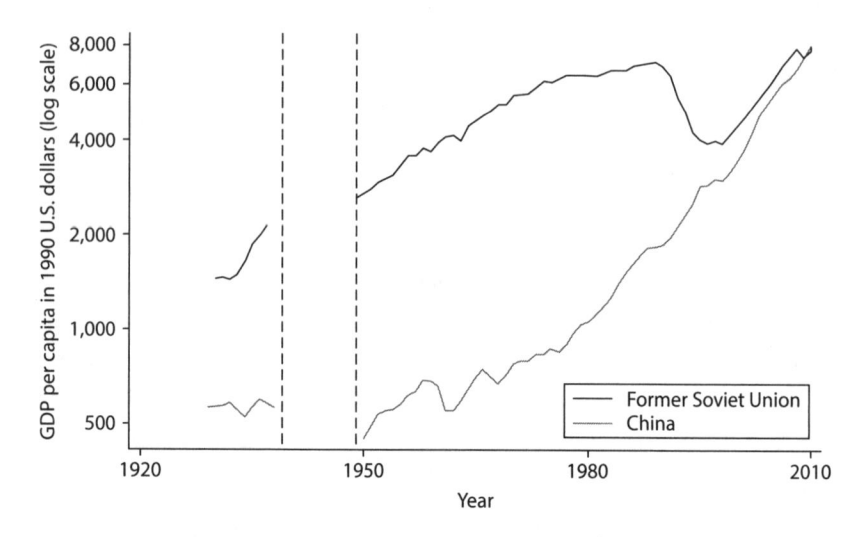

FIGURE 10.2. GDP per capita growth in China and the (former) USSR, 1920–2010
Source: Maddison Project Database, version 2013. Bolt and van Zanden, "The Maddison Project."

(discussed in chapter 11), Deng's willingness to experiment was critical. In the Mao era, ideological red lines meant that local officials did not have much sway in practice. But Deng took a much more adaptable approach. As state-owned enterprises (SOEs) failed to absorb the stream of people from the countryside, families were permitted to form household enterprises (*getihu*) and work for themselves. To support this arrangement, Deng's government obscured a statement by Marx in *Das Kapital* about a capitalist exploiting eight employees to suggest that an entrepreneur with no more than seven workers was not a capitalist. His so-called cat theory—that it does not matter if the cat is black or white, as long as it catches the mouse—became a justification for allowing citizens to accumulate wealth and inequality to rise, as such changes would become the rising tide that lifted all the boats.[97]

Yet in the early days of reform, not everyone was pleased. When Hu Qiaomu—a prominent opponent of such policies—visited Fujian in the 1980s, he compared its SEZs to the nineteenth-century treaty ports imposed on China after the Treaty of Nanking. Indeed, foreign companies initially invested in SEZs mainly to take advantage of China's comparative advantage—namely, a seemingly endless pool of both cheap and skilled labour. In response, the CPC began pressuring local officials to upgrade technology. In 1984, fourteen coastal cities were granted the right to build Economic and Technological Development Zones (ETDZ) to focus more specifically on technology industries. And in the 1990s and 2000s, several ETDZ and High-tech Industry Development Zones (HIDZ) were approved—this time in inland provinces.

Recent research shows that the contribution of these zones to China's economic growth has been significant, underscoring the interplay between decentralized decision-making and centralized directives that have propelled China's success.[98] Entrepreneurs, guided by profit motives, made technology choices, but the impetus for change emanated from the top. Unlike the USSR, China had the institutions to permit local experimentation, fewer vested interests, and the state capacity to get reforms implemented. Hence, while Soviet rulers from Stalin to Brezhnev could afford to patronize their Chinese comrades, who looked to the USSR as an elder brother to be emulated, the Soviet Union would ultimately collapse as China ascended (figure 10.2).

11

The Great Flattening

> The nineteenth century liberal was a radical, both in the etymological sense of going to the root of the matter, and in the political sense of favoring major changes in social institutions. So too must be his modern heir.[1]
>
> —MILTON FRIEDMAN

AS CHINA was beginning to transform in the 1980s, few foreign policy hawks worried about its rise. They were, instead, preoccupied debating Frances Fukuyama's thesis that we had arrived at the end of history—that the arrival of liberal democracy represented the final state of societal evolution. But even when the USSR finally collapsed in 1991 and American technological supremacy was on full display during the widely televised Gulf War, all out euphoria was hampered by the rise of another Asian power. Before the Soviet flag had been lowered from the Kremlin for the final time, *PBS Frontline* aired a new documentary titled "Losing the War to Japan." "The Cold War is over, and Japan won," political scientist Chalmers Johnson remarked in one of its interviews.[2]

This idea was not exactly new. Ezra Vogel had published *Japan As Number One* already in 1979, in which he argued that Japan would soon overtake the United States as the technology leader of the world.[3] However, the experience of the 1980s had, at least on the surface, considerably bolstered his case. For instance, in 1988, the *New York Times* described a group of U.S. computer science experts meeting to assess Japan's tech-

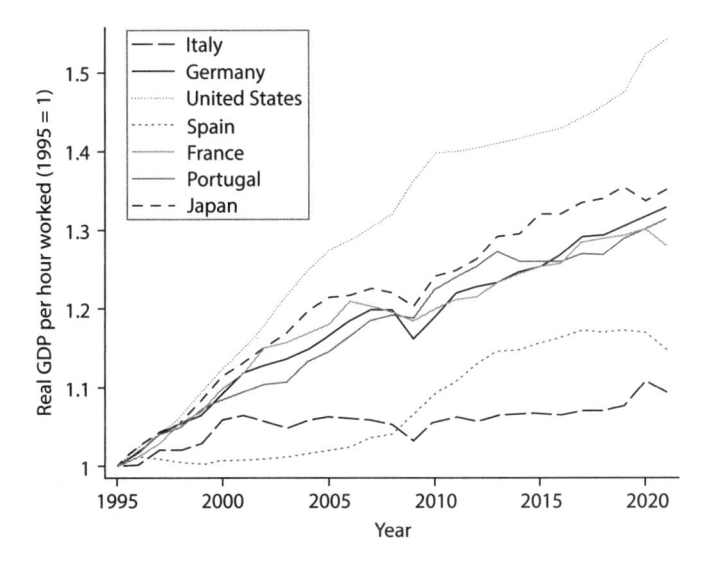

FIGURE 11.1. Productivity growth during the computer revolution by country
Source: Schivardi and Schmitz, "IT Revolution," 2441–2486, Figure 1. Data for Japan from the OECD: https://stats.oecd.org/.

nological capabilities. They concluded that the new generation of computers coming out of Japan dispelled "any illusions that America had maintained its wide lead."[4] There was a sense that Silicon Valley had relinquished the market for semiconductors to the Japanese, just as Boston's Route 128 had done in minicomputers. Commentators frequently compared the situation to Japan's great leap forward in automobiles and the subsequent decline of Detroit.

Yet, the age of computers ended up being an America affair. Around 1995, after two decades of disappointing growth, America experienced a productivity revival (figure 11.1).[5] And while American software was busy eating the world, it was Japan that went through an episode of painful stagnation (figure 11.2).

How did this happen? What made computers ignite an American renaissance? These questions can only be answered by considering how the technology evolved itself—a journey that could never have been fully realized within the confines of any one organization.

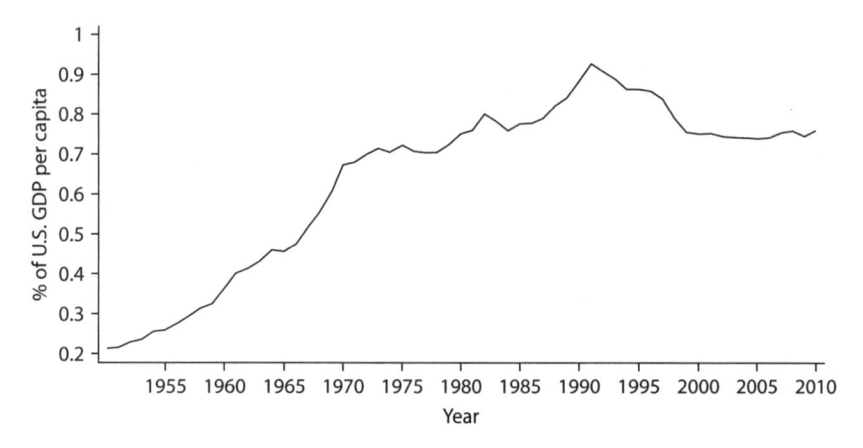

FIGURE 11.2. GDP per capita in Japan relative to the United States, 1950–2010
Source: FRED Graph Observations Federal Reserve Economic Data. https://fred.stlouisfed.org/.

The computer age took off in 1982, when the cover of *Time*'s Person of the Year issue was dedicated not to any human but to the PC, dubbed the "Machine of the Year." Not everyone was pleased. Having expected to be on the cover himself, Steve Jobs allegedly cried.[6] But as the issue noted the personal computer was a collective effort. Too many people had contributed to it for one person to be singled out, which also makes dating its invention notoriously difficult. In *The Innovators,* Walter Isaacsson traces its humble beginnings back to the Victorian era and the days of independent inventors, like Ada Lovlace and Charles Babbage, whose analytical engine conceptualized the first general-purpose computer. Others regard the key milestone to be the ENIAC, or the Electronic Numerical Integrator and Computer, developed by J. Presper Eckert and John Mauchly at the University of Pennsylvania in 1945. Although it was the first fully electronic digital computer, the ENIAC was hardly a general-purpose technology. It was hard-wired to solve a particular set of problems concerned with the computation of firing tables for artillery. Nor were the ideas underpinning the ENIAC conceptually very different from Norbert Wiener's 1940 proposal, which Vannevar Bush turned down for what he deemed to be more urgent military needs (as discussed in chapter 7). In any event, the ENIAC was not fit for personal or even office use. It consisted of 18,000 vacuum tubes, 70,000 resistors, consumed 175 kilowatts of power, had several miles of wires, and weighed thirty tonnes. The sheer size of this colossus led some to joke that when the ENIAC was switched on, the lights of Philadelphia dimmed.[7] Three years earlier, Thomas Watson, the head of IBM, had famously suggested that "there is a world market for maybe five computers."[8] And while this prediction is often ridiculed today, the ENIAC did not give him much reason to reconsider this judgment.

The computer is better understood not as a single discovery, invented at a single point in time, but rather a series of unfolding discoveries and improvements. Wiener's proposal to Bush, for instance, contains a list of at least half a dozen separate inventions that enabled the modern digital computer. Progress in the field would require inventors and scientists to forge all these individual pieces into a unified whole and also make additional breakthroughs along the way.[9] William Nordhaus's seminal study of computer performance over the decades shows that the key discontinuity occurred in the 1980s. Though the cost per computation declined by 37 percent per year between 1945 and 1980, it fell by 64 percent per year thereafter—even faster than Moore's Law predicted.[10] This rapid period of progress can be traced back to 1971, when the invention of the microprocessor by the newly founded Intel Corporation shattered the barriers hindering decentralized computing and opened the floodgates for new contenders, including Apple and Compaq, who emerged to challenge the long-standing dominance of IBM. But it was the arrival of the personal computer, more than anything else, that changed the rules of the game, marking a truly new era of proliferation. As *Time* noted in its 1982 coverage of the PC: "Now, thanks to the transistor and the silicon chip, the computer has been reduced so dramatically in both bulk and price that it is accessible to millions.... In contrast to the $487,000 paid for ENIAC, a top IBM PC today costs about $4,000, and some discounters offer a basic Timex-Sinclair 1000 for $77.95 ... if the automobile business had developed like the computer business, a Rolls-Royce would now cost $2.75 and run 3 million miles on a gallon of gas."[11]

The exponential growth of computing power was undeniably impressive. On its own, however, this breakthrough did not provide much of a boost to economic growth. It took the shotgun marriage of two technologies to transform the economy: the PC and the internet. Before the invention of the World Wide Web, computers were stand-alone devices. Thereafter, they could be linked to the outside world through the internet. By the end of the 1990s, browsers, web surfing, and email had become universal. And over the next two decades, the market for internet services exploded, as new companies like Amazon, Facebook, and Google expanded, while the introduction of Apple's iPhone and Google's Android operating system launched a communications revolution. Suddenly, the average American not only owned a computer, they also carried one around in their pocket, and these tiny computers were all linked together.

The consequences for economies worldwide were profound. As economists Raghuram Rajan and Julie Wulf have shown, in America, there was a strong movement toward flatter, less hierarchical corporations beginning in the 1980s.[12] And those who failed to adjust perished. Decentralized companies were simply more responsive and adaptable and therefore better placed to reap the benefits of the coming Computer Revolution.[13] It was only after these complementary organizational changes were made that productivity growth finally accelerated in the 1990s, with American companies leading the way.[14] Even U.S. firms operating in Europe experienced a productivity miracle that their European competitors did not, with about half of the productivity gap between America and Europe in the decade after 1995 being down to differences in management practices.[15] But these practices did not emerge in a vacuum—they were shaped by the flexibility of American institutions and their commitment to decentralization and competition, which provided the space for experimentation. This institutional background can go some way in explaining why the computer era was U.S. made.

Silicon Valley and Route 128

The Computer Revolution, of course, was not made just anywhere in America. Most of the inventions underpinning the modern world originated from a small, lush valley by the Pacific Ocean.[16] As numerous narratives have emphasized, Silicon Valley benefited from its proximity to military installations and industrial powerhouses like Richmond, Oakland, and San Francisco, which helped secure military funding during and after World War II. Yet, if one had been asked to bet on the region most likely to spearhead the world of computers based solely on government funding, the logical choice would have been Boston, not Silicon Valley.[17]

When Vannevar Bush assumed the role of director at the newly established Office of Scientific Research and Development (OSRD), he solidified the bonds between Washington and his former colleagues at the Massachusetts Institute of Technology (MIT). During the 1940s, the OSRD awarded contracts amounting to $330 million, one-third of which flowed to MIT. Other leading universities in the Boston area, including Harvard and Tufts, also secured significant portions of these contracts.[18] And those ties only grew stronger when war broke out in Korea and the Cold War escalated into a space race with the Soviet Union. Boston-area companies, as well as labs at MIT, continued to capture a disproportionate share of the ever-growing military largesse. In the 1950s, Massachusetts firms signed over $6 billion worth of contracts with the Department of Defense (DOD), and by the early 1960s, half the sales of Route 128 companies—named after the 55-mile Boston beltway that contained this booming tech industry—were to the federal government. In the words of Gene Bylinsky, an early chronicler of the Valley, "Route 128 firms started in the 1950s and 1960s depended on defense and space business to an extent unknown in Silicon Valley."[19]

At the time, it was widely anticipated that Route 128, often called "America's Technology Highway," would maintain its leadership in the industry. Indeed, William Shockley established his company in Palo Alto only after facing rejection from Raytheon in Massachusetts. In addition to enjoying closer proximity to AT&T's Bell Labs in New Jersey, where Shockley originally conceived the transistor, Route 128 boasted a cluster of established electronics companies with tube or transistor operations. Among them were Sylvania, Clevite, CBS-Hytron, and Raytheon, alongside promising start-ups like Transitron, Crystal Onyx, and Solid State Devices. But their reliance on government contracts made them vulnerable. In the early 1960s, when Defense Secretary Robert McNamara abruptly scaled back military spending on high-tech devices, he caused what became known among executives as the "McNamara Depression."[20] And when American troops finally pulled out of Vietnam and the space race slowed down, prompting military contracts to plummet even further, Route 128 experienced a painful downturn. Between 1970 and 1972, approximately 30,000 defense-related jobs vanished, pushing unemployment in the technology sector to a staggering 20 percent.[21]

But while Boston behemoths like Raytheon remained heavily reliant on military contracts, companies in Silicon Valley quickly adjusted their product lines to meet new market demands. Eitel McCullough Corporation (Eimac), originally spun off from Heintz & Kaufman in 1934, developed new power-grid tubes to enhance FM radio. Litton Engineering Laboratories, founded in 1932 by Stanford-educated Charles Litton, shifted its focus from microwave tubes to producing microwave ovens. Varian Associates diversified into scientific and medical instrumentation, reducing its military sales from 90 percent to 40 percent within eight years.[22] And semiconductor pioneers in the Valley similarly forged ahead with minimal dependence on military research and development funding. It was not always easy. Fairchild, for example, initially guarded its independence, particularly from military influence, but over time the company found it increasingly difficult to avoid military contracts.[23] "The competition became so great," recalled Nelson Stone, Fairchild Camera's general counsel, "that we had to back off from our policy." This contributed to the erosion of the firm's autonomy, which together with frustrations over the company's rigid management structure, prompted Gordon Moore and Robert Noyce to leave. Backed by Arthur Rock, the venture capitalist who had helped secure funding for Fairchild, Moore and Noyce cofounded Intel Corporation, which primarily focused on commercial markets.[24]

As venture capital increasingly supplanted military funding as the primary financial engine of Silicon Valley, innovative firms shifted their focus from destructive military applications to productive commercial ones. This led to a chain of successes, as entrepreneurs reinvested their earnings into promising new ventures, propelling further triumphs. Just like Rock, Tom Perkins (who cofounded Kleiner Perkins in 1972 and was an early investor in Genentech), and Don Valentine (who founded Sequoia Capital the same year, and invested in Apple and Cisco Systems) were born and educated on the East Coast but moved westward. They all saw the unique opportunities for founding new enterprises that the West Coast presented. In the Bay Area, founders teamed up with venture capitalists and experienced managers to quickly build start-ups like Intel, Genentech, and Apple.

The West Coast's divergent trajectory compared to the East Coast's was long in the making. Given its close ties to Washington, MIT's leadership focused on retaining relations with federal government agencies, which had contributed some $117 million for the Radiation Lab, the Servomechanism Lab, the High Voltage Lab, and other projects. Stanford, on the other hand, needed to forge relations with industry and was early to invest part of its endowment in new ventures.[25] In the words of Berkeley's AnnaLee Saxenian, "This contrast—between MIT's orientation toward Washington and large, established producers and Stanford's promotion of collaborative relationships among small firms—would fundamentally shape the industrial systems emerging in the two regions."[26]

The HP Way

Santa Clara County was dubbed Silicon Valley in the early 1970s.[27] Its origins as a tech hub, however, are typically traced back to the founding of the Hewlett-Packard Company (HP) in a small Palo Alto garage by two Stanford graduate students in 1939. HP's fortunes, like those of many of its East Coast counterparts, were shaped by the war. But the company's first major sale was a contract with Walt Disney studios for eight audio-oscillators. And although military contracts for its radar detection technology provided a significant boost to the company's bottom line, the sums were small relative to those received by East Coast producers. With a mere 130 employees, HP was dwarfed by GE, RCA, Westinghouse, and Raytheon. And even as they grew, the pioneers of Silicon Valley explicitly sought to avoid the hierarchies of their East Coast competitors.

Long before it was fashionable, William Hewlett and David Packard, and later Intel's Robert Noyce, made openness and autonomy key components of their corporate cultures:

> This management style, which was characterized by trust in individual motivation, a high degree of professional autonomy, and generous employee benefits, came to be known as the HP Way.... They made a point of striking up informal lunch and hallway conversations with employees at all levels, and they encouraged managers to "wander around," spending part of each day initiating unplanned discussions. By institutionalizing the notion that good ideas could come from anywhere, Hewlett and Packard also pioneered a decentralized organizational structure that represented an important departure from traditional corporate organization.[28]

To paraphrase the journalist Tom Wolfe, the atmosphere in these new companies was so democratic that it startled businessmen from the East.[29] Each Thursday, top management at Fairchild and Intel would hold meetings with randomly selected frontline workers to drive grassroots innovation.[30] Furthermore, recognizing that experimentation is chaotic and monitoring is therefore hard and costly, flat organizations in the Bay Area, including Fairchild (1957), Signetics (1961), National Semiconductor (1967), and Intel (1968), introduced profit sharing and equity compensation. As one local venture capitalist remarked, "stock is the mother's milk of Silicon Valley."[31] Fairchild, for example, provided almost all its senior staff with stock options, but when it tried to do the same for its engineers, this move was blocked by its East Coast parent company, which considered profit sharing to be socialist. This response was ironic, since the structure of companies on the East Coast made them look more like their counterparts in the Soviet Union.[32] Just as Soviet line ministries split production branches, East Coast companies separated critical activities, from research and engineering, to manufacturing and marketing. Also like in the USSR, vertical lines of decision-making made it less likely that critical information and heterodox ideas would be shared and realized. On the East Coast, like in Eastern Europe, permission from the senior leadership was needed for almost everything.

The resemblance to the Soviet mode of organization is not surprising. America invented the Taylorism that Lenin and Stalin so vigorously pursued. However, the long dominance of military production in Massachusetts also played its part in reinforcing the quest for corporate autarky and secrecy at the expense of horizontal collaboration. Route 128's technology companies only reluctantly reduced their dependence on defense spending in the 1970s—more than a decade after Silicon Valley had done so—and remained heavily integrated into the industrial-military complex throughout the 1980s. Even after Route 128 was less dependent on military contracts, the legacy would persist, as new technology enterprises inherited organizational structures that were designed for mass production for the military. Companies like Honeywell and Raytheon simply reproduced the traditional hierarchies of RCA, General Electric, and Sylvania, where corporate divisions were subject to the final authority of the central management team.[33] As one employee at a leading technology firm observed at the time: "The CEO ultimately makes all of the important decisions in a Route 128 company."[34] This worked well as long as quantity ruled, but not in an age of technological upheaval. In the words of one executive, "If you were to look at why GE and RCA have failed [in semiconductors], it is because their organization was too disciplined and unable to respond quickly to true innovation."[35]

In the Valley, knowledge flowed not just horizontally within firms but also across them. Entrepreneurs like Charles Litton would casually drop by Varian Associates' research facilities to talk ideas. This culture of collaboration and knowledge exchange among labs and individuals was the fuel of the Valley's entrepreneurial spirit. Xerox's Palo Alto Research Center (PARC) provides a particularly vivid example. Housed within its walls were pioneering researchers who spearheaded innovations like the first PC featuring a graphical user interface, the laser printer, and Ethernet networking technology. And the impact of these ideas permeated throughout the industry. For instance, in 1979, a twenty-four-year-old Steve Jobs paid a visit to the Xerox Center and later incorporated numerous PARC innovations into Apple's Lisa as well as the Macintosh. Similarly, Charles Simonyi, overseeing the development of

Microsoft Office, had previously crafted the first user-friendly word processor during his tenure at PARC, which was only one among many hubs and gather spots for inventors in Silicon Valley. In local watering holes like the Wagon Wheel in Mountain View, technological breakthroughs were sketched on soggy napkins. Meanwhile, the Homebrew Computer Club, established in 1975, swiftly grew to encompass a vibrant community of around 500 members. Apple's cofounder Steve Wozniak describes the significance of their meetings as follows:

> Without computer clubs there would probably be no Apple computers. Our club in the Silicon Valley, the Homebrew Computer Club, was among the first of its kind. It was in early 1975, and a lot of tech-type people would gather and trade integrated circuits back and forth. You could have called it Chips and Dips. We had similar interests and we were there to help other people, but we weren't official and we weren't formal.... During the "random access period" that followed, you would wander outside and find people trading devices or information and helping each other. Occasionally one guy would show up and say, "Is there anyone here from Intel? No? Well, I've got some Intel chips we want to raffle off." This was before big personal computer firms and big money considerations. There was just one personal computer then, the Altair 8800, based around the Intel 8080 microprocessor. The Apple I and II were designed strictly on a hobby, for-fun basis, not to be a product for a company.... Schematics of the Apple I were passed around freely, and I'd even go over to people's houses and help them build their own.[36]

Permission to Compete

The contrasting paths taken by Silicon Valley and Route 128 can be traced back to deep-rooted institutional differences, which shaped the respective cultures of both regions. It is widely recognized, for example, that the Boston area was influenced by the conservative traditions of New England, which placed a stronger emphasis on job stability and unwavering company loyalty than it did on risk-taking and experimentation. New

England had been at the forefront of early American industrialization, but over time, firms became entrenched, and individuals became more fixated on climbing the corporate ladder than striking out on their own or moving between different firms. The notion of leaving a well-established company for an obscure start-up was virtually unheard of. A seasoned employee at Honeywell, who eventually summoned the courage to embark on a new journey with a different firm, recounted the prevailing sentiment in the region: "There is tremendous loyalty to the company [and] pockets of brilliance ... but these individuals never took the leap to go off on their own or join another company.... When I finally left it was like an 8.5 on the Richter scale. Everyone was shocked, they just couldn't believe it!"[37]

On the West Coast, by contrast, job-hopping had become a way of life. The relative ease of setting up a new company in the Valley meant that the fortunes of the region depended less on the decisions of a handful of individuals and corporations, and that many more technological paths were explored than was possible within the hierarchical structures of one company or a less fluid cluster. Notably, many of the Valley's entrepreneurs were engineers who had grown disillusioned by their unsuccessful attempts to pursue their ideas within established corporations. Indeed, in California's computer industry in general, and in Silicon Valley in particular, rates of job-hopping were much higher than in the rest of the country.[38] Famously, for instance, in 1957 eight Mountain View engineers at Shockley Semiconductor—known as the "traitorous eight"—broke away to form Fairchild Semiconductor. Nine years later, as discussed, two of those members, Gordon Moore and Robert Noyce, would leave Fairchild to found Intel.[39]

These moves would not have been possible without the California Civil Code of 1872. By outlawing noncompete agreements in employment contracts, it ensured that engineers were not bound by restrictions that would prevent them from joining competitors or embarking on entrepreneurial ventures. This legal framework had far-reaching implications for the dynamism and vibrancy of the region. In addition to Moore and Noyce, more than thirty talented engineers from Fairchild took advantage of this freedom to establish their own companies. As a result of these defections, the years between 1959 and 1976 witnessed the birth of over forty semiconductor companies in Santa Clara, while Massachusetts only welcomed a comparatively modest five new companies into the world. Perhaps somewhat paradoxically, in a competitive decentralized system, like that of the Valley, a few rigid hierarchies might even facilitate innovation, as people leave incumbents behind to set up their own shops to pursue more radical ideas.[40]

These same forces were once at work in Detroit, which laid some of the critical technological foundations for the golden age of growth.[41] During the first three decades of the car industry, the population of Wayne County, the home of Detroit, swelled from a mere 300,000 to 1.8 million people, as the automotive industry became the largest industry in America.[42] By 1910, seven of the top ten producers of automobiles, including Ford, General Motors, and later Chrysler, were located in the Motor City, which accounted for 65 percent of the market. Economist Stephen Klepper has documented the striking parallels between the two clusters.[43] In both places, non-competes had been long prohibited, and partly as a result, one innovating firm spawned a host of spin-offs as inventors and engineers left to set up their own companies. In Michigan, however, the Antitrust Reform Act of 1985 repealed the ban on the enforcement of such anticompetitive practices and led to a decline in the state's technological dynamism.[44] When barriers to horizontal movement are introduced, knowledge flows are reduced and innovation suffers.

From Taylor to Toyota

Like the Motor City, Japan similarly experienced an arc of growth and stagnation, as the country thrived during the "memory race," only to fall behind in subsequent years. By the mid-1980s, many believed that the practices of open exchange and informal collaboration that had once facilitated the rise of Santa Clara County were no longer apt. Instead of advancing technology, companies now had to mass manufacture standard devices at low cost. In the words of Intel cofounder Andy Grove, the prime objective of his firm was to reduce costs to "market pre-fabricated, mass produced solutions to users." In the wake of this shift from exploration to exploitation, many feared that Japanese firms would soon take over the industry. To make their case, doomsayers pointed out that by 1986, all of Silicon Valley had dropped out of dynamic random access memory (DRAM) production, or that "one in every five local semiconductor employees lost his or her job during the layoffs and plant closings of 1985 and 1986."[45]

As so often is the case, the natural impulse among incumbents was not to raise their game in response to competition but to seek shelter. Beginning in 1978, Silicon Valley executives leveraged the newly formed Semiconductor Industry Association (SIA) to lobby Washington over alleged unfair Japanese trade practices. These efforts were successful in paving the way for the 1986 US–Japan Semiconductor Trade Agreement, designed to prevent "dumping" and to open Japanese markets to American products. At the same time, however, it was becoming clearer that Japan's advantage was not exclusively derived from lower labour costs or government subsidies. When Hewlett-Packard compared Japanese and American 16K DRAMs in 1980, they found that Japanese chips were of higher quality, and not merely the result of better production technology: even when using the same machines, Japanese producers achieved fewer defects.[46] Japanese semiconductor manufacturers worked more closely with suppliers to perfect and modify equipment, which permitted them to attain "lower product costs and faster development times."[47] During its peak in 1977, the American semiconductor industry held a dominant position, catering to 95 percent of the U.S. market and 57 percent of the global market. By 1989, however, the former leader had become a net importer of semiconductors, with Japan supplying a quarter of its demand. The U.S. share of global production also plummeted during this period, dropping from 57 percent to 40 percent, while Japan's share surged from 28 percent to 50 percent.[48]

Economic historians like Peter Lindert have attributed this shift to the relative vigour of U.S. antitrust. To avoid attracting the attention of the authorities, American companies had to grow organically and often diversified into unrelated lines of business. These limitations checked anticompetitive practices within the industry, but they also discouraged scale and coordination.[49] Japanese companies, for instance, could hold partial equity stakes in suppliers. This, in turn, encouraged knowledge and technology transfer, making Japan's collaborative model particularly apt for the changes in production technology that were taking place. Taylorism, which had changed the face of manufacturing in the beginning of the twentieth century, centred on a fixed sequence of steps and specialized machines designed for churning out a single standardized product in extremely large quantities. Yet rapidly shortening product life cycles and growing demand for customization required more flexibility. For example, when Ford ceased producing the Model T, the company had to shut down and redesign the entire plant. The advent of more flexible and reprogrammable machines solved this problem by enabling companies to easily switch from one product to another and thus produce greater variety and smaller batches. The introduction of computers, meanwhile, allowed for better coordination of different activities. Indeed, many companies, including Ford, switched to a parallel rather than sequential approach to design and production, as new technologies, like computer-aided design and manufacturing, allowed them to cut development time by a third. This reduced retooling costs, allowed product designs to use common inputs, and enabled very small inventories. Nowhere was this shift more evident than in Japan, where Toyota's "just-in-time" approach to production revolutionized the industry. In 1950, American car workers had been three times more productive than their closest German rivals. By 1980, when Ford and GM recorded combined losses exceeding $1.3 billion, Japanese car workers had become 17 percent more productive than their American competitors.[50]

Japan's advantage in the exploitation of new technologies was evident in a wide range of industries, and many products invented in the West were suddenly made in Japan. Colour television, for instance, was introduced in America in 1954 with a national colour broadcast of the Rose Parade, whereas colour television would appear in Japan six years later. Yet it was Japan, where governments permitted cartel-like collusion among its seven electronic giants—Hitachi, Matsushita (Panasonic), Mitsubishi, Sanyo, Sharp, Sony, and Toshiba—that would go on to produce the best colour television sets. Even Sony's Walkman—perhaps the greatest consumer success story of the 1980s—was based on the invention of a Dutch company, Philips, which developed the compact audio tape cassette that the Walkman was built to play. Similarly, the technology underlying Sony's hugely successful VCR player, first introduced in Tokyo in September 1971, was invented by the American Ampex Corporation fifteen years earlier.[51] As economist Edwin Mansfield's classic 1988 study showed, Japanese corporations excelled at absorbing and improving foreign technology. According to Mansfield's estimates, two-thirds of U.S. R&D was product-oriented, whereas two-thirds of Japanese R&D was process-oriented.[52] In the words of IBM's chief scientist at the time, Japan's greatest technological strength vis-à-vis the United States was "the speed with which developments [were] translated into improved products and processes."[53]

Eminent observers, like Alfred Chandler Jr., can thus be forgiven for thinking that the computer age had already become one of exploitation rather than exploration. Writing in the late 1980s, Chandler noted that new industries had grown up quickly, following a similar trajectory to the Second Industrial Revolution of the late-nineteenth century. He also felt that most innovation in computing happened inside the walls of long-established firms, like Xerox and IBM in America, or BASF, Mannesmann, and Siemens in Germany. In Japan, he correctly remarked: "all the major computer makers were enterprises that had originally been established by the 1920s."[54]

In America, however, not even Chandler could gloss over new companies like Apple, which was making considerable strides in PCs, or Microsoft, which was doing the same in software. In industries that did not exist before 1940, including computers and biotechnology, new firms were responsible for most significant innovations.[55] As Harvard's Clayton Christensen later noted, no major producer of mainframe computers became a leading player in minicomputers. The Digital Equipment Corporation (DEC), which created the market for minicomputers, was initially joined by Data General, Prime, Wang, Hewlett-Packard, and Nixdorf. However, each of these companies failed to foresee the rise of the PC, so Apple, Commodore, Tandy, and IBM's stand-alone PC division were left to establish the market for desktop computers. Yet even they initially missed the boat for portable computers, where newcomers like Apollo, Sun, and Silicon Graphics would take the lead.[56] Concurrently, on Route 128, producers of minicomputers were particularly slow to recognize the changes taking place. As Saxenian would observe in her comparative study of Silicon Valley and Route 128,

> [the latter] dismissed microcomputers as either irrelevant or silly, much as IBM had dismissed the threat of minicomputers two decades before. DEC's Ken Olsen claimed in the late 1970s that "the personal computer will fall flat on its face in business" and prohibited the use of the term "personal computer" within the company. Five years later he referred to workstations as "snake oil." DG, Wang, and Prime similarly regarded personal computers as toys, rather than as serious competition for their weightier systems. They continued to focus on "pumping iron" for existing customers and defending profitable installed bases, rather than developing products for new markets.[57]

Software and Stagnation

Compared to America's long-standing tradition of competition and support of new companies (going back to the Sherman Antitrust Act of 1890, if not the Constitution itself), the tradition of cooperation across the Pacific Ocean favoured incumbents over start-ups. In Japan, many industries were exempt from antitrust rules, and cartels remained legal. The Japanese Fair Trade Commission (FTC) was weak, antitrust enforcement was lax, and sanctions on criminal behaviour were light.[58] Indeed, by 1989, Japan's FTC had initiated only six criminal prosecutions in the entire forty-two-year history of the Antimonopoly Law. In the same period, the U.S. government filed 2,271 antitrust cases, interventions that research has found boosted both employment and business formation.[59]

To see how antitrust shaped the American Computer Revolution specifically, consider the case of IBM. With the introduction of the IBM 650 in the mid-1950s, the company essentially created the commercial market for computers. And over time, this provided compelling incentives to develop standard software for its architecture. By bundling its software products with its mainframe computers, IBM created significant barriers to entry for independent vendors.[60] This all changed on December 6, 1968, when IBM announced that it was unbundling its sales of hardware and software. To be sure, the role of antitrust in this decision has been the subject of much debate, but the timing of events speaks volumes, as it seems evident the change in policy was meant to get out ahead of coming litigation.[61] Five days after the announcement, the Control Data Corporation (CDC) sued the computer giant for antitrust violations. The following month, the Justice Department filed its landmark suit, charging IBM with monopolizing the market for digital computers. The trial, which began in May 1975, would become so lengthy that Yale law professor Robert Bork dubbed the case "the antitrust division's Vietnam."[62] Regardless of the company's original motives, the never-ending courtroom war of *United States v. International Business Machines Corp.* certainly "prevented IBM from reconsidering its unbundling decision during the 1970s."[63] This, in turn, gave a new generation of start-ups, like Microsoft, the opportunity to enter the scene.

The minicomputer, meanwhile, prompted a shift away from mainframe computers, whose centralized operations made it costlier for users to develop new applications and certainly did its part for the democratization of American software production. But the real take-off came in the 1980s when Sun's workstation, IBM's PC, and Apple's Macintosh proliferated. Suddenly, even smaller companies could afford to own computers. Amid this growth, three emerging software companies—Ashton-Tate, Lotus, and Microsoft—battled to supply the growing PC market. Ultimately, IBM's endorsement of the PC-DOS operating system swung the balance in favour of Microsoft, which quickly became IBM's dominant supplier of software. Meanwhile, the old guard was retreating from the market through different paths. By 1991, the software revenues of Hewlett-Packard, NCR, and Unisys had all fallen below their 1981 level.[64]

The blossoming of the internet (through email, file transfer, and collaborative work applications) was similarly nurtured by America's strong antitrust regime. JCR Licklider, during his time at ARPA, laid the groundwork for what would become the modern internet (chapter 7). To support long-distance collaborations among America's network of universities, these early developments were later entrusted to the National

Science Foundation (NSF). In the early 1990s, the internet was still the domain of researchers, professors, and students; the Web remained in its infancy, barely recognized as a platform for commerce. The NSF, in fact, had never envisioned the internet as a commercial space, but as the network grew, so did its potential applications. This growth was not something that the NSF or any other single organisation was well-equipped to manage. What truly facilitated the explosion of innovation that followed was the remarkable absence of government or corporate oversight dictating the internet's early trajectory. It was instead shaped organically by its users.

Unlike many other countries where foreign carrier services were seamlessly absorbed into state-run telephone monopolies, the United States followed a different path, one that fostered a competitive data carrier business. Had the commercialization of the internet taken place just a decade earlier, the dominant communications giant, AT&T, would have likely absorbed the technology into its existing monopoly, which could have stifled its development altogether if it saw no immediate financial benefit. However, by the time the internet was taken out of the hand of the NSF and privatized, the United States had already undergone significant changes in its telecommunications sector. The 1984 breakup of AT&T, following a decade-long antitrust battle, shattered the monopoly and created a fragmented market with multiple players, each free to pursue their own strategies. Without a single firm wielding unchecked control, the risk of critical decisions being bottlenecked in one boardroom was eliminated.[65]

In the following years, the so-called browser wars ensued after Microsoft, which had initially underestimated the commercial potential of the internet, sought to make up for lost ground to the pioneer, Netscape Navigator, by licensing the Mosaic web browser, upon which it built Internet Explorer. In 1998 when the U.S. Department of Justice filed an antitrust lawsuit against Microsoft for bundling Internet Explorer with its Windows operating system, David Mowery and Nathan Rosenberg observed that the same competition dynamics that had come from deregulating the U.S. telecommunications industry in 1984 would now determine "the future of the U.S. software industry."[66] Indeed, as Internet Explorer's dominance subsequently faded, alternative browsers like Mozilla Firefox and, later, Google Chrome gained traction.

The story of Japan could hardly be more different. While companies like Fujitsu, Hitachi, and NEC had leapt ahead in hardware, Japanese companies fell short in moving into software and failed to tap into the growth of the internet era. The keiretsu system, where companies primarily conducted business within their own group, facilitated anticompetitive practices that excluded outsiders and erected formidable barriers for start-ups attempting to enter the market.[67] Simultaneously, the Japanese government, faced with mounting challenges as Japan approached the technological frontier, struggled to compensate for the private sector's shortcomings. "MITI was unable to 'plan' the geeky university dropout who starts a software firm or an internet business in his parents' garage," to borrow Joe Studwell's memorable phrase.[68] Consequently, compared to the new generation of American companies, Japan's conglomerates produced far fewer software inventions.[69]

Contrast the Japanese experience with that of its former colony, South Korea, which had similar corporatist institutions in the postwar period. While the state checked the power of the chaebol under Park (as discussed in chapter 8), following Korea's transition to democracy in 1987, the power of the state was diffused. As political scientist David C. Kang notes, "This led to increased demands for political payoffs as politicians began to genuinely compete for electoral support and to decreased ability of the state to resist or contain the demands of the business sector."[70] For example, when the Hanbo Steel Company declared bankruptcy in 1997, as the Asian financial crisis took many victims, an inquest uncovered that at least 2 billion dollars were missing. When Hanbo's chairman, Chung Taesoo, was arrested, he privately declared that if pressed he would take the bankers and politicians involved with him. On the bright side, however, the crises paved the way for sweeping reforms, such as a substantial strengthening of antitrust legislation, and many behemoths, including Daewoo, were subsequently culled.

Around that time, observers like Ha-Joon Chang and Jang-Sup Shin suggested that these reforms, which in their view attempted a "transition to an idealised Anglo-American system," would "put the chaebol under serious constraints in operating as business groups, especially through the ban on internal transactions."[71] They did indeed check the operations of the chaebol, but with overwhelmingly positive effects. By dismantling barriers that had previously kept non-chaebol companies out of the market, the Korean antitrust agency delivered a splendid stimulus to competition and innovation. As corrective orders tripled, and financial penalties for anticompetitive behaviour increased twenty-five-fold, Korean patenting surged, and predictably, this acceleration was driven by non-chaebol firms.[72] Like their keiretsu counterparts in Japan, the chaebol had been instrumental to Korea's postwar miracle. But they were not set up to power innovation at the frontier.

In Japan, by contrast, conglomerates maintained their domestic dominance even as competition mounted from abroad, with Silicon Valley specializing in design and innovation while increasingly offshoring its assembly operations. This created an opportunity for Chinese low-cost manufacturers to access Western technology, which eroded the production advantage held by Japanese corporations at the same time. Over the next decades, this shift would redraw the economic and geopolitical landscape of East Asia, and indeed the world. However, it was initially unclear whether China would take advantage of the great flattening by integrating into global value chains, or whether it would attempt to emulate Japan instead.

Forging Chimerica

In 1980, World Bank president Robert McNamara embarked on a trip to Beijing to offer guidance on reform. His visit was part of an extensive three-month study tour and a series of meetings that led the World Bank to prescribe a comprehensive set of free-market policies, later known as the Washington Consensus. Chinese officials were advised to use prices to make investment decisions and to accelerate wide-ranging privatization of state assets. The Chinese government also dispatched bureaucrats to Eastern Europe to study the region's liberalization reforms. However, many of these officials doubted their applicability for China and thought that more could be learned from an example closer to home: Japan.

Indeed, following Deng's first visit to Japan in October 1978, a Japanese advisory group had already been set up. It would continue to meet with Chinese economic officials until 1992. The Chinese were particularly impressed with how Japan's MITI had shaped the modernization of industry. During his visit, Deng marveled over the amount of planning that happened at both the enterprise and government levels.[73] These exchanges convinced many Chinese officials that the Japanese development model was more compatible with Chinese institutions than were those of Western economies. Delegation reports, for instance, frequently highlighted valuable lessons to be learned from Japan's successful high-growth phase from 1956 to 1972.[74]

The allure of Japan's state-led development model is not hard to understand. It seemed to offer something for everyone. On one hand, it embraced private enterprise as the fundamental unit of economic organization, thereby ensuring a space for market dynamics to flourish. On the other hand, it assured planners that their role in guiding the economy toward desired outcomes would persist. When Japanese economists visited China during the 1980s, for example, they took great care to emphasize that Japan was not simply another capitalist country, but rather one where government guidance of markets was critical. This message naturally resonated with Chinese officials. For the State Planning Commission, continuing government intervention meant that it would continue to play a key role, although in reduced form. For the State Economic Commission, the Japanese model also seemed an attractive blend of enterprise and direction. Its Director, Yuan Baohua, who participated in the early inspection tours to Japan, was so impressed with its organization of business that he used Japan's *Keidanren* as a model for China's first industrial association, which aimed to create closer links between government agencies and the corporate sphere.[75]

Yet despite such initiatives, a Tokyo Consensus failed to materialize. Disagreement among Chinese officials, as well as bureaucratic turf wars, led to paralysis in how to drive technological progress. The centralized effort to buy and absorb foreign technology with the proceeds from petroleum exports had failed. Moreover, Deng's "Southern Tour" made clear that localized reform could yield impressive results. Indeed, while

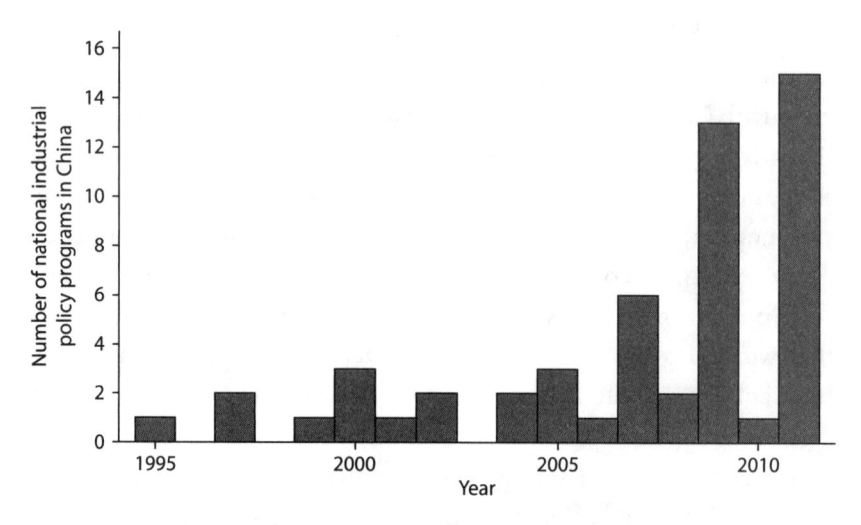

FIGURE 11.3. National industrial policy programs in China, 1995–2012
Source: Heilmann and Shih, "Rise of Industrial Policy in China," Figure 1.

industrial policy early on had primarily focused on Shanghai and Beijing, it was the reformed Guangdong region that emerged as the centre of technology industries like electronics and computers.[76] Sceptics of the Japanese way could point to China's leading computer companies, Legend (now Lenovo) and Great Wall, which were founded in Beijing but soon moved significant production and research operations south.[77] To flourish and gain access to technological know-how, these companies, like so many others, had no choice but to relocate to the provinces of Guangdong or Fujian, which had integrated into global markets.[78] Consequently, before the late 2000s, efforts to support specific technology industries were few (figure 11.3). This retreat reached its nadir during the Premiership of Zhu Rongji (1998–2003), when the most industrial ministries were abolished and the authority to develop industrial policy was withdrawn from the State Planning Commission.[79]

China's technology strategy followed a similar pattern. Initially, the CPC explicitly mandated technology transfer as a quid pro quo for market access, just as Japan had done in its early days. But after joining the World Trade Organization (WTO) in 2001, which prohibits such practices, China formally dropped its joint venture requirement. True, many officials continued to make such demands behind closed doors: when the U.S.–China Business Council surveyed its members in 2012, 36 percent of corporations reported having been asked to transfer technology in return for project approval or to gain market access only in the three previous years.[80] Foreign CEOs thus found themselves in a dilemma: either comply with the requests and share their technologies with potential Chinese competitors, or refuse and miss out on the world's most rapidly expanding market.[81]

As time went on, however, the escalating concerns about technology leakage functioned as a warning sign to Western companies that establishing cutting-edge operations in China carried significant risks. Companies such as Intel, SK Hynix, and Samsung, despite having substantial operations in China, predominantly focused on producing lower-end memory chips for the domestic market, while reserving their most advanced operations for other locations. One keen observer in 2019 noted that with some exceptions, multinationals had become "wary of investing in high-value manufacturing in China for fear of theft."[82] To compensate for this lack of foreign investment in its technology sector, the Chinese government decided to prop up state-owned enterprises (SOEs), but with assured state support, these companies faced few compelling incentives to innovate. Instead, hybrid companies, in part foreign-owned yet with strong links to China, made more meaningful contributions to the country's modernization efforts.[83]

Tapping into the pool of some 20 million Chinese émigrés and their descendants—many of whom were more than willing to provide technology and capital in exchange for access to a billion new customers—turned out to be a better development strategy than propping up lagging SOEs or even forcing joint ventures on multinationals. Extensive research by Harvard's William Kerr highlights the crucial role played by ethnic ties in facilitating technology transfer. In the United States, he found, links between resident talent and their home countries were particularly strong in high-tech sectors and within the Chinese community.[84] The transnational, ethnic Chinese, technology community, in other words, served as "the glue to bind foreign firms to China."[85] The Semiconductor Manufacturing International Corporation (SMIC), for example, was founded in

2000 by Richard Chang Ru-gin—a Taiwanese veteran of Texas Instruments (TI), where he worked alongside Nobel Prize in Physics laureate Jack Kilby, who went on to recruit ethnic Chinese engineers to return from the United States, Taiwan, and Singapore.[86] Despite the admiration that Chinese officials held for Japan's state-led development model, the actual trajectory of China's development was thus more influenced by the events unfolding on its own shores.

Ethnic ties had been no less important for the development of China's runaway province: Taiwan. Since 1955, Taiwan and the United States had been treaty allies, but America's debacle in Vietnam made its security promises uncertain. Anti-Communist governments across Asia, from South Korea to Singapore, sought reassurance and economic investment to prevent Communist influence. Minister K. T. Li saw TI as a solution, with semiconductors at the heart of the plan to bind America to its security commitments. One of its executives, Morris Chang, a mainland-born engineer who had lived in the United States since fleeing Communist China, helped realise this plan by pushing for the first TI plant to be built in Taiwan in 1968. A decade later, Li recruited Chang to run its Industrial Technology Research Institute. With the government providing 48 percent of the start-up capital, Chang went on to found the Taiwan Semiconductor Manufacturing Company (TSMC) in 1987, which soon attracted a host of Silicon Valley customers. During the 1970s and 1980s, the chip industry had been dominated by vertically integrated device manufacturers. TSMC disrupted this model by permitting American companies to offshore production to low-cost, third-party foundries, and focus on chip design.[87]

Indeed, compared to South Korea and Japan, whose economies were dominated by industrial conglomerates, Taiwan, Hong Kong, and Guangdong were more competitively organized. Both the chaebol and the keiretsu relied on the mastery of process technologies to achieve economies of scale, as well as to branch into other lines of business. Few Taiwanese companies, in contrast, were vertically integrated or even developed their own products. Instead, they acted as suppliers to American technology companies. Resembling their counterparts in Silicon Valley, many Taiwanese entrepreneurs embarked on new ventures after departing from their previous companies, and these new companies often focused on specific components or assemblies that catered to the original firm's needs. As a result, by the mid-1990s, Taiwan boasted over four thousand companies engaged in the assembly of PCs and electrical components. According to one prominent economist, Taiwanese firms "have learned how to be fast followers, only a half-step behind the technological frontier."[88] Relative to the chaebol and the keiretsu, they were more responsive to changing economic and technological conditions.

For America, meanwhile, the result was a marriage of convenience. In response to Japan's dominance in process technology, American corporations embraced an alternative approach. They began to devise open, nonproprietary systems that allowed them to tap into global value chains, thereby reducing costs and increasing flexibility. The outcome marked the inception of a new era of integration between America and the so-called China Circle, encompassing the People's Republic of China, Hong Kong, and Taiwan. While Hong Kong and Taiwan had already seen impressive export growth in the 1960s and 1970s, when containers caused shipping costs to plummet, their impact on the U.S. economy was minimal. And as labour costs rose in both places, mainland China became increasingly attractive as a hub for production.[89] Consequently, what Niall Ferguson and Moritz Schularick have aptly called "Chimerica" was forged.[90]

In this process, not just Shenzhen, but the entire Pearl River Delta between Guangzhou and Hong Kong gradually became the factory of the world. Former rice paddies and duck farms were quickly replaced by a vast landscape of factories, often owned by Taiwanese and Hong Kong investors. From alarm clocks to cameras, sweaters to shoes, televisions to disk drives, desktop computers to furniture, and bicycles to stuffed animals, the range of products the region manufactured seemed boundless. In a peacetime migration of historic proportions, workers from interior provinces poured into these factories. This migratory workforce, known as the "floating population" or *liudong renkou*, numbered around 150 million individuals during the early 2000s.[91]

The Computer Revolution, like previous industrial revolutions, led to seismic changes in standards of living and ways of life. Yet unlike its

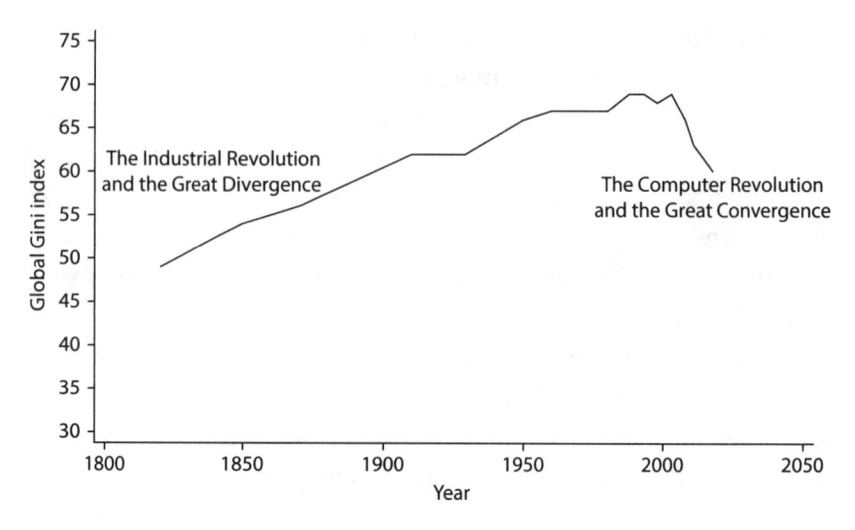

FIGURE 11.4. Global income inequality, 1800–2018
Source: Milanovic, *Capitalism, Alone*, Figure 1.1.

predecessors, which fueled rising inequality around the world, with some exceptions, the Computer Revolution ushered in a new era of convergence.[92] This shift is shown in figure 11.4, which depicts the stunning decline in global inequality accompanying the rise of the computer age. In the 1970s, managers could share documents and blueprints via fax machine, but for many activities, the technology was still inadequate for coordinating complex daily operations. However, as the proliferation of personal computers, email, and the World Wide Web enabled seamless coordination across vast distances, corporations seized the opportunity to offshore a significant number of jobs to the Middle Kingdom. The goods bought by American consumers were no longer made in Dayton, Ohio, but in Shenzhen.

Concurrently, a sprawling network of local firms, numbering in the thousands, emerged alongside foreign producers, amplifying China's industrial prowess. By the turn of the millennium, companies like Motorola found themselves reliant on some 700 suppliers in China, more than 400 of which were domestic.[93] Apple, meanwhile, has spent the past decade and a half sending its top product designers and plant design engineers across the Pacific, where they have played integral roles in advancing production technology. Allegedly, just before the COVID-19 pandemic took its toll, the company reserved fifty first-class seats every day in both directions between San Francisco and China.[94] And having lifted over 800 million people out of poverty, China, like Japan in the 1980s, is now widely regarded as America's peer competitor. Turning to the present, one question looms above all others: Will such extraordinary progress continue?

12

The Great Leap Backward

> With the help of artificial intelligence or multiple intelligence, our perception of the world will be elevated to a new level. As such, big data will make the market smarter and make it possible to plan and predict market forces so as to allow us to finally achieve a planned economy.[1]
>
> —JACK MA

THE ASCENT of China, arguably the most successful poverty reduction programme in history, has cemented Western fears that an authoritarian country will soon become the technological leader of the world. At a time when populism, polarization, and plutocracy are seen as the hallmarks of American capitalism, many see the Chinese model as an increasingly attractive alternative. Not only has the Chinese middle class exploded while the American middle class has withered, but Chinese technology companies have rapidly closed the gap to their American competitors. In separate accounts, political scientist Graham Allison and technologist Kai-Fu Lee have gone as far as to suggest that China has already overtaken the United States in artificial intelligence (AI)—the most important general-purpose technology of our time.[2]

If such a scenario unfolds, the most prosperous people on the planet might one day live under Communist Party rule—quite the opposite of what most predicted when the Berlin Wall fell in 1989. Yet despite high hopes for AI to bolster productivity, the past decade has witnessed sluggish economic growth. In the American context, publications with titles like *The Great Stagnation*, *The Rise and Fall of American Growth*, and "Are Ideas Getting Harder to Find?" underline a productivity slowdown since the mid-2000s that suggests the country has reached a technological plateau. Meanwhile, recent studies show that in China, where the average citizen remains approximately five times poorer than the average American, productivity not only slowed down but turned negative after the Great Recession.[3] Even rosier estimates show a considerable deceleration in the 2010s.[4] To some degree, this is only natural, as the scope for catch-up growth diminishes once foreign technologies have been absorbed. However, China's productivity seems to have plateaued at a level of income considerably lower than other East Asian latecomers, such as Korea, Japan, and Taiwan.[5] Hence, while it has become popular to pitch China and the United States as locked in an economic and technological race, the truth is that both are trending toward stagnation, and further headwinds lie ahead as Chimerica starts to disintegrate. To see why, let's begin by examining the internal dynamics of China itself.

The Privatization Wave

A journey across China's coastal provinces, where burgeoning technological centres thrive and most of the country's riches are generated, provides compelling archaeological evidence of Chinese progress in the post-Mao era. This is even true of parts of the north, like Beijing, where a flourishing technology cluster has emerged around a few spin-offs from leading institutions such as Peking and Tsinghua Universities, the prestigious Chinese Academy of Sciences (CAS), and the Chinese Academy of Engineering (CAE). Just as the founding of Hewlett-Packard, which began as a Stanford offshoot, marked a defining moment in Silicon Valley's history, Lenovo, which was spun-off from CAS, sparked the transformation of the neighbourhood of Zhongguancun into the incubator of China's internet economy.

Take the world's fastest passenger train 1,318 kilometers south and arrive in China's next cluster in a little over four hours: Shanghai. The former treaty port city is the core of the Yangtze River Delta, historically China's most prosperous region, and has attracted a range of foreign technology firms, including Taiwan's leading semiconductor maker, TSMC. Next, stop at Hangzhou, a designated Economic and Technological Development Zone, where Alibaba is headquartered. Further south, Shenzhen, where Deng's economic reforms began, is the land of Huawei—a provider of cutting-edge 5G technology.[6] These clusters have pulled in considerable resources, and not only from abroad: after decades of Maoism, which favoured smokestack industries inland, the eastern region's share of the country's fixed investment jumped from around one-third before 1978 to over 60 percent in the mid-1990s. And foreign investment is even more skewed: in 2001, when China entered the WTO, 86 percent of foreign direct investment targeted its eastern provinces.[7]

Meanwhile, the western regions, which host many of China's state-owned enterprises (SOEs), have attracted assembly companies like Foxconn by providing low-cost labour.[8] However, much of the Chinese Rust Belt, where the resource-hungry state sector is clustered, is yet to recover from the privatization wave of the 1990s.[9] Under the slogan "Grasp the big, let go of the small," many SOEs were either sold to employees or left to go under, while larger ones were corporatized, with private investors becoming part owners alongside the government, which retained a majority stake.[10] This shift surely did much to improve productivity, but for a population accustomed to the iron rice bowl, the social costs were high.[11] As management buyouts multiplied, so did bankruptcies and closures. To cushion the early reforms and make up for the meagre Chinese welfare state, SOE employment had been allowed to expand.[12] After 1993, however, this made their demise all the more painful. Over the next decade, as many SOEs went under, a striking 43 percent of jobs (33 million in total) in government-controlled enterprises were lost.[13] Around that time, in 2001, Premier Zhu Rongji bluntly told laid-off workers to "find jobs on the private labor market."[14]

Most people did. Between 1992 and 2007, urban private employment rose from 11 to 79 million, and in the countryside, it surpassed 110 million, just as the Great Recession broke out in America and a triumphant China made a splash with the Beijing Olympics.[15] By opting for the

Dual-Track System in the 1980s, delaying privatization, and waiting for new jobs to emerge, Beijing might have made the transition less painful than it otherwise would have been. But for SOE workers, who had previously been shielded from competitive forces, the changes were nonetheless dramatic, not least in the northeastern provinces, where giants like the First Automobile Works are headquartered. Ching Kwan Lee's vivid account of the Liaoning Province in this period is telling: "Once the heartland of the socialist planned economy and home to some of China's most prominent state-owned industrial enterprises, Liaoning has declined into a wasteland of bankruptcy and a hotbed of working-class protest by its many unemployed workers and pensioners. Unpaid pensions and wages, defaults on medical subsidies, and inadequate collective consumption are the main grievances triggering labor unrest in Liaoning."[16]

The privatization wave, in short, made China more prosperous but also more unequal. In addition to spawning a new capitalist elite, it created winners and losers in the labour market.[17] In a bestselling and particularly damning account published in the 1990s, Chinese sociologist He Qinglian argued that the early market reforms had brought nothing but "inequality, generalized corruption and the erosion of the moral basis of society."[18] For all the talk about the rise of American plutocracy, the surge in Chinese inequality has been much more dramatic. Between the mid-1980s and 2013, the Gini coefficient in the United States rose by 4 points. In China, over the same period, it rose by almost 20 points.[19] This surge was driven in part by the structural factors that economist Simon Kuznets once emphasized: as China opened up to the world, huge pools of labour moved from low-income agriculture to higher-income manufacturing. According to a 2008 survey of China's 140 million internal migrants, 70 percent had left rural inland provinces, and 62 percent had moved to the urban coastal east, which housed 42 percent of the country's population at the time.[20] However, China's great migration would have been even greater had it not been for the *hokou* system, which ties people to their village of origin by determining where they are eligible to receive public services. In 2019, just before the COVID-19 pandemic, the income ratio between the three richest and the three poorest provinces still stood at four to one. The average Chinese city dweller is as rich as the average Hungarian, while the rural population in China is no better off than the average Vietnamese.[21]

Oligarchy or Autocracy?

Rising inequality in China has also been fueled by the country's increasing share of income from capital, which tends to be more concentrated than income from labour. Between the 1980s and 2015, China's private wealth shot up from 100 percent to 450 percent of national income.[22] This increase was driven in part by the large-scale privatization of housing and SOEs but also the growth of new private enterprises.[23] The rise of China's new business elite is evident from household surveys, which show that in 1988, more than 80 percent of those in the top 5 percent of the income distribution were workers, clerical staff, and government officials. By 2013, their share had almost halved, as they were replaced by entrepreneurs and professionals. Indeed, one indication of Chinese dynamism during this period is that four-fifths of this new professional class had fathers who were either farmers or manual workers.[24]

Yet these figures do not necessarily tell us much about the future. Because the Chinese Revolution of 1949 and the subsequent Cultural Revolution in the 1960s had obliterated the merchant class, such striking social mobility is not surprising. And as wealth becomes more entrenched, as it has in the United States, one might expect China to experience levels of mobility similar to that of the developed world. There is even reason to fear that social mobility will be significantly lower in China than in the West, simply because the role of the Chinese state bureaucracy, whose power has been left unchecked by the rule of law, is so much greater. Indeed, corruption in the 2000s reached extraordinary heights even by Chinese historical standards. According to political scientist Minxin Pei, bureaucratic positions are frequently sold across different levels of government, and payments for these positions increase as one moves up the ranks of the Party apparatus.[25] The overall contribution of such corruption to Chinese inequality is hard to judge, but the sums involved in some corruption cases are truly remarkable. As economist Branko Milanovic recounts:

> Xu Caihou, at the time of his arrest in 2014 the vice chairman of the Central Military Commission and the highest official to be indicted to that date, had the entire basement of his 20,000-square-foot house stocked with cash (renminbis, euros, and dollars) that weighed more than a ton. The precious artifacts filled ten military trucks. [However, the] largest seizure of cash since the founding of the People's Republic concerned a deputy head of the coal department in the National Energy Administration who was found with more than 200 million yuan in cash (about $26 million at the current exchange rate). Sixteen money-counting machines were brought in; four burned out in the process of counting the bills.[26]

Given such widespread corruption, it would be mistaken to assume that China will reach a point when inequality starts to decline due to economic forces, as Kuznets famously argued it would.[27] And this posits a fundamental challenge to the Chinese model itself.

In principle, China can reverse cronyism in two ways: by strengthening the rule of law or strengthening the Party at the expense of Chinese oligarchs and business elites. The trouble with the former approach, of course, is that it threatens to undermine the entire system, which is built on the credibility of the Party being able to reward behaviour that it likes and punish behaviour that it dislikes.[28] The trouble with the latter is that strengthening the party elite risks further public corruption, which threatens the system's legitimacy, not least since its appeal to the broader public has been to deliver common prosperity. Corrupt officials are justly regarded as "termites" gnawing at the foundations of the People's Republic.[29] From time to time, this necessitates anticorruption campaigns, which become more challenging when political and economic power merges to "create a hybrid politico-economic elite."[30] That elite, once firmly established, is unlikely to support anticorruption measures. The government has and will continue to co-opt economic elites through party membership, but doing so risks solidifying the position of incumbents even further, with more power residing in a narrow circle of top CPC and government officials. To paraphrase Milanovic, depending on whether they succeed in checking or merging the power of private sector interests, China will be left with either oligarchy or autocracy.[31]

Rule by Law

In the nineteenth century, America escaped its Gilded Age by bolstering the capacity of the state and strengthening the rule of law to safeguard competition (as discussed in chapter 6). But in China, like in all Leninist political systems, the Party exists outside the legal system. Since Mao Zedong replaced due process with revolutionary committees and arbitrary violence, the Party has certainly done much to bolster the courts, which today manage an increasingly complex economy in a more decentralized manner. Yet it has done so under the wings of the Party. For example, while Xi Jinping's anticorruption drive in 2013—which led to the indictments of more than 100,000 people—sought to depoliticize the judiciary at the provincial and local government levels, hopes for more separation of powers at the national level were dashed in 2015 by an official statement from the Supreme People's Court chief justice Zhou Qiang. The statement made clear that, "All courts shall use the spirit of Xi Jinping's series of major speeches to arm their minds, guide their practice, [and] foster their work."[32]

Even before Xi surged to power, about one-third of China's 150,000 registered lawyers were party members, and almost all law firms had party committees, which assessed not just pay but party loyalty as well.[33] And the CPC consistently reiterated the low rank of law in the political pecking order, with one official report in 2009 noting that "Judges must remain loyal—in order—to the Party, the state, the masses and, finally, the law."[34] According to He Weifang, a former law professor at Peking University, one cannot sue the Party, simply because there is nothing to sue: "As an organization, the Party sits outside, and above the law. It should have a legal identity, in other words, a person to sue, but it is not even registered as an organization. The Party exists outside the legal system altogether."[35] In fact, the judiciary is not a separate branch, but part of the government apparatus. The division of labour between these parts is straightforward. The CPC makes the key decisions on personnel and policy, which are then ratified and codified by the legislature and implemented by the government.[36]

Consider antitrust, which emerged as a crucial check on corporate power during America's Gilded Age. China's first anti-monopoly law was enacted in 2008—more than a century after the Sherman Antitrust Act of 1890 was adopted in the United States. And while the Sherman Act was implemented following agitation by a mobilized society, the introduction of China's anti-monopoly act was a top-down matter. It also served an entirely different purpose: to check competition from foreign companies and punish entrepreneurs who challenged the Party.[37] When Xi came to power, the regulators went into overdrive and enforcement activity surged. Foreign companies found themselves caught in the crosshairs, as a flurry of enforcement actions were initiated by Chinese agencies tasked with administering the nation's anti-monopoly law. Unannounced visits to corporate offices at the break of dawn, relentless verbal admonishments from officials, coerced apologies, and even restrictions of legal representation during interrogations all became commonplace.[38] These anti-monopoly efforts targeted some of the largest foreign companies operating in China, including Johnson & Johnson, Nikon, Audi, Chrysler, Microsoft, and Mercedes-Benz. The most prominent case, however, was lodged against Qualcomm, a global leader in semiconductor design and wireless telecommunications systems.

Following complaints by Chinese cell phone manufacturers, the National Development and Reform Commission (NDRC), formerly the State Planning Commission, launched an investigation into Qualcomm's licensing practices in 2009. The NDRC charged that the American chip designer had gained an unfair advantage by charging its royalty fee based on the price of the end product rather than the smallest saleable unit, the chip itself. Faced with an existential threat to its business model, Qualcomm was prepared to do what other companies would not: challenge the complaint in court. Concerned that a trial might have exposed the weaknesses of the agency, which in the case of an unfavourable judgment would have been held accountable for mismanagement, the NDRC ended up offering concessions and reaching an out-of-court settlement, albeit a face-saving one. They levied a widely televised $975 million record fine, which earned the agency the image of a forceful antitrust regulator, and its director a swift promotion.[39]

The fact that antitrust authorities are rarely challenged in court means that its battles are usually fought within the government bureaucracy.[40] And this gives politically connected behemoths a significant advantage over smaller innovating companies. For instance, though the political influence over SOEs has been diminished, their top executives are still appointed through the nomenklatura system, which determines their bureaucratic ranking and thus the political clout of the company they manage. And because SOE leaders have direct contact with government officials, they can engage in direct lobbying, rather than needing to make such appeals through business associations. The case against China Telecom and China Unicom over alleged price discrimination is instructive in this regard. When the NDRC declared the investigation in November 2011, the public response was overwhelmingly positive. A few days later, two critical editorials were published in newspapers managed by the Ministry of Industry and Information Technology (MIIT). The internal fightback had begun, and from then on the outcome was predetermined. Since the leaders of China Telecom and China Unicom were higher in bureaucratic rank than the head of the NDRC's antitrust bureau, the latter was in no position to give direct orders to the top executives of these two telecommunications companies.[41]

For private companies, in contrast, opposition to the decisions of the bureaucracy has been a road to perdition. In January 2015, the E-Commerce Supervision Department of the State Administration for Industry and Commerce (SAIC) issued a report showcasing counterfeit products on Alibaba's e-commerce platform Taobao. In a bold move, Alibaba put out an open letter, arguing that SAIC's research method was categorically flawed, attacking the SAIC official in charge of the investigation, and claiming that "we are willing to accept your God-like existence, but we cannot agree with the double standard in various sampling procedures and your irrational logic." In response, the SAIC released a White Paper that denounced Alibaba employees for taking bribes and condemned the company for poor supervision of product information and allowing merchants to operate on the platform without business licenses.[42] As Alibaba's share price plummeted, the Chinese media called it the "most expensive quarrel" in history. Little did they know about how things would soon escalate. In 2021, having just forced the cancellation of Alibaba's affiliate Ant's Initial Public Offering (IPO), China's antitrust regulator hit the technology giant with a fine equivalent to $2.8 billion for abusing its dominant position over rivals and merchants on its e-commerce platforms. The only way forward for Alibaba was to fall in line. Indeed, in a public statement, the company announced that it "accepts the penalty with sincerity and will ensure its compliance with determination."[43]

The bottom line is that unlike in the United States, where a rules-based antitrust system serves to check anticompetitive behaviour, Chinese antitrust is based on arbitrary bureaucratic procedure and political power. Often, China's antirust agency need not even resort to formal regulatory tools to enforce its views, as it can use state media to strategically shame companies, which further deters actions countering the agency. This constitutes what legal scholar Angela Zhang aptly has called "Chinese Antitrust Exceptionalism." Fearing retribution, businesses are naturally averse to confronting the antitrust authorities, especially if they have weak connections to the Party. This, in turn, provides formidable barriers to entry for innovating entrepreneurs, while handing an unfair advantage to networked incumbents holding the Party line.

China Inc.

Rather than create a rules-based antitrust framework to check the power of China's new tycoons, the bureaucracy has instead developed tools to co-opt and control them. Of the many astounding revelations in Richard McGregor's *The Party*, the existence of red phones on the desks of powerful Party members stands out. The "red machines," as they are called, are dotted throughout the country, sitting on the desks of ministers and vice-ministers, the chief editors of party newspapers, and the chairmen of large state enterprises. Possession of one of these machines signifies membership of the tight-knit elite club that runs the country, similar to Britain's old boy network, France's *les énarques*, Japan's *Todai elite*, or India's *Gymkhana Club*. But unlike other elite networks, those who possessed a red phone were required to undergo extensive training at Party schools and subsequently needed approval by the Party's Central Organization Department, which evaluates the suitability of candidates, including their political reliability. The machines, in other words, are not meant as a way of giving important officials access to the highest ranks of the Party apparatus. On the contrary, they provide the Party with a hotline into multiple arms of government, including SOEs and companies around the world, and so constitute a means for Beijing to control corporate China. As one Chinese executive puts it, "When the 'red machine' rings, you had better make sure you answer it."[44]

In recent years, however, managing the Party has become an increasingly complex undertaking. For Chinese autocracy, the key challenge is that the growth of China's innovating private sector during the reform years has created enormous wealth outside the system of SOEs, which threatens to undermine Party rule.[45] To address this issue, the Party has expanded its membership to include these innovators—a strategy called "co-opting the capitalists."[46] The Party began its recruitment of entrepreneurs in the mid-1980s, and these efforts accelerated in July 2001, when President Jiang Zemin gave his famous speech calling for the Party to represent the greatest majority of the people, among them the Chinese proletariat and entrepreneurs. Five years later, about one-third of entrepreneurs had become Party members, many of whom have since accumulated vast fortunes.[47] These red tycoons include Jack Ma, the founder of Alibaba; Tencent's founder Ma Huateng, who is also a delegate to the National People's Congress; and Baidu's cofounder Robin Li, who is even a member of the Chinese People's Political Consultative Conference—the central political advisory body to the CPC. With over 90 million members, the Party is today larger than the population of Germany, though as a percentage of the Chinese population, membership still only stands at 6.5 percent.[48]

Despite this relatively small footprint, and even though college campuses remain the main source of new recruits, the Party increasingly penetrates all parts of society: there are more than 4.6 million party cells throughout firms, universities, and neighbourhoods, which means that wherever people live and work, they are subject to the eyes and ears of the CPC. According to *The Economist*, since 2012 the share of private companies with embedded party organisations has increased from around half to more than 70 percent.[49] Journalist Paul Blustein notes that such organisations have become increasingly common and intrusive in foreign-invested companies as well:

> At the Beijing unit of Bosch Rexroth, a German engineering firm, Party members study Xi speeches on Saturdays. The Chinese joint venture of Renault, the French automaker, has organized lectures for new foreign employees on the Party's role. Walt Disney Co.'s Shanghai theme park has about 300 Party members among its staff, who attend Party lectures during business hours at a special Party centre featuring Mickey Mouse decorations. At Cummins Engine, plans to appoint a new manager for one of the company's China businesses were scotched when Party representatives nixed the choice. Doing business in China has long required some sort of Party involvement, but until recently, most Party cells were more symbolic than active.[50]

The CPC is also increasing its leverage over the private sector by taking direct ownership in private companies. Consider the auto manufacturer Cherry, which began in the 1990s as a producer of cheap Volkswagen knockoffs. At the time Chinese authorities were aiming to realize economies of scale by consolidating its state-led giants, like Shanghai Automobile and First Automotive Works. Small competitors like Cherry were not only put at disadvantage but were outright forbidden. However, Shanghai Automobile ended up agreeing to taking a 20 percent equity stake in Cherry, which so became a state-owned subsidiary. Building on this model, China has over the years created a system of politically connected investors, which allows private companies to grow without sacrificing government control. Recently, for example, the Xi government moved to take "golden shares" in local units of the tech giants Alibaba, ByteDance, and Tencent in order to tighten control.[51] More broadly, between 2000 and 2019, the number of private entrepreneurs pursuing joint ventures with state owners increased at a staggering rate, with the share of total assets held by politically connected private owners surging from 14 percent to 34 percent.[52]

Society and Surveillance

In addition to regaining its dominance over entrepreneurs, the CPC is also attempting to exert greater control over civil society, albeit with different tools. Soon after Xi Jinping became Party leader, a secret internal document, known as Document 9, was circulated that outlined seven "malicious" Western values not to be discussed in schools or the media.[53] Among them were constitutional democracy, civil society, and freedom of the press. In March 2020, amid the COVID-19 pandemic, China and Huawei proposed a reinvention of the internet, which the International Telecommunication Union (ITU) warned "will lead to more centralised, top-down control of the internet and potentially even its users." Even before then, some 10 to 15 percent of Chinese users are estimated to have encountered censorship online, and since most probably do not realize that content has been censored, this should be taken as a lower bound.[54] Not only does the government block entire websites—like Google, YouTube, Facebook, and the New York Times—but it also uses the internet as an instrument of omniscient control.[55] Beijing can now monitor the behaviour of some one billion Chinese as they shop, text, and search the Web though WeChat and other applications.[56]

Surveillance, of course, does not only happen in China, as Edward Snowden's revelations of numerous global surveillance programs made painfully evident. China's so-called Great Firewall was, in fact, built with "American bricks."[57] Much of the filtering and surveillance equipment that China uses was first supplied by Cisco Systems in the early 1990s. But since then foreign technology companies have generally been considered insufficiently reliable to run China's digital infrastructure. Its internet service providers remain state-owned, and while platforms like Weibo and WeChat are private, they have strong incentives to abide by the CPC's censorship policies to avoid public criticism, fines, or closure. Indeed, the CPC's Propaganda Department regularly issues directives about news, scandals, and historical events not to be mentioned.[58]

The primary concern of the CPC is naturally collective action and social mobilization that threatens Party rule. According to careful analysis of censored social media posts, state efforts tend to focus on shutting down online attempts to organize street protests or other forms of agitation.[59] And equipped with increasingly powerful AI algorithms, Beijing is now capable of tracking all sorts of anomalies. For example, when netizens used "Winnie the Pooh" as a code name for Xi Jinping, censors soon picked it up and content moderators swiftly banned the phrase. And in addition to tracking online behaviour, the Party now uses facial recognition and mobile software tracking technology to trace physical meetings across the country. In Xinjiang Province, for instance, public security officials have already developed an Integrated Joint Operations Program (IJOP) to track its population. Through the IJOP app, local officials are able to collect and integrate data about people's height, eye colour, the car they drive, and recent purchases—all of which is tied to a national identification number—as well as anything that might seem suspicious, such as using a VPN or getting a new phone number, behaviour which might result in detention in one of Xingang's labour camps. And to help enforce Xi's former zero COVID-19 policy, this program was even rolled out on a national scale.[60]

What makes Chinese surveillance stand out against both past and present competitors, however, is the extent to which it seeks to shape public behaviour. The USSR may have failed to transform *Homo economicus* into *Homo sovieticus*, but China is having another go at it, this time with the aid of modern technology. Just as Americans and Europeans are given a credit score based on their records of paying off previous loans, their Chinese counterparts are now rated through a social credit system, based on information about all sorts of behaviours, ranging from irregular business dealings to traffic violations.[61] And the punitive consequences, as political scientist Bruce Dickson notes, can be severe: "those with poor social credit can be denied access to credit, new jobs and promotions, or travel inside and outside China; even the college prospects of their children can be affected."[62]

Innovation in China

How will Chinese surveillance affect innovation? It is hard to judge. What we do know is that Chinese provinces that report more positive attitudes toward conformism and obedience produce fewer innovations, as documented by a recent study published in the *Proceedings of the National Academy of Science*.[63] What we also know is that access to information matters to science and discovery, and so the proposal to splinter the internet, disconnecting China from the world's collective brain, is likely to create further headwinds, as are the restrictions Chinese researchers face when it comes to participation in international projects and conferences.[64] These latter hurdles are particularly important, because, as Harvard's Qingnan Xie documents, a striking 76 percent of publications from Chinese institutions in the prestigious *Nature* and *Science* journals had an author who had studied abroad before returning to the mainland. Indeed, by all accounts, researchers who were born in China but worked abroad, most notably in the United States, have been critical to China's leap in global science.[65]

In 2013, the inauguration of Schwarzman College at Tsinghua University seemed to symbolize another milestone in U.S.–China relations. The event included the reading of letters from Xi Jinping and President Barack Obama, as well as video testimonials from Henry Kissinger, Colin Powell, and John Kerry. The following year, the Tsinghua-Berkeley Shenzhen Institute was established, alongside partnerships with Microsoft and the University of Washington that resulted in the founding of the Global Innovation Exchange to connect scholars around the world.[66] However, since 2018, U.S.–Chinese collaboration in science has fallen by over 10 percent. This was partly driven by the Trump administration's "China Initiative," which sought to prosecute perceived Chinese spies in American research and industry.[67] However, the lion's share of the decline is due to the decision by Chinese institutions to permit fewer American collaborators.[68]

Much like after 1949, when Mao came to power, the Chinese government is increasingly severing foreign ties and emphasizing national loyalty. Tsinghua, for instance, was recently investigated by the Party's Central

Commission for Discipline Inspection (CCDI), which concluded that its implementation of ideological systems was not sufficiently robust. It also instructed the university to strengthen the Party committees' control over the institution and to divest its commercial assets, a move which would make the university more reliant on state funds, and so the CPC. Meanwhile, prominent scholars, like Xu Zhangrun, have been fired for criticising the government, while Lin Jianhua, the president of Peking University, was abruptly forced into retirement—making him the second Peking University president to be replaced in just three years. This is not yet the literary inquisition of the Qing dynasty, but it marks a significant reversal from the post-Mao era, when universities were granted significant autonomy. Although Peking and Tsinghua Universities still hold impressive positions in the 2023 QS World University Ranking, at twelfth and fourteenth place, respectively, the erosion of university autonomy could rapidly reduce their appeal to scholars around the world and within China itself. The history of Germany's once-leading universities serves as a cautionary tale in this regard. As the Party exerts more control and restricts the independence of academic institutions, the vibrancy that attracted talent and propelled them to international acclaim may be at risk.[69]

As China enters a period of geopolitical competition with the United States, however, slower progress is something it can ill afford. To reduce its reliance on the ingenuity of individual scientists, inventors, and entrepreneurs, China is doubling its efforts to spur innovation through the state. Efforts to check private power, in other words, have been accompanied by a push to recentralize China's innovation ambitions. This effort first began in March 2003, with the creation of the State-owned Assets Supervision and Administration Commission (SASAC), which sought to transform large state-owned companies into national champions.[70] But it really took off in 2006, when the Chinese State Council published its landmark report on "National Medium and Long-Term Plan for the Development of Science and Technology," which called for reducing the country's reliance on foreign technology and promoting "indigenous innovation." Besides pledging to increase R&D spending from 1.3 percent of GDP in 2006 to 2.5 percent of GDP by 2020, it also committed to a revival of industrial policy, with the goal of making the Middle Kingdom the leading science and technology power in the world by the middle of the twenty-first century. Compared to the decentralized, market-based approach embraced during the reform era, the Chinese approach to industrial policy "made a 180 degree turn after 2006."[71]

This reversal in policy and philosophy has only intensified under Xi. Indeed, China observers point to 2015 as another inflection point, when a number of supersized industrial policy programs came into force. Among them, "Made in China 2025" aims to upgrade China's manufacturing capabilities, while the "Internet Plus" strategy seeks to integrate information technology in traditional industries. By channelling trillions of yuan into key technology areas (biotechnology, AI, semiconductors, and advanced robotics) through direct subsidies, tax rebates, state-controlled venture capital firms, and various other instruments, Beijing hopes to supercharge innovation and reduce its reliance on foreign technology. As economic historians have noted, "These huge programs" have achieved a scale "without historical precedent," with government spending exceeding its U.S. rival by some margin.[72] China, in short, is pursuing state-led moonshots as a middle-income economy.

These efforts differ considerably from those of other latecomers. While Japan and Korea steered the economy toward catch-up, Chinese policy since the 2010s is centred on leapfrogging. Beijing is trying to jump into pole position in a number of highly prioritized technology sectors.[73] The sheer novelty of its policies warrants some caution in evaluating them. What we can say with certainty is that the capacity to mobilize vast resources does not automatically translate into innovation, and historically, frontier innovation has been more likely to happen in decentralized economic systems. In the 1970s, the Soviet Union had more scientists and engineers and spent more than the United States on R&D (chapter 10). Furthermore, as the Chinese economy becomes more mission-oriented, SOEs will play an increasingly significant role, because they are easier to instrumentalize for national goals other than making profits.[74] Indeed, empirical studies show that high-performing private companies in China are wary of government involvement, and so are eager to avoid investors with government ties.[75]

Government-sponsored innovation through SOEs did not fail only in the USSR. In China, numerous scholarly papers have documented that SOEs have been a drag on productivity and innovation.[76] For one thing, state firms remain entirely absent from the most dynamic sectors of the Chinese economy. Alibaba's online auction house, Taobao, its online mall, Tmall, and Tencent's Paipai dominate e-commerce. And since its launch by Tencent in 2011, WeChat has crowded out much of China's traditional text messaging services provided by state-owned telecoms.[77] Based on this history, it stands to reason that making SOEs the centrepiece of any innovation strategy diminishes the prospects of success. Yet even if SOEs end up playing a smaller role than many fear, China's emerging private technology giants cannot by themselves push innovation forward. Companies like Huawei, Alibaba, and Tencent might be the Sputniks of the current era, but also like Sputnik, they are no substitute for broad-based dynamism. Smaller and foreign-invested companies are consistently the most innovative in China (figure 12.1), but they are increasingly disadvantaged by a system that heavily favours incumbents.[78]

Despite this, there are good reasons to think that China will continue to drift toward centralization. One is that an economy with a few loyal behemoths is easier for the Party to control. Another is that in the absence of the rule of law, China remains a patronage economy in which entrepreneurs cultivate ties with officials to protect their investments, which makes innovation costly for outsiders.[79] Indeed, since the 2000s, business dynamism has faltered as young companies have given way to old ones, especially in regions where SOEs dominate.[80] And in China, the antitrust action that broke America's vicious cycle of cronyism in the nineteenth century is not feasible, at least not in a rules-based manner. Chinese antitrust is a bureaucratic tool that allows the CPC to punish behaviour it dislikes, and the Party will be loath to abandon this tool, because it is likely to be necessary for its continued survival in the coming years. To avoid the fate of the USSR, which became ungovernable as the credibility of the dictator's ability to punish unwanted action evaporated and lobbies grew stronger, the CPC must suppress vested interests. Well aware of this, politically motivated antitrust, along with

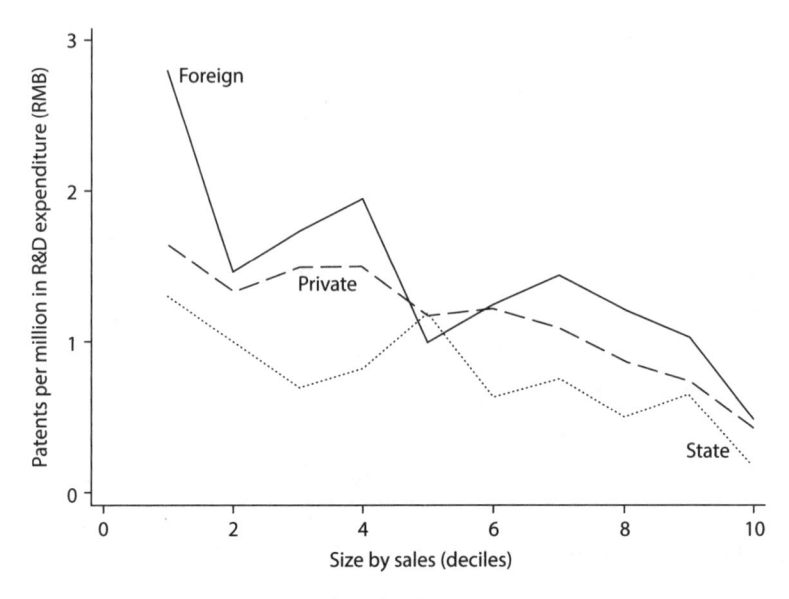

FIGURE 12.1. Innovation in China by firm type
Source: Wei, et al., "From 'Made in China,'" 49–70, Table 4.

Xi's anticorruption campaign, both send a clear message to such interests: conform or risk being imprisoned.

China's rise was aided by its legacy of decentralization, permitting local economic experiments at a time of technological turbulence (chapter 10). Since Xi Jinping became the paramount leader, however, China has become considerably less fragmented while the CPC's role as integrator and coordinator has been bolstered. More decision-making authority has been centralized at the top of the CPC in general, and in the hands of Xi in particular.[81] But as Dickson writes, this comes with a high price, because it makes local officials reluctant to engage in the kinds of policy innovations that were made during the post-Mao reform era: "Without stronger incentives for innovation, the short-term benefits of political stability and loyalty may be outweighed by the long-term stagnation that centralized power leads to."[82]

Moreover, as China approaches the technological frontier, the authoritarian but highly regionally decentralized system that created Chinese prosperity is facing headwinds, even without Xi's centralizing efforts. For this system to function properly, the CPC needs to maintain the capacity to reward and punish local leaders based on set targets. And for outside bureaucrats to monitor performance, targets must be measurable. The trouble with breakthrough innovation is that it requires exploration and so often reduces productivity initially, which makes the benefits of early inventive contrivances notoriously hard to assess. If given the sway to explore with little accountability—since it might take years or even decades to separate out promising technologies from the lemons—local leaders will find ways of taking advantage of this leeway by handing out procurement contracts to cronies. In a system where many local leaders have become used to running their administrations like a franchise, targets that focus on innovation create fertile soil for rent seeking.

One common measure of inventive output is the number of patents produced. Yet when local governments in China were incentivized to increase patent filings, the result was a surge in junk patents. Studies show that where local governments introduced preferential tax policies and subsidies for filing patents, the quality of Chinese patents fell sharply.[83] This explains why Chinese patent applicants are less likely to pay renewal fees, as their patents rarely cover valuable technologies, and why, despite a massive uptick in patent numbers, China continues to lag behind in licensing revenue. For all the talk of China overtaking the United States, when it comes to royalty payments for the use of intellectual property, China still lags by some margin. In 2023, when the United States received $126 billion in royalties from the rest of the world, China received only $11 billion. Chinese innovation, in short, has been less impressive than it is often portrayed.[84]

Thus, in the end, without the rule of law, the future of growth in China depends more on competent bureaucratic management relative to its Western counterparts. And if Deng's pragmatism fades further under Xi, and capable Party insiders are replaced with loyalists, China's bureaucratic capacity will suffer. China's constitution now decrees that "east, west, south, north, the party leads on everything."[85] True, the merit-based civil service examination, reintroduced after the 1978 reforms, remains intact. In 2023, for example, over 3 million people competed for 39,600 civil service positions across the country.[86] And to its credit, China's university system still has competitive entrance requirements for admission, something that many European countries lack. However, in the absence of parliamentary authority, government accountability heavily relies on the capacity of political insiders to remove underperforming executives. And while this has long been one of the politburo's strengths, this crucial accountability mechanism is now under siege.[87]

At the 20th National Congress, Xi was given another five-year term as the Party's general secretary and commander-in-chief of the armed forces, despite a convention that these posts can only be held for two terms. Meanwhile, Li Keqiang, the Party's second highest-ranking member and ally of the former general secretary and president Hu Jintao, was also forced out, while several long-standing comrades of Xi moved up the ranks. The CPC is now a "party of one," in the words of Chun Han Wong.[88] And over time, a nested dictatorship of loyalists could severely reduce the capacity of the Chinese state to drive growth and innovation from the above.

This is how progress in autocracies ends as they approach the technological frontier. To hold on to power, the dictator must exploit divisions in society, making knowledge and ideas less likely to flow horizontally. To divide and rule, more decisions must be made at the top, exacerbating what Hayek called the knowledge problem. As discussed in chapter 2, a strong bureaucratic state can still take an economy some way by developing integrated markets and checking vested interests, but its capacity to drive innovation at the frontier is always limited. And in the absence of an existential threat from the outside, the dictator will likely favour loyalty over competence, undermining the state in the process, and so foreclose the last road to progress. Historically, a strong meritocratic state has been key to Chinese progress, not least under the Song dynasty. The risk is that China is currently edging closer to the days of the Mings and Qings, which weakened the state from within. As previously discussed, emperor Zhu Yuanzhang, who founded the Ming dynasty, abolished the position of prime minister, handed more power to himself, and brought much of the private sector under his own control. The result was a long period of stagnation.

AI-tocracy

China, of course, might bet on AI upending the symbiotic relationship between decentralization and innovation. Indeed, some scholars have argued that AI innovation and autocracy can be mutually reinforcing: autocrats' demand for power-enhancing technologies can act as a catalyst for further innovation in related commercial applications, such as the development of tools that allow parents to track their children, while cementing the power of the dictator. According to recent research, for instance, local unrest in China has led to more government procurement of facial recognition AI, which in turn has suppressed subsequent unrest. This raises the prospect of "AI-tocracy," whereby innovation in AI entrenches the CPC, and the regime's investment in AI for political control spurs further innovation.[89]

One reason to be bullish on such a scenario is that the magnitude and the scope of data held by some governments, not least in China, likely exceeds that of the private sector by some margin. When AI companies act as service providers to the state, thereby gaining access to such data, this can stimulate the development of commercial AI applications. Authoritarian regimes with less regard for data privacy thus have an edge in AI development. Indeed, another recent study found that in China government-held data has contributed to the rise of technology companies working on facial recognition software through public procurement. The data collection efforts by the state, and its procurement policies, seem to have accelerated progress in AI.[90]

Yet even if this positions China as a leader in AI surveillance technology, it does not translate into a similar advantage in areas like drug discovery, autonomous vehicles, or large language models (LLMs). Although many think of data as the new oil and China as "the Saudi Arabia of data," this might well be China's natural resource curse.[91] Consider the case of electric cars. In the early twentieth century, electric cars were broadly on par with their gasoline-powered counterparts. Yet a lack of investment in electricity grids, along with huge oil discoveries, tipped the balance in favour of the internal combustion engine.[92] The result was to lock society into a less promising technology for more than a century. The present focus on data thirsty AI methods, prompted by the abundance of data resulting from the invention of the Web and connected devises, could lead to a similar lock-in into the wrong sort of AI.[93]

We have seen this movie before. Grand promises about the future of AI were made in the 1980s, which led to a funding boom and media hype quite similar to today. Those efforts, however, focused on preprogrammed expert systems, which turned out to be notoriously inflexible, much like a rigid central planner, whose rule book only covers a third of the relevant cases. Eventually, expert systems fell out of favour and funding dried up. Yet the deep learning systems behind the most recent wave of AI, though more flexible and capable of autonomously inferring the rules from large datasets, have their own problems. LLMs, where most progress has been made, remain susceptible to hallucinations, fabricate content and references at times, and sometimes appear to go entirely off the rails. During testing, for example, Microsoft's new AI-powered search engine, incorporating OpenAI's GPT-4, exhibited a range of unsettling behaviours, such as attempting to persuade a *New York Times* reporter to end his marriage or designating certain users as its "enemies." Moreover, it mistakenly implicated a law professor in a case of sexual harassment, apparently misunderstanding statistical associations between unrelated text snippets as significant when they were not. These challenges cannot be easily resolved by merely scaling up models with more parameters. In fact, the current models may already be approaching their upper limit in terms of capabilities.[94]

Even if scaling was the sole path forward, it is uncertain whether sufficient computational resources can be allocated to training ever-bigger LLMs. We have become accustomed to Moore's Law, which states that the number of transistors in an integrated circuit (IC) doubles approximately every two years. Yet many anticipate that this trend will reach its physical limitations in the coming years. And because LLMs have been trained on the bulk of the Web, there is further concern about the scarcity of new valuable data. The flood of content generated by AI on the Web may even degrade the overall quality of online information, which will reduce its utility as a resource for training data over time. One solution to this problem is to generate new data through simulations. For example, in the development of AlphaFold, a system that predicts 3D structures of proteins, DeepMind enhanced its training dataset by incorporating the model's own predictions. However, this approach was contingent on the initial availability of a vast dataset of known protein structures from public repositories like the Protein Data Bank (PDB). In the absence of such data, alternatives with deep neural networks are limited.[95] And ultimately, synthetic data is only as good as our ability to simulate the real world. It is thus not surprising that using such data in training tends to cause irreversible defects in the resulting models.[96]

A deeper concern is that algorithms may have limited capacity to generalize beyond their training data. The stunning results that models like GPT-4 have been able to attain on various tests, ranging from the bar exam to the SAT to introductory sommelier training, largely reflects the model's ability to memorize rather than to generalize. Various experiments show that LLM performance drops dramatically on tests introduced after its most recent update, to which it would not have been exposed during training. Using LeetCode, an online platform for software engineers and computer science students preparing for technical interviews, one experiment found that GPT-4 successfully addressed all straightforward issues and about half of the more challenging issues that were released before its last update. In stark contrast, the model managed to resolve only 69 percent of the new, easier problems that emerged after the update, and none of the hard ones.[97] Other experiments similarly show that when these models are trained on statements like "A is B," they struggle to infer the reciprocal "B is A" automatically. For example, training a model with the statement "John F. Kennedy was the 35th President of the United States" does not ensure it will correctly respond to "Who was the 35th President of the United States?" with "John F. Kennedy." The probability of the model selecting the correct name, it turns out, is no better than chance. Analysis on queries about actual public figures—such as "Who is Tom Cruise's mother?" and inversely "Who is Mary Lee Pfeiffer's son?"—revealed that GPT-4 correctly answers direct questions 79 percent of the time but does so only 33 percent of the time for reversed inquiries. This highlights a fundamental weakness in logical reasoning and pattern generalization—an issue that persists across different sizes and families of models and cannot be mitigated by additional training data.[98]

To see the broader implications of these limitations, consider the game of Go. In 2016, when AI achieved a resounding triumph by defeating the reigning World Champion Lee Sedol 4 to 1 in a five-game match, it demonstrated its capacity to generate innovative moves that caught the attention of experts and spectators alike. For his part, Sedol declared that even if he were to regain the top ranking, there now existed an unbeatable entity that surpassed his abilities. In 2023, however, humanity made a remarkable comeback. It became apparent that deep-learning-driven AI lacks an understanding of certain crucial concepts that humans grasp, such as the significance of groups of stones in the game. Exploiting novel tactics previously unfamiliar to the algorithm, a human amateur, with the help of a basic computer, managed to easily defeat the champion AI.[99] This defeat suggests that the reliability of AI in handling new, unforeseen situations, like a shift in tactics—a key aspect of human creativity—remains uncertain at best.

Similarly, while AI performs well in areas with clear optimization goals, such as in games, it is less obvious how AI will fare when the objective involves creating something entirely new, whether in art or in science. AI systems excel at remixing and recombining music or text in response to specific prompts. However, just as combining Mozart and Schubert's styles will not create music reminiscent of Arvo Pärt, prompting AI to merge impressionist artworks will not lead to conceptual art. Marcel Duchamp's "Fountain," a porcelain urinal acquired from a plumbing supply store, serves as a pertinent example. Although the exact inspiration behind Duchamp's idea remains unknown, clearly it did not stem from analysing a dataset of impressionist paintings. While it is, undoubtedly, impressive that AI can write letters reminiscent of Shakespeare, the reason it can do so is that Shakespeare existed.[100]

The puzzle of AI lies less in the quantity of data an algorithm has access to than in the efficiency with which it learns and is capable of generalizing from that data.[101] The reason we think of James Watt as the inventor of the steam engine rather than Thomas Newcomen, who developed a more rudimentary model decades earlier, is that Watt's separate condenser made the technology energy efficient, and so his engine required much less coal to run. Without this advance, the Industrial Revolution would have been wholly powered by water, and progress would eventually have stalled. The field of AI is still waiting for its separate condenser moment. Ultimately, the race for AI dominance between the United States, China, or any other nation hinges not on who possesses the most extensive data collections but on who will innovate past the current deadlock. And the CPC's efforts to control the innovation process is making this less likely to happen in China. The Cyberspace Administration of China (CAC), for example, has mandated that major technology companies and start-ups alike undergo a compulsory government review of their AI models. According to operational guidelines issued in February 2024, developers of LLMs are now required to compile thousands of sensitive keywords and questions that violate "core socialist values," such as "inciting the subversion of state power" or "undermining national unity."[102]

Even in less politically sensitive domains, China's approach remains heavy handed, as the case of autonomous vehicle development illustrates. China's cybersecurity legislation, by designating vehicle data as "critical information infrastructure," has centralized data collection. This centralization restricts experimental freedom and renders companies reliant on directives from municipal centres that dictate routing and manage traffic centrally. This contrasts with the more decentralized model in the United States, where such choices are made based on data collected by the vehicle itself in dialogue with mapping services that have much more limited information about each vehicle. Different institutions, in other words, have steered technological development in distinct directions.[103]

If the present or the past is any guide to the future, organisations and societies that embrace decentralization are more likely to push the technological frontier in AI. Indeed, as discussed in chapter 2, early dynastic China invested heavily in information and surveillance technologies, which made the economy and society easier to monitor. In doing so, rulers cemented autocracy while giving China an early lead in technology relative to the rest of the world. But they also reduced the prospects for the kind of grassroots innovation that eventually culminated in the Industrial Revolution in Europe. The Chinese trajectory in AI looks similar. Hence, paradoxically, by taking an early lead in AI surveillance, China may miss out on the long-run benefits of the technology. Indeed, when companies experimenting with AI are free to choose, they choose decentralization. Columbia's Tania Babina and collaborators have shown that early adopters are drifting toward flatter organizational structures, just like those that led the way during the computer era in the 1990s, when American companies outperformed the rest.[104]

Growth and Gridlock

For China, however, breakthrough innovation is not necessarily needed for continued growth. The average American is still roughly five times richer than his or her Chinese counterparts, which means that adoption and incremental improvements of existing technologies can still take the Middle Kingdom a long way. And if Xi refrains from filling the bureaucracy with loyalists and preserves meritocratic promotion—a big *if*—his centralizing efforts might enhance China's ability to drive catch-up growth from above. Nor is it always the first movers that reap the greatest benefits from new technologies. The first iPhone was certainly more inventive than the Samsung Galaxy, but Samsung's market share is now bigger than Apple's. China looks to be on a similar trajectory, as it is replicating Korea's success in smartphones across a range of sectors, from telecommunications to solar power and batteries. Tesla, for example, now uses the cobalt-free battery produced by a Chinese company called CATL. Indeed, what Apple did for China's smartphone industry—where Chinese suppliers initially involved with the iPhone eventually started to collaborate with domestic brands—Tesla is now doing for electric cars. As Li Yuan recently reported, Tesla's giant factory in Shanghai is working with "local suppliers to make increasingly sophisticated components that are helping them go head-to-head with Western and Japanese auto suppliers."[105]

The ability of Chinese institutions to support the capacity of companies to swiftly adopt, improve, and scale imported technology is perhaps best exemplified by high-speed rail. Having failed to build a homegrown network by 2002, the Railway Ministry decided that the country's state-owned train manufacturers should instead look abroad. Partnerships were forged with Alstom of France, Bombardier of Canada, and Siemens of Germany, as well as Kawasaki Industries of Japan, which pioneered the iconic shinkansen in the 1960s. In a scene reminiscent of the Tokyo Summer Olympics in 1964 when the shinkansen made its debut, China's first high-speed train, named Hexie, went into operation between Beijing and Tianjin in August 2008, just ahead of the grand opening of the Olympic Games.[106] What followed was even more striking: Chinese companies quickly developed their own capabilities and made significant improvements to existing technology. By 2010, China's Qingdao factory was producing some 200 train sets a year, and by 2015, China had become a technology leader in the field, with the world's fastest trains. The CRRC Corporation, its national champion, exported projects to Turkey, Brazil, Russia, Saudi Arabia, and California. While about 90 percent of the technology is estimated to have been invented in foreign lands, China's high-speed network is now more than twice as long as the rest of the world's combined.[107]

Compare India, where internal barriers to state capacity arise from the competition and rivalry among different actors within the state. This is particularly evident in the capital city Delhi, where municipal functions are spread across multiple state entities with overlapping jurisdictions. These entities include a state-level government, a centrally appointed lieutenant-governor, three locally elected municipal corporations, and the Ministry of Home Affairs, which controls the Delhi Police. As a consequence, when one state actor attempts to undertake a public initiative, such as constructing new public bus depots, they frequently encounter resistance from others. This leads to political gridlock and a lack of accountability, with actors shifting blame to one another for policy failures. Princeton's Kyle Chan has argued that such fragmentation also helps explain the huge inefficiencies of India's rail network and the lack of construction. As late as the early 1990s, China and India had comparable railway networks both in terms of scale and technology. While China's conventional network has doubled in size since then, India's has only grown by 9 percent. Indeed, India only has one high-speed line, connecting Mumbai and Ahmedabad, parts of which are still under construction despite Japanese support.[108]

America, too, suffers from gridlock. The presence of "veto players" exists in all democracies, but the American system is particularly abundant in potential veto points.[109] The Constitution, with its separation, division, and duplication of power, contributes to this complexity. In the American system, a separately elected president holds equal democratic legitimacy to Congress. Congress, meanwhile, is divided into an upper and lower house, each of which must approve almost all legislation. Additionally, an independent judiciary has the authority to overturn legislative acts. The complex Federal system further allocates powers to state and local governments, where functions are again duplicated across branches and along different levels of the bureaucracy. As a result, numerous parties with a vested interest in a project often possess an effective veto, despite representing only a fraction of the population. This intricate web of checks and balances, intended to protect against the abuse of power, has increasingly come to impede swift decision-making and so hinder the adoption of new technologies and needed reforms.[110] As Graham Allison jokingly puts it, "When Americans complain about how long it takes to build a building or repair a road, authorities often reply that 'Rome was not built in a day.' Someone clearly forgot to tell the Chinese."[111]

To be sure, one advantage of being a latecomer is the ability to adopt the latest technologies directly from advanced economies and thus bypass the long and costly intermediary steps. Some latecomers, for example, have prioritized mobile networks over building broadband infrastructure and have embraced mobile banking over traditional consumer banks. Innovations and early adopters, meanwhile, remain locked into old technologies and structures. When John F. Kennedy International Airport was built in 1948 (then called New York International Airport), it was state of the art. Today, it seems particularly antiquated when compared to Chinese airports, like Beijing's Daxing, which features technologies like facial recognition security access, geothermal heat pumps for heating and cooling, and radio frequency identification for baggage tracking.[112] Compared with India, however,

China's leap in high-speed rail, and other critical infrastructure cannot be explained entirely by its relative underdevelopment. China's institutions are simply better suited for catch-up growth. While many decisions remain decentralized at the local and provincial levels, a central coordinating body—the China Railway Corporation (CRC)—streamlines railway construction, ensuring efficiency and execution at scale. This institutional model extends across multiple fields, reinforcing China's ability to scale new technologies at an unmatched pace.[113]

At the same time, China is facing new challenges. For one thing, access to cutting-edge technologies is becoming increasingly difficult. A strategy of imitating and improving existing innovations depends on continued access to them. Yet as the United States and its allies tighten restrictions on advanced semiconductors and other critical technologies, this pathway is narrowing. The initial export controls introduced by the Trump administration largely failed, as China could still acquire the chips it needed from non-American suppliers. However, during its tenure, the Biden administration doubled down with further limits on AI-related semiconductors, such as those designed by Nvidia. Similar measures taken by the Netherlands and Japan, as the *Financial Times* notes, are so broad that they could even disrupt the production of lower-grade silicon used in everything from cars to washing machines.[114]

These controls, to be sure, do not spell the end of China's technological ascent. Chinese firms are likely to achieve some success in reverse engineering foreign technologies, and in semiconductors, Huawei has already made notable progress. Meanwhile, in an effort to reduce reliance on Nvidia's AI chips, the official publication of the Zhejiang Provincial Committee of the CPC recently took the unexpected step of endorsing open-source alternatives. Building on Meta's Llama, the Chinese startup DeepSeek has gained attention with its R1 model, which reportedly rivals OpenAI's leading systems. Although training cost estimates remain uncertain, the R1 was likely developed at a fraction of the cost of its American counterparts. Nevertheless, as AI and semiconductors advance, sustained access to the latest generation of chips will remain crucial, making export controls a major obstacle to China's technological progress.[115]

Importantly, however, the costs of these restrictions are not borne by China alone. While legitimate national security concerns warrant some protective measures, the current restrictions have become excessively broad and counterproductive. At a time when domestic industries are becoming more concentrated and internal competition is dwindling, foreign talent and competition should be a source of renewal. Instead, America is erecting barriers on both fronts. Clampdowns on H-1B visas—which once attracted Elon Musk—hamper contributions from immigrants, who are statistically more likely to become inventors and entrepreneurs (chapter 6). And what began as Trump's economic nationalism was amplified by the Biden administration through additional tariffs and investment restrictions. For instance, the Inflation Reduction Act of 2022, while aiming to boost infrastructure and tackle climate change, also imposes "buy America" provisions—such as tariffs on cheap Chinese EVs—that prioritize domestic protection over innovation and climate concerns. Even if the domestic economic fallout may be less dramatic than postwar Britain's experience with protectionist policies (chapter 8), simply because America's internal market is much larger, these policies ultimately add to the power of incumbent firms to the detriment of continued progress.

America Against Itself

That powerful incumbents will block competition and innovation is, of course, a concern that runs through American history. Consider *Charles River Bridge v. Warren Bridge*, a case heard by the United States Supreme Court in 1837. In 1785, the Charles River Bridge Company had been granted a charter to build a bridge over the river connecting Boston and Charlestown. When the state of Massachusetts authorized another company to build the Warren Bridge in 1828, which would connect the same two cities, the Charles River Bridge proprietors filed a lawsuit arguing that competition undermined their ability to collect tolls. In response, Chief Justice Roger Taney put forward a nightmarish vision, in which incumbent interests would bring American progress to its knees, should the Supreme Court rule in favour of the Charles River Bridge Company:

The proprietors of old turnpike corporations, "awakening from their sleep," might claim similar rights, putting in jeopardy "the millions of property which have been invested in railroads and canals" along adjacent routes. "We shall be thrown back to the improvements of the last century," he warned, held hostage to the claims of these obsolete companies that would prevent states from benefiting from "the lights of modern science" and from partaking "of those improvements which are now adding to the wealth and prosperity, and the convenience and comfort, of every other part of the civilized world."[116]

Taney's concerns were not unfounded. For entrepreneurs building telegraph lines, vested interest in the old system posed a serious challenge. When Samuel Morse tried to build a line in the state of New Jersey, he found that the main routes between New York City and Philadelphia were controlled by the railroads and turnpikes. Morse, who had retained control of his patent in that region, had left the construction to his agent, Amos Kendall. In a letter to Morse, Kendall explained the need to "ascertain who owns the land on each side of the Railroad from Jersey City to New York, see as many of them as you can, and see whether they will permit us to put up our posts on their ground adjoining the railroad."[117] The "exorbitant demands" of the Turnpikes and the New Jersey and Camden and Amboy Railroad Companies, he noted, made line construction difficult and costly. While New Jersey had legislated to allow telegraph lines to be built alongside public roads, this mandate left tollroads and railroads untouched. In New York, on the other hand, the existence of more extensive public roads and liberal legislation made it significantly easier to grant a right-of-way, which solved the holdout problem and encouraged entrepreneurs to roll out the network.[118]

Indeed, while strong property rights are critical to investment, as economists have long emphasized, in times of technological upheaval, flexibility is also important. And herein lies the inherent tension. A theme that runs through this book is that although secure property rights create decentralized incentives to innovate, progress entails creative destruction, and when new technologies replace old ones, they destroy yesterday's rents.[119] Even in America, the government frequently tampered with private property. Yet as legal historian Harry Scheiber pointed out, these interventions did not hold economic development back. In fact, such flexibility has at times acted to facilitate entry and innovation: antitrust played an important role in the rise of American software, unlike in Japan, whose reliance on keiretsu conglomerates thwarted progress as catch-up growth petered out (chapter 11).[120]

The trouble, of course, is that the process of reassigning property easily becomes politicized, just like regulation. In particular, the government tends to interfere with property rights in ways that benefit powerful special interests. In 1852, for example, amid the gold rush, California passed an act making it possible for prospectors to invade private farmland to search for valuable ore resources to support its mining industry. And in perhaps the most notorious case, *Poletown Neighborhood Council v. City of Detroit*, the supreme court of Michigan sanctioned the destruction of a working-class neighbourhood in 1981 to pave the way for the construction of a new factory that General Motors threatened to otherwise build in another state. However, as Naomi Lamoreaux notes, although reallocations have historically favoured the politically powerful, at times "they occurred at the behest of a majority of the voting public."[121] Indeed, in 2004, the *County of Wayne v. Hathcock* case effectively reversed the legal stance established by the Poletown decision following years of extensive legal and public criticism.

The question then is: Under which conditions are reassignments made that support the public good? In an oligarchic society, where powerful interest groups are highly organized, the public is unlikely to end up on top. On the other hand, a highly mobilized society runs the risk of letting expropriation run amok to the detriment of private investment. Progress, in other words, always hangs in the balance. In democratic societies it requires restraint from the public not to undermine private property rights. But it also requires a widespread belief in progress and a society capable of collective action when powerful interests are stifling innovation to enrich themselves at the expense of society at large. In fact, since existing technologies will inevitably spawn interest groups that become more organized over time, societal mobilization is critical to sustain progress and prevent the government from favouring the status quo.

This challenge has become evident in recent years, as special corporate interests have grown stronger at the expense of American dynamism. Not only has there been a striking upsurge in the use of non-compete clauses in technical fields—restricting the kind of job-hopping that made Silicon Valley—three-quarters of U.S. industries are more concentrated today than in the 1990s.[122] Even in the technology sector, often celebrated for its vigour, fewer start-ups are entering the market to challenge dominant incumbents.[123] Once upon a time, start-ups flocked to industries where profits could be made, but in the late 1990s, profits ceased to predict the entry of new firms. This loss of dynamism is particularly worrying since start-ups play an outsized role in commercializing new research.[124] The result has been less creative destruction and less reshuffling of market shares between different companies (figure 12.2).[125]

The reason for this trend, according to economists Germán Gutiérrez and Thomas Philippon, is not rising technological costs or returns to scale but rather the ability of incumbents to successfully lobby for regulation to entrench their position.[126] In fact, some modern corporations are now larger than national governments. The ten biggest companies in the world have annual revenues larger than the governments of Switzerland, Norway, and Russia. Of the 100 largest organizations in the world, 69 are corporations. Not only do these companies have large private security forces rivalling the best secret services, but their public relations offices dwarf U.S. presidential campaign headquarters, with more lawyers than the Justice Department and enough money to win over a majority of elected representatives through campaign donations and lobbying.[127]

The dramatic increase in corporate political spending can be traced back to the landmark case of *Buckley v. Valeo* in 1976, when the Supreme Court, led by Chief Justice Warren Burger, determined that limits on these expenditures infringed on free speech rights.[128] In the following years, between 1980 and 2012, political donations by company executives increased 320-fold in real terms, with 50 percent coming from the top 0.01 percent of corporate donors.[129] However, most of the uptick in corporate political activities came around the new millennia, when America's latest productivity boom petered out. Spending on lobbying, for example, has more than doubled since the late 1990s, mainly due to expenditure by large corporations.[130] In fact, the role of big business is even more outsized in the political system than it is in the economy. On average, the four largest companies in an industry command around

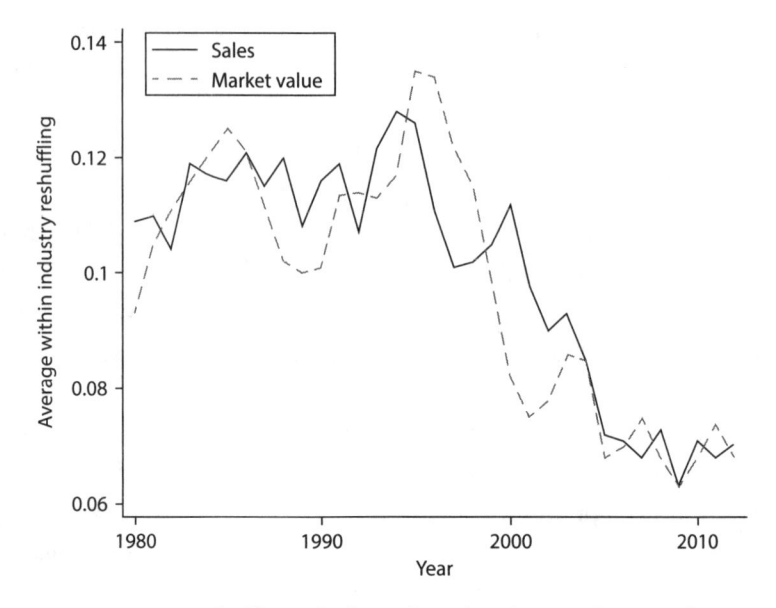

FIGURE 12.2. Reshuffling of sales and market share in the United States, 1980–2012
Source: Philippon, "Case for Free Markets," 707–719, Figure 1.

15 percent of revenues, yet they account for 35 percent of campaign finance contributions and 45 percent of lobbying expenditures.[131]

In light of this, depictions of our time as a "New Gilded Age" seem apt.[132] But while the Gilded Age of the late nineteenth century ultimately paved the way for the world's first antitrust law with the Sherman Act, the sharp increase in lobbying efforts by powerful corporations have meant that the FTC and the DOJ during the 2000s rarely enforced the laws on the books.[133] One wonders, for instance, if the United States government's decision to drop its antitrust case against Google was influenced by the 427 visits that Google employees and associates made to the White House during Obama's presidency, including over twenty meetings with the president. Not least since parallel efforts in the EU led the commission to fine Google some 8.5 billion euros.[134] Indeed, in the eyes of the regulators the case seemed quite compelling: according to a leaked FTC staff report, published by the *Wall Street Journal*, Google had allegedly unlawfully cemented its monopoly over general search and search advertising by scraping content from rival vertical websites and entering restrictive agreements with web publishers preventing them from displaying competing search results or search advertisements.[135] And whatever the merits of the Google case, the trend is clear: between 1970 and the new millennium, the Department of Justice and the FTC brought an annual average of 15.7 cases. Between 2000 and 2014, they brought a meagre 2.8 cases per year.[136]

Of course, some industries naturally lean toward concentration due to network effects—especially in tech. A social media platform with all your friends is far more valuable than one with only a handful of users. However, productive concentration also makes lobbying more lucrative and might become destructive over time. As the University of Chicago's Luigi Zingales points out, "The more an economy becomes winner-take-all, the bigger the incentives to corrupt the political system to gain a small, but often decisive, advantage."[137] The result is a vicious cycle whereby companies use their economic power to cement their position through the political system, and as they grow larger, they are compelled to lobby even more. According to recent research, after a merger, spending on lobbying increases by around 30 percent.[138] And many of these deals are outright "killer acquisitions," whereby an incumbent buys up a promising technology just to terminate it. Questcor Pharmaceutical, for example, enjoyed a monopoly with its Acthar drug, used to treat infantile spasms, among other things. When a synthetic alternative emerged, Questcor acquired the rights in 2013, only to shut it down.[139]

Killer acquisitions are not the only way incumbents block progress. Their lobbying efforts are also bent on making regulation work in their interest. The point is not that regulation itself is bad. But economist George Stigler was surely on to something when he suggested that "as a rule, regulation is acquired by the industry and is designed and operated primarily for its benefit"—a point that is more true today than when Stigler was writing in 1971.[140] For one thing, regulators face increasingly compelling incentives to leave government for jobs at the companies lobbying the very agency for which they once worked.[141] In the 1960s, a partner at a top law firm made about twice as much as an FTC chair. Today, partners make about ten times as much as they did then. Meanwhile, the salaries of the FTC chair, an assistant attorney general, or other DOJ staff have essentially remained flat, adjusted for inflation, as the price of the houses they might be looking to buy in Washington, DC, has quadrupled.[142]

The revolving door between government and big business might not be a problem per se, as serving in one might enhance one's knowledge about how best to perform the role in the other. Yet there are also clear cases of regulatory capture, sometimes with dismal consequences for innovation. For instance, a recent investigation of patent examiners at the U.S. Patent and Trademark Office shows that they are more likely to grant patents to the firms that later hire them, as well as to prospective employers, and that these patents tend to be of lower quality.[143] This also means that innovating start-ups must hire expensive attorneys to survey the patent landscape, which makes it more costly to enter the market. Roger Taney's nightmare is regrettably appearing more real.

A more optimistic take is that unpredictable changes in technology may still dislodge incumbents. How Western Union failed to see the virtues of the telephone and declined to buy Bell's patent was discussed in chapter 6. They had a splendid opportunity to seize control over AT&T yet chose to prioritize dividends over innovation and let their dominant position slip away. In fact, in a striking reversal, AT&T ended up consolidating its power by purchasing a 30 percent stake in Western Union, effectively crafting a new monopoly. Despite the concerted efforts of regulatory intervention, the Postal Telegraph and smaller telephone firms found themselves marginalized in an AT&T-controlled system. The competitive landscape shifted only with Standard Oil's breakup, which lent credibility to the threat of antitrust enforcement. Subsequently, AT&T unveiled the "Kingsbury Commitment," pledging to divest its Western Union telegraph branch and open its network to independent telephone operators.

In similar fashion, OpenAI's unveiling of ChatGPT in November 2023 was a watershed moment that caught incumbents off guard.

Despite developing the Transformer (part of the underlying architecture of all LLMs), Google appears to have hesitated to launch the kind of generative AI that drives ChatGPT, possibly due to concerns that it would divert advertising revenue away from its own search engine and kill its golden goose. Google's CEO Sundar Pichai recently acknowledged, "Scale isn't always good for you," as it makes it harder to "move fast [and] maintain a culture of risk-taking."[144] The incident highlights a recurring pattern where smaller, more agile entities are quicker to adapt to technological advancements, in contrast to their larger counterparts—a reality strongly reflected in recent developments. At the time ChatGPT was put in the hands of the public, OpenAI had a workforce of approximately 375 people, whereas Midjourney, a rising star in image generation, managed its operations with merely eleven full-time employees. Economist Tyler Cowen has even argued that AI might herald the end of big business.[145]

The competition among LLM providers has surely intensified in the past few years. OpenAI, founded in 2015, faces challenges from Elon Musk's xAI, launched in 2023, as well as Yi-Lightning, a Chinese lab led by Kai-Fu Lee, and Anthropic, created by former OpenAI employees who disagreed with the organization's increasingly market-driven direction. Google DeepMind, formed through the merger of Google Brain and DeepMind, remains a major contender as well. Meanwhile, Meta, whose business model relies on advertising revenue from its social media platforms rather than LLM sales, has taken a different approach by adopting an open-source strategy. By offering its Llama models for free, Meta encourages innovation that supports its content creators, in contrast to the proprietary models offered by other labs. As a result, the market now includes over a hundred notable LLMs, with some competing on capabilities and others focusing on smaller, more cost-efficient models, building on Meta's efforts. Among them is Chinese DeepSeek, whose much cheaper high-performance model recently raised concerns in Washington and Silicon Valley, causing the stock prices of American tech firms to plummet.

The question is whether the rise of AI startups is just a blip or the beginning of a new phase in the industry. For decades, the prevailing direction has been one of concentration and consolidation. While the Transformer has accelerated progress—perhaps shaving a few years off the scaling timeline—the fundamental innovations behind today's LLMs, such as neural networks, backpropagation, and gradient descent, were pioneered by academics many decades ago. But the field of AI has changed dramatically since then. In 2004, only 21 percent of AI PhD graduates went into industry; by 2020, that number had soared to 70 percent. At the same time, the share of major AI models developed by large corporations rose from just 11 percent in 2010 to 96 percent by 2021.[146]

As a result, AI—once a field marked by an anarchy of methods—has become increasingly uniform, with a growing emphasis on LLMs, where Microsoft's partnership with OpenAI now gives them joint control over 69 percent of the market, and its investment in the rising startup Mistral AI suggests this trend may continue. A similar pattern exists in the market for chips to train AI models, where Nvidia dominates with a 92 percent share.[147] In fact, OpenAI and Microsoft's decision to partner rather than merge likely reflected growing antitrust scrutiny from the Biden administration rather than a lack of incentive for deeper consolidation. If scaling was all we needed to drive AI progress, further industry concentration might make sense. But it isn't. Between 2019 and 2024, companies scaled LLMs by a factor of 10,000, yet performance on key reasoning benchmarks, such as the ARC test, remained close to zero—OpenAI's GPT-4o, for instance, scored only around 5 percent. Meanwhile, a much simpler approach that relied on program search achieved over 20 percent with minimal computing power. More recently, an inventive method that refines answers while the model is running led to a significant improvement in ARC scores.[148]

Moreover, regardless of how the AI industry itself evolves, its broader economic impact may be dampened by the growing dominance of a few large corporations in the sectors that ultimately adopt the technology. Due to their sheer scale and resources, these corporate giants are best positioned to reap the benefits of automation, while smaller firms often approach technology differently.[149] Large companies typically use AI to optimize and expand existing operations, prioritizing efficiency and scalability, whereas startups are more likely to experiment with new products and business models, pushing innovation in entirely new directions. To see why this matters, imagine the mythical craftsman Daedalus and a team of skilled engineers 3,500 years ago creating machines to automate every task of their time. Sheepherding, pottery making, tunic weaving, horse-drawn cart repairs, and even ritual practices would all be mechanized.[150] Such advancements obviously would not lead to anything like the living standards we enjoy today. This society would still lack vaccines, antibiotics, cars, planes, printing, and computers. Similarly, if all technological innovation since 1800 had been focused on mechanization, we would have productive agriculture and cheap textiles, but not much else. While mimicking human abilities rather than amplifying them may initially boost productivity, it ultimately caps the potential for progress over the long run. Daron Acemoglu estimates that in the absence of AI supercharging scientific discovery or new product development, AI-led automation will boost nationwide productivity by as little as 0.06 percent annually over the next decade.[151]

Yet it is hard to think of a current AI application that goes beyond enhancing productivity in tasks humans are already performing. So it is perhaps not surprising that, despite the launch of generative AI, productivity growth in America remains stuck on its stagnant pre-pandemic trend. Even the poster child of AI in science, AlphaFold, impressive as it is, is about automation: it is folding proteins, as humans long have, albeit at much greater speed. And while many applications of LLMs in scientific research seem promising, such as literature-based discovery, the basic task here—analysing the existing scientific literature for new hypotheses or possible recombination's of existing ideas—has already been greatly aided by the dawn of the personal computer and the Web, which together facilitate instant access to unprecedent amounts of information, aid statistical analysis and simulations, and enable seamless collaboration across the globe. Despite widespread predictions that these new tools would trigger a new scientific revolution in the early twenty-first century—much as Hooke's microscope and Galileo's telescope did in the seventeenth century—computers have largely failed to revive productivity in research and breakthrough innovation more broadly.[152] For instance, maintaining the pace of Moore's Law now requires the efforts of eighteen times as many researchers as it did in the early 1970s. And the same trend is true for the U.S. economy as a whole.[153]

These observations cohere with compelling evidence that while start-ups continue to be the main drivers of innovative breakthroughs, they are increasingly confronted with higher entry barriers.[154] In this context, the recent focus on the national security and extinction risks of AI, whether pushed by Silicon Valley incumbents or actually concerned individuals, serves the interests of established companies by undermining the threat from open-source movements and new market entrants. While it is important that regulators can stress test powerful AI models before their release—ensuring, for instance, that they are not trained on dangerous information—the process must be made more affordable and streamlined than the U.S. Food and Drug Administration's (FDA) approval regime, which has contributed to a pharmaceutical sector controlled by a handful of large companies, stifling entry and medical innovation.[155] The supposedly novel risks presented by AI are not, in fact, very different from those of previous information technologies. In 1996, for instance, *Reuters* suggested that "the Internet, used by millions of Americans every day, has become a virtual textbook for terrorists."[156] And in the 1981, during the ongoing antitrust case against AT&T, which paved the way for the internet era, the company famously argued that a breakup of the Bell System would "jeopardize the military's lines of communication."[157]

The more emphasis we place on AI's dangers over its advantages, the more likely it is that we will drift toward a monopolistic situation that one might think is simpler to control and aligns with the goals of established players. Yet it is far from clear that a powerful AI monopolist, on which we all depend, would be controllable. Despite IBMs striking dominance in computing in the 1930s, its German subsidiary (Dehomag) provided punch card systems that were used for census-taking, record-keeping, and logistics, aiding the Nazi regime in organizing the Holocaust. Meanwhile, such a situation would risk stifling all sorts of progress. Reaping the benefits from technological change requires institutional support to make space for exploration.[158]

13

The Veneer of Progress

Marx thought that the principal conflict to be found in . . . industrialized countries was the deep disparity of interests between owners and employees, but this is a secondary kind of conflict. . . . The primary economic conflict, I think, is between people whose interests are with already-established economic activities, and those whose interests are with the emergence of new economic activities. This is a conflict that can never be put to rest except by economic stagnation.[1]

—JANE JACOBS

THE DECLINE of either China or the United States is by no means inevitable. Over the last two-and-a-half centuries, America has shown an unparalleled ability to adapt its institutions to new technological realities.[2] And some of the Biden administration's antitrust initiatives—such as its attempt to revitalize competition by abolishing non-compete agreements nationwide—can be seen as a welcome development. As for China, improbable as it may seem, Xi Jinping may decide to take a different path, and the experience of Taiwan, the renegade province, shows that a decentralized economic and political system in China is feasible and advantageous.

Yet presently, both the United States and China appear to be on a path toward stagnation. China's property sector, which is estimated to have contributed a staggering 29 percent to its GDP in 2016, is faltering, and technological change is needed to create new opportunities for investment, which the CPC's crackdown on the private sector makes less likely.[3] And although the Federal Trade Commission's aggressive litigation under President Biden marked a shift from the past two decades of U.S. policy, it achieved limited success in court while failing to reverse the trend of venture capital-backed startups favoring acquisition-based exits and industry consolidation over public listings.[4] Nor is the persistence of many freedoms protected by a law-governed state assured, as events on January 6, 2021, when supporters of then-President Donald Trump attacked the Capitol Building in Washington, DC, make clear. This could turn antitrust into a political tool, not unlike in China.[5] In fact, since regaining office, Trump's appointment of loyalists to oversee critical government functions mirrors Xi's approach since the 13th National People's Congress. Likewise, Trump's Department of Government Efficiency (DOGE) initiative—aimed at cutting bureaucracy without easing restrictive regulations on business—is unlikely to deliver better outcomes. Instead, a less competent, politically appointed civil service will weaken America's ability to enforce the rules of the game and carry out essential government functions.

If the two largest economies fade, it will profoundly impact global growth and prosperity. Indeed, since the end of World War II, European growth has heavily depended on the adoption of American technology, and in recent decades China has become an indispensable trading partner, not least as a market for European automobiles. Compounding these challenges, Europe is grappling with the decline of its traditional industries and has pivoted toward protectionist policies under the banner of "strategic autonomy" for national security reasons. This shift involves pushing domestic production targets in key sectors while imposing substantial tariffs—up to 35.3 percent—on Chinese EV makers that offer superior technology at lower prices. Despite massive R&D investments by Europe's squeezed automakers, their EV transition has faltered, as evidenced by Renault's withdrawal of the safety-challenged Zoe and BMW's limited success with the i3.[6]

The EU is not only shielding its industries from foreign competition but is also making it increasingly difficult for European startups to enter the market and build the industries of the future. Regulations such as the General Data Protection Regulation (GDPR) have disproportionately burdened smaller enterprises, inadvertently reinforcing market concentration among large incumbents with the resources to manage compliance costs.[7] And this regulatory trajectory is set to escalate with the coming EU AI Act, which not only designates seemingly beneficial applications like AI tutors as "high-risk" systems requiring extensive compliance measures, but also mandates extreme operational constraints—such as requiring dual human verification for AI banking transactions.[8] Barriers to innovation are being added, while the potential returns—even in the case of success—are subdued compared to those in America and China, due to Europe's fragmented digital services market. The International Monetary Fund (IMF) estimates that Europe's internal barriers make it as costly to do business as if there were a 45 percent tariff on manufactured goods and a 110 percent tariff on services.[9] One might, of course, hope that other parts of the world will provide new engines of innovation. But as China exports its surveillance tech around the globe, many autocracies and weak democracies have new tools to cement centralization, even if doing so results in slower economic growth.[10]

This outcome, while unwelcome, should be no surprise. Tracing the dynamics of progress in time and space, this book has revealed a fundamental tension running through the historical record: technologies that strengthen bureaucratic control later hinder new discoveries and sow the seeds for stagnation. Early dynastic China leveraged technology to achieve its goals, such as tax collection, power consolidation, and warfare (chapter 2). Through the development of advanced soil mapping, for example, its rulers were able to determine agricultural yields and set taxes accordingly, bypassing the need to negotiate with local elites. It is also no coincidence that China's single writing system, which enabled bureaucrats to develop comprehensive population records and communicate via letters across the vast empire, was enforced by a centralized state. By eradicating the information asymmetry between the state and its subjects, the introduction of writing enabled taxation without representation and laid the foundation for centralized political organization.

The Chinese state, in turn, initially leveraged its newfound capacity to push forward technological progress. The construction of the Grand Canal, along with the development of thousands of irrigation and flood control initiatives nationwide, testifies to the ability of the Song dynasty to drive technological progress from above. Over the long run, however, early centralization left many technological trajectories unexplored. According to Joseph Needham's seminal work, China relinquished its position as the global leader in innovation by the fourteenth century, and subsequently, no major breakthroughs were made in the Middle Kingdom. Ultimately, the drive to establish an impersonal and meritocratic system of bureaucratic recruitment led to the suppression of grassroots innovation and diversity of thought. This created political stability but also serious obstacles to reform and continued progress. Skewed incentives encouraged China's most able youths to pursue a career within the government bureaucracy, which significantly weakened its science and technology sector. As a result, China was overtaken by a more fragmented Europe, where intellectuals and inventors could escape the heavy hand of the state.

Unlike in the West, where autonomous cities competed for talent, no such safe havens existed in China (chapter 3). Indeed, as Europe was undergoing a scientific revolution, the Qing government launched a ruthless crackdown on intellectual dissidents in what is known as the "literary inquisition." This suppression of inquiry dealt yet another blow to the already limited scientific pursuits under the Manchu regime, where autocratic state support for technological progress could be withdrawn at will. And as the Middle Kingdom consolidated, the last realm of competition—in the geopolitical arena—faded too. In the annals of Chinese history, the Ming era was a period of relative calm and stability. Devoid of the lurking external security threats that beset other dynasties in Europe, the Ming rulers could focus on consolidating their hold on power. To that end, they pursued an increasingly personalized form of autocracy, which, while shoring up their authority, weakened the state and, in so doing, undermined China's last pathway to progress.

Contrary to the prevailing sentiment among observers that technological progress and state oversight will become increasingly symbiotic in the era of AI, modern China might be on the verge of repeating these historical errors. Indeed, though the CPC's embrace of AI for surveillance has driven innovation in certain areas, like facial recognition technology, beneath the surface this mirrors the pattern of dynastic China, when substantial investment in surveillance secured its technological lead yet ultimately curbed further exploratory advancements.

The central premise of this book is that our ability to think clearly about the possibilities for progress and stagnation today are enhanced by looking backward at the rise and fall of nations around the globe over the past thousand years. This journey has inevitably taken us through a dense forest of detail, and much can be learned from the particulars of each nation's story. Yet important general lessons can be best appreciated by abstracting from much of this detail and comparing how the fundamental institutional arrangements performed over long stretches of time. In this final chapter, I highlight what I see as the most important themes and lessons from our whirlwind tour, some of which recur throughout the book, and others which only become clear by putting the different case studies in dialogue with one another.

Bureaucracy and Scale

One lesson to be learned is that bureaucracy-led development only works when an engineering problem can be clearly defined and executed from the top down, needing minimal exploration. The Rad Lab and the Manhattan Project, for instance, had clearly defined missions that built on earlier scientific exploration, and thus were carried out in a mission-driven manner. By contrast, in the early days of mRNA, Katalin Karikó struggled for years to imagine its possible applications, and several institutions failed to see the promise of the technology (chapter 1). But it was thanks to the groundwork laid by Karikó that the mRNA vaccines could be swiftly deployed once the COVID-19 pandemic spread from Wuhan to Venice. In general, as technologies mature, they become more manageable and amenable to planning and control.

Given this, the question of why the entire world is not developed, despite the potential for latecomers to exploit existing technologies, has long perplexed economists. Part of the answer lies in the prerequisites for scaling: large companies require professional managers to coordinate complex operations and the institutional infrastructure—educational systems and integrated markets—to supply these capabilities.[11] Another reason is that, to avoid turmoil and conflict, rents and privileges in a society must be allocated in rough proportion to the distribution of hard power. To keep their rents, incumbents seek to limit competition and new technologies that might upset the status quo. We saw in chapter 3, for instance, how the guilds fiercely resisted technologies that threatened their incomes, which helps explain why industrialization in China was delayed by two centuries relative to the pathbreaker, England. This book has not had much to say about the developing world today, but as scholars like Gary Cox, Douglas North, and Barry Weingast have shown, similar forces are still at play and partly explain why much of the world remains underdeveloped. Leaving the natural state of rent seeking behind always threatens violence and turmoil, as powerful incumbents are aligned against progress.[12]

In this context it is worth underlining the importance of bureaucratic capacity, first and foremost, to override rent seekers while maintaining political stability, but also to spearhead technological catch-up directly—a point we explored in-depth in the aftermath of the British Industrial Revolution and again after World War II. In the case of Prussia, the Stein-Hardenberg Reforms were a "revolution from above," led by reformist-minded bureaucrats who repressed special interests (and democratic forces) in their pursuit of economic growth. In contrast to England's parliamentary government, which emerged from the Glorious Revolution of 1688–1689, Prussia's Estates were significantly weaker than its state bureaucracy; hence, with fewer checks and balances, Prussia's comparative advantage rested in its ability to quickly adopt and improve on British technologies. The resulting organized capitalism favoured scale, and so Germany emerged as a new technological powerhouse in the late nineteenth century as markets integrated.

German civil service culture also had a profound impact on the process of industrialization (chapter 4). Despite a deep-rooted Prussian scepticism regarding the abilities of private entrepreneurs, Germany's journey toward modernity was fundamentally capitalist, driven by the pursuit of profits. Nevertheless, the imprint of Prussian bureaucratic principles is unmistakable. German corporations, enriched by the disciplined and hierarchical ethos of the Prussian civil service, were distinguished by their rigorous organizational structures, uniform procedures, and efficient communication systems. Industrial giants like BASF, Krupp, and Beyer not only reaped the benefits of incorporating ex-civil servants into their ranks but also thrived amid the burgeoning network of technical universities stretching from Charlottenburg to Karlsruhe and the emergence of business schools in cities like Cologne, Berlin, Mannheim, and Munich.

The distinctive manner in which German institutions facilitated scope and scale can also be seen in its approach to competition law, which differed fundamentally from that of the United States, or indeed Britain. While the Sherman Act made anticompetitive practices illegal, the *Reichsgericht* in Germany ruled that such practices were legal. Consequently, prior to the Allies' dismantling of IG Farben and the subsequent imposition of a more competitive regime after World War II, cartel arrangements between Germany's largest corporations were widespread. By ensuring stable prices and consistent output, which mitigated the financial risks tied to investing in costly machinery, the cartel arrangements smoothed the path for German firms to quickly embrace new technologies. Although cartelization could easily have led to cronyism, Germany's drive to compete in global markets, coupled with escalating geopolitical pressures, helped mitigate these tendencies and channelled investments into productive activities.

Compare this with Tsarist Russia, where the absence of anything like the Stein-Hardenberg Reforms left both the private sector and the state apparatus weak (chapter 5). Peter the Great, who sought to modernize the civil service, undercut his own efforts by personally involving himself in all aspects of state affairs. By the time of the last Tsar, Nicholas II, Russia lacked a civil service examination, and the state remained far more autocratic than other European dynasties. The Tsarist regime maintained power through intense repression, establishing a precarious balance between a weak state and an even weaker society. This dynamic fostered deep suspicion among the aristocracy toward capitalist growth, as they feared both the emergence of wealth beyond royal control and the concentration of potentially rebellious workers in industrial centers.

Hence, unlike in Germany, where a strong state supported industry, Russia's feeble government sought to consolidate its authority by curbing private initiatives. For example, unlike in America, Western Europe, and Japan, where a straightforward process of incorporation by registration facilitated the creation of new businesses, Russia used a concessionary system that prolonged the issuance of corporate charters, thus obstructing the unfettered formation of corporations. As a result, Russia had very few companies, and their success was highly dependent on state support to the detriment of competition.

The success of Meiji Japan reinforces the importance of bureaucratic capacity. The arrival of Commodore Perry's American gunboats in 1853 marked a turning point in Japanese history, exposing the Shogunate's vulnerability and prompting the rapid adoption of Western technology. This led to the establishment of organizations like the Institute of Barbarian Books, which focused on translating and codifying Western science and technology to bolster Japanese industry. Meanwhile, the Meiji Restoration of 1868 fueled comprehensive reforms that ended feudalism, centralized the state, and spurred industrialization, including the development of national rail and telegraph networks. This push, much like in Germany, originated from areas known for their stringent hierarchical structures, notably Chōshū and Satsuma, rather than from the most economically developed regions. And like Germany, the Japanese state used its capacity to source foreign technologies and facilitate corporatist institutions, again supporting scale and coordination. Through the strategic sale of state-operated firms to emerging zaibatsu and the enactment of laws like the Important Industries Control Law, permitting cartels, the Japanese government forged a close partnership with major corporations. While curtailing the rise of democratic and labour movements, this collaboration was instrumental in enabling Japan to rapidly assimilate foreign technologies and emerge as an industrial powerhouse by the early twentieth century.

In the aftermath of World War II, centralizing institutions again proved their usefulness as the world opened up to trade and travel once more, and Western Europe and East Asian allies gained access to accumulated American technological strides (chapter 8). Because of the long period of relative isolation caused by the outbreak of the Great War, the Great Depression, and then again total war, the Second Industrial Revolution, to a large degree, had yet to spread beyond American borders. But thanks to the Marshall Plan, and the reopening of the global economy, Europe swiftly closed the gap, just as it had during the first wave of globalization that followed the British Industrial Revolution. Even Bolshevik progress before the Cold War relied on the flow of American technology: Lenin and Stalin both recognized the United States as the emerging global superpower and tried to emulate her industrial achievements. While there were no formal ties between Washington and Moscow, the latter took full advantage of the Ford Motor Company's open-door policy.

Catch-up, again, was not automatic. The continent, however, was yet again fortuitously equipped with the institutional framework and mechanisms essential for assimilating American innovations, a legacy of its efforts to catch up with Britain during the nineteenth century. To counter British dominance in wireless telegraphy, Kaiser Wilhelm II had ordered the German companies Siemens & Halske and AEG, erstwhile competitors, to collaborate and create a strong German alternative (chapter 4). This led to the formation of Telefunken, a company aimed at breaking the British radio monopoly. Then, in the twentieth century, Europe undertook even larger-scale collaborative efforts in cutting-edge technologies. Airbus, for example, was created as a direct response to the dominance of American aviation manufacturers like Boeing. In 1967, the governments of France, Germany, and the United Kingdom agreed to work together on developing a new aircraft, with Spain soon joining the project. This partnership was then formalized in 1970 with the establishment of *Airbus Industrie*.[13] The result was a formidable competitor to Boeing. Indeed, as discussed in chapter 8, all over Europe, bureaucracies—manifesting as industrial conglomerates, state holding companies, or government planning agencies—stepped forward as the architects of modernization. France's Monnet Plan of 1946, for instance, propelled the nation into a "concerted economy," laying the groundwork for *Les Trente Glorieuses*, thirty years of unprecedented growth. Similarly, in Italy, the *Istituto per la Ricostruzione Industriale*

(IRI) did much to coordinate industrial efforts, as did the *Instituto Nacional de Industria* (INI) in Spain.

In Japan, too, the path to economic triumph was shaped not just by importing American technologies but also by the resilience of its own institutions. The postwar period saw the Ministry of International Trade and Industry (MITI) emerge as a key orchestrator, with its cadre of elite bureaucrats playing a significant role in forcing IBM and Texas Instruments into patent licensing agreements with Japanese firms, and in facilitating the domestic assimilation of foreign technologies. In addition, the close collaboration between governmental and corporate behemoths that characterized the Meiji and Taishō periods endured, with the emergence of keiretsu conglomerates as the modern heirs to the zaibatsu legacy. True, the Antimonopoly Law enacted in 1947, modelled after the Sherman Act, aimed to curtail the zaibatsu as impediments to competition. But Japanese officials soon loosened antitrust laws, once again prioritizing bureaucratic coordination and scale.

Diminishing Returns

The strides made by emerging economies have frequently alarmed established technological leaders, who fear that these rapidly growing countries will soon displace them from pole position. In the nineteenth century, the rise of Imperial Germany stirred anxieties in Britain, leading many to believe that liberal England would soon be outstripped by an autocracy pursuing state-led capitalism. In similar fashion, two decades of extraordinary growth in the Soviet Union, together with the launch of *Sputnik I* in 1957, left many Americans thinking that their country was on the verge of being eclipsed by a Communist regime. And although Soviet fears began to fade in the 1980s, they only did so to be replaced by concerns over the Japanese miracle and the next generation of computers coming out of Fujitsu, NEC, and Hitachi.

These fears are often misplaced. In the field of economic forecasting, one should resist the urge to extrapolate from current growth rates without considering the underlying dynamics of technological development. History shows that periods of centralized bureaucratic management geared toward exploiting low-hanging fruit tend to be accompanied by particularly rapid growth. Yet this growth is dependent on earlier exploratory efforts. Postwar America, for instance, is often cited as a prime example of incredible economic growth that was fueled by centralized institutions, but the foundations for this progress were laid under vastly different conditions during the Second Industrial Revolution in the late nineteenth century (chapter 6). And in America and elsewhere, institutions designed to exploit existing technological breakthroughs encountered significant challenges in the 1970s, as incremental improvements to existing technologies predictably ran into diminishing returns.

In the wake of collapsing smokestack industries, the coordinated economies of Western Europe were put to the test (chapter 10). In the decades following World War II, Europe experienced rapid economic growth through the adoption of American mass production techniques. However, as the dawn of the computer age arrived, the institutions of coordinated capitalism struggled to keep pace with technological change. While bank-based financial systems continued to channel funds into proven technologies, it was decentralized financial markets that proved adept at embracing the risks associated with innovation, which enabled the exploration of new technological trajectories. At the same time, the task of resource allocation became increasingly complex for bureaucrats amid the whirlwind of technological turbulence. In countries like Italy, Spain, and Portugal, stringent state control and competitive constraints ushered in two lost decades of growth during the Computer Revolution. And as usual, Britain stood out as the European exception. Despite facing similar challenges, Britain's decentralized institutional legacy, coupled with Prime Minister Margaret Thatcher's staunch advocacy for competitive markets—a stance further supported by Tony Blair's New Labour—made its economy more adaptable to technological disruption. This flexibility led to a brief economic resurgence, allowing Britain to surpass Germany and France, after falling behind them in the postwar period.

Meanwhile, behind the Iron Curtain, problems were piling up. In the age of mass production, central planning had differential effects on economies depending on their levels of development.[14] Under the shadow of Western rivalry, communist states could achieve impressive feats of modernization—marshaling vast resources to build highways, electrify remote regions, and launch mass education campaigns. The system's ability to mobilize resources under geopolitical pressure temporarily masked its fundamental market deficiencies. But in richer economies, where progress demanded innovation rather than imitation, the absence of market forces proved detrimental. At its core, central planning presented a compromise: it enabled coordination and systematic investments in vital sectors but provided few incentives to innovate, no threat of bankruptcy, and thus limited creative destruction. Initially, the Soviet bloc saw some success with central planning, as it was able to leverage accessible technologies for growth. Yet the system became increasingly inefficient as opportunities for technological catch-up dwindled. Managers were constrained by Party plans and output targets, which left little room for exploration.

These were troubles that could not be fixed by increased spending alone. For the Soviet bureaucracy, the spectre of radical innovation was not just a challenge; it was an existential threat that risked destabilizing the entire system. The pursuit of innovation inevitably made planning harder and exacerbated the already arduous task of monitoring people's productivity. Aware of this challenge, Stalin established the People's Control Commission, which used terror to align individual incentives with state aims—an approach that resulted in the sentencing of 35.8 million people for criminal offenses between 1940 and June 1955. However, under Khrushchev and subsequent leaders, the once ironclad loyalty demanded of Party members waned as disciplinary measures were relaxed, a change that proved fatal to the stability of the existing system. As the era of mass production faded, the imperative for innovation became clear, yet meaningful reform was obstructed by entrenched interests flourishing in the vacuum of state power. And so, the Soviet Union collapsed.

Restoring Competition

Which brings us to the next theme of this book: at the technological frontier, continued progress depends on the power and willingness of governments to override vested interests to restore competition. As outlined in chapter 3, the birth of the Industrial Revolution illustrates this vividly. The revolution first gained momentum in Britain, where inventors such as James Watt and Richard Arkwright turned their ideas into practical applications and gave rise to the factory system that would fuel the global economy for centuries to come. This was in stark contrast to the relatively successful resistance encountered by industrialization in other parts of Europe, where powerful craft guilds saw their interests threatened by this new economic order. In Britain, however, decentralized competition between cities and the early integration of markets helped to undercut the influence of guilds and to unleash the forces of creative destruction. But Parliament's supreme authority also played a crucial role, because it insulated politics from local interests.

Compared with England, the Dutch Republic, often hailed as the first modern economy, was relatively democratic. This meant, however, that its political institutions were more susceptible to being captured by incumbents and special interests, who often sought to impede technological change. The core issue was that, alongside a central assembly for the entire republic, each Dutch town and province maintained its own local assembly. And for any proposal to pass in the higher-level assemblies, it needed approval from every major town. This created gridlock, as powerful interest groups found ways to manipulate trade regulations to their advantage. Over time, as local merchant guilds grew stronger, they used their control to block competition and innovation.

In France, too, the capacity of the government to check vested interests proved critical. Indeed, it was only with the French Revolution and the crowning of Napoleon that the old order was swept away, the guilds were abolished, and a centralized state capable of promoting competition was established and spread its ideas throughout Western Europe. In the Rhineland, where guilds had successfully resisted technological change, the introduction of the French civil code undercut the influence of German local elites, which resulted in the disbandment of guilds and a surge in innovation.

At the dawn of the Industrial Revolution, what truly set Britain apart was the relative lack of power afforded to incumbent economic interests. Unlike in the Dutch Republic, British Members of Parliament were not beholden to strict mandates from their constituents. Instead, they were able to legislate as they saw fit. Britain's industrial revolution thrived not only because Parliament upheld private property rights but also because it was prepared to set them aside when the nation's growth demanded it. The construction of canals and turnpikes, for example, was driven by Parliament's use of private Acts, allowing public infrastructure projects to move forward despite resistance from individual landowners.

America likewise benefited from both the lack of and ability to overcome incumbent interests. As an infant republic, the United States did not have to battle with the legacies of the old regime, and for most of the nineteenth century, inventors did not have to worry about the kind of gilded interests that prevailed on the European continent, where they blocked many technological pathways from being explored. It was, for instance, the absence of gilded restrictions that made Heinrich Steinweg leave his native Germany to set up Steinway & Sons in New York City. True, the expansion of the frontier of free land undoubtedly was a key magnet for much talent, but other nations such as Russia, Argentina, and Chile experienced similar periods of territorial expansion, yet failed to achieve the same level of inventive success as the United States.

The key difference lay in the institutions of each country (chapter 6). In America, the Constitution created a framework of private property rights and free trade, which provided a strong foundation for innovation and entrepreneurship, attracting talent from across the globe. The filing fee for obtaining a patent in the United States was, for example, only a fifth of the price charged in Britain, which enabled a much larger cross section of the population to participate in innovation. It was the work of lone inventors such as Samuel Morse, and not corporations like Western Union, that paved the way for the development of the telegraph. And Morse and others like him were supported by a liquid market for technology that allowed inventors to specialize in exploration.

During the late nineteenth century, the United States remained a small government society compared to its European counterparts. American institutions were developed for an economy where production occurred in small shops and technological progress was fueled by solitary inventors.

But as industrial empires of unprecedented scale emerged to harness the technological opportunities independent inventors had created, new institutions were needed. During the Gilded Age, titans of industry such as Cornelius Vanderbilt, Jay Gould, and John D. Rockefeller made significant investments in the technological advancements that propelled forward the economy of the United States. These industrialists amassed vast fortunes, which in turn, gave them substantial economic and political power. During the period's technology wars, the "robber barons," as they were called by the press, fiercely fought for control of the latest innovations in telegraphy. Vanderbilt and Gould, for instance, locked horns over the control of Western Union.

The combination of weak government and mammoth enterprise created an environment where private interests held disproportionate sway over public policy. From New York City's Tammany Hall to the corridors of Congress in Washington, DC, elected officials were routinely targeted by lobbyists and business leaders looking to secure favourable legislation or access to government contracts. The result was a political system characterized by corruption, cronyism, and ineffectiveness. As Mark Twain supposedly said, "We have the best government that money can buy." Despite states being granted regulatory authority to proceed against mergers by the federal courts, multi-plant corporations could secure a charter in a more favourable jurisdiction or move production altogether, limiting the practicality of state-level antitrust initiatives. As a result, the federal government would have to take the lead on antitrust measures.

In contrast to European nations, which faced the imperative to reform under the threat of foreign invasion, the drive for institutional change in America emerged from grassroots levels. It was the force of social mobilization, rather than the pressures of geopolitical rivalry, that underpinned the enduring nature of American advancement. The passage of the Pendleton Act in 1883 marked a turning point in American politics, when new measures were introduced to combat corruption and create a merit-based bureaucracy, while the Sherman Act of 1890 gave the federal government new powers to proceed against monopolies. True, the process of reining in corporate power was hardly linear, as Supreme Court rulings created loopholes that allowed many entities controlled by trusts to merge into holding companies. Nevertheless, the Progressive movement and its supporters laid down critical institutional groundwork that allowed the federal government to check the robber barons and safeguard competition later in the twentieth century. This, of course, was a fine balancing act, and sometimes the government overstepped. But antitrust policy created a credible deterrent against rent seeking, and thus prompted firms to derive profit from growing organically rather than thwarting competition. A century later, with the computer age on the horizon, this deterrent played a crucial role in facilitating the entry of new companies like Microsoft by prompting IBM to unbundle software and hardware, just as the breakup of AT&T paved the way for the decentralization of the internet (chapter 11).

The divergent approach of America and Japan in the realm of competition policy is particularly instructive. The United States has historically championed decentralized institutions and fostered an environment conducive to new business ventures, a stance markedly different from Japan's preferential treatment of established firms over startups. In postwar Japan, many industries remained exempt from antitrust rules, and cartels were allowed to operate legally. The Japanese Fair Trade Commission (FTC) had limited power and antitrust enforcement was weak. This policy regime enabled Japanese companies like Fujitsu, Hitachi, and NEC to be remarkably successful in hardware, but they, like the old guard in the United States, struggled to keep up with a new generation of America companies moving into software. The keiretsu system, which emphasised trade with other members of their group, continued to allow for anticompetitive practices that held back unrelated startups. As a result, as Silicon Valley ascended, Japan and its conglomerates foundered.

That the Computer Revolution happened in the Bay Area, of all places, is again no mystery. Like Britain's Birmingham and Manchester, which sprang up in formerly rural areas free from guild regulations and became the engines of the Industrial Revolution, Silicon Valley's lack of a prior industrial history and disconnect from established economic and political structures fostered an environment conducive to innovation.

What the Valley's history shows is that a competitive and decentralized system is key to discovery, especially when barriers to horizontal movement are absent. Silicon Valley's rise is attributable in no small part to a culture of job hopping that can be traced back to the California Civil Code of 1872, which outlawed covenants in employment contracts (chapter 11). Nearly a century later, this law would permit the "traitorous eight" to break away from Shockley Semiconductor Laboratory and set up new companies, Fairchild included. So, despite the existence of incumbent, centralized technology clusters in Boston and Detroit, America's federal system created the space for continued experimentation. By allowing for variations in policy and governance at the state and local levels, federalism provided an institutional laboratory, which proved crucial to America's continued progress.

The Dictator's Dilemma

That said, Japan's great stagnation was not a foregone conclusion. Consider the case of South Korea. Under General Park, its government acted as the Chairman of the Board for Korea, Inc. But following Korea's transition to democracy in 1987, the state's power became diffuse, making the chaebol as powerful as their keiretsu counterparts and certainly no less corrupt. When Hanbo Steel Company declared bankruptcy in 1997 during the Asian financial crisis, an investigation revealed that at least $2 billion were missing from its accounts. Yet, on the bright side, the crisis led to significant reforms, including a substantial strengthening of antitrust legislation. Several large conglomerates, such as Daewoo, were subsequently dismantled, leading to an upsurge in innovation powered by non-chaebol companies. As Korea moved away from political centralization under the military, it needed new mechanisms to counterbalance economic centralization, and antitrust provided the answer.

Given such tools, democracy has the edge at the exploration stage. Comparatively, autocratic leaders face a difficult balancing act between granting enough autonomy for experimentation while consolidating their influence and controlling the private sector. This inherent tension lies at the heart of the dictator's dilemma, as rulers seek to drive progress while preserving their hold on power. And it is particularly acute at the cutting-edge of innovation, where the pursuit of new ideas requires the freedom to explore, which makes monitoring costly if not impossible.

In China, in the era of Deng and his successors, this was achieved through local experiments that created transitional institutions to protect entrepreneurs from government interference and preserve market incentives (chapter 10). Local leaders enjoyed autonomy, but the Communist Party retained control over local government personnel. This system, which created incentives for administrative bosses to move up the ranks, required a strong state to enforce and monitor local progress while giving local leaders enough sway to adjust to new technological realities. But closer to the frontier, monitoring became much harder, and so cronyism was an ever-growing concern, not least as the private sector expanded and created a powerful business elite. In China, corruption reached new heights in the 2000s, as bureaucratic positions were frequently sold across all levels of government.

The Party's preference to concentrate economic power in the hands of a select few, so as to maintain control, is understandable. A functioning legal system would undercut the power of the CPC to arbitrarily reward loyalists and punish challengers. However, China's patronage economy comes at a price, as entrepreneurs must build relationships with local officials to ensure protection of their investments. In China's current system, innovation is a costly game for outsiders, a fact underscored by the striking decline in business dynamism since the 2000s. This stands in contrast to America's Gilded Age, where inventors who held patents could trade them in the technology market and earn their investment returns without having to rely on political connections. Given the divergent political and regulatory landscapes between the two nations, the kind of antitrust action that America took in the nineteenth century or that South Korea has used recently to combat cronyism is unlikely to be implemented in the Middle Kingdom. Instead, China's antitrust policy serves primarily as a bureaucratic tool of the government (chapter 12). In the end, the chief priority of the CPC is to avoid the path of the USSR, which fell apart when the dictator's authority could no longer implement policy in the face of competing lobbies. And to do so, the Party must suppress vested interests.

Xi's anticorruption campaign is best understood in this light. To cling to power, the CPC must intentionally check private enterprise and sow division among society. Yet such intervention undermines the security of private property rights to the detriment of investment, while impeding its collective brain in the process. Indeed, political repression, as recent research has shown, reduces the kind of generalized trust a society needs for ideas to flow horizontally between its members.[15] This brings back memories of Stalin's dictatorship, which was highly effective in keeping him in power longer than any other leader. He ensured that subordinates remained loyal to him rather than to each other by creating institutional barriers, including requiring official permission for visits to Moscow and preventing regional leaders from having representative agents in the capital. Stalin also implemented a policy of "divide and rule" to prevent collusion among subordinates, which led to an excessive administrative burden at the top, as nearly every significant decision had to be funneled up the hierarchy. This desire for centralized decision-making is a common problem among dictators, as Vladimir Putin's Russia bears witness to today, and it inevitably exacerbates Hayek's knowledge problem. Yet it is an integral part of the system. As Hannah Arendt observed, "Terror can rule absolutely only over men who are isolated against each other . . . therefore, one of the primary concerns of all tyrannical government is to bring this isolation about."[16]

The dictator's dilemma should not, however, lead one to conclude that state power inevitably retards progress at the technological frontier. While innovation has historically thrived in decentralized systems, the state has often played a crucial role in creating the necessary institutional foundations for such systems to flourish, especially within democracies. In the United States, before independent inventors receded into large corporations, the Morrill Land-Grant Acts provided the means to create new colleges without strings attached, which helped re-establish the role of independent inventors inside universities. Since private enterprise was hesitant to invest in basic science, from which it is hard to capture the returns, the state's investment in decentralized systems of cutting-edge universities was a considerable success. Without a robust system of universities to draw upon, the Advanced Research Projects Agency (ARPA) would not have been a triumph but more likely a fiasco (chapter 7).

The issue arises when the state uses its power to curtail academic autonomy. The rise and fall of the German university system is particularly instructive. Following devastating losses against Napoleon, Prussian modernization took off, and the University of Berlin emerged as a new institution sponsored by the state but not under its control. Influenced by ideas of the Enlightenment era, the Prussian university system embraced academic freedom. As Germany unified, its federalist structure nurtured competition among universities, with Berlin at the top receiving most state funding in Prussia, but cities in other German states, such as Gießen and Leipzig, were also formidable competitors. Such rivalry was largely absent in France, where regional centres and universities were underfunded and simply lacked the resources to compete. As one president of a leading American university remarked in the late nineteenth century: "The German University is today the freest spot on earth.... Nowhere has the passion to push on to the frontier of human knowledge been so general."[17]

The trajectory of Germany's rise to preeminence in higher education seemed to promise a "German century" (chapter 4). However, after much of the university system was mobilized to support the war effort in 1914, the professoriat in Berlin became increasingly conservative, monarchist, and patriotic, with appointments increasingly made on ideological grounds while merit gradually took a backseat. Academic freedom was subject to further constraints in response to the rise of the Social Democratic Party, and it was shattered entirely with the ascent of the Nazi regime. Burning books on the streets of Berlin's Opernplatz in May 1933 by members of the German Student Union marked a dark turning point. What the state had created, it could also take away, especially under autocratic rule.

Although valid worries exist about American elite universities becoming rigid and less diverse in their beliefs, a distinctive advantage of democracy is that competing institutions are able to form to fill any such void. In China, in contrast, the state's increasing control over the university system (a significant departure from the reform era, when universities were granted considerable autonomy) is reminiscent of the trend in Germany during the late Wilhelmine period. Nanjing University, for instance, had aimed to become a world-class institution, aligned with Xi's vision of realizing the Chinese dream. However, its inclusion on the Party's Central Commission for Discipline Inspection list in 2017 led to political interference in its leadership and governance, and ultimately its teaching and research priorities.[18] And as scholars bow down to the doctrine of "Xi Jinping thought" that seeks to strengthen the Marxist–Leninist interpretation of history, the quality of education is bound to deteriorate more broadly. If they read real history instead, they would know that undermining autonomy holds back grassroots innovation.

Epilogue

MORAVEC'S PARADOX

[T]hat most characteristic of human institutions, language, is the best model: a structure of meaning and continuity that is never still and ever open to the improvisations of all its speakers.[1]

—JAMES C. SCOTT

OUR PATHWAY to riches has been paved by technological progress, which has permanently altered the human condition. From 1800 to the present day, the real income of the average person on this planet has grown by a factor of ten, as a steady flow of new technologies has allowed us to produce (much) more with (much) less.[2] And such numbers, impressive as they are, inevitably understate the transformation that has taken place. Many of the products we take for granted today, from Wikipedia to Khan Academy, were once beyond human imagination; yet, because they have zero price, they are not even captured by national income statistics. Our material progress is thus more accurately measured by the disparity between what consumers actually pay and what they would be willing pay for modern-day goods and services.[3]

True, just as many benefits of progress have been left unmeasured, so have some of its perils. The famous hockey-stick blade, which turns upright as the Industrial Revolution takes off in the nineteenth century, after a long flat handle, describes not only the acceleration in incomes per capita and life expectancy, but it is also linked to the rise in atmospheric carbon dioxide and the subsequent rise in temperatures. But although economic growth and carbon emissions have been intimately connected since the eve of the modern world, they have recently decoupled thanks to the development of cleaner technologies.[4] More broadly, technological advancement—whether in the form of lab-based meat, cheaper green energy, more data-efficient AI models, or geoengineering—will be a critical part of the solution to climate change. And while armchair philosophers frequently observe that money cannot buy happiness, empirical evidence continues to show a strong link between income and subjective well-being. Even up to annual incomes of half a million dollars, the correlation between income and happiness remains extremely tight.[5] What remains a tragedy is the unevenness of technological advancement, leaving half the world's population to live on less than US$6 per day. This should serve as a reminder that progress is neither automatic nor even natural. If it was, the Industrial Revolution would have happened much earlier in human history, and the entire world would be equally rich and prosperous today.

As observed throughout this book, a fundamental barrier to technological change is institutional inertia. While discovery thrives in decentralized systems that encourage experimentation, scaling and production benefit from centralized control. Innovation demands breaking rules, but efficient execution relies on following them. Sustained progress, in other words, depends on balancing these forces, shifting between decentralization for exploration and centralization for exploitation. Yet transitioning from a centralized to a decentralized paradigm, as old technologies mature and their benefits are fully realized, is fraught with challenges. Incumbent interests—those decision-makers in government, corporations, and politics—deeply invested in the existing order, often resist change. Although recent advances in AI are impressive, progress is constrained less by intelligence—whether human or artificial—than by the people in power and the incentives that shape their decisions.

Consider the internet, which in the early 1990s was still a research-driven network, never intended as a commercial space. However, its rapid growth soon outpaced the National Science Foundation's ability to manage it, and crucially, no single entity—government or corporate—controlled its trajectory (chapter 11). Unlike countries where telecom state monopolies absorbed foreign carrier services, the United States had already undergone the 1984 breakup of AT&T, fostering a competitive market. Had commercialization occurred a decade earlier, AT&T might have monopolized the internet, and decisions made by a few board members could have stifled its development entirely. Instead, in its early days, a fragmented industry allowed innovation to flourish, free from centralized bottlenecks. In similar fashion, by ensuring that foundational AI models are open source or at least widely available for further refinement, we can avoid the monopolization of AI technology and usher in a golden age of innovation reminiscent of the late nineteenth century, when inventors traded their ideas in the marketplace for technology.

There is, of course, no assurance that past patterns of progress will hold in the future, but despite popular claims to the contrary, AI is still no substitute for decentralized exploration. In 1988, Hans Moravec noted a counterintuitive aspect of AI development that still rings true today: tasks that are simple for humans, such as hiking, are incredibly difficult for robots and AI systems, while activities that require extensive human reasoning, like playing chess at a grandmaster level, can be more easily executed by computers. Much like Hayek, Moravec underscored the limits of centralized processing—whether in the form of a computer or a central planner. The sensorimotor knowledge humans develop through experience is hard to replicate in AI due to its tacit nature and dispersion across society's members. Progress in this domain requires finding ways to codify what was once uncodifiable.

We all know that large language models (LLMs) have been trained on almost the entirety of the Web, an amount of information that it would take a human reading eight hours per day around 170,000 years to consume. Yet, for a four-year-old who has been awake for some 16,000 hours, the amount of information that has reached the visual cortex of that child is around fifty times larger. Most of our knowledge, in other words, is not acquired through speech but through observation and interaction with the real world. Even if everyone uploaded all their life experiences to the Web in a manner that accurately reflects reality, there has been minimal progress over the past decade in developing algorithms that can watch part of a video and predict what happens next.[7]

A key feature of human intelligence is our capacity to predict how the world will evolve in response to an action we might take. And for some activities, like those of inventors, scientists, and entrepreneurs, those results are highly uncertain, which is why successful ones turn a profit in the first place.[8] What successful inventors and scientists do right is a book in itself, but they evidently do more than approximation based on past patterns. In contrast, deep neural networks, such as LLMs, work through statistical associations, whereby frequent mentions of a claim are equated with "truth," a process akin to conducting science by majority vote. Imagine an LLM in the year 1633, trained on all scientific and other texts published by humans to that point. If asked about Galileo's heliocentric view, it would only restate, represent, and mirror the accumulated scientific consensus. The training data would predominantly feature texts supporting a geocentric view, like those of Aristotle and others, placing the Earth at the centre of the universe.

In similar fashion, before the first successful flight, the available data suggested that human air travel was a hopeless endeavour. Some people pointed to birds as "positive" evidence that humans might also fly one day, but sceptics, like the prominent scientist Joseph LeConte, found such arguments easy to dismiss. In 1888, he examined the data on bird species—both those that fly and those that do not—and concluded that there is a size and weight limit for flying animals. LeConte observed that while insects could fly ubiquitously, no bird above the weight of fifty pounds could do so. Large birds like ostriches and emus are flightless, and even the largest flying birds, such as turkeys and bustards, "rise with difficulty" and are "evidently near the limit" of flight capability, he noted.[9] Others, meanwhile, pointed to the numerous failed aviation attempts as evidence that such an endeavour was unlikely to ever succeed. Indeed, just nine weeks before the Wright brothers' success in 1903, Samuel Langley's flight attempts, which were witnessed by large scientific and lay audiences, ended in spectacular failure.[10]

LLMs will surely improve in the coming years, and the latest Chain-of-Thought (CoT) reasoning models, which help AI break down complex problems into step-by-step explanations, already mark a step forward, improving accuracy in tasks like math, logic, and decision-making. Yet they still struggle with novel situations and show no signs of original thinking. The path forward remains uncertain, and it is important to remember that the history of AI is littered with flawed predictions. In the 1970s, for example, AI pioneer Marvin Minsky confidently suggested that within three to eight years, a machine would achieve the general intelligence of an average human being. Despite significant progress over the past fifty years, we are still waiting for that moment. As Demis Hassabis, cofounder of Google DeepMind, recently acknowledged, getting to general artificial intelligence (AGI) will probably require "several more innovations."[11] When those discoveries arrive—if they arrive—and who will then make those leaps is a known unknown. What we do know is that the obstacles to progress are not just technological.

While economic decentralization and political centralization make uneasy partners, autocracies are not inherently incapable of innovation. China, for example, has a deep pool of talent and a government intensely focused on technological advancement. If China continues to support open-source AI while the United States moves to restrict access and competition, the Middle Kingdom could realistically take the lead in the field. But that is not to say that its political system nurtures innovation. As in the West, firms without strong political connections—such as DeepSeek—tend to be the most inventive. And while authorities may allow them to operate freely as long as they serve national objectives, the absence of the rule of law means that they are constantly at risk when priorities change. To survive, they must cultivate political capital, diverting resources away from innovation. And the state's control over critical information technologies creates a persistent temptation to tighten its political grip over society at the expense of grassroots innovation.

Meanwhile, sustained dynamism in liberal democracies presents its own set of challenges. That dynamism, as Joseph Schumpeter emphasized, is largely driven by the process of creative destruction. To Schumpeter, a monopolistic retailer will soon find competition pressures from department stores, mail-order houses, and supermarkets; just as a feudal robber baron building his castle on a river to extract tolls from passing merchants will eventually find his fortress redundant, as traders eventually discover new routes. Today, the prime threat to traditional news media is not the likes of Fox News but online platforms undercutting their whole business model, Schumpeter might have contended. Yet the process of creative destruction is not a universal constant in the modern world. The enduring success of century-old firms in many economies—not least where growth has centred on technological catch-up and centralizing institutions—is, in fact, striking. Unlike the United States, where the five largest companies by market capitalization have an average age of 39 years, this average age soars to 84 years in Japan, 116 years in Britain, 120 years in Germany, 144 years in Italy, and 152 years in France. And while all of America's top firms are in the technology sector, France's big five features no technology companies—four of them are in luxury goods.[12] Meanwhile, Germany's only significant digital company, SAP, was funded in 1972 by five employees from IBM, and most of its leading companies still were created during the Second Industrial Revolution. America, in other words, is a positive outlier in this regard. But as our long historical journey has underscored, no nation, whether Song China, the Dutch Republic, or Victorian Britain, has been at the forefront of technology for very long.[13]

Part of the reason for this is what Schumpeter got right: there are forceful social and political hurdles inherent in technological dynamism. To identify with the capitalist system, as he put it, "the unemployed of today would have to forget his personal fate and the politician of today his personal ambition."[14] As I outlined in my previous book, *The Technology Trap*, sustained progress in liberal democracies relies on a widespread belief that citizens will ultimately benefit from such progress, through rising living standards and the creation of new and better jobs. Without this belief, resistance to change becomes likely.[15] What I did not fully acknowledge is that for new opportunities to emerge, competition must be protected. This sometimes requires collective action, particularly when incumbents obstruct potential challengers from inventing the future. Indeed, most of the jobs held by Americans today did not exist in 1940—they had to be invented.[16]

At a time when large corporations are investing heavily in automation and startups bringing forth new products and jobs are facing surging barriers to entry, it is no surprise that public sentiment toward technological advancement has soured: according to a 2023 Pew Research Survey, 52 percent of Americans are now more concerned than excited about the growing use of artificial intelligence, while only 10 percent say they are more excited than concerned.[17] Meanwhile, intensifying political and economic divisions over recent decades have made collective action more difficult. And while competition from abroad has episodically rocked the foundations of mature economies and forced them to adopt more competitive practices, the impulse of incumbents is generally to seek shelter, with governments finding it straightforward to justify protectionist measures as a way to safeguard national champions and jobs alike. For all of Biden's differences with Trump, his administration did not abolish the Trump tariffs—which we now know actually hurt jobs—but in fact added to them.[18] Trump, in his second term, has done the same. Recognizing the fragility of progress is the first step toward protecting it, with greater public awareness serving as the most important remedy. My hope is that this tome will play a small part in enlisting more citizens to rally to the defense of progress.

ACKNOWLEDGMENTS

THIS BOOK owes its existence to a universe of contributors—sources, editors, fact-checkers, and cherished supporters. My editor Hannah Paul at Princeton University Press, and my development editors Amanda Moon and Thomas LeBien at Moon & Company, offered excellent editorial guidance, while Leopoldo Lazcano, Alex Nannig Larsen, Rubén Nahuelhual, and Chaitanya Rawat provided exceptional research assistance throughout the project. The Dieter Schwarz Foundation and Citigroup provided crucial financial backing, with particular thanks to Andrew Pitt and Robert Garlick for their intellectual engagement and encouragement.

At Oxford many friends and colleagues enriched this work with their comments and suggestions. Special thanks go to Ian Goldin, who brought me to Oxford and has been a constant mentor and source of inspiration. This book was born at the Oxford Martin School and completed at the Oxford Internet Institute, where the intellectual engagement and encouragement of my many colleagues were instrumental in bringing it to fruition. I was also fortunate to spend the early part of my career at the Economic History Department at Lund University and continue to benefit from those ties.

A project of this scope naturally builds on the work of countless scholars. While I cannot hope to pay all my intellectual debts, several works deserve special mention: Daron Acemoglu's and James Robinson's *The Narrow Corridor*, Philippe Aghion's *The Power of Creative Destruction*, Stephen Broadberry's *The Productivity Race*, Nicholas Crafts's *Forging Ahead, Falling Behind and Fighting Back*, Barry Eichengreen's *The European Economy since 1945*, Francis Fukuyama's *Political Order and Political Decay*, Richard von Glahn's *The Economic History of China*, Robert

Gordon's *The Rise and Fall of American Growth*, Mark Harrison's multiple works on the Soviet economy, Douglas Irwin's *Clashing Over Commerce*, Chris Miller's *The Struggle to Save the Soviet Economy*, Joel Mokyr's *A Culture of Growth*, Sheilagh Ogilvie's *The European Guilds*, David Stasavage's *The Decline and Rise of Democracy*, Walter Scheidel's *Escape From Rome*, Richard Tilly's and Michael Kopsidis's *From Old Regime to Industrial State*, Debin Ma's, Loren Brandt's, and Thomas Rawski's many works on China, and Yingyi Qian, Gérard Roland, and Chenggang Xu's scholarship on M-form and U-form hierarchies. Conversations with many of these scholars—the finest in their fields—have been immensely rewarding.

I am particularly grateful to Joel Mokyr—whose work has inspired me since high school—for his thorough review of the full manuscript. I also deeply appreciate the constructive feedback provided by four anonymous reviewers, as well as Giorgio Presidente, Ralph Schroeder, and Chris Russell, who offered detailed comments on various sections. Many scholars also generously responded to my requests. In particular, I would like to thank Ashish Arora, Jonathan Barnett, Daniel Bernhofen, Lee Branstetter, Jaedo Choi, Matias Covarrubias, Matej Drev, Markus Eberhardt, Robert Gordon, German Gutierrez, Bryan Kelly, Jianan Li, Stephen Morgan, Dimitris Papanikolaou, Joan Rosés, Amit Seru, Younghum Shim, David Stasavage, Matt Taddy, and Nikolaus Wolf for sharing data and advise.

Above all, I acknowledge my family's steadfast support of my professional endeavors, including this project. To Claudia, William, Kristian, and Veronica, for always being there. To my children, Victoria and Immanuel, who bring joy and purpose to everything I do. To Sophie, the love of my life, whose support never wavered—thank you for everything. To my amazing parents, Christopher and Britt-Marie, who nurtured my curiosity from the beginning—thank you for setting me on this path. And to my beloved grandmother, Ann-Marie, whose compassion and warmth lives on in all of us, making it all possible.

NOTES

Preface

1. Quoted in Acemoglu and Robinson, *Why Nations Fail*, 125.
2. Von Mises, "Economic Calculation in the Socialist Commonwealth"; Hayek "Socialist Calculation," 125–149; Hayek, "Use of Knowledge in Society," 27–38; Lerner, "Economic Theory and Socialist Economy," 51–61; Lange, "Economic Theory of Socialism," 123–142. For an overview of the socialist calculation debate, see Boettke and Candela, "Feasibility of Technosocialism," 44–54.
3. See Samuelson, *Economics*.
4. Lange and Feinstein, "Computer and the Market," 158–161.
5. On Zelenograd, see Miller, *Chip War*.
6. Friedrich, "Computer Moves In (Machine of the Year)."
7. Cited in Boettke and Candela, "Feasibility of Technosocialism," 44.
8. Harari, "Why Technology Favors Tyranny," 64–73. On surveillance and innovation, see Beraja, et al., "AI-tocracy," 1349–1402.

Chapter 1

1. Baumol and Strom, "'Useful Knowledge' of Entrepreneurship," 527–542.
2. Fisher, "Economics of Prohibition," 5–10.
3. On the ineffectiveness of prohibition, see Miron and Zwiebel, "Alcohol Consumption During Prohibition," 242–247.
4. Ade, *Old-Time Saloon*, 100.
5. Powers, *Faces Along the Bar*, 54.
6. Andrews, "Bar Talk."
7. Marshall, *Principles of Economics*, 271; Marshall and Marshall, *Economics of Industry*, 53.
8. Although coffeehouses expanded and pubs ceased to be the primary meeting place for intellectuals, they remained important for the social networks of commoners. Hailwood, *Alehouses and Good Fellowship*.
9. Cowan, *Social Life of Coffee*.
10. Cowan, *Social Life of Coffee*.
11. It is not without reason that the American tavern has been described not only as a "watering hole but also as a classroom and lecture hall." Sismondo, *America Walks into a Bar*, 42.
12. Montesquieu, *Spirit of the Laws*, 338; cited in Irwin, *Free Trade Under Fire*, 65. On culture and trade, see Felbermayr and Toubal, "Cultural Proximity and Trade," 279–293.
13. On trust and growth, see Algan and Cahuc, "Inherited Trust and Growth," 2060–2092; Algan and Cahuc, "Trust and Growth," 521–549.

14. And in some societies, a Kibbutz or extended family take joint responsibility for raising children.

15. If there is one predictor of who becomes an inventor, it is the proximity to other smart and creative people. In a recent study, Harvard's Raj Chetty and collaborators found that children of inventors and those growing up in neighbourhoods where many inventors live were much more likely to take out patents themselves later in life. Bell, et al., "Who Becomes an Inventor in America?," 647–713. In this regard, Google's founders were the norm rather than the exception. Not only did they benefit from being connected to other smart people at Stanford but both of Brin's parents, Mikhail and Eugenia, were graduates of Moscow State University and had worked in science and technology. His mother would later go on to become a researcher at NASA's Goddard Space Flight Center, while his father became a professor in mathematics at the University of Maryland. Similarly, Page's father was a computer science professor at Michigan State University, where his mother also worked as an instructor in computer programming.

16. Granovetter, "Strength of Weak Ties," 1360–1380. For empirical support for this view, see Rajkumar, et al., "Causal Test of the Strength of Weak Ties," 1304–1310.

17. The term *collective brain* was coined by Muthukrishna and Henrich, "Innovation in the Collective Brain," 20150192. Similar intuitions are also to be found in Weitzman, "Recombinant Growth," 331–360.

18. D. Garde, 2020, "The Story of mRNA: How a Once-Dismissed Idea Became a Leading Technology in the Covid Vaccine Race," *Boston Globe*, November 10.

19. Cited in D. Garde and J. Saltzman, "The Story of mRNA: How a Once-Dismissed Idea Became a Leading Technology in the Covid Vaccine Race." STAT, November 10, 2020, https://www.statnews.com/2020/11/10/the-story-of-mrna-how-a-once-dismissed-idea-became-a-leading-technology-in-the-covid-vaccine-race/.

20. D. Crow, 2021, "How mRNA Became a Vaccine Game-Changer," *Financial Times*, May 13.

21. Crow, "How mRNA Became a Vaccine Game-Changer."

22. Crow, "How mRNA Became a Vaccine Game-Changer."

23. Initial funding for both BioNTech and Moderna came from private capital markets, see S. Linicome, 2021, "Correcting the Record on Operation Warp Speed and Industrial Policy," *National Review*, July 8.

24. Ridley, *How Innovation Works*, 280.

25. Quote from Baumol, *Free-Market Innovation Machine*, 11. Book titles like Henry Petroski's *Invention by Design* captures the essence of the routinization of innovation; Petroski, *Invention by Design*.

26. B. Pancevski and S. Hopkins, 2020, "How Pfizer Partner BioNTech Became a Leader in Coronavirus Vaccine Race," *Wall Street Journal*, October 22.

27. BioNTech also received funding for testing and manufacturing from the German government, but only after the vaccine had been developed.

28. Kerr, et al., "Entrepreneurship as Experimentation," 25–48, 25–26.

29. Kornai compiles a list of 87 "revolutionary" inventions made after 1917. None of them were made in planned economies, about a third are related to computers, and the vast majority came from the United States. This does not include discoveries driven by the military, like *Sputnik I*. However, as we shall see, even more remarkable than Sputnik is that it did nothing to transform commercial telecommunications in the USSR as satellites did in the United States. See Kornai, "Innovation and Dynamism," 14–56.

30. Hayek, "Use of Knowledge in Society," 519–530.

31. Hayek, *Individualism and Economic Order*, 101.

32. Acemoglu, et al., "Technology, Information, and the Decentralization," 1759–1799.

33. Von Mises, *Bureaucracy*, 1.
34. Chandler, *Visible Hand*, 1.
35. On the pin factory example turned into a market, see Munger, "Bosses Don't Wear Bunny Slippers."
36. Coase, "Nature of the Firm," 386–405. See also Williamson, "Economics of Organization," 548–577.
37. Though monopsony power is a concern also in market economies, see Dube, et al., "Monopsony in Online Labor Markets," 33–46.
38. Lamoreaux and Sokoloff, "Inventors, Firms, and the Market," 19–60.
39. On how industries become more footloose when they mature, see Vernon, "International Investment and International Trade," 190–207; Krugman, "Model of Innovation," 253–266.
40. Klepper, "Origin and Growth of Industry Clusters," 15–32; Klepper, "Silicon Valley," 79–115.
41. *New York Times*, 1910, "New Ford Plant," October 4.
42. As the late William Baumol puts it, "One can even offer the plausible conjecture that most revolutionary new ideas have been, and are likely to continue to be, provided preponderantly by independent innovators. But once their initial undertaking proves successful, the inventors or the associated entrepreneurs often establish new firms that in many cases grow large and themselves routinize their innovation. Henry Ford and his automobiles provide only one of many examples." Baumol, *Free-Market Innovation Machine*, 52–53.
43. Link, *Forging Global Fordism*, 2.
44. Freeman, *Behemoth*, 224.
45. Cited in Link, *Forging Global Fordism*, 1.
46. Gerschenkron, *Economic Backwardness in Historical Perspective*.
47. For more recent accounts of catch-up growth, see Acemoglu, et al., "Distance to Frontier," 37–74; Keller, "International Technology Diffusion," 752–782.
48. Lenoir, "Revolution from Above," 22–27.
49. Weber, 1968, *Economy and Society*.
50. On the importance of incremental improvements by incumbents, see Garcia-Macia, et al., "How Destructive Is Innovation?," 1507–1541. Rosenberg was right in pointing out that while routine innovations are less original, they contribute significantly to economic growth; Rosenberg, *Perspectives on Technology*, 66.
51. Mokyr calls this *macroinventions*; Mokyr, "New Economic History," 1–131.
52. In postwar America, young companies played a critical role in biotechnology, semiconductors, as well as computers. For a detailed account, see Mowery and Rosenberg, *Paths of Innovation*.
53. Careful studies show that after listing, the novelty of companies' innovations drop by 40 percent. See Bernstein, "Does Going Public Affect Innovation?," 1365–1403. In addition, because of their sheer scale, large corporations are better placed to benefit from advanced robotics and other production technologies. Indeed, studies show that process R&D is more tightly linked to firm size than product R&D. See Cohen and Klepper, "Reprise of Size and R & D," 925–951.
54. See Akcigit and Kerr, "Growth Through Heterogeneous Innovations," 1374–1443. These findings speak to the span-of-control model of Robert Lucas, which suggests that even the most skilled managers face limits in terms of the number of operations they can effectively oversee. As a result, large companies will invest more in improving existing products rather than developing entirely new ones. These inherent limits on the optimal size of firms create a comparative advantage for smaller companies in breakthrough innovation. Lucas, "Size Distribution of Business Firms," 508–523.

55. Akcigit and Goldschlag, "Where Have All the 'Creative Talents' Gone?"

56. As Jeff Bezos once quipped, "If you can't feed a team with two pizzas, it's too large."

57. On decentralization making it harder to achieve returns to scale, see Thesmar and Thoenig, "Creative Destruction and Firm Organization Choice," 1201–1237.

58. On large vs. small teams, see Wu, et al., "Large Teams," 378–382. On flat vs. hierarchical teams, see Xu, et al., "Flat Teams Drive Scientific Innovation," e2200927119.

59. On Edison and the risk of conservatism stifling progress, see Lamoreaux, "Entrepreneurship," 381. GE, of course, only came into existence following the merger of the Edison Company with the Thomson-Houston Electric Company (THEC), which was also advancing in AC technology and stood as a direct competitor to Westinghouse.

60. On incumbents cannibalizing their own rents, see Reinganum, "Timing of Innovation," 849–908. See also Henderson, "Underinvestment and Incompetence," 248–270.

61. On young inventors filing more creative patents, see Kalyani, "Creativity Decline."

62. On the death of star scientists, see Azoulay, et al., "Does Science Advance?," 2889–2920.

63. On creative destruction, see Aghion and Howitt, "Model of Growth," 323–351; Aghion, et al., *Power of Creative Destruction*.

64. Hymer, "International Operations of National Firms"; Marglin, "What Do Bosses Do?," 33–60.

65. Hobsbawm, *Industry and Empire*, 19.

66. Schumpeter, *Capitalism, Socialism and Democracy*, 76.

67. This is consistent with less productive firms engaging more in lobbying, see Bombardini, et al., "Lobbying Behind the Frontier."

68. On political power and innovation, see Akcigit, et al., "Connecting to Power," 529–564. On destructive entrepreneurship, see Baumol, "Entrepreneurship," 3–22. For an excellent overview of the recent literature, see also Baslandze, "Barriers to Creative Destruction."

69. Olson, *Rise and Decline of Nations*.

70. On the role of competition between states, see Acemoglu and Robinson, "Economic Backwardness in Political Perspective," 115–131.

71. Mokyr, *Culture of Growth*.

72. Together with important information and transportation connections, this resulted in scientific, technological, and artistic ideas spreading rapidly throughout the continent; see North, *Understanding the Process*, 138.

Chapter 2

1. Mokyr, "Cardwell's Law," 561–574.

2. On Macartney's mission, see Cranmer-Byng, *Embassy to China*, 7–9. See also Kissinger, *On China*, 534.

3. As Elman has pointed out, "neither Lord Macartney nor the Qianlong emperor could foresee that the Industrial Revolution in England would produce British military superiority." Elman, *On Their Own Terms*, 254.

4. Cited in Kissinger, *On China*, 42. Privately, however, the Qianlong emperor appears to have been fascinated by Western invention: "[He] had a cherished collection of seventy intricate English clocks gathered over the years, and had written poetry on the loveliness of foreign glass as well as several poems about telescopes. He periodically addressed edicts to the customs commissioner in Canton asking him to send European goods or artisans to the capital." Cited in Koyama and Rubin, *How the World Became Rich*, 70.

5. Peyrefitte, *The Immobile Empire*, xxii.

6. Kissinger, *On China*, 49.

7. On the consequences of the Opium Wars, see Sassoon, *Anxious Triumph*; Osterhammel, "Britain and China 1842–1914," 146–169, Map 8.1.

8. On Chinese technology in this period, see, for example, Shiba, *Commerce and Society in Sung China*; Needham, *Development of Iron and Steel Technology*; McNeill, *Pursuit of Power*, chapter 2.

9. For the Northern Song dynasty, GDP per capita in the Kaifeng Prefecture was more than twice as high as in China as a whole. Broadberry and Guan, "Regional Variation of GDP."

10. On the Kaifeng clock, see Yip and McKern, *China's Next Strategic Advantage*.

11. On Song technology, see Mokyr, *Lever of Riches*, 210, 217; Wagner, *Iron and Steel in Ancient China*, 335–336.

12. Bacon, *Novum Organum*.

13. Acemoglu and Robinson, *Narrow Corridor*, 222–223.

14. Feng, *Bureaucracy and the State*, 89.

15. Comparative analysis reveals that the key distinction setting Qin China apart from European states and empires was its relatively weak aristocracy; see Kiser and Cai, "War and Bureaucratization in Qin China," 511–539. The relatively weak aristocracy, however, was predicated on technologies permitting centralization, where China had a considerable lead.

16. During the Warring States period, 89 years out of 254 were peaceful.

17. On competition and innovation in China, see Huang, *Rise and Fall of the EAST*, Figure 7.1. While the Song era, according to Huang's estimates does not stand out as the most innovative, it arguably still produced the most important discoveries.

18. On political consolidation, see Fukuyama, *Origins of Political Order*, Table 1.

19. Von Glahn, *Economic History of China*, 83.

20. Cited in Acemoglu and Robinson, *Narrow Corridor*, 203.

21. Chinese legalism was wildly unpopular, which probably contributed to the short-lived Qin Empire. But its impact would nonetheless be lasting as it created an ideology that was a hybrid with Confucianism.

22. They also sought to limit the growth of the merchant class, whose fortunes were sometimes rivaling those of kings, deeming it a direct threat to autocratic rule.

23. For an excellent overview of Qin state-building efforts, see Acemoglu and Robinson, *Narrow Corridor*, 202–208.

24. On trading restrictions, see Von Glahn, *Economic History of China*, 91.

25. Von Glahn, *Economic History of China*, 95.

26. This figure includes everyone, down to the lowest ranked clerks; Bielenstein, *Bureaucracy of Han Times*, 156. The bureaucrats' per capita calculation is from Stasavage, *Decline and Rise of Democracy*, 153.

27. On the bureaucratic state reemerging, see Fukuyama, *Origins of Political Order*, 148–149.

28. While China was divided on many occasions, the persistence of its centralized state is unparalleled. On this point, see Ko, et al., "Unified China; Divided Europe," 285–327; Ko and Sng, "Regional Dependence and Political Centralization," 470–483.

29. Huang, *Taxation and Governmental Finance*, 7.

30. On the astrological event, see Pankenier, "Cosmopolitical Background of Heaven's Mandate," 121–176. See also Fen, *Early China*, 117–119.

31. Wittfogel, *Oriental Despotism*.

32. Ostrom, *Governing the Commons*; Ostrom and Gardner, "Coping with Asymmetries in the Commons," 93–112.

33. Stasavage, *Decline and Rise of Democracy*, 145.

34. Indeed, it has been suggested that while fractured land "provides a robust explanation for the political divergence observed at the two ends of Eurasia . . . the presence of a dominant

core region of high land productivity in China—in the form of the North China Plain—and the lack thereof in Europe can also explain political unification in China and division in Europe." Fernández-Villaverde, et al., "Fractured-Land Hypothesis."

35. As Stasavage argues, the more fundamental "explanation [than geographic factors] lies in the fact that Europe was behind in terms of agricultural technology." Stasavage, *Decline and Rise of Democracy*, 108.

36. Stasavage, *Decline and Rise of Democracy*, 12. For a detailed discussion of the tax imperative behind innovation in soil mapping, see Brevik and Hartemink, "Early Soil Knowledge," 23–33; Bockheim and Hartemink, "Soils and Land Appraisal," 213–222; Gong, et al., "Origin and Development of Soil Science," 3–13.

37. Amazingly, the famous Domesday Book in England, recording taxable wealth in the kingdom in 1087, provides hardly any reference to the quality of the soil.

38. This is not to suggest that there was no progress in Europe. The early Middle Ages witnessed important technological advancements in agriculture, including the introduction of crop rotation, enhanced use of animals in farming, and the adoption of the heavy plough, leading to improved agricultural efficiency. But China undisputably had a considerable technological lead.

39. In the words of Georges Duby: "Western Europe is incontestably one of the most varied regions in the world in its local agricultural conditions." Duby, "Medieval Agriculture, 900–1500," 175.

40. On plough adoption in Europe, see White, "Expansion of Technology, 500–1500"; Bloch, *French Rural History*. On China, see Von Glahn, *Economic History of China*, 131–134.

41. Goody, *Logic of Writing*, 103–104. Indeed, excavations at the ancient Sumerian city of Ur show that "85 percent of texts record some sort of an economic transaction"; Stasavage, *Decline and Rise of Democracy*, 81.

42. On China's writing system, see Scheidel, *Escape from Rome*, 312.

43. On population registers, see Von Glahn, *Economic History of China*, 87.

44. Von Glahn, *Economic History of China*, 53.

45. Von Glahn, *Economic History of China*, 18.

46. Put differently, what Michael Mann has called "infrastructural power" required reinforcing technologies; Mann, "Autonomous Power of the State," 185–213; Mann, *Sources of Social Power Volume II*. Throughout the book I use the term "bureaucratic capacity" instead.

47. On the Russian population, see Scheidel, *Escape from Rome*, 32.

48. On Russia having few towns, see Shaw, "Towns and Commerce," 298–316. Difficulties of taxing peasants, landlords, and the business class meant that even by the late nineteenth century the Russian government predominantly relied on indirect taxes on personal consumption; Gatrell, "Russian Fiscal State."

49. On irrigation, see Von Glahn, *Economic History of China*, 236.

50. The lasting importance of the Grand Canal is underlined by the unrest that followed its closure in the nineteenth century; see Cao and Chen, "Rebel on the Canal," 1555–1590.

51. On the role of the state in the introduction of new seed varieties, see Stasavage, *Decline and Rise of Democracy*, 184. The same was true of the Abbasid Caliphate where the unity of governance over a large territory spurred the diffusion of agricultural innovations and technological knowledge; Watson, *Agricultural Innovation in the Early Islamic World*, 2–3. See also Watson, "Arab Agricultural Revolution and Its Diffusion," 8–35.

52. On progress in iron, for example, see Hartwell, 1962, "Revolution in the Chinese Iron and Coal Industries," 153–162; Hartwell, "Markets, Technology, and the Structure of Enterprise," 29–58. On water transport, see Yoshinobu, *Commerce and Society in Sung China*.

53. See Kuhn, *Age of Confucian Rule*, 40–43. On printing during the Tang and Song eras, see also Hymes, "Sung Society and Social Change," 526–664.

54. Lin, "Needham Puzzle," 269–292.

55. Similarly, Elvin famously noted that while China underwent a "medieval economic revolution" between the eighth and thirteenth centuries, this period was followed by a flattening of both growth and innovation; Elvin, *Pattern of the Chinese Past*.

56. This divergence, in other words, happened earlier than scholars like Pomeranz suggested; Pomeranz, *Great Divergence*. For a revised account on the timing of the Great Divergence, see Broadberry, et al., "China, Europe and the Great Divergence," 955–1000; Broadberry, et al., "China, Europe and the Great Divergence," 958–974; Broadberry and Guan, "Regional Variation of GDP."

57. Lin, "Needham Puzzle," 269–292. See also Deng, "Development and Its Deadlock in Imperial China," 479–522.

58. On exam failure rates, see Acemoglu and Robinson, *Narrow Corridor*, 215.

59. For a more detailed overview of the examination system, see also Miyazaki, *China's Examination Hell*; Elman, *Cultural History of Civil Examinations*; Elman, *Civil Examinations and Meritocracy*; Huang, *Rise and Fall of the EAST*. On elite persistence, see Hao, "Social Mobility in China," 233–243.

60. Brandt, et al., "From Divergence to Convergence," 45–123.

61. Chinese organization, as a hierarchical, hub-and-spoke network centred around the emperor, provided an efficient way of ensuring stability across a vast territory, but this also made it highly vulnerable to systemwide collapse; Root, *Network Origins of the Global Economy*.

62. Lin, "Needham Puzzle," 269–92, 110.

63. For a more detailed discussion of ARPA, see chapter 7.

64. Song state building was also aided because kinship ties had become more geographically dispersed, making families more willing to support national goals. On this point, see Wang, "Blood is Thicker Than Water," 896–910.

65. On Wang Anshi, see Von Glahn, *Economic History of China*, 237–239.

66. On the autonomy of ARPA, see Azoulay, et al., "Funding Breakthrough Research," 69–96.

67. Smith, *Taxing Heaven's Storehouse*.

68. Kaifeng's state armoires alone employed more than 13,000 ironworkers, producing swords, lances, and other weapons, along with nails, locks, lamps, and boilers; Von Glahn, *Economic History of China*, 246.

69. On Zhu undermining the state, see Acemoglu and Robinson, *Narrow Corridor*, 210.

70. This rhymes with Elvin's account, pointing to the closing of China's borders under the self-imposed maritime embargo of the Ming dynasty, which greatly diminished trade and contact with foreigners to the detriment of both Smithian and Schumpeterian growth, along with its waning interest for the natural world, precluding progress in science; Elvin, *Pattern of the Chinese Past*. Elvin's argument that the closing of outlets for emigration worsened China's land/labour ratio, making labour-saving innovations less financially attractive, is more speculative.

71. On the Chinese fleet, see Kennedy, *Rise and Fall of the Great Powers*, 6.

72. Kennedy, *Rise and Fall of the Great Powers*, 7. See also Jung-pang, "Emergence of China as a Sea Power," 489–503.

73. For a discussion of factors behind China's decline, see Ho, "Economic and Institutional Factors," 274–276.

74. Kennedy, *Rise and Fall of the Great Powers*, 8.

75. For a detailed discussion of the absence of real threats to the Ming dynasty, see Stasavage, *Decline and Rise of Democracy*, 161.

76. True, there was the Shun dynasty in between the Ming-Qing transition, but it lasted only a few months.

77. Scholars have documented very high rates of elite persistence during Qing era. Indeed, a staggering 87 percent of successful graduates from the province-level civil service examination (*juren*) came from families where members had passed the province-level or highest imperial examination (*jinshi*) in the previous five generations; Hao, "Social Mobility in China," 233–243.

78. On the selling of examination certificates, see Acemoglu and Robinson, *Narrow Corridor*, 217.

79. On the Qing state's decline in tax revenues, see Brandt, et al., "From Divergence to Convergence," 67; Lamouroux and von Glahn, "Public Finance, 1000 to 1800."

80. On distance and taxes, see Sng, "Size and Dynastic Decline," 107–127.

81. On travel time, see Whitney, *China*, 47.

82. Zelin, *Magistrate's Tael*, 255.

83. On the *Censorate* and other mechanisms for monitoring, see Brandt, et al., "From Divergence to Convergence," 45–123.

84. Whether one considers per capita revenue expressed in days' wages for unskilled urban workers, or in grams of silver, the trend is similar. See Brandt, et al., "From Divergence to Convergence," Table 3.

85. On bureaucratic capacity, see Naughton, *Chinese Economy*, 49.

86. Skinner, "Introduction: Urban Development in Imperial China," 19.

87. Acemoglu and Robinson, *Narrow Corridor*, 216.

88. Mayers, *Chinese Government*, 21–22.

89. This paved the way for an authoritarian, and yet decentralized political regime, a topic we shall return to in chapter 10.

90. Sng argues that given the how slim the Chinese bureaucracy had become, officials were forced to delegate responsibility for taxation to the local level. However, because of corruption and local favouritism, much of these revenues never reached the central government; Sng, "Size and Dynastic Decline," 107–27.

91. On palm-leaf guild resistance, see Mann, *Local Merchants and the Chinese Bureaucracy*, 130.

92. Brandt, et al., "From Divergence to Convergence," 45–123. Quote from working paper version, Brandt, et al., "From Divergence to Convergence," 46–47.

93. The legal secretaries who assisted county magistrates, for example, were not part of an official apparatus. They were personally hired and paid by the magistrates.

94. On the legal profession in China, see Macauley, *Social Power and Legal Culture*. See also Chen and Myers, "Customary Law and the Economic Growth," 4–27.

95. Fukuyama, *Origins of Political Order*, 132.

96. Brandt, et al., "From Divergence to Convergence," 45–123.

97. Duara, *Culture, Power, and the State*, 183.

98. Brandt, et al., "From Divergence to Convergence," 45–123.

99. On the weakening of the bureaucracy from within, see Acemoglu and Robinson, *Narrow Corridor*, 227–228.

100. Though the lack of civil society in China might have been overstated, and has been the subject of much controversy, including the concept itself, it is fair to say that kinship acted as a constraint on the growth of what one might call "civil society." See Rowe, "Problem of 'Civil Society,'" 139–157.

101. Gernet argues that the power of merchants in Song China was always checked by the state. Consequently, while they were able to prosper as individuals, they never succeeded in creating a self-conscious "class" pursuing shared interests as was the case in Europe; Gernet, *Daily Life in China*.

102. On Anhui and Hunan guildsmen, see Acemoglu and Robinson, *Narrow Corridor*, 219.

103. Fukuyama, *Origins of Political Order*, 150.

Chapter 3

1. Machiavelli, *The Prince*, 20.
2. Without elaborate irrigation systems, fertilizers, and crop management, bureaucratic rule was untenable in Europe.
3. Scheidel, *Escape from Rome*, 64.
4. In some cases, however, a curia could have up to six hundred members; Jones, *Later Roman Empire*, 724–725.
5. On competition and state formation, see Scheidel, *Escape from Rome*, 88.
6. On Roman governance, see Acemoglu and Robinson, *Narrow Corridor*, 158. On Roman bureaucracy, see Jones, *Later Roman Empire*, 1057. Figures on Han bureaucracy (comprising 130,285 men) from 5th century B.C., see Bielenstein, *Bureaucracy of Han Times*, 156.
7. Gibbon, *History of the Decline and Fall*, 19.
8. Cited in Acemoglu and Robinson, *Narrow Corridor*, 155.
9. On bureaucratic administration, see Bachrach, "Charlemagne and Carolingian Military Administration," 170–196.
10. On positions becoming hereditary, see McKitterick, *Frankish Kingdoms under the Carolingians*, 87–88.
11. On the rise of the feudal order, see Bloch, *Feudal Society Volume 2*, 190–194.
12. On gaining support for war, see Halsall, *Warfare and Society*, 73–77. On how weak rulers made consent necessary more broadly, see Stasavage, "Representation and Consent," 145–162.
13. Krause, "Geschichte Des Institutes Der Missi Dominici," 193–300.
14. Bachrach, "Charlemagne and Carolingian Military Administration," 170–196.
15. On governance, see Reynolds, *Kingdoms and Communities in Western Europe*.
16. For calculation of state revenues, see Stasavage, *Decline and Rise of Democracy*, 11.
17. This stands in contrast to the Roman Empire in the East, where Byzantium started off with a representative assembly. However, under Emperor Leo VI, who ruled from 886 to 912, representative bodies were stripped of their authority and more power was consolidated in the bureaucracy; see Ostrogorsky, *History of the Byzantine State*.
18. On parliamentary activity, see Van Zanden, et al., "Rise and Decline of European Parliaments," 835–861.
19. On the interactions between institutions and Atlantic trade, see Acemoglu, et al., "Rise of Europe," 546–579.
20. While scholars have primarily focused on the role of Parliament in increasing the fiscal capacity of the Crown and spurring investment through a credible commitment to uphold property rights, the diminishing power of incumbent interests to block the rise of modern industry was a no less important factor in explaining why the Industrial Revolution was British in the end. On fiscal capacity and credible commitment, see, for example, North and Weingast, "Constitutions and Commitment," 803–832; North, "Institutions," 97–112.
21. By 1500, in places with longer exposure to such policies, kinship was much less prevalent; see Schulz, et al., "Church, Intensive Kinship, and Global Psychological Variation."
22. On unified Christian identity, see Henrich, *WEIRDest People in the World*, 307.
23. On kinship, cities, and associations, see Henrich, *WEIRDest People in the World*, chapter 9.
24. Empirical work by Schultz, for example, shows that cities with longer exposure to the Church grew much faster between 800 and 1500 CE; Schulz, "Kin Networks and Institutional Development," 2578–2613.
25. For a discussion on borrowing by city-states, see Stasavage, *States of Credit*.
26. On cities in Song China, see Stasavage, *Decline and Rise of Democracy*, 126.

27. Quote from Johnson and data on London and Baghdad from Bosker, et al., "From Baghdad to London," 1418–1437.

28. This point is forcefully made by Harris, *Going the Distance*, 2. A similar point is made in Greif, "Family Structure, Institutions, and Growth," 308–312. On the relative backwardness of Islamic law, see Kuran, *Long Divergence*.

29. Greif and Tabellini, "Cultural and Institutional Bifurcation," 135–140; Greif and Tabellini, "Clan and the Corporation," 1–35. For a detailed discussion of the interaction between state institutions and social organization, see also Mokyr and Tabellini, "Social Organizations and Political Institutions."

30. See Scheidel, *Escape from Rome*, 410.

31. Kuran, *Long Divergence*.

32. Mokyr, *Culture of Growth*, 173.

33. The term *Respublica Literaria* was first attested in 1417 and had become common in use by the 17th century.

34. Later, the 1839 Act of Parliament to replace Britain's expensive system of distance-based postage with a single lower rate increased citations between connected scientists, pointing to important knowledge spillovers between them; Hanlon, et al., "A Penny for Your Thoughts."

35. On the Republic of Letters, see Mokyr, *Culture of Growth*.

36. What Habermas called the emergence of the "public sphere" captures the essence of these developments; Habermas, *Structural Transformation of the Public Sphere*.

37. On the role of coffeehouses, see Cowan, *Social Life of Coffee*.

38. On the link between patents and knowledge societies, see J. Dowey, "Mind over Matter." Research also shows that French cities with knowledge societies, as proxied by subscriber density of Diderot's famous Encyclopaedia before 1750, grew faster in the following century; Squicciarini and Voigtländer, "Human Capital and Industrialization," 1825–1883.

39. Whitehead, *Science and the Modern World*, 96.

40. This share rose steadily to 20 percent by the 1840s and reached almost 30 percent by the 1860s.

41. On engineers in Britain and France, see Hanlon, "Rise of the Engineer."

42. While eighteenth century Britain has been called "Associational Society," the same could be said about other parts of Europe. Newton, Galileo, and Leibniz were read by educated elites from Helsinki to Rome and from Lisbon to St. Petersburg. See, for example, Clark, *British Clubs and Societies*.

43. Using data from membership registers, economic historians have shown that regions with a higher density of members in the late eighteenth century subsequently saw higher inventive activity during the Second Industrial Revolution. A doubling of member density is associated with a 19 percent increase in patents granted between 1877 and 1914 as well as an 11 percent higher number of exhibitors at the 1873 Vienna World's Fair; Koschnick, et al., "Flow of Ideas." Later, in Italy, around the time of unification, the transfer of books and manuscripts from monasteries to public libraries had a strikingly positive effect on innovation; Buonanno, et al., "Books Go Public." On Berlin Monthly, see Clark, *Iron Kingdom*, 249–250.

44. See, for example, Greif, "Cultural Beliefs and the Organization of Society," 912–950; Triandis, *Individualism and Collectivism*. On collectivism in China, see Talhelm, et al., "Large-Scale Psychological Differences," 603–608; and Henrich, "Rice, Psychology, and Innovation," 593–594.

45. Leunig, et al., "Networks in the Premodern Economy," 413–443; de la Croix, et al., "Clans, Guilds, and Markets," 1–70.

46. As van Zanden notes, "In contrast to the relatively closed systems in which the family played a central role, Western Europe had a formal system of apprenticeship—organized by

guilds or similar institutions—and in principle open to all." van Zanden, *Long Road to the Industrial Revolution*. See also Moll-Murata, "Guilds and Apprenticeship in China and Europe."

47. Allen, "Collective Invention," 1–24.

48. In one of his earlier articles, published in 1946, Needham suggested that experimental science might be a fundamentally democratic activity that will only flourish in a decentralized environment; Needham, "On Science and Social Change," 225–251.

49. Mokyr, "Market for Ideas," 3–38.

50. This insight goes back to David Hume, who argued that "the divisions into small states are favorable to learning, by stopping the progress of authority as well as that of power." Hume, "Rise and Progress of the Arts and Sciences," 111–137. More recently, Eric Jones has argued that "the states system was an insurance against economic and technological stagnation." Jones, *European Miracle*, 119.

51. Political fragmentation in the medieval Middle East and in premodern India, for example, seemingly did little to promote innovation in the absence of cultural unity. Qing China, in contrast, achieved political and cultural unity among elites, but it oppressed heterodox thinking and favoured the status quo. See Koyama and Rubin, *How the World Became Rich*, 174.

52. For examples of intellectuals moving around, see Scheidel, *Escape from Rome*, 474. Even when intellectuals could not move as freely, their books and writings did, thanks to the printing press and postal services; Mokyr, *Culture of Growth*, 176–177.

53. On Zhu, see Mokyr, *Culture of Growth*, 311.

54. On religious divisions and the nursery of modernity, see Scheidel, *Escape from Rome*, 9.

55. Bekmann provides a list of forty-six new professions; Bekmann, *Historische Beschreibung der Chur und Mark Brandenburg*, Vol. 1.

56. On Huguenots and fortunes of German towns, see Hornung, "Immigration and the Diffusion of Technology," 84–122.

57. List, *National System of Political Economy*, 153.

58. On Prussian censorship, see Clark, *Iron Kingdom*, 462–464.

59. Serafinelli and Tabellini, "Creativity over Time and Space," 1–43.

60. On the literary inquisition, see Jami, *Emperor's New Mathematics*.

61. On Wang Xihou, see Xue, "Autocratic Rule and Social Capital." See also Reischauer and Fairbank, *East Asia*.

62. Gong, *Gong Zizhen Selected Poems*.

63. On mutual suspicion, see Wang, *Tying the Autocrat's Hands*, 647.

64. On political repression and civil society, see Xue, "Autocratic Rule and Social Capital."

65. On the civil service examination, see Scheidel, *Escape from Rome*, 480.

66. Mokyr, *Culture of Growth*, 317.

67. The adoption of the printing press in the Ottoman Empire was delayed by an astonishing 250 years; Coşgel, et al., "Political Economy of Mass Printing," 357–371.

68. On Roman infrastructure, see Harper, *Fate of Rome*.

69. In the words of Abbott Usher, classical civilizations were "oppressed by tradition," showing little interest in new technology for the advancement for industry; Usher, *History of Mechanical Innovations*, 101.

70. See, for example, Finley, "Technical Innovation and Economic Progress," 29–45; Finley, *Ancient Economy*.

71. On the importance of skills in machine making, see Rosenberg, "Factors Affecting the Diffusion of Technology," 3.

72. For example, Mokyr argues that it was British skilled workers who internalized and realized the ideas of the Enlightenment; Mokyr, *Enlightened Economy*. And British workers were

more skilled than their European neighbours; Kelly, et al., "Precocious Albion," 363–389; Kelly, et al., "Mechanics of the Industrial Revolution," 59–94.

73. Another competing theory is that the Industrial Revolution began in Britain because of its high wages, making it the only country were the adoption of machines paid handsomely; Allen, *British Industrial Revolution*; Allen, "Industrial Revolution in Miniature," 901–927; Allen, "Why the Industrial Revolution Was British," 357–384. However, recent evidence shows that wages in Britain were not as high as previously believed. For revised wages of spinners, see Humphries and Schneider, "Spinning the Industrial Revolution," 126–155. For evidence suggesting that real wages in England in the period 1650–1800 were lower than previously thought, see Stephenson, "'Real' Wages?," 106–132. Another factor that undermines the high wage explanation is that British industrialization relied heavily on cheap child labour; Humphries, "Lure of Aggregates," 693–714; Humphries, *Childhood and Child Labour*.

74. On millwrights, see Van Der Beek, et al., "Wheels of Change," 1894–1926. In a sample of 937 British inventors in the period of the Industrial Revolution and the decades leading up to it, Howes shows that over a quarter were millwrights or similarly trained as mechanics and engineers; Howes, "Relevance of Skills." See also Howes, *Arts and Minds*.

75. On guilds and training in Britain, see Mokyr, "The Holy Land of Industrialism," 223–247. Wallis also notes that apprenticeships in Britain "thrived despite, not because of, the guilds." Wallis, "Apprenticeship and Training in Premodern England," 832–861, 854.

76. On the factory system being a technological event, see Mokyr, "Rise and Fall of the Factory System," 1–45; Jones, "Technology, Transaction Costs," 71–96.

77. James Hargreaves spinning jenny was another key invention, but it did little for the rise of the factory system other than inspiring Samuel Crompton's mule; Allen, *British Industrial Revolution*; Frey, *Technology Trap*, 99–105.

78. On the comparison with France, see Crafts, "British Industrialization in an International Context," 415–428.

79. On steam and productivity, see Crafts, "Steam as a General Purpose Technology," 338–351. Estimates suggest that the social savings from passenger travel amounted to some 5 percent of GDP in 1865 and reached 14 percent by 1912; Leunig, "Time Is Money," 635–673.

80. On the importance of market size and firm size for the Industrial Revolution, see Desmet and Parente, "Evolution of Markets," 205–234.

81. On the demise of the domestic system, see Mantoux, *Industrial Revolution in the Eighteenth Century*; Frey, *Technology Trap*, 109–110.

82. Landes, *Unbound Prometheus*, 12.

83. On guilds helping to resolve the asymmetric information problem, see Richardson, "Brand Names Before the Industrial Revolution." On how tacit knowledge slowly spread throughout Europe via journeymen, see de la Croix, et al., "Clans, Guilds, and Markets," 1–70.

84. New industries, which did not fall under the Apprenticeship Act of the Statute of Artificers, also weakened the guilds; Hibbert, *Influence and Development of English Guilds*, 129.

85. Only Liverpool grew faster, as its port benefited from the rise of the Atlantic economy and booming trade with North America.

86. Ogilvie, *European Guilds*. Epstein also argues that capital-saving technologies were not frowned upon, while labour-saving technologies were more likely to be resisted; Epstein, "Craft Guilds," 684–713.

87. On Papin, see Acemoglu and Robinson, *Why Nations Fail*, 197.

88. In the words of Mokyr, "Guilds, despite their local autonomy, were often allied with kings; hence they were known as *choses du roi*." Mokyr, *Culture of Growth*, 173.

89. On the Leiden riots, see Patterson, "Spinning and Weaving," 151–186. For more examples of bans and resistance, see White, *Modern Capitalist Culture*, 77. For quote and further examples, see also Frey, *Technology Trap*, chapter 3.

90. On travel speed, see Koyama and Rubin, *How the World Became Rich*, 30.

91. In addition, canal construction and waterborne transport linked up the industrial heartland in the northwest with coal deposits, giving a significant boost to Britain's urban economy; Bogart, et al., "Turnpikes, Canals, and Economic Growth."

92. On the shearers guild, see Randall, *Before the Luddites*.

93. On patents and competition, see Desmet, et al., "Spatial Competition, Innovation and Institutions," 1–35. Between 1750 and 1800, the percentage of labour-saving technologies experienced a fourfold increase; MacLeod, *Inventing the Industrial Revolution*, 160.

94. On the Bill of Rights, see Cox, "Glorious Revolution," 567–600; North, "Institutions," 97–112; North and Weingast, "Constitutions and Commitment," 803–832.

95. True, merchants were hardly a majority group in Parliament, but the Whig coalition protected their interests. In addition, the relatively diversified wealth of the landed aristocracy from Britain's trading empire meant that they did not resist mechanization as the landed elites did elsewhere. On the Whig coalition, see Stasavage, *Public Debt*. On the landed elites and mechanization, see Mokyr, *Lever of Riches*, 243.

96. On the turnpikes, see Bogart, "Turnpike Trusts and the Transportation Revolution in 18th Century England," 479–508; Bogart, "Did Turnpike Trusts Increase Transportation," 439–468; Bogart, "Transport Revolution in Industrialising Britain," 368–391.

97. On the role of Parliament in infrastructure investment, see Bogart, "Small Price to Pay"; Bogart and Richardson, "Property Rights and Parliament," 241–274.

98. On internal trade, Koyama and Rubin, *How the World Became Rich*, 161–162.

99. The prevailing winds of change began to erode the foundations of these entrenched interests, compelling them to adopt a more defensive stance; Mokyr and Nye, "Distributional Coalitions," 50–70, 58.

100. Quoted in Mantoux, *Industrial Revolution in the Eighteenth Century*, 403. This rhymes with the view of Rosenthal and Wong, who argue that the growth-enhancing policies introduced were not deliberately growth-enhancing. Rather they were the result of competition between states, which spurred economic development unintentionally; Rosenthal and Wong, *Before and Beyond Divergence*.

101. On the absence of labour repression in France during the revolutionary era, see Horn, *Path Not Taken*, 8.

102. Mokyr, "Technological Inertia in Economic History," 331–332.

103. On Dutch guilds being less restrictive, see Prak and van Zanden, *Pioneers of Capitalism*, 156–158.

104. For examples of resistance, see Davids, *Rise and Decline*, 464–465.

105. On workers in the guild system, see Davids, *Rise and Decline*, 483.

106. On winning essays, see Davids, *Rise and Decline*, 466.

107. On Dutch inventors, see De Vries and Van der Woude, *First Modern Economy*, 344–345. Notable innovations included Archimedes' screw for water pumping in 1634 and significant advancements in industrial windmill technology, including van Uitgeest's mechanical lumber-sawing windmill in 1591 and the introduction of the "Hollander" in papermaking windmills in 1674.

108. On the patent system, see Davids, *Rise and Decline*, 404–405.

109. On mandates, see Price, *Holland and the Dutch Republic*.

110. For a formal model on oligarchy and barriers to entry, see Acemoglu, "Oligarchic Versus Democratic Societies," 1–44.

111. Van Bavel, *Invisible Hand*.

112. On foreign travelers, see Davids, *Rise and Decline*, 473. On protectionist measures, see Davids, *Rise and Decline*, 475.

113. As Jan De Vries and Ad Van Der Woude write, "Once an industry successfully had sunk roots, public policy became noticeably more restrictive. This restriction often was effected via

guild regulations, which generally required municipal confirmation. Guild provisions tended to raise obstacles to the entry of newcomers, certainly to the circle of masters. In their concern for protecting the quality of production and securing stability in the labor market, the guilds habitually turned to protectionism; and this reflex was more readily accommodated by the cities the more business conditions were depressed. Then, the quality controls were more strictly enforced, the departure of skilled workers resisted, and the export of technology forbidden." De Vries and Van der Woude, *First Modern Economy*, 340–341.

114. On the role of mandates, see Stasavage, *Decline and Rise of Democracy*, 219. On the ability of Parliament to override veto players, see Cox, *Marketing Sovereign Promises*.

115. On the economics of *Code Napoléon*, see Acemoglu, et al., "Consequences of Radical Reform," 3286–3307.

116. For examples of guilds preventing innovation in Germany, see Kisch, *From Domestic Manufacture to Industrial Revolution*; Lindberg, "Club Goods and Inefficient Institutions," 604–628; Ogilvie, "Guilds, Efficiency, and Social Capital," 286–333.

117. On French occupation and patenting, see Donges, et al., "Impact of Institutions on Innovation," 1951–1974.

118. On the activities of *kuan-tu shang-pan* enterprises, see Kim, *Japanese Perspectives*, 7–12.

119. On role of government in technology transfer, see Kuo and Liu, "Self-Strengthening," 491–542.

120. On inefficiencies, see Brown, "Transfer of Technology to China," 181–197, 183.

121. Morse, 1909, *Gilds of China*, 1.

122. For examples of resistance, see Desmet, et al., "Spatial Competition, Innovation and Institutions," 1–35.

123. On resistance to silk factories, see Ma, "Between Cottage and Factory," 195–213.

124. On the emergence of local oligarchs, see Brandt, et al., "From Divergence to Convergence," 45–123. See also Motono, *Conflict and Cooperation*, 3–6.

125. On dragon tickets, see Hershatter, *Workers of Tianjin*, 117.

126. Morse, 1932, *Gilds of China*, 24.

127. On distance limiting competition in China relative to Britian, see Desmet, et al., "Spatial Competition, Innovation and Institutions," 1–35.

128. For example, even though a railway from Tientsin to Tongzhou near Peaking had been sanctioned by imperial edict, the project was stopped, reflecting the opposition from officials in Peking who profited from rice being carried by boat through the canal system to the capital; see Kinder, "Railways and Collieries of North China," 278–306, 288. See also Comin and Hobijn, "Lobbies and Technology Diffusion," 229–244.

129. Wang, "Mandarins, Merchants, and the Railway," 31–53.

130. On railroads and the Qing government, see Kinder, "Railways and Collieries of North China," 278–306, 288.

131. On resistance to railroads and telegraph lines in China, see Koyama, et al., "Geopolitics and Asia's Little Divergence," 178–204; Fairbank, *China: A New History*; Baark, *Lightning Wires*.

132. On market integration around 1750, see Shiue and Keller, "Markets in China and Europe," 1189–1216. On Chinese market integration declining thereafter, see Bernhofen, et al., "Assessing Market Integration."

133. On foreign competition and modernization, see Desmet, et al., "Spatial Competition, Innovation and Institutions," 1–35.

134. Brandt and Rawski, "China's Great Boom as a Historical Process," 14.

135. On treaty ports and technology adoption, see Keller and Shiue, "Economic Consequences of the Opium War." See also Jia, "Legacies of Forced Freedom," 596–608.

136. On technology diffusion, see Brandt and Rawski, "China's Great Boom as a Historical Process," 82.
137. The China Merchants Steamship Navigation Company, established in 1872, also added a Chinese dimension to this expansion in trade.
138. On treaty ports, new ideas, and institutional change, see Brandt, et al., "From Divergence to Convergence," 45–123. Quote is in the working paper version, Brandt, et al., "From Divergence to Convergence."
139. On this point, see Acemoglu and Robinson, "Economic Backwardness in Political Perspective," 115–131.
140. Rosenberg and Birdzell, *How the West Grew Rich*, 138.
141. On differences between China and Japan, see Naughton, *Chinese Economy*, 84–86.
142. On reform after the defeat to Japan, see Hao and Wang, "Changing Chinese Views," 142–201.
143. On Cixi and conservatism, see Sassoon, *Anxious Triumph*, 101. See also Hsü, *Rise of Modern China*, 377.
144. Cited in Ichiko, "Political and Institutional Reform," 375–415.
145. On Tsinghua University, see Kirby, *Empires of Ideas*.
146. On scientific translations, Wright, "Yan Fu," 235–255.
147. On continued conservatism, see Sassoon, *Anxious Triumph*, 103. See also Weston, "Founding of the Imperial University," 99–123.
148. Brandt and Rawski, "China's Great Boom as a Historical Process," 17.
149. Naughton, *Chinese Economy*, 87.
150. On the Shanghai Dalong Machinery Company, see Rawski, *Economic Growth in Prewar China*.
151. On paths to industrialization and the Anshan mill, see Naughton, *Chinese Economy*, 88.
152. Weber, 1978, *Economy and Society*, 978.
153. The Qing dynasty collapsed in 1912 after a mutiny in Wuchang, prompting the provinces to declare their independence from Beijing.
154. On central government agencies, see Eastman, *Abortive Revolution*, 219.
155. By the early 1940s, state-run firms accounted for 70 percent of all capital and 32 percent of labour in unoccupied territories; Naughton, *Chinese Economy*, 95.
156. Mokyr, "The Holy Land of Industrialism," 223–247.

Chapter 4

1. Brady, "Industrial Policy," 108–123, 121.
2. Cited in *The Economist*, 1896, "British V. German Trade," August 11.
3. After two decades of declining tariffs, the *Reichstag* introduced import duties on iron, steel, and almost everything else in 1879, raw materials being the exception; Webb, "Tariffs, Cartels, Technology," 309–330.
4. Williams, *Made in Germany*, 8–9.
5. Williams, *Made in Germany*, 10–11.
6. For a word count on "decadence," see Bull, "Decline of Decadence," 83–86.
7. Hoffman, *Great Britain and the German Trade Rivalry*, 255.
8. Cited in Sassoon, *Anxious Triumph*, 175.
9. On "declinism" being exaggerated, see Crafts, "British Relative Economic Decline."
10. On per capita incomes, see Burhop, *Wirtschaftsgeschichte des Kaiserreichs, 1871–1918*.
11. On sectoral differences, see Broadberry, "Anglo-German Productivity Differences 1870–1990," 247–267, Table 4.

12. For example, the dissolution of the monasteries in 1535, which ended feudal land tenure, created a market for monastic land. Parishes affected by the dissolution, saw more people leaving agriculture, paving the way for more rapid industrialization; Heldring, et al., "Long-Run Impact," 2093–2145.

13. This was because Britain's landed elites had relatively diversified wealth and thus stood to gain more from free trade than the aristocracy elsewhere; see Acemoglu and Robinson, "Economic Backwardness in Political Perspective," 115–131. On diversified wealth in Britain, see also Rubinstein, *Men of Property*.

14. On the Prussian political system, see Becker and Hornung, "Political Economy," 1143–1188.

15. Webb, "Agricultural Protection in Wilhelminian Germany," 309–326.

16. For a recent reassessment of the Victorian Climacteric, see Crafts and Mills, "Sooner Than You Think," 736–748.

17. On the failure of Victorian Britain being technological, see Mokyr, *Lever of Riches*, 266.

18. Cited in Landes, *Unbound Prometheus*, 178.

19. Quoted in Jaeger, *Unternehmer in der deutschen Politik (1890–1918)*, 244. See also Sombart, *Der Bourgeois*, 184–185, 189–192.

20. Sombart, *Quintessence of Capitalism*, 150–151.

21. And, of course, Britain itself ended up abandoning laissez-faire as the nineteenth century progressed in response to the economic forces set in motion by the Industrial Revolution, see Hanlon, *Laissez-Faire Experiment*.

22. On the state and catch-up growth, see Sassoon, *Anxious Triumph*.

23. See Pierenkemper and Tilly, *German Economy During the Nineteenth Century*, 19. Kiesewetter also argues that defeat of Napoleon constituted the earliest beginning of industrialization in parts of Germany; Kiesewetter, *Die Industrialisierung Sachsens*.

24. Landes, *Unbound Prometheus*, 148. For a detailed account of technology transfer in this period and the ineffectiveness of British regulation, see Harris, *Industrial Espionage and Technology Transfer*.

25. Landes, *Unbound Prometheus*, 149.

26. Cited in Schnabel, *Deutsche Geschichte im Neunzehnten Jahrhundert*, 287.

27. Landes, *Unbound Prometheus*, 149–150.

28. In Prussia, this entailed a "pro-immigration policy" to attract skilled workers; Hornung, "Immigration and the Diffusion of Technology," 84–122.

29. Landes, *Unbound Prometheus*, 151.

30. Landes, *Unbound Prometheus*, 151.

31. For example, a technical commission was established to evaluate the novelty of inventions. Based on this evaluation, the Ministry of the Interior decided whether a patent should be granted.

32. In Germany, between 1843 and 1877, over 38 percent of all newly issued patents were filed by inventors in other countries; Donges and Selgert, "Technology Transfer via Foreign Patents," 182–208.

33. Nuvolari, et al., "British-French Technology Transfer."

34. On water-power technologies, see Mokyr, *Lever of Riches*, 90–92.

35. While Britain relied predominantly on the Watt engine, the high-pressure Woolf compound engine, which saved more fuel, was more popular in France, and it was this engine that the French improved upon; Nuvolari, "Theory and Practice of Steam Engineering," 177–185.

36. While the Continental Blockade had temporarily shielded local businesses in France from British imports, giving a boost to domestic cotton spinning, access to foreign knowledge rather than protectionism was key to continued progress; on the effects of the blockade, see Juhász, "Temporary Protection and Technology Adoption," 3339–3376. For example, a century later, when the Great War disrupted exports from Britain, suddenly shielded Chinese counties did not see increased domestic activity, simply because they were also cut off from an essential input: British technology; Liu, "Effects of World War I," 246–285. This suggests that the more sophisticated technology becomes, openness to foreign technology becomes ever more important for catch-up; Juhász and Steinwender, "Industrial Policy and the Great Divergence." In the case of France, of course, it also benefited from its relative geographic proximity to Britian and the fact that much British talent settled there, transferring important tacit knowledge as well. As discussed, British inventors were key to France's integration of steam power technology.

37. On the rise of Prussian bureaucracy, see Fukuyama, *Political Order and Political Decay*, 91–92.

38. On Knyphausen, see Clark, *Iron Kingdom*, 85.

39. On the *Generalkriegskommissariat*, see Stasavage, *Decline and Rise of Democracy*, 136; Clark, *Iron Kingdom*, 85–86.

40. On the Waldburg reforms, see Clark, *Iron Kingdom*, 90–91.

41. Clark, *Iron Kingdom*, 148.

42. On the role of Jesuit missionaries, see Jacobsen, "Prussian Emulations," 425–441.

43. The rise of modern bureaucracy was also aided by the Reformation, which increased the availability of skilled potential candidates for the civil service; Figueroa, *Protestant Road to Bureaucracy*. On the link between the Reformation and human capital, see Becker and Woessmann, "Was Weber Wrong?," 531–596.

44. On Jena-Auerstadt, see Fukuyama, *Political Order and Political Decay*, 95–96.

45. Fehrenbach, *Vom Ancien Regime zum Wiener Kongress*, 109.

46. Koselleck, *Preußen zwischen Reform und Revolution*, 160.

47. The dissolution of guilds meant that they could no longer resist the introduction of new technologies; Ogilvie, "Economics of Guilds," 169–192; Ogilvie, *European Guilds*. Moreover, the abolition of serfdom reduced the political clout of local elites, promoted social mobility, and meant that more people where free to innovate; Blum, *End of the Old Order*. Indeed, before the Stein-Hardenberg Reforms, French occupation in parts of Germany led to commercial freedom as the guilds vanished. Analysis of German county-level patent data shows that the occupied regions consequently became more innovative, especially in high-technology sectors; Donges, et al., "Impact of Institutions on Innovation," 1951–1974.

48. On the backgrounds of councillors, see Wehler, *Deutsche Gesellschaftsgeschichte*, Vol. 1, 261–263.

49. Behrens, *Society, Government and the Enlightenment*, 173. Cited in Tilly and Kopsidis, *From Old Regime to Industrial State*, 77.

50. Tilly and Kopsidis, *From Old Regime to Industrial State*, 57–66.

51. Holborn, *History of Modern Germany*, 413.

52. On the civil service, see Fukuyama, *Origins of Political Order*, 96.

53. Rosenberg, *Bureaucracy, Aristocracy and Autocracy*, 161.

54. Tilly, "German Industrialization," 95–125.

55. Tilly and Kopsidis, *From Old Regime to Industrial State*, 25–26.

56. Tilly and Kopsidis, *From Old Regime to Industrial State*, 25, 83.

57. However, in the eighteenth century, up to 90 percent of British public revenue was spent on war; Scheidel, *Escape from Rome*, 382. On comparative fiscal capacity, see Karaman and

Pamuk, "Different Paths to the Modern State," 603–626, Figure 1. See also Koyama and Rubin, *How the World Became Rich*, Figure 3.9.

58. Figure 4.1 only refers to officials working for central government. Though state capacity in Japan might seem low relative to Germany and France, it was considerably higher than other developing economies. Moreover, according to Kyoko Sheridan, government employees (local and central, excluding the military) accounted for 0.6% of the total workforce in 1880, rising to 2.6% in 1910 and 4.8% in 1930 (Sheridan, *Governing the Japanese Economy*, 64n22). However, Sheridan does not explain how these percentages were calculated, and they appear relatively high.

59. For a discussion of these proposed reforms, see Besley, et al., "Bureaucracy and Development," 397–424.

60. Chapman, *Higher Civil Service in Britain*, 18–19. Cited in Fukuyama, *Political Order and Political Decay*, 174.

61. "That Other Public," in Dickens, *Miscellaneous Papers*, 496.

62. On the Crimean War and reform, see Fukuyama, *Political Order and Political Decay*, 175.

63. For an empirical investigation of the negative performance impact of patronage in Britain, see Xu, "Costs of Patronage," 3170–3198.

64. Kocka, "Capitalism and Bureaucracy," 453–468.

65. On coal mines and civil servants, see Tilly and Kopsidis, *From Old Regime to Industrial State*, 122.

66. One simple reason is that few early economic undertakings by the state succeeded. Colonial state projects like the Brandenburg-African Trading Company of 1682, or the *Seehandlung*, founded in 1772, failed spectacularly.

67. This speaks to the findings of Brown and collaborators, who show that the process of privatization in post-communist Russia yielded greater effectiveness in regions characterized by a larger bureaucracy; Brown, et al., "Helping Hand or Grabbing Hand?," 264–283.

68. Kocka, "Capitalism and Bureaucracy," 453–468.

69. In "Economic backwardness in historical perspective," Gerschenkron famously focused on the role in mobilizing material resources for catch-up, but the same idea can also be applied to human capital.

70. Landes, *Unbound Prometheus*, 342.

71. Elementary schools were designed to impart basic skills, while high schools (*Gymnasien*) went beyond rote learning and focused on teaching students how to learn, fostering intellectual independence.

72. On Humboldt, see Kirby, *Empires of Ideas*, 30–35.

73. On Liebig, see Lenoir, "Revolution from Above," 22–27, 23.

74. On Althoff, see Levine, *Allies and Rivals*, 53.

75. On the role of competition, see Levine, *Allies and Rivals*, 14. See also de Ridder-Symoens and Rüegg, *History of the University in Europe*, 227.

76. Cited in Green, "Federal Alternative?," 187–202, 200.

77. On the comparison with France, see Levine, *Allies and Rivals*, 121–122.

78. On the comparison with Britain, see Levine, *Allies and Rivals*, 22.

79. Ben-David and Zloczower, "Universities and Academic Systems," 45–84, 68.

80. True, Britain's landed elites invested in their children's human capital, but they were taught gentlemen skills, like Latin, hunting, fencing, and music, which did little for British industry; see, for example, Doepke and Zilibotti, "Occupational Choice," 747–793.

81. Cited in Landes, *Unbound Prometheus*, 341.

82. On training for industry, see Kocka, "Capitalism and Bureaucracy," 453–468.

83. On engineering enrollment, see Chandler, *Scale and Scope*, 425.
84. On pioneers of industry, see Tilly and Kopsidis, *From Old Regime to Industrial State*, 145.
85. For a detailed discussion of the scientific and educational divergence of Britain and Germany, see Magee, "Manufacturing and Technological Change," 74–98.
86. Becker, et al., "Education and Catch-up," 92–126, 93.
87. Cinnirella and Streb, "Role of Human Capital and Innovation," 193–227.
88. The *Zollverein* facilitated market integration, cutting wheat price gaps across cities by about a third; Keller and Shiue, "Endogenous Formation of Free Trade Agreements," 1168–1204.
89. On Rhine shipping, see Gothein, *Geschichtliche Entwicklung der Rheinschiffahrt im XIX*.
90. On railroad construction and its economic consequences, see Hornung, "Railroads and Growth in Prussia," 699–736.
91. Cited in Tilly and Kopsidis, *From Old Regime to Industrial State*, 116. See also Tilly, *Financial Institutions and Industrialization*.
92. On railroad construction in Chemnitz, see Strauss, *Die Lage und die Bewegung*. On Prussian public finances, see Tilly, "Political Economy of Public Finance," 484–497.
93. On the governance of the German railroads, see Chandler, *Scale and Scope*, 412–415.
94. On the Berlin-Baghdad Railway, see MacMillan, *War that Ended Peace*, 457, 494, 507.
95. On German Ottoman links, see Earle, *Turkey, The Great Powers, and The Bagdad Railway*.
96. On the industrial labour force, see Tilly and Kopsidis, *From Old Regime to Industrial State*, 95.
97. Hornung, "Railroads and Growth in Prussia," 699–736. As factories grew larger, they began to mechanize production and use more horsepower: between 1849 and 1861 the number and horsepower of installed steam engines increased from 28,545 to 137,377; Tilly and Kopsidis, *From Old Regime to Industrial State*, Table 7.5.
98. On firm size, see Tilly and Kopsidis, *From Old Regime to Industrial State*, 186.
99. On employment in the largest corporations, see Kocka and Sigrist, "Die Hundert größten deutschen Industrieunternehmen."
100. Chandler, *Scale and Scope*, 497.
101. On railroad management comparison between Germany and America, see Chandler, *Scale and Scope*, 415.
102. On the largest enterprises, see Burhop, *Wirtschaftsgeschichte des Kaiserreichs, 1871–1918*, 141–42.
103. Cited in Chandler, *Scale and Scope*, 415.
104. In a sample of fourteen major railway companies, it is estimated that the median cost inefficiency was 10.2 percent in 1900, amounting to about 1 percent of GDP; Crafts, et al., "Were British Railway Companies Well Managed?," 842–866.
105. On productivity in transportation, see Broadberry, "How Did the United States and Germany Overtake Britian?," 375–407.
106. Broadberry, *Market Services and the Productivity Race*.
107. On German vs. British firms, see Kocka, "Capitalism and Bureaucracy," 453–468.
108. Only if GE's plants, which were dispersed across space, had been put in one location would America have seen anything like Siemensstadt.
109. On German expansion overseas, see Chandler, *Scale and Scope*, 404.
110. This is not to deny that Germans also made important discoveries as the Siemens-Martin process bears witness to.
111. For steel output between 1865 and 1913, see Tilly and Kopsidis, *From Old Regime to Industrial State*, Table 12.1. Data from Mitchell, *European Historical Statistics*.

112. On vertical integration, see Webb, "Tariffs, Cartels, Technology," 309–330.

113. Among Westphalian industrialists, a rising share of owners and top managers had university and engineering degrees in the late nineteenth century; see Pierenkemper, *Die westfälischen Schwerindustriellen 1852–1913*. This stands in contrast to the English experience; see Berghoff and Möller, "Tired Pioneers and Dynamic Newcomers," 262–287; Nicholas, "Technology, Innovation and Economic Growth."

114. On Britain's disappearing lead in chemicals, see Lindert and Trace, "Yardsticks for Victorian Entrepreneurs," 248–249.

115. Another example is Britain's backward soda manufacturers, who repeatedly refused to scrap the old Leblanc process, despite the obvious benefits of the ammonia process discovered by Ernst Solvay in 1861. "In 1894 over 65 percent of British soda production still came from Leblanc plants, while no other country produced as much as 22 percent by this process." Lindert and Trace, "Yardsticks for Victorian Entrepreneurs," 249.

116. See Lehmann, "Taking Firms to the Stock Market," 92–122.

117. The decline in rates of representation by bank directors on firm supervisory boards further suggests that as an organ of control over industry their role was diminishing by the turn of the century; Fohlin, "Rise of Interlocking Directorates," 307–333. Bank ties also did little to improve firm performance; Fohlin, *Finance Capitalism*. As one review of the literature concludes: "The available evidence does not support the view that universal banks made large contributions to the finance of investment by German industrial joint-stock companies, so that even if one argued that these companies were a leading sector in German industrialization, it would be difficult to assign a central role in industrialization to the universal bank." Edwards and Ogilvie, "Universal Banks and German Industrialization," 427–446.

118. And local stock exchanges also existed in Frankfurt am Main, Leipzig, and Dresden, and Munich; Lehmann-Hasemeyer and Streb, "Berlin Stock Exchange in Imperial Germany," 3558–3576.

119. On the University of Berlin, see Kirby, *Empires of Ideas*, 38.

120. On the connections between research institutions and firms, see Murmann, *Knowledge and Competitive Advantage*, 78–82.

121. Another example is Fritz Haber, who, during his tenure at the University of Karlsruhe, developed what would become known as the Haber–Bosch process. BASF soon acquired the rights and assigned one of their top experts, Carl Bosch, to scale up the project. On companies' cooperation with individual researchers more broadly, see Reinhardt, "Forschung in der chemischen Industrie"; Burhop and Wolf, "German Market for Patents," 69–93.

122. Chandler, *Scale and Scope*, 426.

123. On chemical patents, see Murmann, *Knowledge and Competitive Advantage*, 37–45.

124. On foreign patents granted in the United States, see Pavitt and Soete, "International Dynamics of Innovation," 109.

125. On the composition of patenting, see Cantwell, "Historical Trends." Data on manufacturing exports reveal a similar picture, see Crafts and Thomas, "Comparative Advantage in UK Manufacturing Trade," 629–645; Crafts, "Revealed Comparative Advantage in Manufacturing," 127–137.

126. On German companies accounting only for a fraction of all patents, see Donges and Selgert, "Social Background of Prussian Inventors," 1–41.

127. Despite its resounding success, Otto's enterprise failed to ascend to the echelons of global renown.

128. Streb, et al., "Technological and Geographical Spillover," 347–373.

129. By the end of the Weimar Republic in 1933, Germany was finally economically integrated. Before the Great War it was not; see Wolf, "Was Germany Ever United?," 846–881.

130. On patent transfers, see Burhop and Wolf, "German Market for Patents," 69–93.

131. Although many German inventors moved to large cities, like Berlin, Cologne, and Aachen, there were few interactions between them. On inventor mobility, see Donges and Selgert, "Social Background of Prussian Inventors," 1–41.

132. On the market for technology in Britain, see Nicholas, "Independent Invention," 995–1023.

133. Indeed, as noted, comparisons of British, German and American firms show that British companies were systematically less integrated and diversified; see Kocka and Sigrist, "Die Hundert größten deutschen Industrieunternehmen; Chandler, *Scale and Scope*."

134. Landes, for example, suggested that Britain's Second Industrial Revolution misfired due to the amateurishness and complacency of her entrepreneurs, who made no commitment to systematic research and "lost out for want of knowledge, imagination, and enterprise to Germany, Switzerland, and even France." Landes, *Wealth And Poverty Of Nations*, 457. According to Chandler, on the other hand, the problem was that Britain hung on to personal capitalism, and family-owned companies failed to make the necessary investment in production, distribution and management in order to successfully compete globally; Chandler, *Scale and Scope*. For a comparison of German and British entrepreneurs and their backgrounds, see Berghoff and Möller, "Tired Pioneers and Dynamic Newcomers," 262–287.

135. For an overview of the debate surrounding the late Victorian climacteric, see Crafts, "British Relative Economic Decline"; Crafts, et al., "Climacteric in Late Victorian Britain and France," 103–117; McCloskey and Sandberg, "From Damnation to Redemption," 89–108.

136. Kocka, "Organisierter Kapitalismus oder Staatsmonopolistischer Kapitalismus?," 19–35.

137. Chandler, *Scale and Scope*, 497.

138. For the most part, the larger companies bought shares in the smaller firms, while behemoths held each other's shares. On IGs, see Chandler, *Scale and Scope*, 424.

139. On the Steel Mill Federation, see Hughes and Barbezat, "Basing-Point Pricing," 215–222.

140. On cartels and inefficiency, see McCloskey, *Economic Maturity and Entrepreneurial Decline*.

141. What historian Clive Trebilcock has called "the exuberant German export drive of the 1900s" entailed rigorous export discipline through which the state sought to weed out uncompetitive companies with some success, see Trebilcock, *Industrialization of the Continental Powers*; Studwell, *How Asia Works*, 72.

142. On the effects of cartels and tariffs on steel production, see Webb "Tariffs, Cartels, Technology," 309–330.

143. Chandler, *Scale and Scope*, 472.

144. While the relationship between collusion and entry is a complex one, several studies suggest that cartels deter entry. For an overview of this literature, see Asker and Nocke, "Collusion, Mergers," 177–279.

145. On IG Farben and innovation, see Poege, "Competition and Innovation."

146. Cited in Leone and Robotti, "Guglielmo Marconi," 1–28.

147. On the rise of Marconi, see Brunnermeier, et al., "Beijing's Bismarckian Ghosts," 161–176.

148. For a detailed account of this technology rivalry, see Friedewald, "Telefunken vs. Marconi."

149. Brunnermeier, et al., "Beijing's Bismarckian Ghosts," 161–176.

Chapter 5

1. Inkster, *Science and Technology in History*, 49.
2. Marx, *Das Kapital*.
3. In his work published in 1915, Veblen was early to note that the greater the backwardness of a country relative to the frontier, the faster its potential for growth; Veblen, *Imperial Germany and the Industrial Revolution*.
4. On backwardness and reliance on the state, see Gerschenkron, *Economic Backwardness in Historical Perspective*. For a formal model, see also Findla, "Relative Backwardness," 1–16. For a reassessment of the Gerschenkron thesis, see Sylla and Toniolo, *Patterns of European Industrialisation*.
5. On the estates, see Acemoglu and Robinson, *Why Nations Fail*, 282–283.
6. Crouzet, "France," 36–63.
7. On technology transfer, see Harris, *Industrial Espionage and Technology Transfer*.
8. On the Bureau of Consultation, see Horn, *Path Not Taken*, 174.
9. Cited in Horn, *Path Not Taken*, 188.
10. On industrial exhibitions, see Horn, *Path Not Taken*, 189.
11. On Code Napoléon, see Fukuyama, *Political Order and Political Decay*, 25.
12. This practice had expanded already in the sixteenth century, see Bonney, *Rise of the Fiscal State in France*.
13. On the transition to a merit-based system, see Fukuyama, *Political Order and Political Decay*, 28.
14. On Chaptal, see Horn, *Path Not Taken*, chapter 6. While the prize competitions were privately-run on paper, they included many government officials, who had been handpicked by Chaptal.
15. On SEIN, see Horn, *Path Not Taken*, 209.
16. On SEIN funding, see Khan, *Inventing Ideas*, table 6.1.
17. On patronage and barriers to innovation, see Khan, *Inventing Ideas*, 150.
18. In its initial century, the society's leadership and committees were predominantly composed of the upper echelons, including aristocrats, scientists, politicians, academics, bankers, and affluent industrialists, whereas artisans, machinists, technicians, and regular businesspeople were notably underrepresented. On Chaptal, see Horn, *Path Not Taken*, 209.
19. On the French civil service examination, see Mann, *Sources of Social Power Volume 2*, 463.
20. On railroads in France, see Lévy-Leboyer and Lescure, "France."
21. Lévy-Leboyer and Lescure, "France." Construction efforts were aided because liberal Republicans came to control the National Assembly after 1880, taking over the civil service.
22. Crafts concludes that "it appears probable that labor-productivity in French industry was generally a little below British levels," and that "it would appear likely that French labor productivity was higher than that of "Germany" in 1860." Crafts, "Economic Growth in France and Britain," 49–67.
23. On medals per capita, see Moser, "Determinants of Innovation."
24. On machinery imports, see Bruland, *British Technology and European Industrialization*, table 10.1.
25. On patent reform, see Nuvolari, et al., "British-French Technology Transfer," 833–873.
26. To borrow the terminology of Mann, Tsarist Russia had plenty of "despotic power," but weak "infrastructure power." Meiji Japan, in contrast, had both; Mann, "Autonomous Power of the State," 185–213.
27. Davies, "Industry," 131–157.
28. On patterns of Russian growth, see Broadberry and Korchmina, "Catching-Up and Falling Behind."

29. Cited in Kotkin, *Stalin*, 69–70.

30. That said, Stolypin did manage to push through important land reforms in 1906. This led to land consolidations which "enabled peasants to make independent production decisions from the village commune and take advantage of readily accessible technological advancements." Castañeda and Markevich, "Stolypin Reform," 241–267.

31. On the three schools of thought that competed for influence with the Tsar, see Carstensen and Guroff, "Economic Innovation in Imperial Russia," 347–360.

32. On serfdom and reform, see Hoch, *Serfdom and Social Control in Russia*; Blum, *Lord and Peasant in Russia*.

33. Cited in Kotkin, *Stalin*, 59.

34. On the Stolypin reform, see Castañeda and Markevich, "Stolypin Reform," 241–267.

35. On urbanization, see Bairoch, *Cities and Economic Development*, 221, 290. On Tsarist growth and structural change, see Gregory, *Before Command*. Gregory (p. 29) notes that "the amount of structural change, as measured by the changes in Russia's agriculture and industry shares between 1885 and 1913, was average or slightly below average when compared to the other countries surveyed."

36. On per capita income, see Gregory, "Some Empirical Comments," 654–665.

37. Gregory, "Some Empirical Comments," 57. See also Platonova, "Peter the Great's Government Reforms," 437–464. On the Russian bureaucracy before Peter the Great, see Weickhardt, "Bureaucrats and Boiars," 331–356.

38. On number of officials in Russia and Prussia, see Jones, *Emancipation of the Russian Nobility*, 182.

39. From 1722, the bureaucracy operated under a "system of ranks" where promotions were ostensibly based on abilities and education, but in reality, they were influenced by power and favour, often favouring nobles and ex-military men. True, in 1809, M. M. Speransky, under Tsar Alexander I, successfully lobbied for ranks 5 (state adviser) and 8 (college assessor) to require qualification through examination. However, this reform was highly unpopular and ultimately ineffective, leading to its revocation by 1834 (see Pintner, and Rowney, *Russian Officialdom*; W. M. Pintner, 1975, "The Russian Higher Civil Service on the Eve of the 'Great Reforms'," *Journal of Social History* 8 (3) (Spring 1975): 55–68.

40. On Polity data, see M. G. Marshall and K. Jaggers, 2002, "Political Regime Characteristics and Transitions, 1800–2002," Manual, https://fatcat.wiki/release/vctstuceibhhbgw7geb4coc3fq.

41. Kotkin, *Stalin*, 59.

42. Lieven, *Towards the Flame*, 47.

43. On the suppression of railroads and factories, see Acemoglu and Robinson, *Why Nations Fail*, 221. On the "Tsar's toy," see Metzer, "Railroad Development and Market Integration," 529–550, 535.

44. On spurts of railroad construction, see Rieber, "Formation of La Grande Société," 375–391, 375.

45. On the Siberian Railroad Committee, see Harcave, *Count Sergei Witte*, 54.

46. Contrast colonial India, where the railroads built by the British Raj gave the economy a boost, raising real agricultural income in connected districts, with access to expanded markets, by some 16 percent according to recent estimates. The system however was constructed with locomotives and rail imported from Britain and therefore offered limited stimulus to local steel and engineering industries. On railroads and growth, see Donaldson, "Railroads of the Raj," 899–934.

47. On the expansion of Russian heavy industry, see Allen, *Farm to Factory*, table 2.2.

48. On Russian railroads, Gatrell, *Government, Industry and Rearmament in Russia*; Allen, *Farm to Factory*, 22.

49. Rieber, "Formation of La Grande Société," 375–391, 375.
50. Putnam, *Making Democracy Work*, 152–162.
51. On Russian corporation law, see Carstensen and Guroff, "Economic Innovation in Imperial Russia," 355.
52. Allen, *Farm to Factory*, 23.
53. For a comparison of firm formation in Russia and Germany, see Fohlin and Gregg, "Finance Capitalism in Industrializing Autocracies."
54. Fohlin and Gregg, "Finance Capitalism in Industrializing Autocracies," 10.
55. Jangfeldt, *Nobel Family*.
56. See Fohlin and Gregg, "Finance Capitalism in Industrializing Autocracies." On the benefits of incorporation, see also Gregg, "Factory Productivity and the Concession System," 401–427.
57. Cited in Ferguson, *War of the World*, 120. Ferguson also provides a detailed discussion of the 1904 war and its consequences.
58. On isolation, see Lockwood, *Economic Development of Japan*, 5.
59. Norman, *Japan's Emergence as a Modern State*, 12.
60. Ericson, *Sound of the Whistle*, 4. Cited in Tang, "Railroad Expansion and Industrialization," 863–886.
61. On the railway network, see Free, *Early Japanese Railway*, 11, 85.
62. Sectors that benefited from the codification of Western knowledge saw more rapid productivity and export growth, see Juhász, Sakabe, and Weinstein, "Codification, Technology Absorption, and Globalization."
63. On the Meiji Restoration, see Beasley, *Meiji Restoration*.
64. On the link between railroads and the use of steam power, see Yamasaki, "Railroads, Technology Adoption." On railroads and large-scale enterprise, see Tang, "Railroad Expansion and Industrialization," 863–886. On nationalization, see Eiichi, et al., *History of Japanese Railways*, 15.
65. On the adoption of foreign technologies, see Perkins and Tang, "East Asian Industrial Pioneers"; Tang, "Tale of Two SICs," 174–197.
66. On differences in state capacity, see Koyama, et al., "Geopolitics and Asia's Little Divergence," 178–204. Perkins further writes: "The disparity between Chinese and Japanese effort in this sphere was demonstrated in Japan's overwhelming defeat of the Chinese armies in 1895." Perkins, "Government as an Obstacle to Industrialization," 478–492, 487. See also He, *Paths Toward the Modern Fiscal State*.
67. On overcoming opposition, see Tanaka, *New Times in Modern Japan*.
68. The Tokugawa regime had greater fiscal capacity than the Qing dynasty and differences in the ability of the state to raise revenue would only widen in the Meiji period; see Sng and Moriguchi, "Asia's Little Divergence," 439–470, figure 1. Though the Tokugawa regime was more fragmented than its Qing counterpart, as one reviewer has pointed out, it was more capable in terms of mobilizing resources and overriding impediments to modernization.
69. Lockwood, *Economic Development of Japan*, 10.
70. On state building, see Fukuyama, *Political Order and Political Decay*, 444.
71. On the lack of foreign workers, see Landes, "Japan and Europe," 93–182.
72. Instead, Japanese Meiji entrepreneurs like Shibusawa Eiichi sent Japanese technicians to Manchester to study cotton spinning. This way, backed by a consortium of financiers, he opened a steam-powered factory with 10,000 spindles.
73. On Western enterprise, see Lockwood, *Economic Development of Japan*, 329; Landes, "Japan and Europe," 93.
74. Lockwood, *Economic Development of Japan*, 198.

75. On the role of Tokyo University, see Koh, *Japan's Administrative Elite*, 20.

76. On educational attainment, see Silberman, "Bureaucratic Development," 347–362.

77. On the examination system, see Fukuyama, *Political Order and Political Decay*, 444.

78. Henderson, *Foreign Enterprise in Japan*, 195.

79. In a detailed survey of parallels with the European experience, Landes concluded that the Japanese path to prosperity most closely resembled the German one in defensive nationalism being the driver of modernization, in the existence of a close and cozy relationship between the state and the emerging business elite, and the fact that reform was pushed by conservatives from the above in both cases; Landes, "Japan and Europe," 93–182.

80. Studwell, *How Asia Works*, 68.

81. On Mitsubishi, see Studwell, *How Asia Works*, 68.

82. The three largest factories were owned by the state and produced military equipment. Of the ten largest factories in 1902, only four were private. However, only one state-owned factory (*Shimbashi*) produced civilian technology (railroad cars). See Vries, *Averting a Great Divergence*, table 34a.

83. This figure is for the year 1907 and does not include office personnel, see Vries, *Averting a Great Divergence*, table 34b. Data are from Ohno, *Economic Development of Japan*, 67.

84. These figures exclude military expenditure, see Rosovsky, *Capital Formation in Japan*, 24. Estimates by Minami are even more sizable and suggest an upward trend over this period; Minami, *Economic Development of Japan*, 133.

85. Real wages in early Modern Japan were about half of those in pre-industrial England; Kumon, "Landownership Equality."

86. On Japanese schools, see Platt, *Burning and Building*, 4.

87. On Japanese science and education, see Vries, *Averting a Great Divergence*, chapter 7.

88. On the Japanese cost advantage, see Broadberry, et al., "How Did Japan Catch-Up?" On "discipline capital," see Mokyr and Voth, "Understanding Growth in Europe," 7–42, 32. On Japanese wages, see Yasuba, "Standard of Living in Japan," 217–224.

89. On late colonial Indian factories being slow to adopt automatic looms, see Bagchi, *Private Investment in India*; Banerjee, *Colonialism in Action*. On machines per worker in 1910, see Clark, "Why Isn't the Whole World Developed?" 141–173, table 4. On machines per worker in 1931, see Roy, "Labour Institutions, Japanese Competition," 37–45, table 2.

90. For example, madras workers would accept no more than four automatics per man; see Buchanan, *Development of Capitalistic Enterprise in India*.

91. One British expert hired to reorganise the mills of the Sassoon family in India notes: "The workers in Bombay seem to favour the idea of half work for everybody rather than full work for a few." Cited in Chandavarkar, *Origins of Industrial Capitalism*.

92. Dore, "Comparisons of Latin American and Asian Studies," 18.

93. This rhymes with the observation of Garon, who notes that the Japanese government before the 1920s was "intolerant of the efforts of workers to organize themselves to advance their own interests." Garon, *State and Labor in Modern Japan*, 29. For an overview of this argument, see this excellent post: Pseudoerasmus, "Labour Repression & the Indo-Japanese Divergence," October 2, 2017, https://pseudoerasmus.com/2017/10/02/ijd/.

94. Even after Article 17 was repealed, repression continued under the new Peace Preservation Law, which sanctioned repressive measures and restricted assembly and "dangerous meetings." Gordon, *Evolution of Labor Relations in Japan*, 250.

95. On the English experience, see Frey, *Technology Trap*, chapter 5.

96. Indeed, the impediments to trade unionism and democratic organization in Japan were manifold, stemming also from the prevalence of female workers in the industrial sector as well as the scattered nature of smaller family enterprises dispersed across rural areas.

97. On pilot projects, see Lockwood, *Economic Development of Japan*, 507.

98. On Kishi, see Studwell, *How Asia Works*, 73.

99. On the Important Industries Control Law, see Lockwood, *Economic Development of Japan*, 230.

100. Lockwood, *Economic Development of Japan*, 220.

101. As economist Kōzō Yamamura writes, "In sugar, flour milling, mining and other major industries the pattern was similar." Yamamura, "Japanese Economy, 1911–1930," 299–328, 312.

102. On public–private partnerships, see Lockwood, *Economic Development of Japan*, 221.

103. Lewis, "International Competition in Manufacturers," 578–587.

104. On the zaibatsu, see Tang, "Technological Leadership and Late Development," 99–116.

105. Data from Magee, "Manufacturing and Technological Change," 74–98, table 4.12. Originally complied by Streit, *Union Now*.

106. Landes, "Japan and Europe," 93–182.

Chapter 6

1. Franklin, *Information*.

2. Cited in Klein, *Genesis of Industrial America*, 5.

3. Quote from T. Chaney, K. Cohen, and L. Pelham, 2022, "The Virginia Company of London," *Colonial National Historical Park Virginia*, July 15, https://www.nps.gov/jame/learn/historyculture/the-virginia-company-of-london.htm.

4. On the agriculture employment share, see Carter, et al., *Historical Statistics of the United States*, Ba814 and Ba817.

5. The few cities on the coast, like Boston or New York, grew due to their access to the ocean, making them attractive locations for trade. Further inland, cities emerged at portage sites, again to facilitate trade; Bleakley and Lin, "Portage and Path Dependence," 587–644.

6. A. Gallatin, 1810, American State Papers: Fin 325. D. o. Treasury. ASP010: 425–439, 427. Cited in Atack, et al., "Industrialization and Urbanization," 1–11.

7. Cited in Fukuyama, *Political Order and Political Decay*, 185.

8. See Lipset, *First New Nation*; Lipset, *American Exceptionalism*.

9. Weingast, "Economic Role of Political Institutions," 1–31, 2.

10. Before the mid-nineteenth century, distance to Washington, DC had a moderating effect on the link between manufacturing growth and state presence across geographies, suggesting that monitoring costs were very high in these places. Thereafter, however, this moderating effect was gradually diminished as new technologies, like railroads and the telegraph, reduced communication and monitoring costs; Mastrorocco and Teso, "State Capacity as an Organizational Problem."

11. On forging trading relationships, see Buel, *In Irons*, 69.

12. On trade policy, see Irwin, *Clashing over Commerce*, 54.

13. On tax revenues, see Irwin, *Clashing over Commerce*, 61.

14. The objective of the Federalists—like James Madison and Alexander Hamilton—was never to strengthen people's rights. If anything, they were concerned about too much democracy, which helps explain important institutional features, like indirect election of senators by state legislatures, and indeed the Electoral College to elect the president; see Acemoglu and Robinson, *Narrow Corridor*, 306.

15. On concessions made, see Acemoglu and Robinson, *Narrow Corridor*, 307.

16. Already in 1793, the number of patents filed was so large that the application procedure, which initially required reviews by the attorney general, the secretary of state, and the secretary

of war, essentially became one of registration; see Cain, "Entrepreneurship in the Antebellum United States," 331–366.

17. On import duties as a source of revenue, see Irwin, *Clashing over Commerce*, 7.

18. Syrett, ed., *Papers of Alexander Hamilton*, 226.

19. On America's foreign policy in this period, see Bowman, "Jefferson, Hamilton and American Foreign Policy," 18–41.

20. On the war, see Hickey, *War of 1812*.

21. On the effects of the embargo, see Irwin, "Welfare Cost of Autarky," 631–645; Davis and Irwin, "Trade Disruptions and America's Early Industrialization."

22. Irwin, *Clashing over Commerce*, 155.

23. On the tariff effects on American industry, see Irwin, *Clashing over Commerce*, chapter 2.

24. On Slater, see Jeremy, *Transatlantic Industrial Revolution*. On technology transfer from Britain, see Cain, "Entrepreneurship in the Antebellum United States."

25. On the power loom and productivity, see Bessen, "Technology and Learning by Factory Workers," 33–64; Bessen, *Learning by Doing*.

26. Already by 1820, 86 companies in New England had adopted 1,667 power looms.

27. Irwin, *Clashing over Commerce*, 169.

28. For examples of immigrants, see Cain, "Entrepreneurship in the Antebellum United States," 346. On immigration as a key force behind American innovation over the past 130 years, see Burchardi, et al., "Immigration, Innovation, and Growth." On immigrants being more prolific and productive inventors than natives, see Arkolakis, et al., "European Immigrants"; Akcigit, et al., "Immigration and the Rise," 327–331. On the positive impact of immigration on American industrialization, see Long, et al., "Impact of the Chinese Exclusion Act." On the long-run economic benefits of immigration, including industrialization and innovation, see Sequeira, et al., "Immigrants and the Making of America," 382–419. On the link between immigration and innovation in recent years, see Bernstein, et al., "Contribution of High-Skilled Immigrants."

29. Turner, *Significance of the Frontier*.

30. On the frontier and individualism, see Bazzi, et al., "Frontier Culture," 2329–2368.

31. On measuring individualism, see Hofstede, *Cultures and Organizations*. On data from the World Value Survey, see Haerpfer, et al., *World Values Survey*.

32. On the link between individualism and innovation, see Gorodnichenko and Roland, "Culture, Institutions," 402–416.

33. On mobility, see Khan and Sokoloff, "Schemes of Practical Utility," 289–307.

34. García-Jimeno and Robinson, "Myth of the Frontier," 74.

35. On Heinrich Steinweg, see Torp, "Heinrich Engelhard Steinway."

36. Lincoln received Patent No. 6469 (May 22, 1849). The quotation is from a lecture, "Discoveries and Inventions," which he delivered in Jacksonville, Illinois, on February 11, 1859. Cited in Khan and Sokoloff, "Early Development of Intellectual Property Institutions," 233–246, 244.

37. Cited in Greenspan and Wooldridge, *Capitalism in America*, 48.

38. On patent agencies, see Lamoreaux and Sokoloff, "Inventors, Firms, and the Market," 19–60.

39. On Gatling, see Khan and Sokoloff, "Early Development of Intellectual Property Institutions," 233–246.

40. On the share of patents assigned, see Lamoreaux and Sokoloff, "Inventive Activity and the Market."

41. On patent reform, see Dutton, *Patent System and Inventive Activity*. When the first international patent convention was held in Austria in 1873, it took place at the suggestion of the United States. Indeed, as scholars have noted, "Because the U.S. patent system was recognized

as the most successful, it is not surprising that patent harmonization implied convergence toward that model." Khan and Sokoloff, "Early Development of Intellectual Property Institutions," 233–246.

42. On the American system being more democratic, see Khan and Sokoloff, "Early Development of Intellectual Property Institutions," 233–246; Khan and Sokoloff, "Institutions and Democratic Invention," 395–401.

43. On patent fees, see Nicholas, "Role of Independent Invention," 57–82.

44. On Meucci, see Gordon, *Rise and Fall of American Growth*, 574.

45. On coverture and patenting, see Khan, "Married Women's Property Laws," 356–388.

46. The impact of slavery on the American economy has been hotly debated, but the evidence suggests that the effects were negative. For a detailed account, see Wright, "Slavery," 123–148.

47. It is noteworthy that the allocation of talent improved enormously after the Civil Rights Movement in the 1960s. In 1960, for example, 94 percent of doctors and lawyers were white men. By 2010, this figure had fallen to 62 percent, giving economic growth a considerable boost. See Hsieh, et al., "Allocation of Talent," 1439–1474.

48. Cook, "Violence and Economic Activity," 221–257.

49. On democratized discovery, see Sokoloff and Khan, "Democratization of Invention," 363–378.

50. On inventor backgrounds, see Morison, *From Know-How to Nowhere*.

51. Cain, "Entrepreneurship in the Antebellum United States," 349.

52. On cotton exports, see Irwin, *Clashing over Commerce*, 167.

53. Even after emancipation, the low cost of Black labour held back mechanization; Hornbeck and Naidu, "When the Levee Breaks," 963–990.

54. On the share of patents by individuals, see Lamoreaux and Sokoloff, "Inventors, Firms, and the Market," 19–60.

55. On independent inventors building the most radical technologies, see Hughes, *American Genesis*, 15–16. See also Jewkes, et al., *Sources of Invention*.

56. On Tesla's inventive efforts, see Jewkes, et al., *Sources of Invention*, 66–67. On his many eccentricities, see DeLong, *Slouching Towards Utopia*, 74–79.

57. The share of patents being assigned to entities acquiring more than 10 patents in a given year increased from under 10 percent in 1870 to over 25 percent in 1911, when General Electric alone received over 300 patent assignments.

58. On market integration, see O'Rourke and Williamson, "When Did Globalization Begin?," 23–50. It is also in the 1820s, that American patenting first takes off, see Sokoloff, "Inventive Activity," 813–850, figure 1.

59. On the globalization of services, see Osterhammel, *Transformation of the World*, 36–37.

60. On the telegraph, see Juhász and Steinwender, "Spinning the Web."

61. On the devastating consequences for development in Africa, see Nunn and Wantchekon, "Slave Trade," 3221–3252. There is also evidence that British slave owners invested their profits in modern industry and so contributed to the British Industrial Revolution; Heblich, et al., "Slavery and the British Industrial Revolution." But the magnitude of the contribution is small and ultimately raises the questions of why other European economies, which benefited from stave trade, like Portugal, did not experience anything like an industrial revolution.

62. On exports and colonial markets, see Broadberry, *Productivity Race*, table 7.2.

63. On gravity and trade, see Blum and Goldfarb, "Does the Internet Defy?," 384–405. As Leamer and Levinsohn note, "the effect of distance on trade patterns is not diminishing over time." Leamer and Levinsohn, "International Trade," 1387–1388.

64. On European integration, see Hannah, "Logistics, Market Size, and Giant Plants," 46–79.

65. Many scholars emphasise the importance of America's large and homogenous internal market in creating economies of scale and permitting mass production; see Frankel, *British and American Manufacturing Productivity*; Chandler, *Scale and Scope*; Rostas, *Comparative Productivity*. However, in the early 1900s, when the United States surpassed Britain in terms of productivity leadership, the United States did not possess the same level of dominance in market potential when compared to other leading economies of that time. While the United States exhibited impressive GDP per capita growth, its advantage was not as overwhelming in terms of market potential. See Liu and Meissner, "Market Potential," 72–87.

66. On population comparison, see Hannah, "Logistics, Market Size, and Giant Plants," 46–79.

67. Rothbarth, "Causes of the Superior Efficiency," 383–390, 386. Broadberry similarly notes that institutional and social factors underpinned demand constraints in the British context; see Broadberry, *Productivity Race*, chapter 7.

68. On the American system, see Hounshell, *From the American System to Mass Production*.

69. Quoted in Bryson, *At Home*, 29.

70. On the shipping of American machine tools, see Mowery and Rosenberg, *Paths of Innovation*, 6.

71. Chandler, *Scale and Scope*, 446–448.

72. On Fulton, G. V. Ogden, 1824, "Milestone Documents," *National Archives*, accessed on November 21, 2023, https://www.archives.gov/milestone-documents/gibbons-v-ogden.

73. On land grant colleges and their impact on American engineering, see Maloney and Valencia Caicedo, "Engineering Growth," 1554–1594.

74. On post offices, see Cain, "Entrepreneurship in the Antebellum United States," 344.

75. On rates and news circulation, see John, *Spreading the News*.

76. Tocqueville, *Democracy in America*, 283.

77. Khan, *Democratization of Invention*, 59.

78. On post offices and patenting, see Acemoglu, et al., "State Capacity and American Technology," 61–67. On post office reform further spurring innovation, see Aneja and Xu, "Strengthening State Capacity."

79. John, *Spreading the News*, 10.

80. Even by the 20th century, the opening of air mail routes boosted local innovation; Sohn, et al., "Technology Adoption and Innovation," 3–35.

81. On railroads and patenting, see Perlman, "Connecting the Periphery."

82. On funding, see Hughes, *Governmental Habit Redux*, 68–76. On controversies surrounding the National Road, see Klein, *Genesis of Industrial America*, 58.

83. In the end, the canal was paid for with earmarked taxes, borrowing on state credit, and through toll collection once the canal had opened; Cain, "Entrepreneurship in the Antebellum United States," 340.

84. On the return on the Erie Canal, see Davis, *American Economic Growth*. On the social return, see Atack and Passell, *New Economic View of American History*, 150

85. An open question is: Why? Sokoloff makes the cases that the increase in patenting corresponded to expanded markets but is ultimately unable to disentangle supply and demand factors; Sokoloff, "Inventive Activity," 813–850.

86. Hannah, "Logistics, Market Size, and Giant Plants," 46–79.

87. On different standards, see Usselman, "Patents, Engineering Professionals."

88. Klein, *Genesis of Industrial America*, 13.

89. On the Railroad Act, see Acemoglu and Robinson, *Narrow Corridor*, 317.
90. On the amount of track, see Hannah, "Logistics, Market Size, and Giant Plants," 46–79.
91. Fogel, *Railroads and American Economic Growth*; Fishlow, *American Railroads*.
92. On accounting for market access, see Donaldson and Hornbeck, "Railroads and American Economic Growth," 799–858. The expansion of the rail network also arguably raised the return to innovation by creating a large national market. For a theoretical discussion, see Acemoglu and Linn, "Market Size in Innovation," 1049–1090.
93. On railroads and productivity, see Hornbeck and Rotemberg, "Railroads, Market Access."
94. On government grants, see Goldin, "Governmental Policy," 53–68, 53.
95. On Morse, see Nonnenmacher, "State Promotion and Regulation," 19–36.
96. On mistransmission, see Nonnenmacher, "History of the U.S. Telegraph Industry."
97. On consolidation, see Nonnenmacher, "State Promotion and Regulation," 19–36.
98. On the Telegraph Act, see Bagley, *South Pass*, 245.
99. On Western Union, see Field, "Magnetic Telegraph," 401–413.
100. The telegraph also launched the age of media. The Mexican War in 1846 became the first major conflict to receive coverage though telegraph dispatches, and two years later, in 1848, six leading New York papers joined forces to form the *Associated Press* to share telegraphic news. Most telegraph messages, however, were commercial—in market centres like New Orleans, New York, and Chicago, political and economic news swiftly found their way into commodity and financial asset prices.
101. On single track lines, see Field, "Magnetic Telegraph," 401–413.
102. Estabrook, "First Train Order by Telegraph," 27–29. Cited in Thompson, *Wiring a Continent*, 204.
103. Cited in Lamoreaux and Sokoloff, "Inventors, Firms, and the Market," 19–60.
104. On Theodore N. Vail, see Galambos, "Theodore N. Vail," 95–126.
105. On Westinghouse and Edison Electric/General Electric buying patents from independent inventors, see Wise, *Willis R. Whitney*, 69–70.
106. It was only in the 1920s that Standard Oil began to promote internal R&D on any meaningful scale; Gibb and Knowlton, *Resurgent Years*.
107. Contrary to popular perception, even during the interwar years, when the research lab rose to prominence, behemoth companies were no more focused on R&D than their smaller competitors. Small firms were just as research intensive; see Mowery, "Industrial Research and Firm Size," 953–980. On examples of in-house R&D, see Lamoreaux and Sokoloff, "Inventors, Firms, and the Market," 19–60.
108. Hughes, *American Genesis*, 54.
109. Cited in Hughes, *American Genesis*, 54.
110. Hughes, *American Genesis*, 53
111. On patent inflation, see Lamoreaux and Sokoloff, "Inventors, Firms, and the Market," 19–60.
112. The discussion of railroad companies' practices is based on Usselman, "Patents, Engineering Professionals."
113. In 1887, for example, the ERA was only forced to fence off four minor infringement lawsuits.
114. See the comment by Jeremy Atack on Usselman, "Patents, Engineering Professionals," 101. Other scholars agree, noting that patent pools shifted companies' attitudes toward innovation: "Their previous stance of encouragement gave way to a more conservative effort to control the pace and direction of technological change. Because it was critical to be able to couple cars

owned by one railroad to all of the company's rolling stock, as well as to that of other companies with interconnecting tracks, a change in one part of the system could wreak havoc in the functioning of the whole. Hence, at the same time as they cooperated to exploit more fully technologies that were already in place, railroad executives increasingly worked to channel and even contain the innovations of their subordinates. Productivity increased at a rapid pace, but innovation became more incremental and adaptive in character." Lamoreaux, "Entrepreneurship in the United States," 367–400. Studies of the sewing machines industry also show that patent pools reduced innovation; see Lampe and Moser, "Do Patent Pools Encourage Innovation?," 898–920. On cartels and standardization in the context of the Southern Railway and Steamship Association, see Gross, "Collusive Investments in Technological Compatibility," 5683–5700. The benefits of increased efficiency related to standardization, however, Gross shows, was not passed down to consumers.

115. Employment figures in Tedlow, *Rise of the American Business Corporation*, 14.
116. Chandler, *Visible Hand*.
117. Cited in Klein, *Genesis of Industrial America*, 130.
118. Chandler, *Visible Hand*, 484.
119. On railroads and retail, see Greenspan and Wooldridge, *Capitalism in America*, 136–142.
120. Estimates are from John Moody and cited in Klein, *Genesis of Industrial America*, 128.
121. On Rockefeller and the national debt, see Greenspan and Wooldridge, *Capitalism in America*, 187. On federal employment, see Mastrorocco and Teso, "State Capacity as an Organizational Problem," figure 2A. On comparison with other Great Powers, see Van Riper, *History*, 24; Mosher, *Democracy and the Public Service*, 62. On Washington population, see Gibson, "Population of the 100 Largest Cities." On the U.S. and its limited foreign policy footprint leading up to the Great War, see Tooze, *Deluge*.
122. Crenson, *Federal Machine*, 86–87.
123. On the failure of local-level regulation, see Lamoreaux, "Entrepreneurship in the United States," 367–400. See also McCurdy, "Knight Sugar Decision," 304–342.
124. On personal connections, see Crenson, *Federal Machine*, 72.
125. Mosher refers to the period from 1789 to 1829 as "Government by Gentlemen"; Mosher, *Democracy and the Public Service*.
126. On the percentage of high-ranking positions, see in Fukuyama, *Political Order and Political Decay*, 183.
127. Cited in Theriault, "Patronage, the Pendleton Act," 50–68.
128. On patronage, see Schultz and Maranto, *Politics of Civil Service Reform*, 42; Fukuyama, *Political Order and Political Decay*, 187–197.
129. Cited in Fukuyama, *Political Order and Political Decay*, 192.
130. On the battle over Western Union, see Goldin, "Governmental Policy," 53–68. On the family background of Gould, Carnegie, and Morgan, see Alfani, *As Gods Among Men*, 110–111, 145–116. On Vanderbilt, see Renehan, *Commodore*, 25.
131. Greenspan and Wooldridge, *Capitalism in America*, 167.
132. On personal networks, see Thompson, *Spider Web*.
133. On Senator Douglas, see Cain, "Entrepreneurship in the Antebellum United States," 343.
134. On Crédit Mobilier, see Wahlgren Summers, *Era of Good Stealings*; Lamoreaux, "Entrepreneurship in the United States," 367–400.
135. Greenspan and Wooldridge, *Capitalism in America*, 167.
136. Cited in Fukuyama, *Political Order and Political Decay*, 203.
137. On reform, Fukuyama, *Political Order and Political Decay*, 201–207.

138. Olson, *Logic of Collective Action*.

139. "Mr Pendleton Condemned," *New York Times*, December 28, 1882.

140. On support for the bill, see Theriault, "Patronage, the Pendleton Act," 50–68.

141. Cited in Theriault, "Patronage, the Pendleton Act," 50–68.

142. According to Skowronek, the Pendleton Act "amounted to nothing less than [a] recasting of the foundations of national institutional power." Skowronek, *Building a New American State*, 67. On how the Pendleton Act boosted innovation, see Aneja and Xu, "Strengthening State Capacity."

143. On campaign contributions, see Overacker, *Money in Elections*. For an overview of competition policy in the United States in this period, see Peritz, *Competition Policy in America*; Donges, "Competition and Collusion," 175–183.

144. On strikes, see Greenspan and Wooldridge, *Capitalism in America*, 172.

145. Law and Libecap, "Determinants of Progressive Era Reform," 319–342. On social mobilization being the driver of reform, see Acemoglu and Robinson, *Narrow Corridor*, 324. On the muckrakers, see also Chalmers, "Introduction to the Torchbook Edition"; Trachtenberg, *Incorporation of America*.

146. On muckraking journalists, see Greenspan and Wooldridge, *Capitalism in America*, 176–177.

147. On the merger wave, see Lamoreaux, *Great Merger Movement*, table 1.2; Bittlingmayer, "Antitrust Policy," 77–118.

148. In fact, factories grew more rapidly in size before the merger wave than thereafter, see O'Brien, "Factory Size, Economies of Scale," 639–649.

149. Not to mention Woodrow Wilson, whose administration bolstered the Sherman Act with the passage of the Federal Trade Commission Act and Clayton Antitrust Act in 1914. This explicitly sought to restrict horizontal mergers and also established a separate competition authority: the Federal Trade Commission.

150. Cited in Thorp, "Persistence of the Merger Movement," 77–89.

151. Address at the Annual Convention of the National Paint, Oil and Varnish Association, Inc., Atlantic City, New Jersey, October 28, 1927.

152. Thorp, "Persistence of the Merger Movement," 77–89.

153. On the distribution of net income, see Klein, *Genesis of Industrial America*, 134.

154. On factory size, see Broadberry, *Productivity Race*, table 9.6.

155. Similarly, Usselman argues that the railroads rigid focus on exploiting economies of standardization blinded them to technological changes like the arrival of trucking; Usselman, *Regulating Railroad Innovation*, 327–380).

156. On Western Union, see Nonnenmacher, "History of the U.S. Telegraph Industry."

157. Nonnenmacher, "History of the U.S. Telegraph Industry."

158. Nonnenmacher, "History of the U.S. Telegraph Industry."

159. On Standard Oil's anticompetitive practices, see Lamoreaux, "Problem of Bigness," 94–117.

160. John, *Network Nation*, 359.

Chapter 7

1. Clark and Clark, *Control of Trusts*, 17.

2. Cited in Harrison, "Soviet Industry and the Red Army," 323–342.

3. On the declining percentage of patents granted to individuals, see Nicholas, "Role of Independent Invention," 57–82.

4. True, the seeds of the American military-industrial complex go back to the nineteenth century, but it was then minuscule in comparison before World War II; Baack and Ray, "Political Economy," 369–375.

5. Cited in DeLong, *Slouching Towards Utopia*, 90.

6. On American technological leadership, see Nelson and Wright, "Rise and Fall of American Technological Leadership," 1931–1964.

7. Cited in Tooze, *Wages of Destruction*, 10.

8. On the background of World War II, see Tooze, *Wages of Destruction*, 10–11.

9. On the size of the army, see Overy, *Why the Allies Won*, 233.

10. On the state of U.S military aviation, see Gruber and Johnson, *Jump-Starting America*, 325; Lorell, *U.S. Combat Aircraft Industry*.

11. On rapid technological progress and productivity growth predating the war see, for example, Crafts, "Rise and Fall of American Growth," 57–60.

12. Field, "Most Technologically Progressive Decade," 1399–1413. See also Field, *Great Leap Forward*.

13. On defense jobs, see McCraw, 2009, *American Business Since 1920*, 75. On military expenditure, see Gordon, *Rise and Fall of American Growth*, 536.

14. On car production during the war, see Walton, *Miracle of World War II*, 559; Clive, *State of War*, 22.

15. On the state of the U.S. army, see Atkinson, *Army at Dawn*, 8–9.

16. On mobilization statistics, see Krug, *Production*, 11, 29–32; Smith, *Army and Economic Mobilization*.

17. On the contributions of Ford and GM, see Overy, *Why the Allies Won*, 235.

18. On Willow Run, see Gordon, *Rise and Fall of American Growth*, 533.

19. Cited in Overy, *Why the Allies Won*, 239, 241.

20. While most resource allocation initially happened through the price system, the Roosevelt administration moved to introduce price controls and rationing following Pearl Harbor.

21. Cited in Overy, *Why the Allies Won*, 242.

22. This meant that entrepreneurs and executives had to be convinced to enter the war effort, but many initially resisted. To win them over, Roosevelt moderated his pro-labour rhetoric and rolled back parts of the New Deal.

23. On war mobilization, see Overy, *Why the Allies Won*, 236.

24. On Bush, see R. Reinhold, 1974, "Dr. Vannevar Bush Is Dead at 84," *New York Times*, June 30.

25. On OSRD contracts, see Gross and Sampat, "Inventing the Endless Frontier."

26. These figures include state and federal government spending; see Gruber and Johnson, *Jump-Starting America*, 231.

27. McCraw, *American Business Since 1920*, 65.

28. To describe the chaos, Novick and coauthors uses terms like "administrative anarchy" and "trial-and-error fumbling"; Novick, et al., *Wartime Production Controls*.

29. What the war economy did achieve was to change the outlook and expectations of the nation after the Great Depression, which never seemed to end, leading both pundits and academics to think that the economic machine was irreparably broken. In 1939, for example, Harvard's Alvin Hansen coined the phrase "secular stagnation," suggesting that the American industrial powerhouse had run out of steam; Hansen, "Economic Progress," 10–11.

30. Melman, *Permanent War Economy*, 15.

31. Higgs, "Wartime Prosperity?," 41–60. On the effects of price controls, see also Rockoff, *Drastic Measures*.

32. On working hours, see U.S. War Production Board, *American Industry in War and Transition*, 7, 32.

33. On wartime living conditions, see Polenberg, *War and Society*; Winkler, *Home Front U.S.A.*; Blum, *V Was for Victory*.

34. On the effects of secrecy, see Gross, "Hidden Costs of Securing Innovation," 1935–2545.

35. M. Yglesias, 2020, "The Tech Sector Is Finally Delivering on Its Promise," *Vox*, April 7. Similarly, in *Secrets of the Temple*, Greider argues that World War II forced the government into "rapid development of new productive facilities across many industrial sectors [that] would become the basic industries of America's postwar prosperity" which he suggests laid "the groundwork for an abundant future." Greider, *Secrets of the Temple*. These words also echo those of other scholars, including Sparrow, *Warfare State*; and Klein, *Call to Arms*. However, empirical research on breakthrough innovation shows that it collapsed during World War II and did not recover until the 1980s; Kelly, et al., "Measuring Technological Innovation," 303–320.

36. Bastiat, "That Which Is Seen."

37. "Manhattan Project Background Information and Preservation Work," Office of Legacy Management, https://www.energy.gov/lm/manhattan-project-background-information-and-preservation-work.

38. On Shannon, see Waldrop, *Dream Machine*, 86.

39. Waldrop, *Dream Machine*, 44.

40. On the Manhattan project, see Bachmann and Scherer, *Patents and the Corporation*, 35.

41. On science and technology books published, see Alexopoulos and Cohen, "Volumes of Evidence," 413–450.

42. Of course, some patents are more important than others, but analysis of breakthrough patents reveal a similar decline; Kelly, et al., "Measuring Technological Innovation," 303–320, figure 4, panel A.

43. On immigrants boosting innovation in the United States, see Moser, et al., "German Jewish Émigrés," 3222–3255. Conversely, on the dismissal of scientists in Nazi Germany reducing growth there, see Waldinger, "Bombs, Brains, and Science," 811–831.

44. On productivity, see Field, "Decline of US Manufacturing Productivity," 1163–1190, table 1. Similarly, according to Abramowitz and David, World War II "imposed restrictions on civilian investment, caused a serious reduction in private capital accumulation and retarded normal productivity growth." Abramowitz and David, "American Macroeconomic Growth," 1–92.

45. Stock prices surged in 1945 and again in 1946. In just two years the Standard & Poor's index increased by 37 percent and the value of all shares on registered exchanges by 92 percent; Higgs, "Wartime Prosperity?," 41–60.

46. Careful studies show that OSRD-funded research shaped the trajectory and location of American innovation more directly well beyond the war. But the entire long-run effect was powered by the top 5 percent of clusters that exhibited the highest level of innovation in 1930, prior to securing government contracts. This, in turn, spurred agglomeration forces that exacerbated preexisting disparities in inventive productivity among regions, fueling economic polarization across regions of the country that have persisted to this day; Gross and Sampat, "Inventing the Endless Frontier."

47. Bush, *Science*.

48. Bush, *Science*, 19.

49. On American catch up in science, see MacLeod and Urquiola, "Why Does the United States?," 185–206.

50. MacLeod and Urquiola, "Why Does the United States?," 185–206.

51. On Weber, see Levine, *Allies and Rivals*, 3.
52. On the Bush critics, see Gross and Sampat, "Inventing the Endless Frontier." On NSF funding, see Gruber and Johnson, *Jump-Starting America*, 6.
53. The Soviet Union also caught up in some cutting-edge technologies, like nuclear and long-range rockets.
54. On Sputnik alarmism, see Wang, *In Sputnik's Shadow*, 72.
55. On alarmism over Soviet growth, see Krugman, "The Myth of Asia's Miracle," 62–78.
56. Cited in Erickson, *Into the Unknown Together*, 52.
57. For costs on the Apollo and Manhattan projects, see Stine, *Manhattan Project*. On percentage of federal spending, see Gruber and Johnson, *Jump-Starting America*, 78.
58. On DARPA, see Gallo, "Defense Advanced Research Projects Agency."
59. On productivity spillovers from NASA R&D, see Kantor and Whalley, "Moonshot."
60. R. Solow, 1987, "We'd Better Watch Out," *New York Times Book Review*, July 12.
61. Cited in Waldrop, *Dream Machine*, 200.
62. Cited in Waldrop, *Dream Machine*, 470.
63. On Licklider's pioneering efforts, see also Isaacson, *Innovators*, chapter 7.
64. For quotes and descriptions of Licklider, see Waldrop, *Dream Machine*.
65. Waldrop, *Dream Machine*, 19. On Arpanet, see Waldrop, *Dream Machine*, 223.
66. However, key prerequisites for these technologies were developed long before ARPA. For example, Riemannian geometry enabled the formulation of relativity, which in turn makes accurate GPS technology possible.
67. On the ARPA model, see, for example, Bonvillian, "Connected Science Model for Innovation"; Van Atta, "Testimony."
68. ARPA succeeded by creating an organization capable of drawing in the best talent in the country and providing them with the resources and freedom to explore. If the mission played a role, it was primarily a political one, by enabling the mobilization of resources.
69. Azoulay, et al., "Funding Breakthrough Research," 69–96.
70. Waldrop, *Dream Machine*, 200.
71. On organization and management at ARPA, see Fuchs, "Rethinking the Role," 1133–1147; Colatat, "Organizational Perspective to Funding Science," 874–87; Van Atta, "Testimony"; Roland and Shiman, *Strategic Computing*.
72. On the revolving door and avoiding group think, see Azoulay, et al., "Funding Breakthrough Research," 69–96.
73. On ties with the research community, see Azoulay, et al., "Funding Breakthrough Research," 69–96; Arora, et al., "Changing Structure of American Innovation," 39–93. See also Geiger, *To Advance Knowledge*, 27–29.
74. Cited in Isaacson, *Innovators*, 250.
75. O'Malley, "Drowning in the Net," 78–87, 80. Cited in Gordon, *Rise and Fall of American Growth*, 576.
76. Recent estimates suggest that federally funded R&D in the postwar era might account for one-quarter of business-sector TFP growth; Fieldhouse and Mertens, "The Returns to Government R&D." Given the implied returns between 150 and 300 percent, which are significantly higher than previous findings, their estimates are likely at the higher end. For example, Jones and Summers calculate an average social rate of return on total R&D expenditures of 67 percent; Jones and Summers, "A Calculation of the Social Returns to Innovation."
77. On trends in patenting, see Kelly, et al., "Measuring Technological Innovation," 303–320, figure 4.
78. On the share of patents granted to individuals, see Nicholas, "Role of Independent Invention," 57–82.

79. On social mobility, see Ferrie, "History Lessons," 199–215. Generally, more inventive places were also more socially mobile; see Akcigit, et al., "Rise of American Ingenuity."

80. On Bell Labs, see Gertner, *Idea Factory*. On the rise of in-house R&D, see Arora, et al., "Changing Structure of American Innovation," 39–93.

81. For example, the Chevrolets and Buicks of the early 1940s, which were enabled by the advent of the internal combustion engine, were made inside the walls of GMs research labs, just like many follow-on inventions in computing happened inside the labs of IBM. These improvements were critical to make new discoveries available to a growing middle class at low cost. But as always, incremental improvements ran into diminishing returns. Predictably, the issuance of patents in the automobile, airplane, and radio industries, which emerged in the early twentieth century, showcases an initial surge in activity, eventually reaching a plateau or, in the case of automobiles after 1925, experiencing a marked decline; Gordon, *Rise and Fall of American Growth*, 722. See also Merton, "Fluctuations," 454–474, 462.

82. In addition, the growing complexity of emerging science-based industries arguably made it harder for independent inventors to keep up, not to mention the capital requirements associated with lab-based research; Nicholas, "Role of Independent Invention," 57–82.

83. On the antitrust impacts of the Roosevelt administration, see Hawley, *New Deal*. On the National Industry Recovery Act and collusion, see Vickers and Ziebarth, "National Industrial Recovery Act," 831–862.

84. Barnett, "Great Patent Grab," figure 6.1.

85. Haber and Lamoreaux, *Battle over Patents*, 17.

86. On DuPont, see Hounshell, et al., *Science and Corporate Strategy*.

87. On antitrust and Bell Labs, see Watzinger, et al., "Antitrust Enforcement," 328–359. On how the invalidation of patents owned by larger companies boosts follow-on innovation by smaller companies more broadly, see Galasso and Schankerman, "Patents and Cumulative Innovation," 317–369.

88. On trends in the number of VC-backed IPOs vs. acquisitions, see Ederer and Pellegrino, "The Great Start-up Sellout and the Rise of Oligopoly," 274–278.

89. Gompers and Lerner, *The Money of Invention*, 61–84. A 1988 analysis by Venture Economics revealed that investments in venture-backed IPO firms yielded nearly 1.4 times the returns of those in acquired firms, over comparable holding periods, solidifying the IPO's place as the premier exit strategy in the venture capital playbook, see Nicholas, *VC: An American History*.

90. However, the share of patents taken out by individuals did not increase after 1980; it remained flat at around 15 percent, in large part because entrepreneurs now set up their companies before taking out patents. While it is commonly acknowledged that Bill Gates played a significant role in developing personal computer operating systems for the IBM personal computer, the majority of his patents were acquired after he established Microsoft as a corporation. These patents are then credited to companies in the statistics, but the inventive efforts behind them were driven by individuals rather than giant R&D labs; see Gordon, *Rise and Fall of American Growth*, 724.

91. Lawsuits brought by the Department of Justice between 1971 and 2018 increased both employment and business formation, see Babina, et al., "Antitrust Enforcement Increases Economic Activity."

92. Another example is the invention of television in the 1920s and 1930s, which gradually trickled down to American households in the following decades. The foundations for it were the 1879 invention of wireless transmission combined with Lee De Forest's invention of the vacuum tube in 1907.

93. On electrification and productivity, see David, "Dynamo and the Computer," 355–361.

94. On rural electrification, see Nye, *Electrifying America*.

95. Over the first three decades after its inception, employment in the automobile industry grew 765 percent faster than total manufacturing employment; Lee, "Measuring Agglomeration."

96. Miles per person by air in 1940 was on par with per person miles of car travel in 1904.

97. Gordon, *Rise and Fall of American Growth*, 500.

98. Cited in Leduc and Wilson, "Highway Grants."

99. On highways and productivity, see Nadiri and Mamuneas, "Infrastructure and Public R&D Investments." On the economic effects of highway construction more broadly, see Michaels, "Effect of Trade," 683–701; Baum-Snow, "Did Highways Cause Suburbanization?," 775–805; Duranton and Turner, "Urban Growth and Transportation," 1407–1440.

100. On a tale of two transitions, see Field, "Origins of US Total Factor Productivity," 89. See also Field, *Great Leap Forward*.

101. On early standardization, see Thompson, "Intercompany Technical Standardization," 1–20.

102. For quote and on NBS during World War II, see Dunlavy, *Small, Medium, Large*, 21, 255–257.

103. The number of machine tools produced in the United States doubled between 1940 and 1945; Gordon, "Problems."

104. On Willow Run, see Baime, *Arsenal of Democracy*, 261.

105. On the Kaiser shipyards, see Gordon, *Rise and Fall of American Growth*, 692.

106. Field, *Economic Consequences*.

107. On TWI, see Bianchi and Giorcelli, "Dynamics and Spillovers."

108. Chandler, *Scale and Scope*.

109. Taft and Ross, "American Labor Violence," 221–301.

110. On unions and technological change, see Rothberg, "Adjustment to Automation in Two Firms"; Baldwin and Schultz, "Effects of Automation on Industrial Relations," 47–49.

111. U.S. Congress, *Computerized Manufacturing Automation*.

112. On the role of education for adjustment, see Goldin and Katz, *Race*.

113. On the GI Bill, see Gruber and Johnson, *Jump-Starting America*, 5, 36. On the importance of human capital for the managerial revolution, see Nicholas, "Human Capital."

114. On trade, see Baldwin, "Changing Nature," 5–32.

115. On productivity, see Gollop and Jorgenson, "U.S. Productivity Growth by Industry," 15–136.

Chapter 8

1. Hobsbawm, *Age of Extremes*, 8.

2. Statistics cited and interpretations of the European postwar miracle in this chapter draw heavily on Eichengreen, *European Economy since 1945*; Crafts and Toniolo, *Economic Growth in Europe since 1945*; Crafts, "Golden Age of Economic Growth," 429–447.

3. Though Czechoslovakia and the USSR grew more slowly than Bulgaria, Romania, and Yugoslavia, where GDP per capita was lower from the onset.

4. Cited in Strasser, *Never Done*, 78.

5. On the adoption of household appliances in America, see Greenwood, et al., "Engines of Liberation," 109–133, figure 1; Gordon, *Rise and Fall of American Growth*, figures 4.1 and 4.2. On Europe, see Judt, *Postwar*, 547–548.

6. On automobiles in Europe, see Judt, *Postwar*, 549–550. On America, see Gordon, *Rise and Fall of American Growth*, 211.

7. On travel, see Judt, *Postwar*, 552–553.

8. Judt, *Postwar*, 565.
9. On Fiat, see Fauri, "Role of Fiat," 167–206.
10. On Erhard, see Judt, *Postwar*, 566.
11. This is in line with the seminal account of Hall and Soskice, who argue that the institutions of the coordinated market economies in Europe facilitated incremental rather than radical innovation; Hall and Soskice, *Varieties of Capitalism*.
12. Kennan, "The Sources of Soviet Conduct."
13. On the importance of the Marshall Plan for the development of pro-market institutions in Western Europe, see De Long and Eichengreen, "Marshall Plan"; Casella and Eichengreen, "Can Foreign Aid Accelerate Stabilisation," 605–619; Hogan, *Marshall Plan*.
14. On the economic effects of Marshall aid in Italy, see Giorcelli and Bianchi, "Reconstruction Aid."
15. In addition, military technologies, like guided missiles, were transferred to NATO; Nilsson, "Power of Technology," 127–149.
16. Silberman, et al., "Marshall Plan Productivity Assistance," 443–460.
17. Cited in Giorcelli, "Long-Term Effects," 121–152.
18. On American machines, see Dunning, *American Investment*. On the impact of management and technology transfer, see Giorcelli, "Long-Term Effects," 121–152.
19. On how the container revolutionized trade, see Bernhofen, et al., "Estimating the Effects," 36–50; Levinson, *The Box*.
20. On knowledge exchange, see Fagerberg, "Technology and International Differences," 1147–1175; Nelson and Wright, "Rise and Fall of American Technological Leadership," 1931–1964.
21. On skills, see Krueger and Kumar, "Skill-Specific Rather than General Education," 167–207.
22. Indeed, Abramovitz and David argue European catch-up in this period was based on the "social capability" to take advantage of American technologies; Abramovitz and David, "Convergence and Deferred Catch-Up."
23. Meanwhile, in the United States, the 1950s marked the heyday of union power, which went hand in hand with lower income inequality; Farber, et al., "Unions and Inequality," 1325–1385.
24. Cited in Sassoon, *One Hundred Years of Socialism*, 140.
25. Eichengreen, *European Economy since 1945*, 55.
26. Ross, *Workers and Communists in France*, 31.
27. Of course, in Sweden, industrial peace goes back to the famous Saltsjöbaden Agreement in 1938; Molinder, et al., "Social Democracy," 101420.
28. Eichengreen, *European Economy since 1945*. While there is no clear correlation between centralized collective bargaining and economic growth (Crafts, "Institutions and Economic Growth," 16–38), this is at best a crude test of the Eichengreen thesis; Crafts and Toniolo, "Aggregate Growth," 296–332. Moreover, the function of centralized wage bargaining can have been fulfilled through other institutions. Labour repression achieved the same goal of moderating wage growth and ensuring labour market stability in East Asia.
29. Rosenstein-Rodan, "Problems of Industrialisation," 202–211.
30. On the role of investment, see N. F. Crafts, 1995, "The Golden Age of Economic Growth in Western Europe, 1950–1973," *Economic History Review*: 429–447.
31. On the big-push approach to industrialization, see Rosenstein-Rodan, "Problems of Industrialisation," 202–211; Rosenstein-Rodan, "Notes on the Theory," 57–81. Hirschman famously countered that policymakers better focus on linkages which create knock-on effects on other industries; Hirschman, *Strategy of Economic Development*. Both approaches, however, need bureaucratic coordination.

32. Cited in Huang, et al., "Hayek, Local Information, and Commanding Heights," 2455–2478, 2457.

33. On Wallenberg, see Benner, *Politics of Growth*. On technology transfer to Sweden, see Blomkvist, "Transferring Technology—Shaping Ideology," 273–302; Lundin, "American Numbers Copied!," 303–334.

34. On concentration aiding totalitarianism in the German context, see Crane, "Fascism and Monopoly," 1315. On big business and Hitler, see Turner, "Big Business," 56–70; Turner, *German Big Business*.

35. On ordo-liberalism, see Nicholls, *Freedom with Responsibility*; Labrousse and Weisz, *Institutional Economics*.

36. On Allied influence, see Berghahn, *Americanisation of West German Industry*; Owen, *German Economy*.

37. There were 300 cartels in German manufacturing industry at the turn of the century, but it had risen to 1,000 by 1922 and an astonishing 2,500 by 1925; Wagenfuhr, *Kartelle in Deutschland*. Having declined dramatically, their numbers then increased again from 217 in 1973 to 321 in 1986; Audretsch, "Legalized Cartels in West Germany," 579–600; Broadberry, *Productivity Race*, chapter 9.

38. Carlin, "West German Growth and Institutions," 489.

39. For an overview of France in this period and its long history of mixed enterprises, see Lynch, *France and the International Economy*.

40. In the context of France, Hackett argues that planning made it possible coordinate decision-making across different sectors; Hackett, *Economic Planning in France*.

41. As Eichengreen writes, "If the counterfactual is not market-led investment but an allocation of resources by ministers motivated by political considerations, then delegating power over this decision to a set of independent technocrats could have been efficiency-enhancing"; Eichengreen, *European Economy since 1945*, 108.

42. On the technological backlog and state planning, see Baum, *French Economy and the State*. In addition, Estrin and Holmes argue that indicative planning was easier when it was introduced in 1946 since the French economy was relatively simple and predictable at the time; Estrin and Holmes, *French Planning*.

43. On technology transfer to Spain, see Anduaga, "Autarchy, Ideology, and Technology Transfer," 172–200.

44. Cited in Calvo-González, "American Military Interests and Economic Confidence in Spain."

45. On technical assistance, see Harrison, *Economic History of Modern Spain*, 154.

46. On growth and liberalization, see Prados de la Escosura and Sanz, "Growth and Macroeconomic Performance in Spain."

47. On INI, see Anderson, *Political Economy of Modern Spain*. On INI created companies, see Carreras and Tafunell, "Spain," 246–276.

48. Innovation was also lagging European technology leaders. Even in the 1960s, Italy spent only about one-third of the West German level on R&D and obtained just 3.4 percent of the foreign patents filed in the United States compared to 24.2 percent by German companies; Verspagen, "Technology Indicators and Economic Growth," 215–243. See also Pavitt and Soete, "International Differences in Economic Growth," 105–133.

49. On the Marshall Plan supporting technology adoption at Fiat, see Fauri, "Role of Fiat," 167–206. Cited in Friedman, *Agnelli*, 62.

50. On Italian productivity, see Broadberry, et al., "Productivity." On the role of economies of scale, see Rossi and Toniolo, "Italy," 427–454. On technology and localized learning, see Antonelli and Barbiellini Amidei, "Knowledge, Innovation and Localised Technical Change." On growth figures, see Toniolo, "Overview of Italy's Economic Growth," 22.

51. *The Economist*, April 3, 1993, quoted in Rossi and Toniolo, "Italy." For an overview of Italy's economic performance in the postwar era, see Crafts and Magnani, "Golden Age and the Second Globalization," 69–107.

52. Toniolo, "Overview of Italy's Economic Growth."

53. On bureaucracy, see Bianco and Napolitano, "Italian Administrative System," 541.

54. Resolving the long-standing debate around the importance of German-style banks, as emphasized by Gerschenkron, and the role of infrastructure, as highlighted by Romeo, is not the aim here. Both have their critics. Rather, in line with the literature emphasizing returns to scale in Italy's industrial development (Rossi and Toniolo, "Catching Up or Falling Behind?," 537–563), I argue that both banks and infrastructure played a role in facilitating economies of scale.

55. Cohen, "Financing Industrialization in Italy," 363–382, 378 and 382. Beyond electrical industries, however, there is little evidence for the view that German-style banks played a pivotal role in Italian industrial development; see, for example, Federico, "Italy, 1860–1940," 764–786.

56. Clearly, growth in the North was aided by favourable initial conditions. Indeed, the lasting divide between the South and the North was already visible before unification; Toniolo, "Overview of Italy's Economic Growth."

57. Gerschenkron locates this period between 1896 and 1908; Gerschenkron, "Notes," 360–375, 365. On regional industrial output, see Esposto, "Italian Industrialization," 353–362. On regional patenting, see Nuvolari and Vasta, "Geography of Innovation in Italy," 326–356.

58. Following unification, the civil servant population saw a swift increase, reaching close to 98,000 by 1882; Bianco and Napolitano, "Italian Administrative System," 541.

59. On the railroad network, see Toniolo, "Overview of Italy's Economic Growth," 13.

60. For a detailed discussion of the Italian railroads, see Ciccarelli and Nuvolari, "Technical Change, Non-Tariff Barriers," 860–888.

61. On the importance of foreign technology for Italy's industrial development more broadly, see Barbiellini Amidei, et al., "Innovation and Foreign Technology."

62. In 1906, direct contracts awarded 291 locomotives to domestic manufacturers, while international auctions allocated 112 to foreign manufacturers.

63. The much-debated effect of protective tariffs on Italian railroad development, going back to Gerschenkron, is hard to judge. On the one hand, in the 1880s, the primary locomotive manufacturers—Ansaldo, founded in 1854 near Genoa, and Pietrarsa, established in 1842 near Naples—complained that import duties on iron and other production inputs rendered them uncompetitive. On the other hand, subsequent tariff reform targeting locomotives helped mitigate these costs. As discussed, the Italian state played a constructive role in fostering demand for locally produced locomotives while simultaneously involving foreign companies in international bids. This approach not only supported domestic production but also exposed Italian firms to competitive pressures. Moreover, by the 1880s, Italian locomotive manufacturers had established themselves as technologically competitive; Ciccarelli and Nuvolari, "Technical Change, Non-Tariff Barriers," 860–888.

64. On IRI bureaucrats, see Shonfield, *Changing Balance*. On the Italian model, see Barca, et al., "Postwar Institutional Reform"; Woods, "Crisis (Collapse)," 22–41.

65. On Totsuka Hideo, see Turner, *Japanese Workers in Protest*.

66. On labour repression in East Asia, see Johnson, "Political Institutions and Economic Performance," 149–151. On Korea, see also Cole and Princeton, *Korean Development*, 96, 124–130.

67. On parallels with the nineteenth century, see Chandler, *Scale and Scope*, 616–617.

68. On the political imperative of technology transfer, see Fallows, *Looking at the Sun*, 138.

69. On Allied bombings, see Davis and Weinstein, "Bones, Bombs, and Break Points," 1269–1289; Werrell, *Blankets of Fire*, 32.

70. In addition, Japan already had a significant industrial base, which, despite having suffered from wartime destruction, had made Japan a major power, capable of defeating Tsarist Russia in 1905. This preexisting industrial capacity arguably enabled the country to better absorb cutting-edge technology from abroad in the postwar era.

71. On TWI, see Huntzinger, "Roots of Lean," 14–23.

72. On licensing, see Hirschmeier, *Development of Japanese Business*, 258.

73. On "little Detroits," see Spencer, "External Military Presence," 451–474, 457.

74. On Japanese auto industry during WWII, see Overy, *Why the Allies Won*, 271–272.

75. Indeed, when Freeman developed the concept of "national innovation systems" to support the inward transfer and exploitation of technologies from abroad, he originally did so based on postwar Japan; Freeman, *Technology Policy and Economic Performance*. This approach has also been applied to other economies in more recent work; see, for example, Lundvall, *National Systems of Innovation*; Nelson, *National Innovation Systems*.

76. Inspired by this success, companies like Xerox, Procter & Gamble, and AT&T soon also adopted Japanese management principles with similar outcomes; see Giorcelli, *Professionals and Productivity*, http://www.giorcellimichela.com/uploads/8/3/7/0/83709646/giorcelli_professionals_productivity.pdf.

77. Cited in Johnson, *MITI and the Japanese Miracle*.

78. Johnson, *MITI and the Japanese Miracle*. A mere 2–3 percent of exam takers were admitted to Japan's civil service; Besley, et al., "Bureaucracy and Development," 397–424.

79. On MITI sharing technology domestically, see Mowery and Oxley, "Inward Technology Transfer and Competitiveness," 67–93. The capacity to absorb foreign technology, in turn, depended on the training of scientists and engineers rather than on targeted investments in strategic sectors; Nelson, *National Innovation Systems*, 347–374. Indeed, there is little evidence to suggest that protectionist trade policies or the targeting did much or anything to support Japanese productivity; Beason and Weinstein, "Growth, Economies of Scale," 286–295.

80. On technology sharing requirements, see Steinmueller, "Industry Structure and Government Policies"; Mowery and Steinmueller, "Prospects for Entry by Developing Countries."

81. Studwell, *How Asia Works*, 63.

82. Indeed, business groups, similar to the keiretsu, played a significant role in many developing countries with less developed markets; Granovetter, "Business Groups," chapter 18; Ghemawat and Khanna, "Nature of Diversified Business Groups," 35–61; Khanna and Yafeh, "Business Groups in Emerging Markets," 331–372.

83. On antitrust in Japan, see Hadley, *Antitrust in Japan*.

84. Porter and Sakakibara, "Competition in Japan," 27–50.

85. On keiretsu control, see Caves and Uekusa, *Industrial Organization in Japan*.

86. On barriers to entry, see Lawrence, "Efficient or Exclusionist?," 311–330.

87. On technology transfer, see Mowery and Oxley, "Inward Technology Transfer and Competitiveness," 67–93, table 1.

88. For a detailed account on policy differences and similarities, see Haggard and Cheng, "State and Foreign Capital," 135.

89. Haggard and Cheng, "State and Foreign Capital," 135. Rodrik agrees: "By subsidizing and coordinating investment decisions, government policy managed to engineer a significant increase in the private return to capital." Rodrik, "Getting Interventions Right," 53–107.

90. On "second Japan," see Kim, "The Leviathan," 201.

91. Thus, Palais calls the Yi dynasty "centralized and weak"; Palais, *Politics and Policy*, 5.

92. See Peattie, "Introduction," in Myers and Peattie, *Japanese Colonial Empire*, 29.

93. On government officials, see Kohli, *State-Directed Development*, 34–35.

94. On land surveys, see Kohli, *State-Directed Development*, 42–43.

95. On conflict as an impetus for growth, see Kim, *Big Business, Strong State*; Moon and Lee, "Military Spending and the Arms Race," 69–99. On the Rhee government being preoccupied with political considerations rather than generating economic growth or exports, see Jones and Sakong, *Government, Business, and Entrepreneurship*.

96. Kohli, *State-Directed Development*, 64–68. On the size of the bureaucracy, see Huer, *Marching Orders*, 117.

97. Cited in Amsden, *Asia's Next Giant*, 50.

98. Cited in Studwell, *How Asia Works*, 75.

99. On the examination system, see Kim, "The Leviathan," 204.

100. Cited in Kim, "The Leviathan," Chapter Three, 86.

101. On Korean institutions, see Cheng, et al., "Institutions and Growth in Korea and Taiwan," 87–111. See also Woo-Cumings, "State, Democracy, and the Reform," 116–142.

102. Lane provides empirical support for the notion that South Korea's heavy industrial push had long-lasting impacts on output in the industries targeted, but through investment incentives rather than protectionist measures; Lane, "Manufacturing Revolutions." Other studies document a link between government subsidies and technology adoption in this period; Choi and Shim, "Technology Adoption and Late Industrialization."

103. The value added and employment shares of heavy and chemical industries rose rapidly until the Asian crisis of 1997; Eichengreen, et al., *From Miracle to Maturity*, figures 3.9 and 3.10. Rapidly rising productivity was the result of reforms in the 1960s and again in the 1980s; see Eichengreen, et al., *From Miracle to Maturity*, chapter 3).

104. On conglomerates and GNP, see Kohli, *State-Directed Development*, 97. Between 1962 and 1981, nearly 60 percent of all Korean technology licensing arrangements were with Japan; Sakong, *Korea in the World Economy*, table A48.

105. On accountability, see Kim, "The Leviathan," 216. For statistical evidence on competent bureaucrats boosting exports more, see Barteska and Lee, "Bureaucrats."

106. Mason, et al., *Economic and Social Modernization*, 337.

107. Amsden, *Asia's Next Giant*, 16. Even Krueger, whose work is commonly cited to point to the risks of industrial policy, such as capture by special interests, has distinguished Korea from Latin America in that it was exposed to fierce competition in export markets; Krueger, *Developmental Role of the Foreign Sector*. Survey evidence from Korea in this period also shows that businesses perceived the state compulsion to export as real; Jones and Sakong, *Government, Business, and Entrepreneurship*, 132–139.

108. On the state being the senior partner, see Mason, et al., *Economic and Social Modernization*, 255. In similar spirit, Jones and SaKong also refer to Taiwan and Korea as "hard states"; Jones and Sakong, *Government, Business, and Entrepreneurship*, 132.

109. On the comparison with Latin America, see Kohli, *State-Directed Development*; Johnson, "Political Institutions and Economic Performance," 156.

110. Ireland only became the Celtic Tiger later through a series of policies that facilitated technology transfer and FDI; O'Grada and O'Rourke, "Irish Economic Growth," 388–426.

111. True, growth in Britian was also quite rapid, as generally in Europe in this period, but Britain stands out as an underperformer relative to its European peers; see Crafts, "British Relative Economic Decline Revisited," 17–29, table 5).

112. On decentralized industrial relations, see Crouch, *Industrial Relations and European State Traditions*. On local and sectors specific employer associations, see Flanders, "Industrial Relations," 101–124.

113. Trade unions also continued to enjoy the legal immunities provided by the 1906 Trade Disputes Act, and the 1971 Industrial Relations Act was only a modest attempt to reform.

114. Consequently, manning levels were higher and production runs shorter than in Germany and the United States; Pratten, "Labor Productivity Differentials."

115. Eichengreen, 2006, *European Economy since 1945*, 124–125.

116. On nationalized industry, see Corti, "Perspectives on Public Corporations," 47–86. On productivity gaps, see O'Mahony, *Britain's Productivity Performance*. On subsidies, see Crafts, *Forging Ahead, Falling Behind*.

117. Morris and Stout, "Industrial Policy," 873.

118. On aviation, see Gardner, "Economics of Launching Aid." On computers, see Hendry, *Innovating for Failure*. On and nuclear power, see Cowan, "Nuclear Power Reactors," 541–567. On British Leyland and DeLorean cars, see D. Coyle, 2021, "Dark Side of the Moonshot: Can the State Really Fix Our Broken Capitalism?," *Prospect Magazine*, March.

119. On cartelization and antitrust, see Mercer, *Constructing a Competitive Order*. On protectionism, see Kitson and Solomou, *Protectionism and Economic Revival*; Morgan and Martin, "Tariff Reductions and UK Imports," 38–54.

120. On competition policy, see Clarke, et al., *Monopoly Policy in the UK*.

121. On cartelization, see Broadberry and Crafts, "Competition and Innovation," 97–118. On cartelization and productivity, see Broadberry and Crafts, "British Economic Policy," 65–91. That competition policy could have improved productivity performance is further underlined by the fact that when cartels were abandoned following the 1956 Restrictive Practices Act, labour productivity growth rose in previously cartelized sectors; Symeonidis, "Effects of Competition," 134–146.

122. As Weldon notes of these foreign shipyards, "Their productivity was some 30 to 40 per cent higher [relative to Britain] by the late 1940s and the gap was growing." Weldon, *Two Hundred Years of Muddling Through*, 133–134.

123. On the effect of joining the ECC on the British economy, see Crafts, "Growth Effects of EU Membership." On competition and innovation in Britain in the 1970s, see Geroski, "Innovation," 586–602.

124. Studwell, *How Asia Works*, 62.

Chapter 9

1. H. Arendt, 1970, "Reflections on Civil Disobedience," *The New Yorker*, September 4, 70.

2. In 1889, Witte published a paper titled "National Savings and Friedrich List," citing List to point to the need for a strong domestic industry, protected from foreign competition.

3. Gatrell, *Tsarist Economy*, 161.

4. On sources of growth, see Gregory, *Russian National Income*.

5. On industrial projects, see Lewis, "Technology," 182–197.

6. Cited in Bailes, *Technology and Society*, 49.

7. Lange, "Role of Planning in Socialist Economy," 18.

8. On the models of organization shaping the Soviet economy, see Harrison, "The Soviet Economy, 1917–1991," 199–206.

9. Cited in Bailes, *Technology and Society*, 51. In this spirit, Vladimir Ipatieff, who had been a General-Lieutenant of the Russian army before the October revolution, and was no Bolshevik sympathizer, was made director of the State Scientific Technical Institute.

10. Sutton, *Western Technology and Soviet Economic Development, 1930–1945*, 329. Between 1945 and 1965, Sutton finds another three inventions originating in the USSR; Sutton, *Western Technology and Soviet Economic Development, 1945–1965*.

11. On the sources of foreign technological information, see Harrison, "Soviet Market for Inventions."

12. Harrison, "Soviet Market for Inventions"; Harrison, "Political Economy," 178–212.

13. Harrison, "Political Economy," 178–212.

14. As Harrison writes, "There was no shortage of inventiveness and there were more proposals for radical innovations than the authorities were willing to fund. The main problem for the authorities was to regulate inventive activity, not promote it." Harrison, "Political Economy," 178–212.

15. They included S. A. Aksiutin and N. M. Sinev in Moscow, P. L. Kozhevnikov in Leningrad, and V. T. Tsvetkov in Kharkov.

16. On funding activity, see Harrison, "Political Economy," 178–212.

17. Harrison, "Political Economy," 178–212.

18. On Korolev and Kostikov, see Harrison, "Political Economy," 178–212.

19. On political infighting, see Harrison, "Political Economy," 178–212.

20. On Lysenkoism, see Lewis, "Technology," 182–197.

21. This included the famous botanist Nikolai Vavilov.

22. For an overview of NEP, see Harrison, "Why Did NEP Fail?," 57–67.

23. State Planning Committee, known as Gosplan, was established in February 1921 to create a "unified state plan" for the whole economy and drive harmonization between different departments.

24. While the accuracy of these figures has been subject of much debate, Soviet sources themselves suggest that native inventions in this period were disappointing; Bailes, *Technology and Society*, 341.

25. Cited in Bailes, *Technology and Society*, 343.

26. On American emulation, see Lewis, "Technology," 186.

27. On Harold M. Ware, see R. H. Anderson, 1967, "1917 The Russian Revolution—1967: Americans Played Role in Early Economic Development of the Soviet Union," *New York Times*, November 1.

28. The Autonomous Industrial Colony of Kuzbas lasted from 1921 to 1927. The agreement, which was signed by Lenin himself on the Soviet side, gave the Americans an iron and steel plant in Serov (then Nadezhdinsk), brick plants in Tomsk, a chemical plant, and some leather and shoe factories, along with a timber reserve.

29. On William Haywood, see R. H. Anderson, 1967, "1917—The Russian Revolution—1967: Americans Played Role in Early Economic Development of the Soviet Union," *New York Times*, November 1.

30. Davie, "Logistics of the Combined-Arms Army," 474–501.

31. In addition, American technology was not always a good fit for Soviet conditions. The chairman of the Scientific and Technical Council for the textile industry, A. A. Fedotov, for example, came out strongly against the adoption of American technology and production methods, arguing that they were inappropriate for the USSR with its large reserves of cheap labour.

32. On tank conversion, see Davies, "Industry," 131–157.

33. Overy, *Why the Allies Won*, 258.

34. On army modernization, see Overy, *Why the Allies Won*, 259.

35. On Lend-Lease, see Overy, *Why the Allies Won*, 263.

36. On the share of equipment produced in the USSR, see Harrison, *Soviet Planning in Peace and War*, 264. Western motor transport was important but hardly the sole factor, see Davie, "Logistics of the Combined-Arms Army," 474–501. See also Harrison, "Second World War."

37. On factory evacuation, see Overy, *Why the Allies Won*, 220–221.

38. Link, *Forging Global Fordism*, 205.

39. On Nazi industry, see Buchheim and Scherner, "Role of Private Property," 390–416.

40. On simplicity vs. variety, see Overy, *Why the Allies Won*, chapter 7.

41. On GDP losses, see Eichengreen, *European Economy since 1945*, 131.

42. On state capacity under Communist Party rule, see Hobsbawm, *Age of Extremes*, 64. On how the Great Depression affected attitudes toward planning, see Brus and Laski, *From Marx to the Market*.

43. Even in countries like Poland and Hungary, where some private elements were allowed to exist, entrepreneurs were highly restricted by administrative barrier; see Lipton, et al., "Creating a Market Economy in Eastern Europe," 75–147.

44. On the Soviet planning system, see Eichengreen, 2008, *European Economy since 1945*, 135–136.

45. On socialist enterprise, see B. Milanovic, 2021, "Socialist Enterprise Power Structure and the Soft-Budget Constraint," *gobalinequality*, November 19, https://glineq.blogspot.com/2021/11/socialist-enterprise-power-structure.html.

46. Kornai, "Resource-Constrained," 801–819; Kornai, Maskin, and Roland, "Understanding the Soft Budget Constraint," 1095–1136. The opening of the Soviet archives has vindicated the Kornai view; see Gregory and Harrison, "Allocation Under Dictatorship," 721–761.

47. Berend, *Central and Eastern Europe*, 77.

48. See Heinzen, "Corruption in the Gulag," 456–475.

49. Khlevnyuk, "Economy of the OGPU," 57. On the Gulag, see Gregory and Harrison, "Allocation Under Dictatorship," 721–761, 738.

50. Conveniently, pieces rates could be seen as incapsulating the socialist principle of "to each according to his work," but prices used to value that work were clearly arbitrary.

51. On trade, see Eichengreen, *European Economy since 1945*, 156–160.

52. On German role models, see Brunnermeier, "Beijing's Bismarckian Ghosts," 161–176. On Krupp, see James, *Krupp*, 51. On Chiang Kai-shek, see Wakeman, *Spymaster*, 62. On Chiang Wei-kuo, see Kirby, *Empires of Ideas*.

53. On the NRC, see Studwell, *How Asia Works*, 79.

54. On Mao's reforms, see Perkins, "Centrally Planned Command Economy"; Perkins, "China's Struggle," 565–605.

55. On restricted goods and freedoms, see Dickson, *Party and the People*, 16–17.

56. On the influence of the Prussian system and efforts to attract Western talent, see Kirby, *Empires of Ideas*, 240–241, 306.

57. Not to mention the dissolution of China's once prestigious National Central University.

58. On the effects on Chinese academics, see Dikotter, *Tragedy of Liberation*, 180–182.

59. On Tsinghua under and after Mao, see Kirby, *Empires of Ideas*, 272–276.

60. In fact, the entire organization of Chinese research and innovation came from the Soviets, including the blueprint for the CAS.

61. On Chinese technology policy, see Naughton, *Chinese Economy*, 122–123.

62. On Mao and Stalin, see Dikotter, *Tragedy of Liberation*, 120–125. For an overview of technology transfer activities, see Zhang, et al., *Technology Transfer*.

63. Grow, "Soviet Economic Penetration of China," 262.

64. On Chinese students in the USSR, see Naughton, *Chinese Economy*, 122–123.

65. When Soviet experts arrived at the Daheishan molybdenum plant in the Jilin Province, they soon realized that initial communications had been misinterpreted: the designs didn't fit, and some clarifying letters had been lost. On technology transfer challenges, see Borisov and Koloskov, *Sino-Soviet Relationship*.

66. Quote from G. K. Reddy, "Mr. Nehru Visits Steel Works," *Times of India*, October 25, 1954, 7, cited in Hirata, "Steel Metropolis," PhD diss., Stanford University.

67. On blast furnaces, see Lardy, "Emulating the Soviet Model," 722. On the growth contribution of the 156 Projects, see Giorcelli and Li, "Technology Transfer and Early Industrial Development."

68. On GDP per capita growth, see Brandt and Rawski, "China's Great Boom," 796-801. See also Morawetz, *Twenty-Five Year*, 5. Per capita income estimates are from Penn World Tables v. 9.1, https://www.rug.nl/ggdc/productivity/pwt/pwt-releases/pwt9.1?lang=en, and from Maddison, *Chinese Economic Performance*, 40. On productivity, see Perkins and Rawski, "Forecasting China's Economic Growth," 839.

69. On the Sino-Soviet split, see Whiting, "Sino-Soviet Split," 478-538.

70. Zeitz, "Trade in Equipment," cited in Brandt and Rawski, "China's Great Boom," 798.

71. On the end of technology transfer and project completion, see Yanqiong and Jifeng, "Analysis of Soviet Technology Transfer," 66-110; Naughton, *Chinese Economy*, 536.

72. On Soviet productivity, see Harrison, "Soviet Union after 1945," 103-120, figure 1.

73. On the Soviet military burden, see Barber, et al., "Structure and Development," 3-29. Harrison, "Industrial Expansion under Late Stalinism," 359-378. On postwar militarization, see Harrison, "Soviet Union after 1945," 103-120, 120.

74. Quote from Gordon, *Rise and Fall of American Growth*, 357.

75. On non-monetary inequality, see Harrison, "The Soviet Economy, 1917-1991," 199-206.

76. In the 1950s, for example, Hungary reported 6 percent growth per year net of material product; Poland grew by 7 percent annually; while East Germany and Bulgaria saw astonishing double-digit growth rates of 10 and 11 percent, respectively; Eichengreen, *European Economy since 1945*, table 5.2.

77. On women in government, see Harrison, "The Soviet Economy, 1917-1991," 199-206.

78. Cited in F. M. Hechinger, 1967, "The Russian Revolution," *New York Times*, October 5.

79. Carlin, et al., "Soviet Power Plus Electrification," 116-147.

80. On stagnation and hurdles to innovation in the USSR, see Gomulka, "Soviet Growth Slowdown," 170-174; Gomulka, "Gerschenkron Phenomenon," 451-458. In the words of Broadberry and Klein, "Central planning was able to achieve a satisfactory productivity performance during the era of mass production but could not adapt to the requirements of flexible production technology during the 1980s." Broadberry and Klein, "When and Why," 37-52, 37.

Chapter 10

1. Kornai, "Innovation and Dynamism," 14-56.

2. On the geopolitical environment, see Kotkin, *Armageddon Averted*, chapter 1.

3. Collier, *Future of Capitalism*, 128.

4. On minimills, see Collard-Wexler and De Loecker, "Reallocation and Technology," 131-171.

5. Buss and Redburn, *Shutdown at Youngstown*, 4. See also Strohmeyer, *Crisis in Bethlehem*, 11-14; Bluestone and Harrison, *Deindustrialization of America*; and Rodwin and Sazanami, *Deindustrialization and Regional Economic Transformation*.

6. Kotkin, *Armageddon Averted*, 13-14.

7. On the increasing demand for higher education, see Goldin and Katz, *Race between Education and Technology*; Berger and Frey, "Did the Computer Revolution Shift," 38-45; Berger and Frey, "Industrial Renewal in the 21st Century," 404-413.

8. On postwar institutions becoming inept for the computer age, see Eichengreen, *European Economy since 1945*, chapter 2.

9. Schivardi and Schmitz, "IT Revolution," 2441-2486. In Italy, as economists Bruno Pellegrino and Luigi Zingales have pointed out, "familism and cronyism" made companies unable

to reap the benefits of the computer age, see Pellegrino and Zingales, "Diagnosing the Italian Disease."

10. On import protection, see Ennew, et al., "Further Evidence on Effective Tariffs," 69–78. On subsidies, see Wren, "Grant-Equivalent Expenditure," 317–353.

11. On openness contributing to productivity convergence with the technological leader between 1970 and 1990, see Proudman and Redding, "Summary of the Openness and Growth Project," 1–29.

12. Crafts, 2018, *Forging Ahead, Falling Behind*, 117.

13. Chinitz, "Contrasts in Agglomeration," 279–289, 284. On the backgrounds of inventors, see Bell, et al., "Who Becomes an Inventor in America?," 647–713.

14. Chinitz, "Contrasts in Agglomeration," 279–289, 285.

15. We might just add a footnote to Chinitz's list: Where large incumbents have their stronghold, they are more likely to successfully lobby to erect barriers to entry.

16. Glaeser, et al., "Entrepreneurship and Urban Growth," 498–520.

17. On second-generation migrants, see Franck and Galor, "Flowers of Evil?," 108–128. On how this can create an "obedience trap" in which an economy finds itself in a high-obedience, low-innovation equilibrium, see Campante and Chor, "Just Do Your Job." See also Brezis and Krugman, "Technology," 369–383.

18. Bombardini and Trebbi, "Competition and Political Organization," 18–26.

19. See Kotkin, *Armageddon Averted*, 33.

20. On Stalin and switchboard operators, see Kotkin, *Stalin*, 433.

21. On how repressive technologies can undermine democracy more broadly, see Hariri and Wingender, "Jumping the Gun," 728–760.

22. On Radio transmission, see Kornai, "Innovation and Dynamism," 14–56.

23. On Soviet television, see Kotkin, *Armageddon Averted*, 50.

24. Kotkin, *Armageddon Averted*, 53.

25. For example, while artists and architects briefly joined forces in the 1920s in pursuit of an adventure in Constructivism, by the 1930s their efforts were denounced as decadent and bourgeoisie; A. L. Huxtable, 1967, "1917 The Russian Revolution: Soviet Has Mastered the Industrialized Technology of Low-Cost Mass Building," *New York Times*, October 20.

26. On the role of information from abroad, see Gregory and Harrison, "Allocation under Dictatorship," 721–761.

27. As Allen has noted, the Soviet R&D institutions were long-standing and did not change substantially in the 1970s; Allen, "Rise and Decline," 859–881. In other words, they cannot explain the abrupt decline in productivity; Easterly and Fischer, "Soviet Economic Decline," 341–371.

28. One further possibility is that inventive efforts increasingly came to target destructive ends as the arms race with the United States during the Brezhnev period intensified. However, the diversion of R&D resources from civilian to military innovation was not large enough to account for the decline. Estimates by the CIA suggest that the USSR spent 12 percent of its GDP on defense in the late 1960s relative to 16 percent in the early 1980s. Defense spending estimates are from Davis, "Defense Sector in the Soviet Economy." For an overview of the debates on the magnitude of Soviet defense spending, see also Allen, *Farm to Factory*, 209.

29. Feinstein, "Technical Progress and Technology Transfer," 65.

30. Kotkin, *Armageddon Averted*, 66.

31. Quote from Abouchar, "Postwar Developments in the Cement Industry," 565. On cement, see Allen, *Farm to Factory*, 208.

32. On information and innovation, see Kornai, "Innovation and Dynamism," 14–56.

33. On managers and their incentives, see Berliner, *Factory and Manager in the USSR*, 30–32.

34. On production targets and innovation, see Dearden, et al., "To Innovate or Not to Innovate," 1105–1124.
35. Eichengreen, *European Economy since 1945*, 155.
36. On Karpinski and Jánosi, see Kornai, "Innovation and Dynamism," 14–56.
37. On the absence of spillovers in the USSR, see Kornai, "Innovation and Dynamism," 14–56.
38. On military competition and innovation, see Feinstein, "Technical Progress and Technology Transfer."
39. For empirical evidence on the importance of non-financial incentives, such as public recognition, more broadly, see Ager, et al., "Killer Incentives," 2257–2292.
40. On Ioffe, see Kornai, "Innovation and Dynamism," 14–56.
41. On taxes and Soviet inventors, see Akcigit, et al., "Taxation," 2930–2981.
42. On Soviet scientists and R&D, see Feinstein, "Technical Progress and Technology Transfer," table 3.1; Bergson, "Technological Progress," 54–55.
43. On innovation and planning costs, see Harrison, "Coercion, Compliance, and the Collapse," 397–433. Crafts and Toniolo make a similar point: "innovation drove up monitoring costs which also inhibited moves from mass to flexible production." Crafts and Toniolo, "Aggregate Growth," 296–332. See also Harrison and Simonov, "Voenpriemka," 237–238.
44. On Party membership, see Gershenson and Grossman, "Cooption and Repression."
45. On leniency for connected individuals, see Harrison, "Forging Success," 43–64.
46. On the People's Control Commission, see Markevich, "How Much Control Is Enough?," 1449–1468.
47. On Stalin's atrocities and personal interventions, see Gregory and Harrison, "Allocation under Dictatorship," 721–761.
48. On the loyalty constraint, see Belova and Lazarev, *Funding Loyalty*. On the role of the dictator's reputation, see Harrison, "Coercion, Compliance, and the Collapse," 397–433, 409.
49. The following section draws heavily on Harrison and Ma, "Soaring Dragon, Stumbling Bear"; Miller, *Struggle to Save the Soviet Economy*; Xu, "Fundamental Institutions," 1076–1151.
50. On Deng and Gorbachev, see Vogel, *Deng Xiaoping*, 423.
51. Popov, "Shock Therapy Versus Gradualism," 1–57.
52. On Iziumov, see Miller, *Struggle to Save the Soviet Economy*, 108–109.
53. Cited in Miller, *Struggle to Save the Soviet Economy*, 114.
54. Miller, *Struggle to Save the Soviet Economy*, 118.
55. Cited in Miller, *Struggle to Save the Soviet Economy*, 184.
56. In particular, strong Soviet urban interests, which resisted any change in the state sector, made gradual reform much harder to pursue; Sachs and Woo, "Structural Factors," 101–145. See also Boycko, et al., *Privatizing Russia*.
57. Xu, "Fundamental Institutions," 1076–1151.
58. On the nomenklatura system, see Lewin, "Rebuilding the Soviet Nomenklatura," 219–252.
59. Even in farming the Soviet Union was slow to adjust to new technologies. Tasks like allocating tractors were coordinated by the central government through eleven ministries; see van Atta, "Russian Agriculture Between Plan and Market," 9–24. Any minor change in, for example, grain production, had to involve at least seven ministries: the Ministries of Agriculture, Trade, Cereal and Grain Production, Tractors and Farm Machinery, Food Industry, Rural Construction, and Fertilizer; Qian, et al., "Coordination and Experimentation," 366–402. On M-form vs. U-form hierarchy more generally, see Qian, et al., "Coordination and Experimentation," 366–402; Qian and Xu, "M-form Hierarchy and China's Economic Reform," 541–548.

60. On Stalin's nested dictatorship, see Gregory and Harrison, "Allocation under Dictatorship," 721–761.

61. Cited in Harrison, *Soviet Industry and the Red Army*, 337.

62. We know, for example, that Stalin and his allies allocated motor vehicles, which was the scarcest capital good of the time, for political gain rather than with economic considerations in mind; see Lazarev and Gregory, "Wheels of a Command Economy," 324–348.

63. On the dictator's curse, see Gregory, *Political Economy of Stalinism*.

64. On the Sovnarkhoz system, see Markevich and Zhuravskaya, "M-Form Hierarchy," 1550–1560.

65. See, for example, Hanson, *Rise and Fall of the Soviet Union*.

66. Kotkin, *Armageddon Averted*, 2.

67. Miller, *Struggle to Save the Soviet Economy*, 182.

68. The origins of Chinese decentralization have been traced back to the Qing dynasty; Ma, "Political Institution and Long-run Economic Trajectory," 78–98; Brandt, et al., "From Divergence to Convergence," 45–123. In Russia, in stark contrast, basic decentralized structures were missing before the nineteenth century; Nafziger, "Did Ivan's Vote Matter?," 393–441; Starr, *Decentralization and Self-Government in Russia*.

69. On when yardstick competition works, see Cai and D. Treisman, "State-Corroding Federalism," 819–843.

70. However, some of the negative effects were mitigated by horizontal social networks of regional leaders who had long-standing relationships going back to higher party school; Markevich and Zhuravskaya, "M-Form Hierarchy," 1550–1560.

71. On Chinese diversification vs. Russian specialization, see Xu, "Fundamental Institutions," 1076–1151. This observation naturally raises the question of why East European countries, which were more self-sufficient, and had some freedom to experiment with national economic models, did not more closely track the Chinese pattern of growth. The most plausible explanation is that they too faced considerable resistance from vested interests and that the bureaucratic capacity of their respective states was weaker.

72. For the first time in Chinese history, Mao created a state so strong that it penetrated to the village level. But while the Great Leap Forward, and later the Cultural Revolution, destroyed any organized vested interest groups that might be able to challenge Mao's authority, they also left the "the legitimacy of the CCP . . . deeply shaken" and "severely damaged the national bureaucracy, leaving it weak and divided." While social order remained intact, with no major interruption of food supplies, transport or utility services, "most ministries closed down," rendering Beijing unable to "monitor compliance with many kinds of orders." This brought "the inevitable structural consequence–a drift towards decentralization." Brandt and Rawski, "China's Great Boom," 775–828. In fact, the institutional structures that emerged greatly resembled the millennia old imperial *junxian* system; Xu, "Origin of China's Communist Institutions," 531–564, figures 15.2 and 15.4. This reemergence was then institutionalized in the reform era, when the central government negotiated revenue sharing agreements with each province, which in turn negotiated fiscal relationships with subordinate cities, and so on; see J. C. Oi, 1992, "Fiscal Reform," 99–126. However, as the fiscal revenues of the central government constantly changed and sometimes collapsed, some fiscal consolidation followed in 1994. This reform "established a tax and revenue sharing system that bears similarities with the American federal system." Yao, "Chinese Growth Miracle," 943–1031.

73. In 2008, local governments' share of fiscal revenue and expenditure stood at 40 percent and 73 percent, respectively, compared to the OECD averages of 19 percent and 32 percent; Xu, "Fundamental Institutions," 1076–1151.

74. Strategic industries were an exception. On distance from the centre and local autonomy, see Huang, et al., "Hayek, Local Information, and Commanding Heights," 2455–2478.

75. On the organization of steel production, see Clark, *Economics of Soviet Steel*; Clark, "Soviet Steel Industry," 396–410; Qian, et al., "Coordination and Experimentation," 366–402.
76. On steel output, see Pockney, *Soviet Statistics since 1950*.
77. On the divergence in steel between China and the USSR, see Qian, et al., "Coordination and Experimentation," 366–402.
78. Local governments played a leading role in China's automotive industry, to take one example, albeit with mixed success; Thun, *Changing Lanes in China*.
79. Naughton, *Chinese Economy*, 156.
80. Cited in McMillan and Woodruff, "Central Role of Entrepreneurs," 153–170.
81. This also meant that there could be no clean break with its Communist past and no straightforward copying of Western institutions. To overcome resistance of the social and political groups whose interests were tied to the old institutions while driving modernization, a set contingent institutions were created. In the absence of the rule of law, these institutions depended solely on the willingness of the CCP and Chinese bureaucracy to enforce them. And as long as they did, they provided similar incentives to Western institutions.
82. See Qian and Weingast, "Federalism as a Commitment," 83–92. See also Montinola, et al., "Federalism, Chinese Style," 50–81.
83. Several empirical studies also show a positive relationship between fiscal decentralization and regional economic growth; Jin, et al., "Regional Decentralization and Fiscal Incentives," 1719–1742; Lin and Liu, "Fiscal Decentralization," 1–21.
84. Naughton, *Rise of China's Industrial Policy*, 26.
85. Some have argued that the Chinese system may have encouraged excessive experimentation; Wang and Yang, "Policy Experimentation in China." However, it was surely an improvement on the status quo and an enabler of many reforms.
86. Cai and Treisman, for example, have argued that political centralization was essential to China's growth; Cai and Treisman, "Did Government Decentralization Cause?," 505–535. What is certainly true is that the centre had to be strong enough to discipline and reward regional elites; see Blanchard and Shleifer, "Federalism With and Without Political Centralization," 171–179.
87. Milanovic, *Capitalism, Alone*, 5.
88. On the link between economic growth and promotion, see Yao and Zhang, "Subnational leaders and Economic Growth," 405–436; Li and Zhou, "Political Turnover and Economic Performance," 1743–1762.
89. China's economic miracle has to be explained by the growth-enhancing policies adopted by the central government; see Cai and Treisman, "Did Government Decentralization Cause?," 505–535.
90. Cited in Yao, "Chinese Growth Miracle," 943–1031.
91. On China's technology imports strategy, see Naughton, *Rise of China's Industrial Policy*; Li, "Study of the 1978 State Council Conference." See also Ho, "Technology Transfer to China," 85–106.
92. On migration to Hong Kong, see Liu, "Betting Life to Escape to Hong Kong," 38. See also Du, *Shenzhen Experiment*, 51–52.
93. Vogel, *Deng Xiaoping*, 397.
94. On the Guangdong experiment, see Vogel, *Deng Xiaoping*, chapter 14.
95. Cited in Du, *Shenzhen Experiment*, 87.
96. On the rise of Shenzhen, see Du, *Shenzhen Experiment*.
97. On Deng's intellectual flexibility, see Vogel, *Deng Xiaoping*, 392.
98. On tech zones boosting growth, see Alder, et al., "Economic Reforms and Industrial Policy," 305–349.

Chapter 11

1. Friedman, *Capitalism and Freedom*, 6.
2. PBS, "Frontline: Losing the War with Japan," Season 1991, Episode 6, aired 1991.
3. Vogel, *Japan as Number One*.
4. D.E. Sanger, 1988, "A High-Tech Lead in Danger," *New York Times*, December 18.
5. As Jorgenson and Nomura writes, "The Japanese computer industry led its US counterpart until the early 1990s, when US TFP growth accelerated sharply." Jorgenson and Nomura, "Industry Origins," 315–341.
6. On Steve Jobs, see Isaacson, *Steve Jobs*.
7. On the ENIAC, see Gordon, *Rise and Fall of American Growth*, 448.
8. Cited in Ridley, *How Innovation Works*, 203.
9. On Wiener and the computer, see Waldrop, *Dream Machine*.
10. Nordhaus, "Two Centuries of Productivity Growth," 128–159.
11. Friedrich, "Computer Moves In," *Time*, January 3, 1983, 15. Cited in Frey, *Technology Trap*, 404.
12. Rajan and Wulf, "Flattening Firm," 759–773.
13. On the link between decentralization and ICT, see Caroli and Van Reenen, "Skill-Biased Organizational Change?," 1449–1492; Bresnahan, et al., "Information Technology," 339–376. On how delegation becomes more attractive closer to the technological frontier, see Acemoglu, et al., "Distance to Frontier," 37–74.
14. For a survey, see also Brynjolfsson and Yang, "Information Technology and Productivity," 179–214.
15. These management practices include "Managing human capital," "Rewarding high performance," "Removing poor performers," and "Promoting high performers." Bloom, et al., "Americans Do IT Better," 167–201. Good management, in turn, thrives in competitive environments, where labour markets are flexible and hereditary family firms are few. On competition and family firms, see Bloom and Van Reenen, "Measuring and Explaining," 1351–1408. On labour market regulation, see Bloom, et al., "Management Practices," 12–33.
16. This section draws heavily on Saxenian, *Regional Advantage*.
17. Between 1941 and 1948, the state of Massachusetts received 32 percent of all OSRD contracts, followed by California (21 percent) and New York (20 percent). Among the top ten companies receiving OSRD contracts not a single one was located in California; see Gross and Sampat, "Inventing the Endless Frontier," table 2.
18. The universities in California receiving the bulk of OSRD contracts were not in the Bay Area, but in Los Angeles, see Gross and Sampat, "Inventing the Endless Frontier," table 2. On funding for Boston universities, see also Rosegrant and Lampe, *Route 128*, 80.
19. Bylinsky, *Innovation Millionaires*. In the early 1950s, the Department of Defense predominantly relied on sole-source contracts, favoring a select group of well-connected companies. However, by the 1960s, the department had shifted toward competitive bidding, which led to a diversification of the defense industry. This transition was also marked by a significant relocation of contracts to California, especially as the Korean War escalated and the American war effort demanded ships and aircraft from the region. However, the majority of contracts were concentrated in Los Angeles, not in the Valley. In 1959, Los Angeles secured 61 percent of these contracts, while Santa Clara received only 13 percent. See Clayton, "Defense Spending," 280–293, Table 3.
20. On the McNamara Depression, see Lécuyer, *Making Silicon Valley*, 171–172, 283.
21. On defense jobs, see Saxenian, *Regional Advantage*, 17.
22. On how Silicon Valley firms adjusted, see Nicholas, *VC*, 190.

23. Between 1951 and 1968, new firms, like Fairchild, were responsible for most product innovations in semiconductors. Despite receiving only 22 percent of government R&D funding in 1959 (compared to the 78 percent allocated to the nine largest incumbents), these new firms astonishingly accounted for 66 percent of the innovations. That said, government procurement contracts hovered between one-quarter and one-half of all sales during the 1950s and 1960s, providing stable demand; Tilton, *International Diffusion of Technology*, tables 4.3, 4.7, 4.10. We lack government procurement data for semiconductors by company, but as Tilton points out, William Shockley developed the first transistor with Bell Lab's own funds, and Texas Instruments only gained a government contract with the Air Force *after* it achieved a working model of an integrated circuit. On the role of military funding, see also Mowery and Rosenberg, *Paths of Innovation*, chapter 6; Kleiman, "Integrated Circuit Industry," 173–174.

24. For Nelson quote, see Lécuyer, "Silicon for Industry," 186; and the role of VC funding, see Nicholas, *VC*.

25. On MIT funding, see Waldrop, *Dream Machine*, 18.

26. Saxenian, *Regional Advantage*, 12.

27. The term was coined by the journalist Don Hoefler after the main ingredient in the semiconductor.

28. Saxenian, *Regional Advantage*, 50.

29. T. Wolfe, 1983, "The Tinkerings of Robert Noyce," *Esquire*, December 1.

30. On firm size and the absence of hierarchical management, see Nicholas and Lee, "Origins and Development of Silicon Valley."

31. Quoted in R. Wolf, 1992, "Valley Execs Take Stock—and Moderate Salaries," *San Jose Mercury News*, June 29.

32. Lécuyer, *Making Silicon Valley*, 164.

33. William Foster interview, Jan. 9, 1991, in Saxenian, *Regional Advantage*, 76.

34. Saxenian, *Regional Advantage*, 76.

35. Wilson, et al., *Innovation, Competition, and Government Policy*, 55. Cited in Saxenian, *Regional Advantage*, 187.

36. Wozniak, "Homebrew."

37. Quote from Saxenian, *Regional Advantage*, 63.

38. On worker mobility, see Fallick, et al., "Job-Hopping in Silicon Valley," 472–481.

39. A year later Jerry Sanders III followed in Moore's and Noyce's footsteps, leaving Fairchild to launch Advanced Micro Devices (AMD).

40. On semiconductor companies established, see Nicholas and Lee, "Origins and Development of Silicon Valley."

41. On parallels with Detroit, see Klepper, "Silicon Valley," 79–115.

42. In the three decades following the inception of the industry, some hundred semiconductor companies sprang up, just like over a hundred auto makers had in the Motor City during the first three decades of the car industry.

43. Klepper, "Origin and Growth of Industry Clusters," 15–32.

44. Berger and Frey, "Regional Technological Dynamism," 655–668. See also Marx, et al., "Mobility," 875–889.

45. Saxenian, *Regional Advantage*, 89.

46. On the quality of Japanese goods, see Stowsky, "Weakest Link."

47. Hass, "Applying the Lessons," 40–41.

48. On market shares, see Lindert, "Twentieth-Century Foreign Trade," 448.

49. On how American antitrust in the postwar era promoted diversification rather than consolidation, see Langlois, *Corporation and the Twentieth Century*, chapter 6.

50. On flexible production, see Milgrom and Roberts, "Economics of Modern Manufacturing," 511–528. On just-in-time, see Abegglen and Stalk, *Japanese Corporation*. On productivity, see Lindert, "Twentieth-Century Foreign Trade," 432, 435.

51. On examples of Japan commercializing Western technologies, see Gorodnichenko and Roland, "Culture, Institutions, and the Wealth of Nations," 402–416.

52. Mansfield, "Speed and Cost of Industrial Innovation," 1157–1279.

53. Cited in Mansfield, "Speed and Cost of Industrial Innovation," 1157. The eminent Regis McKenna made a similar observation: "Mature markets are those that give advantages to our Japanese competitors because of the latter's greater skills in, and attention to, marketing and manufacturing. Product standardization, process innovation, high-quality production, and incremental improvements are all Japanese strengths." Cited in Norton, "Industrial Policy and American Renewal," 1–40.

54. Chandler, *Scale and Scope*, 612.

55. On the importance of small firms in computers and semiconductors, see Flamm, *Creating the Computer*; Malerba, *Semiconductor Business*; Tilton, *International Diffusion of Technology*; Mowery, "Boundaries of the US Firm," 147–182. For an account emphasizing the role of small companies in biotech, see Pisano, et al., "Joint Ventures and Collaboration."

56. Christensen, *Innovator's Dilemma*, chapter 1.

57. Saxenian, *Regional Advantage*, 100.

58. On Japanese antitrust practices, see Porter and Sakakibara, "Competition in Japan," 27–50.

59. On cases filed, see First, "Antitrust Enforcement in Japan," 137–182; Porter and Sakakibara, "Competition in Japan," 27–50. On impacts on employment and business formation, Babina, et al., "Antitrust Enforcement Increases Economic Activity."

60. In 1953, John W. Backus had submitted a proposal to his IBM superiors to develop a better assembly language for programming their IBM 704 mainframe computer. The result was FORTRAN—a high-level language that could be used for accounting and other business applications. Subsequent efforts to develop a more general language yielded some advances, like COBOL, but these programming languages still required substantial investments in training for buyers of mainframe computers. Thus, when IBM introduced the 1401 model in 1960, which was a less expensive general-purpose machine designed to serve the needs of the medium size user, it "sold with a new high-level software language RPG, whose operations resembled those of punched card systems, and thus could be used by individuals without costly retraining in the more abstract FORTRAN and COBOL languages." Still, while software existed, there was no software industry. For companies buying mainframe computers, it was part of the package. See Steinmueller, "U.S. Software Industry."

61. For an overview of this debate, see Steinmueller, "U.S. Software Industry." For a careful account based on legal records, see Fisher, *IBM and the U.S. Data Processing Industry*.

62. "US vs. IBM," 1981, *New York Times*, February 15. It concluded on January 8, 1982, when William Baxter, the Assistant Attorney General overseeing the Antitrust Division of the Department of Justice at the time, dismissed the case.

63. Steinmueller, "U.S. Software Industry." This point is also made by Mowery and Rosenberg, *Paths of Innovation*.

64. On emerging software companies, see Mowery and Rosenberg, *Paths of Innovation*.

65. On the history of the privatization of the internet and the importance of the AT&T breakup, see Greenstein, *How the Internet Became Commercial*.

66. Mowery and Rosenberg, *Paths of Innovation*. Gordon agrees with this assessment: "progress started with the 1983 breakup of the Bell Telephone monopoly into nonoverlapping regional monopolies. After a series of mergers, landline service was provided primarily by a new

version of AT&T and by Verizon, soon to be joined by major cable television companies, such as Comcast and Time-Warner, that offered landline phone service as part of their cable TV and Internet packages." Gordon, *Rise and Fall of American Growth*, 577.

67. On anticompetitive practices, see Lawrence, "Efficient or Exclusionist?," 311–330. There is also empirical evidence that the keiretsu erected considerable barriers to trade; see Fung, "Characteristics of Japanese Industrial Groups," 137–164.

68. Studwell, *How Asia Works*, 121.

69. On software patents, see Arora, et al., "Going Soft," 757–775.

70. Kang, *Crony Capitalism*, 10. On the role of state cohesion in compelling corporates to fall in line with national objectives, see also Kohli, *State-Directed Development*.

71. Chang and Shin, "Evaluating the Post-Crisis Corporate Restructuring," 301, 304.

72. Aghion, et al., "Chaebols," 593–626. On antitrust penalties, see Shin, "Competition Law and Policy."

73. On Japan, Deng, and Chinese economic policy, see Vogel, *Deng Xiaoping*, 462–464.

74. On Chinese views on the Japanese model, see Heilmann and Shih, "Rise of Industrial Policy," 5.

75. On the influence of Japanese economists, see Heilmann and Shih, "Rise of Industrial Policy," 5.

76. On the contrasts between Beijing, Shanghai, and Guangdong, see Naughton, "Emergence of the China Circle," 27.

77. Legend was originally a spin-off from the Chinese Academy of Science and Great Wall was set up within the Ministry of Electronics.

78. The engine of Chinese growth decisively shifted toward the south in the process. In 1985, the Guangdong and Fujian provinces accounted for a mere 12 percent of electronics value added in the country. By 1997, it had surged to 31 percent. The main reason was foreign investment, which was more prominent in electronics than in other mainland industries. This shift reflects the failure of the CCP to foster indigenous technological capabilities and build national champions through state-owned enterprises in the Beijing area; see Naughton, "Emergence of the China Circle," 28.

79. On industrial policy, see Jung, "Retreat of the State?," 105–125.

80. US–China Business Council, "USCBC 2012." Cited in Blustein, *Schism*.

81. Hout and Ghemawat, "China vs the World," 94–103.

82. VerWey, "Chinese Semiconductor Industrial Policy."

83. On SOEs vs. hybrid companies, see Wei, et al., "From 'Made in China,'" 49–70.

84. Kerr, "Ethnic Scientific Communities," 518–537, 519.

85. On the importance of hybrid companies, see Fuller, *Paper Tigers, Hidden Dragons*.

86. VerWey, "Chinese Semiconductor Industrial Policy."

87. Miller, *Chip War*, chapters 12 and 29.

88. Naughton, "Emergence of the China Circle," 22.

89. Between 1985 and 1995, Hong Kong and Taiwan lost almost a million manufacturing jobs between them, while the Guangdong and Fujian provinces added 4.5 million manufacturing jobs, see Naughton, "Emergence of the China Circle," 13.

90. Ferguson and Schularick, "Chimerica," 215–239.

91. On the transformation of the Pearl River delta, see Blustein, *Schism*.

92. On the Computer Revolution and convergence, see the seminal account of Baldwin, *Great Convergence*.

93. On Motorola, see Jiang, *FDI in China*, 29.

94. On Apple, see P. McGee, 2023, "How Apple Tied Its Fortunes to China," *Financial Times*, January 17; DeLong, *Slouching Towards Utopia*, 496.

Chapter 12

1. Cited in Boettke and Candela, "On the Feasibility of Technosocialism," 44–54, 44.
2. Lee, *AI Superpowers*; G. Allison and E. Schmidt, 2020, "Is China Beating America to AI Supremacy?," *The National Interest*, December 22.
3. Cowen, *Great Stagnation*; Bloom, et al., "Are Ideas Getting Harder to Find?," 1104–1144; Gordon, *Rise and Fall of American Growth*. On American productivity decline, see Byrne, et al., "Does the United States?," 109–182; Goldin, et al., "Why Is Productivity Slowing Down?," 196–268. On the decline of American science and innovation, see also Park, et al., "Papers and Patents," 138–144.
4. On negative productivity in China, see Wei, et al., "From 'Made in China,'" 49–70, figure 1. For more optimistic estimates, see Brandt, et al., "China's Productivity Slowdown."
5. On the productivity comparison with other East Asian economies, see Rajah and Leng, "Revising Down the Rise of China," figure 7.
6. On the geography of Chinese technology industries, see Naughton, *Chinese Economy*, 552.
7. On the geography of Chinese investment, see Brandt and Rawski, "China's Great Boom," 812. On FDI, see Jiang, *FDI in China*, 82.
8. On Foxconn, see Freeman, *Behemoth*, 272.
9. Productivity in SOEs at the time was by some estimates around half of that in private firms; see Jefferson and Rawski, "Enterprise Reform in Chinese Industry," 47–70.
10. Slogan cited in Blustein, *Schism*.
11. On privatization and productivity, see Lardy, *Markets over Mao*.
12. On China's welfare state, see Naughton, "Is China Socialist?," 3–24.
13. On jobs shredded, see Naughton, *Chinese Economy*, 179.
14. Q. W. Zhu, 2001, "Domestic Market Fuels Growth," *China Daily*, August 6, 4.
15. On the expansion of private sector employment, see Brandt and Rawski, "China's Great Boom," 810-11.
16. Lee, *Against the Law*, 8–9.
17. Unsurprisingly, wage inequality rose faster in the private sector than among SOEs; Ding, et al., "Transition and Inequality." On winners and losers, see Milanovic, *Capitalism, Alone*, 101–103.
18. Cited in Arrighi, *Adam Smith in Beijing*, 15.
19. For a comparison of U.S. and Chinese inequality as well as the factors underpinning it, see Xie and Zhou, "Income Inequality in Today's China," 6928–6933.
20. On internal migration, see Brandt and Rawski, "China's Great Boom," 810.
21. On Chinese income comparisons, see B. Milanovic, 2021, "China's Inequality Will Lead It to a Stark Choice," *Foreign Affairs*, February 11.
22. On Chinese wealth, see Piketty, et al., "Capital Accumulation," 2469–2496.
23. On the growing importance of capital income in Chinese inequality, see Chi, "Capital Income and Income Inequality," 228–239.
24. On Chinese social mobility, see Yang, et al., "From Workers to Capitalists," 478–513.
25. Pei, *China's Trapped Transition*; Pei, *China's Crony Capitalism*.
26. Milanovic, *Capitalism, Alone*, 109.
27. Ravallion and Chen, "Is that Really a Kuznets Curve?."
28. Corruption, in other words, is built into the system.
29. Vito Tanzi cited in Milanovic, *Capitalism, Alone*, 107.
30. B. Milanovic, "China's Inequality Will Lead It to a Stark Choice," *Foreign Affairs*, February 11, 2021. Ang aptly calls this China's Gilded Age; Ang, *China's Gilded Age*.
31. Milanovic, "China's Inequality Will Lead It to a Stark Choice,"

32. Cited in Blustein, *Schism*. See also R. Liao, 2017, "Judicial Reform in China," *Foreign Affairs*, February 2.
33. Figures on registered lawyers are from May 2009.
34. McGregor, *The Party*, 59.
35. Cited in McGregor, *The Party*, 56.
36. On the structure of policy making in China, Lieberthal and Oksenberg, *Policy Making in China*. On the division of labour, see Dickson, *Party and the People*, 28–30.
37. This section draws heavily on Zhang, *Chinese Antitrust Exceptionalism*.
38. Blustein, *Schism*, 199.
39. Zhang, *Chinese Antitrust Exceptionalism*, 29–32.
40. In fact, even the courts favour Chinese companies. In cases heard in Chinese IP courts, for example, domestic plaintiffs are substantially more likely to receive favourable judgments; Long and Wang, "Judicial Local Protectionism in China," 48–59.
41. On the China Telecom case, see Zhang, *Chinese Antitrust Exceptionalism*, 55.
42. On SAIC report, see Zhang, *Chinese Antitrust Exceptionalism*, 87. On the White Paper, see Z. Huage, 2015, "The Chinese Government Has Erased a Damning Report on Alibaba, But You Can Read It," *Quartz*, January 29.
43. Zhai, "Alibaba."
44. Cited in McGregor, *The Party*, 37.
45. To borrow Lardy's words, as some companies grew very rapidly, there was a fear that entrepreneurs might "organize outside of the party, perhaps by aligning with pro-democracy political activists, as appeared to be the case in 1989." Lardy, *Markets over Mao*, 120.
46. On co-opting the capitalists, see Dickson, *Wealth into Power*, chapter 3.
47. On entrepreneurs becoming Party members, see Dickson, *Wealth into Power*, 70.
48. However, while party membership grew at almost 3 percent annually under Hu Jintao, it has only grown by 1 percent per year under Xi; Dickson, *Party and the People*, 33–35.
49. *The Economist*, 2021, "The Party Is Eager to Expand Its Influence Within Business," June 26.
50. Blustein, *Schism*, 202.
51. On golden shares, see R. McMorrow, Q. Liu, and C. Leng, 2023, "China moves to take 'golden shares' in Alibaba and Tencent units," *Financial Times*, January 13.
52. On politically connected owners, see Bai, et al., "Special Deals," table 2.
53. An English translation of Document 9 is available here: https://www.chinafile.com/document-9-chinafile-translation. Accessed April 5, 2022.
54. On online censorship, see Roberts, *Censored*; Dickson, *Dictator's Dilemma*.
55. Even VPNs, which permitted access to these websites in the past, are becoming much more heavily restricted.
56. For data on the number of Chinese internet users, see https://ourworldindata.org/internet. Accessed December 12, 2024.
57. Goldsmith and Wu, *Who Controls the Internet?*, 93.
58. On Cisco, see Griffiths, *Great Firewall of China*, 76–77.
59. On Social media censorship, see King, et al., "Censorship in China," 326–343.
60. On the code name for Xi, see Dickson, *Party and the People*, 155. On IJOP, see Dickson, *Party and the People*, 141–142. According to the *New York Times*, Chinese scientists are even in the process of developing technology capable of reconstructing human faces based on DNA samples; see S. L. Wee and P. Mozur, 2019, "China Uses DNA to Map Faces, with Help from the West," *New York Times*, December 10.
61. Businesses similarly receive a social credit score which customers can look up before using their services.
62. Dickson, *Party and the People*, 143.

63. Chua, et al., "Mapping Cultural Tightness," 6720–6725.

64. On Chinese restrictions on books and conference participation, see *The Economist*, 2020, "MBAs with Chinese Characteristics," February 15. On the importance of information for innovation, see Berkes and Nencka, "Knowledge Access."

65. Figure on publications cited in E. Olcott, C. Cookson, and A. Smith, 2023, "China's Fake Science Industry: How 'Paper Mills' Threaten Progress," *Financial Times*, March 28. For further research on this point, see Xie and Freeman, "Contribution of Chinese Diaspora."; Xie and Freeman, "Creating and Connecting." On home bias in Chinese citations, see Qiu, et al., "Paper Tiger?"

66. On the Schwarzman College at Tsinghua University, see Kirby, *Empires of Ideas*, 297–300.

67. Although the Biden administration scrapped Trump's China Initiative, concerns about national security have persisted, as is evident from the 2022 CHIPS and Science Act, designed to counter China's influence.

68. On the reversal in U.S–China scientific collaboration, see Xie and Freeman, "Creating and Connecting," figure 5.

69. On political interference in education, see Kirby, *Empires of Ideas*.

70. To paraphrase Mark Wu, SASAC is the equivalent to a would-be U.S. government agency controlling General Electric, General Motors, Ford, Boeing, U.S. Steel, DuPont, AT&T, Verizon, Honeywell, and United Technologies, behaving like an activist private equity fund rather than a passive shareholder, where the performance metric is not just profit, but the Chinese state's interest more broadly; Wu, "China, Inc.," 261.

71. Naughton, *Rise of China's Industrial Policy*. On China promoting indigenous innovation, see also Blustein, *Schism*.

72. Brandt and Rawski, "China's Great Boom," 817. On the magnitude of Chinese industrial policy spending, see DiPippo, et al., "Red Ink."

73. On China and leapfrogging, see Naughton, *Rise of China's Industrial Policy*.

74. As Naughton notes, "the overall impact of industrial policies still favors SOEs. This is because SOEs are more easily assigned "missions" and given resources in pursuit of national goals." Naughton, *Rise of China's Industrial Policy*, 93.

75. For empirical evidence on firms disliking investors with government ties, see Colonnelli, et al., "Investing with the Government."

76. For an overview of productivity in SOEs, see Wei, et al., "From 'Made in China,'" 49–70.

77. On China's leading companies being private, see Lardy, *Markets over Mao*, chapter 4.

78. Also, of China's vast Industrial Guidance Funds (IGFs), only 4 percent target SMEs; Naughton, *Rise of China's Industrial Policy*, figure 5.1.

79. On the role of political connections for entrepreneurship in China, see McNally, et al., "Entrepreneurship and Political Guanxi Networks"; McNally, "China's Changing Guanxi Capitalism," 1–29.

80. Cerdeiro and Ruane, "China's Declining Business Dynamism."

81. As one recent survey of the literature concludes, "China scholars almost unanimously agree that policymaking and implementation saw a tangible re-centralization under the Xi Jinping administration after 2013." Ahlers and Schubert, "Nothing New," 2150017.

82. Dickson, *Party and the People*, 98.

83. On low quality patents, see Long and Wang, "Evaluating Patent Promotion."

84. Data on royalties from the World Bank: https://data.worldbank.org/indicator/BX.GSR.ROYL.CD?end=2021&locations=US-CN&start=199. Accessed August 19, 2024. On trends in royalty payments, see Peake and Santacreu, "China's Innovation."

85. N. Grünberg and K. Drinhausen, 2019, "The Party Leads on Everything," *MERICS China Monitor*, September 24, 10; cited in Brandt and Rawski, "China's Great Boom," 821.

86. B. Orr, 2023, "Record Numbers Sit for China Civil Service Exam, Hoping for Job Security," *Reuters*, November 27, www.reuters.com/world/china/record-numbers-sit-china-civil-service-exam-hoping-job-security-2023-11-27/.

87. Besley and Kudamatsu, "Making Autocracy Work," 452–510. On the role of political insiders in selecting leaders, see Bueno de Mesquita et al., *The Logic of Political Survival*.

88. Wong, *Party of One*.

89. Beraja, et al., "AI-tocracy," 1349–1402.

90. Beraja, et al., "Data-Intensive Innovation."

91. Lee, *AI Superpowers*. However, as AI expert Jeffery Ding points out, "Western observers consistently overinflate Chinese AI capabilities." J. Ding, 2019, "ChinAI #48: Year 1 of ChinAI," *ChinAI Newsletter*, April 1, https://chinai.substack.com/p/chinai-48-year-1-of-chinai?s=r. For example, one Alibaba employee reports that its "AI labs have already fizzled out." J. Ding, 2021, "ChinAI #126: Alibaba's AI Lab Fizzles Out," *ChinAI Newsletter*, January 11, https://chinai.substack.com/p/chinai-126-alibabas-ai-lab-fizzles?s=r.

92. On performance comparisons between gasoline, steam, and electric cars, as well as the role of the electric grid, see Taalbi and Nielsen, "Role of Energy Infrastructure," 970–976.

93. On the wrong kind of AI, see Acemoglu and Restrepo, "Wrong Kind of AI?," 25–35; Johnson and Acemoglu, *Power and Progress*.

94. On scaling running into diminishing returns, see Udandarao, et al., "No 'Zero-Shot.'"

95. AlphaFold was designed with a specific purpose in mind, lacking versatility for broader applications.

96. On headwinds for progress in LLMs, see Frey and Osborne, "Generative AI," 1–17. On model failure, see Shumailov, et al., "Curse of Recursion."

97. A. Svetkin, 2023, "ChatGPT-4 Solves 85% of Leetcode Easy Problems," *Hackernoon*, June 21, https://hackernoon.com/chatgpt-4-solves-85percent-of-leetcode-easy-problems. See also Roberts, et al., "Data Contamination."

98. Berglund, et al., "Reversal Curse."

99. R. Waters, 2023, "Man Beats Machine at Go in Human Victory over AI," *Financial Times*, February 17.

100. On AI and creativity, see Frey and Osborne, "Generative AI," 1–17.

101. C. B. Frey and M. Osborne, 2020, "China Won't Win the Race for AI Dominance," *Foreign Affairs*, June 19.

102. On LLMs, see R. McMorrow and T. Hu, 2024, "China Deploys Censors to Create Socialist AI," *Financial Times*, July 17.

103. On autonomous vehicles, see Kennedy, "China's Uneven High-Tech Drive." See also Frey, "How Culture Gives the US," 55–61.

104. Babina, et al., "Firm Investments in Artificial Intelligence."

105. L. Yuan, 2021, "In China, Tesla Is a Catfish, and Turns Auto Companies Into Sharks," *The New York Times*, November 30.

106. On high-speed rail, see Blustein, *Schism*, 130–132.

107. On the share of the technology invented abroad, see J. Anderlini and M. Dickie, 2010, "China: A Future on Track," *Financial Times*, September 24.

108. Chan, "Fast Track."

109. Tsebelis, *Veto Players*.

110. On the institutional hurdles to American infrastructure development, see F. Fukuyama, 2016, "Too Much Law and Too Little Infrastructure," *The American Interest*, November 8.

111. Allison, *Destined for War*, 25.

112. On airport comparison, see Jin, *New China Playbook*, 206.

113. On railway organization, see Chan, "Fast Track."

114. Q. Liu, K. Inagaki, and A. Gross, 2023, "China Fears Japan's Chipmaking Curbs Go Further Than US Restrictions," *Financial Times*, May 23.

115. Z. Wang, 2025, "Official Provincial Commentary on DeepSeek," Pekingnology, January 29, https://www.pekingnology.com/p/official-provincial-commentary-on.

116. Some early disputes over watermills often pitted manufacturers against farmers, as they began to operate on the same rivers, interfering with each other's water resources. In these cases, governments responded by reallocating property rights through statutes known as Mill Acts, which transferred powers of eminent domain to manufacturers, often without adequate compensation for farmers. But as Lamoreaux writes, "the courts gradually felt their way toward a new set of rules that struck a balance between the efficiency gains from technological innovation and the need to provide mill owners with greater security for their investments." Lamoreaux, "Mystery of Property Rights," 275–306.

117. Nonnenmacher, "State Promotion and Regulation," 19–36.

118. On Morse, see Nonnenmacher, "State Promotion and Regulation," 19–36.

119. On the importance of flexibility in times of technological change, see also Aghion, et al., *Power of Creative Destruction*.

120. Scheiber, "Property Law," 23.

121. Lamoreaux, "Mystery of Property Rights," 275–306.

122. On rising concentration, see Grullon, et al., "US Industries," 697–743; Autor, et al., "Fall of the Labor Share," 645–709. Engineering and computer science positions show the highest adoption rates of non-competes at 38 and 36 percent respectively, see Rothstein and Starr, "Noncompete Agreements, Bargaining, and Wages," https://www.bls.gov/opub/mlr/2022/article/noncompete-agreements-bargaining-and-wages-evidence-from-the-national-longitudinal-survey-of-youth-1997.htm.

123. On declining dynamism, see Decker, et al., "Declining Business Dynamism," 203–207; Haltiwanger, et al., "Top Ten Signs,"; Decker, et al., "Declining Dynamism, Allocative Efficiency, and the Productivity Slowdown," 322–326. Guzman and Stern argue that the quality-adjusted decline in dynamism is less pronounced, but even so, following an increase in the 1990s, they document a sharp decline in the 2000s; Guzman and Stern, "State of American Entrepreneurship," 212–243.

124. On start-ups and new research, see Kolev, et al., "Of Academics and Creative Destruction."

125. On reshuffling, see Philippon, "Case for Free Markets," 707–719.

126. Gutiérrez and Philippon, "Failure of Free Entry."

127. On the size and power of large corporations relative to nations, see Zingales, "Towards a Political Theory," 113–130.

128. For a discussion of *Buckley v. Valeo* and its effects on lobbying, see Kruse and Zelizer, *Fault Lines*.

129. On donations, see Rockey and Zakir, "Power and the Money."

130. On lobbying expenditure, see Philippon, *Great Reversal*, figure 9.1.

131. On four largest companies, see Philippon, *Great Reversal*, 167–168.

132. Wu, *Curse of Bigness*.

133. On the decline in enforcement, see Gutiérrez and Philippon, "How European Markets Became Free." For further discussion of lobbying as the driver behind the decline in antitrust enforcement, see Philippon, *Great Reversal*, 173; Lancieri, et al., "Political Economy of the Decline."

134. On Google meetings at the White House, see the Google Transparency Project at http://googletransparencyproject.org/articles/googles-white-house-meetings. Accessed June 12, 2022.

135. This document is available via the *Wall Street Journal* website at https://graphics.wsj.com/google-ftc-report/img/ftc-ocr-watermark.pdf. Accessed June 12, 2022. See also Zingales, "Towards a Political Theory," 113–130.

136. On cases filed, see Grullon, et al., "US Industries," 697–743.
137. Zingales, "Towards a Political Theory," 113–130.
138. On the merger effect on lobbying, see Cowgill, et al., "Political Power and Market Power."
139. On killer acquisitions, see Cunningham, et al., "Killer Acquisitions," 649–702.
140. Stigler, "Theory of Economic Regulation," 3–21.
141. Having served as chairman at the FCC in the early 2000s, Michael Powell went on to become CEO of the National Cable and Telecommunications Association (NCTA), just like FCC commissioner Meredith Baker left for a top lobbying job at Comcast. For examples on the revolving door, see Philippon, *Great Reversal*, 200.
142. On growing salary differentials, see Lancieri, et al., "Political Economy of the Decline."
143. On patent examiners, see Tabakovic and Wollmann, "From Revolving Doors."
144. M. Murgia and R. Waters, 2005, "How Google Lost Ground in the AI Race," *Financial Times*, April 5.
145. For employment figures, see Cowen, "AI Could Spell the End."
146. On the shift toward industry, see Ahmed, et al., "Growing Influence of Industry," 884–886.
147. On the narrowing down on deep learning, see Klinger, et al., "Narrowing of AI Research?" On the market concentration, see Korinek and Vipra, "Concentrating Intelligence," 225–256.
148. These scores as well as the ARC competition itself have been established by computer scientist François Chollet.
149. On process R&D being more tightly correlated with firm size relative to product R&D, see Cohen and Klepper, "Reprise of Size and R & D," 925–951. On the decline in product introduction with growing firm size, see Argente, et al., "Patents to Products," figure 4. The picture becomes even more dramatic when products are quality adjusted. As Argente, et al. note: "The fact that the quality-adjusted introduction rate declines more steeply than the simple product introduction rate indicates that, on average, new products introduced by larger firms are more likely to represent incremental improvements over existing products and are thus less novel."
150. On Daedalus, see Brynjolfsson, "Turing Trap," 272–287.
151. Acemoglu, "Simple Macroeconomics of AI."
152. Science and technology tend to feed off each other, creating a virtuous cycle, see Mokyr, "Building Taller Ladders," 1–4.
153. Bloom, et al., "Are Ideas Getting Harder to Find?" On the decline in breakthrough innovation, see Park, et al., "Papers and Patents," 138–144.
154. Kolev, et al., "Of Academics and Creative Destruction."
155. FDA deregulation events boosted both entry and innovation, see Rogers, "Regulating the Innovators."
156. Cited in J. Schwartz, 1996, "Restricting the Internet Is Not the Way to Stem the Tide of Terror," *The Washington Post*, August 5.
157. Broad, "AT&T," 990–991.
158. Black, *IBM and the Holocaust*.

Chapter 13

1. Jacobs, *Economy of Cities*, 248–249.
2. While the post-pandemic economy has experienced an increase in new business formation, this has been seemingly driven by temporary factors, like the shift from downtown areas

to suburbs. On business formation, see Decker and Haltiwanger, "High Tech Business Entry"; Decker and Haltiwanger, "Business Entry and Exit."

3. On housing, see Rogoff and Yang, "Peak China Housing."

4. On fewer antitrust cases won by the Buden administration in percentage terms, see S. Indap, 2024, "Wall Street Wants Harris to Turn the Antitrust Tide," *Financial Times*, July 28. Strong antitrust enforcement under the Biden administration might also partly explain why many business leaders have donated to the Trump campaign, see A. Rogers, T. Kinder, H. Murphy, and G. Hammond, 2024, "Silicon Valley's Tech Titans Line Up to Donate to Donald Trump," *Financial Times*, July 16.

5. On this point, see C. B. Frey, 2024, "The US Should Beware of Regulation as Retribution," *Financial Times*, August 23.

6. On Chinese EVs, see M. Draghi, 2024, "The Future of European Competitiveness: In-Depth Analysis and Recommendations," European Commission, https://commission.europa.eu/topics/strengthening-european-competitiveness/eu-competitiveness-looking-ahead_en. Accessed November 30, 2024.

7. On the GDPR, see Peukert, et al., "Regulatory Spillovers and Data Governance"; Johnson, et al., "Privacy and Market Concentration"; Frey and Presidente, "Privacy Regulation and Firm Performance."

8. On the EU AI Act, see L. Garicano, 2024, "The Strange Kafka World of the EU AI Act: The Regulation Needs Repealing," Silicon Continent, October 30, https://www.siliconcontinent.com/p/the-strange-kafka-world-of-the-eu. Accessed November 30, 2024.

9. International Monetary Fund, Europe's Declining Productivity Growth.

10. On facial recognition AI exports, see Beraja, et al., "Exporting the Surveillance State."

11. On the link between skills and managerial capitalism, see Engbom, et al., "Economic Development According to Chandler."

12. Cox, et al., "Violence Trap," 3–19. See also North, et al., *Shadow of Violence*.

13. Ahrens, "The Importance of Being European," 63–78.

14. Carlin, et al., "Soviet Power Plus Electrification," 116–147.

15. Xue, "Autocratic Rule and Social Capital."

16. Arendt, *Origins of Totalitarianism*, 474.

17. Cited in Kirby, *Empires of Ideas*, 24.

18. On Nanjing University, see Kirby, *Empires of Ideas*, 326.

Epilogue

1. Scott, *Seeing Like a State*, 357.

2. On global growth, see McCloskey, "The Great Enrichment," 583–598.

3. Brynjolfsson, et al., "Using Massive Online Choice Experiments," 7250–7255.

4. On growth and emissions decoupling, see H. Ritchie, 2021, "Many Countries Have Decoupled Economic Growth from CO_2 Emissions, Even if We Take Offshored Production into Account," *Our World in Data*, December 1, https://ourworldindata.org/co2-gdp-decoupling; McAfee, *More from Less*.

5. On the persistent link between income and well-being, see Stevenson and Wolfers, "Subjective Well-Being and Income," 598–604.

6. F. Maglione and P. Cachero, 2023, "Wealthy Parents are Spending $1.2m to Get Kids into Top Unis," *Financial Review*, September 29.

7. On sensory input relative to language input as well as AI prediction on video, see Y. Lecun, 2024, "Meta AI, Open Source, Limits of LLMs, AGI & the Future of AI," Lex Fridman Podcast #416.

8. On uncertainty and profit, see Knight, *Risk, Uncertainty and Profit*.

9. LeConte, "Problem of a Flying Machine," 69–77.
10. On LLMs, Galileo and the Wright Brothers, see Felin and Holweg, "Theory Is All You Need."
11. H. Mance, 2024, "AI Keeps Going Wrong. What If It Can't Be Fixed?," *Financial Times*, April 6.
12. Market Cap data from https://companiesmarketcap.com. Taken on March 26, 2024. Calculations exclude former state-owned, privatized companies, and spin-offs of major companies.
13. On Cardwell's Law, see Mokyr, "Cardwell's Law," 561–574.
14. Schumpeter, *Capitalism, Socialism and Democracy*, 145.
15. Frey, *Technology Trap*.
16. Autor, et al., "New Frontiers," 1399–1465.
17. Pew Research Center, 2023, "Growing public concern about the role of artificial intelligence in daily life," https://www.pewresearch.org/short-reads/2023/08/28/growing-public-concern-about-the-role-of-artificial-intelligence-in-daily-life/. Accessed August 28, 2024.
18. Autor, et al., "Help for the Heartland?."

BIBLIOGRAPHY

Abegglen, J., and G. Stalk Jr. 1985. *The Japanese Corporation*. New York: Basic Books.
Abouchar, A. 1976. "Postwar Developments in the Cement Industry." In *Soviet Economy in a New Perspective: A Compendium of Papers Submitted to the Joint Economic Committee of the Congress of the United States*, 558–574. Washington: U.S. Government Printing Office.
Abramovitz, M., and P. A. David. 1996. "Convergence and Deferred Catch-Up: Productivity Leadership and the Waning." In *The Mosaic of Economic Growth*, edited by R. Landau, T. Taylor, and G. Wright. Stanford: Stanford University Press.
Abramovitz, M., and P. David. 2000. "American Macroeconomic Growth in the Era of Knowledge-Based Progress: The Long Run Perspective." In *The Cambridge Economic History of the United States Volume III: The Twentieth Century*, edited by S. Engerman and R. Gallman, 1–92. Cambridge: Cambridge University Press.
Acemoglu, D. 2008. "Oligarchic Versus Democratic Societies." *Journal of the European Economic Association* 6 (1): 1–44.
Acemoglu, D. 2024. "The Simple Macroeconomics of AI." Working Paper 32487, National Bureau of Economic Research.
Acemoglu, D., P. Aghion, C. Lelarge, J. Van Reenen, and F. Zilibotti. 2007. "Technology, Information, and the Decentralization of the Firm." *The Quarterly Journal of Economics* 122 (4): 1759–1799.
Acemoglu, D., P. Aghion, and F. Zilibotti. 2006. "Distance to Frontier, Selection, and Economic Growth." *Journal of the European Economic Association* 4 (1): 37–74.
Acemoglu, D., D. Cantoni, S. Johnson, and J. A. Robinson. 2011. "The Consequences of Radical Reform: The French Revolution." *American Economic Review* 101 (7): 3286–3307.
Acemoglu, D., S. Johnson, and J. Robinson. 2005. "The Rise of Europe: Atlantic Trade, Institutional Change, and Economic Growth." *American Economic Review* 95 (3): 546–79.
Acemoglu, D., and J. Linn. 2004. "Market Size in Innovation: Theory and Evidence from the Pharmaceutical Industry." *The Quarterly Journal of Economics* 119 (3): 1049–1090.
Acemoglu, D., J. Moscona, and J. A. Robinson. 2016. "State Capacity and American Technology: Evidence from the Nineteenth Century." *American Economic Review* 106 (5): 61–67.
Acemoglu, D., and P. Restrepo. 2020. "The Wrong Kind of AI? Artificial Intelligence and the Future of Labour Demand." *Cambridge Journal of Regions, Economy and Society* 13 (1): 25–35.
Acemoglu, D., and J. A. Robinson. 2006. "Economic Backwardness in Political Perspective." *American Political Science Review* 100 (1): 115–131.
Acemoglu, D., and J. Robinson. 2012. *Why Nations Fail: The Origins of Power, Prosperity, and Poverty*. London: Profile Books.
Acemoglu, D., and J. A. Robinson. 2019. *The Narrow Corridor: How Nations Struggle for Liberty*. London: Penguin Books.

Ade, G. 1931. *The Old-Time Saloon: Not Wet—Not Dry, Just History*. Chicago: University of Chicago Press.

Ager, P., L. Bursztyn, L. Leucht, and H. J. Voth. 2022. "Killer Incentives: Rivalry, Performance and Risk-Taking among German Fighter Pilots, 1939–45." *The Review of Economic Studies* 89 (5): 2257–2292.

Aghion, P., C. Antonin, and S. Bunel. 2021. *The Power of Creative Destruction*. Cambridge, MA: Harvard University Press.

Aghion, P., S. Guriev, and K. Jo. 2021. "Chaebols and Firm Dynamics in Korea." *Economic Policy* 36 (108): 593–626.

Aghion, P., and P. Howitt. 1992. "A Model of Growth Through Creative Destruction." *Econometrica* 60 (2): 323–351.

Ahlers, A. L., and G. Schubert. 2022. "Nothing New Under 'Top-Level Design'? A Review of the Conceptual Literature on Local Policymaking in China." *Issues & Studies* 58 (01): 2150017.

Ahmed, N., M. Wahed, and N. C. Thompson. 2023. "The Growing Influence of Industry in AI Research." *Science* 379 (6635): 884–886.

Ahrens, R. 2020. "The Importance of Being European: Airbus and West German Industrial Policy from the 1960s to the 1980s." *Journal of Modern European History* 18 (1): 63–78.

Akcigit, U., S. Baslandze, and F. Lotti. 2023. "Connecting to Power: Political Connections, Innovation, and Firm Dynamics." *Econometrica* 91 (2): 529–564.

Akcigit, U., S. Baslandze, and S. Stantcheva. 2016. "Taxation and the International Mobility of Inventors." *American Economic Review* 106 (10): 2930–2981.

Akcigit, U., and N. Goldschlag. 2023. "Where Have All the 'Creative Talents' Gone? Employment Dynamics of US Inventors." NBER Working Paper No. 31085. National Bureau of Economic Research.

Akcigit, U., J. Grigsby, and T. Nicholas. 2017. "Immigration and the Rise of American Ingenuity." *American Economic Review* 107 (5): 327–331.

Akcigit, U., and W. R. Kerr. 2018. "Growth Through Heterogeneous Innovations." *Journal of Political Economy* 126 (4): 1374–1443.

Alder, S., L. Shao, and F. Zilibotti. 2016. "Economic Reforms and Industrial Policy in a Panel of Chinese Cities." *Journal of Economic Growth* 21 (4): 305–349.

Alexopoulos, M., and J. Cohen. 2011. "Volumes of Evidence: Examining Technical Change in the Last Century through a New Lens." *Canadian Journal of Economics/Revue Canadienne d'économique* 44 (2): 413–450.

Alfani, G. 2023. *As Gods Among Men: A History of the Rich in the West*. Princeton: Princeton University Press.

Algan, Y., and P. Cahuc. 2010. "Inherited Trust and Growth." *American Economic Review* 100 (5): 2060–2092.

Algan, Y., and P. Cahuc. 2013. "Trust and Growth." *Annual Review of Economics* 5 (1): 521–549.

Allen, R. C. 1983. "Collective Invention." *Journal of Economic Behavior & Organization* 4 (1): 1–24.

Allen, R. C. 2001. "The Rise and Decline of the Soviet Economy." *Canadian Journal of Economics* 34 (4): 859–881.

Allen, R. C. 2009. *The British Industrial Revolution in Global Perspective*. Cambridge: Cambridge University Press.

Allen, R. C. 2009. "The Industrial Revolution in Miniature: The Spinning Jenny in Britain, France, and India." *The Journal of Economic History* 69 (4): 901–927.

Allen, R. C. 2011. "Why the Industrial Revolution Was British: Commerce, Induced Invention, and the Scientific Revolution." *The Economic History Review* 64 (2): 357–384.

Allen, R. C. 2021. *Farm to Factory: A Reinterpretation of the Soviet Industrial Revolution*. Princeton: Princeton University Press.

Allison, G. 2018. *Destined for War: Can America and China Escape Thucydides's Trap?*. Boston: Houghton Mifflin Harcourt.

Amsden, A. H. 1992. *Asia's Next Giant: South Korea and Late Industrialization*. Oxford: Oxford University Press.

Anderson, C. W. 1970. *The Political Economy of Modern Spain: Policy Making in an Authoritarian System*. Madison: University of Wisconsin Press.

Andrews, M. 2019. "Bar Talk: Informal Social Networks, Alcohol Prohibition, and Invention." Working Paper 3489466, Social Science Research Network.

Anduaga, A. 2009. "Autarchy, Ideology, and Technology Transfer in the Spanish Oil Industry, 1939–1960." *Comparative Technology Transfer and Society* 7 (2): 172–200.

Aneja, A., and G. Xu. 2022. "Strengthening State Capacity: Postal Reform and Innovation during the Gilded Age." Working Paper 29852, National Bureau of Economic Research.

Ang, Y. Y. 2020. *China's Gilded Age: The Paradox of Economic Boom and Vast Corruption*. Cambridge: Cambridge University Press.

Antonelli, C., and F. Barbiellini Amidei. 2009. "Knowledge, Innovation and Localised Technical Change in Italy, 1950–1990." Working Paper 200913, University of Turin.

Arendt, H. 1951. *The Origins of Totalitarianism*. New York: Schocken.

Argente, D., S. Baslandze, D. Hanley, and S. Moreira. 2020. "Patents to Products: Product Innovation and Firm Dynamics." Working Paper 14692, CEPR Discussion Paper.

Arkolakis, C., S. K. Lee, and M. Peters. 2020. "European Immigrants and the United States' Rise to the Technological Frontier." Working Paper 1420, 2019 Meeting Papers, Society for Economic Dynamics.

Arora, A., S. Belenzon, A. Patacconi, and J. Suh. 2020. "The Changing Structure of American Innovation: Some Cautionary Remarks for Economic Growth." *Innovation Policy and the Economy* 20 (1): 39–93.

Arora, A., L. G. Branstetter, and M. Drev. 2013. "Going Soft: How the Rise of Software-Based Innovation Led to the Decline of Japan's IT Industry and the Resurgence of Silicon Valley." *Review of Economics and Statistics* 95 (3): 757–775.

Arrighi, G. 2007. *Adam Smith in Beijing: Lineages of the Twenty-First Century*. London: Verso.

Asker, J., and V. Nocke. 2021. "Collusion, Mergers, and Related Antitrust Issues." In *Handbook of Industrial Organization Volume 5*, edited by K. Ho, A. Hortacsu and A. Lizzeri, 177–279. Amsterdam: North Holland.

Atack, J., R. A. Margo, and P. W. Rhode. 2022. "Industrialization and Urbanization in Nineteenth Century America." *Regional Science and Urban Economics* 94 (103678): 1–11.

Atack, J., and P. Passell. 1994. *A New Economic View of American History: From Colonial Times to 1940*. New York: W. W. Norton.

Atkinson, R. 2002. *An Army at Dawn*. New York: Henry Holt.

Audretsch, D. B. 1989. "Legalized Cartels in West Germany." *Antitrust Bulletin* 34: 579–600.

Autor, D., A. Beck, D. Dorn, and G. H. Hanson. 2024. "Help for the Heartland? The Employment and Electoral Effects of the Trump Tariffs in the United States." Working Paper 32082, National Bureau of Economic Research.

Autor, D., C. Chin, A. Salomons, and B. Seegmiller. 2024. "New Frontiers: The Origins and Content of New Work, 1940–2018." *Quarterly Journal of Economics* 139(3): 1399–1465.

Autor, D., D. Dorn, L. F. Katz, C. Patterson, and J. Van Reenen. 2020. "Fall of the Labor Share and the Rise of Superstar Firms." *The Quarterly Journal of Economics* 135 (2): 645–709.

Azoulay, P., C. Fons-Rosen, and J. S. Graff Zivin. 2019. "Does Science Advance One Funeral at a Time?." *American Economic Review* 109 (8): 2889–2920.

Azoulay, P., E. Fuchs, A. P. Goldstein, and M. Kearney. 2019. "Funding Breakthrough Research: Promises and Challenges of the 'ARPA Model.'" *Innovation Policy and the Economy* 19 (1): 69–96.

Baack, B., and E. Ray. 1985. "The Political Economy of the Origins of the Military-Industrial Complex in the United States." *The Journal of Economic History* 45 (2): 369–375.

Baark, E. 1997. *Lightning Wires: The Telegraph and China's Technological Modernization, 1860–1890.* Westport: Greenwood Press.

Babina, T., S. Barkai, J. Jeffers, E. Karger and E. Volkova. 2023. "Antitrust Enforcement Increases Economic Activity." Working Paper 31597, National Bureau of Economic Research.

Babina, T., A. Fedyk, A. X. He, and J. Hodson, 2022. "Firm Investments in Artificial Intelligence Technologies and Changes in Workforce Composition." Working Paper 31325, National Bureau of Economic Research.

Bachmann, O., and F. M. Scherer. 1959. *Patents and the Corporation.* Boston: James Galvin & Associates.

Bachrach, B. S. 2016. "Charlemagne and Carolingian Military Administration." In *Empires and Bureaucracy in World History: From Late Antiquity to the Twentieth Century,* edited by P. Crooks and T. H. Parsons, 170–196. Cambridge: Cambridge University Press.

Bacon, F. 1620. *Novum Organum.* Oxford: Clarendon Press.

Bagchi, A. K. 2000. *Private Investment in India, 1900–1939 Volume 5.* London: Taylor & Francis.

Bagley, W. 2014. *South Pass: Gateway to a Continent.* Norman: University of Oklahoma Press.

Bai, C. E., C. T. Hsieh, Z. M. Song, and X. Wang. 2020. "Special Deals from Special Investors: The Rise of State-Connected Private Owners in China." Working Paper 28170, National Bureau of Economic Research.

Bailes, K. E. 1978. *Technology and Society under Lenin and Stalin: Origins of the Soviet Technical Intelligentsia, 1917–1941.* Princeton: Princeton University Press.

Baime, A. J. 2014. *The Arsenal of Democracy: FDR, Detroit, and an Epic Quest to Arm an America at War.* Boston: Houghton Mifflin Harcourt.

Bairoch, P. 1982. "International Industrialization Levels from 1750 to 1980." *Journal of European Economic History* 11 (2): 269–333.

Bairoch, P. 1988. *Cities and Economic Development: From the Dawn of History to the Present.* Chicago: University of Chicago Press.

Baldwin, G. B., and G. P. Schultz. 1960. "The Effects of Automation on Industrial Relations." In *Impact of Automation: A Collection of 20 Articles about Technological Change, from the Monthly Labor Review,* edited by U.S. Government Printing Office. Washington, DC: Bureau of Labor Statistics.

Baldwin, R. 2019. *The Great Convergence.* Cambridge, MA: Harvard University Press.

Baldwin, R. E. 2008. "The Changing Nature of US Trade Policy since World War II." In *The Structure and Evolution of Recent US Trade Policy,* edited by R. E. Baldwin and A. O. Krueger, 5–32. Chicago: University of Chicago Press.

Banerjee, D. 1999. *Colonialism in Action: Trade, Development, and Dependence in Late Colonial India.* Hyderabad: Orient Blackswan.

Barber, J., M. Harrison, N. Simonov, and B. Starkov. 2000. "The Structure and Development of the Defence-Industry Complex." In *The Soviet Defence-Industry Complex from Stalin to Khrushchev,* edited by J. Barber and M. Harrison, 3–29. Cambridge, MA: MIT Press.

Barbiellini Amidei, F., J. Cantwell, and A. Spadavecchia. 2013. "Innovation and Foreign Technology." In *The Oxford Handbook of the Italian Economy Since Unification,* edited by G. Toniolo. Oxford: Oxford University Press.

Barca, F., K. Iwai, U. Pagano, and S. Trento. 1998. "Postwar Institutional Reform: The Divergence of Italian and Japanese Corporate Governance Models." Working Paper 234, Università degli Studi di Siena, Dipartimento di Economia Politica.

Barnett, J. M. 2021. "The Great Patent Grab." In *The Battle over Patents: History and Politics of Innovation,* edited by S. H. Haber and N. R. Lamoreaux. Oxford: Oxford University Press.

Barteska, P., and J. E. Lee. 2023. "Bureaucrats and the Korean Export Miracle." NICEP Working Paper 2024–11.

Baslandze, S. 2021. "Barriers to Creative Destruction: Large Firms and Non-Productive Strategies." Working Paper 3927528, Social Science Research Network.

Bastiat, F. 1850. "That Which Is Seen, and That Which Is Not Seen." *Mises Institute*, November 25. https://mises.org/library/which-seen-and-which-not-seen.

Baum, W. C. 1958. *The French Economy and the State*. Princeton: Princeton University Press.

Baumol, W. J. 1996. "Entrepreneurship: Productive, Unproductive, and Destructive." *Journal of Business Venturing* 11 (1): 3–22.

Baumol, W. J. 2014. *The Free-Market Innovation Machine*. Princeton: Princeton University Press.

Baumol, W. J., and R. J. Strom. 2010. "'Useful Knowledge' of Entrepreneurship: Some Implications of the History." In *The Invention of Enterprise: Entrepreneurship from Ancient Mesopotamia to Modern Times*, edited by D. S. Landes, J. Mokyr and W. J. Baumol, 527–542. Princeton: Princeton University Press.

Baum-Snow, N. 2007. "Did Highways Cause Suburbanization?." *The Quarterly Journal of Economics* 122 (2): 775–805.

Bazzi, S., M. Fiszbein, and M. Gebresilasse. 2020. "Frontier Culture: The Roots and Persistence of 'Rugged Individualism' in the United States." *Econometrica* 88 (6): 2329–2368.

Beasley, W. G. 1972. *The Meiji Restoration*. Stanford: Stanford University Press.

Beason, R., and D. E. Weinstein. 1996. "Growth, Economies of Scale, and Targeting in Japan (1955–1990)." *The Review of Economics and Statistics* 78 (2): 286–295.

Becker, S. O., and E. Hornung. 2020. "The Political Economy of the Prussian Three-Class Franchise." *The Journal of Economic History* 80 (4): 1143–1188.

Becker, S. O., E. Hornung, and L. Woessmann. 2011. "Education and Catch-up in the Industrial Revolution." *American Economic Journal: Macroeconomics* 3 (3): 92–126, 93.

Becker, S. O., and L. Woessmann. 2009. "Was Weber Wrong? A Human Capital Theory of Protestant Economic History." *Quarterly Journal of Economics* 124 (2): 531–596.

Behrens, C. B. A. 1985. *Society, Government and the Enlightenment: The Experiences of Eighteenth-Century France and Prussia*. London: Thames & Hudson.

Bekmann, J. C. 1751. *Historische Beschreibung der Chur und Mark Brandenburg*, Vol. 1. Berlin: Voss.

Bell, A., R. Chetty, X. Jaravel, N. Petkova, and J. Van Reenen. 2019. "Who Becomes an Inventor in America? The Importance of Exposure to Innovation." *The Quarterly Journal of Economics* 134 (2): 647–713.

Belova, E., and V. Lazarev. 2013. *Funding Loyalty: The Economics of the Communist Party*. New Haven, CT: Yale University Press.

Ben-David, J., and A. Zloczower. 1962. "Universities and Academic Systems in Modern Societies." *European Journal of Sociology/Archives Européennes de Sociologie* 3 (1): 45–84, 68.

Benner, M. 1997. *The Politics of Growth: Economic Regulation in Sweden, 1930–1994*. Stockholm: Arkiv Forlag.

Beraja, M. A., Kao, D. Y. Yang, and N. Yuchtman. 2021. "AI-tocracy." *The Quarterly Journal of Economics* 138 (3): 1349–1402.

Beraja, M., A. Kao, D. Y. Yang, and N. Yuchtman. 2023. "Exporting the Surveillance State via Trade in AI." Working Paper 31676, National Bureau of Economic Research.

Beraja, M., D. Y. Yang, and N. Yuchtman. 2020. "Data-Intensive Innovation and the State: Evidence from AI Firms in China." Working Paper 27723, National Bureau of Economic Research.

Berend, I. 1996. *Central and Eastern Europe, 1944–1993: Detour from the Periphery to the Periphery*. Cambridge: Cambridge University Press.

Berger, T., and C. B. Frey. 2016. "Did the Computer Revolution Shift the Fortunes of U.S. Cities? Technology Shocks and the Geography of New Jobs." *Regional Science and Urban Economics* 57: 38–45.

Berger, T., and C. B. Frey. 2017. "Industrial Renewal in the 21st Century: Evidence from U.S. Cities." *Regional Studies* 51 (3): 404–413.

Berger, T., and C. B. Frey. 2017. "Regional Technological Dynamism and Noncompete Clauses: Evidence from a Natural Experiment." *Journal of Regional Science* 57 (4): 655–668.

Berghahn, V. R. 1986. *The Americanisation of West German Industry, 1945–1973*. Leamington Spa: Berg.

Berghoff, H., and R. Moller. 1994. "Tired Pioneers and Dynamic Newcomers? A Comparative Essay on English and German Entrepreneurial History, 1870–1914." *Economic History Review* 47 (2): 262–287.

Berglund, L., M. Tong, M. Kaufmann, M. Balesni, A. C. Stickland, T. Korbak, and O. Evans. 2023. "The Reversal Curse: LLMs trained on 'A is B' fail to learn 'B is A.'" Working Paper 2309.12288, arXiv.

Bergson, A. 1983. "Technological Progress." In *The Soviet Economy: Toward the Year 2000*, edited by A. Bergson and H. S. Levine. London: Taylor & Francis.

Berkes, E., and P. Nencka. 2020. "Knowledge Access: The Effects of Carnegie Libraries on Innovation." Working Paper 3629299, Social Science Research Network.

Berliner, J. S. 1957. *Factory and Manager in the USSR*. Cambridge, MA: Harvard University Press.

Bernhofen, D. M., Z. El-Sahli, and R. Kneller. 2016. "Estimating the Effects of the Container Revolution on World Trade." *Journal of International Economics* 98: 36–50.

Bernhofen, D. M., J. Li, M. Eberhardt, and S. L. Morgan. 2022. "Assessing Market Integration in the Early Modern Period." Working Paper 4190880, Social Science Research Network.

Bernstein, S. 2015. "Does Going Public Affect Innovation?." *The Journal of Finance* 70 (4): 1365–1403.

Bernstein, S., R. Diamond, A. Jiranaphawiboon, T. McQuade, and B. Pousada. 2022. "The Contribution of High-Skilled Immigrants to Innovation in the United States." Working Paper 30797, National Bureau of Economic Research.

Besley, T., R. Burgess, A. Khan, and G. Xu. 2021. "Bureaucracy and Development." *Annual Review of Economics* 14: 397–424.

Besley, T., and M. Kudamatsu. 2008. "Making Autocracy Work." In *Institutions and Economic Performance*, edited by E. Helpman, 452–510. Cambridge, MA: Harvard University Press.

Bessen, J. 2003. "Technology and Learning by Factory Workers: The Stretch-Out at Lowell, 1842." *The Journal of Economic History* 63 (1): 33–64.

Bessen, J. 2015. *Learning by Doing: The Real Connection between Innovation, Wages, and Wealth*. New Haven, CT: Yale University Press.

Bianchi, N., and M. Giorcelli. 2021. "The Dynamics and Spillovers of Management Interventions: Evidence from the Training Within Industry Program." Working Paper 28833, National Bureau of Economic Research.

Bianco, M., and G. Napolitano. 2013. "The Italian Administrative System: Why a Source of Competitive Disadvantage?." In *The Oxford Handbook of the Italian Economy Since Unification*, edited by G. Toniolo. Oxford: Oxford University Press.

Bielenstein, H. 1980. *The Bureaucracy of Han Times*. Cambridge: Cambridge University Press.

Bittlingmayer, G. 1985. "Did Antitrust Policy Cause The Great Merger Wave?." *The Journal of Law and Economics* 28 (1): 77–118.

Black, E. 2001. *IBM and the Holocaust: The Strategic Alliance between Nazi Germany and America's Most Powerful Corporation*. New York: Crown Publishing Group.

Blanchard, O., and A. Shleifer. 2001. "Federalism With and Without Political Centralization: China Versus Russia." *IMF Staff Papers* 48 (1): 171–179.
Bleakley, H., and J. Lin. 2012. "Portage and Path Dependence." *The Quarterly Journal of Economics* 127 (2): 587–644.
Bloch, M. 1961. *Feudal Society Volume 2.* Chicago: University of Chicago Press.
Bloch, M. 1966. *French Rural History.* Berkeley: University of California Press.
Blomkvist, P. 2004. "Transferring Technology—Shaping Ideology: American Traffic Engineering and Commercial Interests in the Establishment of a Swedish Car Society, 1945–1965." *Comparative Technology Transfer and Society* 2 (3): 273–302.
Bloom, N., C. Genakos, R. Sadun, and J. Van Reenen. 2012. "Management Practices Across Firms and Countries." *Academy of Management Perspectives* 26 (1): 12–33.
Bloom, N., C. I. Jones, J. Van Reenen, and M. Webb. 2020. "Are Ideas Getting Harder to Find?." *American Economic Review* 110 (4): 1104–1144.
Bloom, N., R. Sadun, and J. Van Reenen. 2012. "Americans Do IT Better: US Multinationals and the Productivity Miracle." *American Economic Review* 102 (1): 167–201.
Bloom, N., and J. Van Reenen. 2007. "Measuring and Explaining Management Practices across Firms and Countries." *Quarterly Journal of Economics* 122 (4): 1351–1408.
Bluestone, B., and B. Harrison. 1982. *The Deindustrialization of America.* New York: Basic Books.
Blum, B. S., and A. Goldfarb. 2006. "Does the Internet Defy the Law of Gravity?." *Journal of International Economics* 70 (2): 384–405.
Blum, J. 1971. *Lord and Peasant in Russia: From the Ninth to the Nineteenth Century.* Princeton: Princeton University Press.
Blum, J. 1978. *The End of the Old Order in Rural Europe.* Princeton: Princeton University Press.
Blum, J. M. 1976. *V Was for Victory: Politics and American Culture During World War II.* Boston: Houghton Mifflin Harcourt.
Blustein, P. 2020. "Schism: China, America, and the Fracturing of the Global Trading System." *International Journal: Canada's Journal of Global Policy Analysis* 75 (1): 112–114.
Bockheim, J. G., and A. E. Hartemink. 2017. "Soils and Land Appraisal." In *The Soils of Wisconsin,* edited by J. G. Bockheim and A. E. Hartemink, 213–222. Madison, University of Wisconsin Press.
Boettke, P. J., and R. A. Candela. 2023. "On the Feasibility of Technosocialism." *Journal of Economic Behavior & Organization* 205: 44–54.
Bogart, D. 2005. "Did Turnpike Trusts Increase Transportation Investment in Eighteenth-Century England?." *The Journal of Economic History* 65 (2): 439–468.
Bogart, D. 2005. "Turnpike Trusts and the Transportation Revolution in 18th Century England." *Explorations in Economic History* 42 (4): 479–508.
Bogart, D. 2012. "A Small Price to Pay: A Historical Perspective on Infrastructure Regulation during Britain's Industrialization." Working Paper, University of California Irvine.
Bogart, D. 2014. "The Transport Revolution in Industrialising Britain." In *The Cambridge Economic History of Modern Britain Volume 1, 1700–1870,* edited by R. Floud, J. Humphries, and P. Johnson, 368–391. Cambridge: Cambridge University Press.
Bogart, D., and G. Richardson. 2011. "Property Rights and Parliament in Industrializing Britain." *Journal of Law and Economics* 54 (2): 241–274.
Bogart, D., M. Satchell, E. J. Alvarez-Palau, X. You, and L. S. Taylor. 2017. "Turnpikes, Canals, and Economic Growth in England and Wales, 1800–1850." Working Paper, University of California Irvine.
Bolt, J., and J. L. van Zanden. 2014. "The Maddison Project: Collaborative Research on Historical National Accounts." *Economic History Review* 67 (3): 627–651.

Bombardini, M., O. C. Rendina, and F. Trebbi. 2021. "Lobbying Behind the Frontier." Working Paper 2912, National Bureau of Economic Research.

Bombardini, M., and F. Trebbi. 2012. "Competition and Political Organization: Together or Alone in Lobbying for Trade Policy?." *Journal of International Economics* 87 (1): 18–26.

Bonney, R. 2012. *The Rise of the Fiscal State in France, 1500–1914*. Cambridge: Cambridge University Press.

Bonvillian, W. B. 2009. "The Connected Science Model for Innovation—The DARPA Role." In *21st Century Innovation Systems for Japan and the United States: Lessons from a Decade of Change*, edited by S. Nagaoka, M. Kondo, K. Flamm, and C. Wessner. Washington, DC: National Academies Press.

Borisov, I., and A. Koloskov. 1980. *The Sino-Soviet Relationship*. Moscow: Mysl.

Bosker, M., E. Buringh, and J. L. Van Zanden. 2013. "From Baghdad to London: Unraveling Urban Development in Europe, the Middle East, and North Africa, 800–1800." *Review of Economics and Statistics* 95 (4): 1418–1437.

Bowman, A. H. 1956. "Jefferson, Hamilton and American Foreign Policy." *Political Science Quarterly* 71 (1): 18–41.

Boycko, M., A. Shleifer, and R. Vishny. 1997. *Privatizing Russia*. Cambridge, MA: MIT Press.

Brady, R. A. 1943. "Industrial Policy." *The Journal of Economic History* 3 (S1): 108–123.

Brandt, L., J. Litwack, E. Mileva, L. Wang, Y. Zhang, and L. Zhao. 2020. "China's Productivity Slowdown and Future Growth Potential." Working Paper 9298, World Bank, Washington, DC.

Brandt, L., D. Ma, and T. G. Rawski. 2012. "From Divergence to Convergence: Reevaluating the History behind China's Economic Boom." Working Papers 158/12, London School of Economics, Department of Economic History.

Brandt, L., D. Ma, and T. G. Rawski. 2014. "From Divergence to Convergence: Reevaluating the History behind China's Economic Boom." *The Journal of Economic Literature* 52 (1): 45–123.

Brandt, L., and T. G. Rawski. 2022. "China's Great Boom as a Historical Process." In *The Cambridge Economic History of China*, edited by D. Ma and R. von Glahn, 775–828. Cambridge: Cambridge University Press.

Bresnahan, T. F., E. Brynjolfsson, and L. M. Hitt. 2002. "Information Technology, Workplace Organization, and the Demand for Skilled Labor: Firm-Level Evidence." *The Quarterly Journal of Economics* 117 (1): 339–376.

Brevik, E. C., and A. E. Hartemink. 2010. "Early Soil Knowledge and the Birth and Development of Soil Science." *Catena* 83 (1): 23–33.

Brezis, E. S., and P. R. Krugman. 1997. "Technology and the Life Cycle of Cities." *Journal of Economic Growth* 2 (4): 369–383.

Broad, W. J. 1981. "AT&T Tries to Put Antitrust Suit on Hold: Bell Says Breakup of Empire Would be "Lethal" to National Security, But Courtroom Inquiry Casts Doubt on Credibility of Arguments." *Science* 213 (4511): 990–991.

Broadberry, S. 2006. *Market Services and the Productivity Race, 1850–2000: British Performance in International Perspective* Cambridge: Cambridge University Press.

Broadberry, S. N. 1997. "Anglo-German productivity differences 1870–1990: A Sectoral Analysis." *European Review of Economic History* 1 (2): 247–267, Table 4.

Broadberry, S. N. 1997. *The Productivity Race: British Manufacturing in International Perspective, 1850–1990*. Cambridge: Cambridge University Press.

Broadberry, S. N. 1998. "How Did the United States and Germany Overtake Britian? A Sectoral Analysis of Comparative Productivity Levels, 1870–1990." *The Journal of Economic History* 58 (2): 375–407.

Broadberry, S., and N. Crafts. 2001. "Competition and Innovation in 1950s Britain." *Business History* 43: 97–118.

Broadberry, S. N., and N. Crafts. 1996. "British Economic Policy and Industrial Performance in the Early Postwar Period." *Business History* 38: 65–91.

Broadberry, S., K. Fukao, and N. Zammit. 2015. "How Did Japan Catch-Up on The West? A Sectoral Analysis of Anglo-Japanese Productivity Differences, 1885–2000." Working Paper 231, University of Warwick, CAGE Research Centre.

Broadberry, S. N., C. Giordano, and F. Zollino. 2013. "Productivity." In *The Oxford Handbook of the Italian Economy since Unification*, edited by G. Toniolo. New York: Oxford University Press.

Broadberry, S., and H. Guan. 2022. "Regional Variation of GDP per Head Within China, 1080–1850: Implications for the Great Divergence Debate." Working Paper 196, Oxford Economic and Social History.

Broadberry, S., H. Guan, and D. D. Li. 2018. "China, Europe and the Great Divergence: A Study in Historical National Accounting." *Journal of Economic History* 78 (4): 955–1000.

Broadberry, S., G. Hanhui, and D. D. Li. 2021. "China, Europe and the Great Divergence: A Restatement." *Journal of Economic History* 81 (3): 958–974.

Broadberry, S., and A. Klein. 2011. "When and Why Did Eastern European Economies Begin to Fail? Lessons from a Czechoslovak/UK Productivity Comparison, 1921–1991." *Explorations in Economic History* 48 (1): 37–52.

Broadberry, S., and E. Korchmina. 2022. "Catching-Up and Falling Behind: Russian Economic Growth, 1960s-1880s." Working Paper 626, University of Warwick, CAGE Research Centre.

Brown, J. D., J. S. Earle, and S. Gehlbach. 2009. "Helping Hand or Grabbing Hand? State Bureaucracy and Privatization Effectiveness." *American Political Science Review* 103 (2): 264–283.

Brown, S. R. 1979. "The Transfer of Technology to China in the Nineteenth Century: The Role of Direct Foreign Investment." *The Journal of Economic History* 39 (1): 181–197.

Bruland, K. 1989. *British Technology and European Industrialization. The Norwegian Textile Industry in the Mid Nineteenth Century*. Cambridge: Cambridge University Press.

Brunnermeier, M., R. Doshi, and H. James. 2018. "Beijing's Bismarckian Ghosts: How Great Powers Compete Economically." *The Washington Quarterly* 41 (3): 161–176.

Brus, W., and K. Laski. 1989. *From Marx to the Market: Socialism in Search of an Economic System*. Oxford: Clarendon Press.

Brynjolfsson, E. 2022. "The Turing Trap: The Promise & Peril of Human-Like Artificial Intelligence." *Daedalus* 151 (2): 272–287.

Brynjolfsson, E., A. Collis, and F. Eggers. 2019. "Using Massive Online Choice Experiments to Measure Changes in Well-Being." *Proceedings of the National Academy of Sciences* 116 (15): 7250–7255.

Brynjolfsson, E., and S. Yang. 1996. "Information Technology and Productivity: A Review of the Literature." *Advances in Computers* 43: 179–214.

Bryson, B. 2010. *At Home: A Short History of Private Life*. Toronto: Doubleday Canada.

Bueno de Mesquita, M., A. Smith, R. Siverson, and J. Morrow. 2003. *The Logic of Political Survival*. Cambridge, MA: MIT Press.

Buonanno, P., F. Cinnirella, E. Harka, and M. Puca. 2024. Books Go Public: The Consequences of the Expropriation of Monastic Libraries on Innovation. CEPR Discussion Paper 18926.

Buchanan, D. H. 2013. *The Development of Capitalistic Enterprise in India*. London: Routledge.

Buchheim, C., and J. Scherner. 2006. "The Role of Private Property in the Nazi Economy: The Case of Industry." *The Journal of Economic History* 66 (2): 390–416.

Buel, R. 1998. *In Irons: Britain's Naval Supremacy and the American Revolutionary Economy*. New Haven, CT: Yale University Press.
Bull, M. 2015. "The Decline of Decadence." *New Left Review* 94: 83–86.
Burchardi, K. B., T. Chaney, T. A. Hassan, L. Tarquinio, and S. J. Terry. 2020. "Immigration, Innovation, and Growth." Working Paper 27075, National Bureau of Economic Research.
Burhop, C. 2011. *Wirtschaftsgeschichte des Kaiserreichs, 1871–1918*. Göttingen: Vandenhoeck & Ruprecht.
Burhop, C., and N. Wolf. 2013. "The German Market for Patents during the 'Second Industrialization' 1884–1913: A Gravity Approach." *Business History Review* 87 (1): 69–93.
Bush, V. 1945. *Science: The Endless Frontier*. Washington, DC: U.S. Government Printing Office.
Buss, T. F., and F. S. Redburn. 1983. *Shutdown at Youngstown: Public Policy for Mass Unemployment*. Albany: State University of New York Press.
Bylinsky, G. 1976. *The Innovation Millionaires: How They Succeed*. New York: Scribner.
Byrne, D. M., J. G. Fernald, and M. B. Reinsdorf. 2016. "Does the United States Have a Productivity Slowdown or a Measurement Problem?." *Brookings Papers on Economic Activity* (1): 109–182.
Cai, H., and D. Treisman. 2004. "State-Corroding Federalism." *Journal of Public Economics* 88 (3–4): 819–843.
Cai, H., and D. Treisman. 2006. "Did Government Decentralization Cause China's Economic Miracle?." *World Politics* 58 (4): 505–535.
Cain, L. P. 2012. "Entrepreneurship in the Antebellum United States." In *The Invention of Enterprise*, edited by D. S. Landes, J. Mokyr, and W. J. Baumol. Princeton: Princeton University Press.
Calvo-González, O. 2007. "American Military Interests and Economic Confidence in Spain under the Franco Dictatorship." *The Journal of Economic History* 67(3): 740–767.
Campante, F. R., and D. Chor. 2017. "Just Do Your Job: Obedience, Routine Tasks, and the Pattern of Specialization." Discussion Paper 2016-36, Economic Research Institute for ASEAN and East Asia.
Cantwell, J. 1987. "Historical Trends in International Patterns of Technological Innovation." Working Paper, Department of Economics, University of Reading.
Cao, Y., and S. Chen. 2022. "Rebel on the Canal: Disrupted Trade Access and Social Conflict in China, 1650–1911." *American Economic Review* 112 (5): 1555–1590.
Carlin, W. 1995. "West German Growth and Institutions, 1945–90." In *Economic Growth in Europe since 1945*, edited by N. Crafts and G. Toniolo. Cambridge: Cambridge University Press.
Carlin, W., M. Schaffer, and P. Seabright. 2013. "Soviet Power Plus Electrification: What Is the Long-Run Legacy of Communism?." *Explorations in Economic History* 50 (1): 116–147.
Caroli, E., and J. Van Reenen. 2001. "Skill-Biased Organizational Change? Evidence from A Panel of British and French Establishments." *The Quarterly Journal of Economics* 116 (4): 1449–1492.
Carreras, A., and X. Tafunell. 1997. "Spain: Big Manufacturing Firms between State and Market." In *Big Business and the Wealth of Nations*, edited by A. Chandler, F. Amatori, and T. Hikino, 236–276. Cambridge: Cambridge University Press.
Carstensen, F. V., and G. Guroff. 1983. "Economic Innovation in Imperial Russia and the Soviet Union: Observations." In *Entrepreneurship in Imperial Russia and the Soviet Union*, edited by G. Guroff and F. V. Carstensen, 347–360. Princeton: Princeton University Press.
Carter, S. B., S. S. Gartner, M. R. Haines, A. L. Olmstead, R. Sutch, G. Wright, and L. P. Cain, eds. 2006. *Historical Statistics of the United States Millennial Edition Online*. Cambridge: Cambridge University Press.
Casella, A., and B. Eichengreen. 1996. "Can Foreign Aid Accelerate Stabilisation." *Economic Journal* 106 (436): 605–619.

Castañeda, P., and A. Markevich. 2019. "The Stolypin Reform and Agricultural Productivity in Late Imperial Russia." *European Review of Economic History* 23 (3): 241–267.

Caves, R. E., and M. Uekusa. 1976. *Industrial Organization in Japan*. Washington, DC: Brookings Institution.

Cerdeiro, D. A., and C. Ruane. 2022. "China's Declining Business Dynamism." Working Paper 22/32, International Monetary Fund.

Chalmers, D. M. 1966. "Introduction to the Torchbook Edition." In *The History of the Standard Oil Company*, edited by M. Tarbell and D. Schechter. New York: Harper and Row.

Chan, K. 2023. "Fast Track: State Capacity and Railway Bureaucracies in China and India." PhD diss., Princeton University.

Chandavarkar, R. 1994. *The Origins of Industrial Capitalism in India Business Strategies and the Working Classes in Bombay, 1900–1940*. Cambridge: Cambridge University Press.

Chandler, A. D. 1977. *The Visible Hand: The Managerial Revolution in American Business*. Cambridge, MA: Harvard University Press.

Chandler, A. D., Jr. 1994. *Scale and Scope: The Dynamics of Industrial Capitalism*. Cambridge, MA: Harvard University Press.

Chang, H. J., and J. S. Shin. 2006. "Evaluating the Post-crisis Corporate Restructuring in Korea." In *The East Asian Development Experience*, edited by H. J. Chang. London: Zed Books.

Chapman, R. A. 1971. *Higher Civil Service in Britain*. London: Constable & Co. Ltd.

Chen, F. C. and R. H. Myers. 1978. "Customary Law and the Economic Growth of China during the Ch'ing Period." *Ch'ing-shih wen-t'i* 3 (10): 4–27.

Cheng, T. J., S. Haggard, and D. Kang. 1998. "Institutions and Growth in Korea and Taiwan: The Bureaucracy." *The Journal of Development Studies* 34 (6): 87–111.

Chi, W. 2012. "Capital Income and Income Inequality: Evidence from Urban China." *Journal of Comparative Economics* 40 (2): 228–239.

Chinitz, B. 1961. "Contrasts in Agglomeration: New York and Pittsburgh." *The American Economic Review* 51 (2): 279–289.

Choi, J., and Y. Shim. 2022. "Technology Adoption and Late Industrialization." Working Paper 4308957, Social Science Research Network.

Christensen, C. M. 1997. *The Innovator's Dilemma: When New Technologies Cause Great Firms to Fail*. Cambridge, MA: Harvard Business Review Press.

Chua, R. Y., K. G. Huang, and M. Jin. 2019. "Mapping Cultural Tightness and Its Links to Innovation, Urbanization, and Happiness Across 31 Provinces in China." *Proceedings of the National Academy of Sciences* 116 (14): 6720–6725.

Ciccarelli, C., and A. Nuvolari. 2015. "Technical Change, Non-Tariff Barriers, and the Development of the Italian Locomotive Industry, 1850–1913." *The Journal of Economic History* 75 (3): 860–888.

Cinnirella, F., and J. Streb. 2017. "The Role of Human Capital and Innovation in Economic Development: Evidence from Post-Malthusian Prussia." *Journal of Economic Growth* 22 (2): 193–227.

Clark, C. M. 2006. *Iron Kingdom: The Rise and Downfall of Prussia, 1600–1947*. Cambridge, MA: Harvard University Press.

Clark, G. 1987. "Why Isn't the Whole World Developed? Lessons from the Cotton Mills." *The Journal of Economic History* 47 (1): 141–173.

Clark, J. B., and J. M. Clark. 1912. *The Control of Trusts*. New York: Macmillan.

Clark, M. G. 1952. "The Soviet Steel Industry." *The Journal of Economic History* 12 (4): 396–410.

Clark, M. G. 1956. *The Economics of Soviet Steel*. Cambridge, MA: Harvard University Press.

Clark, P. 2000. *British Clubs and Societies, 1580–1800: The Origins of an Associational World*. Oxford: Clarendon Press.

Clarke, R., S. Davies, and N. Driffield. 1998. *Monopoly Policy in the UK: Assessing the Evidence*. Cheltenham: Edward Elgar.

Clayton, J. L. 1962. "Defense Spending: Key to California's Growth." *Western Political Quarterly* 15 (2): 280–293.

Clive, A. 1979. *State of War: Michigan in World War II*. Ann Arbor: University of Michigan Press.

Coase, R. 1937. "The Nature of the Firm." *Economica* 4 (16): 386–405.

Cohen, J. S. 1967. "Financing Industrialization in Italy, 1894–1914: The Partial Transformation of a Late-Comer." *The Journal of Economic History* 27 (3): 363–382.

Cohen, W. M., and S. Klepper. 1996. "A Reprise of Size and R & D." *The Economic Journal* 106 (437): 925–951.

Colatat, P. 2015. "An Organizational Perspective to Funding Science: Collaborator Novelty at DARPA." *Research Policy* 44 (4): 874–887.

Cole, D. C., and Princeton N. Lyman. 1971. *Korean Development: The Interplay of Politics and Economics*. Cambridge, MA: Harvard University Press.

Collard-Wexler, A., and J. De Loecker. 2015. "Reallocation and Technology: Evidence from the US Steel Industry." *American Economic Review* 105 (1): 131–171.

Collier, P. 2018. *The Future of Capitalism: Facing the New Anxieties*. New York: Harper.

Colonnelli, E., B. Li, and E. Liu. 2022. "Investing with the Government: A Field Experiment in China." Working Paper 30161, National Bureau of Economic Research.

Comin, D., and B. Hobijn. 2009. "Lobbies and Technology Diffusion." *The Review of Economics and Statistics* 91 (2): 229–244.

Cook, L. D. 2014. "Violence and Economic Activity: Evidence from African American Patents, 1870–1940." *Journal of Economic Growth* 19 (2): 221–257.

Corti, G. 1976. "Perspectives on Public Corporations and Public Enterprises in Five Nations." *Annals of Collective Economy* 47 (1): 47–86.

Coşgel, M. M., T. J. Miceli, and J. Rubin. 2012. "The Political Economy of Mass Printing: Legitimacy and Technological Change in the Ottoman Empire." *Journal of Comparative Economics* 40 (3): 357–371.

Cowan, B. 2005. *The Social Life of Coffee: The Emergence of the British Coffeehouse*. New Haven, CT: Yale University Press.

Cowan, R. 1990. "Nuclear Power Reactors: A Study in Technological Lock-In." *Journal of Economic History* 50: 541–567.

Cowen, T. 2011. *The Great Stagnation: How America Ate All the Low-Hanging Fruit of Modern History, Got Sick, and Will (Eventually) Feel Better*. New York: Dutton.

Cowen, T. 2023. "AI Could Spell the End of Big Business." *Bloomberg*, April 26.

Cowgill, B., A. Prat, and T. Valletti. 2022. "Political Power and Market Power." Working Paper 17178, CEPR Discussion Paper.

Cox, G. W. 2012. "Was the Glorious Revolution a Constitutional Watershed?." *Journal of Economic History* 72 (3): 567–600.

Cox, G. W. 2016. *Marketing Sovereign Promises: Monopoly Brokerage and the Growth of the English State*. Cambridge: Cambridge University Press.

Cox, G. W., D. C. North, and B. R. Weingast. 2019. "The Violence Trap: A Political-Economic Approach to the Problems of Development." *Journal of Public Finance and Public Choice* 34 (1): 3–19.

Crafts, N. 1984. "Economic Growth in France and Britain, 1830–1910: A Review of the Evidence." *The Journal of Economic History* 44 (1): 49–67.

Crafts, N. 1989. "British Industrialization in an International Context." *Journal of Interdisciplinary History* 19 (3): 415–428.

Crafts, N. 1989. "Revealed Comparative Advantage in Manufacturing, 1899–1950." *Journal of European Economic History* 18 (1): 127–137.
Crafts, N. 1992. "Institutions and Economic Growth: Recent British Experience in an International Context." *West European Politics* 15: 16–38.
Crafts, N. 1995. "The Golden Age of Economic Growth in Western Europe, 1950–1973." *Economic History Review* 48 (3): 429–447.
Crafts, N. 2004. "Steam as a General Purpose Technology: A Growth Accounting Perspective." *Economic Journal* 114 (495): 338–351.
Crafts, N. 2012. "British Relative Economic Decline Revisited: The Role of Competition." *Explorations in Economic History* 49 (1): 17–29.
Crafts, N. 2016. "The Growth Effects of EU Membership for the UK: A Review of the Evidence." Working Paper 280, University of Warwick CAGE.
Crafts, N. 2016. "The Rise and Fall of American Growth: Exploring the Numbers." *American Economic Review* 106 (5): 57–60.
Crafts, N. 2018. *Forging Ahead, Falling Behind and Fighting Back: British Economic Growth from the Industrial Revolution to the Financial Crisis*. Cambridge: Cambridge University Press.
Crafts, N. 2020. "British Relative Economic Decline in the Aftermath of German Unification." Working Paper 1295, University of Warwick, Department of Economics.
Crafts, N., T. Leunig, and A. Mulatu. 2008. "Were British railway companies well managed in the early twentieth century?." *The Economic History Review* 61 (4): 842–866.
Crafts, N. S. J. Leybourne, and T. C. Mills. 1989. "The Climacteric in Late Victorian Britain and France: A Reappraisal of the Evidence." *Journal of Applied Econometrics* 4 (2): 103–117.
Crafts, N., and M. Magnani. 2013. "The Golden Age and the Second Globalization in Italy." In *The Oxford Handbook of the Italian Economy Since Unification*, edited by G. Toniolo, 69–107. Oxford: Oxford University Press.
Crafts, N., and T. C. Mills. 2020. "Sooner Than You Think: The Pre-1914 UK Productivity Slowdown was Victorian not Edwardian." *European Review of Economic History* 24 (4): 736–748.
Crafts, N., and M. Thomas. 1986. "Comparative Advantage in UK Manufacturing Trade, 1910–1935." *Economic Journal* 96 (383): 629–645.
Crafts, N., and G. Toniolo, eds. 1996. *Economic Growth in Europe since 1945*. Cambridge: Cambridge University Press.
Crafts, N., and G. Toniolo. 2010. "Aggregate Growth, 1950–2005." In *The Cambridge Economic History of Modern Europe Volume 2*, edited by S. Broadberry and K.H.O. Rourke, 296–322. Cambridge: Cambridge University Press.
Crane, D. A. 2019. "Fascism and Monopoly." *Michigan Law Review* 118 (7): 1315–1370.
Cranmer-Byng, J. L., ed. 1962. *An Embassy to China: Being the Journal Kept by Lord Macartney During His Embassy to the Emperor Ch'ien-lung 1793–1794*. London: Longmans, Green & Co.
Crenson, M. A. 1975, *The Federal Machine: Beginnings of Bureaucracy in Jacksonian America*. Baltimore: Johns Hopkins University Press.
Crouch, C. 1993. *Industrial Relations and European State Traditions*. Oxford: Clarendon Press.
Crouzet, F. 1996. "France." In *The Industrial Revolution in National Context: Europe and the USA*, edited by M. Teich and R. Porter, 36–63. Cambridge: Cambridge University Press.
Cunningham, C., F. Ederer, and S. Ma. 2021. "Killer Acquisitions." *Journal of Political Economy* 129 (3): 649–702.

David, P. A. 1990. "The Dynamo and the Computer: An Historical Perspective on the Modern Productivity Paradox." *The American Economic Review* 80 (2): 355–361.

Davids, K. 2008. *The Rise and Decline of Dutch Technological Leadership (2 Vols): Technology, Economy and Culture in the Netherlands, 1350–1800 Volume 1*. Boston: Brill.

Davie, H. G. W. 2018. "Logistics of the Combined-Arms Army—Motor Transport." *The Journal of Slavic Military Studies* 31 (4): 474–501.

Davies, R. W. 1994. "Industry." In *The Economic Transformation of the Soviet Union, 1913–1945*, edited by R. W. Davies, M. Harrison, and S. G. Wheatcroft, 131–157. Cambridge: Cambridge University Press.

Davis, C. 1992. "The Defense Sector in the Soviet Economy during Perestroika: From Expansion to Disarmament to Disintegration." In *The Macroeconomic Dimensions of Arms Reduction*, edited by F. G. Adams. Oxford: Westview Press.

Davis, D. R., and D. E. Weinstein. 2002. "Bones, Bombs, and Break Points: The Geography of Economic Activity." *American Economic Review* 92 (5): 1269–1289.

Davis, J. H., and D. A. Irwin. 2003. "Trade Disruptions and America's Early Industrialization." Working Paper 9944, National Bureau of Economic Research.

Davis, L. E. 1972. *American Economic Growth: An Economist's History of the United States, 468–547*. New York: Harper & Row.

De la Croix, D., M. Doepke, and J. Mokyr. 2018. "Clans, Guilds, and Markets: Apprenticeship Institutions and Growth in the Preindustrial Economy." *The Quarterly Journal of Economics* 133 (1): 1–70.

De Long, J. B., and B. Eichengreen. 1993. "The Marshall Plan: History's Most Successful Structural Adjustment Program." In *Postwar Economic Reconstruction and its Lessons for East Today*, edited by R. Dornbusch, W. Nolling, and R. Layard. Cambridge, MA: MIT Press.

De Vries, J., and A. Van der Woude. 1997. *The First Modern Economy: Success, Failure, and Perseverance of the Dutch Economy, 1500–1815*. Cambridge: Cambridge University Press.

Dearden, J., B. Ickes, and L. Samuelson. 1990. "To Innovate or Not to Innovate: Incentives and Innovation in Hierarchies." *American Economic Review* 80: 1105–1124.

Decker, R., and J. Haltiwanger. 2024. "High Tech Business Entry in the Pandemic Era." *FEDS Notes*, April 19.

Decker, R. A., and J. Haltiwanger. 2022. "Business Entry and Exit in the COVID-19 Pandemic: A Preliminary Look at Official Data." *FEDS Notes*, May 06.

Decker, R. A., J. Haltiwanger, R. S. Jarmin, and J. Miranda. 2016. "Declining Business Dynamism: What We Know and the Way Forward." *American Economic Review* 106 (5): 203–207.

Decker, R. A., J. Haltiwanger, R. S. Jarmin, and J. Miranda. 2017. "Declining Dynamism, Allocative Efficiency, and the Productivity Slowdown." *American Economic Review* 107 (5): 322–326.

DeLong, J. B. 2022. *Slouching Towards Utopia: An Economic History of the Twentieth Century*. New York: Basic Books.

Deng, K. G. 2003. "Development and Its Deadlock in Imperial China, 221 B.C.–1840 A.D.." *Economic Development and Cultural Change* 51 (2): 479–522.

Desmet, K., A. Greif, and S. L. Parente. 2020. "Spatial Competition, Innovation and Institutions: The Industrial Revolution and the Great Divergence." *Journal of Economic Growth* 25 (1): 1–35.

Desmet, K., and S. L. Parente. 2012. "The Evolution of Markets and the Revolution of Industry: A Unified Theory of Growth." *Journal of Economic Growth* 17 (3): 205–234.

Dickens, C. 1914. *Miscellaneous Papers*. London: Chapman & Hall.

Dickson, B. 2008. *Wealth into Power: The Communist Party's Embrace of China's Private Sector*. Cambridge: Cambridge University Press.

Dickson, B. 2016. *The Dictator's Dilemma: The Chinese Communist Party's Strategy for Survival.* Oxford: Oxford University Press.

Dickson, B. J. 2021. *The Party and the People.* Princeton: Princeton University Press.

Dikotter, F. 2015. *The Tragedy of Liberation: A History of the Chinese Revolution 1945–1957.* New York: Bloomsbury.

Ding, H., Z. Fu, and H. He. 2018. "Transition and Inequality." Unpublished Manuscript, IMF Seminar 22.

DiPippo, G., I. Mazzocco, and S. Kennedy. 2022. "Red Ink: Estimating Chinese Industrial Policy Spending in Comparative Perspective." *Center for Strategic and International Studies,* May 23. https://csis-website-prod.s3.amazonaws.com/s3fs-public/publication/220523_DiPippo_Red_Ink.pdf?LH8ILLKWz4o.bjrwNS7csuX_C04FyEre.

Doepke, M., and F. Zilibotti. 2008. "Occupational Choice and the Spirit of Capitalism." *The Quarterly Journal of Economics* 123 (2): 747–793.

Donaldson, D. 2018. "Railroads of the Raj: Estimating the Impact of Transportation Infrastructure." *American Economic Review* 108 (4–5): 899–934.

Donaldson, D., and R. Hornbeck. 2016. "Railroads and American Economic Growth: A 'Market Access' Approach." *The Quarterly Journal of Economics* 131 (2): 799–858.

Donges, A. 2018. "Competition and Collusion." In *An Economist's Guide to Economic History,* edited by M. Blum and C. L. Colvin. Basingstoke: Palgrave Macmillan.

Donges, A., J. M. Meier, and R. C. Silva. 2022. "The Impact of Institutions on Innovation." *Management Science* 69 (4): 1951–1974.

Donges, A., and F. Selgert. 2019. "Technology Transfer via Foreign Patents in Germany, 1843–77." *The Economic History Review* 72 (1): 182–208.

Donges, A., and F. Selgert, 2021. "The Social Background of Prussian Inventors and Entrepreneurs during the First Industrial Revolution." *Zeitschrift für Unternehmensgeschichte* 66 (1): 1–41.

Dore, R. P. 1963. "Some Comparisons of Latin American and Asian Studies with Special Reference to Research on Japan." Working Paper, Social Science Research Council.

Dowey, J. 2017. "Mind over Matter: Access to Knowledge and the British Industrial Revolution." PhD diss., London School of Economics and Political Science.

Du, J. 2020. *The Shenzhen Experiment: The Story of China's Instant City.* Cambridge, MA: Harvard University Press.

Duara, P. 1988. *Culture, Power, and the State: Rural North China, 1900–1942.* Stanford: Stanford University Press.

Dube, A., J. Jacobs, S. Naidu, and S. Suri. 2020. "Monopsony in Online Labor Markets." *American Economic Review: Insights* 2 (1): 33–46.

Duby, G. 1972. "Medieval Agriculture, 900–1500." In *The Fontana Economic History of Europe,* edited by C. Cipolla. Glasgow: Collins.

Dunlavy, C. A. 2024. *Small, Medium, Large: How Government Made the US into a Manufacturing Powerhouse.* John Wiley & Sons.

Dunning, J. H. 1998. *American Investment in British Manufacturing Industry.* 2nd ed. London: Routledge.

Duranton, G., and M. A. Turner. 2012. "Urban Growth and Transportation." *Review of Economic Studies* 79 (4): 1407–1440.

Dutton, H. I. 1984. *The Patent System and Inventive Activity During the Industrial Revolution 1750–1852.* Manchester: Manchester University Press.

Earle, E. M. 1923. *Turkey, The Great Powers, and The Bagdad Railway A Study in Imperialism.* London: Macmillan.

Easterly, W., and S. Fischer. 1995. "The Soviet Economic Decline." *The World Bank Economic Review* 9 (3): 341–371.

Eastman, L. E. 1974. *The Abortive Revolution: China Under Nationalist Rule, 1927–1937.* Cambridge, MA: Harvard University Press.

Ederer, F., and B. Pellegrino. 2023. "The Great Start-up Sellout and the Rise of Oligopoly." *AEA Papers and Proceedings* 113: 274–278.

Edwards, J., and S. Ogilvie. 1996. "Universal Banks and German Industrialization: A Reappraisal." *Economic History Review* 49 (3): 427–446.

Eichengreen, B. 2008. *The European Economy since 1945: Coordinated Capitalism and Beyond.* Princeton: Princeton University Press.

Eichengreen, B., D. H. Perkins, and K. Shin. 2012. *From Miracle to Maturity: The Growth of the Korean Economy.* Cambridge, MA: Harvard University Press.

Eiichi, A., M. Imashiro, S. Kato, and Y. Wakuda. 2000. *A History of Japanese Railways.* Tokyo: East Japan Railway Culture Foundation.

Elman, B. A. 2000. *A Cultural History of Civil Examinations in Late Imperial China.* Berkeley: University of California Press.

Elman, B. A. 2005. *On Their Own Terms: Science in China, 1550–1900.* Cambridge, MA: Harvard University Press.

Elman, B. A. 2013. *Civil Examinations and Meritocracy in Late Imperial China.* Cambridge, MA: Harvard University Press.

Elvin, M. 1973. *The Pattern of the Chinese Past: A Social and Economic Interpretation.* Stanford: Stanford University Press.

Engbom, N., H. Malmberg, T. Porzio, F. Rossi, and T. Schoellman. 2024. "Economic Development According to Chandler." Working paper, New York University.

Ennew, C., D. Greenaway, and G. Reed. 1990. "Further Evidence on Effective Tariffs and Effective Protection in the UK." *Oxford Bulletin of Economics and Statistics* 52: 69–78.

Epstein, R. 1998. "Craft Guilds, Apprenticeship and Technological Change in Preindustrial Europe." *Journal of Economic History* 58 (3): 684–713.

Erickson, M. 2005. *Into the Unknown Together: The DOD, NASA, and Early Spaceflight.* Montgomery: Air University Press.

Ericson, S. 1996. *The Sound of the Whistle: Railroads and the State in Meiji Japan.* Cambridge, MA: Council on East Asian Studies, Harvard University Press.

Esposto, A. G. 1992. "Italian Industrialization and the Gerschenkronian 'Great Spurt': A Regional Analysis." *The Journal of Economic History* 52 (2): 353–362.

Estabrook, H. D. 1913. "The First Train Order by Telegraph." *Baltimore Magazine* 1: 27–29.

Estrin, S., and P. Holmes. 1983. *French Planning in Theory and Practice.* European Bank for Reconstruction. London: Allen & Unwin.

Fagerberg, J. 1994. "Technology and International Differences in Growth Rates." *Journal of Economic Literature* 32 (3): 1147–1175.

Fairbank, J. 1992. *China: A New History.* Cambridge, MA: Belknap Press.

Fallick, B., C. A. Fleischman, and J. B. Rebitzer. 2006. "Job-Hopping in Silicon Valley: Some Evidence Concerning the Microfoundations of a High-Technology Cluster." *Review of Economics and Statistics* 88 (3): 472–481.

Fallows, J. 1994. *Looking at the Sun: The Rise of the New East Asian Economic and Political System* New York: Pantheon.

Farber, H. S., D. Herbst, I. Kuziemko, and S. Naidu. 2021. "Unions and Inequality over the Twentieth Century: New Evidence from Survey Data." *The Quarterly Journal of Economics* 136 (3): 1325–1385.

Fauri, F. 1996. "The Role of Fiat in the Development of the Italian Car Industry in the 1950s." *Business History Review* 70: 167–206.

Federico, G. 1996. "Italy, 1860–1940: A Little-Known Success Story." *The Economic History Review* 49 (4): 764–786.
Fehrenbach, E. 2008. *Vom Ancien Regime zum Wiener Kongress*. Munich: Oldenbourg.
Feinstein, C. H. 1997. "Technical Progress and Technology Transfer in a Centrally Planned Economy: The Experience of the USSR, 1917–87." In *Chinese Technology Transfer in the 1990s*, edited by C. Feinstein and C. Howe. Cheltenham: Edward Elgar.
Felbermayr, G. J., and F. Toubal. 2010. "Cultural Proximity and Trade." *European Economic Review* 54 (2): 279–293.
Felin, T., and M. Holweg. 2024. "Theory Is All You Need: AI, Human Cognition, and Decision Making." Working Paper 4737265, Social Science Research Network.
Fen, L. 2013. *Early China: A Social and Cultural History*. Cambridge: Cambridge University Press.
Feng, L. 2008. *Bureaucracy and the State in Early China*. Cambridge: Cambridge University Press.
Ferguson, N. 2012. *The War of the World: Twentieth-Century Conflict and the Descent of the West*. New York: Penguin Press.
Ferguson, N., and M. Schularick. 2007. "Chimerica and the Global Asset Market Boom." *International Finance* 10 (3): 215–239.
Fernández-Villaverde, J., M. Koyama, Y. Lin, and T. H. Sng. 2020. "The Fractured-Land Hypothesis." Working Paper 27774, National Bureau of Economic Research.
Ferrie, J. P. 2005. "History Lessons: The End of American Exceptionalism? Mobility in the United States Since 1850." *Journal of Economic Perspectives* 19 (3): 199–215.
Field, A. J. 1992. "The Magnetic Telegraph, Price and Quantity Data, and the New Management of Capital." *The Journal of Economic History* 52 (2): 401–413.
Field, A. J. 2003. "The Most Technologically Progressive Decade of the Century." *American Economic Review* 93 (4): 1399–1413.
Field, A. J. 2007. "The Origins of US Total Factor Productivity Growth in the Golden Age." *Cliometrica* 1 (1): 89.
Field, A. J. 2011. *A Great Leap Forward: 1930s Depression and U.S. Economic Growth*. New Haven, CT: Yale University Press.
Field, A. J. 2022. "The Decline of US Manufacturing Productivity between 1941 and 1948." *The Economic History Review* 76: 1163–1190.
Field, A. J. 2022. *The Economic Consequences of U.S. Mobilization for the Second World War*. New Haven, CT: Yale University Press.
Fieldhouse, A. J., and K. Mertens. 2023. "The Returns to Government R&D: Evidence from US Appropriations Shocks." Working Paper, Federal Reserve Bank of Dallas, Research Department.
Figueroa, V. 2021. "The Protestant Road to Bureaucracy." Working Paper 20230006, Pontificia Universidad Católica de Chile.
Findla, R. 1978. "Relative Backwardness, Direct Foreign Investment, and the Transfer of Technology: A Simple Dynamic Model." *The Quarterly Journal of Economics* 92 (1): 1–16.
Finley, M. I. 1965. "Technical Innovation and Economic Progress in the Ancient World." *Economic History Review* 18 (1): 29–45.
Finley, M. I. 1973. *The Ancient Economy*. Berkeley: University of California Press.
First, H. 1995. "Antitrust Enforcement in Japan." *Antitrust Law Journal* 64: 137–182.
Fisher, F. M. 1983. *IBM and the U.S. Data Processing Industry: An Economic History*. New York: Praeger.
Fisher, I. 1927. "The Economics of Prohibition." *The American Economic Review* 17 (1): 5–10.

Fishlow, A. 1965, *American Railroads and the Transformation of the Ante-bellum Economy*. Cambridge, MA: Harvard University Press.
Flamm, K. 1988. *Creating the Computer: Government, Industry and High Technology*. Washington, DC: Brookings Institution Press.
Flanders, A. 1952. "Industrial Relations." In *The British Economy, 1945–1950*, edited by G. D. N. Worswick and P. H. Ady, 101–124. Oxford: Clarendon Press.
Fogel, R. W. 1964. *Railroads and American Economic Growth*. Baltimore: Johns Hopkins Press.
Fohlin, C. 1999. "The Rise of Interlocking Directorates in Imperial Germany." *Economic History Review* 52 (2): 307–333.
Fohlin, C. 2007. *Finance Capitalism and Germany's Rise to Industrial Power*. Cambridge: Cambridge University Press.
Fohlin, C., and A. Gregg. 2022. "Finance Capitalism in Industrializing Autocracies: Evidence from Corporate Balance Sheets in Imperial Germany and Russia." Working Paper 17029, CEPR Discussion Paper.
Franck, R., and O. Galor. 2019. "Flowers of Evil? Industrialization and Long Run Development." *Journal of Monetary Economics* 117: 108–128.
Frankel, M. 1957. *British and American Manufacturing Productivity*. Champaign: University of Illinois Press.
Franklin, B. 1784. *Information to Those Who Would Remove to America*. Passy: Printed by Benjamin Franklin.
Free, D. 2008. *Early Japanese Railways, 1853–1914*. Tokyo: Tuttle.
Freeman, C. 1987. *Technology Policy and Economic Performance: Lessons from Japan*. London: Frances Pinter.
Freeman, J. B. 2018. *Behemoth: A History of the Factory and the Making of the Modern World*. New York: W. W. Norton.
Frey, C. B. 2019. *The Technology Trap: Capital, Labour, and Power in the Age of Automation*. Princeton: Princeton University Press.
Frey, C. B. 2021. "How Culture Gives the US an Innovation Edge Over China." *MIT Sloan Management Review* 62 (3): 55–61.
Frey, C. B., and M. Osborne. 2023. "Generative AI and the Future of Work: A Reappraisal." *Brown Journal of World Affairs* 30 (1): 1–17.
Frey, C. B., and G. Presidente. 2024. "Privacy Regulation and Firm Performance: Estimating the GDPR Effect Globally." *Economic Inquiry* 62 (3): 1074–89.
Friedewald, M. 2012. "Telefunken vs. Marconi, or the Race for Wireless Telegraphy at Sea, 1896–1914." Working Paper 2375755, Social Science Research Network.
Friedman, A. 1988. *Agnelli: Fiat and the Network of Italian Power*. New York: New American Library.
Friedman, M. 1982. *Capitalism and Freedom: Fortieth Anniversary Edition*. Chicago: University of Chicago.
Friedrich, O. 1983. "The Computer Moves In (Machine of the Year)." *Time*, January 3, 15.
Fuchs, E. R. H. 2010. "Rethinking the Role of the State in Technology Development: DARPA and the Case for Embedded Network Governance." *Research Policy* 39: 1133–1147.
Fukuyama, F. 2011. *Origins of Political Order: From Prehuman Times to the French Revolution*. London: Profile Books.
Fukuyama, F. 2014. *Political Order and Political Decay: From the Industrial Revolution to the Globalisation of Democracy*. London: Profile Books.
Fuller, D. B. 2016. *Paper Tigers, Hidden Dragons: Firms and the Political Economy of China's Technological Development*. Oxford: Oxford University Press.

Fung, K. C. 1991. "Characteristics of Japanese Industrial Groups and Their Potential Impact on U.S.-Japanese Trade." In *Empirical Studies of Commercial Policy*, edited by R. E. Baldwin. Chicago: University of Chicago Press.

Galambos, L. 1992. "Theodore N. Vail and the Role of Innovation in the Modern Bell System." *Business History Review* 66: 95–126.

Galasso, A., and M. Schankerman. 2015. "Patents and Cumulative Innovation: Causal Evidence from the Courts." *The Quarterly Journal of Economics* 130 (1): 317–369.

Gallatin, A. 1810. "American State Papers: Fin 325. D. o. Treasury." ASP010: 425–439, 427.

Gallo, M. E. 2018. "Defense Advanced Research Projects Agency: Overview and Issues for Congress - CRS Report for Congress R45088." Congressional Research Service.

García-Jimeno, C., and J. A. Robinson. 2011. "The Myth of the Frontier." In *Understanding Long-Run Economic Growth*, edited by D. L. Costa and N. R. Lamoreaux. Chicago: University of Chicago Press.

Garcia-Macia, D., C. T. Hsieh, and P. J. Klenow. 2019. "How Destructive Is Innovation?." *Econometrica* 87 (5): 1507–1541.

Gardner, N. 1976. "The Economics of Launching Aid." In *The Economics of Industrial Subsidies*, edited by A. Whiting. London: HMSO.

Garon, S. 1987. *The State and Labor in Modern Japan*. Berkeley: University of California Press.

Gatrell, P. 1986. *The Tsarist Economy, 1850–1917*. London: Palgrave Macmillan.

Gatrell, P. 1994. *Government, Industry and Rearmament in Russia, 1900–1914: The Last Argument of Tsarism*. Cambridge: Cambridge University Press.

Gatrell, P. 2012. "The Russian Fiscal State, 1600–1914." In *The Rise of Fiscal States: A Global History, 1500–1914*, edited by B. Yun-Casalilla, P. K. O'Brien, and F. C. Comín. Cambridge: Cambridge University Press.

Geiger, R. L. 1986. *To Advance Knowledge: The Growth of American Research Universities, 1900–1940*. New York: Oxford University Press.

Gernet, J. 1962. *Daily Life in China on the Eve of Mongol Invasion, 1250–1276*. New York: Macmillan.

Geroski, P. A. 1990. "Innovation, Technological Opportunity, and Market Structure." *Oxford Economic Papers* 42 (3): 586–602.

Gerschenkron, A. 1955. "Notes on the Rate of Industrial Growth in Italy, 1881–1913." *The Journal of Economic History* 15 (4): 360–375, 365.

Gerschenkron, A. 1962. *Economic Backwardness in Historical Perspective*. Cambridge, MA: Harvard University Press.

Gershenson, D., and H. I. Grossman. 2000. "Cooption and Repression in the Soviet Union." Working Paper 00/201, International Monetary Fund Washington, DC.

Gertner, J. 2012. *The Idea Factory: Bell Labs and the Great Age of American Innovation*. New York: Penguin Books.

Ghemawat, P., and T. Khanna. 1998. "The Nature of Diversified Business Groups: A Research Design and Two Case Studies." *Journal of Industrial Economics* 46 (1): 35–61.

Gibb, G. S., and E. H. Knowlton. 1956. *The Resurgent Years, 1911–1927: History of Standard Oil Company*. New York: Harper & Brothers.

Gibbon, E. 1788. *The History of the Decline and Fall of the Roman Empire Volume 5*. Rockville: Wildside Press.

Gibson, C. 1998. "Population of the 100 Largest Cities and Other Urban Places in the United States: 1790 to 1990." Working Paper POP-WP027, US Census Bureau.

Giorcelli, M. 2019. "The Long-Term Effects of Management and Technology Transfers." *American Economic Review* 109 (1): 121–152.

Giorcelli, M. 2022. *Professionals and Productivity: The Diffusion of Soft Technologies during and after WWII*. Princeton: Princeton University Press. Forthcoming.

Giorcelli, M., and N. Bianchi. 2021. "Reconstruction Aid, Public Infrastructure, and Economic Development: The Case of the Marshall Plan in Italy." Working Paper 29537, National Bureau of Economic Research.

Giorcelli, M., and B. Li. 2021. "Technology Transfer and Early Industrial Development: Evidence from the Sino-Soviet Alliance." Working Paper 29455, National Bureau of Economic Research.

Glaeser, E. L., S. P. Kerr, and W. R. Kerr. 2015. "Entrepreneurship and Urban Growth: An Empirical Assessment with Historical Mines." *Review of Economics and Statistics* 97 (2): 498–520.

Goldin, C., and L. F. Katz. 2008. *The Race Between Education and Technology*. Cambridge, MA: Harvard University Press.

Goldin, H. H. 1947. "Governmental Policy and the Domestic Telegraph Industry." *The Journal of Economic History* 7 (1): 53–68.

Goldin, I., P. Koutroumpis, F. Lafond, and J. Winkler. 2024. "Why Is Productivity Slowing Down?." *Journal of Economic Literature* 62 (1): 196–268.

Goldsmith, J., and T. Wu. 2008. *Who Controls the Internet?: Illusions of a Borderless World*. Oxford: Oxford University Press.

Gollop, F., and D. Jorgenson. 1980. "U.S. Productivity Growth by Industry, 1947–73." In *New Developments in Productivity Measurement*, edited by J. W. Kendrick and B. N. Vaccara, 15–136. Chicago: University of Chicago Press.

Gompers, P. A., and J. Lerner. 2001. *The Money of Invention: How Venture Capital Creates New Wealth*. Boston: Harvard Business School Press.

Gomulka, S. 1986. "Soviet Growth Slowdown: Duality, Maturity, and Innovation." *The American Economic Review* 76 (2): 170–174.

Gomulka, S. 1988. "The Gerschenkron Phenomenon and Systemic Factors in the Post-1975 Growth Slowdown." *European Economic Review* 32 (2–3): 451–458.

Gong, Z. 1991. *Gong Zizhen Selected Poems*. Shanghai: Shanghai Ancient Books Publishing House.

Gong, Z., Z. Xuelei, J. Chen, and G. Zhang. 2003. "Origin and Development of Soil Science in Ancient China." *Geoderma* 115 (1–2): 3–13.

Goody, J. 1986. *The Logic of Writing and the Organization of Society*. Cambridge: Cambridge University Press.

Gordon, A. 1988. *The Evolution of Labor Relations in Japan: Heavy Industry, 1853–1955*. Cambridge, MA: Harvard University Asia Center.

Gordon, R. J. 1967. "Problems in the Measurement of Real Investment in the US Private Economy." PhD diss., Massachusetts Institute of Technology.

Gordon, R. J. 2016. *The Rise and Fall of American Growth: The U.S. Standard of Living since the Civil War*. Princeton: Princeton University Press.

Gorodnichenko, Y., and G. Roland. 2017. "Culture, Institutions, and the Wealth of Nations." *Review of Economics and Statistics* 99 (3): 402–416.

Gothein, E. 1903. *Geschichtliche Entwicklung der Rheinschiffahrt im XIX. Jahrhundert*. Leipzig: Duncker & Humblot.

Granovetter, M. 1994. "Business Groups." In *Handbook of Economic Sociology*, edited by N. J. Smelser and R. Swedberg. Princeton: Princeton University Press.

Granovetter, M. 1973. "The Strength of Weak Ties." *American Journal of Sociology* 78 (6): 1360–1380.

Green, A. 2003. "The Federal Alternative? A New View of Modern German History." *The Historical Journal* 46 (1): 187–202, 200.

Greenspan, A., and A. Wooldridge. 2018. *Capitalism in America: An Economic History of the United States*. London: Penguin Books.

Greenstein, S. 2015. *How the Internet Became Commercial: Innovation, Privatization, and the Birth of a New Network*. Princeton: Princeton University Press.

Greenwood, J., A. Seshadri, and M. Yorukoglu. 2005. "Engines of Liberation." *The Review of Economic Studies* 72 (1): 109–133.

Gregg, A. G. 2020. "Factory Productivity and the Concession System of Incorporation in Late Imperial Russia, 1894–1908." *American Economic Review* 110 (2): 401–427.

Gregory, P. R. 1974. "Some Empirical Comments on the Theory of Relative Backwardness: The Russian Case." *Economic Development and Cultural Change* 22 (4): 654–665.

Gregory, P. R. 1982. *Russian National Income, 1885–1913*. Cambridge: Cambridge University Press.

Gregory, P. R. 1994. *Before Command: An Economic History of Russia from Emancipation to the First Five-Year Plan*. Princeton: Princeton University Press.

Gregory, P. R. 2003. *The Political Economy of Stalinism: Evidence from the Soviet Secret Archives*. Cambridge: Cambridge University Press.

Gregory, P. R., and M. Harrison. 2005. "Allocation Under Dictatorship: Research in Stalin's Archives." *Journal of Economic Literature* 43 (3): 721–761.

Greider, W. 1989. *Secrets of the Temple: How the Federal Reserve Runs the Country*. New York: Simon and Schuster.

Greif, A. 1994. "Cultural Beliefs and the Organization of Society: A Historical and Theoretical Reflection on Collectivist and Individualist Societies." *Journal of Political Economy* 102 (5): 912–950.

Greif, A. 2006. "Family Structure, Institutions, and Growth: The Origins and Implications of Western Corporations." *American Economic Review* 96 (2): 308–312.

Greif, A., and G. Tabellini. 2010. "Cultural and Institutional Bifurcation: China and Europe Compared." *American Economic Review* 100 (2): 135–140.

Greif, A., and G. Tabellini. 2017. "The Clan and the Corporation: Sustaining Cooperation in China and Europe." *Journal of Comparative Economics* 45 (1): 1–35.

Griffiths, J. 2021. *The Great Firewall of China: How to Build and Control an Alternative Version of the Internet*. London: Bloomsbury.

Gross, D. P. 2020. "Collusive Investments in Technological Compatibility: Lessons from US Railroads in the Late 19th Century." *Management Science* 66 (12): 5683–5700.

Gross, D. P. 2022. "The Hidden Costs of Securing Innovation: The Manifold Impacts of Compulsory Invention Secrecy." *Management Science* 69 (4): 1935–2545.

Gross, D. P., and B. N. Sampat. 2020. "Inventing the Endless Frontier: The Effects of the World War II Research Effort on Post-War Innovation." Working Paper 27375, National Bureau of Economic Research.

Grow, R. F. 1984. "Soviet Economic Penetration of China, 1945–1960: 'Imperialism' as a Level of Analysis Problem." In *Testing Theories of Economic Imperialism*, edited by S. J. Rosen and J. R. Keith. Lexington: Lexington Books.

Gruber, J., and S. Johnson. 2019. *Jump-Starting America: How Breakthrough Science Can Revive Economic Growth and the American Dream*. New York: PublicAffairs.

Grullon, G., Y. Larkin, and R. Michaely. 2019. "Are US Industries Becoming More Concentrated?." *Review of Finance* 23 (4): 697–743.

Gutiérrez, G., and T. Philippon. 2018. "How European Markets Became Free: A Study of Institutional Drift." Working Paper 24700, National Bureau of Economic Research.

Gutiérrez, G., and T. Philippon. 2019. "The Failure of Free Entry." Working Paper 26001, National Bureau of Economic Research.

Guzman, J., and S. Stern. 2020. "The State of American Entrepreneurship: New Estimates of the Quantity and Quality of Entrepreneurship for 32 US States, 1988–2014." *American Economic Journal: Economic Policy* 12 (4): 212–243.

Haber, S. H., and N. R. Lamoreaux. 2021. *The Battle over Patents: History and Politics of Innovation*. Oxford: Oxford University Press.

Habermas, J. 1989. *The Structural Transformation of the Public Sphere*. Cambridge, MA: MIT Press.

Hackett, J. 1965. *Economic Planning in France: Its Relation to the Policies of the Developed Countries of Western Europe*. Bombay: Asian Publishing House.

Hadley, E. M. 1970. *Antitrust in Japan*. Princeton: Princeton University Press.

Haerpfer, C., R. Inglehart, A. Moreno, C. Welzel, K. Kizilova, J. Diez-Medrano, M. Lagos, P. Norris, E. Ponarin, and B. Puranen, eds. 2020. *World Values Survey: Round Seven*. Madrid, Spain & Vienna, Austria: JD Systems Institute and WVSA Secretariat.

Haggard, S., and T. J. Cheng. 1987. "State and Foreign Capital in the East Asian NICs." In *The Political Economy of the New Asian Industrialism*. Cornell: Cornell University Press.

Hailwood, M. 2014. *Alehouses and Good Fellowship in Early Modern England*. Woodbridge: Boydell Press.

Hall, P., and D. Soskice, eds. 2001. *The Varieties of Capitalism: The Institutional Foundations of Comparative Advantage*. New York: Oxford University Press.

Halsall, G. 2003. *Warfare and Society in the Barbarian West, 450–900*. London: Routledge.

Haltiwanger, J., R. Decker, and R. Jarmin. 2015. "Top Ten Signs of Declining Business Dynamism and Entrepreneurship in the U.S." Kauffman Foundation New Entrepreneurial Growth Conference.

Hanlon, W. W. 2022. "The Rise of the Engineer: Inventing the Professional Inventor During the Industrial Revolution." Working Paper 29751, National Bureau of Economic Research.

Hanlon, W. W. 2024. *The Laissez-Faire Experiment: Why Britain Embraced and Then Abandoned Small Government, 1800–1914*. Princeton: Princeton University Press.

Hanlon, W. W., S. Heblich, F. Monte, and M. B. Schmitz. 2022. "A Penny for Your Thoughts." Working Paper 30076, National Bureau of Economic Research.

Hannah, L. 2008. "Logistics, Market Size, and Giant Plants in the Early Twentieth Century: A Global View." *The Journal of Economic History* 68 (1): 46–79.

Hansen, A. H. 1939. "Economic Progress and Declining Population Growth." *American Economic Review* 29 (1): 10–11.

Hanson, P. 2003. *The Rise and Fall of the Soviet Union*. London: Longman.

Hao, Y. 2021. "Social Mobility in China, 1645–2012: A Surname Study." *China Economic Quarterly International* 1 (3): 233–243.

Hao, Y. P., and E. M. Wang. 1980. "Changing Chinese Views of Western Relations." In *The Cambridge History of China Volume 11*, edited by J. Fairbank and K. C. Liu, 142–201. Cambridge: Cambridge University Press.

Harari, Y. N. 2018. "Why Technology Favors Tyranny." *The Atlantic* 322 (3): 64–73.

Harcave, S. 2015. *Count Sergei Witte and the Twilight of Imperial Russia: A Biography*. London: Routledge.

Hariri, J. G., and A. M. Wingender. 2023. "Jumping the Gun: How Dictators Got Ahead of Their Subjects." *The Economic Journal* 133 (650): 728–760.

Harper, K. 2017. *The Fate of Rome*. Princeton: Princeton University Press.

Harris, J. R. 2017. *Industrial Espionage and Technology Transfer: Britain and France in the 18th Century*. Abingdon: Taylor & Francis.

Harris, R. 2020. *Going the Distance: Eurasian Trade and the Rise of the Business Corporation, 1400–1700*. Princeton: Princeton University Press.

Harrison, J. 1978. *An Economic History of Modern Spain*. Manchester: Manchester University Press.

Harrison, M. 1980. "Why Did NEP Fail?." *Economics of Planning* 16 (2): 57–67.

Harrison, M. 1985. *Soviet Planning in Peace and War, 1938–1945*. Cambridge: Cambridge University Press.

Harrison, M. 1989. "Industrial Expansion under Late Stalinism (1945–1955): the Short-Run Dynamic of Civilian Output from Demobilisation to Rearmament." *Journal of European Economic History* 17 (2): 359–378.

Harrison, M. 1994. "The Second World War." In *The Economic Transformation of the Soviet Union, 1913–1945*, edited by R. W. Davies, M. Harrison, and S. G. Wheatcroft. Cambridge: Cambridge University Press.

Harrison, M. 2001. "The Soviet Market for Inventions: The Case of Jet Propulsion, 1932 to 1944." Working Paper 2068–2018–1335, Warwick Economic Research Papers.

Harrison, M. 2002. "Coercion, Compliance, and the Collapse of the Soviet Command Economy." *Economic History Review* 55: 397–433.

Harrison, M. 2002. "Economic Growth and Slowdown." In *Brezhnev Reconsidered*, edited by Edwin Bacon and Mark Sandle, 38–67. London: Palgrave Macmillan.

Harrison, M. 2003. "The Political Economy of a Soviet Military R&D Failure: Steam Power for Aviation, 1932 to 1939." *The Journal of Economic History* 63 (1): 178–212.

Harrison, M. 2003. "Soviet Industry and the Red Army under Stalin: A Military-Industrial Complex?." *Cahiers Du Monde Russe* 44 (2/3): 323–342.

Harrison, M. 2011. "Forging Success: Soviet Managers and Accounting Fraud, 1943–1962." *Journal of Comparative Economics* 39 (1): 43–64.

Harrison, M. 2011. "The Soviet Union after 1945: Economic Recovery and Political Repression." *Past and Present* 210 (6): 103–120.

Harrison, M. 2017. "The Soviet Economy, 1917–1991: Its Life and Afterlife." *The Independent Review* 22 (2): 199–206.

Harrison, M., and D. Ma. 2013. "Soaring Dragon, Stumbling Bear China's Rise in a Comparative Context." The CAGE–Chatham House Series (6). https://www.chathamhouse.org/sites/default/files/public/Research/International%20Economics/0313bp_chinarise.pdf.

Harrison, M., and N. S. Simonov. 2000. "Voenpriemka: Prices, Costs, and Quality in Defence Industry." In *The Soviet Defence Industry Complex from Stalin to Krushchev*, edited by M. Harrison and J. D. Barber, 237–238. New York: St. Martin's Press.

Hartwell, R. 1962. "A Revolution in the Chinese Iron and Coal Industries." *Journal of Asian Studies* 21 (2): 153–162.

Hartwell, R. 1966. "Markets, Technology, and the Structure of Enterprise in the Development of the Eleventh-Century Chinese Iron and Steel Industry." *Journal of Economic History* 26 (1): 29–58.

Hass, E. A. 1987. "Applying the Lessons: Networking Semiconductor Companies." *Entrepreneurial Economy* 6 (1): 40–41.

Hawley, E. W. 1966. *The New Deal and the Problem of Monopoly: A Study in Economic Ambivalence*. Princeton: Princeton University Press.

Hayek, F. A. 1940. "Socialist Calculation: The Competitive 'Solution.'" *Economica* 7 (26): 125–149.

Hayek, F. A. 1945. "The Use of Knowledge in Society." *The American Economic Review* 35 (4): 519–530.

Hayek, F. A. 1948. *Individualism and Economic Order*. Chicago: University of Chicago Press.

Hayek, F. A. 2013. "The Use of Knowledge in Society." In *Modern Understandings of Liberty and Property*, edited by R. A. Epstein, 27–38. New York: Routledge.

He, W. 2013. *Paths toward the Modern Fiscal State*. Cambridge, MA: Harvard University Press.
Headrick, D. R. 1988. *The Tentacles of Progress: Technology Transfer in the Age of Imperialism, 1850–1940*. Oxford: Oxford University Press.
Heblich, S., S. J. Redding, and H. J. Voth. 2022. "Slavery and the British Industrial Revolution." Working Paper 30451, National Bureau of Economic Research.
Heilmann, S., and L. Shih. 2013. "The Rise of Industrial Policy in China, 1978–2012." Working Paper, Harvard-Yenching Institute Working Paper Series 17 (7).
Heinzen, J. W. 2005. "Corruption in the Gulag: Dilemmas of Officials and Prisoners." *Comparative Economic Studies* 47 (2): 456–475.
Heldring, L., J. A. Robinson, and S. Vollmer. 2021. "The Long-Run Impact of the Dissolution of the English Monasteries." *The Quarterly Journal of Economics* 136 (4): 2093–2145.
Henderson, D. F. 1975. *Foreign Enterprise in Japan: Laws and Policies*. Tokyo: Tuttle.
Henderson, R. 1993. "Underinvestment and Incompetence as Responses to Radical Innovation: Evidence from the Photolithographic Alignment Equipment Industry." *The RAND Journal of Economics* 24 (2): 248–270.
Hendry, J. 1989. *Innovating for Failure: Government Policy and the Early British Computer Industry*. Cambridge, MA: MIT Press.
Henrich, J. 2014. "Rice, Psychology, and Innovation." *Science* 344 (6184): 593–594.
Henrich, J. 2020. *The WEIRDest People in the World: How the West Became Psychologically Peculiar and Particularly Prosperous*. London: Penguin Books.
Hershatter, G. 1986. *The Workers of Tianjin, 1900–1949*. Stanford: Stanford University Press.
Hibbert, F. A. 1891. *The Influence and Development of English Guilds*. New York: Sentry.
Hickey, D. R. 2012. *The War of 1812: A Forgotten Conflict*. Champaign: University of Illinois Press.
Higgs, R. 1992. "Wartime Prosperity? A Reassessment of the US Economy in the 1940s." *The Journal of Economic History* 52 (1): 41–60.
Hirata, K. 2018. "Steel Metropolis: Industrial Manchuria and the Making of Chinese Socialism, 1916–1964." PhD diss., Stanford University.
Hirschman, A. O. 1958. *The Strategy of Economic Development*. New Haven, CT: Yale University Press.
Hirschmeier, J., and T. Yui. 2018. *The Development of Japanese Business, 1600–1980*. Abingdon: Routledge.
Ho, P. 1970. "Economic and Institutional Factors in the Decline of the Chinese Empire." In *The Economic Decline of Empires*, edited by C. Cipolla, 274–276. London: Methuen Young Books.
Ho, S. P. 1997. "Technology Transfer to China During the 1980s-How Effective? Some Evidence from Jiangsu." *Pacific Affairs* (1997): 85–106.
Hobsbawm, E. J. 1995. *The Age of Extremes: The Short Twentieth Century 1914–1991*. London: Abacus.
Hobsbawm, E. J. 1968. *Industry and Empire: The Making of Modern English Society, 1750 to the Present Day*. New York: Pantheon Books.
Hoch, S. L. 1989. *Serfdom and Social Control in Russia: Petrovskoe, a Village in Tambov*. Chicago: University of Chicago Press.
Hoffman, R. J. 2019. *Great Britain and the German Trade Rivalry: 1875–1914 Volume 23*. London: Routledge.
Hofstede, G. 1991. *Cultures and Organizations: Software of the Mind*. New York: McGraw-Hill.
Hogan, M. J. 1987. *The Marshall Plan. America, Britain and the Reconstruction of Western Europe, 1947–1952*. Cambridge: Cambridge University Press.
Holborn, H. 1982. *A History of Modern Germany: 1840–1945 Volume 3*. Princeton: Princeton University Press.

Horn, J. 2008. *The Path Not Taken: French Industrialization in the Age of Revolution, 1750–1830*. Cambridge, MA: MIT Press.

Hornbeck, R., and M. Rotemberg. 2021. "Railroads, Market Access, and Aggregate Productivity Growth." Working Paper 26594, National Bureau of Economic Research.

Hornbeck, R., and S. Naidu. 2014. "When the Levee Breaks: Black Migration and Economic Development in the American South." *American Economic Review* 104 (3): 963–990.

Hornung, E. 2014. "Immigration and the Diffusion of Technology: The Huguenot Diaspora in Prussia." *American Economic Review* 104 (1): 84–122.

Hornung, E. 2015. "Railroads and Growth in Prussia." *Journal of the European Economic Association* 13 (4): 699–736.

Hounshell, D. 1985. *From the American System to Mass Production, 1800–1932: The Development of Manufacturing Technology in the United States*. Baltimore: Johns Hopkins University Press.

Hounshell, D. A., J. K. Smith, and J. V. Smith. 1988. *Science and Corporate Strategy: Du Pont R and D, 1902–1980*. Cambridge: Cambridge University Press.

Hout, T. M., and P. Ghemawat. 2010. "China vs the World." *Harvard Business Review* 88 (12): 94–103.

Howes, A. 2017. "The Relevance of Skills to Innovation During the British Industrial Revolution, 1547–1851." Working Paper, Brown University.

Howes, A. 2020. *Arts and Minds: How the Royal Society of Arts Changed a Nation*. Princeton: Princeton University Press.

Hsieh, C. T., E. Hurst, C. I. Jones, and P. J. Klenow. 2019. "The Allocation of Talent and U.S. Economic Growth." *Econometrica* 87 (5): 1439–1474.

Hsü, I. C. Y. 1990. *The Rise of Modern China*. Oxford: Oxford University Press.

Huang, R. 1974. *Taxation and Governmental Finance in Sixteenth-Century Ming China*. Cambridge: Cambridge University Press.

Huang, Y. 2023. *The Rise and Fall of the EAST: How Exams, Autocracy, Stability, and Technology Brought China Success, and Why They Might Lead to Its Decline*. New Haven, CT: Yale University Press.

Huang, Z., L. Li, G. Ma, and L. C. Xu. 2017. "Hayek, Local Information, and Commanding Heights: Decentralizing State-Owned Enterprises in China." *American Economic Review* 107 (8): 2455–2478.

Huer, J. 1989. *Marching Orders: The Role of the Military in South Korea's "Economic Miracle," 1961–1971*. New York: Greenwood Press.

Hughes, J. R. 1991. *The Governmental Habit Redux: Economic Controls from Colonial Times to the Present*. Princeton: Princeton University Press.

Hughes, J. W., and D. P. Barbezat. 1996. "Basing-Point Pricing and the Stahlwerksverband: An Examination of the 'New Competitive School.'" *The Journal of Economic History* 56 (1): 215–222.

Hughes, T. P. 1989. *American Genesis: A Century of Invention and Technological Enthusiasm, 1870–1970*. Chicago: University of Chicago Press.

Hume, D. 1777. "Of the Rise and Progress of the Arts and Sciences." In *Essays: Moral, Political and Literary*, edited by F. Eugene, 111–137. Indianapolis: Liberty Fund.

Humphries, J. 2010. *Childhood and Child Labour in the British Industrial Revolution*. Cambridge: Cambridge University Press.

Humphries, J. 2013. "The Lure of Aggregates and the Pitfalls of the Patriarchal Perspective: A Critique of the High Wage Economy Interpretation of the British Industrial Revolution." *Economic History Review* 66 (3): 693–714.

Humphries, J., and B. Schneider. 2019. "Spinning the Industrial Revolution." *The Economic History Review* 72 (1): 126–155.

Huntzinger, J. 2002. *The Roots of Lean: Training Within Industry: The Origin of Kaizen, Association for manufacturing Excellence.* Cicero: LeanFrontiers.

Hymer, S. H. 1974. "The International Operations of National Firms: A Study of Direct Foreign Investment." PhD diss., Massachusetts Institute of Technology.

Hymes, R. 2015. "Sung Society and Social Change." In *The Cambridge History of China Volume 5, Part 2: Sung China, 960–1279*, edited by J. Chaffee and D. Twitchett, 526–664. Cambridge: Cambridge University Press.

Ichiko, C. 1980. "Political and Institutional Reform, 1901–11." In *The Cambridge History of China Volume 11*, edited by J. Fairbank and K. C. Liu, 375–415. Cambridge: Cambridge University Press.

Inkster, I. 1991. *Science and Technology in History: An Approach to Industrial Development.* London: Macmillan.

International Monetary Fund. 2024. Europe's Declining Productivity Growth: Diagnoses and Remedies (Note No. 2024/001). International Monetary Fund.

Irwin, D. A. 2005. "The Welfare Cost of Autarky: Evidence from the Jeffersonian Trade Embargo, 1807–09." *Review of International Economics* 13 (4): 631–645.

Irwin, D. A. 2017. *Clashing over Commerce: A History of US Trade Policy.* Chicago: University of Chicago Press.

Irwin, D. A. 2020. *Free Trade Under Fire.* Princeton: Princeton University Press.

Isaacson, W. 2014. *The Innovators: How a Group of Hackers, Geniuses, and Geeks Created the Digital Revolution.* New York: Simon and Schuster.

Isaacson, W. 2015. *Steve Jobs: The Exclusive Biography.* New York: Simon & Schuster.

Jacobs, J. 1969. *The Economy of Cities.* New York: Random House.

Jacobsen, S. G. 2015. "Prussian Emulations of a Chinese Meritocratic Ideal? Early Modern Europe Debating How China Selected Civil Servants." *Journal for Eighteenth-Century Studies* 38 (3): 425–441.

Jaeger, H. 1967. *Unternehmer in der deutschen Politik (1890 - 1918).* Bonn: Rohrscheid Verlag.

James, H. 2012. *Krupp: A History of the Legendary British Firm.* Princeton: Princeton University Press.

Jami, C. 2012. *The Emperor's New Mathematics: Western Learning and Imperial Authority during the Kangxi Reign (1662–1722).* Oxford: Oxford University Press.

Jangfeldt, B. 2023. *The Nobel Family: Swedish Geniuses in Tsarist Russia.* London: Bloomsbury.

Jefferson, G. H., and T. G. Rawski. 1994. "Enterprise Reform in Chinese Industry." *Journal of Economic Perspectives* 8 (2): 47–70.

Jeremy, D. J. 1981. *Transatlantic Industrial Revolution: The Diffusion of Textile Technologies between Britain and America, 1790–1830s.* Cambridge, MA: MIT Press.

Jewkes, J., D. Sawers, and R. Stillerman. 1958. *The Sources of Invention.* London: Macmillan Publishers.

Jia, R. 2014. "The Legacies of Forced Freedom: China's Treaty Ports." *Review of Economics and Statistics* 96 (4): 596–608.

Jiang, X. J. 2004. *FDI in China: Contributions to Growth, Restructuring and Competitiveness.* New York: Nova Science.

Jin, H., Y. Qian, and B. R. Weingast. 2005. "Regional Decentralization and Fiscal Incentives: Federalism, Chinese Style." *Journal of Public Economics* 89 (9–10): 1719–1742.

Jin, K. 2023. *The New China Playbook: Beyond Socialism and Capitalism.* London: Swift Press.

John, R. R. 1995. *Spreading the News: The American Postal System from Franklin to Morse.* Cambridge, MA: Harvard University Press.

John, R. R. 2010. *Network Nation.* Cambridge, MA: Harvard University Press.

Johnson, C. 1982. *MITI and the Japanese Miracle: The Growth of Industrial Policy, 1925–1975.* Stanford: Stanford University Press.

Johnson, C. 1987. "Political Institutions and Economic Performance: The Government-Business Relationship in Japan, South Korea, and Taiwan." In *The Political Economy of the New Asian Industrialism*, edited by F. C. Deyo, 149–151. Cornell: Cornell University Press.

Johnson, G. A., S. K. Shriver, and S. G. Goldberg. 2023. "Privacy and Market Concentration: Intended and Unintended Consequences of the GDPR." *Management Science* 69 (10): 5695–721.

Johnson, S., and D. Acemoglu. 2023. *Power and Progress: Our Thousand-Year Struggle Over Technology and Prosperity*. London: Hachette.

Jones, A. H. M. 1964. *The Later Roman Empire*. Oxford: Basil Blackwell.

Jones, E. L. 1981. *The European Miracle*. Cambridge: Cambridge University Press.

Jones, L. P., and I. Sakong. 1980. *Government, Business, and Entrepreneurship in Economic Development: The Korean Case*. Cambridge, MA: Council on East Asian Studies, Harvard University.

Jones, R. E. 1973. *The Emancipation of the Russian Nobility, 1762–1785*. Princeton: Princeton University Press.

Jones, S. R. H. 1987. "Technology, Transaction Costs, and the Transition to Factory Production in the British Silk Industry, 1700–1870." *The Journal of Economic History*, 47 (1): 71–96.

Jones, B. H., and L. H. Summers. 2020. "A Calculation of the Social Returns to Innovation." Working Paper 27863, National Bureau of Economic Research.

Jorgenson, D. W., and K. Nomura. 2007. "The Industry Origins of the US–Japan Productivity Gap." *Economic Systems Research* 19 (3): 315–341.

Judt, T. 2006. *Postwar: A History of Europe Since 1945*. London: Penguin.

Juhász, R. 2018. "Temporary Protection and Technology Adoption: Evidence from the Napoleonic Blockade." *American Economic Review* 108 (11): 3339–3376.

Juhász, R., S. Sakabe, and D. Weinstein. 2024. "Codification, Technology Absorption, and the Globalization of the Industrial Revolution." Working Paper 32667, National Bureau of Economic Research.

Juhász, R., and C. Steinwender. 2018. "Spinning the Web: The Impact of ICT on Trade in Intermediates and Technology Diffusion." Working Paper 24589, National Bureau of Economic Research.

Juhász, R., and C. Steinwender. 2023. "Industrial Policy and the Great Divergence." Working Paper 31736, National Bureau of Economic Research.

Jung, J. Y. 2008. "Retreat of the State? Restructuring the Chinese Central Bureaucracies in the Era of Economic Globalization." *The China Review* 8 (1): 105–125.

Jung-pang, L. 1995. "The Emergence of China as a Sea Power During the Late Sung and Early Yuan Periods." *Far Eastern Quarterly* 14: 489–503.

Kalyani, A. 2022. "The Creativity Decline: Evidence from US Patents." Working Paper 4318158, Social Science Research Network.

Kang, D. C. 2002. *Crony Capitalism: Corruption and Development in South Korea and the Philippines*. Cambridge: Cambridge University Press.

Kantor, S., and A. Whalley. 2023. "Moonshot: Public R&D and Growth." Working Paper 31471, National Bureau of Economic Research.

Karaman, K. K., and S. Pamuk. 2013. "Different Paths to the Modern State in Europe: The Interaction Between Warfare, Economic Structure, and Political Regime." *American Political Science Review* 107 (3): 603–626.

Keller, W. 2004. "International Technology Diffusion." *Journal of Economic Literature* 42 (3): 752–782.

Keller, W., and C. H. Shiue. 2014. "Endogenous Formation of Free Trade Agreements: Evidence from the Zollverein's Impact on Market Integration." *The Journal of Economic History* 74 (4): 1168–1204.

Keller, W., and C. H. Shiue. 2023. "The Economic Consequences of the Opium War." Working Paper: 29404, National Bureau of Economic Research.

Kelly, B., D. Papanikolaou, A. Seru, and M. Taddy. 2021. "Measuring Technological Innovation over the Long Run." *American Economic Review Insights* 3 (3): 303–320.

Kelly, M., J. Mokyr, and C. Ó. Gráda. 2014. "Precocious Albion: A New Interpretation of the British Industrial Revolution." *Annual Review of Economics* 6 (1): 363–389.

Kelly, M., J. Mokyr, and C. Ó. Gráda. 2023. "The Mechanics of the Industrial Revolution." *Journal of Political Economy* 131 (1): 59–94.

Kennan, G. F. 1947. "The Sources of Soviet Conduct." *Foreign Affairs* 25 (4): 566–582.

Kennedy, P. 1987. *The Rise and Fall of the Great Powers*. New York: HarperCollins.

Kennedy, S., ed. 2020. "China's Uneven High-Tech Drive: Implications for the United States." Center for Strategic and International Studies. https://csis-prod.s3.amazonaws.com/s3fs-public/publication/200227_Kennedy_ChinaUnevenDrive_v2.pdf?U.l3GWz1BbzIgMQM0FLXqj.Ph1OmOKb8.

Kerr, W. R. 2008. "Ethnic Scientific Communities and International Technology Diffusion." *The Review of Economics and Statistics* 90 (3): 518–537.

Kerr, W. R., R. Nanda, and M. Rhodes-Kropf. 2014. "Entrepreneurship as Experimentation." *Journal of Economic Perspectives* 28 (3): 25–48.

Khan, B. Z. 1996. "Married Women's Property Laws and Female Commercial Activity: Evidence from United States Patent Records, 1790–1895." *The Journal of Economic History* 56 (2): 356–388.

Khan, B. Z. 2005. *The Democratization of Invention: Patents and Copyrights in American Economic Development, 1790–1920*. Cambridge: Cambridge University Press.

Khan, B. Z. 2020. *Inventing Ideas: Patents, Prizes, and the Knowledge Economy*. Oxford: Oxford University Press.

Khan, B. Z., and K. L. Sokoloff. 1993. "'Schemes of Practical Utility': Entrepreneurship and Innovation Among 'Great Inventors' in the United States, 1790–1865." *The Journal of Economic History* 53 (2): 289–307.

Khan, B. Z., and K. L. Sokoloff. 2001. "History Lessons: The Early Development of Intellectual Property Institutions in the United States." *Journal of Economic Perspectives* 15 (3): 233–246.

Khan, B. Z., and K. L. Sokoloff. 2004. "Institutions and Democratic Invention in 19th-Century America: Evidence from 'Great Inventors,' 1790–1930." *American Economic Review* 94 (2): 395–401.

Khanna, T., and Y. Yafeh. 2007. "Business Groups in Emerging Markets: Paragons or Parasites?." *Journal of Economic Literature* 45 (2): 331–372.

Khlevnyuk, O. V. 2003. "The Economy of the OGPU, NKVD, and MVD of the USSR, 1930–1953: The Scale, Structure, and Trends of Development." In *The Economics of Forced Labor: The Soviet Gulag*, edited by P. R. Gregory and V. Lazarev. Stanford: Hoover Institution Press.

Kiesewetter, H. 2007. *Die Industrialisierung Sachsens: Ein regional-vergleichendes Erklärungsmodell*. Stuttgart: Steiner.

Kim, B. K. 2013. "The Leviathan: Economic Bureaucracy under Park." In *The Park Chung Hee Era*, edited by B. K. Kim and E. F. Vogel. Cambridge, MA: Harvard University Press.

Kim, E. M. 1997. *Big Business, Strong State: Collusion and Conflict in South Korean Development, 1960–1990*. Albany: State University of New York Press.

Kim, K. H. 1974. *Japanese Perspectives on China's Early Modernization: The Self-Strengthening Movement, 1860–1895*. Ann Arbor: University of Michigan for Chinese Studies.

Kinder, C. W. 1891. "Railways and Collieries of North China." *Minutes of the Proceedings of the Institution of Civil Engineers* 103: 278–306.

King, G., J. Pan, and M. E. Roberts. 2013. "How Censorship in China Allows Government Criticism but Silences Collective Expression." *American Political Science Review* 107 (2): 326–343.

Kirby, W. C. 2022. *Empires of Ideas: Creating the Modern University from Germany to America to China*. Cambridge, MA: Harvard University Press.

Kisch, H. 1989. *From Domestic Manufacture to Industrial Revolution: The Case of the Rhineland Textile Districts*. Oxford: Oxford University Press.

Kiser, E., and Y. Cai. 2003. "War and Bureaucratization in Qin China: Exploring an Anomalous Case." *American Sociological Review* 68 (4): 511–539.

Kissinger, H. 2011. *On China*. London: Penguin Books.

Kitson, M., and S. Solomou. 1990. *Protectionism and Economic Revival*. Cambridge: Cambridge University Press.

Kleiman, H. 1966. "The Integrated Circuit Industry: A Case Study of Product Innovation in the Electronics Industry." D.B.A. diss., George Washington University.

Klein, M. 2007. *The Genesis of Industrial America, 1870–1920*. Cambridge: Cambridge University Press.

Klein, M. 2013. *A Call to Arms: Mobilizing America for World War II*. London: Bloomsbury.

Klepper, S. 2009. "Silicon Valley—A Chip off the Old Detroit Bloc." In *Entrepreneurship, Economic Growth and Public Policy*, edited by Z. J. Ács, D. B. Audretsch, and R. J. Strom. Cambridge, MA: Cambridge University Press.

Klepper, S. 2010. "The Origin and Growth of Industry Clusters: The Making of Silicon Valley and Detroit." *Journal of Urban Economics* 67 (1): 15–32.

Klinger, J., J. Mateos-Garcia, and K. Stathoulopoulos. 2020. "A Narrowing of AI Research?." Working Paper 2009.10385, arXiv.

Knight, F. H. 1921. *Risk, Uncertainty and Profit*. New York: Houghton Mifflin.

Ko, C.Y., M. Koyama, and T. H. Sng. 2018. "Unified China and Divided Europe." *International Economic Review* 59 (1): 285–327.

Ko, C.Y., and T.H. Sng. 2013. "Regional Dependence and Political Centralization in Imperial China." *Eurasian Geography and Economics* 54 (5-6): 470–483.

Kocka, J. 1974. "Organisierter Kapitalismus oder Staatsmonopolistischer Kapitalismus?: Begriffliche Vorbemerkungen." In *Organisierter Kapitalismus: Voraussetzungen und Anfänge*, edited by H. A. Winkler and G. D. Feldman, 19–35. Göttingen: Vandenhoeck & Ruprecht.

Kocka, J. 1981. "Capitalism and Bureaucracy in German Industrialization before 1914." *The Economic History Review* 34 (3): 453–468.

Kocka, J., and H. Sigrist. 1979. "Die Hundert größten deutschen Industrieunternehmen im späten 19. und frühen 20. Jahrhundert. Expansion, Diversifikation und Integration im internationalen Vergleich." In *Recht und Entwicklung der Grossunternehmen im 19. und frühen 20. Jahrhundert*, edited by N. Horn and J. Kocka. Göttingen: Vandenhoeck & Ruprecht.

Koh, B. C. 1989. *Japan's Administrative Elite*. Berkeley: University of California Press.

Kohli, A. 2004. *State-Directed Development: Political Power and Industrialization in the Global Periphery*. Cambridge: Cambridge University Press.

Kolev, J., A. Haughey, F. Murray, and S. Stern. 2022. "Of Academics and Creative Destruction: Startup Advantage in the Process of Innovation." Working Paper 30362, National Bureau of Economic Research.

Korinek, A., and J. Vipra. 2025. "Concentrating Intelligence: Scaling and Market Structure in Artificial Intelligence." *Economic Policy* 40 (121): 225–256.

Kornai, J. 1979. "Resource-Constrained Versus Demand-Constrained Systems." *Econometrica* 47 (4): 801–19.

Kornai, J. 2012. "Innovation and Dynamism: Interaction between Systems and Technical Progress." In *Economies in Transition*, edited by G. Roland, 14–56. London: Palgrave Macmillan.

Kornai, J., E. Maskin, and G. Roland. 2003. "Understanding the Soft Budget Constraint." *Journal of Economic Literature* 41 (4): 1095–1136.

Koschnick, J., E. Hornung, and F. Cinnirella. 2022. "Flow of Ideas: Economic Societies and the Rise of Useful Knowledge." Working Paper 9836, Center for Economic Studies.

Koselleck, R. 1967. *Preußen zwischen Reform und Revolution. Allgemeines Landrecht, Verwaltung und soziale Bewegung von 1791–1848*. Stuttgart: Klett Cotta.

Kotkin, S. 2008. *Armageddon Averted: The Soviet Collapse, 1970–2000*. Oxford: Oxford University Press.

Kotkin, S. 2014. *Stalin Volume 1: The Paradoxes of Power, 1878–1928*. London: Penguin Press.

Koyama, M., and J. Rubin. 2022. *How the World Became Rich: The Historical Origins of Economic Growth*. Hoboken: John Wiley & Sons.

Koyama, M., C. Moriguchi, and T. H. Sng. 2018. "Geopolitics and Asia's Little Divergence: State Building in China and Japan after 1850." *Journal of Economic Behavior & Organization* 155: 178–204.

Krause, V. 1890. "Geschichte Des Institutes Der Missi Dominici." *Mitteilungen des Instituts für Österreichische Geschichtsforschung* 11: 193–300.

Krueger, A. O. 1979. *The Developmental Role of the Foreign Sector and Aid Volume 87*. Cambridge, MA: Harvard University Asia Center.

Krueger, D., and K. Kumar. 2002. "Skill-Specific Rather than General Education: A Reason for US–Europe Growth Differences?." Working Paper 9408, National Bureau of Economic Research.

Krug, J. A. 1945. *Production: Wartime Achievements and the Reconversion Outlook*. Special report prepared for the U.S. War Production Board. Washington, DC: Washington Press.

Krugman, P. 1979. "A Model of Innovation, Technology Transfer, and the World Distribution of Income." *Journal of Political Economy* 87 (2): 253–266.

Krugman, P. 1994. "The Myth of Asia's Miracle." *Foreign Affairs* 73 (6): 62–78.

Kruse, K. M., and J. E. Zelizer. 2019. *Fault Lines: A History of the United States Since 1974*. New York: W. W. Norton.

Kuhn, D. 2009. *The Age of Confucian Rule: The Song Transformation of China*. Cambridge, MA: Harvard University Press.

Kumon, Y. 2022. "How Landownership Equality Created a Low Wage Society: Pre-industrial Japan, 1600–1870." Working Paper 138, Institute for Advanced Study in Toulouse.

Kuo, T., and K. C. Liu. 1978. "Self-Strengthening: The Pursuit of Western Technology." In *The Cambridge History of China Volume 10*, edited by J. K. Fairbank, 491–542. Cambridge: Cambridge University Press.

Kuran, T. 2012. *The Long Divergence: How Islamic Law Held Back the Middle East*. Princeton: Princeton University Press.

Labrousse, A., and J. D. Weisz, eds. 2001. *Institutional Economics in France and Germany: German Ordoliberalism versus the French Regulation School*. Berlin: Springer.

Lamoreaux, N. R. 1988. *The Great Merger Movement in American Business, 1895–1904*. Cambridge: Cambridge University Press.

Lamoreaux, N. R. 2010. "Entrepreneurship in the United States, 1865–1920." In *The Invention of Enterprise: Entrepreneurship from Ancient Mesopotamia to Modern Times*, edited by D. S. Landes, J. Mokyr, and W. J. Baumol, 367–400. Princeton: Princeton University Press.

Lamoreaux, N. R. 2011. "The Mystery of Property Rights: A U.S. Perspective." *The Journal of Economic History* 71 (2): 275–306.

Lamoreaux, N. R. 2019. "The Problem of Bigness: From Standard Oil to Google." *Journal of Economic Perspectives* 33 (3): 94–117.

Lamoreaux, N. R., and K. L. Sokoloff. 1999. "Inventive Activity and the Market for Technology in the United States, 1840–1920." Working Paper 7107, National Bureau of Economic Research.

Lamoreaux, N. R., and K. L. Sokoloff. 1999. "Inventors, Firms, and the Market for Technology in the Late Nineteenth and Early Twentieth Centuries." In *Learning by Doing in Markets, Firms, and Countries*, edited by N. R. Lamoreaux, D. M. G. Raff, and P. Temin, 19–60. Chicago: University of Chicago Press.

Lamouroux, C., and R. von Glahn. 2022. "Public Finance, 1000 to 1800." In *The Cambridge Economic History of China Volume 1*, edited by D. Ma and R. von Glahn, 244–269. Cambridge: Cambridge University Press.

Lampe, R., and P. Moser. 2010. "Do Patent Pools Encourage Innovation? Evidence from the 19th-Century Sewing Machine Industry." *The Journal of Economic History* 70 (4): 898–920.

Lancieri, F., E. A. Posner, and L. Zingales. 2022. "The Political Economy of the Decline in Antitrust Enforcement in the United States." Working Paper 30326, National Bureau of Economic Research.

Landes, D. S. 1965. "Japan and Europe: Contrasts in Industrialization." In *State and Economic Enterprise in Japan: Essays in the Political Economy of Growth*, edited by W. W. Lockwood, 93–182. Princeton: Princeton University Press.

Landes, D. S. 1999. *Wealth And Poverty Of Nations*. New York: W. W. Norton.

Landes, D. S. 2003. *The Unbound Prometheus: Technological Change and Industrial Development in Western Europe from 1750 to the Present*. Cambridge: Cambridge University Press.

Lane, N. 2022. "Manufacturing Revolutions: Industrial Policy and Industrialization in South Korea." Working Paper 3890311, Social Science Research Network.

Lange, O. 1937. "On the Economic Theory of Socialism: Part Two." *The Review of Economic Studies* 4 (2): 123–142.

Lange, O. 1962. "Role of Planning in Socialist Economy." In *Problems of Political Economy of Socialism*, edited by O. Lange. Delhi: People's Publishing House.

Lange, O., and C. H. Feinstein. 1967. "The Computer and the Market." In *Socialism, Capitalism and Economic Growth: Essays Presented to Maurice Dobb*, edited by C. H. Feinstein, 158–161. Cambridge: Cambridge University Press.

Langlois, R. N. 2023. *The Corporation and the Twentieth Century: The History of American Business Enterprise*. Princeton: Princeton University Press.

Lardy, N. 1995. "Emulating the Soviet Model, 1949–1957." In *The Cambridge History of China Volume 14: The People's Republic of China: The Emergence of Revolutionary China, 1949–1965*, edited by R. MacFarquhar and J. K. Fairbank. Cambridge: Cambridge University Press.

Lardy, N. 2014. *Markets Over Mao: The Rise of Private Business in China*. New York: Columbia University Press.

Law, M., and G. D. Libecap. 2006. "The Determinants of Progressive Era Reform. The Pure Food and Drugs Act of 1906." In *Corruption and Reform: Lessons from America's Economic History*, edited by E. L. Glaeser and C. Goldin. Chicago: University of Chicago Press.

Lawrence, R. Z. 1991. "Efficient or Exclusionist? The Import Behavior of Japanese Corporate Groups." *Brookings Papers on Economic Activity* 1991 (1): 311–330.

Lazarev, V., and P. R. Gregory. 2002. "The Wheels of a Command Economy: Allocating Soviet Vehicles." *The Economic History Review* 55 (2): 324–348.

Leamer, E., and J. Levinsohn. 1995. "International Trade: The Evidence." In *Handbook of International Economics Volume 3*, edited by G. M. Grossman and K. Rogoff, 1387–1388. Amsterdam: North-Holland.

LeConte, J. 1888. "The Problem of a Flying Machine." *Science Monthly* 34: 69–77.

Lécuyer, C. 1999. "Silicon for Industry: Component Design, Mass Production, and the Move to Commercial Markets at Fairchild Semiconductor, 1960–1967." *History and Technology* 16 (2): 179–216.

Lécuyer, C. 2006. *Making Silicon Valley: Innovation and the Growth of High Tech, 1930–1970*. Cambridge, MA: MIT Press.

Leduc, S., and D. Wilson. 2012. "Highway Grants: Roads to Prosperity?." *FRBSF Economic Letter* 35 (November): 1–6.

Lee, C. K. 2007. *Against the Law: Labor Protests in China's Rustbelt and Sunbelt*. Berkeley: University of California Press.

Lee, J. 2014. "Measuring Agglomeration: Products, People, and Ideas in U.S. Manufacturing, 1880–1990." Job Market Paper, Harvard University.
Lee, K. F. 2018. *AI Superpowers: China, Silicon Valley, and the New World Order*. Boston: Houghton Mifflin.
Lehmann, S. H. 2014. "Taking Firms to the Stock Market: IPOs and the Importance of Large Banks in Imperial Germany 1896–1913." *The Economic History Review* 67 (1): 92–122.
Lehmann-Hasemeyer, S., and J. Streb. 2016. "The Berlin Stock Exchange in Imperial Germany: A Market for New Technology?." *American Economic Review* 106 (11): 3558–3576.
Lenoir, T. 1998. "Revolution from Above: The Role of the State in Creating the German Research System, 1810–1910." *The American Economic Review* 88 (2): 22–27.
Leone, M., and N. Robotti. 2021. "Guglielmo Marconi, Augusto Righi and the Invention of Wireless Telegraphy." *The European Physical Journal H* 46 (1): 1–28.
Lerner, A. P. 1934. "Economic Theory and Socialist Economy." *The Review of Economic Studies* 2 (1): 51–61.
Lerner, J., M. Sorensen, and P. Strömberg. 2011. "Private Equity and Long-Run Investment: The Case of Innovation." *The Journal of Finance* 66 (2): 445–477.
Leunig, T. 2006. "Time Is Money: A Re-Assessment of the Passenger Social Savings from Victorian British Railways." *Journal of Economic History* 66 (3): 635–73.
Leunig, T., C. Minns, and P. Wallis. 2011. "Networks in the Premodern Economy: The Market for London Apprenticeships, 1600–1749." *Journal of Economic History* 71 (2): 413–443.
Levine, E. J. 2021. *Allies and Rivals: German-American Exchange and the Rise of the Modern Research University*. Chicago: University of Chicago Press.
Levinson, M. 2016. *The Box: How the Shipping Container Made the World Smaller and the World Economy Bigger*. Princeton: Princeton University Press.
Lévy-Leboyer, M., and M. Lescure. 1991. "France." In *Patterns of European Industrialisation: The Nineteenth Century*, edited by R. Sylla and G. Toniolo. London: Routledge.
Lewin, M. 2003. "Rebuilding the Soviet Nomenklatura 1945–1948." *Cahiers du monde russe. Russie-Empire russe-Union soviétique et États indépendants* 44 (44/2–3): 219–252.
Lewis, R. 1994. "Technology and the Transformation of the Soviet Economy." In *The Economic Transformation of the Soviet Union, 1913–1945*, edited by R. W. Davies, M. Harrison, and S. G. Wheatcroft, 182–197. Cambridge: Cambridge University Press.
Lewis, W. A. 1957. "International Competition in Manufacturers." *The American Economic Review* 47 (2): 578–587.
Li, H., and L. A. Zhou. 2005. "Political Turnover and Economic Performance: The Incentive Role of Personnel Control in China." *Journal of Public Economics* 89 (9–10): 1743–1762.
Li, Z. 2015. "A Study of the 1978 State Council Conference to Discuss Principles." In *Selected Essays on the History of Contemporary China*, edited by X. Zhang. Leiden: Brill.
Lieberthal, K., and M. Oksenberg. 1988. *Policy Making in China*. Princeton: Princeton University Press.
Lieven, D. 2015. *Towards the Flame: Empire, War and the End of Tsarist Russia*. London: Penguin Books.
Lin, J. 1995. "The Needham Puzzle: Why the Industrial Revolution Did Not Originate in China." *Economic Development and Cultural Change* 43 (2): 269–292.
Lin, J. Y., and Z. Liu. 2000. "Fiscal Decentralization and Economic Growth in China." *Economic Development and Cultural Change* 49 (1): 1–21.
Lindberg, E. 2009. "Club Goods and Inefficient Institutions: Why Danzig and Lübeck Failed in the Early Modern Period." *Economic History Review* 62 (3): 604–628.
Lindert, P. H. 2000. "Twentieth-Century Foreign Trade and Trade Policy." In *The Cambridge Economic History of the United States Volume 3: The Twentieth Century*, edited by S. Engerman and R. Gallman. Cambridge: Cambridge University Press.

Lindert, P. H., and K. Trace. 2015. "Yardsticks for Victorian Entrepreneurs." In *Essays on a Mature Economy: Britain after 1840*, edited by D. N. McCloskey. Princeton: Princeton University Press.

Link, S. J. 2020. *Forging Global Fordism: Nazi Germany, Soviet Russia, and the Contest over the Industrial Order* Vol. 33. Princeton: Princeton University Press.

Lipset, S. M. 1963. *The First New Nation: The United States in Historical and Comparative Perspective*. New York: W. W. Norton.

Lipset, S. M. 1997. *American Exceptionalism: A Double-Edged Sword*. New York: W. W. Norton.

Lipton, D., J. Sachs, S. Fischer, and J. Kornai. 1990. "Creating a Market Economy in Eastern Europe: The Case of Poland." *Brookings Papers on Economic Activity* (1): 75–147.

List, F. 1856. *National System of Political Economy*. Philadelphia: J. B. Lippincott.

Liu, C. 2020. "The Effects of World War I on the Chinese Textile Industry: Was the World's Trouble China's Opportunity?." *The Journal of Economic History* 80 (1): 246–285.

Liu, D., and C. M. Meissner. 2015. "Market Potential and the Rise of US Productivity Leadership." *Journal of International Economics* 96 (1): 72–87.

Liu, H. 2010. "Betting Life to Escape to Hong Kong: The Great Exodus that Shook the Central Government." *History Reference* 13 (2010): 38.

Liu, W. G. 2005. "Wrestling for Power: The State and Economy in Later Imperial China, 1000–1770." PhD thesis, Harvard University.

Lockwood, W. W. 1954. *The Economic Development of Japan: Growth and Structural Change, 1868–1938*. Princeton: Princeton University Press.

Long, C. X., and J. Wang. 2015. "Judicial Local Protectionism in China: An Empirical Study of IP Cases." *International Review of Law and Economics* 42: 48–59.

Long, C. X., and J. Wang. 2016. "Evaluating Patent Promotion Policies in China: Consequences for Patent Quantity and Quality." In *Economic Impacts of Intellectual Property-Conditioned Government Incentives*, edited by D. Prud'homme and H. Song. Singapore: Springer.

Long, J., C. Medici, N. Qian, and M. Tabellini. 2023. "The Impact of the Chinese Exclusion Act on the US Economy." Working Paper 23008, Harvard Business School Working Paper Series.

Lorell, M. A. 2003. *The U.S. Combat Aircraft Industry, 1909–2000*. Santa Monica: Rand Corporation.

Lucas, R. E. 1978. "On the Size Distribution of Business Firms." *The Bell Journal of Economics* 9 (2): 508–523.

Lundin, P. 2004. "American Numbers Copied! Shaping the Swedish." *Comparative Technology Transfer and Society* 2 (3): 303–334.

Lundvall, B. A., ed. 1992. *National Systems of Innovation: Towards a Theory of Innovation Interactive Learning*. London: Francis Pinter.

Lynch, F. 1997. *France and the International Economy: From Vichy to the Treaty of Rome*. Abingdon: Routledge.

Ma, D. 2005. "Between Cottage and Factory: The Evolution of Chinese and Japanese Silk-Reeling Industries in the Latter Half of the Nineteenth Century." *Journal of the Asia Pacific Economy* 10 (2): 195–213.

Ma, D. 2012. "Political Institution and Long-Run Economic Trajectory: Some Lessons from Two Millennia of Chinese Civilization." In *Institutions and Comparative Economic Development*, edited by M. Aoki and J. Wu, 78–98. Basingstoke: Palgrave Macmillan.

Macauley, M. 1998. *Social Power and Legal Culture: Litigation Masters in Late Imperial China*. Stanford: Stanford University Press.

Machiavelli, N. 1532. *The Prince*. Translated by W. K. Mariott. Leawood: Digireads.com.

MacLeod, C. 1998. *Inventing the Industrial Revolution: The English Patent System, 1660–1800*. Cambridge: Cambridge University Press.

MacLeod, W. M., and M. Urquiola. 2021. "Why Does the United States Have the Best Research Universities? Incentives, Resources, and Virtuous Circles." *Journal of Economic Perspectives* 35 (1): 185–206.

MacMillan, M. 2013. *The War that Ended Peace: How Europe Abandoned Peace for the First World War.* London: Profile Books.

Maddison, A. 1998. *Chinese Economic Performance in the Long Run.* Paris: OECD.

Magee, G. B. 2004. "Manufacturing and Technological Change." In *The Cambridge Economic History of Modern Britain Volume II: Economic Maturity, 1860–1939,* edited by Roderick Floud and Paul Johnson, 74–98. Cambridge: Cambridge University Press.

Malerba, F. 1985. *The Semiconductor Business: The Economics of Rapid Growth and Decline.* Madison: University of Wisconsin Press.

Maloney, W. F., and F. Valencia Caicedo. 2022. "Engineering Growth." *Journal of the European Economic Association* 20 (4): 1554–1594.

Mann, M. 1984. "The Autonomous Power of the State: Its Origins, Mechanisms and Results." *European Journal of Sociology* 25 (2): 185–213.

Mann, M. 1993. *The Sources of Social Power: Volume II The Rise of Classes and Nation-States,* 1st ed. Cambridge: Cambridge University Press.

Mann, M. 2012. *The Sources of Social Power: Volume 2 The Rise of Classes and Nation-States, 1760–1914,* new ed. Cambridge: Cambridge University Press.

Mann, S. 1987. *Local Merchants and the Chinese Bureaucracy, 1750–1950.* Stanford: Stanford University Press.

Mansfield, E. 1988. "The Speed and Cost of Industrial Innovation in Japan and the United States: External vs. Internal Technology." *Management Science* 34 (10): 1157–1279.

Mantoux, P. 1961. *The Industrial Revolution in the Eighteenth Century.* London: Routledge.

Marglin, S. 1974. "What Do Bosses Do? The Origins and Functions of Hierarchy in Capitalist Production." *Review of Radical Political Economics* 6 (2): 33–60.

Markevich, A. 2011. "How Much Control Is Enough? Monitoring and Enforcement under Stalin." *Europe-Asia Studies* 63 (8): 1449–1468.

Markevich, A., and E. Zhuravskaya. 2011. "M-Form Hierarchy with Poorly-Diversified Divisions: A Case of Khrushchev's Reform in Soviet Russia." *Journal of Public Economics* 95 (11–12): 1550–1560.

Marshall, A. 1920. *Principles of Economics,* 8th ed. London: Macmillan.

Marshall, A., and P. M. Marshall. 1879. *The Economics of Industry.* London: Macmillan.

Marx, K. 1867. "Preface." *Das Kapital,* 1st ed. Hamburg: Otto Meissner.

Marx, M., D. Strumsky and L. Fleming. 2009. "Mobility, Skills, and the Michigan Non-Compete Experiment." *Management Science* 55 (6): 875–889.

Mason, E. S., M. J. Kim, D. H. Perkins, K. S. Kim, and D. C. Cole. 1980. *The Economic and Social Modernization of the Republic of Korea,* Volume 47. Cambridge, MA: Harvard University Press.

Mastrorocco, N., and E. Teso. 2023. "State Capacity as an Organizational Problem. Evidence from the Growth of the U.S. State Over 100 Years." Working Paper 31591, National Bureau of Economic Research.

Mayers, W. F. 1886. *The Chinese Government: A Manual of Chinese Titles, Categorically Arranged and Explained, with an Appendix.* Shanghai: Kelly & Walsh.

McAfee, A. 2019. *More from Less: The Surprising Story of How We Learned to Prosper Using Fewer Resources—And What Happens Next.* New York: Scribner.

McCloskey, D. 1973. *Economic Maturity and Entrepreneurial Decline: British Iron and Steel, 1870–1913.* Cambridge, MA: Harvard University Press.

McCloskey, D. 2016. "The Great Enrichment: A Humanistic and Social Scientific Account." *Social Science History* 40 (4): 583–598.

McCloskey, D., and L. G. Sandberg. 1971. "From Damnation to Redemption: Judgments on the late Victorian Entrepreneur." *Explorations in Economic History* 9: 89–108.

McCraw, T. K. 2009. *American Business Since 1920: How It Worked*. Hoboken: Wiley-Blackwell.

McCurdy, C. W. 1979. "The Knight Sugar Decision of 1895 and the Modernization of American Corporate Law, 1869–1903." *Business History Review* 53: 304–342.

McGregor, R. 2010. *The Party: The Secret World of China's Communist Rulers*. London: Penguin Books.

McKitterick, R. 1983. *The Frankish Kingdoms under the Carolingians, 751–987*. Harlow: Longman.

McMillan, J., and C. Woodruff. 2002. "The Central Role of Entrepreneurs in Transition Economies." *Journal of Economic Perspectives* 16 (3): 153–170.

McNally, C. A. 2011. "China's Changing Guanxi Capitalism: Private Entrepreneurs between Leninist Control and Relentless Accumulation." *Business and Politics* 13 (2): 1–29.

McNally, C. A., H. Guo, and G. Hu. 2007. "Entrepreneurship and Political Guanxi Networks in China's Private Sector." Working Paper 19, East-West Center Working Papers.

McNeill, W. H. 1983. *The Pursuit of Power: Technology, Armed Forces and Society Since 1000 A.D.* Chicago: University of Chicago Press.

Melman, S. 1974. *The Permanent War Economy: American Capitalism in Decline*. New York: Simon & Schuster.

Mercer, H. 1995. *Constructing a Competitive Order: The Hidden History of British Antitrust Policies*. Cambridge: Cambridge University Press.

Merton, R. K. 1935. "Fluctuations in the Rate of Industrial Invention." *Quarterly Journal of Economics* 49 (3): 454–474.

Metzer, J. 1974. "Railroad Development and Market Integration in Tsarist Russia: Evidence on Oil Products and Grain." *The Journal of Economic History* 34 (3): 529–550.

Michaels, G. 2008. "The Effect of Trade on the Demand for Skill: Evidence from the Interstate Highway System." *The Review of Economics and Statistics* 90 (4): 683–701.

Milanovic, B. 2019. *Capitalism, Alone: The Future of the System That Rules the World*. Cambridge, MA: Harvard University Press.

Milgrom, P., and J. Roberts. 1990. "The Economics of Modern Manufacturing: Technology, Strategy, and Organization." *The American Economic Review* 80 (3): 511–528.

Miller, C. 2016. *The Struggle to Save the Soviet Economy: Mikhail Gorbachev and the Collapse of the USSR*. Chapel Hill: University of North Carolina Press.

Miller, C. 2022. *Chip War: The Fight for the World's Most Critical Technology*. New York: Simon & Schuster.

Minami, R. 1986. *The Economic Development of Japan: A Quantitative Study*. New York: St. Martin's Press.

Miron, J. A., and J. Zwiebel. 1991. "Alcohol Consumption During Prohibition." *American Economic Review Papers and Proceedings* 81 (2): 242–247.

Mitchell, B. A. 1975. *European Historical Statistics, 1750–1970*. London: Macmillan.

Miyazaki, I. 1981. *China's Examination Hell: The Civil Service Examinations of Imperial China*. New Haven, CT: Yale University Press.

Mokyr, J. 1992. *The Lever of Riches: Technological Creativity and Economic Progress*. Oxford: Oxford University Press.

Mokyr, J. 1992. "Technological Inertia in Economic History." *Journal of Economic History* 52 (2): 331–332.

Mokyr, J. 1994. "Cardwell's Law and the Political Economy of Technological Progress." *Research Policy* 23 (5): 561–574.

Mokyr, J. 1999. "The New Economic History and the Industrial Revolution." In *The British Industrial Revolution: An Economic Perspective*, 1–131. Boulder: Westview Press.

Mokyr, J. 2001. "The Rise and Fall of the Factory System: Technology, Firms, and Households Since the Industrial Revolution." *Carnegie-Rochester Conference Series on Public Policy* 55 (1): 1–45.

Mokyr, J. 2007. "The Market for Ideas and the Origins of Economic Growth. TSEG-The Low Countries." *Journal of Social and Economic History* 4 (1): 3–38.

Mokyr, J. 2011. *The Enlightened Economy: An Economic History of Britain 1700–1850*. London: Penguin Books.

Mokyr, J. 2011. "The Intellectual Origins of Modern Economic Growth." *Economic History Review* 64 (2): 357–384.

Mokyr, J. 2016. *A Culture of Growth: The Origins of the Modern Economy*. Princeton: Princeton University Press.

Mokyr, J. 2018. "Building Taller Ladders." *Finance & Development* 55 (2): 1–4.

Mokyr, J. 2021. "'The Holy Land of Industrialism': Rethinking the Industrial Revolution." *Journal of the British Academy* 9: 223–247.

Mokyr J., and J. V. Nye. 2007. "Distributional Coalitions, the Industrial Revolution, and the Origins of Economic Growth in Britain." *Southern Economic Journal* 74 (1): 50–70.

Mokyr, J., and G. Tabellini. 2023. "Social Organizations and Political Institutions: Why China and Europe Diverged." Working Paper 18143, CEPR Discussion Paper Series.

Mokyr, J., and H. J. Voth. 2010. "Understanding Growth in Europe, 1700–1870: Theory and Evidence." In *The Cambridge Economic History of Modern Europe*, edited by S. Broadberry and K. H. O'Rourke, 7–42. Cambridge: Cambridge University Press.

Molinder, J., T. Karlsson, and K. Enflo. 2022. "Social Democracy and the Decline of Strikes." *Explorations in Economic History* 83: 101420.

Moll-Murata, C. 2013. "Guilds and Apprenticeship in China and Europe: The Jingdezhen and European Ceramics Industries." In *Technology, Skills and the Pre-Modern Economy in the East and the West*, edited by J. L. van Zanden and M. Prak, 225–257. Boston: Brill.

Montesquieu, L. de S. 1989. *The Spirit of the Laws*. Translated by A. M. Cohler, B. C. Miller, and H. S. Stone. Cambridge: Cambridge University Press.

Montinola, G., Y. Qian, and B. R. Weingast. 1995. "Federalism, Chinese Style: The Political Basis for Economic Success in China." *World Politics* 48 (1): 50–81.

Moon, C., and S. Lee. 2009. "Military Spending and the Arms Race on the Korean Peninsula." *Asian Perspective* 33 (4): 69–99.

Morawetz, D. 1977. *Twenty-Five Years of Economic Development, 1950 to 1975*. Baltimore: Johns Hopkins University Press.

Morgan, A. D., and D. Martin. 1975. "Tariff Reductions and UK Imports of Manufactures, 1955–1971." *National Institute Economic Review* 72: 38–54.

Morison, E. E. 1974. *From Know-How to Nowhere. The Development of American Technology*. New York: Basic Books.

Morris, D. J., and D. Stout. 1985. "Industrial Policy." In *The Economic System in the UK*, edited by D. J. Morris. Oxford: Oxford University Press.

Morse, H. B. 1909. *The Gilds of China*. London: Longmans, Green and Co.

Morse, H. B. 1932. *The Gilds of China: With an Account of the Gild Merchant of Co-Hong of Canton*, 2nd ed. New York: Longmans, Green, and Co.

Moser, P. 2002. "The Determinants of Innovation. New Evidence from Nineteenth-Century World Fairs." PhD diss., University of California, Berkeley.

Moser, P., A. Voena, and F. Waldinger. 2014. "German Jewish Émigrés and US Invention." *American Economic Review* 104 (10): 3222–3255.

Mosher, F. C. 1982. *Democracy and the Public Service*. Oxford: Oxford University Press.

Motono, E. 2000. *Conflict and Cooperation in Sino-British Business, 1860–1911: The Impact of the Pro-British Commercial Network in Shanghai.* London: Palgrave Macmillan.

Mowery, D. C. 1983. "Industrial Research and Firm Size, Survival, and Growth in American Manufacturing, 1921–1946: An Assessment." *The Journal of Economic History* 43 (4): 953–980.

Mowery, D. C. 1997. "The Boundaries of the US Firm in R&D." In *Coordination and Information: Historical Perspectives on the Organization of Enterprise*, edited by S. B. Adams. Chicago: University of Chicago Press.

Mowery, D. C., and J. E. Oxley. 1995. "Inward Technology Transfer and Competitiveness: The Role of National Innovation Systems." *Cambridge Journal of Economics* 19 (1): 67–93.

Mowery, D. C., and N. Rosenberg. 1999. *Paths of Innovation: Technological Change in 20th-Century America.* Cambridge: Cambridge University Press.

Mowery, D. C., and W. E. Steinmueller. 1991. "Prospects for Entry by Developing Countries into the Global Integrated Circuit Industry: Lessons from the US, Japan, and the NIEs." Working Paper 91-8, Center for Research in Management, University of California, Berkeley.

Munger, M. 2008. "Bosses Don't Wear Bunny Slippers: If Markets Are So Great, Why Are There Firms?." The Library of Economics and Liberty. https://www.econlib.org/library/Columns/y2008/Mungerfirms.html.

Murmann, J. P. 2003. *Knowledge and Competitive Advantage: The Coevolution of Firms, Technology, and National Institutions.* Cambridge: Cambridge University Press.

Muthukrishna, M., and J. Henrich. 2016. "Innovation in the Collective Brain." *Philosophical Transactions of the Royal Society B: Biological Sciences* 371 (1690): 20150192.

Myers R. H., and M. R. Peattie, eds. 1984. *The Japanese Colonial Empire, 1895–1945.* Princeton: Princeton University Press.

Nadiri, M. I., and T. P. Mamuneas. 1994. "Infrastructure and Public R&D Investments, and the Growth of Factor Productivity in U.S. Manufacturing Industries." Working Paper 4845, National Bureau of Economic Research.

Nafziger, S. 2011. "Did Ivan's Vote Matter? The Political Economy of Local Democracy in Tsarist Russia." *European Review of Economic History* 15 (3): 393–441.

Naughton, B. 1997. "The Emergence of the China Circle." In *The China Circle: Economics and Technology in the PRC, Taiwan, and Hong Kong*, edited by B. Naughton. Washington, DC: Brookings Institution Press.

Naughton, B. 2017. "Is China Socialist?." *Journal of Economic Perspectives* 31 (1): 3–24.

Naughton, B. 2021. *The Rise of China's Industrial Policy, 1978 to 2020.* Boulder: Lynne Rienner Publishers.

Naughton, B. J. 2018. *The Chinese Economy: Adaptation and Growth.* Cambridge, MA: MIT Press.

Needham, J. 1946. "On Science and Social Change." *Science and Society* 10: 225–251.

Needham, J. 1961. *The Development of Iron and Steel Technology in China.* Cambridge: Cambridge University Press.

Nelson, R. R. 1992. "National Innovation Systems: A Retrospective on a Study." *Industrial and Corporate Change* 1 (2): 347–374.

Nelson, R. R., ed. 1993. *National Innovation Systems: A Comparative Analysis.* Oxford: Oxford University Press.

Nelson, R. R., and G. Wright. 1992. "The Rise and Fall of American Technological Leadership: The Post War Era in Historical Perspective." *Journal of Economic Literature* 30 (4): 1931–1964.

Nicholas, T. 2010. "The Role of Independent Invention in U.S. Technological Development, 1880–1930." *The Journal of Economic History* 70 (1): 57–82.

Nicholas, T. 2011. "Independent Invention During the Rise of the Corporate Economy in Britain and Japan." *The Economic History Review* 64 (3): 995–1023.

Nicholas, T. 2014. "Technology, Innovation and Economic Growth in Britain since 1870." In *The Cambridge Economic History of Modern Britain Volume 2: Growth and Decline, 1870 to the Present*, edited by R. Floud, J. Humphries, and P. Johnson. Cambridge: Cambridge University Press.

Nicholas, T. 2019. *VC: An American History*. Cambridge, MA: Harvard University Press.

Nicholas, T. 2022. "Human Capital and the Managerial Revolution in the United States." Working Paper 23015, Harvard Business School Working Paper Series.

Nicholas, T., and J. Lee. 2013. "The Origins and Development of Silicon Valley." Harvard Business School Case 813–098. https://www.hbs.edu/faculty/Pages/item.aspx?num=43895.

Nicholls, A. J. 1994. *Freedom with Responsibility*. Oxford: Oxford University Press.

Nilsson, M. 2008. "The Power of Technology: US Hegemony and the Transfer of Guided Missiles to Nato During the Cold War, 1953–1962." *Comparative Technology Transfer and Society* 6 (2): 127–149.

Nonnenmacher, T. 2001. "History of the U.S. Telegraph Industry." *EH.Net Encyclopedia*, August 14. http://eh.net/encyclopedia/history-of-the-u-s-telegraph-industry/.

Nonnenmacher, T. 2001. "State Promotion and Regulation of the Telegraph Industry, 1845–1860." *The Journal of Economic History* 61 (1): 19–36.

Nordhaus, W. D. 2007. "Two Centuries of Productivity Growth in Computing." *The Journal of Economic History* 67 (1): 128–159.

Norman, E. H. 1940. *Japan's Emergence as a Modern State: Political and Economic Problems of the Meiji Period*. Vancouver: UBC Press.

North, D. C. 1991. "Institutions." *Journal of Economic Perspectives* 5 (1): 97–112.

North, D. C. 2010. *Understanding the Process of Economic Change*. Princeton: Princeton University Press.

North, D. C., J. J. Wallis, S. B. Webb, and B. R. Weingast, B. R., eds. 2013. *In the Shadow of Violence: Politics, Economics and the Problem of Development*. Cambridge: Cambridge University Press.

North, D. C., and B. R. Weingast. 1989. "Constitutions and Commitment: The Evolution of Institutions Governing Public Choice in Seventeenth-Century England." *Journal of Economic History* 49 (4): 803–832.

Norton, R. D. 1986. "Industrial Policy and American Renewal." *Journal of Economic Literature* 24 (1): 1–40.

Novick, D., M. Anshen, and W. C. Truppner. 1949. *Wartime Production Controls*. New York: Columbia University Press.

Nunn, N., and L. Wantchekon. 2011. "The Slave Trade and the Origins of Mistrust in Africa." *American Economic Review* 101 (7): 3221–3252.

Nuvolari, A. 2010. "The Theory and Practice of Steam Engineering in Britain and in France, 1800–1850." *Documents pour l'histoire des techniques* 19 (2): 177–185.

Nuvolari, A., G. Tortorici, and M. Vasta. 2020. "British-French Technology Transfer from the Revolution to Louis Philippe (1791–1844): Evidence from Patent Data." Working Paper 15620, CEPR Discussion Paper.

Nuvolari, A., G. Tortorici, and M. Vasta. 2023. "British-French Technology Transfer from the Revolution to Louis Philippe (1791–1844): Evidence from Patent Data." *The Journal of Economic History* 83 (3): 833–873.

Nuvolari, A., and M. Vasta. 2017. "The Geography of Innovation in Italy, 1861–1913: Evidence from Patent Data." *European Review of Economic History* 21 (3): 326–356.

Nye, D. 1992. *Electrifying America: Social Meanings of a New Technology, 1880–1940*. Cambridge, MA: MIT Press.

O'Brien, A. P. 1988. "Factory Size, Economies of Scale, and the Great Merger Wave of 1898–1902." *The Journal of Economic History* 48 (3): 639–649.
Ogilvie, S. 2004. "Guilds, Efficiency, and Social Capital: Evidence from German Proto-industry." *Economic History Review* 57 (2): 286–333.
Ogilvie, S. 2014. "The Economics of Guilds." *Journal of Economic Perspectives* 28 (4): 169–192.
Ogilvie, S. 2019. *The European Guilds*. Princeton: Princeton University Press.
O'Grada, C., and K. H. O'Rourke. 1996. "Irish Economic Growth, 1945–88." In *Economic Growth in Europe since 1945*, edited by N. Crafts and G. Toniolo, 388–426. Cambridge: Cambridge University Press.
Ohno, K. 2006. *The Economic Development of Japan: The Path Travelled by Japan as a Developing Country*. Tokio: GRIPS Development Forum.
Oi, J. C. 1992. "Fiscal Reform and the Economic Foundations of Local State Corporatism in China." *World Politics* 45 (1): 99–126.
Olson, M. 1984. *The Rise and Decline of Nations: Economic Growth, Stagflation, and Social Rigidities*. New Haven, CT: Yale University Press.
Olson, M. 2009. *The Logic of Collective Action*. Cambridge, MA: Harvard University Press.
O'Mahony, M. 1999. *Britain's Productivity Performance, 1950–1996*. London: NIESR.
O'Malley, C. 1995. "Drowning in the Net." *Popular Science* 246 (6): 78–87.
O'Rourke, K. H., and J. G. Williamson. 2002. "When Did Globalization Begin?." *European Review of Economic History* 6 (1): 23–50.
Osterhammel, J. 1999. "Britain and China 1842–1914." In *The Oxford History of the British Empire Volume III: The Nineteenth Century*, edited by A. Porter and W. R. Louis, 146–169. Oxford: Oxford University Press.
Osterhammel, J. 2014. *The Transformation of the World: A Global History of the Nineteenth Century*. Princeton: Princeton University Press.
Ostrogorsky, G. 1969. *History of the Byzantine State*. New Brunswick: Rutgers University Press.
Ostrom, E. 1990. *Governing the Commons*. Cambridge: Cambridge University Press.
Ostrom, E., and R. Gardner. 1993. "Coping with Asymmetries in the Commons: Self Governing Irrigation Systems Can Work." *Journal of Economic Perspectives* 7 (4): 93–112.
Overacker, L. 1932. *Money in Elections*. New York: Macmillan.
Overy, R. 1997. *Why the Allies Won*. New York: W. W. Norton.
Owen, S. E. 1994. *The German Economy* London: Routledge.
Palais, J. B. 1991. *Politics and Policy in Traditional Korea*, Volume 82. Cambridge, MA: Harvard University Asia Center.
Pankenier, D. 1995. "The Cosmopolitical Background of Heaven's Mandate." *Early China* 20: 121–176.
Park, M., E. Leahey, and R. J. Funk. 2023. "Papers and Patents Are Becoming Less Disruptive over Time." *Nature* 613 (7942): 138–144.
Patterson, R. 1957. "Spinning and Weaving." In *A History of Technology Volume 3: From the Renaissance to the Industrial Revolution, c. 1500–c. 1750*, edited by C. Singer, E. J. Holmyard, A. R. Hall, and T. I. Williams, 151–186. Oxford: Oxford University Press.
Pavitt, K., and L. L. Soete. 1981. "International Dynamics of Innovation." In *Emerging Technologies: Consequences for Economic Growth, Structural Change, and Employment*, edited by H. Giersch. Tübingen: Mohr.
Pavitt, K., and L. Soete. 1982. "International Differences in Economic Growth and the International Location of Innovation." In *Emerging Technologies*, edited by H. Giersch, 105–133. Tübingen: Mohr.
Peake, M., and A. M. Santacreu. 2019. "China's Innovation and Global Technology Diffusion." *Economic Synopses* 2019 (7). https://doi.org/10.20955/es.2019.7.

Pei, M. 2006. *China's Trapped Transition.* Cambridge, MA: Harvard University Press.
Pei, M. 2016. *China's Crony Capitalism.* Cambridge, MA: Harvard University Press.
Pellegrino, B., and L. Zingales. 2017. "Diagnosing the Italian Disease." Working Paper 23964, National Bureau of Economic Research.
Peritz, R. 1996. *Competition Policy in America, 1888–1892: History, Rhetoric, Law.* Oxford: Oxford University Press.
Perkins, D. H. 1987. "Government as an Obstacle to Industrialization." *Journal of Economic History* 27 (4): 478–492.
Perkins, D. H. 2014. "The Centrally Planned Command Economy." In *Routledge Handbook of the Chinese Economy*, edited by G. C. Chow and D. H. Perkins. London: Routledge.
Perkins, D. H. 2022. "China's Struggle with the Soviet Growth Model, 1949–1978." In *The Cambridge Economic History of China*, edited by D. Ma and R. von Glahn, 565–605. Cambridge: Cambridge University Press.
Perkins, D. H., and T. G. Rawski. 2008. "Forecasting China's Economic Growth over the Next Two Decades." In *China's Great Economic Transformation*, edited by L. Brandt and T. G. Rawski. Cambridge: Cambridge University Press.
Perkins, D. H., and J. P. Tang. 2017. "East Asian Industrial Pioneers: Japan, Korea, and Taiwan." In *The Spread of Modern Industry to the Periphery since 1871*, edited by K. H. O'Rourke and J. G. Williamson. Oxford: Oxford University Press.
Perlman, E. R. 2016. "Connecting the Periphery: Three Papers on the Developments Caused by Spreading Transportation and Information Networks in the Nineteenth Century United States." PhD diss., Boston University.
Petroski, H. 1996. *Invention by Design: How Engineers Get from Thought to Thing.* Cambridge, MA: Harvard University Press.
Peukert, C., S. Bechtold, M. Batikas, and T. Kretschmer. 2022. "Regulatory Spillovers and Data Governance: Evidence from the GDPR." *Marketing Science* 41 (4): 746–768.
Peyrefitte, A. 2013. *The Immobile Empire.* New York: Vintage Books.
Philippon, T. 2019. *The Great Reversal: How America Gave Up on Free Markets.* Cambridge, MA: Harvard University Press.
Philippon, T. 2021. "The Case for Free Markets." *Oxford Review of Economic Policy* 37 (4): 707–719.
Pierenkemper, T. 1979. *Die westfälischen Schwerindustriellen 1852–1913. Soziale Struktur und unternehmerischer Erfolg.* Göttingen: Vandenhoeck & Ruprecht.
Pierenkemper, T., and R. H. Tilly. 2004. *The German Economy During the Nineteenth Century.* New York: Berghahn Books.
Piketty, T., L. Yang, and G. Zucman. 2019. "Capital Accumulation, Private Property, and Rising Inequality in China, 1978–2015." *American Economic Review* 109 (7): 2469–2496.
Pintner, W. M., and D. K. Rowney, eds. 1980. *Russian Officialdom: The Bureaucratization of Russian Society from the Seventeenth to the Twentieth Century.* Chapel Hill: The University of North Carolina Press.
Pisano, G., W. Shan, and D. J. Teece. 1988. "Joint Ventures and Collaboration in the Biotechnology Industry." In *International Collaborative Ventures in U.S. Manufacturing*, edited by D. C. Mowery. Washington, DC: American Enterprise Institute.
Platonova, N. 2009. "Peter the Great's Government Reforms and Accounting Practice in Russia." *Accounting History* 14: 437–464.
Platt, B. 2004. *Burning and Building: Schooling and State Formation in Japan, 1750–1890.* Cambridge MA: Harvard University Press.
Pockney, B. P. 1991. *Soviet Statistics since 1950.* Aldershot: Dartmouth.
Poege, F. 2022. "Competition and Innovation: The Breakup of IG Farben." Working Paper 15517, IZA Discussion Papers.

Polenberg, R. 1972. *War and Society: The United States, 1941–45*. Santa Barbara: Praeger.
Pomeranz, K. 2021. *The Great Divergence*. Princeton: Princeton University Press.
Popov, V. 2000. "Shock Therapy Versus Gradualism: The End of the Debate." *Comparative Economic Studies* 42 (1): 1–57.
Porter, M. E., and M. Sakakibara. 2004. "Competition in Japan." *Journal of Economic Perspectives* 18 (1): 27–50.
Powers, M. 1998. *Faces Along the Bar: Lore and Order in the Workingman's Saloon, 1870–1920*. Chicago: University of Chicago Press.
Prados de la Escosura, L., and J. C. Sanz. 1996. "Growth and Macroeconomic Performance in Spain 1939–1993." In *Economic Growth in Europe since 1945*, edited by N. Crafts and G. Toniolo. Cambridge: Cambridge University Press.
Prak, M., and J. L. van Zanden. 2022. *Pioneers of Capitalism: The Netherlands 1000–1800*. Princeton: Princeton University Press.
Pratten, C. F. 1976. "Labor Productivity Differentials within International Companies." Occasional Paper 50, Department of Applied Economics, University of Cambridge.
Price, J. L. 1994. *Holland and the Dutch Republic in the Seventeenth Century: The Politics of Particularism*. Oxford: Clarendon Press.
Proudman, J., and S. Redding. 1998. "A Summary of the Openness and Growth Project." In *Openness and Growth*, edited by J. Proudman and S. Redding, 1–29. London: Bank of England.
Putnam, R. B. 1993. *Making Democracy Work: Civic Traditions in Modern Italy*. Princeton: Princeton University Press.
Qian, Y., G. Roland, and C. Xu. 2006. "Coordination and Experimentation in M-Form and U-Form Organizations." *Journal of Political Economy* 114 (2): 366–402.
Qian, Y., and B. R. Weingast. 1997. "Federalism as a Commitment to Reserving Market Incentives." *Journal of Economic Perspectives* 11 (4): 83–92.
Qian, Y. and C. Xu. 1993. "The M-form Hierarchy and China's Economic Reform." *European Economic Review* 37 (2–3): 541–548.
Qiu, S., C. Steinwender, and P. Azoulay. 2024. "Paper Tiger? Chinese Science and Home Bias in Citations." Working Paper 32468, National Bureau of Economic Research.
Rajah, R., and A. Leng. 2022. "Revising Down the Rise of China." *Lowy Institute Analysis*, March 14. https://www.lowyinstitute.org/publications/revising-down-rise-china.
Rajan, R. G., and J. Wulf. 2006. "The Flattening Firm: Evidence from Panel Data on the Changing Nature of Corporate Hierarchies." *The Review of Economics and Statistics* 88 (4): 759–773.
Rajkumar, K., G. Saint-Jacques, I. Bojinov, E. Brynjolfsson, and S. Aral. 2022. "A Causal Test of the Strength of Weak Ties." *Science* 377 (6612): 1304–1310.
Randall, A. 1991. *Before the Luddites: Custom, Community and Machinery in the English Woollen Industry, 1776–1809*. Cambridge: Cambridge University Press.
Ravallion, M., and S. Chen. 2021. "Is that Really a Kuznets Curve? Turning Points for Income Inequality in China." Working Paper 29199, National Bureau of Economic Research.
Rawski, T. 1989. *Economic Growth in Prewar China*. Berkeley: University of California Press.
Reinganum, J. F. 1989. "The Timing of Innovation: Research, Development, and Diffusion." In *Handbook of Industrial Organization*, edited by R. Schmalensee, M. Armstrong, and R. D. Willig, 849–908. Amsterdam: Elsevier.
Reinhardt, C. 1997. "Forschung in der chemischen Industrie: Die Entwicklung synthetischer Farbstoffe bei BASF und Hoechst, 1863–1914." PhD diss., Technische Universität der Bergakademie Freiberg.
Reischauer, E. O., and J. K. Fairbank. 1958. *East Asia: The Great Tradition*. Boston: Houghton Mifflin.
Renehan, E. J., Jr. 2009. *Commodore: The Life of Cornelius Vanderbilt*. New York: Basic Books.

Reynolds, S. 1984. *Kingdoms and Communities in Western Europe, 900–1300*. Oxford: Oxford University Press.
Richardson, G. 2008. "Brand Names Before the Industrial Revolution." Working Paper 13930, National Bureau of Economic Research.
Ridder-Symoens, H., and W. Rüegg, eds. 1996. *A History of the University in Europe Volume 2: Universities in Early Modern Europe*. Cambridge: Cambridge University Press.
Ridley, M. 2020. *How Innovation Works: And Why It Flourishes in Freedom*. New York: Harper.
Rieber, A. J. 1973. "The Formation of La Grande Société des Chemins de Fer Russes." *Jahrbücher für Geschichte Osteuropas* 21 (3): 375–391.
Roberts, M., H. Thakur, C. Herlihy, C. White, and S. Dooley. 2023. "Data Contamination Through the Lens of Time." Working Paper 2310.10628, arXiv.
Roberts, M. E. 2018. *Censored: Distraction and Diversion inside China's Great Firewall*. Princeton: Princeton University Press.
Rockey, J., and N. Zakir. 2021. "Power and the Money, Money and the Power: A Network Analysis of Donations from American Corporate to Political Leaders." Working Paper 3808668, Social Science Research Network.
Rockoff, H. 1984. *Drastic Measures: A History of Wage and Price Controls in the United States*. Cambridge: Cambridge University Press.
Rodrik, D. 1995. "Getting Interventions Right: How South Korea and Taiwan Grew Rich." *Economic Policy* 10 (20): 53–107.
Rodwin, L., and H. Sazanami, eds. 1989. *Deindustrialization and Regional Economic Transformation: The Experience of the United States*. London: Routledge.
Rogers, P. 2023. "Regulating the Innovators: Approval Costs and Innovation in Medical Technologies." Working Paper 336, CATO Research Briefs in Economic Policy.
Rogoff, K. S., and Y. Yang. 2020. "Peak China Housing." Working Paper 27697, National Bureau of Economic Research.
Roland, A., and P. Shiman. 2002. *Strategic Computing: DARPA and the Quest for Machine Intelligence 1983–1993*. Cambridge, MA: MIT Press.
Root, H. L. 2020. *Network Origins of the Global Economy: East vs. West in a Complex Systems Perspective*. Cambridge: Cambridge University Press.
Rosegrant, S., and D. R. Lampe. 1992. *Route 128: Lessons from Boston's High Tech Community*. New York: Basic Books.
Rosenberg, H. 1958. *Bureaucracy, Aristocracy and Autocracy: The Prussian Experience 1660–1815*. Cambridge, MA: Harvard University Press.
Rosenberg, N. 1972. "Factors Affecting the Diffusion of Technology." *Explorations in Economic History* 10 (1): 3–33.
Rosenberg, N. 1976. *Perspectives on Technology* Cambridge: Cambridge University Press.
Rosenberg, N., and L. E. Birdzell. 1986. *How the West Grew Rich: The Economic Transformation of the Western World*. New York: Basic Books.
Rosenstein-Rodan, P. N. 1943. "Problems of Industrialisation of Eastern and South-Eastern Europe." *The Economic Journal* 53: 202–211.
Rosenstein-Rodan, P. N. 1961. "Notes on the Theory of the 'Big Push.'" In *Economic Development for Latin America*, edited by F. Benham, 57–81. London: Palgrave Macmillan.
Rosenthal, J. L., and R. B. Wong. 2011. *Before and Beyond Divergence: The Politics of Economic Change in China and Europe*. Cambridge, MA: Harvard University Press.
Rosés, J., and N. Wolf. 2021. "Regional Growth and Inequality in the Long-Run: Europe, 1900–2015." *Oxford Review of Economic Policy* 37 (1): 17–48.
Rosovsky, H. 1968. *Capital Formation in Japan 1868–1940*. Charleston: Literary Licensing, LLC.
Ross, G. 1982. *Workers and Communists in France*. Berkeley: University of California Press.

Rossi, N., and G. Toniolo. 1992. "Catching Up or Falling Behind? Italy's Economic Growth, 1895–1947." *Economic History Review* 45 (3): 537–563.

Rossi, N., and G. Toniolo. 1996. "Italy." In *Economic Growth in Europe since 1945*, edited by N. Crafts and G. Toniolo. Cambridge: Cambridge University Press.

Rostas, L. 1948. *Comparative Productivity in British and American Industry*. Cambridge: Cambridge University Press.

Rothbarth, E. 1946. "Causes of the Superior Efficiency of U.S.A. Industry as Compared with British Industry." *The Economic Journal* 56 (223): 383–390.

Rothberg, H. J. 1960. "Adjustment to Automation in Two Firms." In *Impact of Automation: A Collection of 20 Articles about Technological Change, from the Monthly Labor Review*, edited by U.S. Government Printing Office. Washington, DC: Bureau of Labor Statistics.

Rothstein, D.S., and E. Starr. 2022. "Noncompete Agreements, Bargaining, and Wages: Evidence from the National Longitudinal Survey of Youth 1997." *Monthly Labor Review*, U.S. Bureau of Labor Statistics.

Rowe, W. T. 1993. "The Problem of 'Civil Society' in Late Imperial China." *Modern China* 19 (2): 139–157.

Roy, T. 2008. "Labour Institutions, Japanese Competition, and the Crisis of Cotton Mills in Interwar Mumbai." *Economic and Political Weekly* 43 (1): 37–45.

Rubinstein, W. D. 1981. *Men of Property: The Very Wealthy in Britain Since the Industrial Revolution*. London: Croom Helm.

Sachs, J., and W. T. Woo. 1994. "Structural Factors in the Economic Reforms of China, Eastern Europe, and the Former Soviet Union." *Economic Policy* 9 (18): 101–145.

Sakong, I. 1993. *Korea in the World Economy*. Washington, DC: Peterson Institute for International Economics.

Samuelson, P. A. 1961. *Economics: An Introductory Analysis*. 5th ed., reprint. New York: McGraw-Hill.

Sassoon, D. 1996. *One Hundred Years of Socialism: The West European Left in the Twentieth Century*. London: IB Tauris.

Sassoon, D. 2019. *The Anxious Triumph: A Global History of Capitalism, 1860–1914*. London: Penguin Books.

Saxenian, A. 1996. *Regional Advantage: Culture and Competition in Silicon Valley and Route 128*. Cambridge, MA: Harvard University Press.

Scheiber, H. N. 1973. "Property Law, Expropriation, and Resource Allocation by Government: The United States, 1789–1910." *The Journal of Economic History* 33 (1): 23.

Scheidel, W. 2019. *Escape from Rome: The Failure of Empire and the Road to Prosperity*. Princeton: Princeton University Press.

Schivardi, F., and T. Schmitz. 2020. "The IT Revolution and Southern Europe's Two Lost Decades." *Journal of the European Economic Association* 18 (5): 2441–2486.

Schnabel, F. 1954. *Deutsche Geschichte im Neunzehnten Jahrhundert*. Freiburg: Herder.

Schultz, D. A., and R. Maranto. 1998. *The Politics of Civil Service Reform*. New York: Peter Lang.

Schulz, J. 2022. "Kin Networks and Institutional Development." *The Economic Journal* 132 (647): 2578–2613.

Schulz, J. F., D. Bahrami-Rad, J. P. Beauchamp, and J. Henrich. 2019. "The Church, Intensive Kinship, and Global Psychological Variation." *Science* 366 (6466): 1–12. https://pubmed.ncbi.nlm.nih.gov/31699908/.

Schumpeter, J. A. 1976. *Capitalism, Socialism and Democracy*, 3rd ed. New York: Harper Torchbooks.

Scott, J. C. 2020. *Seeing like a State: How Certain Schemes to Improve the Human Condition Have Failed*. New Haven, CT: Yale University Press.

Sequeira, S., N. Nunn, and N. Qian. 2020. "Immigrants and the Making of America." *The Review of Economic Studies* 87 (1): 382–419.
Serafinelli, M., and G. Tabellini. 2022. "Creativity over Time and Space: A Historical Analysis of European Cities." *Journal of Economic Growth* 27 (1): 1–43.
Shaw, D. 2006. "Towns and Commerce." In *The Cambridge History of Russia Volume 1: From Early Rus' to 1689*, edited by M. Perrie, 298–316. Cambridge: Cambridge University Press.
Sheridan, K. 1993. *Governing the Japanese Economy*. Cambridge: Cambridge University Press.
Shiba, Y. 1970. *Commerce and Society in Sung China*. Ann Arbor: University of Michigan Press.
Shin, K. 2003. "Competition Law and Policy." In *Economic Crisis and Corporate Restructuring in Korea: Reforming the Chaebol*, edited by S. Haggard, W. Lim, and E. Kim. Cambridge: Cambridge University Press.
Shiue, C. H., and W. Keller. 2007. "Markets in China and Europe on the Eve of the Industrial Revolution." *American Economic Review* 97 (4): 1189–1216.
Shonfield, A. 1965. *The Changing Balance of Public and Private Power*. New York: Oxford University Press.
Shumaylov, I. Z., Y. Zhao, Y. Gal, N. Papernot, and R. Anderson. 2023. "The Curse of Recursion: Training on Generated Data Makes Models Forget." Working Paper 2305.17493, arXiv.
Silberman, B. S. 1970. "Bureaucratic Development and the Structure of Decision-Making in Japan: 1868–1925." *Journal of Asian Studies* 29 (2): 347–362.
Silberman, J. M., C. Weiss, and M. Dutz. 1996. "Marshall Plan Productivity Assistance: A Unique Program of Mass Technology Transfer and a Precedent for the Former Soviet Union." *Technology in Society* 18 (4): 443–460.
Sismondo, C. 2011. *America Walks into a Bar: A Spirited History of Taverns and Saloons, Speakeasies and Grog Shops*. Oxford: Oxford University Press.
Skinner, G. W. 1977. "Introduction: Urban Development in Imperial China." In *The City in Late Imperial China*, edited by G. W. Skinner, 3–32. Stanford: Stanford University Press.
Skowronek, S. 1982. *Building a New American State: The Expansion of National Administrative Capacities, 1877–1920*. Cambridge: Cambridge University Press.
Smith, P. J. 2020. *Taxing Heaven's Storehouse: Horses, Bureaucrats, and the Destruction of the Sichuan Tea Industry 1074–1224*. Cambridge, MA: Council on East Asian Studies, Harvard University.
Smith, R. E., ed. 1959. *The Army and Economic Mobilization*. Washington, DC: Office of the Chief of Military History, Department of the Army.
Smith, T. C. 1955. *Political Change and Industrial Development in Japan: Government Enterprise, 1868–1880*. Stanford: Stanford University Press.
Sng, T. H. 2014. "Size and Dynastic Decline: The Principal-Agent Problem in Late Imperial China, 1700–1850." *Explorations in Economic History* 54: 107–27.
Sng, T. H., and C. Moriguchi. 2014. "Asia's Little Divergence: State Capacity in China and Japan Before 1850." *Journal of Economic Growth* 19 (4): 439–470, Figure 1.
Sohn, E., R. Seamans, and D. Sands. 2023. "Technology Adoption and Innovation: The Establishment of Airmail and Aviation Innovation in the United States, 1918–1935." *Strategic Management Journal* 45 (1): 3–35.
Sokoloff, K. L. 1988. "Inventive Activity in Early Industrial America: Evidence From Patent Records, 1790–1846." *The Journal of Economic History* 48 (4): 813–850.
Sokoloff, K. L., and B. Z. Khan. 1990. "The Democratization of Invention During Early Industrialization: Evidence from the United States, 1790–1846." *The Journal of Economic History* 50 (2): 363–378.
Sombart, W. 1913. *Der Bourgeois*. München und Leipzig: Duncker & Humblot.

Sombart, W. 1967. *Quintessence of Capitalism: A Study of the History and Psychology of the Modern Business Man*. New York: Howard Fertig.

Sparrow, J. T. 2011. *Warfare State: World War II Americans and the Age of Big Government*. Oxford: Oxford University Press.

Spencer, D. L. 1965. "An External Military Presence, Technological Transfer, and Structural Change." *Kyklos* 18 (3): 451–474.

Squicciarini, M. P., and N. Voigtländer. 2015. "Human Capital and Industrialization: Evidence from the Age of Enlightenment." *The Quarterly Journal of Economics* 130 (4): 1825–1883.

Starr, S. F. 1972. *Decentralization and Self-Government in Russia, 1830–1870*. Princeton: Princeton University Press.

Stasavage, D. 2003. *Public Debt and the Birth of the Democratic State: France and Great Britain 1688–1789*. Cambridge: Cambridge University Press.

Stasavage, D. 2011. *States of Credit: Size, Power, and the Development of European Polities*. Princeton: Princeton University Press.

Stasavage, D. 2016. "Representation and Consent: Why They Arose in Europe and Not Elsewhere." *Annual Review of Political Science* 19: 145–162.

Stasavage, D. 2020. *The Decline and Rise of Democracy: A Global History from Antiquity to Today*. Princeton: Princeton University Press.

Steinmueller, W. E. 1988. "Industry Structure and Government Policies in the US and Japan Integrated-Circuit Industries." In *Government Policy Towards Industry in United States and Japan*, edited by J. B. Shoven. Cambridge: Cambridge University Press.

Steinmueller, W. E. 1996. "The U.S. Software Industry: An Analysis and Interpretive History." In *The International Computer Software Industry*, edited by D. C. Mowery. New York: Oxford University Press.

Stephenson, J. Z. 2018. "'Real' Wages? Contractors, Workers, and Pay in London Building Trades, 1650–1800." *Economic History Review* 71 (1): 106–132.

Stevenson, B., and J. Wolfers. 2013. "Subjective Well-Being and Income: Is There Any Evidence of Satiation?." *American Economic Review* 103 (3): 598–604.

Stigler, G. J. 1971. "The Theory of Economic Regulation." *Bell Journal of Economics and Management Science* 2 (1): 3–21.

Stine, D. D. 2009. *The Manhattan Project, the Apollo Program, and Federal Energy Technology R&D Programs: A Comparative Analysis*. Washington, DC: Congressional Research Service.

Stowsky, J. 1987. "The Weakest Link: Semiconductor Equipment, Linkages, and the Limits to International Trade." Working Paper, 27, Berkeley Roundtable on the International Economy, University of California, Berkeley.

Strasser, S. 1982. *Never Done: A History of American Housework*. New York: Pantheon.

Strauss, R. 1960. *Die Lage und die Bewegung der Chemnitzer Arbeiter in der ersten Hälfte des 19. Jahrhunderts*. Berlin: Akademie Verlag.

Streb, J., J. Baten, and S. Yin. 2006. "Technological and Geographical Spillover." *Economic History Review* 59 (2): 347–373.

Streit, C. K. 1949. *Union Now: A Proposal for an Atlantic Federal Union of the Free*. New York: Harper & Brothers.

Strohmeyer, J. 1986. *Crisis in Bethlehem: Big Steel's Struggle to Survive*. London: Penguin Books.

Studwell, J. 2013. *How Asia Works: Success and Failure in the World's Most Dynamic Region*. New York: Grove/Atlantic.

Sutton, A. C. 1971. *Western Technology and Soviet Economic Development, 1930–1945*. Stanford: Hoover Institution on War, Revolution and Peace, Stanford University.

Sutton, A. C. 1973. *Western Technology and Soviet Economic Development, 1945–1965*. Stanford: Hoover Institution on War, Revolution and Peace, Stanford University.

Sylla, R., and G. Toniolo, eds. 1991. *Patterns of European Industrialisation: The Nineteenth Century.* London: Routledge.

Symeonidis, G. 2008. "The Effects of Competition on Wages and Productivity: Evidence from the United Kingdom." *Review of Economics and Statistics* 90: 134–146.

Syrett, H. C., ed. 1962. *The Papers of Alexander Hamilton.* New York: Columbia University Press.

Taalbi, J., and H. Nielsen. 2021. "The Role of Energy Infrastructure in Shaping Early Adoption of Electric and Gasoline Cars." *Nature Energy* 6 (10): 970–976.

Tabakovic, H., and T. G. Wollmann. 2018. "From Revolving Doors to Regulatory Capture? Evidence from Patent Examiners." Working Paper 24638, National Bureau of Economic Research.

Taft, P., and P. Ross. 1969. "American Labor Violence: Its Causes, Character, and Outcome." In *Violence in America: Historical and Comparative Perspectives*, edited by H. D. Graham and T. R. Gurr, 221–301. London: Corgi Books.

Talhelm, T., X. Zhang, S. Oishi, C. Shimin, D. Duan, X. Lan, and S. Kitayama. 2014. "Large-Scale Psychological Differences Within China Explained by Rice Versus Wheat Agriculture." *Science* 344 (6184): 603–608.

Tanaka, S. 2004. *New Times in Modern Japan.* Princeton: Princeton University Press.

Tang, J. P. 2011. "Technological Leadership and Late Development: Evidence from Meiji Japan, 1868–1912." *The Economic History Review* 64: 99–116.

Tang, J. P. 2014. "Railroad Expansion and Industrialization: Evidence from Meiji Japan." *The Journal of Economic History* 74 (3): 863–886.

Tang, J. P. 2016. "A Tale of Two SICs: Japanese and American Industrialisation in Historical Perspective." *Australian Economic History Review* 56 (2): 174–197.

Tedlow, R. 2013. *The Rise of the American Business Corporation.* Abingdon: Taylor & Francis.

Theriault, S. M. 2003. "Patronage, the Pendleton Act, and the Power of the People." *The Journal of Politics* 65 (1): 50–68.

Thesmar, D., and M. Thoenig. 2000. "Creative Destruction and Firm Organization Choice." *The Quarterly Journal of Economics* 115 (4): 1201–1237.

Thompson, G. V. 1954. "Intercompany Technical Standardization in the Early American Automobile Industry." *The Journal of Economic History* 14 (1): 1–20.

Thompson, M. S. 1980. *The Spider Web: Congress and Lobbying in the Age of Grant.* Madison: University of Wisconsin.

Thompson, R. L. 1947. *Wiring a Continent.* Princeton: Princeton University Press.

Thorp, W. L. 1931. "The Persistence of the Merger Movement." *The American Economic Review* 21 (1): 77–89.

Thun, E. 2006. *Changing Lanes in China: Foreign Direct Investment, Local Governments, and Auto Sector Development.* Cambridge: Cambridge University Press.

Tilly, R. H. 1966. *Financial Institutions and Industrialization in the Rhineland.* Madison: University of Wisconsin Press.

Tilly, R. H. 1966. "The Political Economy of Public Finance and the Industrialization of Prussia, 1815–1866." *The Journal of Economic History* 26 (4): 484–497.

Tilly, R. H. 1996. "German Industrialization." In *The Industrial Revolution in National Context: Europe and the USA*, edited by M. Teich and R. Porter, 95–125. Cambridge: Cambridge University Press.

Tilly, R. H., and M. Kopsidis. 2020. *From Old Regime to Industrial State: A History of German Industrialization from the Eighteenth Century to World War I.* Chicago: University of Chicago Press.

Tilton, J. L. 1971. *International Diffusion of Technology: The Case of Semiconductors.* Washington, DC: Brookings Institution.

Tocqueville, A. 1863. *Democracy in America*, edited by Francis Bowen. 2nd ed. Garden City: Doubleday & Co.
Toniolo, G. 2013. "An Overview of Italy's Economic Growth." In *The Oxford Handbook of the Italian Economy Since Unification*, edited by G. Toniolo. Oxford: Oxford University Press.
Tooze, A. 2006. *The Wages of Destruction: The Making and Breaking of the Nazi Economy*. London: Penguin Books.
Tooze, A. 2015. *The Deluge: The Great War, America and the Remaking of the Global Order, 1916–1931*. London: Penguin Books.
Torp, C. 2012. "Heinrich Engelhard Steinway." In *Immigrant Entrepreneurship: German-American Business Biographies, 1720 to the Present*, edited by P. Erben and M. S. Wokeck. Washington, DC: German Historical Institute.
Trachtenberg, A. 1982. *The Incorporation of America: Culture and Society in the Gilded Age*. New York: Hill and Wang.
Trebilcock, C. 1982. *The Industrialization of the Continental Powers, 1780–1914*. London: Longman.
Triandis, H. C. 1995. *Individualism and Collectivism*. Boulder: Westview Press.
Tsebelis, G. 2002. *Veto Players: How Political Institutions Work*. Princeton: Princeton University Press.
Turner, C. L. 1995. *Japanese Workers in Protest: An Ethnography of Consciousness and Experience*. Berkeley: University of California Press.
Turner, F. J. 2008. *The Significance of the Frontier in American History*. London: Penguin Books.
Turner, H. A. 1969. "Big Business and the Rise of Hitler." *The American Historical Review* 75 (1): 56–70.
Turner, H. A. 1985. *German Big Business and the Rise of Hitler*. Oxford: Oxford University Press.
Udandarao, V., A. Prabhu, A. Ghosh, Y. Sharma, P. H. S. Torr, A. Bibi, S. Albanie, and M. Bethge. 2024. "No 'Zero-Shot' Without Exponential Data: Pretraining Concept Frequency Determines Multimodal Model Performance." Working Paper 2404.04125, arXiv.
Urquiola, M. 2020. *Markets, Minds, and Money: Why America Leads the World in University Research*. Cambridge, MA: Harvard University Press.
US–China Business Council. 2012. "USCBC 2012 China Business Environment Survey Results." http://www.uschina.org/sites/default/files/uscbc-2012-member-survey-results.pdf.
U.S. Congress. 1984. *Computerized Manufacturing Automation: Employment, Education, and the Workplace*. Washington, DC: Office of Technology Assessment.
U.S. Patent and Trademark Office (USPTO). 1977. US Patent Statistics Report, US Technology Assessment and Forecast Seventh Report. Washington, DC: USPTO.
U.S. War Production Board. 1945. *American Industry in War and Transition, 1940–1950. Part II: The Effect of the War on the Industrial Economy*. Washington, DC: U.S. Government Printing Office.
Usher, A. P. 1954. *A History of Mechanical Innovations*. Cambridge, MA: Harvard University Press.
Usselman, S. W. 2002. *Regulating Railroad Innovation: Business, Technology, and Politics in America, 1840–1920*. Cambridge: Cambridge University Press.
Usselman, S. W. 2007. "Patents, Engineering Professionals, and the Pipelines of Innovation: The Internalization of Technical Discovery by Nineteenth Century American Railroads." In *Learning by Doing in Markets, Firms, and Countries*, edited by N. R. Lamoreaux, D. M. G. Raff, and P. Temin. Chicago: University of Chicago Press.
Van Atta, D. 1993. "Russian Agriculture Between Plan and Market." In *The Farmer Threat*, edited by D. van Atta, 9–24. Boulder: Westview Press.

Van Atta, R. H. 2007. Testimony before the Hearing on "Establishing the Advanced Research Projects Agency- Energy (ARPA- E)." Subcommittee on Energy and Environment, Committee on Science and Technology, United States House of Representatives, Washington, DC.
Van Bavel, B. 2016. *The Invisible Hand: How Market Economies Have Emerged and Declined since 500*. Oxford: Oxford University Press.
Van Der Beek, K., J. Mokyr, and A. Sarid. 2022. "The Wheels of Change: Technology Adoption, Millwrights and the Persistence in Britain'S Industrialisation." *The Economic Journal* 132 (645): 1894–1926.
Van Riper, P. 1958. *History of the United States Civil Service*. Evanston: Row, Peterson and Company.
Van Zanden, J. L. 2009. *The Long Road to the Industrial Revolution: The European Economy in a Global Perspective 1000–1800*. Boston: Brill.
Van Zanden, J. L., E. Buringh, and M. Bosker. 2012. "The Rise and Decline of European Parliaments, 1188–1789." *Economic History Review* 65 (3): 835–861.
Veblen, T. 1915. *Imperial Germany and the Industrial Revolution*. London: Macmillan.
Vernon, R. 1966. "International Investment and International Trade in the Product Cycle." *Quarterly Journal of Economics* 80 (2): 190–207.
Verspagen, B. 1996. "Technology Indicators and Economic Growth in the European Area: Some Empirical Evidence." In *Quantitative Aspects of Post-War European Economic Growth*, edited by B. van Ark and N. Crafts, 215–243. Cambridge: Cambridge University Press.
VerWey, J. 2019. "Chinese Semiconductor Industrial Policy: Past and Present." *Journal of International Commerce and Economics* 2019 (1): 1–29.
Vickers, C., and N. L. Ziebarth. 2014. "Did the National Industrial Recovery Act Foster Collusion? Evidence from the Macaroni Industry." *The Journal of Economic History* 74 (3): 831–862.
Vogel, E. F. 1979. *Japan As Number One: Lessons for America*. Cambridge, MA: Harvard University Press.
Vogel, E. F. 2011. *Deng Xiaoping and the Transformation of China*. Cambridge, MA: Belknap Press.
Von Glahn, R. 2016. *The Economic History of China: From Antiquity to the Nineteenth Century*. Cambridge: Cambridge University Press.
Von Mises, L. 1944. *Bureaucracy*. New Haven, CT: Yale University Press.
Von Mises, L. 1990. "Economic Calculation in the Socialist Commonwealth." *Ludwig von Mises Institute*. Auburn, AL: Mises Institute.
Vries, P. 2019 *Averting a Great Divergence: State and Economy in Japan, 1868–1937*. London: Bloomsbury.
Wagenfuhr, H. 1931. *Kartelle in Deutschland*. Nurnberg: Krische Verlag.
Wagner, D. 1993. *Iron and Steel in Ancient China*. Leiden: Brill Academic.
Wahlgren Summers, M. 1993. *The Era of Good Stealings*. Oxford: Oxford University Press.
Wakeman, F. 2003. *Spymaster: Dai Li and the Chinese Secret Service*. Berkeley: University of California Press.
Waldinger, F. 2016. "Bombs, Brains, and Science: The Role of Human and Physical Capital for the Creation of Scientific Knowledge." *Review of Economics and Statistics* 98 (5): 811–831.
Waldrop, M. M. 2001. *The Dream Machine: J.C.R. Licklider and the Revolution That Made Computing Personal*. New York: Viking Penguin.
Wallis, P. 2008. "Apprenticeship and Training in Premodern England." *Journal of Economic History* 68 (3): 832–861.
Walton, F. 1956. *Miracle of World War II: How American Industry Made Victory Possible*. New York: Macmillan.
Wang, H. C. 2015. "Mandarins, Merchants, and the Railway: Institutional Failure and the Wusong Railway, 1874–1877." *International Journal of Asian Studies* 12 (1): 31–53.

Wang, S., and D. Y. Yang. 2021. "Policy Experimentation in China: the Political Economy of Policy Learning." Working Paper 29402, National Bureau of Economic Research.
Wang, Y. 2015. *Tying the Autocrat's Hands*. Cambridge: Cambridge University Press.
Wang, Y. 2022. "Blood is Thicker Than Water: Elite Kinship Networks and State Building in Imperial China." *American Political Science Review* 116 (3): 896–910.
Wang, Z. 2008. *In Sputnik's Shadow: The President's Science Advisory Committee and Cold War America*. New Brunswick: Rutgers University Press.
Watson, A. M. 1974. "The Arab Agricultural Revolution and Its Diffusion, 700–1100." *Journal of Economic History* 34 (1): 8–35.
Watson, A. M. 1983. *Agricultural Innovation in the Early Islamic World*. Cambridge: Cambridge University Press.
Watzinger, M., T. A. Fackler, M. Nagler, and M. Schnitzer. 2020. "How Antitrust Enforcement Can Spur Innovation: Bell Labs and the 1956 Consent Decree." *American Economic Journal: Economic Policy* 12 (4): 328–359.
Webb, S. B. 1980. "Tariffs, Cartels, Technology, and Growth in the German Steel Industry, 1879 to 1914." *The Journal of Economic History* 40 (2): 309–330.
Webb, S. B. 1982. "Agricultural Protection in Wilhelminian Germany: Forging an Empire with Pork and Rye." *The Journal of Economic History* 42 (2): 309–326.
Weber, M. 1968. *Economy and Society: An Outline of Interpretive Sociology*. Berkeley: University of California Press.
Weber, M. 1978. *Economy and Society: An Outline of Interpretive Sociology Volume 2*. Berkeley: University of California Press.
Wehler, H. U. 1987. *Deutsche Gesellschaftsgeschichte*. Vol. 1: *Vom Feudalismus des Alten Reiches bis zur Defensiven Modernisierung der Reformära 1700–1815*. Munich: C. H. Beck.
Wei, S. J., Z. Xie, and X. Zhang. 2017. "From 'Made in China' to 'Innovated in China': Necessity, Prospect, and Challenges." *Journal of Economic Perspectives* 31 (1): 49–70.
Weickhardt, G. G. 1983. "Bureaucrats and Boiars in the Muscovite Tsardom." *Russian History* 10 (1): 331–356.
Weingast, B. 1995. "The Economic Role of Political Institutions: Market-Preserving Federalism and Economic Development." *Journal of Law, Economics, and Organization* 11 (19): 1–31.
Weitzman, M. L. 1998. "Recombinant Growth." *The Quarterly Journal of Economics* 113 (2): 331–360.
Weldon, D. 2021. *Two Hundred Years of Muddling Through: The Surprising Story of Britain's Economy from Boom to Bust and Back Again*. London: Hachette.
Werrell, K. P. 1996. *Blankets of Fire: U.S. Bombers over Japan During World War II*. Washington, DC: Smithsonian Institution Press.
Weston, T. B. 2002. "The Founding of the Imperial University and the Emergence of Chinese Modernity." In *Rethinking the 1898 Reform Period: Political and Cultural Change in Late Qing China*, edited by R. E. Karl and P. Zarrow, 99–123. Cambridge, MA: Harvard University Asia Center.
White, L. 1972. "The Expansion of Technology, 500–1500." In *The Fontana Economic History of Europe*, edited by C. Cipolla. Glasgow: Collins.
White, L. A. 2016. *Modern Capitalist Culture*. New York: Routledge.
Whitehead, A. N. 1925. *Science and the Modern World*. London: Free Press.
Whiting, A. S. 1987. "The Sino-Soviet Split." In *The Cambridge History of China Volume 14: The People's Republic of China: The Emergence of Revolutionary China, 1949–1965*, edited by R. MacFarquhar and J. K. Fairbank. Cambridge: Cambridge University Press.
Whitney, J. B. R. 1970. *China: Area, Administration, and Nation Building*. Chicago: University of Chicago Press.

Williams, E. E. 1896. *Made in Germany*. London: W. Heinemann.
Williamson, O. E. 1981. "The Economics of Organization: The Transaction Cost Approach." *American Journal of Sociology* 87 (3): 548–577.
Wilson, R. W., P. K. Ashton, and T. P. Egan. 1980. *Innovation, Competition, and Government Policy in the Semiconductor Industry*. Lexington: Lexington Books.
Winkler, A. M. 2000. *Home Front U.S.A.: America during World War II*. Wheaton: Harlan Davidson.
Wise, G. 1985. *Willis R. Whitney, General Electric, and the Origins of U.S. Industrial Research*. New York: Columbia University Press.
Wittfogel, K. A. 1957. *Oriental Despotism: A Comparative Study of Total Power*. New Haven, CT: Yale University Press.
Wolf, N. 2009. "Was Germany Ever United? Evidence from Intra- and International Trade, 1885–1933." *The Journal of Economic History* 69 (3): 846–881.
Wong, C. H. 2023. *Party of One: The Rise of Xi Jinping and China's Superpower Future*. New York: Simon and Schuster.
Woo-Cumings, M. 1999. "The State, Democracy, and the Reform of the Corporate Sector in Korea." In *The Politics of the Asian Economic Crisis*, edited by T. J. Pempel, 116–142. Ithaca, NY: Cornell University Press.
Woods, D. 1998. "The Crisis (Collapse) of Italy's Public Enterprise System: A Revised Property Rights Perspective." *Journal of Modern Italian Studies* 3 (1): 22–41.
Wozniak, S. 1984. "Homebrew and How the Apple Came To Be." In *Digital Deli: The Comprehensive, User-Lovable Menu of Computer Lore, Culture, Lifestyles and Fancy*, edited by S. Ditlea. New York: Workman.
Wren, C. 1996. "Grant-Equivalent Expenditure on Industrial Subsidies in the Postwar United Kingdom." *Oxford Bulletin of Economics and Statistics* 58: 317–353.
Wright, D. 2001. "Yan Fu and the Tasks of the Translator." In *New Terms for New Ideas: Western Knowledge and Lexical Change in Late Imperial China*, edited by M. Lackner, I. Amelung, and J. Kurz, 235–255. Leiden: Brill.
Wright, G. 2022. "Slavery and the Rise of the Nineteenth-Century American Economy." *Journal of Economic Perspectives* 36 (2): 123–148.
Wu, L., D. Wang, and J. A. Evans. 2019. "Large Teams Develop and Small Teams Disrupt Science and Technology." *Nature* 566 (7744): 378–382.
Wu, M. 2016. "The 'China, Inc.' Challenge to Global Trade Governance." *Harvard International Law Journal* 57: 261.
Wu, T. 2018. *The Curse of Bigness: Antitrust in the New Gilded Age*. New York: Columbia Global Reports.
Xie, Q., and R. B. Freeman. 2020. "The Contribution of Chinese Diaspora Researchers to Global Science and China's Catching Up in Scientific Research." Working Paper 27169, National Bureau of Economic Research.
Xie, Q., and R. B. Freeman. 2023. "Creating and Connecting US and China Science: Chinese Diaspora and Returnee Researchers." Working Paper 31306, National Bureau of Economic Research.
Xie, Y., and X. Zhou. 2014. "Income Inequality in Today's China." *Proceedings of the National Academy of Sciences* 111 (19): 6928–6933.
Xu, C. 2011. "The Fundamental Institutions of China's Reforms and Development." *Journal of economic literature* 49 (4): 1076–1151.
Xu, C. 2022. "The Origin of China's Communist Institutions." In *The Cambridge Economic History of China*, edited by D. Ma and R. von Glahn, 531–564. Cambridge: Cambridge University Press.

Xu, F., L. Wu, and J. Evans. 2022. "Flat Teams Drive Scientific Innovation." *Proceedings of the National Academy of Sciences* 119 (23): e2200927119.

Xu, G. 2018. "The Costs of Patronage: Evidence from the British Empire." *American Economic Review* 108 (11): 3170–3198.

Xue, M. M. 2021. "Autocratic Rule and Social Capital: Evidence from Imperial China." Working Paper 2856803, Social Science Research Network.

Yamamura, K. 1974. "The Japanese Economy, 1911–1930: Concentration, Conflicts and Crises." In *Japan in Crisis. Essays in Taisho Democracy*, edited by B. S. Silberman and H. D. Harootunian, 299–328. Princeton: Princeton University Press.

Yamasaki, J. 2019. "Railroads, Technology Adoption, and Modern Economic Development: Evidence from Japan." Working Paper 3432796, Social Science Research Network.

Yang, L., F. Novokmet, and B. Milanovic. 2021. "From Workers to Capitalists in Less Than Two Generations: A Study of Chinese Urban Top Group Transformation Between 1988 and 2013." *The British Journal of Sociology* 72 (3): 478–513.

Yanqiong, L., and L. Jifeng. 2009. "Analysis of Soviet Technology Transfer in the Development of China's Nuclear Weapons." *Comparative Technology Transfer and Society* 7 (1): 66–110.

Yao, Y. 2014. "The Chinese Growth Miracle." In *Handbook of Economic Growth*, edited by S. Ogilvie and A. W. Carus, 943–1031. Amsterdam: North-Holland.

Yao, Y., and M. Zhang. 2015. "Subnational Leaders and Economic Growth: Evidence from Chinese Cities." *Journal of Economic Growth* 20 (4): 405–436.

Yasuba, Y. 1986. "Standard of Living in Japan Before Industrialization: From What Level Did Japan Begin? A Comment." *The Journal of Economic History* 46 (1): 217–224.

Yip, S. G., and B. McKern. 2016. *China's Next Strategic Advantage from Imitation to Innovation*. Cambridge, MA: MIT Press.

Yoshinobu, S. 1970. *Commerce and Society in Sung China*. Ann Arbor: University of Michigan Press.

Zeitz, P. 2011. "Trade in Equipment and Technological Development: Evidence from the Sino-Soviet Split." PhD diss., University of California, Los Angeles.

Zelin, M. 1984. *The Magistrate's Tael: Rationalizing Fiscal Reform in Eighteenth-Century Ch'ing China*. Berkeley: University of California Press.

Zhai, K. 2021. "Alibaba Hit With Record $2.8 Billion Antitrust Fine in China." *Wall Street Journal*, April 10.

Zhang, A. 2021. *Chinese Antitrust Exceptionalism: How the Rise of China Challenges Global Regulation*. Oxford: Oxford University Press.

Zhang, B., F. Yao, J. Zhang, and L. Jiang. 2003. *The Technology Transfer from Soviet Union to China, 1949–1966*. Shandong: Shandong Education Press.

Zingales, L. 2017. "Towards a Political Theory of the Firm." *Journal of Economic Perspectives* 31 (3): 113–130.

INDEX

Page numbers ending in f refer to figures and those ending in t refer to tables.

Abouchar, Alan, 285
Abromovitz, Moses, 438n22
Accumulatoren-Fabrik Aktiengesellschaft (AFA), 122
Acemoglu, Daron, 10, 27, 369, 399
Acheson, Dean, 233
Adams, Arthur, 259
Adams, John, 149, 176
Adams, Samuel, 149
Adenauer, Konrad, 226
Advanced Micro Devices (AMD), 452n39
Advanced Research Projects Agency (ARPA), 38–39, 200–205, 221, 390, 435n66, 435n68
AEG, 113, 118, 122–24, 379
Afeyan, Noubar, 8
Aganbegyan, Abel, 284
Agfa, 116, 121
Airbus Industrie, 379
A. J. Brandt Co., 260
Akcigit, Ufuk, 16
Albert Kahn Associates, 260
Alexander II (tsar), 132, 135–36
Alibaba, 332, 338–41, 347
Allen, Paul, 210, 447n27
Allen, Robert, 59
Allison, Graham, 330, 358
Althoff, Friedrich, 104–5, 197
Amazon, 16, 209–10, 306
American Ampex Corporation, 317
American Economic Association (AEA), 2–3, 6
American Tobacco Company, 181
Amsden, Alice H., 242, 246
Andreessen, Marc, 210
Andrews, Michael, 3

Apple, 202, 210, 305–6, 309, 311–12, 317, 319, 328, 356
Appleton, Nathan, 154
Arco, Georg von, 123
Arendt, Hannah, 389
Arkwright, Richard, 66–67, 91, 154, 383
Armstrong, Edwin, 159
Arnold, Matthew, 107
Arnold, Thurmond, 207
artificial intelligence (AI) and large language models (LLMs), 351–55, 367–70, 394–96, 398, 458n95
Ashton-Tate, 319
AT&T, 13, 120, 169–71, 183, 206–8, 320, 366, 370, 386, 394, 453n66
Atack, Jeremy, 172
Attlee, Clement, 228, 248
Audi, 337
Austria, 83, 91, 125, 221–22, 225, 231, 238
Azoulay, Pierre, 203

Babbage, Charles, 304
Babina, Tania, 356
Backus, John W., 453n60
Baeyer, Adolf, 117
Barnett, Jonathan, 207
BASF, 109, 116–17, 121, 317, 377, 420n121
Bassermann, Ernst, 90
Bastiat, Fredric, 192
Baumol, William, 403n42
Baxter, William, 453n62
Bayer, 109, 116, 121
Bayle, Pierre, 61
Beck, Thomas, 63
Becker, Sacha, 109
Bell, Alexander Graham, 158–59, 183

Bell Labs, 207–8, 307
Bell Telephone Company. *See* AT&T
Ben-David, Joseph, 107
Bendix, Vincent, 214
Benz, Karl, 211
Berger, Samuel D., 244
Beriia, Lavrenty, 256, 265
Bernard, Claude, 106
Berners-Lee, Tim, 205
Berthollet, Claude Louis, 126
Bessemer, Henry, 115
Beyer, 377
Bezos, Jeff, 209–10, 404n55
Bicycle Thieves (film), 222
Bidault, Georges, 226
Biden, Joseph, 359–60, 368, 371–72, 398, 457n67, 461n4
BioNTech, 6, 8–9, 402n27
Birdzell, L. E., Jr., 82
Bismarck, Otto von (Iron Chancellor), 15, 86, 90, 111, 113, 119, 131, 141, 227, 242, 267
Björnståhl, J. J., 76
Black, Joseph, 57
Blaine, James, 177
Blair, Tony, 381
Blustein, Paul, 341
Boeing, 16, 212, 379
Bombardini, Matilde, 281
Borsig, August, 108
Bosack, Leonard, 210
Bosch, Carl, 420n121
Bosch Rexroth, 341
Boston Manufacturing Company, 154
Bottino, Vittori Bonadè, 14
Boulton, Matthew, 57, 67–68
Boulton & Watt Company, 57, 68
Brandeis, Louis, 180
Brandenburg-African Trading Company of 1682, 418n66
Brandt, Loren, 45, 80
Braun, Karl Ferdinand, 122–23
Brezhnev, Leonid, 293–94, 301, 447n28
Brin, Sergey, 5, 9–10, 210, 402n15
British Iron and Coal Trades Review, 121
Broadberry, Stephen, 114, 249
Bronstein, Lev Davidovich, 185
Brozek, Jan, 57
Brunel, Marc Isambard, 20, 58
Buckley v. Valeo (1976), 363
Burdon, Henry, 155

Burger, Warren, 363
Bush, George H. W., 291
Bush, Vanevar, 189, 192, 195–98, 304–5, 307
Bylinsky, Gene, 307
Bystrova, Irina, 292
ByteDance, 341

Cai Yuanpei, 268, 450n86
Campanella, Tommaso, 61
Carl, Friedrich, 110
Carlin, Wendy, 274
Carnegie, Andrew, 176
Carnegie Steel, 180
Cartwright, Edmund, 67
Cassella, 121
Catholic Church and Reformation, 61–62
centralized bureaucracy, 286, 292, 295, 380, 449n68, 450n86
Chalgrin, François, 127
Chan, Kyle, 357
Chandler, Alfred, Jr., 11, 91, 113, 119–20, 173, 215, 317, 421n134
Chang, Morris, 326
Chang Ru-gin, Richard, 326
Chapman, Richard, 100
Chaptal, Jean-Antoine, 128–29, 422n14
Charles River Bridge v. Warren Bridge (1837), 360–61, 459n116
Chemische Febrik Kalle, 121
Chen Duxiu, 268
Cherry (automobile company), 341
Chetty, Raj, 402n15
Chiang Kai-shek, 85, 267, 298
China: agriculture, 31–33, 35, 405n34, 406n35, 406n51; bureaucracy of, 20, 29–35, 41–43, 45–47, 405n26, 407n61, 407n68, 408n89; civil service in, 28–29, 36–39, 64, 83, 268, 408n77; civil society in, 46, 408nn100–101; foreign trade, 40, 80, 82; guilds in, 78–79; innovation in, 36, 39, 45, 407n55; kinship and, 55–56, 59–60, 407n64, 408n100; maritime embargo, 39, 407n70; naval warfare and shipping in, 39–40; taxation in, 29, 33, 41–43, 45, 405n22, 408n90; technology of, 26–30, 36, 79, 404n4; transportation in, 35, 79–80, 406n50, 414n129, 415n138
China, computer age, 300, 323–27, 330–52, 356–59, 387–89, 454nn77–78, 455n9,

455n17, 456n40, 456n45, 456n55, 456n60, 456n61, 457n70, 457n74, 457n81
China, People's Republic of, 267–72, 290–301, 374, 390, 445n57, 445n60, 445n65, 449n68, 449n72, 449n74, 450n78, 450n81, 450nn85–86, 450n89
Chinitz, Benjamin, 280–81, 447n15
Christensen, Clayton, 317
Chrysler, 314, 337
Chung Taesoo, 321
Chun Han Wong, 350
Churchill, Winston, 112, 187, 228, 247
Cisco Systems, 210, 342
Citroën, 223
civil service comparisons, 99, 101
Clark, Christopher, 96
Clark, Jim, 210
Cleveland, Grover, 180
Clinton, De Witt, 165
Coase, Ronald, "The Nature of the Firm," 12, 18
Cockerill, James, 92
Cockerill, John, 93
Colbert, Jean-Baptiste, 95
Coleridge, Samuel Taylor, 105
Colfax, Schuyler, 177
Collier, Paul, 277
Colt, Samuel, 162–63
Comcast, 454n66
Commodore, 317
Communist Party of China (CPC), 267–68, 270, 297, 301, 324–26, 337, 339–42, 350, 389, 391, 449n72, 456n48
Compaq, 305
Compton, A. H., 204
Computer Revolution, 23, 205, 209–10, 279, 284, 306, 318, 327–28, 381, 386
computers and computing, 202, 204–5, 286–87, 304–6, 350
"Concentration of Economic Power" (Arnold), 207
Congress of Vienna (1815), 92, 109
Conquest, Robert, 256
Control Data Corporation (CDC), 319
Control of Manufactures Act (1932, 1934) (Ireland), 247
Cook, Lisa, 158
Cooke, William, 168
Coolidge, Calvin, 181, 259
Country, the Revolution and I, The (Park), 244

County of Wayne v. Hathcock (Mich. 2004), 362
Cowan, Brian, 4
Cox, Gary, 376
Crafts, Nicholas, 249, 280, 422n22, 448n43
creative destruction, 17, 20, 56, 66, 76, 82, 172, 216, 274, 362–63, 381, 383, 396–97
Crouzet, François, 126
Crystal Palace Exhibition (1851), 90, 130, 162, 213
Culvert, Herbert, 259
Cummins Engine, 341
Czechoslovakia, 263, 266, 283, 286, 437n3

Daewoo, 245–46, 321, 387
Dai-Ichi, 241
Daimler, Gottlieb, 118
Darby, Abraham, 41
Das Kapital (Marx), 300
David, Paul A., 438n22
David Copperfield (TV serial), 283
Davies, R. W., 131
Defense Advanced Research Projects Agency (DARPA), 200, 221
de Forest, Lee, 159
de Freycinet, Charles, 130
de Gasperi, Alcide, 228
de Gaulle, Charles, 230, 232
De Gérando, Joseph-Marie, 129
de Groot, Johan, 74
Deindustrialization of America, The (Bluestone, Harrison), 278
Dell, Michael, 210
Dell Technologies, 210
Deming, W. Edwards, 240
de Neufchâteau, Nicolas-Louis François, 127
Deng Xiaoping, 269, 290–91, 294, 296–300, 323, 332, 349, 388
Department of Government Efficiency (DOGE), 372
Descartes, René, 61
Detour (film), 222
Deutsche Bank, 114, 117, 162
Deutsch-Luxemburg, 115
De Vries, Jan, 414n114
De Wendel, 162
Dewey, John, 268
Dickens, Charles, 101, 157
Dickson, Bruce, 343, 348
Diderot, Denis, *Encyclopaedia*, 410n38

Digital Equipment Corporation (DEC), 317–18
Dixon, Job, 92
"Doctrine of Fascism, The," 14
Donovan, William J., 181
Dore, Ronald, 143
Douglas, Hugo, 118
Douglas, Norman, 93
Douglas, Stephen, 177
Doyle, Thomas, 259
Dryden, Hugh, 200
Duara, Prasenjit, 45
DuPont, 13, 170, 181, 185, 206, 208, 218, 280
Duruy, Victor, 106
Dutch Republic, 73–76, 383, 414n114

Eastern and Central Europe, post WWII, 263–66, 286, 445n43
Eastern Railroad Association (ERA), 172, 430n113
East Germany, 286
Eastman Kodak, 17, 181, 207
Eckert, J. Presper, 304
Economist, The, 233, 341
Edison, Thomas Alva, 17, 119, 159, 170–71, 207, 210, 224
Edison Electric. *See* General Electric (GE)
Edwards, Humphrey, 94
Ehrlich, Paul, 105
Eichengreen, Barry, 230, 236, 286, 438n28, 439n42
Eisenhower, Dwight D., 184, 200, 212
Eitel McCullough Corporation (Eimac), 308
Elvin, Mark, 407n55, 407n70
Empress Cixi, 83
Encyclopaedia (Diderot), 410n38
Engel, Rolf, 253
Engelbart, Douglas, 202
Engels, Friedrich, 63, 252
Enlightenment and Scientific Revolution, 20, 60, 96–97, 105, 111, 390, 411n72
Epstein, S. R., 412n86
Erhard, Ludwig, 224
Estabrook, H. D., 169
Estrin, Saul, 439n43
Et Dieu . . . créa la femme (film), 223
Eucken, Walter, 231
Europe, 32–34, 48, 51–58, 60–64, 68–77, 91, 111–13, 162, 221, 406n38, 409n17, 410n33, 410n34, 410n38, 410nn42–43, 410n46, 411n50
Europe, post WWII, 219–25, 227–28, 230, 236–37, 249–50, 278–79, 281–82f, 316, 380–81, 437n3, 438n11, 438n22, 438n28, 438n31, 439n48
European Union (EU), 279, 364, 372–73

Fairchild, 308, 310, 386, 452n23, 452n39
Fairchild Semiconductor, 313
Fano, Robert, 202
"Federalist Papers, The" (Hamilton), 149
Fedotov, A. A., 444n31
Fehrenbach, Elisabeth, 97
Feigenbaum, Mitchell, 202
Ferdinand, Franz (Archduke), 135
Ferguson, Niall, 327
Fessenden, Reginald, 159
Fiat, 14, 223–24, 233–34
Field, Alexander, 187, 213
Financial Times, 359
Finley, Moses I., 65
First Automobile Works, 333
Fisher, Irving, 2, 5
Fishlow, Albert, 167–68
Fitzgerald, F. Scott, *The Great Gatsby*, 3
Flammermont, Jules, 106
Fogel, Robert, 167–68
Ford, Henry, 182, 211, 214–15, 221, 223–24, 252–53, 403n42
Ford Motor Company, 13–14, 185, 188, 239–40, 259–60, 314, 316, 379
Foreign Affairs, 199, 225
Foxconn, 332
France, 52, 72–73, 76, 98, 106, 125–30, 162–63, 229, 383, 422n12, 422n18, 422n21, 422n22
France, post WWII, 219, 221, 231–33, 378, 439n43
Franco, Francisco, 232–33
Franco-Prussian War of 1870, 87
Frederick the Great, 95, 107, 133
Frederick William (king of Prussia), 62, 95, 98
Frederick William I, 95
Frederick William III, 103
Freeman, Christopher, 441n75
French Planning (Estrin, Holmes), 439n43
Frey, Carl Bennett, 354
Freyn, H. J., 14
Fuji, 241
Fukuyama, Frances, 45, 302

Full Monty, The (film), 278
Fulton, Robert, 129, 163, 165

Galbraith, John Kenneth, 185, 209
Galileo, 56
Gallatin, Albert, 148, 154
Gao Chongxi, 269
Garfield, James A., 177–78
Garibaldi, Giuseppe, 234
Garnett, George, 72
Garon, Sheldon M., 425n94
Gates, Bill, 210, 436n90
Gatling, Richard, 157
Gatrell, Peter, 252
Gelsenberg, 115
Genentech, 309
General Electric (GE), 17, 114, 120, 170–71, 207, 217, 221–22, 237, 260, 311
General Motors, 188, 314, 362
Genneté, Leopold, 73
Germany: agriculture in, 89–90; antitrust and cartels, 120–21, 377, 421n144; banking and finance, 114–15, 117, 420nn117–118; bureaucracy of, 417n43; censorship in, 62–63; civil service in, 96–97, 101–2, 105, 113, 376, 418nn66–67; collaborative efforts, 378; comparison of states, 98–99; fragmentation and unification of, 86–87, 105–6, 111, 119, 420n129; Haber–Bosch process, 420n121; immigration of skilled workers, 93, 416n28; import tariffs, 87, 415n3; industrialization, 15, 89–91, 112–14, 419n97, 421n141; knowledge societies, 58; labour unions in, 229–30; Ottoman Empire and, 112; Siemensstadt industrial complex, 114; steel industry, 115–16, 121; three class franchise system, 89–90; wireless telegraphy, 123–24; *Zollverein*, customs union, 109, 118, 163, 418n58, 419n88
Germany (Nazi era), 186, 193, 260–62
Germany, educational system, 102–9, 117, 390, 418n69, 418n71, 420n113
Germany, post WWII, 229–32, 277, 439n38
Germany, transportation, 94, 109–13
Gernet, Jacques, 408n101
Gerschenkron, Alexander, 15, 54, 117, 418n69, 440n57, 440n63
Ghetaldi, Marino, 57
Gibbon, Edward, 49

Gilchrist, Sidney, 115
Gilman, George Francis, 173
Glaeser, Edward L., 281
global comparisons, 37f, 46, 100f, 217f, 219–20f, 263f, 274f, 303f, 328, 328f
globalization, 160–61, 226–27
Gompers, Paul, 209
Gong Zizhen, 64
Goodyear, Charles, 158
Google, 5, 9–10, 16, 209–10, 306, 342, 364–65, 367, 402n15
Gorbachev, Mikhail, 290–91, 294, 297
Gordon, Robert, 210, 212, 453n66
Gorodnichenko, Yuriy, 155
Gould, Jay, 176–77, 385
Gramsci, Antonio, 253
Granovetter, Mark, 5
Grant, Ulysses administration, 178
Great Atlantic & Pacific Tea Company (A&P), 173
Great Britain: Apprenticeship Act, 412n84; banking and finance, 116–17; Benoit Fourneyron water-turbine, 94; Birmingham Lunar Society, 57; Calico Act of 1721, 71; chemical industry, 116; civil service in, 99–101, 418n58; Corn Laws repeal (1846), 89; Crimean War (1853–1856), 101; decentralization in, 55, 383–84; Domesday Book, 406n37; Dominions and trade, 161; economic liberalism of, 91, 416n21; export ban on machinery, 154; free trade, 416n13; German imports, 87–89; German industrial comparison, 114–15, 117–20, 419n108, 421n131, 421n133; Germany competition, 380; Glorious Revolution of 1688, 71, 76, 94; guilds and progress, 382, 412n84, 412n86; Indian Civil Service, 99; industrialists, 91–92; Industrial Revolution, 20, 43, 58, 66–69, 404n3, 409n20, 410n40, 411nn72–73; London Chapter Coffee House, 57; Luddite riots of 1811–1816, 72, 413n101; Magna Carta, 51; merchant class, 71; millwrights, 66, 412n74; modernity in, 89, 416n12; Municipal Corporations Act (1835), 70; Northcote–Trevelyan Report (1854), 99–100, 178; Parliament and power, 71, 413n96; patents and patent law, 58, 94, 118–19, 158, 417n36; private Acts and progress, 384; slave trade and, 161, 428n61;

Great Britain (*continued*)
spinning jenny, 412n77; steel technology, 115–16; taxation and tax revenue in, 51, 417n57; technology of, 90–91, 114; textile industry, 66–67, 116, 420n115; transportation and canal construction, 413n91; Victorian Climacteric, 90; Warren Fisher Reform (1930), 101; wireless telegraphy, 122–24

Great Britain, computers and computing: decentralized economy, 381; disruptive technology, 279–80

Great Britain, educational system, 100, 103, 106–8, 418n80

Great Britain, post WWII: automobile industry in, 248–49; comparison to European neighbors, 246–48, 442n111; deindustrialization, 277; EU membership, 279; GDP per capita comparison, 248f; growth deceleration in, 279; labour unions in, 247, 442nn113–114; mass production in, 250; Monopolies and Mergers Commission, 249; Monopolies and Restrictive Practices Commission, 249; nationalizations in, 248; Restrictive Practices Act (1956), 249–50, 443n121; shipbuilding industry, 250, 443n122

Great Britain, transportation, 67–68, 70, 94, 114, 416n35, 419n104

Great Depression, 145, 159, 183, 216, 236, 257–58, 264, 379, 433n29

Great Stagnation, The, 331

Greider, William, 434n35

Grove, Andy, 314

Gu Mu, 299

Gutehoffnungshütte, 115

Gutiérrez, Germán, 363

Haber, Fritz, 420n121
Haber, Stephen, 207
Ha-Joon Chang, 321
Halske, Johann Georg, 119
Hamilton, Alexander, 148–49, 151–52, 426n14
Hanbo Steel Company, 321, 387
Hansen, Alvin, 433n29
Hardenberg, Karl August von, 15, 98
Harding, Warren G., 3
Hargreaves, James, 412n77
Harkort, Fritz, 91
Harnack, Adolf von, 105
Harrison, Mark, 254–55, 289, 444n14
Hassenfratz, Jean Henri, 126
Haussmann, Georges-Eugène, 106
Hayek, Friedrich von, 10–11, 13, 24, 42, 232, 295, 350, 389, 394
Haywood, William, 259
Hegel, Georg Wilhelm Friedrich, 97
Henckel, Ole, 76
Henrich, Joseph, 53
Henry, Patrick, 149
He Qinglian, 333
He Weifang, 336
Hewlett, William, 310
Hewlett-Packard Company (HP), 309–10, 315, 317, 319, 331
Higgs, Robert, 191
Hirata Tosuke, 141
Hirschman, Albert O., 438n31
Hirubumi, Ito, 242
Hitachi, 316
Hitler, Adolf, 104, 185–86
Hobbes, Thomas, *The Elements of Law*, 61
Hobsbawm, Eric, 18
Hoechst, 116, 121
Hoffman, Ross, 88
Hofmann, August Wilhelm von, 116
Holmes, Peter, 439n43
Honeywell, 311, 313
Hong Kong, 26, 78, 82, 269, 290, 298–99, 326–27, 454n89
Hoover, Calvin, 199
Hoover, Herbert, 216, 258
Hörder-Verein, 115
horizontal or vertical learning, 5, 402nn14–15
horizontal or vertical relationships, 9–10, 12–16, 59, 115, 121, 144, 180, 292, 310–11, 314, 326, 350, 386, 389, 449n70
Hornung, Erik, 109
Howes, Anton, 412n74
Huang, Jensen, 210
Huang, Ray, 31
Huang Yasheng, 405n17
Huawei, 332, 342, 347, 359
Hughes, Thomas P., 170
Hu Jintao, 350, 456n48
Humboldt, Alexander von, 104
Humboldt, Wilhelm von, 103–5, 107
Hume, David, 411n50
Hungary, 266, 286, 446n76

Huntington, Samuel, 138
Hu Qiaomu, 300
Hu Shi, 268
Hymer, Stephen, 18
Hyundai, 245, 291

IBM, 207, 218, 227, 240–41, 287, 305, 317–19, 379, 386, 397, 436n81, 453n60
IG Farben, 120–22, 231, 262, 377
India, 143, 357–58, 423n46, 425nn91–92
Industrial Efficiency (Shadwell), 89
Innovators, The (Isacsson), 304
Inoue Kaoru, 140
institutional inertia, 393
Intel Corporation, 305, 308–10, 312–13
International Harvester, 181
International Monetary Fund (IMF), 373
International Patent Convention (1873), 428n41
International Rail Traffic Association, 161
International Telecommunication Union (ITU), 342
International Telegraph Union, 161
Ioffe, Abram, 287
Ipatieff, Vladimir, 443n9
Iran, 277
Ireland, 87, 247, 442n110
Irwin, Douglas, 153–54
Isacsson, Walter, 304
Italy, post WWII, 224–25, 233–36, 378, 410n43, 440nn54–56, 440n57, 440nn62–63, 446n9
Ito Hirobumi, 140–41, 243
Ivanov, E.A., 255
Iwasaki Yataro, 142
Iziumov, A. I., 290

J. & P. Coats, 162
Jackson, Henry M., 198
Jackson, James, 91
Jacobi, Jacob, 73
Jacquard, Joseph Marie, 130
Jang-Sup Shin, 321
Jánosi, Marcell, 286
Japan: Bank of Japan, 145; Black Ships incident, 138; bureaucracy of, 140–41; cartels and competition in, 144, 386; censorship in, 64; civil service in, 139, 141; comparisons to Germany, 139, 141, 144; comparison to China, 139, 424n66, 424n68; foreign talent and technology, 140; government role in industrialization, 142, 425nn82–85; Important Industries Control Law, 144; Institute of Barbarian Books (Bansho Torishirabesho), 138; international trade in, 137; Korea and, 239, 242–43; labour in, 143–44, 425n86, 425n94, 425n97; management principles of, 240, 441n76; manufacturing in, 138, 424n72; Meiji Constitution, 141; Meiji Restoration (1868), 13, 83, 138–39, 237, 242, 378; Peace Preservation Law, 426n95; Public Order & Police Law, 143, 426n95; railroads in, 137–38; Satsuma Rebellion (1877), 139; state owned enterprises (SOEs), 425n82; technology of, 138, 142; *zaibatsu* (vertically integrated conglomerates), 144–45, 240, 378, 380, 426n102
Japan, computer age: antitrust and, 318; cartels in, 318; foreign technology, 316; great stagnation, 387; Japanese Fair Trade Commission (FTC), 318, 386; keiretsu (zaibatsu successors), 441n82, 454n67; software and internet, 321; United States comparison, 302–3, 451n5; US–Japan Semiconductor Trade Agreement, 315
Japan, educational system, 142–43
Japan, industry: automotive industry, 239–40; foreign technology, 317
Japan, post WWII: Antimonopoly Law (1947), 241, 380; GDP per capita comparison, 304f; *kaizen* (continuous improvement), 239; keiretsu (zaibatsu successors), 241–42, 321, 380, 386; Korean War and, 239; labour force in, 237; Military Assistance Program (MAP), 238; Ministry of International Trade and Industry (MITI), 240–41, 380, 441nn78–79; technology and, 237–38; Training Within Industry (TWI) Service, 239; Treaty of San Francisco (1945), 237; Vehicle Exchange programs, 239; wartime devastation and recovery, 238–39, 441n70, 441n75
Japan As Number One (Vogel), 302
Japanese National Diet Library (NDL), 138
Jardine, Matheson and Co., 79
Jefferson, Thomas, 149–50, 152–53, 176
Jiang Zemin, 340
Jobs, Steve, 210, 304, 311

Johnson, Chalmers, 240, 302
Johnson, Lyndon B. (senator), 199
Johnson, Samuel, 55
Johnson & Johnson, 337
Jorgenson, Dale W., 451n5
Judt, Tony, 223

Kaiser, Henry, 214
Kanai Noboru, 141
Kang, David C., 321
Kant, Immanuel, 58, 60
Karikó, Katalin, 6–8, 10, 375
Karpinski, Jacek, 286
Kendall, Amos, 361
Kennan, George, 224–25, 266
Kennedy, John F., 200
Kerr, Sari Pekkala, 281
Kerr, William, 16, 281, 325
Kerry, John, 344
Khan, Zorina, 164
Khrushchev, Nikita, 199, 266, 271, 273, 289, 293–94, 382
Kilby, Jack, 326
Kilgore, Harley M., 198
Kishi Nobosuke, 144
Kissinger, Henry, 298, 344
Klein, Maury, 166
Kleiner Perkins Caufield & Byers, 209
Klepper, Stephen, 314
Koch, Robert, 105
Kocka, Jürgen, 101–2, 120, 228
Koepsel, Adolf, 123
Kohli, Atul, 243
Kopsidis, Michael, 98–99
Korea. *See* South Korea
Korean War, 233, 239, 243, 272, 451n19
Korea Shipbuilding and Engineering Company, 246
Kornai, János, 265
Kornhardt, Wilhelm, 118
Korolev, Sergei, 256
Koselleck, Reinhart, 97
Kostikov, Andrey, 256
Kosygin, Alexei, 293
Kotkin, Stephen, 278, 283
Kōzō Yamamura, 426n102
Krause, Victor, 51
Krueger, A. O., 442n107
Krupp, 377

Krupp, Alfred, 108, 112–13, 115, 267
Kuran, Timur, 56
Kuznets, Simon, 333, 335

Lagrange, Jean-Louis, 126
Lamoreaux, Naomi, 208, 362, 459n116
Lamprecht, Karl, 268
Lanchester, Frederick, 119
Landes, David, 68, 119, 146, 421n134, 425n79
Lane, Nathan, 442n102
Lang, Fritz, 189
Lange, Oskar, 252
Langemak, Georgy, 256
Langley, Samuel, 396
Lanz, Heinrich, 163
Laplace, Pierre-Simon de, 126–27
Lavoisier, Antoine, 126
Law, Marc, 180
Lawrence, Ernest, 204
Leblanc, Nicolas, 127
LeConte, Joseph, 395
Lee, Ching Kwan, 333
Lee, Kai-Fu, 330
Lee, William, 70
Legend (Lenovo), 324, 454n77
Leibniz, Gottfried, 69
Lenin, Vladimir, 134, 252–53, 256, 258–59, 273, 282, 292, 311, 378, 444n28
Lenovo, 331
Lerner, Josh, 209
Lerner, Sandy, 210
Leroy, Jean-Baptiste, 127
Les Thibault (TV serial), 283
Le Turc, Bonaventure, 76
Levine, Emily, 106
Li, K. T., 326
Li, Robin, 340
Liard, Louis, 106
Libecap, Gary, 180
Licklider, J. C. R., 201–3, 205, 319
Li Dazhao, 268
Liebig, Justus von, 104–5
Li Hongzhang, 267
Li Keqiang, 350
Limits of State Action, The (Humboldt), 103
Lin, Justin, 36, 38
Lincoln, Abraham, 156–57, 166–67, 176, 427n36
Lindbergh, Charles, 189, 212

Linde, Carl von, 118
Lindert, Peter, 116, 315
Lingfei Wu, 17
Lin Jianhua, 345
Link, Stephan, 262
Li Pingxin, 269
Lipset, Seymour Martin, 149
List, Friedrich, 62, 91, 111, 135, 251, 443n2
Litton, Charles, 308, 311
Litton Engineering Laboratories, 308
Livien, Dominic, 133
Li Yuan, 356
Locke, John, 61
Lockwood, T. D., 169
Lockwood, William, 142, 144
Loewe, Ludwig, 112, 163
Lord of Rosebery, Archibald Primrose, 87
"Losing the War to Japan," 302
Lotus, 319
Louisiana Purchase, 148
Louis XIV (king of France), 62
Lovlace, Ada, 304
Lowell, Francis Cabot, 154
Lowell Machine Shop, 169
Ludendorf, Erich, 252
Luo Jialun, 268
Luo Rong'an, 269
Luther, Martin, 61–62
Lysenko, Trofim, 257

Ma, Debin, 45
Ma, Jack, 340
MacArthur, Douglas, 238–40
Macartney, George, 25–26, 404n3
MacLeod, W. Bentley, 196
Macmillan, Harold, 247
macroinventions, 403n51
Made in Germany (Williams), 87
Madison, James, 153, 165, 426n14
Ma Huateng, 340
Malachowsky, Chris, 210
Malenkov, Georgy, 293
Mann, Michael, 34, 406n46
Mannesmann, 317
Mansfield, Edwin, 317
Mao Zedong, 30, 266, 268, 270–71, 289, 294, 298, 336, 344, 449n72
Marconi, Guglielmo, 122–23
Marconi Company, 123–24

Marglin, Stephen, 18
Markevich, Andrei, 295
Marshall, Alfred, 4, 227
Marx, Karl, 125, 160, 252, 300
Mason, Edward, 245
Massachusetts Institute of Technology (MIT), 189, 197, 204, 307
Matsushita, 316
Mauchly, John, 304
Maxim, Hiram, 159
Maybach, Wilhelm, 118
Mazzucato, Mariana, 187
McCarthy, John, 202
McClure's Magazine, 180
McCormick, Cyrus, 158
McCraw, Thomas, 190
McGregor, Richard, 339
McKenna, Regis, 453n53
McNamara, Robert, 201, 308, 322
Melman, Seymour, 190
Mercedes-Benz, 337
Meta, 16, 367
Metropolis (film), 189
Meucci, Antonio, 158
Microsoft, 23, 210, 311–12, 317, 319–20, 337, 344, 352, 368, 386, 436n90
Middle East, business corporations in, 56
Milanovic, Branko, 297, 335–36
Miller, Chris, 291, 294
Mills, C. Wright, 185
Minxin Pei, 334
Mitsubishi, 142–45, 241, 316
Mitsui, 144–45, 237, 241
Moderna, 6, 8–9, 402n23
Mokyr, Joel, 60, 64, 85, 403n51, 411n72
Monnet, Jean, 232, 379
Montecatini company, 224
Moody, Paul, 154
Moore, Gordon, 308, 313, 452n39
Moore's Law, 305, 352, 370
Morgan, J. P., 176–77
Morris (automobile company), 223
Morse, Hosea Ballou, 78–79
Morse, Samuel, 158, 168, 361, 384
Mosaddegh, Mohammad, 277
Mowery, David, 320
Mulvany, William, 92
Münchhausen, Gerlach Adolph von, 105
Munn and Company, 157

Musk, Elon, 16, 360
Mussolini, Benito, "The Doctrine of Fascism," 14–15, 236

Napoleon Bonaparte, 76–77, 97, 102, 127, 129, 132, 383, 416n23
Napoleon III, 106
"National Research Program for Space Technology, A" (Dryden), 200
National Science Foundation (NSF), 319–20
Nature, 344
Naughton, Barry, 270, 296, 457n74
NCR, 319
Needham, Joseph, *Science and Civilization in China*, 27, 36, 374, 411n48
Needham puzzle, 36
Nehru, Jawaharlal, 271
Nelson, Donald, 189
Nernst, Walther, 105
Nestlé & Anglo-Swiss, 162
Netscape Communications Corporation, 210
Newcomen, Thomas, 67, 354
New Industrial State, The (Galbraith), 185
Newton, Isaac, *Principia*, 57
New York Times, 14, 178, 212, 302, 352
New York Times Magazine, 278
New York Tribune, 160
Nicholas I (tsar), 133
Nicholas II (tsar), 133
Nikon, 337
Nixon, Richard, 245, 273, 298
Nobel, Immanuel, 136
Nobel Dynamite (company), 162
Nomura, Koji, 451n5
Nordhaus, William, 305
Norman, E. Herbert, 137
North, Douglas, 376
North Atlantic Treaty Organization (NATO), 438n15
Noyce, Robert, 308, 310, 313, 452n39
Nuvolari, Alessandro, 94
NVIDIA, 210, 359
Nvidia, 368

Obama, Barack, 344, 364
Ogilvie, Sheilagh, 69
Ohno, Taiichi, 239
Okubo Toshimichi, 142
Olsen, Ken, 318
Olson, Mancur, 19, 178

OpenAI, 16, 352, 366–68
Opium War (1839–1842), 26, 80
Oppenheimer, Robert, 204
Ordzhonikidze, Sergo, 257
Organization of Petroleum Exporting Countries (OPEC), 276
Osborne, Michael, 354
Ostrom, Elinor, 32
Otis Elevator, 181
Otto, Nikolaus, 118, 420n127
Ottoman Empire, 64–65, 112, 411n67
Our Nation's Path (Park), 244

Packard, David, 310
Page, Larry, 5, 9–10, 210, 402n15
Papin, Denis, 69, 71
Paris Peace Treaties (1947), 193, 205
Park, Chung Hee, 243–46, 321, 387
Party, The (McGregor), 339
Pasteur, Louis, 106
patents and patent law, 74, 93–94, 118, 157, 413n108, 416nn31–32
PBS Frontline, 302
Peattie, Mark, 242
Pellegrino, Bruno, 446n9
People's Republic of China, 338
Pepperell Manufacturing Company, 173
Périer, Jacques-Constantin, 127
Perkin, William, 116
Perkins, Dwight H., 424n66
Perkins, Tom, 309
Perlis, Alan, 202
Perry, Matthew C., 137–38, 242, 377
Peter the Great (tsar), 131, 133
Pew Research Survey, 398
Peyrefitte, Alain, 26
Pfizer, 9
Philippon, Thomas, 363
Philips, 227, 317
Pichai, Sundar, 367
Pig Iron Syndicate, 121
Pius IX (pope), 119
Planck, Max, 17, 105
planned economies, 10–11, 22, 221, 266, 286, 402n29
Plehve, Vyacheslav von, 132
Pliny the Elder, 65
Plumb, Preston B., 179
Poland, 52, 61, 91, 188, 220, 251, 263, 266, 445n43, 446n76

Polanyi, Karl, 14
Poletown Neighborhood Council v. City of Detroit (Mich. 1981), 361
Pomeranz, Kenneth, 407n56
Pompidou, Georges, 226
Porsche (company), 223
Porsche, Ferdinand, 14
Portugal, 79, 221, 279, 381, 428n61
Powell, Colin, 344
Powell, Michael, 460n141
Power Elite, The (Mills), 185
Priem, Curtis, 210
Priestley, J. B., 223
private enterprise, profit and, 18
private property rights, 20–21, 45, 76, 91, 97, 128, 151, 156, 158, 361–62
Proceedings of the National Academy of Science, 344
protectionism, 75–76, 89, 152, 154
Prussia, 21, 92, 94–99, 102, 104–5, 417n47
Putin, Vladimir, 292, 389
Putnam, Robert, 135

Qingnan Xie, 344
Qualcomm, 337–38
Questcor Pharmaceutical, 365

railroads, 68, 94, 110–14, 130, 134–35, 137–38, 230, 235–36, 252, 419n104, 422n21
railroads, China, 79–80, 414n129, 415n138
railroads, United States, 166–68, 171–72, 430n92, 432n155
Rajan, Raghuram, 306
Rathenau, Walther, 252
Rawski, Thomas, 45, 80
Raytheon, 189, 307–9, 311
RCA, 309, 311
Renault, 223, 341, 372
Rennie, John, 94
"Report on the Subject of Manufactures" (Hamilton), 152
Respublica Literaria, 410n33
Reuters, 370
revolutionary inventions, 10, 402n29
Rhee, Syngman, 237, 243–44
Rheinische Stahlwerke, 115
Richthofen, Ferdinand von, 105
Ridley, Matt, 8
Rieber, Alfred, 135

Rio Tinto, 162
Rise and Fall of American Growth, The (Gordon), 210
Robert, Nicolas-Louis, 129
Robinson, James, 27
Rock, Arthur, 308
Rockefeller, John D., 173, 176, 385
Rode, Carl, 123
Roebuck, Alvah, 173
Roland, Gerard, 155
Roosevelt, Franklin D., 187, 189–90, 207, 211, 216, 232, 433n20
Roosevelt, Theodore, 137, 181
Rosenberg, Nathan, 82, 320, 403n50
Rosenstein-Rodan, Paul, 230
Rosenthal, Jean-Laurent, 413n101
Rossi, Derrick, 7–8
Rothbarth, Erwin, 162
Rother, Christian von, 93
Rothschild, 162
Royal Dutch Shell, 162
Ruina, Jack, 201–2
Russell, William Howard, 160
Russia, 21, 34, 130–36, 251–52, 377–78, 406n48, 423n26, 423n30, 423n35, 423n39
Russia, transportation in, 134–35
Ryabushinsky, Pavel, 259

Sahin, Ugur, 8
Saltsjöbaden Agreement (1938), 438n27
Samsung, 245, 325, 356
Sanwa, 241
Sanyo, 316
Saturday Night Fever (film), 278
Saxenian, AnnaLee, 309, 318
Scheiber, Harry, 361
Scheidel, Walter, 49
Schijf, Daam, 73
Schiller, Friedrich, 103
Schofield brothers, 154
Schularick, Moritz, 327
Schulz, Jonathan, 53
Schumacher, Kurt, 228
Schumpeter, Joseph, 18, 396–97
Science, 344
"Science: The Endless Frontier" (Bush), 195
Scientific American, 157, 214
Sears, Richard Warren, 173
Second Book (Hitler), 185–86

Second Industrial Revolution, 22–23, 109, 116, 140, 143, 145, 159, 161, 182, 205–6, 213, 219, 284, 317, 378, 381, 397, 410n43, 421n134
Secrets of the Temple (Greider), 434n35
Sedol, Lee, 354
Semiconductor Manufacturing International Corporation (SMIC), 325–26
Serafinelli, Michel, 63
Shadwell, Arthur, 89
Shakhurin, Aleksey, 254
Shanghai Automobile, 341
Shannon, Claude, 192–93
Sharp, 316
Sheffield, John Lord, 150
Shenzong (emperor), 38
Shibusawa Eiichi, 424n72
Shigeru Sahashi, 240
Shinjin, 246
Shockley, William, 307
Shockley Semiconductor, 313
Shockley Semiconductor Laboratory, 386
Shutdown at Youngstown, Crisis in Bethlehem (Buss, Redburn), 278
Siemens, 109, 114, 117–18, 120–21, 162, 237, 317
Siemens, Georg, 117
Siemens, Werner, 102, 108, 119
Siemens & Halske, 102, 123–24, 378
Siemens-Martin process, 419n110
Siemens-Schuckert, 113
Silberman, James, 225–26
Silicon Graphics, 318
Simonyi, Charles, 311
Sinclair, Upton, 180
Singapore, 242, 299, 326
Singer, Isaac, 158
Slaby, Adolf, 123
Slater, Samuel, 154
Smeaton, John, 20, 58, 94
Smith, Adam, *The Wealth of Nations*, 11, 84, 128
Smith, Thomas G., 425n85
Smokey and the Bandit (film), 212
Sng, Tuan-Hwee, 408n90
Sobchak, Anatoly, 290
social networks, 3–5, 29, 39, 44, 46–47, 53, 55, 57, 156, 401n8, 401n11, 409n21, 409n24
solo inventors and decentralized teams, 16–17, 170, 175, 185, 196, 209, 212, 384, 394
Solow, Robert, 201
Solvay, Ernst, 420n115
Sombart, Werner, 91, 113
Sony, 316–17
Sorensen, Charles, 188
South Korea, 11, 39, 136, 237, 241–46, 307, 321–22, 326–27, 346, 387–88, 441n91, 442nn102–103, 442n107
South Manchuria Railway, 145
Space X, 16
Spain, 52, 60, 70, 221–22, 232–33, 236, 279, 379, 381
Speer, Albert, 262
Speransky, M. M., 423n39
Sperry, Elmer Ambrose, 159, 170
Springfield Armory, 155
Stalin, Joseph, 253, 256–57, 265–66, 270, 273, 282, 289, 292, 382, 389
Standard Oil, 170, 174, 180–81, 183, 367, 430n106
Stanford University, 196, 204, 309
Stasavage, David, 32, 406n35
Steffens, Lincoln, 258
Stein, Karl vom und zum, 15, 97
Stein-Hardenberg Reforms, 83, 97–98, 132, 376–77, 417n47
Steinway & Sons, 156
Steinweg, Heinrich, 156
Stephenson, George, 68, 114
St. Gotthard rail tunnel, 162
Stigler, George, 365
Stimson, Henry, 189
Stolypin, Pyotr, 132, 423n30
Stone, Nelson, 308
Streit, Clarence, 145
Studwell, Joe, 250, 321
"Study of Administration, The" (W. Wilson), 178
Suez Canal completion (1869), 80
Sukhoi, P.O., 255
Sultan Bayezid II, 64
Sumitomo, 144, 241
Sumner, Charles, 176
Sun, 318–19
Sun Yat-sen, 85
Suslov, Mikhail, 283
Su Song, 38
Sutton, Anthony, 253, 443n10
Swan, Joseph, 119
Sweden, 61, 221, 230–31, 250, 438n27
Sylvania, 307, 311
Symbiosis, 201
System Althoff, 104

Tabellini, Guido, 63
Tacitus, *The Germania*, 50
Taft, William Howard, 181
Taiwan, 237, 242, 250, 269, 297, 299, 326–27, 331–32, 371, 454n89
Tandy, 317
Taney, Roger, 360–61, 366
Tarbell, Ida, 180
Taylor, Bob, 201, 205
Taylor, Henry Winslow and Taylorism, 14, 253, 311, 316, 443n9
Taylor, Zachary, 176
Taylor Society, 14
team size, 16, 404n55
Technology Trap, The (Frey), 397
Telefunken, 124
Teller, Edward, 199
Tencent, 340–41, 347
Tesla (company), 16, 356
Tesla, Nikola, 159–60
Texas Instruments (TI), 208, 240, 326, 379, 452n23
textile industry, Great Britain, 66–67, 116, 420n115
textile industry, India, 143, 425nn91–92
textile industry, United States, 154–55, 158–59, 427n26
Thatcher, Margaret, 279–80, 381
"That Which Is Seen, and That Which Is Not Seen" (Bastiat), 192
Thomas, David, 155
Thomas, Edward, 92
Thomas, Sidney Gilchrist, 115
Thomas Cook, 162
Thomson, Elihu, 159, 170
Thomson-Houston Electric Company (THEC), 404n58
Thorp, Willard, 181–82
Thyssen, Fritz, 231
Tilly, Richard H., 98–99
Time "Machine of the Year," 304
Time Magazine, 199, 305
Times, The (London), 88, 112, 160
Time-Warner, 454n66
Tocqueville, Alexis de, 128, 164, 174
Tokyo Streetcar Company, 143
Tolstoy, Leo, *War and Peace*, 34
Toniolo, Gianni, 448n43
Torricelli, Evangelista, 67
Toshiba, 316

Totsuka, Hideo, 236
Toyota Motor Corporation, 239–40, 316
Trance, Keith, 116
Treaty of Ghent (1814), 153
Trebbi, Francesco, 281
Trebilcock, Clive, 421n141
Treisman, Daniel, 450n86
Trevelyan, Charles, 99
Trevithick, Richard, 68, 114
Trotsky, Leon, 137, 185, 256–57
Truman, Harry, 198, 218, 225
Trump, Donald, 9, 344, 359–60, 372, 398, 457n67
Tukhachevskii, Mikhail, 255
Turner, Frederick Jackson, 155–56

Ulyanov, Vladimir Ilyich. *See* Lenin, Vladimir
Uncapher, Keith, 202
Unisys, 319
United Airlines, 212
United States: African Americans and, 158, 428nn46–47, 428n53; agriculture in, 148; American Relief Administration of 1921, 258; antitrust, cartels and mergers, 180–83, 207–9, 361, 436n91; Articles of Confederation, of, 150; automobiles, 14, 182, 185, 188, 211, 214–15, 314, 437nn95–96; aviation industry, 211–12; Bill of Rights, 151; bureaucracy in, 149; civil service in, 179; Civil Service Reform League, 178; Civil War, 159; Clayton Antitrust Act (1914), 179, 432n149; Constitutional Convention (1787), 150; Constitution of, 149–51; corporations and management, 172–73; corporations and trusts, 174–76; Department of Justice, 230, 365–66, 436n91; entrepreneurship in, 147, 280–81, 447n15; federal government powers, 151; Federalists and, 150, 426n14; Federal Trade Commission Act (1914), 179, 432n149; France and, 149–50; frontier influence, 155–56; "Gilded Age" and "robber barons," 176; government patronage scandals and reform, 176–80; Hepburn Act (1906), 179; individualism in, 155–56; Interstate Commerce Act (1887), 179; Interstate Commerce Clause, 163; Interstate Highway System, 212–13; labour relations, 180, 215–16; manufacturing in, 151, 153, 194f, 211f; mass production in, 162, 188, 211, 214–15,

United States (*continued*)
429n65; military industrial complex, 433n4; National Bureau of Standards (NBS), 213–14; National Industrial Recovery Act (1933), 207; National Labor Relations Act (1935), 216; national prohibition, 2–5; patents and patent law, 21, 148, 156–58, 164, 170–72, 193–94f, 205, 207–8f, 384, 427n16, 428n41, 428n57, 429n85, 436n89; Pendleton Act (1883), 179, 385, 432n142; Postal Service Act (1792), 164–65, 390; postwar corporations and innovation, 16, 403nn52–54; "Progress of the Nation," 155; public-private partnerships, 163, 177; research in corporations, 169–70, 430nn106–107, 430n114; Rural Electrification Act (1936), 211; Sherman Antitrust Act (1890), 120, 179–82, 207, 241, 337, 364, 377, 380, 385, 432n149; slavery in the, 158–59; South America comparison, 156; Tariff of 1816, 154; tariffs and taxation, 151, 153–54, 175; taxation in, 150; technological restrictions, 383; technology in, 21–22, 158–59, 226, 384; trade embargo (1807–1809), 152–53; trade policy, 149–50, 218; trucking industry, 212–13

United States, communication, 149, 160–61, 164–65, 168–69, 180, 182–83, 426n10, 429n80, 430n100

United States, computer age: American success, 23; American university system and, 203, 307; antitrust and cartels, 318–20, 365–69, 386, 453n66, 460n150; Antitrust Reform Act of 1985 (Michigan), 314; Boston-area universities and, 307; California Civil Code of 1872, 386; "Chimerica," 327, 331, 360; corporate size and influence, 363; East and West Coast, 310, 312–14, 318, 452n42; Federal Trade Commission (FTC), 364–66, 372; Homebrew Computer Club, 202, 312; immigration and H-1B visas, 360; management practices in, 306, 451n15; Open AI and ChatGPT, 366; Open AI and ChatGPT collaboration, 368–69; Palo Alto Research Center (PARC), 311–12; post-pandemic economy, 461n2; profit sharing and equity compensation, 310; regulatory capture, 366; revival of, 303; Silicon Valley, 13, 23, 303, 306–9, 311–13, 367, 370, 386–87,

452n27; technological plateau, 330; *United States v. International Business Machines Corp.* (1996), 319, 453n62; "veto players" and gridlock, 358

United States, education, 163, 216, 389–90

United States, post WWII: Apollo program, 200, 221, 318; corporations and innovation, 206–9, 436n81; Department of Defense (DOD), 201, 203–5, 307, 451n19; government funding of science, 197–98, 435n76; Marshall Plan, 217, 225–27, 234, 379, 438n15; mass production in, 276–77; National Advisory Committee for Aeronautics (NACA), 199–200; National Aeronautics and Space Act (1958), 200; National Science Foundation (NSF), 197–98; National Science Foundation Act (1950), 198; Rad Lab, 195, 200, 204, 375; science-based industries, 436n82; space race, 198–200; steel industry in, 277–78; stock market, 195, 343n45; television invention, 436n92; universities' research role, 196–98, 204–5; venture capital (VC) and initial public offerings (IPO), 209, 436n89

United States, transportation, 129, 165–66, 177–80, 212, 429n83

United States, wars, 152, 186–93, 195–96, 200, 204, 214–17, 307, 433n20, 433n22, 433n26, 433nn28–29, 434n35, 434n42, 434n44, 434n46, 451nn17–18

United States v. United States Steel Corp (1920), 181

Universal Postal Union, 161

Urey, Harold, 204

Urquiola, Miguel, 196

Usher, Abbott, 411n69

Usselman, Steven W., 432n155

USSR, 199, 225, 252–60, 262–63, 281, 285, 287, 295, 380–82, 435n53, 443n10, 444n14, 444n21, 444n24, 444n28, 444n31, 449n71. *See also* Russia

USSR, post WWII, 38, 198, 200, 257, 266–67, 272–77, 282–95, 347, 380, 382, 402n29, 444n23, 445n50, 447n25, 447nn27–28, 447n28, 448n56, 448n59, 449n62, 449n70

USSR, wartime, 260–62, 444n36

U.S. Steel, 181, 280, 295

Vail, Theodore N., 170
Valentine, Don, 309

Vanderbilt, Cornelius, 176–77, 385
Van Der Woude, Ad, 414n114
van Zanden, Jan Luiten, 410n46
Varian Associates, 308, 311
Vavilov, Nikolai, 444n21
Veblen, Thorstein, 422n3
Verizon, 454n66
Vesalius, Andreas, 56
Virginia Company of London, 147
Vogel, Ezra, 298, 302
Volkswagen, 14, 16, 341
Voltaire, 61
von Ense, Karl Varnhagen, 62
von Glahn, Richard, 28
von Knyphausen, Dodo, 95
von Mises, Ludwig, *Bureaucracy*, 11
von Struensee, Carl August, 98
Voznesensky, Nikolai, 254
Vries, Peer, 143

Waddington, Richard, 92
Waldrop, Mitchell, 202–3
Wallenberg family, 231
Wall Street Journal, 364
Walt Disney Co., 309, 341
Wang Anshi, 35, 38–39
Wang Xihou, 63
Ward, Aaron Montgomery, 173
Ward, Artemus, 176
Ware, Harold M., 258–59
Washington, George, 150, 152
Watson, Thomas, 305
Watt, James, 20, 57–58, 67, 354–55, 383
Weber, Max, 15–16, 85, 94, 197
Weingast, Barry, 149, 296, 375–76
Weissman, Drew, 7–8, 10
Wells, H. G., 107
Western Railroad Association (WRA), 172
Western Union, 159, 169, 177, 182–83, 366, 385
Westinghouse, 114, 120, 160, 170, 174, 185, 237, 404n58
Westinghouse, George, 17, 119, 159
Wheatstone, Charles, 168
Whitehead, Alfred North, 57
Whitney, Eli, 158–59, 162
Wiener, Norbert, 192–93, 304–5
Wilhelm II (kaiser), 90, 123–24
William I of Prussia (German Emperor), 86
Williams, Ernest Edwin, 87–88

Williamson, Oliver, 18
Wilson, Henry, 177
Wilson, Woodrow, 3, 178, 432n149
Witte, Sergei, 131–35, 251–52, 443n2
Wittfogel, Karl, *Oriental Despotism*, 31
Woessmann, Ludger, 109
Wojcicki, Susan, 9
Wolfe, Tom, 310
Wong, R. Bin, 413n101
World Bank, 322
World Trade Organization (WTO), 324
World Value Survey, 155
Wozniak, Steve, 210, 312
Wright brothers, 159, 211, 395
Wu, Mark, 457n70
Wulf, Julie, 306
Wundt, Wilhelm, 268

X (formerly Twitter), 16
Xerox, 311, 317, 441n76
Xi Jinping, 19, 24, 336, 341–44, 348–50, 371, 389, 391, 457n81
Xi Zhongxun, 294, 298
Xu Caihou, 335
Xu Chenggang, 291
Xu Zhangrun, 345

Yakovlev, Alexander, 262
Yamagata, Aritomo, 140
Yamanaka Shinya, 7–8
Yasuda, 144–45
Yawata Steel Works, 143, 145
Yezhov, Nikolai, 255–56
Yingyi Qian, 296
Yokohama Specie Bank, 145
YouTube, 16
Yuan Baohua, 323

Zelin, Madeleine, 42
Zhang, Angela, 339
Zheng He, 40
Zhenzong (emperor), 35
Zhou Enlai, 298
Zhou Qiang, 336
Zhuravskaya, Ekaterina, 295
Zhu Rongji, 324, 332
Zhu Shunshui, 61
Zhu Yuanzhang, 39, 350
Zingales, Luigi, 365, 446n9
Zwingli, Ulrich, 61

A NOTE ON THE TYPE

This book has been composed in Arno, an Old-style serif typeface in the classic Venetian tradition, designed by Robert Slimbach at Adobe.